THE BROADVIEW
Introduction to
Literature
CONCISE EDITION
Second Edition

THE BROADVIEW
Introduction to
Literature

CONCISE EDITION
Second Edition

General Editors
Lisa Chalykoff
Neta Gordon
Paul Lumsden

broadview press

BROADVIEW PRESS – www.broadviewpress.com
Peterborough, Ontario, Canada

Founded in 1985, Broadview Press remains a wholly independent publishing house. Broadview's focus is on academic publishing; our titles are accessible to university and college students as well as scholars and general readers. With over 600 titles in print, Broadview has become a leading international publisher in the humanities, with world-wide distribution. Broadview is committed to environmentally responsible publishing and fair business practices.

Library and Archives Canada Cataloguing in Publication

Title: The Broadview introduction to literature / general editors, Lisa Chalykoff, Neta Gordon,
    Paul Lumsden.
Other titles: Introduction to literature
Names: Chalykoff, Lisa, editor. | Gordon, Neta, 1971- editor. | Lumsden, Paul, 1961- editor.
Description: Concise second edition. | Includes bibliographical references and index.
Identifiers: Canadiana 20190083263 | ISBN 9781554814756 (softcover)
Subjects: LCSH: Literature—Collections.
Classification: LCC PN6014 .B66 2019 | DDC 808—dc23

Broadview Press handles its own distribution in North America:
PO Box 1243, Peterborough, Ontario K9J 7H5, Canada
555 Riverwalk Parkway, Tonawanda, NY 14150, USA
Tel: (705) 743-8990; Fax: (705) 743-8353
email: customerservice@broadviewpress.com

Distribution is handled by Eurospan Group in the UK, Europe, Central Asia, Middle East, Africa, India, Southeast Asia, Central America, South America, and the Caribbean. Distribution is handled by Footprint Books in Australia and New Zealand.

Broadview Press acknowledges the financial support of the
Government of Canada for our publishing activities.

Canada

Interior design and typeset by Eileen Eckert
Cover design by Michel Vrana

PRINTED IN CANADA

Contributors to *The Broadview Introduction to Literature*

MANAGING EDITOR	Marjorie Mather
MANAGING EDITOR, FIRST EDITION	Don LePan
DEVELOPMENTAL AND TEXTUAL EDITOR	Laura Buzzard
EDITORIAL COORDINATOR	Tara Bodie
CONTRIBUTING EDITORS AND TRANSLATORS	Lisa Chalykoff
	Neta Gordon
	Ian Johnston
	David Swain
CONTRIBUTING WRITERS	Laura Buzzard
	Andrew Reszitnyk
	Paul Johnston Byrne
	Tara Bodie

EDITORIAL CONTRIBUTORS

Tara Bodie	Bryanne Manveiler
Alicia Christianson	Amanda Mullen
Joel DeShaye	Virginia Philipson
Victoria Duncan	Anja Pujic
Rose Eckert-Jantzie	David Ross
Emily Farrell	Nora Ruddock
Travis Grant	Kate Sinclair
Karim Lalani	Jack Skeffington
Phil Laven	Helena Snopek
Kellen Loewen	Kaitlyn Till
Melissa MacAulay	Morgan Tunzelmann

PRODUCTION

PRODUCTION COORDINATOR:	Tara Lowes
PROOFREADERS:	Joe Davies
	Judith Earnshaw
	Michel Pharand
DESIGN AND TYPESETTING:	Eileen Eckert
PERMISSIONS COORDINATOR:	Merilee Atos
COVER DESIGN:	Michel Vrana

Contents

Preface   xvii
Acknowledgements   xix
The Study of Literature   xxi

SHORT FICTION

Introduction   1
Sir Thomas Malory (c. 1415–1471)
    from *Le Morte Darthur* (sites.broadviewpress.com/BIL)
Edgar Allan Poe (1809–1849)   16
    "The Black Cat"   16
Kate Chopin (1850–1904)   25
    "The Story of an Hour"   25
Guy de Maupassant (1850–1893)
    "The False Gems" (sites.broadviewpress.com/BIL)
Joseph Conrad (1857–1924)
    "The Secret Sharer" (sites.broadviewpress.com/BIL)
Anton Pavlovich Chekhov (1860–1904)
    "An Upheaval" (sites.broadviewpress.com/BIL)
Charlotte Perkins Gilman (1860–1935)   28
    "The Yellow Wallpaper"   28
Edith Wharton (1862–1937)   43
    "Atrophy"   43
Susan Glaspell (1876–1948)
    "A Jury of Her Peers" (sites.broadviewpress.com/BIL)
James Joyce (1882–1941)   53
    "Araby"   53
    "The Dead" (sites.broadviewpress.com/BIL)
Franz Kafka (1883–1924)
    "Metamorphosis" (sites.broadviewpress.com/BIL)
Katherine Mansfield (1888–1923)   59
    "The Garden Party"   59
Ernest Hemingway (1899–1961)   72
    "A Clean, Well-Lighted Place"   73
    "Hills Like White Elephants" (sites.broadviewpress.com/BIL)
Flannery O'Connor (1925–1964)   77
    "A Good Man Is Hard to Find"   77
Ursula K. Le Guin (1929–2018)   91
    "The Ones Who Walk Away from Omelas"   92
Chinua Achebe (1930–2013)   98
    "Dead Men's Path"   98

ALICE MUNRO (B. 1931)   102
    "Friend of My Youth"   102
ALISTAIR MACLEOD (1936–2014)   120
    "As Birds Bring Forth the Sun"   120
MARGARET ATWOOD (B. 1939)   127
    "Happy Endings"   127
THOMAS KING (B. 1943)   131
    "A Short History of Indians in Canada"   131
OCTAVIA BUTLER (1947–2006)   134
    "Speech Sounds"   134
HARUKI MURAKAMI (B. 1949)   147
    "On Seeing the 100% Perfect Girl One Beautiful April Morning"   147
IAN MCEWAN (B.1948)
    "Last Day of Summer" (sites.broadviewpress.com/BIL)
BARBARA GOWDY (B. 1950)   152
    "We So Seldom Look on Love"   152
ROHINTON MISTRY (B. 1952)   163
    "Squatter"   163
KAZUO ISHIGURO (B. 1954)   185
    "A Family Supper"   185
EDEN ROBINSON (B. 1968)   194
    "Terminal Avenue"   194
LYNN COADY (B. 1970)   202
    "Hellgoing"   202
LEANNE BETASAMOSAKE SIMPSON (B. 1971)   209
    "Big Water"   210
DAVID BEZMOZGIS (B. 1973)   213
    "Tapka"   213
HASSAN BLASIM (B. 1973)   225
    "The Nightmare of Carlos Fuentes"   225
ANDERS NILSEN (B. 1973)   232
    "Toward a Conceptual Framework for Understanding Your Individual
        Relationship to the Totality of the Universe in Four Simple Diagrams" 233
JONATHAN SAFRAN FOER (B. 1977)
    "A Primer for the Punctuation of Heart Disease" (sites.broadviewpress.com/BIL)

DRAMA

INTRODUCTION   239
SOPHOCLES (C. 496–C. 406 BCE)
    Oedipus the King (sites.broadviewpress.com/BIL)
WILLIAM SHAKESPEARE (1564–1616)
    Twelfth Night (sites.broadviewpress.com/BIL)
HENRIK IBSEN (1828–1906)   248
    A Doll's House   249
OSCAR WILDE (1854–1900)   309
    The Importance of Being Earnest   310

SHARON POLLOCK (B. 1936)   364
  Blood Relations   365
GEOFF KAVANAGH (B. 1961)
  Ditch (sites.broadviewpress.com/BIL)
HANNAH MOSCOVITCH (B. 1978)   413
  Essay   414

POETRY

INTRODUCTION   443
GEOFFREY CHAUCER (C. 1343–1400)
  from *The Canterbury Tales* (sites.broadviewpress.com/BIL)
SIR THOMAS WYATT (C. 1503–1542)   468
  ["The long love that in my thought doth harbour"]   468
  ["They flee from me that sometime did me seek"]   469
  ["Whoso list to hunt, I know where is an hind"]   470
SIR WALTER RALEGH (C. 1554–1618)   471
  "The Nymph's Reply to the Shepherd"   472
CHRISTOPHER MARLOWE (1564–1593)   473
  "The Passionate Shepherd to His Love"   473
WILLIAM SHAKESPEARE (1564–1616)   475
  Sonnets
    18 ["Shall I compare thee to a summer's day?"]   475
    29 ["When in disgrace with fortune and men's eyes"]   476
    73 ["That time of year thou mayst in me behold"]   476
    116 ["Let me not to the marriage of true minds"]   477
    130 ["My mistress' eyes are nothing like the sun"]   477
JOHN DONNE (1572–1631)   478
  "The Flea"   478
  from *Holy Sonnets*
    10 ["Death be not proud, though some have called thee"]   479
    14 ["Batter my heart, three personed God; for you"]   480
  "A Valediction: Forbidding Mourning"   480
LADY MARY WROTH (1587–1653?)   482
  from *Pamphilia to Amphilanthus*
    Song ["Love, a child, is ever crying"]   482
    77 ["In this strange labyrinth how shall I turn?"]   483
GEORGE HERBERT (1593–1633)   484
  "The Altar"   485
  "Easter Wings"   486
JOHN MILTON (1608–1674)   487
  "On Shakespeare"   487
  ["When I consider how my light is spent"]   488
  "Lycidas" (sites.broadviewpress.com/BIL)
ANNE BRADSTREET (1612–1672)   489
  "The Author to Her Book"   489

ANDREW MARVELL (1621–1678)   491
   "To His Coy Mistress"   491
ANNA LAETITIA BARBAULD (1743–1825)   494
   "The Caterpillar"   494
PHILLIS WHEATLEY (1753–1784)   496
   "On Being Brought from Africa to America"   496
WILLIAM BLAKE (1757–1827)   497
   from *Songs of Innocence*
      "The Lamb"   497
   from *Songs of Experience*
      "London"   499
WILLIAM WORDSWORTH (1770–1850)   500
   "Lines Written a Few Miles above Tintern Abbey" 501
   ["The world is too much with us"]   505
SAMUEL TAYLOR COLERIDGE (1772–1834)   506
   "Frost at Midnight"   506
   "Kubla Khan"   508
   "The Rime of the Ancient Mariner" (sites.broadviewpress.com/BIL)
GEORGE GORDON, LORD BYRON (1788–1824)
   "Darkness" (sites.broadviewpress.com/BIL)
PERCY BYSSHE SHELLEY (1792–1822)   511
   "Ozymandias"   511
   "Ode to the West Wind"   512
JOHN KEATS (1795–1821)   516
   "When I Have Fears that I May Cease to Be"   516
   "La Belle Dame sans Merci: A Ballad"   517
   "Ode to a Nightingale"   519
   "Ode on a Grecian Urn"   521
   "To Autumn"   523
ELIZABETH BARRETT BROWNING (1806–1861)   525
   from *Sonnets from the Portuguese*
      Sonnet 22 ["When our two souls stand up erect and strong"] 525
      Sonnet 24 ["Let the world's sharpness like a clasping knife"] 526
      Sonnet 43 ["How do I love thee? Let me count the ways"] 526
EDGAR ALLAN POE (1809–1849)   527
   "The Raven"   527
ALFRED, LORD TENNYSON (1809–1892)   531
   "The Lady of Shalott"   531
   "Ulysses"   537
   "The Charge of the Light Brigade"   539
ROBERT BROWNING (1812–1889)   542
   "My Last Duchess"   543
EMILY BRONTË (1818–1848)   545
   ["Ah! why, because the dazzling sun"]   545
   ["No coward soul is mine"]   547
   ["Often rebuked, yet always back returning"] 548

["I'll come when thou art saddest"] 549
WALT WHITMAN (1819–1892) 550
    from *Song of Myself*
      1 ["I celebrate myself, and sing myself"] 550
      "I Hear America Singing" 551
      "When I Heard the Learn'd Astronomer" 551
EMILY DICKINSON (1830–1886) 552
    249 ["Wild Nights—Wild Nights!"] 552
    288 ["I'm Nobody! Who are you?"] 553
    341 ["After great pain, a formal feeling comes"] 553
    465 ["I heard a Fly buzz—when I died"] 554
    712 ["Because I could not stop for Death"] 554
    754 ["My Life had stood—a Loaded Gun"] 555
    1129 ["Tell all the Truth but tell it slant"] 556
CHRISTINA ROSSETTI (1830–1894) 557
    "Goblin Market" 557
GERARD MANLEY HOPKINS (1844–1889) 574
    "God's Grandeur" 574
    "The Windhover" 575
W.B. YEATS (1865–1939) 576
    "Easter 1916" 576
    "The Second Coming" 579
    "Leda and the Swan" 580
    "Sailing to Byzantium" 580
PAUL LAURENCE DUNBAR (1872–1906) 582
    "We Wear the Mask" 582
ROBERT FROST (1874–1963) 583
    "The Road Not Taken" 583
    "Stopping by Woods on a Snowy Evening" 584
WALLACE STEVENS (1879–1955) 585
    "Thirteen Ways of Looking at a Blackbird" 585
MINA LOY (1882–1966)
    "Human Cylinders"
    "Gertrude Stein" (sites.broadviewpress.com/BIL)
WILLIAM CARLOS WILLIAMS (1883–1963) 588
    "The Red Wheelbarrow" 588
    "Spring and All" 589
    "This Is Just to Say" 589
    "Landscape with the Fall of Icarus" 590
EZRA POUND (1885–1972) 591
    "The River-Merchant's Wife: A Letter" 591
    "In a Station of the Metro" 592
MARIANNE MOORE (1887–1972) 593
    "Poetry" 593
    "Poetry" (revised version) 594

T.S. ELIOT (1888–1965)   595
   "The Love Song of J. Alfred Prufrock"   596
   "Journey of the Magi"   600
EDNA ST. VINCENT MILLAY (1892–1950)   602
   ["I, being born a woman and distressed"]   602
   ["What lips my lips have kissed, and where, and why"]   603
WILFRED OWEN (1893–1918)   604
   "Anthem for Doomed Youth"   604
   "Dulce et Decorum Est"   605
E.E. CUMMINGS (1894–1962)   606
   ["in Just–"]   606
   ["somewhere i have never travelled,gladly beyond"]   607
   ["anyone lived in a pretty how town"]   608
LANGSTON HUGHES (1902–1967)   610
   "The Negro Speaks of Rivers"   610
   "Harlem (2)"   611
STEVIE SMITH (1902–1971)   612
   "Not Waving but Drowning"   612
EARLE BIRNEY (1904–1995)   613
   "Vancouver Lights"   613
   "The Bear on the Delhi Road"   615
W.H. AUDEN (1907–1973)   616
   "Funeral Blues"   617
   "Musée des Beaux Arts"   617
   "September 1, 1939"   618
   "The Unknown Citizen"   621
THEODORE ROETHKE (1908–1963)   623
   "My Papa's Waltz"   623
   "I Knew a Woman"   624
ELIZABETH BISHOP (1911–1979)   626
   "Sestina"   626
   "First Death in Nova Scotia"   628
   "One Art"   629
DYLAN THOMAS (1914–1953)   631
   "Do Not Go Gentle into That Good Night"   631
P.K. PAGE (1916–2010)   633
   "The Stenographers"   633
   "Stories of Snow"   635
AL PURDY (1918–2000)   637
   "Trees at the Arctic Circle"   637
   "Lament for the Dorsets"   639
ALLEN GINSBERG (1926–1997)   642
   "A Supermarket in California"   642
ADRIENNE RICH (1929–2012)   644
   "Aunt Jennifer's Tigers"   644
   "Living in Sin"   645

"Diving into the Wreck" 645
TED HUGHES (1930–1998) 649
  "The Thought-Fox" 649
  "Pike" 650
DEREK WALCOTT (1930–2017) 652
  "A Far Cry from Africa" 652
ARUN KOLATKAR (1932–2004) 654
  "Yeshwant Rao" 654
  "Pictures from a Marathi Alphabet Chart" 657
SYLVIA PLATH (1932–1963) 659
  "Daddy" 660
  "Lady Lazarus" 662
LUCILLE CLIFTON (1936–2010) 666
  "miss rosie" 666
  "the lost baby poem" 667
MARGARET ATWOOD (B. 1939) 668
  "Death of a Young Son by Drowning" 668
  ["you fit into me"] 669
  "Variation on the Word *Sleep*" 670
FRANK BIDART (B. 1939) 671
  "Queer" 671
  "Half-Light" 673
SEAMUS HEANEY (1939–2013) 675
  "Digging" 675
  "Mid-Term Break" 677
  "The Grauballe Man" 678
  "Cutaways" 680
GWENDOLYN MACEWEN (1941–1987) 682
  "Dark Pines Under Water" 682
  "The Discovery" 683
SHARON OLDS (B. 1942) 684
  "The One Girl at the Boys Party" 684
  "Sex without Love" 685
EAVAN BOLAND (B. 1944) 686
  "Night Feed" 686
  "Against Love Poetry" 688
bpNICHOL (1944–1988) 689
  "Blues" 689
  ["dear Captain Poetry"] 690
TOM WAYMAN (B. 1945) 691
  "Did I Miss Anything?" 691
ROBERT BRINGHURST (B. 1946) 693
  "Leda and the Swan" 693
MARILYN NELSON (B. 1946) 696
  "Minor Miracle" 696

LORNA CROZIER (B. 1948)   698
    from *The Sex Lives of Vegetables*
        "Carrots"   698
        "Onions"   699
    "When I Come Again to My Father's House"   699
AGHA SHAHID ALI (1949–2001)   701
    "Postcard from Kashmir"   701
    "The Wolf's Postscript to 'Little Red Riding Hood'"   702
ANNE CARSON (B. 1950)   704
    from *Short Talks*
        "On Rain"   704
        "On Sylvia Plath"   705
        "On Walking Backwards"   705
LILLIAN ALLEN (B. 1951)   706
    "One Poem Town"   706
DIONNE BRAND (B. 1953)   708
    from *thirsty*
        30 ["Spring darkness is forgiving. It doesn't descend"]   708
        32 ["Every smell is now a possibility, a young man"]   709
LOUISE BERNICE HALFE (B. 1953)   710
    "*wêpinâson*"   711
    "*ê-kwêskît* — Turn-Around Woman"   711
HARRYETTE MULLEN (B. 1953)   714
    "Dim Lady"   714
    "Black Nikes"   715
    from *Muse & Drudge*
        ["marry at a hotel, annul 'em"]   716
KIM ADDONIZIO (B. 1954)   717
    "First Poem for You"   717
CAROL ANN DUFFY (B. 1955)   718
    "Drunk"   718
    "Crush"   719
MARILYN DUMONT (B. 1955)   720
    "Not Just a Platform for My Dance"   720
    "The White Judges"   721
RICHARD HARRISON (B. 1957)
    "On Not Losing My Father's Ashes in the Flood"
    "Cell Phone" (sites.broadviewpress.com/BIL)
LI-YOUNG LEE (B. 1957)   723
    "Persimmons"   723
GEORGE ELLIOTT CLARKE (B. 1960)   726
    from *Whylah Falls*
        "Blank Sonnet"   726
        "Look Homeward, Exile"   727
    "Casualties"   728

JACKIE KAY (B. 1961)   730
   "In My Country"   730
   "Her"   731
GREGORY SCOFIELD (B. 1966)   732
   "Not All Halfbreed Mothers"   733
   "Aunty"   734
   "Wrong Image"   736
KAREN SOLIE (B. 1966)   738
   "Sturgeon"   738
   "Nice"   739
   "Self-Portrait in a Series of Professional Evaluations"   740
ARUNDHATHI SUBRAMANIAM (B. 1967)   741
   "To the Welsh Critic Who Doesn't Find Me Identifiably Indian"   741
RITA WONG (B. 1968)   744
   "opium"   745
   "nervous organism"   746
VICTORIA CHANG (B. 1970)   747
   "Mr. Darcy"   747
SHARON HARRIS (B. 1972)   749
   "99. Where Do Poems Come From?"   749
   "70. Why Do Poems Make Me Cry?"   750
D'BI.YOUNG ANITAFRIKA (B. 1977)   751
   "self-esteem (ii)"   752
   "foreign mind/local body"   752
   "love speak"   754
HAI-DANG PHAN (B. 1980)   755
   "My Father's 'Norton Introduction to Literature,' Third Edition (1981)"   755
JORDAN ABEL (B. 1985)   758
   from *The Place of Scraps*   759

LITERARY NON-FICTION

INTRODUCTION   773
LUCIUS ANNAEUS SENECA (C. 4 BCE–65 CE)
   from Moral Letters to Lucilius (sites.broadviewpress.com/BIL)
MICHEL DE MONTAIGNE (1533–1592)
   "On Cannibals" (sites.broadviewpress.com/BIL)
JONATHAN SWIFT (1667–1745)   781
   "A Modest Proposal"   781
VIRGINIA WOOLF (1882–1941)   790
   "The Death of the Moth"   790
ZORA NEALE HURSTON (1891–1960)   793
   "How It Feels to Be Coloured Me"   794
GEORGE ORWELL (1903–1950)   798
   "Shooting an Elephant"   798
   "Politics and the English Language" (sites.broadviewpress.com/BIL)

RICHARD WAGAMESE (1955–2017)   805
    "Finding Father"   805
SCOTT MCCLOUD (B. 1960)   809
    from *Understanding Comics*   810
KAMAL AL-SOLAYLEE (B. 1964)   816
    from *Brown: What Being Brown in the World Today Means (to Everyone)*   816
MIRIAM TOEWS (B. 1964)   826
    "A Father's Faith"   827
IVAN COYOTE (B. 1969)   832
    "Tomboys Still"   832

GLOSSARY   837
PERMISSIONS ACKNOWLEDGEMENTS   863
INDEX OF FIRST LINES   871
INDEX OF AUTHORS AND TITLES   875

Preface

On hearing that Broadview was planning a new anthology designed to provide an overview of literature at the first-year level, more than a few people expressed surprise. What could a new anthology have to offer that really is different—that gives something new and valuable to academics and students alike? We hope that you will find your own answers to that question once you have looked through this volume. Certainly our intent has been to offer something that is in many ways different. We have brought fresh eyes to the process of choosing a table of contents; you'll find selections here that have not been widely anthologized elsewhere. You'll also find more visual material than in competing anthologies—including graphic literature such as Anders Nilsen's "Towards a Conceptual Framework." You'll also find a selection of literary non-fiction—a form that is increasingly being taken seriously as a literary genre, but that is passed over in most anthologies which purport to offer an overview of literature.

Although the emphasis of the anthology is very much on literature in English (in recognition of the reality that most "introduction to literature" courses in Canada are taught in English departments), we have included rather more literature in translation than is to be found in most competing anthologies.

Not everything about *The Broadview Introduction to Literature* is entirely new, of course. Many of the selections will, we hope, be familiar to instructors; as to which of the "old chestnuts" continue to work well in a teaching context, we have in large part been guided by the advice provided to us by academics at a variety of institutions across Canada. But even where familiar authors and selections are concerned, we think you'll find quite a bit here that is different. We have worked hard to pitch both the author introductions and the explanatory notes at a consistent level throughout—and, in both introductions and notes, to give students more by way of background.

For the second edition, we wanted to keep the same balance of fresh and familiar texts while making the anthology as a whole more contemporary and relevant. We have added more literature from the last twenty years in all genres, with a particular focus on contemporary Canadian writers; more world literature, both in English and in translation; more literature by Indigenous writers; more science fiction; and more graphic and illustrated literature.

Finally, you'll find fresh material posted on the companion website associated with the anthology. The site <http://sites.broadviewpress.com/BIL/> features additional material on many literary sub-genres and movements (from the sonnet to sound poetry, and from speculative fiction to microfiction); material on reading poetry (including exercises that will help those unfamiliar with the patterns of accentual-syllabic metre in English); material on writing essays about literature—and on referencing and citation; a much fuller glossary of literary terms than it is possible to include in these pages; self-test quizzes on the information provided in the introductions to the various genres; and several additional selections that we were unable to find space for in the bound book. Those looking to incorporate more long poems into a course will find several options on the website (including Milton's "Lycidas" and Coleridge's "The Rime of the Ancient Mariner"). Similarly, those looking to explore the borders of short fiction may find further examples of long short stories (or short novels) on the website—including Kafka's "Metamorphosis," Conrad's "The Secret Sharer," and Joyce's "The Dead." All are introduced and annotated according to the same principles and presented in the same format as the selections in the bound-book anthology. Those wishing to go beyond these choices for fiction—or for drama—may assign any one of the more than 300 volumes in the acclaimed Broadview Editions series, and we can arrange to have that volume bundled together with the bound-book anthology in a shrink-wrapped package, at little or no additional charge to the student.

Any of the genre volumes of the anthology may also be bundled together in special-price shrink-wrapped packages; whatever genres your course covers, and whatever works you would like to cover within those genres, we will do our best to put together a package that will suit your needs. (Instructors should note that, in addition to the main companion website of materials that may be of interest both to students and to instructors, we have posted instructor-related materials on a separate website.)

I do hope you will like what you see—and I hope as well that you will be in touch with any questions or suggestions; we will always be on the lookout for good ideas as to what we should add to the anthology's companion website—and/or for what we should look to include in the next edition of *The Broadview Introduction to Literature*.

[D.L., M.M.]

Acknowledgements

The General Editors, managing editors, and all of us at Broadview owe a debt of gratitude to the academics who have offered assistance and feedback at various stages of the project:

Thomas Allen
Rhonda Anderson
Trevor Arkell
Veronica Austen
John C. Ball
David Bentley
Gregory Betts
Shashi Bhat
Linda Van Netten Blimke
Nicholas Bradley
Chris Bundock
Sheila Burgar
Hilary Clark
David Clark
Jocelyn Coates
Richard Cole
Alison Conway
David Creelman
Heidi J. Tiedemann Darroch
Carrie Dawson
Celeste Daphne Derksen
Joel DeShaye
Lorraine DiCicco
Kerry Doyle
Monique Dumontet
Christopher Fanning
Sarah Fanning
Michelle Faubert
Triny Finlay
Rebecca Gagan
Jay Gamble

Dana Hansen
Alexander Hart
Ceilidh Hart
Linda Harwood
Chandra Hodgson
Kathryn Holland
Ashton Howley
Renee Hulan
Suzanne James
Kathleen James-Cavan
Karl Jirgens
Michelle Jordan
Kirk Layton
Diana Frances Lobb
Kathryn MacLennan
Shelley Mahoney
Rohan Maitzen
Laura Manning
Joanna Mansbridge
Mark McDayter
Elisabeth MacDonald-Murray
Lindsey McMaster
Susan McNeill-Bindon
Alexis McQuigge
Craig Melhoff
Bob Mills
Stephanie Morley
Maureen Moynagh
Andrew Murray
David Parkinson
Russell Perkin

Allan Pero

Mike Perschon

Kait Pinder

John Pope

Phyllis Rozendal

Cory Rushton

The Study of Literature

The Nobel Prize-winning physicist Paul Dirac reportedly said, "The aim of science is to make difficult things understandable in a simple way; the aim of poetry is to state simple things in an incomprehensible way." More recently, noted Language poet Charles Bernstein—whose work typically challenges the limits of simple comprehension—published the poem "Thank you for saying thank you," in which he explicitly takes up the issue of how poetry "states" things:

> This is a totally
> accessible poem.
> There is nothing
> in this poem
> that is in any
> way difficult.
> All the words
> are simple &
> to the point.

Though Bernstein's work is undoubtedly meant to register as ironic, both his poem and Dirac's comment draw attention to the idea that literature uses language in a peculiar way, and that one of the most fundamental questions readers of literature must ask themselves is: "How is this said?" Or—with apologies to Dirac—the question might be: "How do the language choices in this text make a seemingly simple thing—for example, a statement about love, or family, or justice, or grief—not incomprehensible, but rather more than just something simple?"

Another way of approaching the question of how literature works is to consider the way this anthology of literature is organized around the idea of genre, with texts chosen and categorized according to the way they fit into the classifications of poetry, short fiction, drama, and literary non-fiction. One way of organizing an introductory anthology of literature is the historical, in which selections are sorted from oldest to most recent, usually grouped together according to what have become acknowledged as distinctive historical periods of literary output. Another is the topical or thematic, in which historically and generically diverse selections are grouped together according to subject matter, so that students may compare differing attitudes toward, for example, gender relations, personal loss, particular historical events, or the process of growing up. The decision by an editor of an anthology—or the instructor of a course—to select one organizing principle over another is not arbitrary, but reflects a choice in terms of teaching students how to approach the reading of literature. In very simple terms, one might regard the three options thus: the historical configuration emphasizes discovering the "what" and "when" of literature—what is the body of written work that has come to be considered "literature" (especially in terms of tracing the outlines of a national literature), and when were examples from this distinguished corpus written? The thematic configuration emphasizes sorting through the "why" of literature—why do writers turn to literature to work through complex ideas, and what can we make of our complex responses to differing, often competing, stances on various topics? The generic configuration, finally, emphasizes the "how" of literature—how is the text put together? What are its working parts? How does an attention to the formal attributes of a literary piece help the reader understand the way it achieves its intellectual and emotional—its more than just simple—effects?

What do literary critics mean when they refer to genre? The word was introduced into the English language sometime in the late eighteenth century, borrowed from the French word *genre*, which means "kind" or "style" of art, as when the British agricultural reformer Arthur Young refers in his travel narratives to the "genre" of Dutch painting, which he finds wanting in comparison to the work of the Italian masters. We can look back further to the Latin root *genus*, or even the Greek γένος (*génos*), a term which also refers to the idea of a distinct family or clan; thus, the notion of "kind" might helpfully be thought of as a way of thinking about resemblances, relationships, and keys to recognition among the literary genres. Another helpful analogy is the way biologists have taken up the term *genus* as part of the taxonomy of organisms. The term *genus felis*, for example, refers to a particular order of small cats, including such species as the domestic cat (*felis catus*) and the wildcat (*felis silvestris*); both species share common generic attributes, such as a similar size and a preferred diet of small rodents. For biologists and literary critics alike, the concept of genus or genre, respectively, is used to group things together according to a system of shared, identifiable features, with both terms allowing for the idea that larger groupings can be further broken down into even more specific ones (thus we can refer to the various breeds of domestic cats, or the distinctions among the Petrarchan, Shakespearean, and Spenserian sonnets).

Biologists tend to use the word "characteristics" to designate the features of a genus; literary critics, on the other hand, make use of the word "convention," a somewhat more complicated term. Like *characteristics*, the term *conventions* refers to distinguishing elements of a genre, which is why the study of literature requires a thorough understanding of the specialized descriptive vocabulary used to discuss such elements as a text's metre, its narrative point of view, its use of figurative language, etc. The introductions to each section of this anthology will draw attention to this specialized vocabulary, and students will also want to refer to the extensive glossary of literary terms located at the end of the anthology. The idea of convention, though, has additional conceptual importance relating to the way texts are built to be read. While a domestic cat is simply born with retractable claws and a taste for mice, a literary text is constructed, written in a particular way, often with the aim of eliciting a particular response from a reader. The word convention, in this sense, harks back to the legal concept of agreement, so that when writers make use of conventions associated with a genre, they set up a kind of contract with the reader whereby the reader has a sense of what to expect from the text. For example: when the first five minutes of a film include a long shot of the Pentagon, along with a few quickly edited shots of grim-looking military personnel moving quickly through underground hallways, and perhaps a shot of someone in a dark suit yelling into a cellphone, "Operation Silvestris has been aborted!" the audience understands that they are in for some sort of political thriller. They need not know anything about the details of Operation Silvestris to make this interpretive leap, as the presence of a few conventions of the political thriller (the shot of the Pentagon, the phrase "Operation [blank] has been aborted!") are enough to provide the general outline of a contract entered into between film and audience. Likewise, recognizing that a poem has 14 lines and makes use of a rhyming couplet at the end will provide knowledgeable readers of literature with an inkling as to what they should expect, as these readers will be familiar with the structural conventions of the Shakespearean sonnet.

Whereas a legal contract is a fairly straightforward affair—it outlines the terms of agreement for both sides and more or less explicitly refers to the penalties for undermining those terms—the contract between text and reader is multifaceted. One of the most fascinating things about the way writers make use of literary convention is that the terms of agreement are constantly subject to further consideration, thoughtful challenge, or outright derision. Thus, when the speaker of Shakespeare's sonnet 130 refers to his lady's "dun" breasts and "reek[ing]" breath, the point is not to insult his mistress, or even to admire her in a new, more realistic way; rather, the point is to ridicule the way other poets slavishly adhere to the convention that sonnets glorify a woman's beauty, comparing her eyes to the sun and her breath to the smell of roses. This reading is available for the reader who knows that by the time

Shakespeare decided to try his hand at the genre, translations and imitations of the Petrarchan sonnet had been circulating at the Elizabethan court for many decades. Like organisms, or even laws, conventions of literature evolve over time as writers seek to rethink the rules of the form they wish to explore. The speaker in Lillian Allen's "One Poem Town," warns an imaginary writer: "keep it kool! kool! kool! / on the page / 'cause, if yu bring one in / any other way / we'll shoot you with metaphors." Here, Allen—a writer of experimental poetry—both shows and reflects on the way the conventions of genre can create a set of expectations about what constitutes "proper" literature, and how those expectations can be tested.

Is it somehow problematic to inquire too tenaciously into the working parts of a literary text? Does one risk undermining the emotional force of a poem, the sharp wit of a play, or the exciting plot of an adventure tale if one pays too much attention to seemingly mundane issues of plot structure or metre? To paraphrase a common grievance of the distressed student: by examining the way literature works, are we, somehow, just wrecking it? These questions might, paradoxically, recall Dirac's complaint that literature makes simple things incomprehensible: while we know that literature can manage to communicate difficult notions, making what is mysterious more comprehensible, it is often difficult to articulate or make a viable argument about how it does so. By paying attention to the way a text is built and to the way an author constructs his or her end of the contract, the reader can begin to understand and respond explicitly to the question of how literature produces its particular effects.

Consider the following two textual excerpts:

> Come live with me and be my love,
> And we will all the pleasures prove.
> (Christopher Marlowe, 1590)

> Boom, boom, boom, let's go back to my room,
> And we can do it all night, and you can make me feel right.
> (Paul Lekakis, 1987)

Based on a quick reading, which excerpt is more appropriate for inclusion in a Valentine's Day card? A poll of employees at Hallmark, not to mention the millions of folks invested in the idea that Valentine's Day is a celebration of romance, would likely make an overwhelming case for the Marlowe excerpt. But why? Answering that question might involve a methodological inquiry into how each excerpt produces a particular response, one which might be broken down into five stages:

Level One: Evaluation—Do I like this text? What is my gut reaction to it?
No doubt, most students of literature have heard an instructor proclaim, with
more or less vitriol, "It doesn't matter if you like the poem/story/play! This
is a literature class, not a book club!" And, while it is true that the evaluative
response does not constitute an adequate final critical response to a text, it's
important to acknowledge one's first reaction. After all, the point of literature
is to produce an effect, sometimes an extreme response. When a text seems
confusing, or hilarious, or provocative, or thrilling, it prompts questions: How
are such effects produced using mere words in particular combinations? Why
would an author want to generate feelings of confusion, hilarity, provocation,
etc.? How am I—the reader—being positioned on the other end of such effects?

Level Two: Interpretation—What is the text about? This is a trickier level
of reading than it might seem. Students sometimes think, mistakenly, that
all literature—and especially poetry—is "open to interpretation," and that all
interpretations are therefore correct. This line of thinking leads to snap, top-
down interpretations, in which the general "mood" of the text is felt at a gut
level (see above), and the ensuing reading of the poem is wrangled into shape
to match that feeling. It is sometimes helpful to think about interpretation
as a kind of translation, as in the way those who work at the United Nations
translating talking points from Arabic to Russian are called "interpreters."
Though no translation is flawless, the goal of simultaneous translation is to
get as close as possible to the meaning of the original. Thus, an interpretation
should be thought of as a carefully paraphrased summary or, for particularly
dense works, a line by line explication of the literary text, both of which may
require several rereadings and some meticulous use of a dictionary. As with
reading for evaluation, reading for interpretation can help generate useful critical questions, such as: How does the way this text is written affect my attitude
toward the subject matter? What is the point of all the fancy language, which
makes this text more or less difficult to interpret? Now that I've figured out
what this text is about—at least in terms of its subject matter—can I begin to
determine what sorts of themes are being tackled?

A note about the distinction between subject matter and **theme**: while
these terms are sometimes used interchangeably, the notion of theme differs
from subject matter in that it implies an idea about or attitude toward the
subject matter. A good rule of thumb to remember is that theme can never be
summed up in just one word (so, there is no such thing as the theme of "Love"
or "Family" or "Women"). Whereas the subject matter of Shakespeare's sonnet
"Shall I compare thee to a summer's day" is admiration or the nature of beauty,
one theme of the poem, arguably, is that the beloved's good qualities are best

made apparent in poetry, and that art is superior to nature. Another theme of the poem, arguably, is that the admiration of youth is best accomplished by someone older. Thus, identifying a text's subject matter via interpretation aims to pinpoint a general topic, while the process of contemplating a text's theme is open to elaboration and argumentation.

Level Three: Description—What does the text look like, at least at first glance? Can you give a quick account of its basic formal features? At this level of reading, one starts to think about how a text is built, especially in terms of basic generic features. For example, are we dealing with poetry? Short fiction? Drama? If poetry, can we identify a sub-genre the text fits into—for instance, the sonnet, the ode, or the elegy—and can we begin to assess whether the author is following or challenging conventions associated with that genre? Of course, answering these questions requires prior knowledge of what, for example, a conventional ode is supposed to look like, which is why the student of literature must have a thorough understanding of the specific terminology associated with the discipline. At this level of reading, one might also begin to think about and do some preliminary research on when and where the text was written, so that the issues of literary history and cultural context are broached; likewise, one might begin to think about who is writing the poem, as the matter of the author's societal position might prove a fruitful avenue for further investigation. Thus, a consequent objective at this level of reading is to map the terrain of inquiry, establishing some general facts about the text as building blocks that underpin critical analysis.

Level Four: Analysis—How are particular formal features working, especially as they interact with content? The word analysis comes from the Greek terms ανά- (ana-), meaning "throughout," and λύειν (lysis), meaning "to loose." Thus, the procedure for analysis involves taking a text and shaking it apart in order to see more clearly all its particular bits and pieces. This level of reading is akin to putting a text under a microscope. First, one has to identify individual formal features of the text. Then one needs to consider how all the parts fit together. It is at this level that one's knowledge of generic conventions and particular literary techniques—the way figurative language works, the ways in which rhythm and rhyme affect our response to language, the way plotting and point of view can be handled, and so on—is crucial. It may be the case that not everything one notices will find its way into an essay. But the goal at this level of reading should be to notice as much as possible (and it is usually when working at this level that an instructor will be accused of "reading too much into a text," as if that image of a moth beating its wings against a window means nothing more than that the moth is trapped, and that it just happens to have been included in a work). Careful analysis shows that nothing in a text "just happens" to be there. A text is constructed out of special uses of language that beg to be "read into." Reading at this level takes time and a certain amount of expertise so as to tease out how the work is built and begin to understand the connections between form and content.

Level Five: Critical Analysis—How do the formal elements of a literary work connect with what the work has to say to the reader? It is at this level of reading that one begins to make an argument, to develop a thesis. In order to construct a viable thesis, one needs to answer a question, perhaps one of the questions that arose at an earlier level of reading. For example, why does this poem, which seems on the surface to be about love, make use of so many images that have to do with science? What is up with this narrator, who seems to be addressing another character without in any way identifying who he is speaking to? What is significant about the fact that the climax of this play hangs on the matter of whether a guy is willing to sell a portrait? It is at this level of reading, rather than at the level of interpretation, that the literary critic is able to flex his or her creative muscles, as a text poses any number of viable questions and suggests any number of viable arguments. Note, however, that the key word here is "viable." In order to make an argument—in order to convincingly answer a question posed—one must have the textual evidence to make the case, evidence that has been gleaned through careful, meticulous, and thoughtful reading.

Returning now to the two texts, let's see if we can come up with one viable argument as to why Marlowe's text seems more likely to show up in a Valentine's Day card, going through each level of reading to build the foundation—the case—for making that argument.

Level One: Evaluation. At first glance, the Marlowe text just seems more romantic than the Lekakis text: it uses flowery words and has a nice flow to it, while the phrase "do it all night" is kind of blunt and unromantic. On a gut level, one might feel that a Valentine's Day card should avoid such blunt language (although this gut reaction might suggest a first useful research question: why should romance be associated with flowery language rather than blunt expressions?).

Moving on to **Level Two: Interpretation.** Well, the Lekakis text is certainly the more straightforward one when it comes to interpretation, though one has to know that the phrase "do it" refers to having sex as opposed to some other activity (and it is interesting to note that even in the more straightforward text, the author has used a common euphemism). The phrase "Boom boom boom" seems to be untranslatable, which begs the question of why the author used it. Is the phrase still meaningful, even if it's just a series of sounds?

As for the Marlowe text, a careful paraphrase would go something like this: "Move in with me and be my lover, and we can enjoy all kinds of pleasures together." Hmmm—wait a minute: what does the author mean by "pleasures"? Eating good food? Playing card games? Though the word is arguably vague, the references in the first line to moving in together and love make it pretty clear that "pleasures" is another euphemism for having sex (though perhaps a more elegant one than "doing it").

If both texts can be interpreted similarly—both are the words of a would-be lover trying to convince the object of his/her affection to have sex—why does it matter which phrase ends up in a Valentine's Day card? What are the significant differences between each text that cause them to generate distinct gut responses?

Level Three: Description. The Marlowe text, at least this piece of it, is a **couplet**, written in iambic **tetrameter** (or eight syllables in each line that follow the rhythmic pattern of unstressed/stressed). The language is flowery, or, to use a slightly more technical phrase, the **diction** is elevated, which means that this is not the way people normally talk in everyday life. In fact, there seems to have been a lot of attention paid to making the words sound pleasing to the ear, through patterns of rhythm and rhyme, and also through patterns of alliteration in the consonants (of the soft "l" sound in the first line, and then of powerful plosives at the end of the second).

The Lekakis text also makes use of rhyme, but in a different way: each line includes an **internal rhyme**, so that "boom" rhymes with "room" and "night" rhymes with "right." The rhythmic pattern is harder to make sense of, as there is a different number of syllables in each line and a lot of short, sharp words that undermine a sing-song effect. The sound effects of the text are comparatively harsher than in the Marlowe text, with many "b" and "k" and "t" sounds.

The Marlowe text was written in the 1590s, while the Lekakis text is a popular dance song from the 1980s; it might be interesting to follow up on the distinct cultural contexts out of which each work emerges. It might also be interesting to examine how each text thematizes the subject of having sex: whereas the Marlowe text seems to promote the attitude that the "pleasures" of sex should be tried out (to "prove" in sixteenth-century English meant to test or to try out) within the context of "living with" someone, or that love and sex go hand-in-hand, the Lekakis text seems to suggest that even sex on one "night" in someone's "room" can make one feel "right." Or, good sex has nothing at all to do with love.

Because these texts are so short and are fairly simple, much of the work of **Level Four: Analysis** has already been touched on. A closer inspection of the use of rhyme and **alliteration** in the Marlowe text demonstrates the way the poem insists on the idea that love can be "proved" by sex, while the internal rhyming of the words "me," "be," and "we" further indicates a strong emphasis on how the joining of two people represents a significant change. The use of elevated diction is consistent, suggesting that discussions of love and sex are worthy of serious consideration.

As for the Lekakis text, a major point to analyze is the phrase "Boom boom boom." Is this **onomatopoeia**? If so, what "sense" is the sound trying to express? The sound of sex? If so, what kind of sex are we talking about here? Or is it the sound of something else, perhaps dancing (as is suggested by the cultural context out of which the text emerges)? Maybe the phrase is simply meant to express excitement? What do we make of the plain speech the text employs? Does the use of such diction debase notions of sex, or is it simply more candid about the way sex and love might be separated?

As you can see, the level of **Critical Analysis**, or argument, is quickly and organically developing. If the research question one decides on is, What is interesting about the distinct way each text thematizes the relationship between love and sex?, a viable argument, based on evidence gleaned from close reading, might be: "Whereas Marlowe's text suggests that the pleasures of sex are best discovered within the context of a stable, long-term relationship, the text by Lekakis asserts that sex can be enjoyed in and of itself, undermining the importance of the long-term relationship." One might take this argument further. Why is what you have noted significant or particularly interesting? A possible answer to that question—and an even more sophisticated thesis—might be: "Thus, while the Lekakis text is, on the surface, less romantic, its attitude toward sex is much less confining than the attitude presented in Marlowe's text." Or, one might pursue an entirely different argument: "Whereas Marlowe's text indicates that sex is to be enjoyed mutually by two people, the Lekakis text implies that sex is something one 'does' to another person. Further, it implies that sex is a fairly meaningless and potentially aggressive activity."

The above description of the steps taken toward critical analysis shows how students of literature are meant to approach the works they read. What the description does not convey is why one would bother to make the effort at all, or why the process of critical literary analysis is thought to be a meaningful activity. In order to answer that question, it is helpful to consider how the discipline of literary studies came to be considered a worthwhile course of study for university and college students.

The history of literary studies is both very old and, in terms of the study of English literature, very fresh. In the fifth century, Martianus Capella wrote the allegory *De nuptiis Philologiae et Mercurii* ("The Marriage of Philology and Mercury"), in which he described the seven pillars of learning: grammar, dialectic, rhetoric, geometry, arithmetic, astronomy, and musical harmony. Collectively, such subjects came to be referred to as the liberal arts; as such, they were taken up by many of the high medieval universities as constituting the core curriculum. During the Early Modern period, the study of the so-called *trivium* (grammar, dialectic, rhetoric) was transformed to include the critical analysis of classical texts, i.e., the study of literature. As universities throughout Europe, and later in North America, proliferated and flourished between the sixteenth and nineteenth centuries, the focus remained on classical texts. As Gerald Graff explains, "In theory, the study of Greek and Latin was supposed to inspire the student with the nobility of his cultural heritage." Somewhat paradoxically, classical texts were studied primarily in terms of their language use as opposed to their literary quality, perhaps because no one read or spoke Greek or Latin outside the classroom. Until the late nineteenth century, the university system did not consider literary works written in English (or French or German or Italian) to be worthy of rigorous study, but only of *appreciation*. As Terry Eagleton notes in *Literary Theory: An Introduction*, the reading of works of English Literature was thought best left to working-class men, who might attend book clubs or public lectures, and to women; it was "a convenient sort of non-subject to palm off on the ladies, who were in any case excluded from science and the professions." It was only in the early twentieth century—hundreds of years after the founding of the great European universities—that literature came to be taken seriously as a university or college subject.

Over the past century and more, the discipline of literary studies has undergone a number of shifts. In the very early twentieth century, literature was studied largely for the way in which it embodied cultural tradition; one would learn something about being American or British by reading so-called great works of literature. As British subjects, Canadians were also taught what it was to be a part of the British tradition. By mid-century the focus had shifted to the aesthetic properties of the work itself. This fresh approach was known as Formalism and/or the New Criticism. Its proponents advocated paying close attention to literary form—in some cases, for an almost scientific approach to close reading. They tended to de-emphasize authorial biography and literary history. The influence of this approach continues to be felt in university and college classrooms (giving rise to such things as, for example, courses organized around the concept of literary genre). But it is important to keep in mind here that the emphasis on form—on generic conventions, on literary terminology, on the aesthetic as opposed to the cultural, philosophical, or moral qualities of literature—is not the only way to approach the study of literature, but was, rather, institutionalized as the best, most scholarly way. The work of close reading and producing literary criticism is not in any way "natural," but is how the study of literature has been "disciplined"; thus the student in a literature classroom should not feel discouraged if the initial steps of learning what it is he or she is supposed to be doing are challenging or seem strange.

The most recent important shift to have occurred in the "disciplining" of literary studies was the rise in the 1960s and 1970s of what became known as "literary theory." There is not room enough here to adequately elucidate the range of theories that have been introduced into literary studies, but a crude comparison between how emerging methods were set in opposition to New Criticism (which is itself a type of literary theory) may be useful. John Crowe Ransom's *The World's Body*—a sort of manifesto for New Criticism—argues that the work of the literary critic must strenuously avoid, among other things, "Any other special studies which deal with some abstract or prose content taken out of the work ... [such as] Chaucer's command of medieval sciences ... [or] Shakespeare's understanding of the law." In other words, the New Critic should focus solely on the text itself. In contrast, those today who make use of such theoretical frameworks as New Historicism, Gender Studies, or Postcolonial Studies will strenuously *embrace* all manner of "special studies" in order to consider how the text interacts with context. As Anne Stevens points out in *Literary Theory and Criticism*, "A cornerstone of literary theory is a belief in the cultural construction of knowledge ... literary theory gives you a way to step back and think about the constructedness of culture and reflect upon your own preconceptions." For the student of literature trying to work out how to answer the question: "Why is what I have noticed in the text significant?", literary theory provides an extensive set of vocabularies and methodologies. For example: a New Historicist or a Marxist approach might help a student inquire into how a particular poem illuminates historical notions of class divisions. A Gender Studies approach might be useful for an examination of what a particular play can tell us about changing conceptions of masculinity. A Semiotic approach might consider the complex set of meaning systems gestured toward in the image of a police uniform described in a science fiction story. And, though it might seem that the focus on form that so defines the New Critical approach becomes irrelevant once Literary Theory arrives on the disciplinary scene, the fact is that most field practitioners (i.e., writers of literary criticism) still depend heavily on the tools of close reading; formal analysis becomes the foundation on which a more theoretical analysis is built.

Thus, we might consider a sixth level of reading: advanced critical analysis. At this level the stakes are raised as arguments about why a text's formal construction is meaningful are set within a larger conceptual framework. The work of advanced critical analysis requires that the literary critic think about and research whatever conceptual framework is being pursued. For example, after noticing that the Marlowe text and the Lekakis text are written about 400 years apart, one might further research cultural attitudes toward sex in the two time periods to come up with another, even more sophisticated layer of argumentation, one which would not only provide insight into two literary texts, but show how the comparative analysis of such texts tells us something about how viewpoints on sex have shifted. Or, after noticing that both texts are written by male authors, one might further research and consider what they reveal about masculine approaches to sex and seduction. Or, after discovering that Marlowe's poem follows the conventions of **pastoral** poetry, or that "Boom boom boom, let's go back to my room" became popular within the LGBT community, one might contemplate and develop an argument about the implications of the way sex is idealized and/or becomes part of a complex cultural fantasy. Or, after discovering that Marlowe presented homoerotic material frequently in his other writing (in his poem "Hero and Leander," for example, he writes of one of the male protagonists that "in his looks were all that men desire"), one might inquire into the ways in which the author's or narrator's sexual orientation may or may not be relevant to a discussion of a love poem. To put it bluntly (and anachronistically), does it matter if Marlowe was gay?

Because the reading of literature entails a painstaking, thoughtful interaction with some of the most multifaceted, evocative, and provocative uses of language humans have produced, thinking about such work critically may tell us something about what it means to be human.

[N.G.]

Short Fiction

History

It's hard to imagine a time when people didn't tell stories. There is something close-to-magical about their capacity to capture and transport us. The Cherokee-Greek author Thomas King makes an even bolder claim about stories in his 2003 Lecture Series, *The Truth about Stories*, when he declares, "the truth about stories is that that's all we are." Although this may sound extreme, King has a point: stories are indeed a key way we root ourselves to the past and establish our identities in the present. King, for example, shares an "Earth Diver" story, which is a kind of story that has been passed orally between First Nations for millennia to explain not only how the earth came to be, but the relationships between the various beings who make up the world. As he points out, Earth Diver stories are an oral version of the more general origin story, and all people have these. King illustrates how his Earth Diver story, for example, is both similar to and different from the earliest books of the Bible. These stories, credited to Moses and dating back to around 400 BCE, also explain how the world came to be (in Genesis) and how the Jewish people escaped slavery (in Exodus). Every culture, like most families and most individuals, has its foundational stories, stories that are used to establish origins and explain what makes us who we are.

The short stories collected here are a modern incarnation of this fundamental story-telling impulse, one with a history that is both shorter and more culturally specific than that of the origin story. The short story—if we understand it as a genre of prose fiction that authors have been conscious of producing and consciously trying to understand—came into being quite rapidly in the nineteenth century, in both America and Europe, with writers such as Washington Irving, Nathaniel Hawthorne, and Edgar Allan Poe (in America), and Honoré de Balzac, Anton Chekhov, and E.T.A. Hoffmann (in Europe). Why would this genre have come into being so suddenly in both America and Europe? For one thing, more and more people were learning to read, and were reading for pleasure; not surprisingly, easily accessible and affordable forms of writing, such as newspapers and magazines, rose to feed this new readership's hunger. The short story was ideally suited to these venues: it is compact, discrete, and entertaining. This history reflects the fact that short fiction is a dynamic literary form, one that quickly echoes social and cultural change.

The flexibility of short fiction may also explain why this genre has, from its earliest years, accommodated so many literary styles and forms of experimentation. In the early 1800s Hoffmann used it as a means of giving expression to surrealism—a movement that sought to channel the unconscious mind, with its myriad images and seemingly nonsensical connections. The modernists Virginia Woolf and Katherine Mansfield both used short fiction to express the modernist's fascination with human consciousness, making a close study of the many levels of perception—conscious, unconscious, sensual, emotional—in a style of writing that sought to capture the full "stream" of human consciousness, as the philosopher William James put it (see "The Garden Party" for an example of this form of writing). The American writer Edgar Allan Poe used short fiction to bring forth some of the darkest elements and impulses of the human mind, anticipating Freud's theories of guilt and the unconscious in ways that lead quite rapidly to the flourishing traditions of the mystery and the psychological thriller (see "The Black Cat" for a macabre study of psychological guilt). Another field of literature with deep roots in short fiction is regionalism, a kind of writing that focuses on the particular characteristics of a place and the human culture it helps shape. Some of the best-loved examples of literary regionalism are short stories; Flannery O'Connor's "A Good Man Is Hard to Find" and Alistair MacLeod's "As Birds Bring Forth the Sun" are two excellent examples. Authors have also used this genre to think through and ask us to imagine worlds other than our own—a kind of writing broadly termed speculative fiction. We include several examples here: Ursula K. Le Guin's "The Ones Who Walk Away from Omelas," Octavia Butler's "Speech Sounds," Eden Robinson's "Terminal Avenue," and Leanne Betasamosake Simpson's "Big Water" all imagine alternate worlds in ways that encourage us to view our own worlds anew, and often in newly-critical ways.

Short Fiction: Some Defining Characteristics

No one has ever fixed on a tidy definition of short fiction (or the novel), and this is largely because of the genre's diversity. The only characteristics a piece of writing *must* have to be classified as short fiction are the two captured in its name: it must be relatively *short*, and it must be *fiction*.

How short is short? There is no rule for this, but there is a great rule of thumb, one that Poe introduced in his review of Hawthorne's *Twice-Told Tales* in the genre's early days: one of the quintessential features of short fiction is that readers can consume it in a single sitting; if we can't read a story all at once (barring breaks to answer the telephone or make a cup of tea), then it isn't really a short story: it's moving toward the novella or, more typically, the novel. The longest story we've included here is Rohinton Mistry's "Squatter," at about 10,000 words.

The brevity of short fiction also helps to explain what many—including Poe—see as another key characteristic of a successful short story: that it possess a certain singularity of purpose. Poe thought that a proper short story should be crafted from its first sentence to create a very specific effect on the reader. As he put it back in 1842,

> A skilful literary artist has constructed a tale. If wise, he has not fashioned his thoughts to accommodate his incidents; but having conceived, with deliberate care, a certain unique or single effect to be wrought out, he then invents such incidents—he then combines such events as may best aid him in establishing this preconceived effect. If his very initial sentence tend [sic] not to the out-bringing of this effect, then he has failed in his first step. In the whole composition there should be no word written, of which the tendency, direct or indirect, is not to the one pre-established design.

These days few would claim that *all* short story writers begin with an effect they want to create and then choose characters, events, and language to bring it about. And we're certainly less preoccupied with an author's intentions these days than people were back in Poe's time (critics now being more likely to think of a text as a thing with a life of its own that extends beyond the author's thoughts about it). But there is something in Poe's statement that remains as true today as it was then: good short stories tend to have a relatively tight focus. While a novel can develop many characters and include many plot lines, the brevity of the short story encourages a much tidier approach. To give just one example, many short stories focus on the development of a single human relationship over time; in this collection, Alice Munro's "Friend of My Youth," Octavia Butler's "Speech Sounds," and Lynn Coady's "Hellgoing" all have a human relationship at their centre.

Yet my characterization of these stories as being about a specific relationship is an act of critical judgement: there is always more than one way to articulate the focus of a story. Such efforts are attempts to isolate a central theme in a work, a **theme** being an abstract concept that is made concrete in fiction through characters, actions, images, dialogue, etc. In order to be fully developed, however, a theme must go beyond naming the concept (e.g., "love") and assert what the work is saying about it (e.g., "love hurts"). Though some themes are more central than others, it's important to note that no work of literature has just one. To illustrate this, let's take another look at two of the stories mentioned above. While many might argue that the human ability (or inability) to communicate is central to "Speech Sounds," others might prioritize themes relating to gender, the environment, memory, and hope. Similarly, while Lynn Coady explores the nature of family obligations in "Hellgoing," she also asks us to think about feminism, friendship, aging, and academic life. In sum, though short stories often gain some of their elegance and artistic unity through a singularity of focus, the business of articulating this focus very quickly moves us from description to thematic analysis.

We've now considered some of the ways the "short" of "short fiction" gives this genre certain distinctive characteristics. The "fiction" element of "short fiction" clearly isn't as important in trying to understand the distinctive features of this genre—novels are fiction, too. But the fictional element is at least as important in helping us understand how short stories create meaning and inspire responses in readers. A key element in almost all prose **fiction**, whether we're dealing with a novel or a short story, is that it tells a story, and an invented one at that. For many years fictional narratives were defined in opposition to non-fictional narratives: while fiction tells us made-up stories, the theory went, non-fiction is based on real historical events. Over the last few decades, literary critics and historians alike have become more aware of how much is shared by fictional and non-fictional narratives: for example, both rely on the author's imagination to select, arrange, and prioritize events and the "characters" who enact them in very particular ways. In other words, there is much invention at play in any narrative, whether based on real or made-up events. The line separating the fictional and the non-fictional is one that continues to be questioned and debated by theorists, critics, and writers of our own day. Here we include works that purposefully trouble the line between fiction and non-fiction, and in both, the non-fictional content comes from the writers' own lives. For example, in "Towards a Conceptual Framework for Understanding Your Relationship to the Entire Universe in Four Simple Diagrams," Anders Nilsen presents what he calls a "universal memoir" that takes events from his own life and situates them within an imaginative, graphic context that asks some fascinating questions about where a life begins and ends. This work makes bold use of form to draw attention to the various parts that compose their totalities, and in so doing, Nilsen encourages us to go beyond simply absorbing stories, and to think about how they are made.

Making Short Stories:
The Selection and Manipulation of Events

Most of us have probably encountered friends who aren't particularly good storytellers; maybe they leave out necessary details or, conversely, ramble on at such length that we lose interest in the story. Short story writers need many of the same skills as those of us who can spin a good tale orally. They need to be particularly adept at two things: selecting which events to include and ordering them in a way that sparks and sustains a reader's interest.

Over the years authors and scholars have developed a number of terms and distinctions to name the ways writers organize narratives. For example, novelist E.M. Forster came up with the useful distinction between **story** and **plot** to help us think about how we use time to organize narrative information: while a story is the chronological unfolding of the events that compose a narrative, the plot is the result of an author's manipulation of these events. Thus we say that the events of a narrative are *plotted*. Sometimes the plot follows the chronological order of the story. This is the case in Katherine Mansfield's "The Garden Party": we follow the day's happenings as they unfold, beginning with breakfast and preparations for the party, proceeding to the party itself (which gets quite brief treatment, interestingly), and ending with Laura's evening trip to the grieving widow (notice how wonderfully the fading of day coincides with the darkening of mood here). In contrast, Barbara Gowdy's "We So Seldom Look on Love" moves back and forth from the protagonist's childhood to her recent past and present. Such plotting almost always emphasizes causality—it uses the past to in some way *explain* the present.

Another effect that can be created by manipulating the order in which we receive information is **suspense**, our anticipation of an outcome of events. Think of how Flannery O'Connor's "A Good Man Is Hard to Find" pulls readers along by first presenting The Misfit as a notorious figure in the newspaper—hardly more than an idea, really—and slowly but surely drawing him closer and closer into the lives of the Grandmother and her family. As is often the case, ambiguity is a key ingredient in the creation of suspense here: it's our uncertainty, first about the identity of the stranger—*is* he The Misfit? No, surely not—and then about the nature of this man's character—just how good or bad a man is he? Would he do that? No, surely not—that propels us forward in anticipation that answers will be given.

A field of literary criticism called narratology has developed a number of useful terms for naming particular ways that authors organize and present the events in a narrative. **Analepsis**, for example, is a shift backward in time (a technique also known as a flashback) and is routinely used by short story writers to create history for characters and events. **Prolepsis**—a sudden movement ahead to future time, also known as a flashforward—is used less frequently in short fiction. We see an interesting example of it in Eden Robinson's "Terminal Avenue": as the narrator describes the family's last potlatch on Monkey Beach, this voice states, "This will happen in four hours when they land." In this seemingly simple statement we in fact see analepsis and prolepsis combined—we're being given a flashforward within a memory. Here Robinson provides a great illustration of the paradox that, while it's sometimes complex to clearly express how time is manipulated in narratives, such shifts in time are a simple facet of life: the human mind is wonderfully adept at roving back and forth through time, putting events together for itself.

Sometimes authors choose to embed one story within another, thus creating what is called an **embedded narrative**: a story within a story. Rohinton Mistry's "Squatter" is an embedded narrative: what we encounter in the story is an unidentified narrator telling us the story of Nariman Hansotia, who is himself telling various stories, but centrally the story of the migrant Sarosh, to the boys of Firozsha Baag (an apartment complex in Mumbai). As this description illustrates, embedded narratives are more structurally complex, and this complexity can create certain effects. For example, embedding one narrative within another inevitably makes storytelling itself a theme worth thinking about. Embedding one narrative within another can also reveal information about character: in "Squatter," for instance, we might well ask ourselves why the narrator didn't just take over the telling of Sarosh's stories for himself; why give Nariman such pride of place? If you were to read the full collection from which "Squatter" is taken—*Tales from Firozsha Baag*—you would learn that our narrator is in fact a man named Kersi, who was once one of the boys whom Nariman Hansotia delighted with his tales. Thus the fact that Kersi, our narrator, chooses to weave Nariman's storytelling so closely within his own might suggest, for example, his desire to honour his mentor, thereby lending a story that uses comedy to advance a biting critique of racism a gentle emotional warmth.

Freytag's Pyramid

Another tool that can enhance our ability to stand back from a story and see how authors distribute narrative information and tension levels to create a good story is **Freytag's Pyramid**. This tool was invented by German novelist and playwright Gustav Freytag to analyze the classical, five-act plays from ancient Greece and Renaissance England in the late nineteenth century. However, these days Freytag's Pyramid is just as commonly used to analyze short fiction. The tool was invented when Freytag noticed that many of the classical plays he studied arranged narrative events in a similar way, which he sought to systematize in his "pyramid." The five stages he named correspond to the five acts in many classical plays. Not all short stories—or for that matter, plays—include the five parts and, even when they do, they're sometimes not so tidily or discretely arranged as they used to be. However, Freytag's Pyramid is useful precisely because it gives us a model to apply: whether a short story conforms to the five stages or not, examining its structure against this standard allows us to gain some critical distance from the plotting of events; we can begin to step back from the work and see the choices that have gone into crafting the story.

The five stages Freytag identified were, first, **exposition**, in which some context is established and the conflict that will be examined and resolved in some way over the course of the work is introduced. Second comes the **rising action** in which both the conflict and the central characters are more thoroughly developed. Third is the **climax**, which can be understood in a couple of ways: it can be the moment of highest drama or tension in a work or, slightly differently, the moment that marks a turning point in the protagonist's life. Fourth comes what Freytag called the **falling action**, where the conflict between protagonist and antagonist is resolved; this often involves a moment of tension during which the protagonist is again tested or altered, though not so dramatically as in the climax. Finally, the fifth element is the **dénouement**, wherein events are concluded.

Stories conform to the expectations of Freytag's Pyramid to differing degrees. A short story that is well served by Freytag's schema is Achebe's "Dead Men's Path." There isn't any right way of drawing the lines between the five stages, but thinking about how to do so nicely opens up the story. One possibility is to say the exposition begins with our introduction to Michael Obi, a young teacher known to be an "outspoken" champion of the new ways, who has arrived to run the "unprogressive" Ndume Central school, and ends when we learn of Michael and Nancy's plans to make the school "*modern* and delightful," inside and out (p. 99). The rising action, in which the characters and conflict come into clearer focus, would then begin when we learn about the existence of the "dead men's path," and of Michael's decision to seal it off (p. 100). From here, the tension rises quickly: the climax might well be the uncomfortable meeting between Michael and the village priest, who arrives to reach a compromise—which Obi refuses—and leaves with the ominous statement, "I have no more words" (p. 101). The consequences of Obi's actions become clear when a village woman dies in childbirth and Michael awakens to find his school a shambles; this interval would then constitute the falling action in that the priest's authority seems to have been affirmed over that of Michael (and thus the conflict between protagonist and antagonist is resolved). At this point, there is only the dénouement left: Achebe uses his final sentence to establish the rich irony that Michael, having taken on the agenda of the colonial powers, is condemned for exercising these powers too crudely.

You may well have different ideas about where to draw the lines between these five stages, particularly in a story such as "Dead Men's Path," where there is a progressive stepping up of tension rather than a sudden leap. The very process of drawing these lines asks us to consider many questions, such as whether Michael's authority is lost when his school is destroyed (which represents his authority over the villagers), or when he is reprimanded by the "white" Supervisor (which represents his authority within the colonial administration). And this is precisely why Freytag's Pyramid is such a useful analytic tool: it sparks thought, and often debate. Moreover, there are certainly cases in which we could argue convincingly that stories lack some of the elements. For example, stories that conclude with a shocking sudden event—known as an "O. Henry" or a "surprise ending"—such as Kate Chopin's "The Story of an Hour," could be said to lack both falling action and dénouement: the narrative simply ends with the disclosure of a climactic revelation or event. The point of Freytag's Pyramid is not so much to label the parts of a story as it is to enable us to stand back and recognize that there are discernible stages in the plotting of events, the development of character, and the distribution of narrative tension.

Character and Characterization

There is perhaps no feature of storytelling that more powerfully draws us into a narrative than character: the simple fact is that we human beings find each other (and ourselves) endlessly interesting. Fiction, whether of the long or short variety, gives us an opportunity to indulge and indeed examine this interest. The development of literary characters is quite sensibly termed **characterization**. And for all the power that characters have to pull us out of ourselves, to pull us into stories, and to make us care about the figments of someone else's imagination, they are constructed with surprisingly few tools. Characters are developed in three basic ways: through narrative description (which can include suggestive physical description as well as direct statements about character), through actions (including dialogue) that implicitly suggest traits, and by giving us access to characters' feelings and thought processes.

The basic vocabulary surrounding character is quite simple: characters are said to be **round** when they have enough complexity to give them a three-dimensional likeness to human beings; characters are said to be **flat** when they lack such complexity. It's important to bear in mind that these aren't evaluative terms: flat characters are not inferior to or less useful than round characters; rather, these character types serve different purposes. The characters in fables, for example, are *necessarily* flat because it is their task to stand in for or symbolize things. Had Aesop given his tortoise complexity, the additional traits would only have lessened his capacity both to oppose the hare and stand in for the benefits of slow and steady work. And it isn't just fables that require flat characters to achieve their ends: many short stories require them as well: think of Thomas King's "A Short History of Indians in Canada" and Le Guin's "The

Ones Who Walk Away from Omelas": as in Aesop's fable, the flat characters in these stories do the work of standing in for certain social categories. Giving them idiosyncratic characteristics would only detract from their ability to do this work.

One other distinction commonly used to categorize characters is stasis versus dynamism. While **static characters** (whether round or flat) remain essentially unchanged over the course of a work, **dynamic characters** undergo some kind of development, either experiencing a shift in character or revealing new dimensions of their character as the narrative unfolds (it's not always easy to distinguish between these two processes). Static characters can be round or flat: for instance, Flora from Alice Munro's "Friend of My Youth" seems to be a round character since she reveals a number of interesting traits (we might think of cheerfulness, adaptability, competence, fierce independence, a seemingly forgiving nature, patience, and industriousness). And you might say it's the very consistency of these traits in the face of such a remarkable series of life events that makes Flora so compelling a character: we keep waiting for the emotional calculus to complete itself, for some hint of bitterness or anger to come into view—for her to *become* a dynamic character. But does she? In fact, as the story proceeds, Flora's status as a character comes to the fore as the narrator offers different ways Flora's actions might be interpreted and contemplates the varying motivations we might have for "reading" her one way or another.

Setting

Because the events in stories have to occur somewhere, it is inevitable that all fiction has a setting or, more often than not, settings. While this is also the case with drama, it's not with poetry: for example, a lyric can articulate ideas and feelings without specifying a locale. Fiction writers are a little freer to imagine setting than playwrights since they're not constrained by the need to choose settings that can be physically created on a stage. Given this freedom, it's not surprising that writers of short and long fiction craft all kinds of imaginary geographies, which achieve a variety of ends.

The most basic of these ends is to help create a convincing fictional world. This aim is a constant regardless of whether authors are attempting to construct a world that resembles one that exists or has existed or are seeking to create a world that is different from our own. There are no rules about how much description is necessary to establish setting, or how this material should be incorporated into a story; but more often than not authors avoid overt, sustained descriptions of setting and instead delineate it gradually through the use of small, seemingly unnecessary details. It's typically the accumulation of details that allows the reader's imagination to create the locations in which actions occur.

Yet the work accomplished by setting goes well beyond the creation of a convincing fictional world. It also does tremendous work of other sorts, in echoing theme, shaping character, establishing mood, and creating symbols, for example. Take Alistair MacLeod's decision to begin "As Birds Bring Forth the Sun" with the vague claim, "Once there was a family with a highland name who lived beside the sea" (p. 120). Although the narrator might have begun by telling us where and when this tale is set, he withholds these details, as well as his own personal connection to the story. Not only does this withholding of information help to create a mood of mystery and even tension in the story, it also helps to develop our narrator's character by revealing his own desire to maintain the mythic qualities of this family story. This is one example of the general fact that authors choose the details of their imaginary geographies carefully, often making them accomplish multiple tasks. Think, for instance, of Joyce's decision in "Araby" to describe the street where the neighbourhood children play as "blind." How might we link this word choice with themes or the development of our narrator's character? Similarly, the house in Poe's "The Black Cat" accomplishes some great work in creating symbols: as our narrator falls further and further from his better nature, so his home undergoes a parallel degradation; in the end, the ugly secret in his heart seems to be disturbingly paralleled by the ugly secret in the cellar. In contrast, in Munro's "Friend of My Youth" it's the stability of Flora's house, echoing the stability and indeed stasis of her own life, that seems to give it symbolic qualities. Not only do the two sides of the house echo the contrasting lives of its inhabitants, they also serve as a social statement that the outside world reads and interprets. In all of these cases setting helps to contribute to mood, whether through the choice of the adjective "blind" or through the use of strong images, of a house quite literally divided in Munro, or of a house undergoing a process of decay in Poe. Setting works so effectively to create mood and echo theme because it gives expression to the fact that we can never neutrally view or inhabit the places we interact with: our geographies are always, to some extent, emotional geographies. Fiction highlights and intensifies this fact, allowing us to savour it and, if we look closely into the matter, interrogate it.

Point of View and Narration

All short fiction comes from a certain **point of view**, a very roomy expression that generally refers to the perspective from which a story is told. This includes both the kind of narrator an author utilizes and, more challengingly, the narrator's attitude toward events and characters.

The vast majority of short stories utilize either a first- or a third-person narrator (there are examples of second-person narration, but they are relatively rare). In the case of **third-person narration**, we usually don't know the identity of the narrator, who refers to all characters in the third person ("he," "she," "Peter," etc.) but generally makes no reference to him or herself (indeed, it's only the demands of English that require us to ascribe a sex to such anonymous voices). The opposite is true of a **first-person narrator** (sometimes also called a **character narrator**): we typically do know the narrator's identity, and such a voice tends to refer to him or herself in the first person ("I").

So long as a writer is using the realist style, only omniscient narrators can exhibit the power called **omniscience**. We know we have an **omniscient narrator** when we are given access to the thoughts and feelings of different characters as well as the details of their past and even future lives. Sometimes it is only one or two characters whose inner worlds we gain access to—this is called **limited omniscience**. Perhaps not surprisingly, omniscient narrators often give priority to the thoughts of the protagonist, as in Chinua Achebe's "Dead Men's Path," where we see Michael Obi's view of events. But we also glimpse the thoughts and emotions of his wife, Nancy, and briefly see Michael from her perspective.

Determining the narrator's attitude toward events may sometimes be a real challenge for readers. This is especially the case with third-person narrators, who are often imagined to be objective purveyors of information. Though we have little choice but to take the basic facts delivered by third-person narrators as truthful, we should be alert for signs of the particular attitudes such narrators exhibit toward characters and events. As an example, consider Mansfield's "The Garden Party," where some close reading reveals that the narrator gives more sympathetic treatment to Laura, who is initially horrified to carry on with the party after learning of the neighbour's death, than to her sisters or mother, who show impatience with Laura's sensitivity. Notice, for instance, how the narrator's final comment undermines Jose's words as she responds to Laura's horror at continuing with plans for the party:

> "If you're going to stop a band playing every time someone has an accident, you'll lead a very strenuous life. I'm every bit as sorry about it as you. I feel just as sympathetic." Her eyes hardened.

The narrator's decision to add that last sentence—"Her eyes hardened"—suggests that this voice isn't simply describing the characters and events (which it is indeed doing): it's also revealing a certain attitude toward them. Jose's eyes could have "glazed over" or "stared at her sister" rather than "harden," a term that so efficiently suggests her lack of sympathy and the fact that she is not "every bit as sorry" about the man's death as is Laura.

Many readers have an easier time discerning the narrator's attitude toward characters and events in the case of first-person narratives; this is perhaps because there is no guise of objectivity clinging to first-person narrators: it is clear that all of our information is being filtered through a consciousness that has its own particular way of viewing the world. As readers, our task is to try to discern how events and characters might appear to us were we able to correct for the narrator's biases. Sometimes this is relatively easy: in "Cathedral," for instance, Carver makes use of a male narrator whose prejudices toward and jealousy of Robert, his wife's blind friend, are difficult to miss. Such prejudices mean that, when it comes to assessing our narrator's view of characters and events, we must account for the effects of an **unreliable narrator**, a narrator whose understandings or information may be called into question.

Free Indirect Discourse

Though authors have to make decisions about what kind of narrator to use, a specific style of writing, known as **free indirect discourse**, represents something of a middle ground between first- and third-person narration. Developed by nineteenth-century authors (from Jane Austen through to Gustave Flaubert and Anton Chekhov), this style of writing allows an author to imbue a third-person perspective with some of the characteristics of first-person writing. Flaubert inspired moral outrage for his use of free indirect discourse to give expression to Emma Bovary's adulterous desires precisely because this style of writing makes it difficult to discern whether the ideas we are reading are those of the narrator or those of the character being described by the narrator. Flaubert's reading public objected to this ambiguity, believing that it was the narrator's duty to unequivocally condemn Emma's unfaithfulness. Happily for us, this style of writing has long outlasted Flaubert's initial experimentation and is widely found in third-person writing today. Edith Wharton makes fine use of free indirect discourse to sketch out Nora Frenway's thoughts about her own adulterous desires in "Atrophy":

> Not that she was a woman to be awed by the conventions. She knew she wasn't. She had always taken their measure, smiled at them—and conformed. On account of poor George Frenway, to begin with. Her husband, in a sense, was a man to be pitied; his weak health, his bad temper, his unsatisfied vanity, all made him a rather forlornly comic figure. But it was chiefly on account of the two children that she had always resisted the temptation to do anything reckless. The least self-betrayal would have been the end of everything. Too many eyes were watching her, and her husband's family was so strong, so

united—when there was anybody for them to hate—and at all times so influential, that she would have been defeated at every point, and her husband would have kept the children.

At the mere thought she felt herself on the brink of an abyss.

Though the **voice** delivering these words to us is clearly that of the narrator—Nora is referred to as "she," not "I"—it is difficult to determine whether we are accessing Nora's thoughts or the knowledge and opinions of the omniscient narrator. Once we reach the first sentence of the second paragraph—"At the mere thought she felt herself on the brink of an abyss"—we receive confirmation that at least those ideas coming to us near the end of the first paragraph must have originated in Nora's mind. But ambiguity remains regarding the earlier statements. Also note the stylistic advantages that come from free indirect discourse: Wharton varies the rhythm of some of her sentences to *suggest* that we are accessing Nora's thought processes. Intentionally ungrammatical "run-on" sentences (or comma splices) are often used in free indirect discourse, as are double dashes—the purpose being to try to capture the somewhat chaotic flow of human thought. Here we seem to see Nora adjust her initial claim that the family is united, to the more precise and critical idea that they are united "when there was anybody for them to hate." When we think to ourselves (as opposed to when we write for others), our ideas are often refined through such gradual processes of self-correction and adjustment.

Metafiction

Metafiction is writing that draws a reader's attention to the fact that he or she is engaged in the process of reading a piece of writing. It's best understood in opposition to the specific style of writing known as realism. When successful, realism induces what is sometimes called the realist illusion, an expression for that delightful way in which a story can allow us to lose awareness of the fact that we are reading, thus enabling us to fall into the textual world the author has created for us. A key characteristic of metafiction is that it disrupts the realist illusion and renders us self-conscious readers.

One way authors encourage self-consciousness within their readers is by making reference to some facet of literature within the literary work itself. For example, Mistry makes storytelling itself a theme in "Squatter" both by creating an embedded narrative (see the discussion of this in "Making Short Stories: The Selection and Manipulation of Events" above) and, more boldly, by crafting a character, Jehangir, who discusses the literary styles and techniques (such as humour) used by Nariman, one of the two storytellers we encounter. Margaret Atwood gives us another variation on this kind of metafiction in

"Happy Endings" when she discusses endings and plots, even referring at one instance to a weak point in her own story's plotting. Reading a story that itself talks about weak plotting or the use of humour makes many readers conscious of what they themselves are reading and of how it is plotted or makes use of humour, for example. This is one of metafiction's most common impacts: it alters our perspective on the story, encouraging us to regard it more analytically.

There is nothing new about metafiction. A famous example is found in Chaucer's medieval verse narrative "Troilus and Criseyde." In his Epilogue, Chaucer addresses the text itself, saying "go litel book," and expresses his hopes that it won't be misunderstood by the world. However, metafiction has become much more popular and experimental since the 1970s and is now a significant component of contemporary fiction, short and long. The question of why authors wish to break the realist illusion and render us self-conscious readers is a complex and difficult one, but one that deserves at least brief consideration here. Some see the popularity of metafiction as an inevitable consequence of the fact that readers are highly literate these days and can become bored by a given set of literary conventions. By definition, conventions become familiar, and they can begin to strike readers as tired and trite. Authors seek to **defamiliarize** fiction—to make that which was familiar *unfamiliar* and fresh—by breaking rules and pushing boundaries. New forms of metafiction come along to renew the literary genre and for a time seem fresh, exciting, challenging. We see Murakami's efforts to refresh the love story in "On Seeing the 100% Perfect Girl One Beautiful April Morning": on the one hand, this story challenges the suspension of disbelief requisite to most stories about romantic love, while on the other, it manifests some of the love story's most cherished ideals: the genre's conventions exist in a bracing state of tension.

A final point: just because a work is broadly classified as realist does not mean that it is devoid of metafictional elements. Coady's "Hellgoing," for example, is a story that is realist in virtually all regards, but could well take a metafictional turn were readers to focus their attention on the theme of storytelling, and more specifically on the protagonist's efforts to manipulate the story of her visit home to best suit her audience of women friends (an effort that becomes more noticeable as we sense how poorly the brother conforms to the pattern of gender relations the group seeks to affirm). Munro's "Friend of My Youth" invites a similar metafictional turn when the narrator veers from her task of narrating the story of Flora for us and begins to consider the differing ways she and her mother interpreted these characters, and indeed, the motivations they had for "reading" these people in different ways. Both of these stories are gently encouraging us to think about how the past is made into a story, about the multiple ways the past can be narrated, about the impossibility of a definitive version of events—more generally, about how life is turned into history. These are some of the many ways authors use small stories to ask rather large questions about neutrality, authority, and history. However briefly, these examples suggest the role metafictional elements can play in making us more critical readers. Many have argued that the rise of metafiction reflects the needs of our own times: in a world in which so many competing interests seek to convince us of the truth of their claims, or to destabilize the possibility of truth, people need critical skills. Metafiction provides a means by which authors can tell a good story, one that can even move us emotionally, while also offering readers the opportunity to deepen their thinking about story, history, and truth.

[L.C.]

Edgar Allan Poe
1809–1849

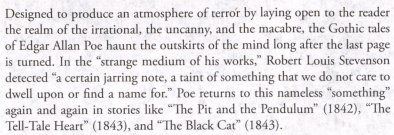

Designed to produce an atmosphere of terror by laying open to the reader the realm of the irrational, the uncanny, and the macabre, the Gothic tales of Edgar Allan Poe haunt the outskirts of the mind long after the last page is turned. In the "strange medium of his works," Robert Louis Stevenson detected "a certain jarring note, a taint of something that we do not care to dwell upon or find a name for." Poe returns to this nameless "something" again and again in stories like "The Pit and the Pendulum" (1842), "The Tell-Tale Heart" (1843), and "The Black Cat" (1843).

However one defines the "suggestive indefinitiveness" at the core of his most characteristic tales—a fascination with death, the iron grip of the past, or what Poe called "the human thirst for self-torture" perhaps come close— its presence reflects his pursuit of "a unity of effect or impression," a quality he considered the form of short fiction uniquely well suited to support. Poe held that the very brevity of the tale enlarges its power: because such works may be read at a sitting, the soul of the reader is fully at the writer's control, with neither weariness nor distraction to compromise the totality of the effect. But if the compactness of the tale allows the writer to realize "the fulness [sic] of his intention," it also demands perfect craft: for Poe, every word must advance "the one pre-established design."

Although Poe was among the first major theorists of the modern short story, his fictional practice has always been controversial, particularly among fellow American writers. Some object to his baroque prose and highly wrought formalism; others dismiss him as a hack who, having spent much of his life in poverty, indulged a lurid sensationalism in the hope of securing a wider readership. But as D.H. Lawrence observed, Poe was above all "an adventurer into vaults and cellars and horrible underground passages of the human soul," an author who not only founded detective fiction but who invested familiar forms with enormous power and psychological complexity.

The Black Cat

For the most wild, yet most homely narrative which I am about to pen, I neither expect nor solicit belief. Mad indeed would I be to expect it, in a case where my very senses reject their own evidence. Yet, mad am I not—and very surely do I not dream. But to-morrow I die, and to-day I would unburden my soul. My immediate purpose is to place before the world, plainly, succinctly, and without comment, a series of mere household events. In their consequences, these events have terrified—have tortured—have destroyed me. Yet I will not attempt to expound them. To me, they have presented little but Horror—to many they will seem less terrible than *barroques*.[1] Hereafter, perhaps, some intellect may be found which will reduce my phantasm[2] to the common-place—some intellect more calm, more logical, and far less excitable than my own, which will perceive, in the circumstances I detail with awe, nothing more than an ordinary succession of very natural causes and effects.

From my infancy I was noted for the docility and humanity of my disposition. My tenderness of heart was even so conspicuous as to make me the jest of my companions. I was especially fond of animals, and was indulged by my parents with a great variety of pets. With these I spent most of my time, and never was so happy as when feeding and caressing them. This peculiarity of character grew with my growth, and in my manhood, I derived from it one of my principal sources of pleasure. To those who have cherished an affection for a faithful and sagacious dog, I need hardly be at the trouble of explaining the nature or the intensity of the gratification thus derivable. There is something in the unselfish and self-sacrificing love of a brute, which goes directly to the heart of him who has had frequent occasion to test the paltry friendship and gossamer fidelity of mere *Man*.

I married early, and was happy to find in my wife a disposition not uncongenial with my own. Observing my partiality for domestic pets, she lost no opportunity of procuring those of the most agreeable kind. We had birds, gold-fish, a fine dog, rabbits, a small monkey, and *a cat*.

This latter was a remarkably large and beautiful animal, entirely black, and sagacious to an astonishing degree. In speaking of his intelligence, my wife, who at heart was not a little tinctured with superstition, made frequent allusion to the ancient popular notion, which regarded all black cats as witches in disguise. Not that she was ever *serious* upon this point—and I mention the matter at all for no better reason than that it happens, just now, to be remembered.

Pluto[3]—this was the cat's name—was my favourite pet and playmate. I alone fed him, and he attended me wherever I went about the house. It was even with difficulty that I could prevent him from following me through the streets.

Our friendship lasted, in this manner, for several years, during which my general temperament and character—through the instrumentality of the Fiend Intemperance[4]—had (I blush to confess it) experienced a radical alteration for the worse. I grew, day by day, more moody, more irritable, more regardless of the feelings of others. I suffered myself to use intemperate language to my

1   *barroques* French: weird, strange.
2   *phantasm* Delusion or frightening apparition.
3   *Pluto* In classical mythology, Pluto is the lord of the underworld.
4   *Fiend Intemperance* The narrator demonizes the excessive consumption of alcohol.

wife. At length, I even offered her personal violence. My pets, of course, were made to feel the change in my disposition. I not only neglected, but ill-used them. For Pluto, however, I still retained sufficient regard to restrain me from maltreating him, as I made no scruple of maltreating the rabbits, the monkey, or even the dog, when by accident, or through affection, they came in my way. But my disease grew upon me—for what disease is like Alcohol!—and at length even Pluto, who was now becoming old, and consequently somewhat peevish—even Pluto began to experience the effects of my ill temper.

One night, returning home, much intoxicated, from one of my haunts about town, I fancied that the cat avoided my presence. I seized him; when, in his fright at my violence, he inflicted a slight wound upon my hand with his teeth. The fury of a demon instantly possessed me. I knew myself no longer. My original soul seemed, at once, to take its flight from my body and a more than fiendish malevolence, gin-nurtured, thrilled every fibre of my frame. I took from my waistcoat-pocket a pen-knife, opened it, grasped the poor beast by the throat, and deliberately cut one of its eyes from the socket! I blush, I burn, I shudder, while I pen the damnable atrocity.

When reason returned with the morning—when I had slept off the fumes of the night's debauch—I experienced a sentiment half of horror, half of re-morse, for the crime of which I had been guilty; but it was, at best, a feeble and equivocal feeling, and the soul remained untouched. I again plunged into excess, and soon drowned in wine all memory of the deed.

In the meantime the cat slowly recovered. The socket of the lost eye pre-sented, it is true, a frightful appearance, but he no longer appeared to suffer any pain. He went about the house as usual, but, as might be expected, fled in extreme terror at my approach. I had so much of my old heart left, as to be at first grieved by this evident dislike on the part of a creature which had once so loved me. But this feeling soon gave place to irritation. And then came, as if to my final and irrevocable overthrow, the spirit of PERVERSENESS. Of this spirit philosophy takes no account. Yet I am not more sure that my soul lives, than I am that perverseness is one of the primitive impulses of the human heart—one of the indivisible primary faculties, or sentiments, which give direction to the character of Man. Who has not, a hundred times, found himself committing a vile or a silly action, for no other reason than because he knows he should not? Have we not a perpetual inclination, in the teeth of our best judgment, to violate that which is *Law*, merely because we understand it to be such? This spirit of perverseness, I say, came to my final overthrow. It was this unfathom-able longing of the soul *to vex itself*—to offer violence to its own nature—to do wrong for the wrong's sake only—that urged me to continue and finally to consummate the injury I had inflicted upon the unoffending brute. One morning, in cool blood, I slipped a noose about its neck and hung it to the limb of a tree;—hung it with the tears streaming from my eyes, and with the bitterest remorse at my heart;—hung it *because* I knew that it had loved me, and *because* I felt it had given me no reason of offence;—hung it *because* I knew that in so doing I was committing a sin—a deadly sin that would so jeopardize my immortal soul as to place it—if such a thing were possible—even beyond the reach of the infinite mercy of the Most Merciful and Most Terrible God.

On the night of the day on which this cruel deed was done, I was aroused from sleep by the cry of fire. The curtains of my bed were in flames. The whole house was blazing. It was with great difficulty that my wife, a servant, and myself, made our escape from the conflagration.[1] The destruction was complete. My entire worldly wealth was swallowed up, and I resigned myself thenceforward to despair.

I am above the weakness of seeking to establish a sequence of cause and effect, between the disaster and the atrocity. But I am detailing a chain of facts—and wish not to leave even a possible link imperfect. On the day succeeding the fire, I visited the ruins. The walls, with one exception, had fallen in. This exception was found in a compartment wall, not very thick, which stood about the middle of the house, and against which had rested the head of my bed. The plastering had here, in great measure, resisted the action of the fire—a fact which I attributed to its having been recently spread. About this wall a dense crowd were collected, and many persons seemed to be examining a particular portion of it with very minute and eager attention. The words "strange!" "singular!" and other similar expressions, excited my curiosity. I approached and saw, as if graven in *bas relief*[2] upon the white surface, the figure of a gigantic *cat*. The impression was given with an accuracy truly marvellous. There was a rope about the animal's neck.

When I first beheld this apparition—for I could scarcely regard it as less—my wonder and my terror were extreme. But at length reflection came to my aid. The cat, I remembered, had been hung in a garden adjacent to the house. Upon the alarm of fire, this garden had been immediately filled by the crowd—by some one of whom the animal must have been cut from the tree and thrown, through an open window, into my chamber. This had probably been done with the view of arousing me from sleep. The falling of other walls had compressed the victim of my cruelty into the substance of the freshly-spread plaster; the lime of which, with the flames, and the *ammonia* from the carcass, had then accomplished the portraiture as I saw it.

---

1   *conflagration* Destructive fire.
2   *bas relief* Relief sculpture characterized by slightly raised features that project from a flat background.

Although I thus readily accounted to my reason, if not altogether to my conscience, for the startling fact just detailed, it did not the less fail to make a deep impression upon my fancy. For months I could not rid myself of the phantasm of the cat; and, during this period, there came back into my spirit a half-sentiment that seemed, but was not, remorse. I went so far as to regret the loss of the animal, and to look about me, among the vile haunts which I now habitually frequented, for another pet of the same species, and of somewhat similar appearance, with which to supply its place.

One night as I sat, half stupefied, in a den of more than infamy, my attention was suddenly drawn to some black object, reposing upon the head of one of the immense hogsheads[1] of Gin, or of Rum, which constituted the chief furniture of the apartment. I had been looking steadily at the top of this hogshead for some minutes, and what now caused me surprise was the fact that I had not sooner perceived the object thereupon. I approached it, and touched it with my hand. It was a black cat—a very large one—fully as large as Pluto, and closely resembling him in every respect but one. Pluto had not a white hair upon any portion of his body; but this cat had a large, although indefinite splotch of white, covering nearly the whole region of the breast. Upon my touching him, he immediately arose, purred loudly, rubbed against my hand, and appeared delighted with my notice. This, then, was the very creature of which I was in search. I at once offered to purchase it of the landlord; but this person made no claim to it—knew nothing of it—had never seen it before.

I continued my caresses, and, when I prepared to go home, the animal evinced a disposition to accompany me. I permitted it to do so; occasionally stooping and patting it as I proceeded. When it reached the house it domesticated itself at once, and became immediately a great favourite with my wife.

For my own part, I soon found a dislike to it arising within me. This was just the reverse of what I had anticipated; but—I know not how or why it was—its evident fondness for myself rather disgusted and annoyed. By slow degrees, these feelings of disgust and annoyance rose into the bitterness of hatred. I avoided the creature; a certain sense of shame, and the remembrance of my former deed of cruelty, preventing me from physically abusing it. I did not, for some weeks, strike, or otherwise violently ill use it; but gradually—very gradually—I came to look upon it with unutterable loathing, and to flee silently from its odious presence, as from the breath of a pestilence.

What added, no doubt, to my hatred of the beast, was the discovery, on the morning after I brought it home, that, like Pluto, it also had been deprived of one of its eyes. This circumstance, however, only endeared it to my wife, who, as I have already said, possessed, in a high degree, that humanity of feel-

---

1   *hogsheads* Casks.

ing which had once been my distinguishing trait, and the source of many of my simplest and purest pleasures.

With my aversion to this cat, however, its partiality for myself seemed to increase. It followed my footsteps with a pertinacity which it would be difficult to make the reader comprehend. Whenever I sat, it would crouch beneath my chair, or spring upon my knees, covering me with its loathsome caresses. If I arose to walk it would get between my feet and thus nearly throw me down, or, fastening its long and sharp claws in my dress, clamber, in this manner, to my breast. At such times, although I longed to destroy it with a blow, I was yet withheld from so doing, partly by a memory of my former crime, but chiefly—let me confess it at once—by absolute dread of the beast.

This dread was not exactly a dread of physical evil—and yet I should be at a loss how otherwise to define it. I am almost ashamed to own—yes, even in this felon's cell, I am almost ashamed to own—that the terror and horror with which the animal inspired me, had been heightened by one of the merest chimaeras[1] it would be possible to conceive. My wife had called my attention, more than once, to the character of the mark of white hair, of which I have spoken, and which constituted the sole visible difference between the strange beast and the one I had destroyed. The reader will remember that this mark, although large, had been originally very indefinite; but, by slow degrees—degrees nearly imperceptible, and which for a long time my Reason struggled to reject as fanciful—it had, at length, assumed a rigorous distinctness of outline. It was now the representation of an object that I shudder to name—and for this, above all, I loathed, and dreaded, and would have rid myself of the monster *had I dared*—it was now, I say, the image of a hideous—of a ghastly thing—of the GALLOWS!—oh, mournful and terrible engine of Horror and of Crime—of Agony and of Death!

And now was I indeed wretched beyond the wretchedness of mere Humanity. And a brute beast—whose fellow I had contemptuously destroyed—*a brute beast* to work out for *me*—for me a man, fashioned in the image of the High God—so much of insufferable woe! Alas! neither by day nor by night knew I the blessing of Rest any more! During the former the creature left me no moment alone; and, in the latter, I started, hourly, from dreams of unutterable fear, to find the hot breath of *the thing* upon my face, and its vast weight—an incarnate Night-Mare that I had no power to shake off—incumbent eternally upon my *heart*!

Beneath the pressure of torments such as these, the feeble remnant of the good within me succumbed. Evil thoughts became my sole intimates—the darkest and most evil of thoughts. The moodiness of my usual temper in-

---

1   *chimaeras* Illusory or monstrous things.

creased to hatred of all things and of all mankind; while, from the sudden, frequent, and ungovernable outbursts of a fury to which I now blindly abandoned myself, my uncomplaining wife, alas! was the most usual and the most patient of sufferers.

One day she accompanied me, upon some household errand, into the cellar of the old building which our poverty compelled us to inhabit. The cat followed me down the steep stairs, and, nearly throwing me headlong, exasperated me to madness. Uplifting an axe, and forgetting, in my wrath, the childish dread which had hitherto stayed my hand, I aimed a blow at the animal which, of course, would have proved instantly fatal had it descended as I wished. But this blow was arrested by the hand of my wife. Goaded, by the interference, into a rage more than demoniacal, I withdrew my arm from her grasp and buried the axe in her brain. She fell dead upon the spot, without a groan.

This hideous murder accomplished, I set myself forthwith, and with entire deliberation, to the task of concealing the body. I knew that I could not remove it from the house, either by day or by night, without the risk of being observed by the neighbours. Many projects entered my mind. At one period I thought of cutting the corpse into minute fragments, and destroying them by fire. At another, I resolved to dig a grave for it in the floor of the cellar. Again, I deliberated about casting it in the well in the yard—about packing it in a box, as if merchandize, with the usual arrangements, and so getting a porter to take it from the house. Finally I hit upon what I considered a far better expedient than either of these. I determined to wall it up in the cellar—as the monks of the middle ages are recorded to have walled up their victims.

For a purpose such as this the cellar was well adapted. Its walls were loosely constructed, and had lately been plastered throughout with a rough plaster, which the dampness of the atmosphere had prevented from hardening. Moreover, in one of the walls was a projection, caused by a false chimney, or fireplace, that had been filled up, and made to resemble the rest of the cellar. I made no doubt that I could readily displace the bricks at this point, insert the corpse, and wall the whole up as before, so that no eye could detect any thing suspicious. And in this calculation I was not deceived. By means of a crow-bar I easily dislodged the bricks, and, having carefully deposited the body against the inner wall, I propped it in that position, while, with little trouble, I re-laid the whole structure as it originally stood. Having procured mortar, sand, and hair,[1] with every possible precaution, I prepared a plaster which could not be distinguished from the old, and with this I very carefully went over the new brickwork. When I had finished, I felt satisfied that all was right. The wall did

---

1   *hair* The addition of animal hair to mortar increases its durability.

not present the slightest appearance of having been disturbed. The rubbish on the floor was picked up with the minutest care. I looked around triumphantly, and said to myself—"Here at least, then, my labour has not been in vain."

My next step was to look for the beast which had been the cause of so much wretchedness; for I had, at length, firmly resolved to put it to death. Had I been able to meet with it, at the moment, there could have been no doubt of its fate; but it appeared that the crafty animal had been alarmed at the violence of my previous anger, and forbore to present itself in my present mood. It is impossible to describe, or to imagine, the deep, the blissful sense of relief which the absence of the detested creature occasioned in my bosom. It did not make its appearance during the night—and thus for one night at least, since its introduction into the house, I soundly and tranquilly slept; aye, slept even with the burden of murder upon my soul!

The second and the third day passed, and still my tormentor came not. Once again I breathed as a freeman. The monster, in terror, had fled the premises forever! I should behold it no more! My happiness was supreme! The guilt of my dark deed disturbed me but little. Some few inquiries had been made, but these had been readily answered. Even a search had been instituted—but of course nothing was to be discovered. I looked upon my future felicity as secured.

Upon the fourth day of the assassination, a party of the police came, very unexpectedly, into the house, and proceeded again to make rigorous investigation of the premises. Secure, however, in the inscrutability of my place of concealment, I felt no embarrassment whatever. The officers bade me accompany them in their search. They left no nook or corner unexplored. At length, for the third or fourth time, they descended into the cellar. I quivered not in a muscle. My heart beat calmly as that of one who slumbers in innocence. I walked the cellar from end to end. I folded my arms upon my bosom, and roamed easily to and fro. The police were thoroughly satisfied and prepared to depart. The glee at my heart was too strong to be restrained. I burned to say if but one word, by way of triumph, and to render doubly sure their assurance of my guiltlessness.

"Gentlemen," I said at last, as the party ascended the steps, "I delight to have allayed your suspicions. I wish you all health, and a little more courtesy. By the bye, gentlemen, this—this is a very well constructed house." [In the rabid desire to say something easily, I scarcely knew what I uttered at all.]—"I may say an *excellently* well constructed house. These walls—are you going, gentlemen?—these walls are solidly put together"; and here, through the mere phrenzy of bravado, I rapped heavily, with a cane which I held in my hand, upon that very portion of the brick-work behind which stood the corpse of the wife of my bosom.

But may God shield and deliver me from the fangs of the Arch-Fiend! No sooner had the reverberation of my blows sunk into silence, than I was answered by a voice from within the tomb!—by a cry, at first muffled and broken, like the sobbing of a child, and then quickly swelling into one long, loud, and continuous scream, utterly anomalous and inhuman—a howl—a wailing shriek, half of horror and half of triumph, such as might have arisen only out of hell, conjointly from the throats of the dammed in their agony and of the demons that exult in the damnation.

Of my own thoughts it is folly to speak. Swooning, I staggered to the opposite wall. For one instant the party upon the stairs remained motionless, through extremity of terror and of awe. In the next, a dozen stout arms were toiling at the wall. It fell bodily. The corpse, already greatly decayed and clotted with gore, stood erect before the eyes of the spectators. Upon its head, with red extended mouth and solitary eye of fire, sat the hideous beast whose craft had seduced me into murder, and whose informing voice had consigned me to the hangman. I had walled the monster up within the tomb!

—1843

Kate Chopin
1850–1904

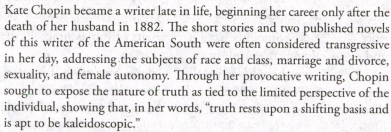

Kate Chopin became a writer late in life, beginning her career only after the death of her husband in 1882. The short stories and two published novels of this writer of the American South were often considered transgressive in her day, addressing the subjects of race and class, marriage and divorce, sexuality, and female autonomy. Through her provocative writing, Chopin sought to expose the nature of truth as tied to the limited perspective of the individual, showing that, in her words, "truth rests upon a shifting basis and is apt to be kaleidoscopic."

The controversy that Chopin's ideas incited is perhaps best exemplified by the reception of her most recognized work, *The Awakening* (1899). The novel, which depicts one woman's sensual awakening and her defiance of societal expectations of women, received high praise from a few reviewers, but a larger number dismissed it as "morbid," "sordid," and "sex fiction." It took scholars roughly 50 years after Chopin's death to acknowledge *The Awakening* as a novel of enduring importance—a work of historical value for its critical engagement with the role of women at the turn of the nineteenth century, but also a work that would continue to resonate for generations of readers.

Like *The Awakening*, "The Story of an Hour," first published in the December 1894 issue of *Vogue*, probes the marked tension between what Chopin referred to as the "outward existence which conforms, [and] the inward life which questions."

The Story of an Hour

Knowing that Mrs. Mallard was afflicted with a heart trouble, great care was taken to break to her as gently as possible the news of her husband's death.

It was her sister Josephine who told her, in broken sentences; veiled hints that revealed in half concealing. Her husband's friend Richards was there, too, near her. It was he who had been in the newspaper office when intelligence of the railroad disaster was received, with Brently Mallard's name leading the list of "killed." He had only taken the time to assure himself of its truth by a second telegram, and had hastened to forestall any less careful, less tender friend in bearing the sad message.

She did not hear the story as many women have heard the same, with a paralyzed inability to accept its significance. She wept at once, with sudden, wild abandonment, in her sister's arms. When the storm of grief had spent itself she went away to her room alone. She would have no one follow her.

There stood, facing the open window, a comfortable, roomy armchair. Into this she sank, pressed down by a physical exhaustion that haunted her body and seemed to reach into her soul.

She could see in the open square before her house the tops of trees that were all aquiver with the new spring life. The delicious breath of rain was in the air. In the street below a peddler was crying his wares. The notes of a distant song which someone was singing reached her faintly, and countless sparrows were twittering in the eaves.

There were patches of blue sky showing here and there through the clouds that had met and piled one above the other in the west facing her window.

She sat with her head thrown back upon the cushion of the chair, quite motionless, except when a sob came up into her throat and shook her, as a child who has cried itself to sleep continues to sob in its dreams.

She was young, with a fair, calm face, whose lines bespoke repression and even a certain strength. But now there was a dull stare in her eyes, whose gaze was fixed away off yonder on one of those patches of blue sky. It was not a glance of reflection, but rather indicated a suspension of intelligent thought.

There was something coming to her and she was waiting for it, fearfully. What was it? She did not know; it was too subtle and elusive to name. But she felt it, creeping out of the sky, reaching toward her through the sounds, the scents, the colour that filled the air.

Now her bosom rose and fell tumultuously. She was beginning to recognize this thing that was approaching to possess her, and she was striving to beat it back with her will—as powerless as her two white slender hands would have been.

When she abandoned herself a little whispered word escaped her slightly parted lips. She said it over and over under her breath: "free, free, free!" The vacant stare and the look of terror that had followed it went from her eyes. They stayed keen and bright. Her pulses beat fast, and the coursing blood warmed and relaxed every inch of her body.

She did not stop to ask if it were or were not a monstrous joy that held her. A clear and exalted perception enabled her to dismiss the suggestion as trivial.

She knew that she would weep again when she saw the kind, tender hands folded in death; the face that had never looked save with love upon her, fixed and grey and dead. But she saw beyond that bitter moment a long procession of years to come that would belong to her absolutely. And she opened and spread her arms out to them in welcome.

There would be no one to live for her during those coming years; she would live for herself. There would be no powerful will bending hers in that blind persistence with which men and women believe they have a right to impose a private will upon a fellow-creature. A kind intention or a cruel intention made the act seem no less a crime as she looked upon it in that brief moment of illumination.

And yet she had loved him—sometimes. Often she had not. What did it matter! What could love, the unsolved mystery, count for in face of this possession of self-assertion which she suddenly recognized as the strongest impulse of her being!

"Free! Body and soul free!" she kept whispering.

Josephine was kneeling before the closed door with her lips to the keyhole, imploring for admission. "Louise, open the door! I beg; open the door—you will make yourself ill. What are you doing, Louise? For heaven's sake open the door."

"Go away. I am not making myself ill." No; she was drinking in a very elixir of life through that open window.

Her fancy was running riot along those days ahead of her. Spring days, and summer days, and all sorts of days that would be her own. She breathed a quick prayer that life might be long. It was only yesterday she had thought with a shudder that life might be long.

She arose at length and opened the door to her sister's importunities. There was a feverish triumph in her eyes, and she carried herself unwittingly like a goddess of Victory. She clasped her sister's waist, and together they descended the stairs. Richards stood waiting for them at the bottom.

Some one was opening the front door with a latchkey. It was Brently Mallard who entered, a little travel-stained, composedly carrying his grip-sack and umbrella. He had been far from the scene of accident, and did not even know there had been one. He stood amazed at Josephine's piercing cry; at Richards' quick motion to screen him from the view of his wife.

But Richards was too late.

When the doctors came they said she had died of heart disease—of joy that kills.

—1894

Charlotte Perkins Gilman
1860–1935

Charlotte Perkins Gilman was born into a family prominent for activism and reform; her great-aunt was Harriet Beecher Stowe, author of *Uncle Tom's Cabin*. As a young woman she embraced the idea that a single woman could be a useful member of society and she resolved to dedicate her life to her work. Circumstances intervened, however: she fell in love, married, and plunged into a severe depression after the birth of her only child in 1885. She received treatment from the "nerve doctor" S. Weir Mitchell, who prescribed his famous "rest cure"—isolation, quiet domesticity, and abstention from intellectual endeavours—which greatly worsened her condition. In 1892, she published the short story "The Yellow Wallpaper," in which the protagonist is treated according to similar principles.

By this time, Gilman had left her husband, moved to California, and began again to work outside the home, forging a career as a feminist writer and lecturer. She won admiration from women reformers such as Jane Addams (1860–1935) and Elizabeth Cady Stanton (1815–1902). Her non-fiction work *Women and Economics* (1898) was a bestseller. From 1909 to 1916, she wrote for and edited her own magazine, *The Forerunner*; in 1915, the magazine serialized her novel *Herland*, about a utopia populated solely by women. In a statement that she made about the composition of "The Yellow Wallpaper," Gilman expressed the belief that informed all of her writing: "Work, in which is joy and growth and service, without which one is a pauper and a parasite," was essential for women.

The Yellow Wallpaper

It is very seldom that mere ordinary people like John and myself secure ancestral halls for the summer.

A colonial mansion, a hereditary estate, I would say a haunted house and reach the height of romantic felicity—but that would be asking too much of fate!

Still I will proudly declare that there is something queer about it.

Else, why should it be let so cheaply? And why have stood so long untenanted?

John laughs at me, of course, but one expects that.

John is practical in the extreme. He has no patience with faith, an intense horror of superstition, and he scoffs openly at any talk of things not to be felt and seen and put down in figures.

John is a physician, and *perhaps*—(I would not say it to a living soul, of course, but this is dead paper and a great relief to my mind)—*perhaps* that is one reason I do not get well faster.

You see, he does not believe I am sick! And what can one do?

If a physician of high standing, and one's own husband, assures friends and relatives that there is really nothing the matter with one but temporary nervous depression—a slight hysterical tendency—what is one to do?

My brother is also a physician, and also of high standing, and he says the same thing.

So I take phosphates or phosphites—whichever it is—and tonics, and air and exercise, and journeys, and am absolutely forbidden to "work" until I am well again.

Personally, I disagree with their ideas.

Personally, I believe that congenial work, with excitement and change, would do me good.

But what is one to do?

I did write for a while in spite of them, but it *does* exhaust me a good deal—having to be so sly about it, or else meet with heavy opposition.

I sometimes fancy that in my condition, if I had less opposition and more society and stimulus—but John says the very worst thing I can do is to think about my condition, and I confess it always makes me feel bad.

So I will let it alone and talk about the house.

The most beautiful place! It is quite alone, standing well back from the road, quite three miles from the village. It makes me think of English places that you read about, for there are hedges and walls and gates that lock, and lots of separate little houses for the gardeners and people.

There is a *delicious* garden! I never saw such a garden—large and shady, full of box-bordered paths, and lined with long grape-covered arbours with seats under them.

There were greenhouses, but they are all broken now.

There was some legal trouble, I believe, something about the heirs and co-heirs; anyhow, the place has been empty for years.

That spoils my ghostliness, I am afraid, but I don't care—there is something strange about the house—I can feel it.

I even said so to John one moonlight evening, but he said what I felt was a draught, and shut the window.

I get unreasonably angry with John sometimes. I'm sure I never used to be so sensitive. I think it is due to this nervous condition.

But John says if I feel so, I shall neglect proper self-control; so I take pains to control myself—before him, at least, and that makes me very tired.

I don't like our room a bit. I wanted one downstairs that opened on the piazza and had roses all over the window, and such pretty old-fashioned chintz hangings! But John would not hear of it.

He said there was only one window and not room for two beds, and no near room for him if he took another.

He is very careful and loving, and hardly lets me stir without special direction.

I have a schedule prescription for each hour in the day; he takes all care from me, and so I feel basely ungrateful not to value it more.

He said we came here solely on my account, that I was to have perfect rest and all the air I could get. "Your exercise depends on your strength, my dear," said he, "and your food somewhat on your appetite; but air you can absorb all the time." So we took the nursery at the top of the house.

It is a big, airy room, the whole floor nearly, with windows that look all ways, and air and sunshine galore. It was nursery first and then playroom and gymnasium, I should judge; for the windows are barred for little children, and there are rings and things in the walls.

The paint and paper look as if a boys' school had used it. It is stripped off—the paper—in great patches all around the head of my bed, about as far as I can reach, and in a great place on the other side of the room low down. I never saw a worse paper in my life. One of those sprawling flamboyant patterns committing every artistic sin.

It is dull enough to confuse the eye in following, pronounced enough to constantly irritate and provoke study, and when you follow the lame uncertain curves for a little distance they suddenly commit suicide—plunge off at outrageous angles, destroy themselves in unheard-of contradictions.

The colour is repellent, almost revolting; a smouldering unclean yellow, strangely faded by the slow-turning sunlight. It is a dull yet lurid orange in some places, a sickly sulphur tint in others.

No wonder the children hated it! I should hate it myself if I had to live in this room long.

There comes John, and I must put this away—he hates to have me write a word.

We have been here two weeks, and I haven't felt like writing before, since that first day.

I am sitting by the window now, up in this atrocious nursery, and there is nothing to hinder my writing as much as I please, save lack of strength.

John is away all day, and even some nights when his cases are serious.

I am glad my case is not serious!

But these nervous troubles are dreadfully depressing.

John does not know how much I really suffer. He knows there is no reason to suffer, and that satisfies him.

Of course it is only nervousness. It does weigh on me so not to do my duty in any way!

I mean to be such a help to John, such a real rest and comfort, and here I am a comparative burden already!

Nobody would believe what an effort it is to do what little I am able—to dress and entertain, and order things.

It is fortunate Mary is so good with the baby. Such a dear baby!

And yet I *cannot* be with him, it makes me so nervous.

I suppose John never was nervous in his life. He laughs at me so about this wallpaper!

At first he meant to repaper the room, but afterwards he said that I was letting it get the better of me, and that nothing was worse for a nervous patient than to give way to such fancies.

He said that after the wallpaper was changed it would be the heavy bedstead, and then the barred windows, and then that gate at the head of the stairs, and so on.

"You know the place is doing you good," he said, "and really, dear, I don't care to renovate the house just for a three months' rental."

"Then do let us go downstairs," I said. "There are such pretty rooms there."

Then he took me in his arms and called me a blessed little goose, and said he would go down cellar, if I wished, and have it whitewashed into the bargain.

But he is right enough about the beds and windows and things.

It is as airy and comfortable a room as anyone need wish, and, of course, I would not be so silly as to make him uncomfortable just for a whim.

I'm really getting quite fond of the big room, all but that horrid paper.

Out of one window I can see the garden—those mysterious deep-shaded arbours, the riotous old-fashioned flowers, and bushes and gnarly trees.

Out of another I get a lovely view of the bay and a little private wharf belonging to the estate. There is a beautiful shaded lane that runs down there from the house. I always fancy I see people walking in these numerous paths and arbours, but John has cautioned me not to give way to fancy in the least. He says that with my imaginative power and habit of story-making, a nervous weakness like mine is sure to lead to all manner of excited fancies, and that I ought to use my will and good sense to check the tendency. So I try.

I think sometimes that if I were only well enough to write a little it would relieve the press of ideas and rest me.

But I find I get pretty tired when I try.

It is so discouraging not to have any advice and companionship about my work. When I get really well, John says we will ask Cousin Henry and Julia down for a long visit; but he says he would as soon put fireworks in my pillow-case as to let me have those stimulating people about now.

I wish I could get well faster.

But I must not think about that. This paper looks to me as if it *knew* what a vicious influence it had!

There is a recurrent spot where the pattern lolls like a broken neck and two bulbous eyes stare at you upside down.

I get positively angry with the impertinence of it and the everlastingness. Up and down and sideways they crawl, and those absurd unblinking eyes are everywhere. There is one place where two breadths didn't match, and the eyes go all up and down the line, one a little higher than the other.

I never saw so much expression in an inanimate thing before, and we all know how much expression they have! I used to lie awake as a child and get more entertainment and terror out of blank walls and plain furniture than most children could find in a toy-store.

I remember what a kindly wink the knobs of our big old bureau used to have, and there was one chair that always seemed like a strong friend.

I used to feel that if any of the other things looked too fierce I could always hop into that chair and be safe.

The furniture in this room is no worse than inharmonious, however, for we had to bring it all from downstairs. I suppose when this was used as a playroom they had to take the nursery things out, and no wonder! I never saw such ravages as the children have made here.

The wallpaper, as I said before, is torn off in spots, and it sticketh closer than a brother[1]—they must have had perseverance as well as hatred.

Then the floor is scratched and gouged and splintered, the plaster itself is dug out here and there, and this great heavy bed which is all we found in the room, looks as if it had been through the wars.

But I don't mind it a bit—only the paper.

There comes John's sister. Such a dear girl as she is, and so careful of me! I must not let her find me writing.

She is a perfect and enthusiastic housekeeper, and hopes for no better profession. I verily believe she thinks it is the writing which made me sick!

But I can write when she is out, and see her a long way off from these windows.

---

1   *sticketh ... brother* From Proverbs 18.24.

There is one that commands the road, a lovely shaded winding road, and one that just looks off over the country. A lovely country, too, full of great elms and velvet meadows.

This wallpaper has a kind of sub-pattern in a different shade, a particularly irritating one, for you can only see it in certain lights, and not clearly then.

But in the places where it isn't faded and where the sun is just so—I can see a strange, provoking, formless sort of figure that seems to skulk about behind that silly and conspicuous front design.

There's sister on the stairs!

Well, the Fourth of July is over! The people are all gone, and I am tired out. John thought it might do me good to see a little company, so we just had Mother and Nellie and the children down for a week.

Of course I didn't do a thing. Jennie sees to everything now.

But it tired me all the same.

John says if I don't pick up faster he shall send me to Weir Mitchell in the fall.

But I don't want to go there at all. I had a friend who was in his hands once, and she says he is just like John and my brother, only more so!

Besides, it is such an undertaking to go so far.

I don't feel as if it was worthwhile to turn my hand over for anything, and I'm getting dreadfully fretful and querulous.

I cry at nothing, and cry most of the time.

Of course I don't when John is here, or anybody else, but when I am alone.

And I am alone a good deal just now. John is kept in town very often by serious cases, and Jennie is good and lets me alone when I want her to.

So I walk a little in the garden or down that lovely lane, sit on the porch under the roses, and lie down up here a good deal.

I'm getting really fond of the room in spite of the wallpaper. Perhaps because of the wallpaper.

It dwells in my mind so!

I lie here on this great immovable bed—it is nailed down, I believe—and follow that pattern about by the hour. It is as good as gymnastics, I assure you. I start, we'll say, at the bottom, down in the corner over there where it has not been touched, and I determine for the thousandth time that I *will* follow that pointless pattern to some sort of conclusion.

I know a little of the principle of design, and I know this thing was not arranged on any laws of radiation, or alternation, or repetition, or symmetry, or anything else that I ever heard of.

It is repeated, of course, by the breadths, but not otherwise.

Looked at in one way, each breadth stands alone; the bloated curves and flourishes—a kind of "debased Romanesque"[1] with delirium tremens[2]—go waddling up and down in isolated columns of fatuity.

But, on the other hand, they connect diagonally, and the sprawling outlines run off in great slanting waves of optic horror, like a lot of wallowing sea-weeds in full chase.

The whole thing goes horizontally, too, at least it seems so, and I exhaust myself trying to distinguish the order of its going in that direction.

They have used a horizontal breadth for a frieze, and that adds wonderfully to the confusion.

There is one end of the room where it is almost intact, and there, when the crosslights fade and the low sun shines directly upon it, I can almost fancy radiation after all—the interminable grotesque seems to form around a common centre and rush off in headlong plunges of equal distraction.

It makes me tired to follow it. I will take a nap, I guess.

I don't know why I should write this.

I don't want to.

I don't feel able.

And I know John would think it absurd. But I *must* say what I feel and think in some way—it is such a relief!

But the effort is getting to be greater than the relief.

Half the time now I am awfully lazy, and lie down ever so much.

John says I mustn't lose my strength, and has me take cod liver oil and lots of tonics and things, to say nothing of the ale and wine and rare meat.

Dear John! He loves me very dearly, and hates to have me sick. I tried to have a real earnest reasonable talk with him the other day, and tell him how I wish he would let me go and make a visit to Cousin Henry and Julia.

But he said I wasn't able to go, nor able to stand it after I got there; and I did not make out a very good case for myself, for I was crying before I had finished.

It is getting to be a great effort for me to think straight. Just this nervous weakness, I suppose.

And dear John gathered me up in his arms, and just carried me upstairs and laid me on the bed, and sat by me and read to me till it tired my head.

He said I was his darling and his comfort and all he had, and that I must take care of myself for his sake, and keep well.

---

1   *Romanesque* Medieval architectural style involving columns and round arches similar to those found in Roman architecture.

2   *delirium tremens* Condition resulting from extreme alcohol withdrawal; its symptoms include tremors, hallucinations, and random physical movements.

He says no one but myself can help me out of it, that I must use my will and self-control and not let any silly fancies run away with me.

There's one comfort—the baby is well and happy, and does not have to occupy this nursery with the horrid wallpaper.

If we had not used it, that blessed child would have! What a fortunate escape! Why, I wouldn't have a child of mine, an impressionable little thing, live in such a room for worlds.

I never thought of it before, but it is lucky that John kept me here after all, I can stand it so much easier than a baby, you see.

Of course I never mention it to them any more—I am too wise—but I keep watch for it all the same.

There are things in that paper that nobody knows about but me, or ever will.

Behind that outside pattern the dim shapes get clearer every day.

It is always the same shape, only very numerous.

And it is like a woman stooping down and creeping about behind that pattern. I don't like it a bit. I wonder—I begin to think—I wish John would take me away from here!

It is so hard to talk with John about my case, because he is so wise, and because he loves me so.

But I tried it last night.

It was moonlight. The moon shines in all around just as the sun does.

I hate to see it sometimes, it creeps so slowly, and always comes in by one window or another.

John was asleep and I hated to waken him, so I kept still and watched the moonlight on that undulating wallpaper till I felt creepy.

The faint figure behind seemed to shake the pattern, just as if she wanted to get out.

I got up softly and went to feel and see if the paper *did* move, and when I came back John was awake.

"What is it, little girl?" he said. "Don't go walking about like that—you'll get cold."

I thought it was a good time to talk, so I told him that I really was not gaining here, and that I wished he would take me away.

"Why, darling!" said he. "Our lease will be up in three weeks, and I can't see how to leave before.

"The repairs are not done at home, and I cannot possibly leave town just now. Of course if you were in any danger, I could and would, but you really are better, dear, whether you can see it or not. I am a doctor, dear, and I know.

You are gaining flesh and colour, your appetite is better, I feel really much easier about you."

"I don't weigh a bit more," said I, "nor as much; and my appetite may be better in the evening when you are here but it is worse in the morning when you are away!"

"Bless her little heart!" said he with a big hug. "She shall be as sick as she pleases! But now let's improve the shining hours[1] by going to sleep, and talk about it in the morning!"

"And you won't go away?" I asked gloomily.

"Why, how can I, dear? It is only three weeks more and then we will take a nice little trip of a few days while Jennie is getting the house ready. Really, dear, you are better!"

"Better in body perhaps—" I began, and stopped short, for he sat up straight and looked at me with such a stern, reproachful look that I could not say another word.

"My darling," said he, "I beg of you, for my sake and for our child's sake, as well as your own, that you will never for one instant let that idea enter your mind! There is nothing so dangerous, so fascinating, to a temperament like yours. It is a false and foolish fancy. Can you not trust me as a physician when I tell you so?"

So of course I said no more on that score, and we went to sleep before long. He thought I was asleep first, but I wasn't, and lay there for hours trying to decide whether that front pattern and the back pattern really did move together or separately.

On a pattern like this, by daylight, there is a lack of sequence, a defiance of law, that is a constant irritant to a normal mind.

The colour is hideous enough, and unreliable enough, and infuriating enough, but the pattern is torturing.

You think you have mastered it, but just as you get well under way in following, it turns a back-somersault and there you are. It slaps you in the face, knocks you down, and tramples upon you. It is like a bad dream.

The outside pattern is a florid arabesque,[2] reminding one of a fungus. If you can imagine a toadstool in joints, an interminable string of toadstools, budding and sprouting in endless convolutions—why, that is something like it.

That is, sometimes!

---

1   *improve the ... hours* See Isaac Watts's popular children's poem "Against Idleness and Mischief" (1715): "How doth the little busy bee / Improve each shining hour."

2   *arabesque* Complex decorative design.

There is one marked peculiarity about this paper, a thing nobody seems to notice but myself, and that is that it changes as the light changes.

When the sun shoots in through the east window—I always watch for that first long, straight ray—it changes so quickly that I never can quite believe it.

That is why I watch it always.

By moonlight—the moon shines in all night when there is a moon—I wouldn't know it was the same paper.

At night in any kind of light, in twilight, candlelight, lamplight, and worst of all by moonlight, it becomes bars! The outside pattern, I mean, and the woman behind it is as plain as can be.

I didn't realize for a long time what the thing was that showed behind, that dim sub-pattern, but now I am quite sure it is a woman.

By daylight she is subdued, quiet. I fancy it is the pattern that keeps her so still. It is so puzzling. It keeps me quiet by the hour.

I lie down ever so much now. John says it is good for me, and to sleep all I can.

Indeed he started the habit by making me lie down for an hour after each meal.

It is a very bad habit I am convinced, for you see, I don't sleep.

And that cultivates deceit, for I don't tell them I'm awake—O no!

The fact is I am getting a little afraid of John.

He seems very queer sometimes, and even Jennie has an inexplicable look.

It strikes me occasionally, just as a scientific hypothesis, that perhaps it is the paper!

I have watched John when he did not know I was looking, and come into the room suddenly on the most innocent excuses, and I've caught him several times *looking at the paper*! And Jennie too. I caught Jennie with her hand on it once.

She didn't know I was in the room, and when I asked her in a quiet, a very quiet voice, with the most restrained manner possible, what she was doing with the paper—she turned around as if she had been caught stealing, and looked quite angry—asked me why I should frighten her so!

Then she said that the paper stained everything it touched, that she had found yellow smooches on all my clothes and John's, and she wished we would be more careful!

Did not that sound innocent? But I know she was studying that pattern, and I am determined that nobody shall find it out but myself!

Life is very much more exciting now than it used to be. You see I have something more to expect, to look forward to, to watch. I really do eat better, and am more quiet than I was.

John is so pleased to see me improve! He laughed a little the other day, and said I seemed to be flourishing in spite of my wallpaper.

I turned it off with a laugh. I had no intention of telling him it was *because* of the wallpaper—he would make fun of me. He might even want to take me away.

I don't want to leave now until I have found it out. There is a week more, and I think that will be enough.

I'm feeling so much better!

I don't sleep much at night, for it is so interesting to watch developments; but I sleep a good deal during the daytime.

In the daytime it is tiresome and perplexing.

There are always new shoots on the fungus, and new shades of yellow all over it. I cannot keep count of them, though I have tried conscientiously.

It is the strangest yellow, that wallpaper! It makes me think of all the yellow things I ever saw—not beautiful ones like buttercups, but old, foul, bad yellow things.

But there is something else about that paper—the smell! I noticed it the moment we came into the room, but with so much air and sun it was not bad. Now we have had a week of fog and rain, and whether the windows are open or not, the smell is here.

It creeps all over the house.

I find it hovering in the dining-room, skulking in the parlour, hiding in the hall, lying in wait for me on the stairs.

It gets into my hair.

Even when I go to ride, if I turn my head suddenly and surprise it—there is that smell!

Such a peculiar odour, too! I have spent hours in trying to analyze it, to find what it smelled like.

It is not bad—at first—and very gentle, but quite the subtlest, most enduring odour I ever met.

In this damp weather it is awful, I wake up in the night and find it hanging over me.

It used to disturb me at first. I thought seriously of burning the house—to reach the smell.

But now I am used to it. The only thing I can think of that it is like is the *colour* of the paper! A yellow smell.

There is a very funny mark on this wall, low down, near the mopboard. A streak that runs round the room. It goes behind every piece of furniture, except the bed, a long, straight, even *smooch*, as if it had been rubbed over and over.

I wonder how it was done and who did it, and what they did it for. Round and round and round—round and round and round—it makes me dizzy!

I really have discovered something at last.

Through watching so much at night, when it changes so, I have finally found out.

The front pattern *does* move—and no wonder! The woman behind shakes it!

Sometimes I think there are a great many women behind, and sometimes only one, and she crawls around fast, and her crawling shakes it all over.

Then in the very bright spots she keeps still, and in the very shady spots she just takes hold of the bars and shakes them hard.

And she is all the time trying to climb through. But nobody could climb through that pattern—it strangles so; I think that is why it has so many heads.

They get through, and then the pattern strangles them off and turns them upside down, and makes their eyes white!

If those heads were covered or taken off it would not be half so bad.

I think that woman gets out in the daytime!

And I'll tell you why—privately—I've seen her!

I can see her out of every one of my windows!

It is the same woman, I know, for she is always creeping, and most women do not creep by daylight.

I see her in that long shaded lane, creeping up and down. I see her in those dark grape arbours, creeping all around the garden.

I see her on that long road under the trees, creeping along, and when a carriage comes she hides under the blackberry vines.

I don't blame her a bit. It must be very humiliating to be caught creeping by daylight!

I always lock the door when I creep by daylight. I can't do it at night, for I know John would suspect something at once.

And John is so queer now that I don't want to irritate him. I wish he would take another room! Besides, I don't want anybody to get that woman out at night but myself.

I often wonder if I could see her out of all the windows at once.

But, turn as fast as I can, I can only see out of one at one time.

And though I always see her, she *may* be able to creep faster than I can turn! I have watched her sometimes away off in the open country, creeping as fast as a cloud shadow in a wind.

If only that top pattern could be gotten off from the under one! I mean to try it, little by little.

I have found out another funny thing, but I shan't tell it this time! It does not do to trust people too much.

There are only two more days to get this paper off, and I believe John is beginning to notice. I don't like the look in his eyes.

And I heard him ask Jennie a lot of professional questions about me. She had a very good report to give.

She said I slept a good deal in the daytime.

John knows I don't sleep very well at night, for all I'm so quiet!

He asked me all sorts of questions, too, and pretended to be very loving and kind.

As if I couldn't see through him!

Still, I don't wonder he acts so, sleeping under this paper for three months.

It only interests me, but I feel sure John and Jennie are affected by it.

Hurrah! This is the last day, but it is enough. John is to stay in town over night, and won't be out until this evening.

Jennie wanted to sleep with me—the sly thing; but I told her I should undoubtedly rest better for a night all alone.

That was clever, for really I wasn't alone a bit! As soon as it was moonlight and that poor thing began to crawl and shake the pattern, I got up and ran to help her.

I pulled and she shook, I shook and she pulled, and before morning we had peeled off yards of that paper.

A strip about as high as my head and half around the room.

And then when the sun came and that awful pattern began to laugh at me, I declared I would finish it today!

We go away tomorrow, and they are moving all my furniture down again to leave things as they were before.

Jennie looked at the wall in amazement, but I told her merrily that I did it out of pure spite at the vicious thing.

She laughed and said she wouldn't mind doing it herself, but I must not get tired.

How she betrayed herself that time!

But I am here, and no person touches this paper but Me—not *alive*!

She tried to get me out of the room—it was too patent! But I said it was so quiet and empty and clean now that I believed I would lie down again and sleep all I could; and not to wake me even for dinner—I would call when I woke.

So now she is gone, and the servants are gone, and the things are gone, and there is nothing left but that great bedstead nailed down, with the canvas mattress we found on it.

We shall sleep downstairs tonight, and take the boat home tomorrow.

I quite enjoy the room, now it is bare again.

How those children did tear about here!

This bedstead is fairly gnawed!

But I must get to work.

I have locked the door and thrown the key down into the front path.

I don't want to go out, and I don't want to have anybody come in, till John comes.

I want to astonish him.

I've got a rope up here that even Jennie did not find. If that woman does get out, and tries to get away, I can tie her!

But I forgot I could not reach far without anything to stand on!

This bed will *not* move!

I tried to lift and push it until I was lame, and then I got so angry I bit off a little piece at one corner—but it hurt my teeth.

Then I peeled off all the paper I could reach standing on the floor. It sticks horribly and the pattern just enjoys it! All those strangled heads and bulbous eyes and waddling fungus growths just shriek with derision!

I am getting angry enough to do something desperate. To jump out of the window would be admirable exercise, but the bars are too strong even to try.

Besides I wouldn't do it. Of course not. I know well enough that a step like that is improper and might be misconstrued.

I don't like to *look* out of the windows even—there are so many of those creeping women, and they creep so fast.

I wonder if they all come out of that wallpaper as I did?

But I am securely fastened now by my well-hidden rope—you don't get me out in the road there!

I suppose I shall have to get back behind the pattern when it comes night, and that is hard!

It is so pleasant to be out in this great room and creep around as I please!

I don't want to go outside. I won't, even if Jennie asks me to.

For outside you have to creep on the ground, and everything is green instead of yellow.

But here I can creep smoothly on the floor, and my shoulder just fits in that long smooch around the wall, so I cannot lose my way.

Why there's John at the door!

It is no use, young man, you can't open it!

How he does call and pound!

Now he's crying to Jennie for an axe.

It would be a shame to break down that beautiful door!

"John dear!" said I in the gentlest voice. "The key is down by the front steps, under a plantain leaf!"

That silenced him for a few moments.

Then he said—very quietly indeed, "Open the door, my darling!"

"I can't," said I. "The key is down by the front door under a plantain leaf!"

And then I said it again, several times, very gently and slowly, and said it so often that he had to go and see, and he got it of course, and came in. He stopped short by the door.

"What is the matter?" he cried. "For God's sake, what are you doing!"

I kept on creeping just the same, but I looked at him over my shoulder.

"I've got out at last," said I, "in spite of you and Jane! And I've pulled off most of the paper, so you can't put me back!"

Now why should that man have fainted? But he did, and right across my path by the wall, so that I had to creep over him every time!

—1892

Edith Wharton

1862–1937

Edith Wharton was born in New York into a life of wealth and privilege, but, from an early age, she perceived that her peers, particularly women, were imprisoned by the social constraints of her class. Her novels and short stories would become known for their keen, often satiric observation of social mores—especially those of the high society world of her youth—and the ways in which those mores complicated and stifled the lives of her characters. As the novelist Francine Prose has said, "no one has written more incisively not just about a historical period and a particular social milieu but about something more timeless—the ardor with which we flee and return to the prison of conditioning and convenience."

Like most girls of her class, Wharton was educated at home by governesses, but she augmented her education by reading widely. As she reveals in her autobiography, *A Backward Glance*, she also loved "making up" stories and began to write when very young, even though her family disapproved of the activity as beneath her class—"something between a black art and a form of manual labor." In fact, she was so strapped for writing paper she was often reduced to using the wrapping from packages for her compositions. In 1879, *The Atlantic Monthly* published some of her poems; 25 novels, 86 short stories, and numerous works of non-fiction were to follow, with her 1920 novel, *The Age of Innocence*, winning a Pulitzer Prize.

By 1913, Wharton had moved permanently to France and, like her good friend, the writer Henry James (1843–1916), she capitalized on her knowledge of the differences between American and European society to write novels like *The Custom of the Country* (1913) with settings on both sides of the Atlantic.

Atrophy

1

Nora Frenway settled down furtively in her corner of the Pullman[1] and, as the express plunged out of the Grand Central Station, wondered at herself for being where she was. The porter came along. "Ticket?" "Westover." She had instinctively lowered her voice and glanced about her. But neither the porter nor her nearest neighbours—fortunately none of them known to her—seemed in the least surprised or interested by the statement that she was travelling to Westover.

---

1   *Pullman* Luxurious railway carriage.

Yet what an earth-shaking announcement it was! Not that she cared, now; not that anything mattered except the one overwhelming fact which had convulsed her life, hurled her out of her easy velvet-lined rut, and flung her thus naked to the public scrutiny.... Cautiously, again, she glanced about her to make doubly sure that there was no one, absolutely no one, in the Pullman whom she knew by sight.

Her life had been so carefully guarded, so inwardly conventional in a world where all the outer conventions were tottering, that no one had ever known she had a lover. No one—of that she was absolutely sure. All the circumstances of the case had made it necessary that she should conceal her real life—her only real life—from everyone about her; from her half-invalid irascible husband, his prying envious sisters, and the terrible monumental old chieftainess, her mother-in-law, before whom all the family quailed and humbugged and fibbed and fawned.

What nonsense to pretend that nowadays, even in big cities, in the world's greatest social centres, the severe old-fashioned standards had given place to tolerance, laxity and ease! You took up the morning paper, and you read of girl bandits, movie-star divorces, "hold-ups" at balls, murder and suicide and elopement, and a general welter of disjointed disconnected impulses and appetites; then you turned your eyes onto your own daily life, and found yourself as cribbed and cabined, as beset by vigilant family eyes, observant friends, all sorts of embodied standards, as any white-muslin novel heroine of the 'sixties![1]

In a different way, of course. To the casual eye Mrs. Frenway herself might have seemed as free as any of the young married women of her group. Poker playing, smoking, cocktail drinking, dancing, painting, short skirts, bobbed hair and the rest—when had these been denied to her? If by any outward sign she had differed too markedly from her kind—lengthened her skirts, refused to play for money, let her hair grow, or ceased to make-up—her husband would have been the first to notice it, and to say: "Are you ill? What's the matter? How queer you look! What's the sense of making yourself conspicuous?" For he and his kind had adopted all the old inhibitions and sanctions, blindly transferring them to a new ritual, as the receptive Romans did when strange gods were brought into their temples....

The train had escaped from the ugly fringes of the city, and the soft spring landscape was gliding past her: glimpses of green lawns, budding hedges, pretty irregular roofs, and miles and miles of alluring tarred roads slipping away into

---

1   *white-muslin ... 'sixties* Refers to the 1860s trend of the sensation novel, characterized by lurid plots involving crime and shocking family secrets. Among the most popular of these novels was Wilkie Collins's *The Woman in White* (1860), in which the title character is unjustly committed to an asylum.

mystery. How often she had dreamed of dashing off down an unknown road with Christopher!

Not that she was a woman to be awed by the conventions. She knew she wasn't. She had always taken their measure, smiled at them—and conformed. On account of poor George Frenway, to begin with. Her husband, in a sense, was a man to be pitied; his weak health, his bad temper, his unsatisfied vanity, all made him a rather forlornly comic figure. But it was chiefly on account of the two children that she had always resisted the temptation to do anything reckless. The least self-betrayal would have been the end of everything. Too many eyes were watching her, and her husband's family was so strong, so united—when there was anybody for them to hate—and at all times so influential, that she would have been defeated at every point, and her husband would have kept the children.

At the mere thought she felt herself on the brink of an abyss. "The children are my religion," she had once said to herself; and she had no other.

Yet here she was on her way to Westover.... Oh, what did it matter now? That was the worst of it—it was too late for anything between her and Christopher to matter! She was sure he was dying. The way in which his cousin, Gladys Brincker, had blurted it out the day before at Kate Salmer's dance: "You didn't know—poor Kit?[1] Thought you and he were such pals! Yes, awfully bad, I'm afraid. Return of the old trouble! I know there've been two consultations— they had Knowlton down. They say there's not much hope; and nobody but that forlorn frightened Jane mounting guard...."

Poor Christopher! His sister Jane Aldis, Nora suspected, forlorn and frightened as she was, had played in his life a part nearly as dominant as Frenway and the children in Nora's. Loyally, Christopher always pretended that she didn't; talked of her indulgently as "poor Jenny." But didn't she, Nora, always think of her husband as "poor George"? Jane Aldis, of course, was much less self-assertive, less demanding, than George Frenway; but perhaps for that very reason she would appeal all the more to a man's compassion. And somehow, under her unobtrusive air, Nora had—on the rare occasions when they met—imagined that Miss Aldis was watching and drawing her inferences. But then Nora always felt, where Christopher was concerned, as if her breast were a pane of glass through which her trembling palpitating heart could be seen as plainly as holy viscera in a reliquary. Her sober after-thought was that Jane Aldis was just a dowdy self-effacing old maid whose life was filled to the brim by looking over the Westover place for her brother, and seeing that the fires were lit and the rooms full of flowers when he brought down his friends for a week-end.

---

1   *Kit* Short for Christopher.

Ah, how often he had said to Nora: "If I could have you to myself for a week-end at Westover"—quite as if it were the easiest thing imaginable, as far as his arrangements were concerned! And they had even pretended to discuss how it could be done. But somehow she fancied he said it because he knew that the plan, for her, was about as feasible as a week-end in the moon. And in reality her only visits to Westover had been made in the company of her husband, and that of other friends, two or three times, at the beginning.... For after that she wouldn't. It was three years now since she had been there.

Gladys Brincker, in speaking of Christopher's illness, had looked at Nora queerly, as though suspecting something. But no—what nonsense! No one had ever suspected Nora Frenway. Didn't she know what her friends said of her? "Nora? No more temperament than a lamp-post. Always buried in her books.... Never very attractive to men, in spite of her looks." Hadn't she said that of other women, who perhaps, in secret, like herself...?

The train was slowing down as it approached a station. She sat up with a jerk and looked at her wrist-watch. It was half-past two, the station was Ockham; the next would be Westover. In less than an hour she would be under his roof, Jane Aldis would be receiving her in that low panelled room full of books, and she would be saying—what would she be saying?

She had gone over their conversation so often that she knew not only her own part in it but Miss Aldis's by heart. The first moments would of course be painful, difficult; but then a great wave of emotion, breaking down the barriers between the two anxious women, would fling them together. She wouldn't have to say much, to explain; Miss Aldis would just take her by the hand and lead her upstairs to the room.

That room! She shut her eyes, and remembered other rooms where she and he had been together in their joy and their strength.... No, not that; she must not think of that now. For the man she had met in those other rooms was dying; the man she was going to was someone so different from that other man that it was like a profanation to associate their images.... And yet the man she was going to was her own Christopher, the one who had lived in her soul; and how his soul must be needing hers, now that it hung alone on the dark brink! As if anything else mattered at such a moment! She neither thought nor cared what Jane Aldis might say or suspect; she wouldn't have cared if the Pullman had been full of prying acquaintances, or if George and all George's family had got in at that last station.

She wouldn't have cared a fig for any of them. Yet at the same moment she remembered having felt glad that her old governess, whom she used to go and see twice a year, lived at Ockham—so that if George did begin to ask questions, she could always say: "Yes, I went to see poor old Fraulein; she's absolutely crippled now. I shall have to get her a Bath chair.[1] Could you get me a catalogue of prices?" There wasn't a precaution she hadn't thought of—and now she was ready to scatter them all to the winds....

Westover—"Junction!"

She started up and pushed her way out of the train. All the people seemed to be obstructing her, putting bags and suit-cases in her way. And the express stopped for only two minutes. Suppose she should be carried on to Albany?

Westover Junction was a growing place, and she was fairly sure there would be a taxi at the station. There was one—she just managed to get to it ahead of a travelling man with a sample case and a new straw hat. As she opened the door a smell of damp hay and bad tobacco greeted her. She sprang in and gasped: "To Oakfield. You know? Mr. Aldis's place near Westover."

2

It began exactly as she had expected. A surprised parlour maid—why surprised?—showed her into the low panelled room that was so full of his presence, his books, his pipes, his terrier dozing on the shabby rug. The parlour maid said she would go and see if Miss Aldis could come down. Nora wanted to ask if she were with her brother—and how he was. But she found herself unable to speak the words. She was afraid her voice might tremble. And why should she question the parlour maid, when in a moment, she hoped, she was to see Miss Aldis?

The woman moved away with a hushed step—the step which denotes illness in the house. She did not immediately return, and the interval of waiting in that room, so strange yet so intimately known, was a new torture to Nora. It was unlike anything she had imagined. The writing table with his scattered pens and letters was more than she could bear. His dog looked at her amicably from the hearth, but made no advances; and though she longed to stroke him, to let her hand rest where Christopher's had rested, she dared not for fear he should bark and disturb the peculiar hush of that dumb watchful house. She stood in the window and looked out at the budding shrubs and the bulbs pushing up through the swollen earth.

"This way, please."

Her heart gave a plunge. Was the woman actually taking her upstairs to his room? Her eyes filled, she felt herself swept forward on a great wave of passion and anguish.... But she was only being led across the hall into a stiff lifeless drawing-room—the kind that bachelors get an upholsterer to do for them, and then turn their backs on forever. The chairs and sofas looked at her with an undisguised hostility, and then resumed the moping expression

---

1   *Bath chair* Wheelchair.

common to furniture in unfrequented rooms. Even the spring sun slanting in through the windows on the pale marquetry of a useless table seemed to bring no heat or light with it.

The rush of emotion subsided, leaving in Nora a sense of emptiness and apprehension. Supposing Jane Aldis should look at her with the cold eyes of this resentful room? She began to wish she had been friendlier and more cordial to Jane Aldis in the past. In her intense desire to conceal from everyone the tie between herself and Christopher she had avoided all show of interest in his family; and perhaps, as she now saw, excited curiosity by her very affectation of indifference.

No doubt it would have been more politic to establish an intimacy with Jane Aldis; and today, how much easier and more natural her position would have been! Instead of groping about—as she was again doing—for an explanation of her visit, she could have said: "My dear, I came to see if there was anything in the world I could do to help you."

She heard a hesitating step in the hall—a hushed step like a parlour maid's—and saw Miss Aldis pause near the half-open door. How old she had grown since their last meeting! Her hair, untidily pinned up, was grey and lanky. Her eyelids, always reddish, were swollen and heavy, her face sallow with anxiety and fatigue. It was odd to have feared so defenceless an adversary. Nora, for an instant, had the impression that Miss Aldis had wavered in the hall to catch a glimpse of her, take the measure of the situation. But perhaps she had only stopped to push back a strand of hair as she passed in front of a mirror.

"Mrs. Frenway—how good of you!" She spoke in a cool detached voice, as if her real self were elsewhere and she were simply an automaton wound up to repeat the familiar forms of hospitality. "Do sit down," she said.

She pushed forward one of the sulky arm-chairs, and Nora seated herself stiffly, her hand-bag clutched on her knee, in the self-conscious attitude of a country caller.

"I came——"

"So good of you," Miss Aldis repeated. "I had no idea you were in this part of the world. Not the slightest."

Was it a lead she was giving? Or did she know everything, and wish to extend to her visitor the decent shelter of a pretext? Or was she really so stupid—

"You're staying with the Brinckers, I suppose. Or the Northrups? I remember the last time you came to lunch here you motored over with Mr. Frenway from the Northrups'. That must have been two years ago, wasn't it?" She put the question with an almost sprightly show of interest.

"No—three years," said Nora mechanically.

"Was it? As long ago as that? Yes—you're right. That was the year we moved the big fern-leaved beech. I remember Mr. Frenway was interested in tree moving, and I took him out to show him where the tree had come from. He IS interested in tree moving, isn't he?"

"Oh, yes; very much."

"We had those wonderful experts down to do it. 'Tree doctors,' they call themselves. They have special appliances, you know. The tree is growing better than it did before they moved it. But I suppose you've done a great deal of transplanting on Long Island."

"Yes. My husband does a good deal of transplanting."

"So you've come over from the Northrups'? I didn't even know they were down at Maybrook yet. I see so few people."

"No; not from the Northrups'."

"Oh—the Brinckers'? Hal Brincker was here yesterday, but he didn't tell me you were staying there."

Nora hesitated. "No. The fact is, I have an old governess who lives at Ockham. I go to see her sometimes. And so I came on to Westover——" She paused, and Miss Aldis interrogated her brightly: "Yes?" as if prompting her in a lesson she was repeating.

"Because I saw Gladys Brincker the other day, and she told me that your brother was ill."

"Oh." Miss Aldis gave the syllable its full weight, and set a full stop after it. Her eyebrows went up, as if in a faint surprise. The silent room seemed to close in on the two speakers, listening. A resuscitated fly buzzed against the sunny window pane. "Yes; he's ill," she conceded at length.

"I'm so sorry; I ... he has been ... such a friend of ours ... so long...."

"Yes; I've often heard him speak of you and Mr. Frenway." Another full stop sealed this announcement. ("No, she knows nothing," Nora thought.) "I remember his telling me that he thought a great deal of Mr. Frenway's advice about moving trees. But then you see our soil is so different from yours. I suppose Mr. Frenway has had your soil analyzed?"

"Yes; I think he has."

"Christopher's always been a great gardener."

"I hope he's not—not very ill? Gladys seemed to be afraid——"

"Illness is always something to be afraid of, isn't it?"

"But you're not—I mean, not anxious ... not seriously?"

"It's so kind of you to ask. The doctors seem to think there's no particular change since yesterday."

"And yesterday?"

"Well, yesterday they seemed to think there might be."

"A change, you mean?"

"Well, yes."

"A change—I hope for the better?"

"They said they weren't sure; they couldn't say."

The fly's buzzing had become so insistent in the still room that it seemed to be going on inside of Nora's head, and in the confusion of sound she found it more and more difficult to regain a lead in the conversation. And the minutes were slipping by, and upstairs the man she loved was lying. It was absurd and lamentable to make a pretense of keeping up this twaddle. She would cut through it, no matter how.

"I suppose you've had—a consultation?"

"Oh, yes; Dr. Knowlton's been down twice."

"And what does he——"

"Well; he seems to agree with the others."

There was another pause, and then Miss Aldis glanced out of the window. "Why, who's that driving up?" she enquired. "Oh, it's your taxi, I suppose, coming up the drive."

"Yes, I got out at the gate." She dared not add: "For fear the noise might disturb him."

"I hope you had no difficulty in finding a taxi at the Junction?"

"Oh, no; I had no difficulty."

"I think it was so kind of you to come—not even knowing whether you'd find a carriage to bring you out all this way. And I know how busy you are. There's always so much going on in town, isn't there, even at this time of year?"

"Yes; I suppose so. But your brother——"

"Oh, of course my brother won't be up to any sort of gaiety; not for a long time."

"A long time; no. But you do hope——"

"I think everybody about a sick bed ought to hope, don't you?"

"Yes; but I mean——"

Nora stood up suddenly, her brain whirling. Was it possible that she and that woman had sat thus facing each other for half an hour, piling up this conversational rubbish, while upstairs, out of sight, the truth, the meaning of their two lives hung on the frail thread of one man's intermittent pulse? She could not imagine why she felt so powerless and baffled. What had a woman who was young and handsome and beloved to fear from a dowdy and insignificant old maid? Why, the antagonism that these very graces and superiorities would create in the other's breast, especially if she knew they were all spent in charming the being on whom her life depended. Weak in herself, but powerful from her circumstances, she stood at bay on the ruins of all that Nora had ever loved. "How she must hate me—and I never thought of it," mused Nora, who had imagined that she had thought of everything where her relation to her lover was concerned. Well, it was too late now to remedy her omission; but at least she must assert herself, must say something to save the precious minutes that remained and break through the stifling web of platitudes which her enemy's tremulous hand was weaving around her.

"Miss Aldis—I must tell you—I came to see——"

"How he was? So very friendly of you. He would appreciate it, I know. Christopher is so devoted to his friends."

"But you'll—you'll tell him that I——"

"Of course. That you came on purpose to ask about him. As soon as he's a little bit stronger."

"But I mean—now?"

"Tell him now that you called to enquire? How good of you to think of that too! Perhaps tomorrow morning, if he's feeling a little bit brighter...."

Nora felt her lips drying as if a hot wind had parched them. They would hardly move. "But now—now—today." Her voice sank to a whisper as she added: "Isn't he conscious?"

"Oh, yes; he's conscious; he's perfectly conscious." Miss Aldis emphasized this with another of her long pauses. "He shall certainly be told that you called." Suddenly she too got up from her seat and moved toward the window. "I must seem dreadfully inhospitable, not even offering you a cup of tea. But the fact is, perhaps I ought to tell you—if you're thinking of getting back to Ockham this afternoon there's only one train that stops at the Junction after three o'clock." She pulled out an old-fashioned enamelled watch with a wreath of roses about the dial, and turned almost apologetically to Mrs. Frenway. "You ought to be at the station by four o'clock at the latest; and with one of those old Junction taxis.... I'm so sorry; I know I must appear to be driving you away." A wan smile drew up her pale lips.

Nora knew just how long the drive from Westover Junction had taken, and understood that she was being delicately dismissed. Dismissed from life—from hope—even from the dear anguish of filling her eyes for the last time with the face which was the one face in the world to her! ("But then she does know everything," she thought.)

"I mustn't make you miss your train, you know."

"Miss Aldis, is he—has he seen any one?" Nora hazarded in a painful whisper.

"Seen any one? Well, there've been all the doctors—five of them! And then the nurses. Oh, but you mean friends, of course. Naturally." She seemed to reflect. "Hal Brincker, yes; he saw our cousin Hal yesterday—but not for very long."

Hal Brincker! Nora knew what Christopher thought of his Brincker cousins—blighting bores, one and all of them, he always said. And in the extremity of his illness the one person privileged to see him had been—Hal Brincker! Nora's eyes filled; she had to turn them away for a moment from Miss Aldis's timid inexorable face.

"But today?" she finally brought out.

"No. Today he hasn't seen any one; not yet." The two women stood and looked at each other; then Miss Aldis glanced uncertainly about the room. "But couldn't I—Yes, I ought at least to have asked if you won't have a cup of tea. So stupid of me! There might still be time. I never take tea myself." Once more she referred anxiously to her watch. "The water is sure to be boiling, because the nurses' tea is just being taken up. If you'll excuse me a moment I'll go and see."

"Oh, no, no!" Nora drew in a quick sob. "How can you?... I mean, I don't want any...."

Miss Aldis looked relieved. "Then I shall be quite sure that you won't reach the station too late." She waited again, and then held out a long stony hand. "So kind—I shall never forget your kindness. Coming all this way, when you might so easily have telephoned from town. Do please tell Mr. Frenway how I appreciated it. You will remember to tell him, won't you? He sent me such an interesting collection of pamphlets about tree moving. I should like him to know how much I feel his kindness in letting you come." She paused again, and pulled in her lips so that they became a narrow thread, a mere line drawn across her face by a ruler. "But, no; I won't trouble you; I'll write to thank him myself." Her hand ran out to an electric bell on the nearest table. It shrilled through the silence, and the parlour maid appeared with a stage-like promptness.

"The taxi, please? Mrs. Frenway's taxi."

The room became silent again. Nora thought: "Yes; she knows everything." Miss Aldis peeped for the third time at her watch, and then uttered a slight unmeaning laugh. The blue-bottle banged against the window, and once more it seemed to Nora that its sonorities were reverberating inside her head. They were deafeningly mingled there with the explosion of the taxi's reluctant starting-up and its convulsed halt at the front door. The driver sounded his horn as if to summon her.

"He's afraid too that you'll be late!" Miss Aldis smiled.

The smooth slippery floor of the hall seemed to Nora to extend away in front of her for miles. At its far end she saw a little tunnel of light, a miniature maid, a toy taxi. Somehow she managed to travel the distance that separated her from them, though her bones ached with weariness, and at every step she seemed to be lifting a leaden weight. The taxi was close to her now, its door open, she was getting in. The same smell of damp hay and bad tobacco greeted her. She saw her hostess standing on the threshold. "To the Junction, driver—back to the Junction," she heard Miss Aldis say. The taxi began to roll toward the gate. As it moved away Nora heard Miss Aldis calling: "I'll be sure to write and thank Mr. Frenway."

—1927

James Joyce
1882–1941

James Joyce was born in Dublin, and although he left the city for good in 1904, it provided the background for all his major works. His best-known novel, *Ulysses* (1922), describes a day in the life of three of the city's inhabitants, with the various incidents paralleling episodes from Homer's *Odyssey*. It is written in an intricately constructed combination of literary styles, including long sections of stream-of-consciousness narration.

Joyce and Nora Barnacle, a woman whom he met on a Dublin street and who would become his wife and lifelong companion, lived in Trieste, Zurich, and Paris, where Joyce made his living by teaching English. In 1914, the modernist poet Ezra Pound arranged for Joyce's autobiographical novel *A Portrait of the Artist as a Young Man* to be serialized in *The Egoist*, a British magazine. The same year, Joyce's collection of short stories, *Dubliners*, was published. In each story, the protagonist experiences what Joyce called an "epiphany," a moment of revelation that he described as "a sudden spiritual manifestation, whether in the vulgarity of speech or of gesture or in a memorable phase of the mind itself."

Shortly after, Joyce began work on *Ulysses*. In 1918, *The Egoist* and an American magazine, *The Little Review,* began serializing the work, but charges that passages were obscene led to the suspension of serialization. Joyce is said to have retorted, "If *Ulysses* isn't fit to read, life isn't fit to live." It was finally published in book form in Paris in 1922.

By this time, friends and admirers were supporting Joyce financially, allowing him to concentrate on his writing; he began work on his last book, *Finnegans Wake*, an extremely complex work of dream imaginings and linguistic invention, which was published in 1939.

Araby[1]

North Richmond Street, being blind,[2] was a quiet street except at the hour when the Christian Brothers' School set the boys free. An uninhabited house of two storeys stood at the blind end, detached from its neighbours in a square ground. The other houses of the street, conscious of decent lives within them, gazed at one another with brown imperturbable faces.

The former tenant of our house, a priest, had died in the back drawing-room. Air, musty from having been long enclosed, hung in all the rooms, and

---

1   *Araby* Charity bazaar held in Dublin in 1894; it was advertised as a "grand, Oriental fête."

2   *being blind* I.e., being a dead-end street.

the waste room behind the kitchen was littered with old useless papers. Among these I found a few paper-covered books, the pages of which were curled and damp: *The Abbot*, by Walter Scott, *The Devout Communicant* and *The Memoirs of Vidocq*.[1] I liked the last best because its leaves were yellow. The wild garden behind the house contained a central apple-tree and a few straggling bushes under one of which I found the late tenant's rusty bicycle-pump. He had been a very charitable priest; in his will he had left all his money to institutions and the furniture of his house to his sister.

When the short days of winter came dusk fell before we had well eaten our dinners. When we met in the street the houses had grown sombre. The space of sky above us was the colour of ever-changing violet and towards it the lamps of the street lifted their feeble lanterns. The cold air stung us and we played till our bodies glowed. Our shouts echoed in the silent street. The career of our play brought us through the dark muddy lanes behind the houses where we ran the gantlet of the rough tribes from the cottages, to the back doors of the dark dripping gardens where odours arose from the ash-pits, to the dark odorous stables where a coachman smoothed and combed the horse or shook music from the buckled harness. When we returned to the street light from the kitchen windows had filled the areas.[2] If my uncle was seen turning the corner we hid in the shadow until we had seen him safely housed. Or if Mangan's sister came out on the doorstep to call her brother in to his tea we watched her from our shadow peer up and down the street. We waited to see whether she would remain or go in and, if she remained, we left our shadow and walked up to Mangan's steps resignedly. She was waiting for us, her figure defined by the light from the half-opened door. Her brother always teased her before he obeyed and I stood by the railings looking at her. Her dress swung as she moved her body and the soft rope of her hair tossed from side to side.

Every morning I lay on the floor in the front parlour watching her door. The blind was pulled down to within an inch of the sash so that I could not be seen. When she came out on the doorstep my heart leaped. I ran to the hall, seized my books and followed her. I kept her brown figure always in my eye and, when we came near the point at which our ways diverged, I quickened my pace and passed her. This happened morning after morning. I had never spoken to her, except for a few casual words, and yet her name was like a summons to all my foolish blood.

---

1   *The Abbot* 1820 historical novel by Sir Walter Scott about Mary, Queen of Scots; *The Devout Communicant* Title common to several nineteenth-century religious tracts; *The Memoirs of Vidocq* Autobiography of François Vidocq, a nineteenth-century Parisian criminal turned police detective.

2   *areas* Spaces between the railings and the fronts of houses, below street level.

Her image accompanied me even in places the most hostile to romance. On Saturday evenings when my aunt went marketing I had to go to carry some of the parcels. We walked through the flaring streets, jostled by drunken men and bargaining women, amid the curses of labourers, the shrill litanies of shop-boys who stood on guard by the barrels of pigs' cheeks, the nasal chanting of street-singers, who sang a *come-all-you* about O'Donovan Rossa,[1] or a ballad about the troubles in our native land. These noises converged in a single sensation of life for me: I imagined that I bore my chalice safely through a throng of foes. Her name sprang to my lips at moments in strange prayers and praises which I myself did not understand. My eyes were often full of tears (I could not tell why) and at times a flood from my heart seemed to pour itself out into my bosom. I thought little of the future. I did not know whether I would ever speak to her or not or, if I spoke to her, how I could tell her of my confused adoration. But my body was like a harp and her words and gestures were like fingers running upon the wires.

One evening I went into the back drawing-room in which the priest had died. It was a dark rainy evening and there was no sound in the house. Through one of the broken panes I heard the rain impinge upon the earth, the fine incessant needles of water playing in the sodden beds. Some distant lamp or lighted window gleamed below me. I was thankful that I could see so little. All my senses seemed to desire to veil themselves and, feeling that I was about to slip from them, I pressed the palms of my hands together until they trembled, murmuring: *O love! O love!* many times.

At last she spoke to me. When she addressed the first words to me I was so confused that I did not know what to answer. She asked me was I going to *Araby*. I forget whether I answered yes or no. It would be a splendid bazaar, she said; she would love to go.

—And why can't you? I asked.

While she spoke she turned a silver bracelet round and round her wrist. She could not go, she said, because there would be a retreat that week in her convent.[2] Her brother and two other boys were fighting for their caps and I was alone at the railings. She held one of the spikes, bowing her head towards me. The light from the lamp opposite our door caught the white curve of her neck, lit up her hair that rested there and, falling, lit up the hand upon the railing. It fell over one side of her dress and caught the white border of a petticoat, just visible as she stood at ease.

—It's well for you, she said.

---

1   *come-all-you* Ballad, so called because many ballads started with this phrase; *O'Donovan Rossa* Jeremiah O'Donovan Rossa (1831–1915), an activist for Irish independence.

2   *convent* I.e., convent school.

—If I go, I said, I will bring you something.

What innumerable follies laid waste my waking and sleeping thoughts after that evening! I wished to annihilate the tedious intervening days. I chafed against the work of school. At night in my bedroom and by day in the classroom her image came between me and the page I strove to read. The syllables of the word *Araby* were called to me through the silence in which my soul luxuriated and cast an Eastern enchantment over me. I asked for leave to go to the bazaar on Saturday night. My aunt was surprised and hoped it was not some Freemason[1] affair. I answered few questions in class. I watched my master's face pass from amiability to sternness; he hoped I was not beginning to idle. I could not call my wandering thoughts together. I had hardly any patience with the serious work of life which, now that it stood between me and my desire, seemed to me child's play, ugly monotonous child's play.

On Saturday morning I reminded my uncle that I wished to go to the bazaar in the evening. He was fussing at the hallstand, looking for the hatbrush, and answered me curtly:

—Yes, boy, I know.

As he was in the hall I could not go into the front parlour and lie at the window. I left the house in bad humour and walked slowly towards the school. The air was pitilessly raw and already my heart misgave me.

When I came home to dinner my uncle had not yet been home. Still it was early. I sat staring at the clock for some time and, when its ticking began to irritate me, I left the room. I mounted the staircase and gained the upper part of the house. The high cold empty gloomy rooms liberated me and I went from room to room singing. From the front window I saw my companions playing below in the street. Their cries reached me weakened and indistinct and, leaning my forehead against the cool glass, I looked over at the dark house where she lived. I may have stood there for an hour, seeing nothing but the brown-clad figure cast by my imagination, touched discreetly by the lamplight at the curved neck, at the hand upon the railings and at the border below the dress.

When I came downstairs again I found Mrs. Mercer sitting at the fire. She was an old garrulous woman, a pawnbroker's widow, who collected used stamps for some pious purpose. I had to endure the gossip of the tea-table. The meal was prolonged beyond an hour and still my uncle did not come. Mrs. Mercer stood up to go: she was sorry she couldn't wait any longer, but it was after eight o'clock and she did not like to be out late, as the night air was bad for her. When she had gone I began to walk up and down the room, clenching my fists. My aunt said:

---

1   *Freemason* In reference to the Freemasons, a secret society believed by many in Ireland to be anti-Catholic.

—I'm afraid you may put off your bazaar for this night of Our Lord.

At nine o'clock I heard my uncle's latchkey in the halldoor. I heard him talking to himself and heard the hallstand rocking when it had received the weight of his overcoat. I could interpret these signs. When he was midway through his dinner I asked him to give me the money to go to the bazaar. He had forgotten.

—The people are in bed and after their first sleep now, he said.

I did not smile. My aunt said to him energetically:

—Can't you give him the money and let him go? You've kept him late enough as it is.

My uncle said he was very sorry he had forgotten. He said he believed in the old saying: *All work and no play makes Jack a dull boy.* He asked where I was going and, when I had told him a second time he asked me did I know *The Arab's Farewell to his Steed.*[1] When I left the kitchen he was about to recite the opening lines of the piece to my aunt.

I held a florin tightly in my hand as I strode down Buckingham Street towards the station. The sight of the streets thronged with buyers and glaring with gas recalled to me the purpose of my journey. I took my seat in a third-class carriage of a deserted train. After an intolerable delay the train moved out of the station slowly. It crept onward among ruinous houses and over the twinkling river. At Westland Row Station a crowd of people pressed to the carriage doors; but the porters moved them back, saying that it was a special train for the bazaar. I remained alone in the bare carriage. In a few minutes the train drew up beside an improvised wooden platform. I passed out on to the road and saw by the lighted dial of a clock that it was ten minutes to ten. In front of me was a large building which displayed the magical name.

I could not find any sixpenny entrance and, fearing that the bazaar would be closed, I passed in quickly through a turnstile, handing a shilling to a weary-looking man. I found myself in a big hall girdled at half its height by a gallery. Nearly all the stalls were closed and the greater part of the hall was in darkness. I recognized a silence like that which pervades a church after a service. I walked into the centre of the bazaar timidly. A few people were gathered about the stalls which were still open. Before a curtain, over which the words *Café Chantant* were written in coloured lamps, two men were counting money on a salver.[2] I listened to the fall of the coins.

Remembering with difficulty why I had come I went over to one of the stalls and examined porcelain vases and flowered tea-sets. At the door of the

---

1   *The Arab's ... his Steed* Popular Romantic poem by Caroline Norton (1808–77).

2   *Café Chantant* Café that provides musical entertainment; *salver* Tray.

stall a young lady was talking and laughing with two young gentlemen. I remarked their English accents and listened vaguely to their conversation.

—O, I never said such a thing!

—O, but you did!

—O, but I didn't!

—Didn't she say that?

—Yes. I heard her.

—O, there's a ... fib!

Observing me the young lady came over and asked me did I wish to buy anything. The tone of her voice was not encouraging; she seemed to have spoken to me out of a sense of duty. I looked humbly at the great jars that stood like eastern guards at either side of the dark entrance to the stall and murmured:

—No, thank you.

The young lady changed the position of one of the vases and went back to the two young men. They began to talk of the same subject. Once or twice the young lady glanced at me over her shoulder.

I lingered before her stall, though I knew my stay was useless, to make my interest in her wares seem the more real. Then I turned away slowly and walked down the middle of the bazaar. I allowed the two pennies to fall against the sixpence in my pocket. I heard a voice call from one end of the gallery that the light was out. The upper part of the hall was now completely dark.

Gazing up into the darkness I saw myself as a creature driven and derided by vanity; and my eyes burned with anguish and anger.

—1914

Katherine Mansfield

1888–1923

In her short life, Katherine Mansfield managed to secure a reputation as one of the world's most gifted writers of short fiction. Her later stories in particular are important for their experimentation with style and atmosphere; instead of a conventional storyline, these stories present a series of loosely linked moments, portraying the small details of human life as a means of illuminating a specific character at a specific point of crisis or epiphany. Through such small details, Mansfield addresses grand themes such as the evolution of the self and the reality of death. Malcolm Cowley, a contemporary of Mansfield, wrote that her stories "have a thesis: namely, that life is a very wonderful spectacle, but disagreeable for the actors."

Born as Kathleen Mansfield Beauchamp in Wellington, New Zealand, in 1908 Mansfield moved permanently to Europe, where she could live the bohemian life she craved. In London, she cultivated several close—if sometimes tumultuous—friendships within literary circles, most notably with D.H. Lawrence, Virginia Woolf, and Aldous Huxley.

Mansfield grieved profoundly when her youngest brother Leslie was killed in 1915 as a soldier in France. In an effort to console herself she began writing stories about her childhood in New Zealand; thus began her most productive and successful period as a writer. Her long story *Prelude*, first published by Woolf's Hogarth Press in 1918, draws on her memories of New Zealand, as do several of her other stories, some of which return to the characters she introduces in *Prelude*. *Prelude* was reprinted in *Bliss and Other Stories* (1920); this and her following collection, *The Garden Party and Other Stories* (1922), established her importance as a modernist writer.

Troubled by ill health for most of her adult life, Mansfield died of tuberculosis at 34. After her death, her husband John Middleton Murry published two more collections of her stories, as well as editions of her poems, journals, and letters; her letters in particular are valued almost as highly as her short stories for their wit, perceptiveness, and sincerity.

The Garden Party

And after all the weather was ideal. They could not have had a more perfect day for a garden party if they had ordered it. Windless, warm, the sky without a cloud. Only the blue was veiled with a haze of light gold, as it is sometimes in early summer. The gardener had been up since dawn, mowing the lawns and sweeping them, until the grass and the dark flat rosettes where the daisy plants had been seemed to shine. As for the roses, you could not help feeling they understood that roses are the only flowers that impress people at garden parties; the only flowers that everybody is certain of knowing. Hundreds, yes, literally hundreds, had come out in a single night; the green bushes bowed down as though they had been visited by archangels.

Breakfast was not yet over before the men came to put up the marquee.[1]

"Where do you want the marquee put, mother?"

"My dear child, it's no use asking me. I'm determined to leave everything to you children this year. Forget I am your mother. Treat me as an honoured guest."

But Meg could not possibly go and supervise the men. She had washed her hair before breakfast, and she sat drinking her coffee in a green turban, with a dark wet curl stamped on each cheek. Jose, the butterfly, always came down in a silk petticoat and a kimono jacket.

"You'll have to go, Laura, you're the artistic one."

Away Laura flew, still holding her piece of bread-and-butter. It's so delicious to have an excuse for eating out of doors and, besides, she loved having to arrange things; she always felt she could do it so much better than anybody else.

Four men in their shirt-sleeves stood grouped together on the garden path. They carried staves[2] covered with rolls of canvas, and they had big tool-bags slung on their backs. They looked impressive. Laura wished now that she was not holding that piece of bread-and-butter, but there was nowhere to put it, and she couldn't possibly throw it away. She blushed and tried to look severe and even a little bit short-sighted as she came up to them.

"Good morning," she said, copying her mother's voice. But that sounded so fearfully affected that she was ashamed, and stammered like a little girl, "Oh—er—have you come—is it about the marquee?"

"That's right, miss," said the tallest of the men, a lanky, freckled fellow, and he shifted his tool-bag, knocked back his straw hat, and smiled down at her. "That's about it."

His smile was so easy, so friendly, that Laura recovered. What nice eyes he had, small, but such a dark blue! And now she looked at the others, they were smiling too. "Cheer up, we won't bite," their smile seemed to say. How very nice workmen were! And what a beautiful morning! She mustn't mention the morning; she must be businesslike. The marquee.

"Well, what about the lily-lawn? Would that do?"

And she pointed to the lily-lawn with the hand that didn't hold the bread-and-butter. They turned, they stared in the direction. A little fat chap thrust out his underlip, and the tall fellow frowned.

---

1   *marquee* Tent.
2   *staves* Rods.

"I don't fancy it," said he. "Not conspicuous enough. You see, with a thing like a marquee," and he turned to Laura in his easy way, "you want to put it somewhere where it'll give you a bang slap in the eye, if you follow me."

Laura's upbringing made her wonder for a moment whether it was quite respectful of a workman to talk to her of bangs slap in the eye. But she did quite follow him.

"A corner of the tennis court," she suggested. "But the band's going to be in one corner."

"H'm, going to have a band, are you?" said another of the workmen. He was pale. He had a haggard look as his dark eyes scanned the tennis court. What was he thinking?

"Only a very small band," said Laura gently. Perhaps he wouldn't mind so much if the band was quite small. But the tall fellow interrupted.

"Look here, miss, that's the place. Against those trees. Over there. That'll do fine."

Against the karakas. Then the karaka trees would be hidden. And they were so lovely, with their broad, gleaming leaves, and their clusters of yellow fruit. They were like trees you imagined growing up on a desert island, proud, solitary, lifting their leaves and fruits to the sun in a kind of silent splendour. Must they be hidden by a marquee?

They must. Already the men had shouldered their staves and were making for the place. Only the tall fellow was left. He bent down, pinched a sprig of lavender, put his thumb and forefinger to his nose and snuffed up the smell. When Laura saw that gesture she forgot all about the karakas in her wonder at him caring for things like that—caring for the smell of lavender. How many men that she knew would have done such a thing. *Oh, how extraordinarily nice workmen were*, she thought. Why couldn't she have workmen for friends rather than the silly boys she danced with and who came to Sunday night supper? She would get on much better with men like these.

It's all the fault, she decided, as the tall fellow drew something on the back of an envelope, something that was to be looped up or left to hang, of these absurd class distinctions. Well, for her part, she didn't feel them. Not a bit, not an atom.... And now there came the chock-chock of wooden hammers. Someone whistled, someone sang out, "Are you right there, matey?" "Matey!" The friendliness of it, the—the—Just to prove how happy she was, just to show the tall fellow how at home she felt, and how she despised stupid conventions, Laura took a big bite of her bread-and-butter as she stared at the little drawing. She felt just like a work-girl.

"Laura, Laura, where are you? Telephone, Laura!" a voice cried from the house.

"Coming!" Away she skimmed, over the lawn, up the path, up the steps, across the veranda, and into the porch. In the hall her father and Laurie were brushing their hats ready to go to the office.

"I say, Laura," said Laurie very fast, "you might just give a squiz[1] at my coat before this afternoon. See if it wants pressing."

"I will," said she. Suddenly she couldn't stop herself. She ran at Laurie and gave him a small, quick squeeze. "Oh, I do love parties, don't you?" gasped Laura.

"Ra-ther," said Laurie's warm, boyish voice, and he squeezed his sister too, and gave her a gentle push. "Dash off to the telephone, old girl."

The telephone. "Yes, yes; oh yes. Kitty? Good morning, dear. Come to lunch? Do, dear. Delighted of course. It will only be a very scratch[2] meal—just the sandwich crusts and broken meringue-shells and what's left over. Yes, isn't it a perfect morning? Your white? Oh, I certainly should. One moment—hold the line. Mother's calling." And Laura sat back. "What, mother? Can't hear."

Mrs. Sheridan's voice floated down the stairs. "Tell her to wear that sweet hat she had on last Sunday."

"Mother says you're to wear that *sweet* hat you had on last Sunday. Good. One o'clock. Bye-bye."

Laura put back the receiver, flung her arms over her head, took a deep breath, stretched, and let them fall. "Huh," she sighed, and the moment after the sigh she sat up quickly. She was still, listening. All the doors in the house seemed to be open. The house was alive with soft, quick steps and running voices. The green baize door[3] that led to the kitchen regions swung open and shut with a muffled thud. And now there came a long, chuckling absurd sound. It was the heavy piano being moved on its stiff castors. But the air! If you stopped to notice, was the air always like this? Little faint winds were playing chase in at the tops of the windows, out at the doors. And there were two tiny spots of sun, one on the inkpot, one on a silver photograph frame, playing too. Darling little spots. Especially the one on the inkpot lid. It was quite warm. A warm little silver star. She could have kissed it.

The front door bell pealed, and there sounded the rustle of Sadie's print skirt on the stairs. A man's voice murmured; Sadie answered, careless, "I'm sure I don't know. Wait. I'll ask Mrs. Sheridan."

"What is it, Sadie?" Laura came into the hall.

"It's the florist, Miss Laura."

---

1   *squiz* New Zealand slang: a quick, close look.

2   *scratch* Quickly thrown together.

3   *green baize door* Swinging door that separated the servants' quarters from the rest of the house. Baize, a felt-like fabric, was often tacked to the inside of doors to insulate against noise.

It was, indeed. There, just inside the door, stood a wide, shallow tray full of pots of pink lilies. No other kind. Nothing but lilies—canna lilies, big pink flowers, wide open, radiant, almost frighteningly alive on bright crimson stems.

"O-oh, Sadie!" said Laura, and the sound was like a little moan. She crouched down as if to warm herself at that blaze of lilies; she felt they were in her fingers, on her lips, growing in her breast.

"It's some mistake," she said faintly. "Nobody ever ordered so many. Sadie, go and find mother."

But at that moment Mrs. Sheridan joined them.

"It's quite right," she said calmly. "Yes, I ordered them. Aren't they lovely?" She pressed Laura's arm. "I was passing the shop yesterday, and I saw them in the window, and I suddenly thought for once in my life I shall have enough canna lilies. The garden party will be a good excuse."

"But I thought you said you didn't mean to interfere," said Laura. Sadie had gone. The florist's man was still outside at his van. She put her arm round her mother's neck and gently, very gently, she bit her mother's ear.

"My darling child, you wouldn't like a logical mother, would you? Don't do that. Here's the man."

He carried more lilies still, another whole tray.

"Bank them up, just inside the door, on both sides of the porch, please," said Mrs. Sheridan. "Don't you agree, Laura?"

"Oh, I *do*, mother."

In the drawing room Meg, Jose, and good little Hans had at last succeeded in moving the piano.

"Now, if we put this chesterfield against the wall and move everything out of the room except the chairs, don't you think?"

"Quite."

"Hans, move these tables into the smoking room, and bring a sweeper to take these marks off the carpet and—one moment, Hans—" Jose loved giving orders to the servants, and they loved obeying her. She always made them feel they were taking part in some drama. "Tell Mother and Miss Laura to come here at once."

"Very good, Miss Jose."

She turned to Meg. "I want to hear what the piano sounds like, just in case I'm asked to sing this afternoon. Let's try over 'This Life is Weary'."

Pom! Ta-ta-ta *Tee*-ta! The piano burst out so passionately that Jose's face changed. She clasped her hands. She looked mournfully and enigmatically at her mother and Laura as they came in.

This Life is *Wee*-ary,
A Tear—a Sigh.

A Love that *Chan*-ges,
    This Life is *Wee*-ary,
A Tear—a Sigh.
A Love that *Chan*-ges,
And then ... Good-bye!

But at the word "Good-bye", and although the piano sounded more desperate than ever, her face broke into a brilliant, dreadfully unsympathetic smile.

"Aren't I in good voice, mummy?" she beamed.

This Life is *Wee*-ary,
Hope comes to Die,
A Dream—a *Wa*-kening.

But now Sadie interrupted them. "What is it, Sadie?"

"If you please, m'm, cook says have you got the flags for the sandwiches?"

"The flags for the sandwiches, Sadie?" echoed Mrs. Sheridan dreamily. And the children knew by her face that she hadn't got them. "Let me see." And she said to Sadie firmly, "Tell cook I'll let her have them in ten minutes."

Sadie went.

"Now, Laura," said her mother quickly, "come with me into the smoking room. I've got the names somewhere on the back of an envelope. You'll have to write them out for me. Meg, go upstairs this minute and take that wet thing off your head. Jose, run and finish dressing this instant. Do you hear me, children, or shall I have to tell your father when he comes home tonight? And—and, Jose, pacify cook if you do go into the kitchen, will you? I'm terrified of her this morning."

The envelope was found at last behind the dining-room clock, though how it had got there Mrs. Sheridan could not imagine.

"One of you children must have stolen it out of my bag, because I remember vividly—cream-cheese and lemon-curd. Have you done that?"

"Yes."

"Egg and—" Mrs. Sheridan held the envelope away from her. "It looks like mice. It can't be mice, can it?"

"Olive, pet," said Laura, looking over her shoulder.

"Yes, of course, olive. What a horrible combination it sounds. Egg and olive."

They were finished at last, and Laura took them off to the kitchen. She found Jose there pacifying the cook, who did not look at all terrifying.

"I have never seen such exquisite sandwiches," said Jose's rapturous voice. "How many kinds did you say there were, cook? Fifteen?"

"Fifteen, Miss Jose."

"Well, cook, I congratulate you."

Cook swept up crusts with the long sandwich knife, and smiled broadly.

"Godber's has come," announced Sadie, issuing out of the pantry. She had seen the man pass the window.

That meant that cream puffs had come. Godber's were famous for their cream puffs. Nobody ever thought of making them at home.

"Bring them in and put them on the table, my girl," ordered cook.

Sadie brought them in and went back to the door. Of course Laura and Jose were far too grown-up to really care about such things. All the same, they couldn't help agreeing that the puffs looked very attractive. Very. Cook began arranging them, shaking off the extra icing sugar.

"Don't they carry one back to all one's parties?" said Laura.

"I suppose they do," said practical Jose, who never liked to be carried back. "They look beautifully light and feathery, I must say."

"Have one each, my dears," said cook in her comfortable voice. "Yer ma won't know."

Oh, impossible. Fancy cream puffs so soon after breakfast. The very idea made one shudder. All the same, two minutes later Jose and Laura were licking their fingers with that absorbed inward look that only comes from whipped cream.

"Let's go into the garden, out by the back way," suggested Laura. "I want to see how the men are getting on with the marquee. They're such awfully nice men."

But the back door was blocked by cook, Sadie, Godber's man and Hans. Something had happened.

"Tuk-tuk-tuk," clucked cook like an agitated hen. Sadie had her hand clapped to her cheek as though she had a toothache. Hans's face was screwed up in the effort to understand. Only Godber's man seemed to be enjoying himself; it was his story.

"What's the matter? What happened?"

"There's been a horrible accident," said cook. "A man killed."

"A man killed! Where? How? When?"

But Godber's man wasn't going to have his story snatched from under his very nose.

"Know those little cottages just below here, miss?" Know them? Of course, she knew them. "Well, there's a young chap living there, name of *Scott*, a carter.[1] His horse shied at a traction-engine,[2] corner of Hawke Street this morning, and he was thrown out on the back of his head. Killed."

---

1   *carter* Driver of a horse-drawn vehicle used to transport goods.

2   *traction-engine* Steam locomotive used on roads.

"Dead!" Laura stared at Godber's man.

"Dead when they picked him up," said Godber's man with relish. "They were taking the body home as I come up here." And he said to the cook, "He's left a wife and five little ones."

"Jose, come here." Laura caught hold of her sister's sleeve and dragged her through the kitchen to the other side of the green baize door. There she paused and leaned against it. "Jose!" she said, horrified, "however are we going to stop everything?"

"Stop everything, Laura!" cried Jose in astonishment. "What do you mean?"

"Stop the garden party, of course." Why did Jose pretend?

But Jose was still more amazed. "Stop the garden party? My dear Laura, don't be so absurd. Of course we can't do anything of the kind. Nobody expects us to. Don't be so extravagant."

"But we can't possibly have a garden party with a man dead just outside the front gate."

That really was extravagant, for the little cottages were in a lane to themselves at the very bottom of a steep rise that led up to the house. A broad road ran between. True, they were far too near. They were the greatest possible eyesore and they had no right to be in that neighbourhood at all. They were little mean dwellings painted a chocolate brown. In the garden patches there was nothing but cabbage stalks, sick hens and tomato cans. The very smoke coming out of their chimneys was poverty-stricken. Little rags and shreds of smoke, so unlike the great silvery plumes that uncurled from the Sheridans' chimneys. Washerwomen lived in the lane and sweeps and a cobbler and a man whose house-front was studded all over with minute bird-cages. Children swarmed. When the Sheridans were little they were forbidden to set foot there because of the revolting language and of what they might catch. But since they were grown up, Laura and Laurie on their prowls sometimes walked through. It was disgusting and sordid. They came out with a shudder. But still one must go everywhere; one must see everything. So through they went.

"And just think of what the band would sound like to that poor woman," said Laura.

"Oh, Laura!" Jose began to be seriously annoyed. "If you're going to stop a band playing every time someone has an accident, you'll lead a very strenuous life. I'm every bit as sorry about it as you. I feel just as sympathetic." Her eyes hardened. She looked at her sister just as she used to when they were little and fighting together. "You won't bring a drunken workman back to life by being sentimental," she said softly.

"Drunk! Who said he was drunk?" Laura turned furiously on Jose. She said just as they had used to say on those occasions, "I'm going straight up to tell mother."

"Do, dear," cooed Jose.

"Mother, can I come into your room?" Laura turned the big glass door-knob.

"Of course, child. Why, what's the matter? What's given you such a colour?" And Mrs. Sheridan turned round from her dressing-table. She was trying on a new hat.

"Mother, a man's been killed," began Laura.

"*Not* in the garden?" interrupted her mother.

"No, no!"

"Oh, what a fright you gave me!" Mrs. Sheridan sighed with relief, and took off the big hat and held it on her knees.

"But listen, mother," said Laura. Breathless, half-choking, she told the dreadful story. "Of course, we can't have our party, can we?" she pleaded. "The band and everybody arriving. They'd hear us, mother; they're nearly neighbours!"

To Laura's astonishment her mother behaved just like Jose; it was harder to bear because she seemed amused. She refused to take Laura seriously. "But, my dear child, use your common sense. It's only by accident we've heard of it. If someone had died there normally—and I can't understand how they keep alive in those poky little holes—we should still be having our party, shouldn't we?"

Laura had to say "yes" to that, but she felt it was all wrong. She sat down on her mother's sofa and pinched the cushion frill.

"Mother, isn't it really terribly heartless of us?" she asked.

"Darling!" Mrs. Sheridan got up and came over to her, carrying the hat. Before Laura could stop her she had popped it on. "My child!" said her mother, "the hat is yours. It's made for you. It's much too young for me. I have never seen you look such a picture. Look at yourself!" And she held up her hand-mirror.

"But, mother," Laura began again. She couldn't look at herself; she turned aside.

This time Mrs. Sheridan lost patience just as Jose had done.

"You are being very absurd, Laura," she said coldly. "People like that don't expect sacrifices from us. And it's not very sympathetic to spoil everybody's enjoyment as you're doing now."

"I don't understand," said Laura, and she walked quickly out of the room into her own bedroom. There, quite by chance, the first thing she saw was this charming girl in the mirror, in her black hat trimmed with gold daisies and a long black velvet ribbon. Never had she imagined she could look like that. Is mother right? she thought. And now she hoped her mother was right. Am I being extravagant? Perhaps it was extravagant. Just for a moment she had another glimpse of that poor woman and those little children, and the body being carried into the house. But it all seemed blurred, unreal, like a picture in the newspaper. I'll remember it again after the party's over, she decided. And somehow that seemed quite the best plan....

Lunch was over by half-past one. By half-past two they were all ready for the fray. The green-coated band had arrived and was established in a corner of the tennis court.

"My dear!" trilled Kitty Maitland, "aren't they too like frogs for words? You ought to have arranged them round the pond with the conductor in the middle on a leaf."

Laurie arrived and hailed them on his way to dress. At the sight of him Laura remembered the accident again. She wanted to tell him. If Laurie agreed with the others, then it was bound to be all right. And she followed him into the hall.

"Laurie!"

"Hallo!" He was halfway upstairs, but when he turned round and saw Laura he suddenly puffed out his cheeks and goggled his eyes at her. "My word, Laura! You do look stunning," said Laurie. "What an absolutely topping hat!"

Laura said faintly "Is it?" and smiled up at Laurie, and didn't tell him after all.

Soon after that people began coming in streams. The band struck up; the hired waiters ran from the house to the marquee. Wherever you looked there were couples strolling, bending to the flowers, greeting, moving on over the lawn. They were like bright birds that had alighted in the Sheridans' garden for this one afternoon, on their way to—where? Ah, what happiness it is to be with people who all are happy, to press hands, press cheeks, smile into eyes.

"Darling Laura, how well you look!"

"What a becoming hat, child!"

"Laura, you look quite Spanish. I've never seen you look so striking."

And Laura, glowing, answered softly, "Have you had tea? Won't you have an ice? The passion-fruit ices really are rather special." She ran to her father and begged him: "Daddy darling, can't the band have something to drink?"

And the perfect afternoon slowly ripened, slowly faded, slowly its petals closed.

"Never a more delightful garden party ..." "The greatest success ..." "Quite the most ..."

Laura helped her mother with the good-byes. They stood side by side on the porch till it was all over.

"All over, all over, thank heaven," said Mrs. Sheridan. "Round up the others, Laura. Let's go and have some fresh coffee. I'm exhausted. Yes, it's been very successful. But oh, these parties, these parties! Why will you children insist on giving parties!" And they all of them sat down in the deserted marquee.

"Have a sandwich, daddy dear. I wrote the flag."

"Thanks." Mr. Sheridan took a bite and the sandwich was gone. He took another. "I suppose you didn't hear of a beastly accident that happened today?" he said.

"My dear," said Mrs. Sheridan, holding up her hand, "we did. It nearly ruined the party. Laura insisted we should put it off."

"Oh, mother!" Laura didn't want to be teased about it.

"It was a horrible affair all the same," said Mr. Sheridan. "The chap was married too. Lived just below in the lane, and leaves a wife and half a dozen kiddies, so they say."

An awkward little silence fell. Mrs. Sheridan fidgeted with her cup. Really, it was very tactless of father....

Suddenly she looked up. There on the table were all those sandwiches, cakes, puffs, all uneaten, all going to be wasted. She had one of her brilliant ideas.

"I know," she said. "Let's make up a basket. Let's send that poor creature some of this perfectly good food. At any rate, it will be the greatest treat for the children. Don't you agree? And she's sure to have neighbours calling in and so on. What a point to have it all ready prepared. Laura!" She jumped up. "Get me the big basket out of the stairs cupboard."

"But, mother, do you really think it's a good idea?" said Laura.

Again, how curious, she seemed to be different from them all. To take scraps from their party. Would the poor woman really like that?

"Of course! What's the matter with you today? An hour or two ago you were insisting on us being sympathetic."

Oh well! Laura ran for the basket. It was filled, it was now heaped by her mother.

"Take it yourself, darling," said she. "Run down just as you are. No, wait, take the arum lilies too. People of that class are so impressed by arum lilies."

"The stems will ruin her lace frock," said practical Jose.

So they would. Just in time. "Only the basket, then. And, Laura!"—her mother followed her out of the marquee—"don't on any account—"

"What, mother?"

No, better not put such ideas into the child's head! "Nothing! Run along."

It was just growing dusky as Laura shut their garden gates. A big dog ran by like a shadow. The road gleamed white, and down below in the hollow the little cottages were in deep shade. How quiet it seemed after the afternoon. Here she was going down the hill to somewhere where a man lay dead, and she couldn't realize it. Why couldn't she? She stopped a minute. And it seemed to her that kisses, voices, tinkling spoons, laughter, the smell of crushed grass were somehow inside her. She had no room for anything else. How strange!

She looked up at the pale sky, and all she thought was, "Yes, it was the most successful party."

Now the broad road was crossed. The lane began, smoky and dark. Women in shawls and men's tweed caps hurried by. Men hung over the palings; the children played in the doorways. A low hum came from the mean little cottages. In some of them there was a flicker of light, and a shadow, crab-like, moved across the window. Laura bent her head and hurried on. She wished now she had put on a coat. How her frock shone! And the big hat with the velvet streamer—if only it was another hat! Were the people looking at her? They must be. It was a mistake to have come; she knew all along it was a mistake. Should she go back even now?

No, too late. This was the house. It must be. A dark knot of people stood outside. Beside the gate an old, old woman with a crutch sat in a chair, watching. She had her feet on a newspaper. The voices stopped as Laura drew near. The group parted. It was as though she was expected, as though they had known she was coming here.

Laura was terribly nervous. Tossing the velvet ribbon over her shoulder, she said to a woman standing by, "Is this Mrs. Scott's house?" and the woman, smiling queerly, said, "It is, my lass."

Oh, to be away from this! She actually said, "Help me, God," as she walked up the tiny path and knocked. To be away from those staring eyes, or to be covered up in anything, one of those women's shawls even. I'll just leave the basket and go, she decided. I shan't even wait for it to be emptied.

Then the door opened. A little woman in black showed in the gloom.

Laura said, "Are you Mrs. Scott?" But to her horror the woman answered, "Walk in, please, miss," and she was shut in the passage.

"No," said Laura, "I don't want to come in. I only want to leave this basket. Mother sent—"

The little woman in the gloomy passage seemed not to have heard her. "Step this way, please, miss," she said in an oily voice, and Laura followed her.

She found herself in a wretched little low kitchen, lighted by a smoky lamp. There was a woman sitting before the fire.

"Em," said the little creature who had let her in. "Em! It's a young lady." She turned to Laura. She said meaningly, "I'm 'er sister, miss. You'll excuse 'er, won't you?"

"Oh, but of course!" said Laura. "Please, please don't disturb her. I—I only want to leave—"

But at that moment the woman at the fire turned round. Her face, puffed up, red, with swollen eyes and swollen lips, looked terrible. She seemed as though she couldn't understand why Laura was there. What did it mean? Why was this stranger standing in the kitchen with a basket? What was it all about? And the poor face puckered up again.

"All right, my dear," said the other. "I'll thenk the young lady."

And again she began, "You'll excuse her, miss, I'm sure," and her face, swollen too, tried an oily smile.

Laura only wanted to get out, to get away. She was back in the passage. The door opened. She walked straight through into the bedroom where the dead man was lying.

"You'd like a look at 'im, wouldn't you?" said Em's sister, and she brushed past Laura over to the bed. "Don't be afraid, my lass,"—and now her voice sounded fond and sly, and fondly she drew down the sheet—"'e looks a picture. There's nothing to show. Come along, my dear."

Laura came.

There lay a young man, fast asleep—sleeping so soundly, so deeply, that he was far, far away from them both. Oh, so remote, so peaceful. He was dreaming. Never wake him up again. His head was sunk in the pillows, his eyes were closed; they were blind under the closed eyelids. He was given up to his dream. What did garden parties and baskets and lace frocks matter to him? He was far from all those things. He was wonderful, beautiful. While they were laughing and while the band was playing, this marvel had come to the lane. Happy ... happy.... All is well, said that sleeping face. This is just as it should be. I am content.

But all the same you had to cry, and she couldn't go out of the room without saying something to him. Laura gave a loud childish sob.

"Forgive my hat," she said.

And this time she didn't wait for Em's sister. She found her way out of the door, down the path, past all those dark people. At the corner of the lane she met Laurie.

He stepped out of the shadow. "Is that you, Laura?"

"Yes."

"Mother was getting anxious. Was it all right?"

"Yes, quite. Oh, Laurie!" She took his arm, she pressed up against him.

"I say, you're not crying, are you?" asked her brother.

Laura shook her head. She was.

Laurie put his arm round her shoulder. "Don't cry," he said in his warm, loving voice. "Was it awful?"

"No," sobbed Laura. "It was simply marvellous. But, Laurie—" She stopped, she looked at her brother. "Isn't life," she stammered, "isn't life—" But what life was she couldn't explain. No matter. He quite understood.

"*Isn't* it, darling?" said Laurie.

—1922

Ernest Hemingway

1899–1961

Ernest Hemingway is considered one of the great American authors of the twentieth century. His influence can be seen in the objective style of writing he propagated, characterized by sparse sentences devoid of embellishment. Hemingway famously argues for his technique in *Death in the Afternoon* (1932): "If a writer of prose knows enough about what he is writing about he may omit things that he knows and the reader, if the writer is writing truly enough, will have a feeling of those things as strongly as though the writer had stated them. The dignity of movement of an iceberg is due to only one-eighth of it being above water." In 1952, Hemingway was awarded the Pulitzer Prize for his novel *The Old Man and the Sea*, the story of a Cuban fisherman's quest to reel in a giant marlin. In 1954, he was awarded the Nobel Prize in Literature for his "mastery of the art of narrative, most recently demonstrated in *The Old Man and the Sea*, and for the influence that he has exerted on contemporary style."

In 1918, Hemingway travelled to Italy as an ambulance driver for the American Red Cross. His injury and recuperation later that year removed him from service, but the experience inspired his 1929 novel, *A Farewell to Arms*. His first novel, *The Sun Also Rises* (1926), drew from his life as an expatriate in Paris in the 1920s. During the Spanish Civil War (1936–39), Hemingway raised money for the Republican cause and travelled throughout Spain as a journalist. This inspired his greatest commercial success, the 1939 novel *For Whom the Bell Tolls*, a semi-autobiographical story of a young American who fights fascism.

Hemingway's writing reflects his passion for pursuits such as bullfighting, fishing, and hunting, and often examines the cruel legacy of war. In presenting the Nobel Prize to Hemingway, Anders Osterling said: "It may be true that Hemingway's earlier writings display brutal, cynical, and callous sides which may be considered at variance with the Nobel Prize's requirement for a work of an ideal tendency. But on the other hand, he also possesses a heroic pathos which forms the basic element in his awareness of life, a manly love of danger and adventure with a natural admiration for every individual who fights the good fight in a world of reality overshadowed by violence and death."

Hemingway committed suicide in Idaho in 1961, after a period of serious depression.

A Clean, Well-Lighted Place

It was very late and every one had left the café except an old man who sat in the shadow the leaves of the tree made against the electric light. In the day time the street was dusty, but at night the dew settled the dust and the old man liked to sit late because he was deaf and now at night it was quiet and he felt the difference. The two waiters inside the café knew that the old man was a little drunk, and while he was a good client they knew that if he became too drunk he would leave without paying, so they kept watch on him.

"Last week he tried to commit suicide," one waiter said.

"Why?"

"He was in despair."

"What about?"

"Nothing."

"How do you know it was nothing?"

"He has plenty of money."

They sat together at a table that was close against the wall near the door of the café and looked at the terrace where the tables were all empty except where the old man sat in the shadow of the leaves of the tree that moved slightly in the wind. A girl and a soldier went by in the street. The street light shone on the brass number on his collar. The girl wore no head covering and hurried beside him.

"The guard will pick him up," one waiter said.

"What does it matter if he gets what he's after?"

"He had better get off the street now. The guard will get him. They went by five minutes ago."

The old man sitting in the shadow rapped on his saucer with his glass. The younger waiter went over to him.

"What do you want?"

The old man looked at him. "Another brandy," he said.

"You'll be drunk," the waiter said. The old man looked at him. The waiter went away.

"He'll stay all night," he said to his colleague. "I'm sleepy now. I never get into bed before three o'clock. He should have killed himself last week."

The waiter took the brandy bottle and another saucer from the counter inside the café and marched out to the old man's table. He put down the saucer and poured the glass full of brandy.

"You should have killed yourself last week," he said to the deaf man. The old man motioned with his finger. "A little more," he said. The waiter poured on into the glass so that the brandy slopped over and ran down the stem into the top saucer of the pile. "Thank you," the old man said. The waiter took the bottle back inside the café. He sat down at the table with his colleague again.

"He's drunk now," he said.

"He's drunk every night."

"What did he want to kill himself for?"

"How should I know."

"How did he do it?"

"He hung himself with a rope."

"Who cut him down?"

"His niece."

"Why did they do it?"

"Fear for his soul."

"How much money has he got?"

"He's got plenty."

"He must be eighty years old."

"Anyway I should say he was eighty."

"I wish he would go home. I never get to bed before three o'clock. What kind of hour is that to go to bed?"

"He stays up because he likes it."

"He's lonely. I'm not lonely. I have a wife waiting in bed for me."

"He had a wife once too."

"A wife would be no good to him now."

"You can't tell. He might be better with a wife."

"His niece looks after him."

"I know. You said she cut him down."

"I wouldn't want to be that old. An old man is a nasty thing."

"Not always. This old man is clean. He drinks without spilling. Even now, drunk. Look at him."

"I don't want to look at him. I wish he would go home. He has no regard for those who must work."

The old man looked from his glass across the square, then over at the waiters.

"Another brandy," he said, pointing to his glass. The waiter who was in a hurry came over.

"Finished," he said, speaking with that omission of syntax stupid people employ when talking to drunken people or foreigners. "No more tonight. Close now."

"Another," said the old man.

"No. Finished." The waiter wiped the edge of the table with a towel and shook his head.

The old man stood up, slowly counted the saucers, took a leather coin purse from his pocket and paid for the drinks, leaving half a peseta tip.

The waiter watched him go down the street, a very old man walking unsteadily but with dignity.

"Why didn't you let him stay and drink?" the unhurried waiter asked. They were putting up the shutters. "It is not half-past two."

"I want to go home to bed."

"What is an hour?"

"More to me than to him."

"An hour is the same."

"You talk like an old man yourself. He can buy a bottle and drink at home."

"It's not the same."

"No, it is not," agreed the waiter with a wife. He did not wish to be unjust. He was only in a hurry.

"And you? You have no fear of going home before your usual hour?"

"Are you trying to insult me?"

"No, hombre,[1] only to make a joke."

"No," the waiter who was in a hurry said, rising from pulling down the metal shutters. "I have confidence. I am all confidence."

"You have youth, confidence, and a job," the older waiter said. "You have everything."

"And what do you lack?"

"Everything but work."

"You have everything I have."

"No. I have never had confidence and I am not young."

"Come on. Stop talking nonsense and lock up."

"I am of those who like to stay late at the café," the older waiter said. "With all those who do not want to go to bed. With all those who need a light for the night."

"I want to go home and into bed."

"We are of two different kinds," the older waiter said. He was now dressed to go home. "It is not only a question of youth and confidence although those things are very beautiful. Each night I am reluctant to close up because there may be some one who needs the café."

"Hombre, there are bodegas[2] open all night long."

"You do not understand. This is a clean and pleasant café. It is well lighted. The light is very good and also, now, there are shadows of the leaves."

---

1   *hombre* Spanish: man, dude.

2   *bodegas* Wine sellers, cheap drinking establishments.

"Good night," said the younger waiter.

"Good night," the other said. Turning off the electric light he continued the conversation with himself. It is the light of course but it is necessary that the place be clean and pleasant. You do not want music. Certainly you do not want music. Nor can you stand before a bar with dignity although that is all that is provided for these hours. What did he fear? It was not a fear or dread. It was a nothing that he knew too well. It was all a nothing and a man was nothing too. It was only that and light was all it needed and a certain cleanness and order. Some lived in it and never felt it but he knew it all was nada y pues nada[1] y nada y pues nada. Our nada who art in nada, nada be thy name thy kingdom nada thy will be nada in nada as it is in nada. Give us this nada our daily nada and nada us our nada as we nada our nadas and nada us not into nada but deliver us from nada; pues nada. Hail nothing full of nothing, nothing is with thee.[2] He smiled and stood before a bar with a shining steam pressure coffee machine.

"What's yours?" asked the barman.

"Nada."

"Otro loco más,"[3] said the barman and turned away.

"A little cup," said the waiter.

The barman poured it for him.

"The light is very bright and pleasant but the bar is unpolished," the waiter said.

The barman looked at him but did not answer. It was too late at night for conversation.

"You want another copita?"[4] the barman asked.

"No, thank you," said the waiter and went out. He disliked bars and bodegas. A clean, well-lighted café was a very different thing. Now, without thinking further, he would go home to his room. He would lie in the bed and finally, with daylight, he would go to sleep. After all, he said to himself, it is probably only insomnia. Many must have it.

—1933

---

1   *nada … nada* Spanish: nothing and then nothing.
2   *Our nada … with thee* Parodies the Lord's Prayer, which is included in the New Testament (see Matthew 6:9–13) and used in most Christian churches.
3   *Otro loco más* Spanish: One more madman.
4   *copita* Spanish: glass.

Flannery O'Connor
1925–1964

Born in Savannah, Georgia, Mary Flannery O'Connor spent most of her life in the American South, where her novels and most of her short stories are set. Participating in the tradition of the "Southern Gothic," her writing blends humour and the grotesque, often incorporating bleak or violent events and physically deformed or morally twisted characters. O'Connor approached the "Southern Gothic" through the lens of her intensely deep Catholic faith; indeed, she writes that "the meaning of life is centered in our Redemption by Christ and what I see in the world I see in its relation to that."

After graduating from the Georgia State College for Women in 1945, O'Connor spent three years at the prestigious Writers' Workshop at the University of Iowa. She probably would have remained in the northern United States if she were not struck in 1950 by the first signs of lupus. Weakened by the disease and the debilitating cortisone treatments it required, she went to live with her mother in Milledgeville, Georgia, where she would remain for the rest of her life.

Although O'Connor was a deeply committed Catholic, her fiction is set in the Southern "Bible Belt" where Protestantism was predominant, and her characters are often Protestant fundamentalists who are both materially and spiritually poor. Her stories focus on terrible events befalling such characters, she said, in order to portray "the action of grace in territory held largely by the devil." She described her short story collection *A Good Man Is Hard to Find* (1955), which received the O. Henry first prize for short fiction, as a book of "stories about original sin."

In addition to *A Good Man Is Hard to Find*, O'Connor published two novels—*Wise Blood* (1952) and *The Violent Bear It Away* (1960)—before her early death in 1964 as a result of lupus. Her last short story collection, *Everything that Rises Must Converge*, was published posthumously the following year.

A Good Man Is Hard to Find

The grandmother didn't want to go to Florida. She wanted to visit some of her connections in east Tennessee and she was seizing at every chance to change Bailey's mind. Bailey was the son she lived with, her only boy. He was sitting on the edge of his chair at the table, bent over the orange sports section of the *Journal*. "Now look here, Bailey," she said, "see here, read this," and she stood with one hand on her thin hip and the other rattling the newspaper at his bald head. "Here this fellow that calls himself The Misfit is aloose from the Federal Pen and headed toward Florida and you read here what it says he did to these people. Just you read it. I wouldn't take my children in any direction with a criminal like that aloose in it. I couldn't answer to my conscience if I did."

Bailey didn't look up from his reading so she wheeled around then and faced the children's mother, a young woman in slacks, whose face was as broad and innocent as a cabbage and was tied around with a green head-kerchief that had two points on the top like rabbit's ears. She was sitting on the sofa, feeding the baby his apricots out of a jar. "The children have been to Florida before," the old lady said. "You all ought to take them somewhere else for a change so they would see different parts of the world and be broad. They never have been to east Tennessee."

The children's mother didn't seem to hear her but the eight-year-old boy, John Wesley, a stocky child with glasses, said, "If you don't want to go to Florida, why dontcha stay at home?" He and the little girl, June Star, were reading the funny papers on the floor.

"She wouldn't stay at home to be queen for a day," June Star said without raising her yellow head.

"Yes and what would you do if this fellow, The Misfit, caught you?" the grandmother asked.

"I'd smack his face," John Wesley said.

"She wouldn't stay at home for a million bucks," June Star said. "Afraid she'd miss something. She has to go everywhere we go."

"All right, Miss," the grandmother said. "Just remember that the next time you want me to curl your hair."

June Star said her hair was naturally curly.

The next morning the grandmother was the first one in the car, ready to go. She had her big black valise that looked like the head of a hippopotamus in one corner, and underneath it she was hiding a basket with Pitty Sing, the cat, in it. She didn't intend for the cat to be left alone in the house for three days because he would miss her too much and she was afraid he might brush against one of the gas burners and accidentally asphyxiate himself. Her son, Bailey, didn't like to arrive at a motel with a cat.

She sat in the middle of the back seat with John Wesley and June Star on either side of her. Bailey and the children's mother and the baby sat in front and they left Atlanta at eight forty-five with the mileage on the car at 55890. The grandmother wrote this down because she thought it would be interesting to say how many miles they had been when they got back. It took them twenty minutes to reach the outskirts of the city.

The old lady settled herself comfortably, removing her white cotton gloves and putting them up with her purse on the shelf in front of the back window. The children's mother still had on slacks and still had her head tied up in a green kerchief, but the grandmother had on a navy blue straw sailor hat with a bunch of white violets on the brim and a navy blue dress with a small white dot in the print. Her collars and cuffs were white organdy trimmed with lace and at her neckline she had pinned a purple spray of cloth violets containing a sachet. In case of an accident, anyone seeing her dead on the highway would know at once that she was a lady.

She said she thought it was going to be a good day for driving, neither too hot nor too cold, and she cautioned Bailey that the speed limit was fifty-five miles an hour and that the patrolmen hid themselves behind billboards and small clumps of trees and sped out after you before you had a chance to slow down. She pointed out interesting details of the scenery: Stone Mountain; the blue granite that in some places came up to both sides of the highway; the brilliant red clay banks slightly streaked with purple; and the various crops that made rows of green lace-work on the ground. The trees were full of silver-white sunlight and the meanest of them sparkled. The children were reading comic magazines and their mother had gone back to sleep.

"Let's go through Georgia fast so we won't have to look at it much," John Wesley said.

"If I were a little boy," said the grandmother, "I wouldn't talk about my native state that way. Tennessee has the mountains and Georgia has the hills."

"Tennessee is just a hillbilly dumping ground," John Wesley said, "and Georgia is a lousy state too."

"You said it," June Star said.

"In my time," said the grandmother, folding her thin veined fingers, "children were more respectful of their native states and their parents and everything else. People did right then. Oh look at the cute little pickaninny!"[1] she said and pointed to a Negro child standing in the door of a shack. "Wouldn't that make a picture, now?" she asked and they all turned and looked at the little Negro out of the back window. He waved.

"He didn't have any britches on," June Star said.

"He probably didn't have any," the grandmother explained. "Little niggers[2] in the country don't have things like we do. If I could paint, I'd paint that picture," she said.

The children exchanged comic books.

The grandmother offered to hold the baby and the children's mother passed him over the front seat to her. She set him on her knee and bounced him and told him about the things they were passing. She rolled her eyes and screwed up her mouth and stuck her leathery thin face into his smooth bland

---

1   *pickaninny* Derogatory term for an African American child.
2   *niggers* This pejorative term remained in frequent use by many white Americans in the South until well into the 1960s.

one. Occasionally he gave her a faraway smile. They passed a large cotton field with five or six graves fenced in the middle of it, like a small island. "Look at the graveyard!" the grandmother said, pointing it out. "That was the old family burying ground. That belonged to the plantation."

"Where's the plantation?" John Wesley asked.

"Gone With the Wind," said the grandmother. "Ha. Ha."

When the children finished all the comic books they had brought, they opened the lunch and ate it. The grandmother ate a peanut butter sandwich and an olive and would not let the children throw the box and the paper napkins out the window. When there was nothing else to do they played a game by choosing a cloud and making the other two guess what shape it suggested. John Wesley took one the shape of a cow and June Star guessed a cow and John Wesley said, no, an automobile, and June Star said he didn't play fair, and they began to slap each other over the grandmother.

The grandmother said she would tell them a story if they would keep quiet. When she told a story, she rolled her eyes and waved her head and was very dramatic. She said once when she was a maiden lady she had been courted by a Mr. Edgar Atkins Teagarden from Jasper, Georgia. She said he was a very good-looking man and a gentleman and that he brought her a watermelon every Saturday afternoon with his initials cut in it, E.A.T. Well, one Saturday, she said, Mr. Teagarden brought the watermelon and there was nobody at home and he left it on the front porch and returned in his buggy to Jasper, but she never got the watermelon, she said, because a nigger boy ate it when he saw the initials, E.A.T.! This story tickled John Wesley's funny bone and he giggled and giggled but June Star didn't think it was any good. She said she wouldn't marry a man that just brought her a watermelon on Saturday. The grandmother said she would have done well to marry Mr. Teagarden because he was a gentleman and had bought Coca-Cola stock when it first came out and that he had died only a few years ago, a very wealthy man.

They stopped at The Tower for barbecued sandwiches. The Tower was a part stucco and part wood filling station and dance hall set in a clearing outside of Timothy. A fat man named Red Sammy Butts ran it and there were signs stuck here and there on the building and for miles up and down the highway saying, TRY RED SAMMY'S FAMOUS BARBECUE. NONE LIKE FAMOUS RED SAMMY'S! RED SAM! THE FAT BOY WITH THE HAPPY LAUGH. A VETERAN! RED SAMMY'S YOUR MAN!

Red Sammy was lying on the bare ground outside The Tower with his head under a truck while a grey monkey about a foot high, chained to a small chinaberry tree, chattered nearby. The monkey sprang back into the tree and got on the highest limb as soon as he saw the children jump out of the car and run toward him.

Inside, The Tower was a long dark room with a counter at one end and tables at the other and dancing space in the middle. They all sat down at a board table next to the nickelodeon and Red Sam's wife, a tall burnt-brown woman with hair and eyes lighter than her skin, came and took their order. The children's mother put a dime in the machine and played "The Tennessee Waltz," and the grandmother said that tune always made her want to dance. She asked Bailey if he would like to dance but he only glared at her. He didn't have a naturally sunny disposition like she did and trips made him nervous. The grandmother's brown eyes were very bright. She swayed her head from side to side and pretended she was dancing in her chair. June Star said play something she could tap to so the children's mother put in another dime and played a fast number and June Star stepped out onto the dance floor and did her tap routine.

"Ain't she cute?" Red Sam's wife said, leaning over the counter. "Would you like to come be my little girl?"

"No I certainly wouldn't," June Star said. "I wouldn't live in a broken-down place like this for a million bucks!" and she ran back to the table.

"Ain't she cute?" the woman repeated, stretching her mouth politely.

"Ain't you ashamed?" hissed the grandmother.

Red Sam came in and told his wife to quit lounging on the counter and hurry up with these people's order. His khaki trousers reached just to his hip bones and his stomach hung over them like a sack of meal swaying under his shirt. He came over and sat down at a table nearby and let out a combination sigh and yodel. "You can't win," he said. "You can't win," and he wiped his sweating red face off with a grey handkerchief. "These days you don't know who to trust," he said. "Ain't that the truth?"

"People are certainly not nice like they used to be," said the grandmother.

"Two fellers come in here last week," Red Sammy said, "driving a Chrysler. It was a old beat-up car but it was a good one and these boys looked all right to me. Said they worked at the mill and you know I let them fellers charge the gas they bought? Now why did I do that?"

"Because you're a good man!" the grandmother said at once.

"Yes'm, I suppose so," Red Sam said as if he were struck with this answer.

His wife brought the orders, carrying the five plates all at once without a tray, two in each hand and one balanced on her arm. "It isn't a soul in this green world of God's that you can trust," she said. "And I don't count nobody out of that, not nobody," she repeated, looking at Red Sammy.

"Did you read about that criminal, The Misfit, that's escaped?" asked the grandmother.

"I wouldn't be a bit surprised if he didn't attact this place right here," said the woman. "If he hears about it being here, I wouldn't be none surprised to see him. If he hears it's two cent in the cash register, I wouldn't be a tall surprised if he...."

"That'll do," Red Sam said. "Go bring these people their Co'-Colas," and the woman went off to get the rest of the order.

"A good man is hard to find," Red Sammy said. "Everything is getting terrible. I remember the day you could go off and leave your screen door unlatched. Not no more."

He and the grandmother discussed better times. The old lady said that in her opinion Europe was entirely to blame for the way things were now. She said the way Europe acted you would think we were made of money and Red Sam said it was no use talking about it, she was exactly right. The children ran outside into the white sunlight and looked at the monkey in the lacy chinaberry tree. He was busy catching fleas on himself and biting each one carefully between his teeth as if it were a delicacy.

They drove off again into the hot afternoon. The grandmother took cat naps and woke up every few minutes with her own snoring. Outside of Toombsboro she woke up and recalled an old plantation that she had visited in this neighbourhood once when she was a young lady. She said the house had six white columns across the front and that there was an avenue of oaks leading up to it and two little wooden trellis arbours on either side in front where you sat down with your suitor after a stroll in the garden. She recalled exactly which road to turn off to get to it. She knew that Bailey would not be willing to lose any time looking at an old house, but the more she talked about it, the more she wanted to see it once again and find out if the little twin arbours were still standing. "There was a secret panel in this house," she said craftily, not telling the truth but wishing that she were, "and the story went that all the family silver was hidden in it when Sherman[1] came through but it was never found ..."

"Hey!" John Wesley said. "Let's go see it! We'll find it! We'll poke all the woodwork and find it! Who lives there? Where do you turn off at? Hey Pop, can't we turn off there?"

"We never have seen a house with a secret panel!" June Star shrieked. "Let's go to the house with the secret panel! Hey, Pop, can't we go see the house with the secret panel!"

"It's not far from here, I know," the grandmother said. "It wouldn't take over twenty minutes."

Bailey was looking straight ahead. His jaw was as rigid as a horseshoe. "No," he said.

---

1   *Sherman* American Union commander William Tecumseh Sherman.

The children began to yell and scream that they wanted to see the house with the secret panel. John Wesley kicked the back of the front seat and June Star hung over her mother's shoulder and whined desperately into her ear that they never had any fun even on their vacation, that they could never do what THEY wanted to do. The baby began to scream and John Wesley kicked the back of the seat so hard that his father could feel the blows in his kidney.

"All right!" he shouted and drew the car to a stop at the side of the road. "Will you all shut up? Will you all just shut up for one second? If you don't shut up, we won't go anywhere."

"It would be very educational for them," the grandmother murmured.

"All right," Bailey said, "but get this: this is the only time we're going to stop for anything like this. This is the one and only time."

"The dirt road that you have to turn down is about a mile back," the grandmother directed. "I marked it when we passed."

"A dirt road," Bailey groaned.

After they had turned around and were headed toward the dirt road, the grandmother recalled other points about the house, the beautiful glass over the front doorway and the candle-lamp in the hall. John Wesley said that the secret panel was probably in the fireplace.

"You can't go inside this house," Bailey said. "You don't know who lives there."

"While you all talk to the people in front, I'll run around behind and get in a window," John Wesley suggested.

"We'll all stay in the car," his mother said.

They turned onto the dirt road and the car raced roughly along in a swirl of pink dust. The grandmother recalled the times when there were no paved roads and thirty miles was a day's journey. The dirt road was hilly and there were sudden washes in it and sharp curves on dangerous embankments. All at once they would be on a hill, looking down over the blue tops of trees for miles around, then the next minute, they would be in a red depression with the dust-coated trees looking down on them.

"This place had better turn up in a minute," Bailey said, "or I'm going to turn around."

The road looked as if no one had travelled on it in months.

"It's not much farther," the grandmother said and just as she said it, a horrible thought came to her. The thought was so embarrassing that she turned red in the face and her eyes dilated and her feet jumped up, upsetting her valise in the corner. The instant the valise moved, the newspaper top she had over the basket under it rose with a snarl and Pitty Sing, the cat, sprang onto Bailey's shoulder.

The children were thrown to the floor and their mother, clutching the baby, was thrown out the door onto the ground; the old lady was thrown into the front seat. The car turned over once and landed right-side-up in a gulch off the side of the road. Bailey remained in the driver's seat with the cat—grey-striped with a broad white face and an orange nose—clinging to his neck like a caterpillar.

As soon as the children saw they could move their arms and legs, they scrambled out of the car, shouting, "We've had an ACCIDENT!" The grand-mother was curled up under the dashboard, hoping she was injured so that Bailey's wrath would not come down on her all at once. The horrible thought she had had before the accident was that the house she had remembered so vividly was not in Georgia but in Tennessee.

Bailey removed the cat from his neck with both hands and flung it out the window against the side of a pine tree. Then he got out of the car and started looking for the children's mother. She was sitting against the side of the red gutted ditch, holding the screaming baby, but she only had a cut down her face and a broken shoulder. "We've had an ACCIDENT!" the children screamed in a frenzy of delight.

"But nobody's killed," June Star said with disappointment as the grand-mother limped out of the car, her hat still pinned to her head but the broken front brim standing up at a jaunty angle and the violet spray hanging off the side. They all sat down in the ditch, except the children, to recover from the shock. They were all shaking.

"Maybe a car will come along," said the children's mother hoarsely.

"I believe I have injured an organ," said the grandmother, pressing her side, but no one answered her. Bailey's teeth were clattering. He had on a yellow sport shirt with bright blue parrots designed in it and his face was as yellow as the shirt. The grandmother decided that she would not mention that the house was in Tennessee.

The road was about ten feet above and they could see only the tops of the trees on the other side of it. Behind the ditch they were sitting in there were more woods, tall and dark and deep. In a few minutes they saw a car some distance away on top of a hill, coming slowly as if the occupants were watching them. The grandmother stood up and waved both arms dramatically to attract their attention. The car continued to come on slowly, disappeared around a bend and appeared again, moving even slower, on top of the hill they had gone over. It was a big black battered hearse-like automobile. There were three men in it.

It came to a stop just over them and for some minutes, the driver looked down with a steady expressionless gaze to where they were sitting, and didn't speak. Then he turned his head and muttered something to the other two and they got out. One was a fat boy in black trousers and a red sweat shirt with a silver stallion embossed on the front of it. He moved around on the right side of them and stood staring, his mouth partly open in a kind of loose grin. The other had on khaki pants and a blue striped coat and a grey hat pulled down very low, hiding most of his face. He came around slowly on the left side. Neither spoke.

The driver got out of the car and stood by the side of it, looking down at them. He was an older man than the other two. His hair was just beginning to grey and he wore silver-rimmed spectacles that gave him a scholarly look. He had a long creased face and didn't have on any shirt or undershirt. He had on blue jeans that were too tight for him and was holding a black hat and a gun. The two boys also had guns.

"We've had an ACCIDENT!" the children screamed.

The grandmother had the peculiar feeling that the bespectacled man was someone she knew. His face was as familiar to her as if she had known him all her life but she could not recall who he was. He moved away from the car and began to come down the embankment, placing his feet carefully so that he wouldn't slip. He had on tan and white shoes and no socks, and his ankles were red and thin. "Good afternoon," he said. "I see you all had you a little spill."

"We turned over twice!" said the grandmother.

"Oncet," he corrected. "We seen it happen. Try their car and see will it run, Hiram," he said quietly to the boy with the grey hat.

"What you got that gun for?" John Wesley asked. "Whatcha gonna do with that gun?"

"Lady," the man said to the children's mother, "would you mind calling them children to sit down by you? Children make me nervous. I want all you all to sit down right together there where you're at."

"What are you telling US what to do for?" June Star asked.

Behind them the line of woods gaped like a dark open mouth. "Come here," said their mother.

"Look here now," Bailey began suddenly, "we're in a predicament! We're in...."

The grandmother shrieked. She scrambled to her feet and stood staring. "You're The Misfit!" she said. "I recognized you at once!"

"Yes'm," the man said, smiling slightly as if he were pleased in spite of himself to be known, "but it would have been better for all of you, lady, if you hadn't of reckernized me."

Bailey turned his head sharply and said something to his mother that shocked even the children. The old lady began to cry and The Misfit reddened.

"Lady," he said, "don't you get upset. Sometimes a man says things he don't mean. I don't reckon he meant to talk to you thataway."

"You wouldn't shoot a lady, would you?" the grandmother said and removed a clean handkerchief from her cuff and began to slap at her eyes with it.

The Misfit pointed the toe of his shoe into the ground and made a little hole and then covered it up again. "I would hate to have to," he said.

"Listen," the grandmother almost screamed, "I know you're a good man. You don't look a bit like you have common blood. I know you must come from nice people!"

"Yes mam," he said, "finest people in the world." When he smiled he showed a row of strong white teeth. "God never made a finer woman than my mother and my daddy's heart was pure gold," he said. The boy with the red sweat shirt had come around behind them and was standing with his gun at his hip. The Misfit squatted down on the ground. "Watch them children, Bobby Lee," he said. "You know they make me nervous." He looked at the six of them huddled together in front of him and he seemed to be embarrassed as if he couldn't think of anything to say. "Ain't a cloud in the sky," he remarked, looking up at it. "Don't see no sun but don't see no cloud neither."

"Yes, it's a beautiful day," said the grandmother. "Listen," she said, "you shouldn't call yourself The Misfit because I know you're a good man at heart. I can just look at you and tell."

"Hush!" Bailey yelled. "Hush! Everybody shut up and let me handle this!" He was squatting in the position of a runner about to sprint forward but he didn't move.

"I pre-chate that, lady," The Misfit said and drew a little circle in the ground with the butt of his gun.

"It'll take a half a hour to fix this here car," Hiram called, looking over the raised hood of it.

"Well, first you and Bobby Lee get him and that little boy to step over yonder with you," The Misfit said, pointing to Bailey and John Wesley. "The boys want to ast you something," he said to Bailey. "Would you mind stepping back in them woods there with them?"

"Listen," Bailey began, "we're in a terrible predicament! Nobody realizes what this is," and his voice cracked. His eyes were as blue and intense as the parrots in his shirt and he remained perfectly still.

The grandmother reached up to adjust her hat brim as if she were going to the woods with him but it came off in her hand. She stood staring at it and after a second she let it fall on the ground. Hiram pulled Bailey up by the arm as if he were assisting an old man. John Wesley caught hold of his father's hand and Bobby Lee followed. They went off toward the woods and just as they reached the dark edge, Bailey turned and supporting himself against a grey naked pine trunk, he shouted, "I'll be back in a minute, Mamma, wait on me!"

"Come back this instant!" his mother shrilled but they all disappeared into the woods.

"Bailey Boy!" the grandmother called in a tragic voice but she found she was looking at The Misfit squatting on the ground in front of her. "I just know you're a good man," she said desperately. "You're not a bit common!"

"Nome, I ain't a good man," The Misfit said after a second as if he had considered her statement carefully, "but I ain't the worst in the world neither. My daddy said I was a different breed of dog from my brothers and sisters. 'You know,' Daddy said, 'it's some that can live their whole life out without asking about it and it's others has to know why it is, and this boy is one of the latters. He's going to be into everything!'" He put on his black hat and looked up suddenly and then away deep into the woods as if he were embarrassed again. "I'm sorry I don't have on a shirt before you ladies," he said, hunching his shoulders slightly. "We buried our clothes that we had on when we escaped and we're just making do until we can get better. We borrowed these from some folks we met," he explained.

"That's perfectly all right," the grandmother said. "Maybe Bailey has an extra shirt in his suitcase."

"I'll look and see terrectly," The Misfit said.

"Where are they taking him?" the children's mother screamed.

"Daddy was a card himself," The Misfit said. "You couldn't put anything over on him. He never got in trouble with the Authorities though. Just had the knack of handling them."

"You could be honest too if you'd only try," said the grandmother. "Think how wonderful it would be to settle down and live a comfortable life and not have to think about somebody chasing you all the time."

The Misfit kept scratching in the ground with the butt of his gun as if he were thinking about it. "Yes'm, somebody is always after you," he murmured.

The grandmother noticed how thin his shoulder blades were just behind his hat because she was standing up looking down on him. "Do you ever pray?" she asked.

He shook his head. All she saw was the black hat wiggle between his shoulder blades. "Nome," he said.

There was a pistol shot from the woods, followed closely by another. Then silence. The old lady's head jerked around. She could hear the wind move through the tree tops like a long satisfied insuck of breath. "Bailey Boy!" she called.

"I was a gospel singer for a while," The Misfit said. "I been most everything. Been in the arm service, both land and sea, at home and abroad, been twict married, been an undertaker, been with the railroads, plowed Mother Earth, been in a tornado, seen a man burnt alive oncet," and he looked up at the children's mother and the little girl who were sitting close together, their faces white and their eyes glassy; "I even seen a woman flogged," he said.

"Pray, pray," the grandmother began, "pray, pray...."

"I never was a bad boy that I remember of," The Misfit said in an almost dreamy voice, "but somewheres along the line I done something wrong and got sent to the penitentiary. I was buried alive," and he looked up and held her attention to him by a steady stare.

"That's when you should have started to pray," she said. "What did you do to get sent to the penitentiary that first time?"

"Turn to the right, it was a wall," The Misfit said, looking up again at the cloudless sky. "Turn to the left, it was a wall. Look up it was a ceiling, look down it was a floor. I forget what I done, lady. I set there and set there, trying to remember what it was I done and I ain't recalled it to this day. Oncet in a while, I would think it was coming to me, but it never come."

"Maybe they put you in by mistake," the old lady said vaguely.

"Nome," he said. "It wasn't no mistake. They had the papers on me."

"You must have stolen something," she said.

The Misfit sneered slightly. "Nobody had nothing I wanted," he said. "It was a head-doctor at the penitentiary said what I had done was kill my daddy but I known that for a lie. My daddy died in nineteen ought nineteen of the epidemic flu and I never had a thing to do with it. He was buried in the Mount Hopewell Baptist churchyard and you can go there and see for yourself."

"If you would pray," the old lady said, "Jesus would help you."

"That's right," The Misfit said.

"Well then, why don't you pray?" she asked trembling with delight suddenly.

"I don't want no hep," he said. "I'm doing all right by myself."

Bobby Lee and Hiram came ambling back from the woods. Bobby Lee was dragging a yellow shirt with bright blue parrots in it.

"Thow me that shirt, Bobby Lee," The Misfit said. The shirt came flying at him and landed on his shoulder and he put it on. The grandmother couldn't name what the shirt reminded her of. "No, lady," The Misfit said while he was buttoning it up, "I found out the crime don't matter. You can do one thing or you can do another, kill a man or take a tire off his car, because sooner or later you're going to forget what it was you done and just be punished for it."

The children's mother had begun to make heaving noises as if she couldn't get her breath. "Lady," he asked, "would you and that little girl like to step off yonder with Bobby Lee and Hiram and join your husband?"

"Yes, thank you," the mother said faintly. Her left arm dangled helplessly and she was holding the baby, who had gone to sleep, in the other. "Hep that lady up, Hiram," The Misfit said as she struggled to climb out of the ditch, "and Bobby Lee, you hold onto that little girl's hand."

"I don't want to hold hands with him," June Star said. "He reminds me of a pig."

The fat boy blushed and laughed and caught her by the arm and pulled her into the woods after Hiram and her mother.

Alone with The Misfit, the grandmother found that she had lost her voice. There was not a cloud in the sky nor any sun. There was nothing around her but woods. She wanted to tell him that he must pray. She opened and closed her mouth several times before anything came out. Finally she found herself saying, "Jesus. Jesus," meaning, Jesus will help you, but the way she was saying it, it sounded as if she might be cursing.

"Yes'm," The Misfit said as if he agreed. "Jesus thrown everything off balance. It was the same case with Him as with me except He hadn't committed any crime and they could prove I had committed one because they had the papers on me. Of course," he said, "they never shown me my papers. That's why I sign myself now. I said long ago, you get you a signature and sign everything you do and keep a copy of it. Then you'll know what you done and you can hold up the crime to the punishment and see do they match and in the end you'll have something to prove you ain't been treated right. I call myself The Misfit," he said, "because I can't make what all I done wrong fit what all I gone through in punishment."

There was a piercing scream from the woods, followed closely by a pistol report. "Does it seem right to you, lady, that one is punished a heap and another ain't punished at all?"

"Jesus!" the old lady cried. "You've got good blood! I know you wouldn't shoot a lady! I know you come from nice people! Pray! Jesus, you ought not to shoot a lady. I'll give you all the money I've got!"

"Lady," The Misfit said, looking beyond her far into the woods, "there never was a body that give the undertaker a tip."

There were two more pistol reports and the grandmother raised her head like a parched old turkey hen crying for water and called, "Bailey Boy, Bailey Boy!" as if her heart would break.

"Jesus was the only One that ever raised the dead," The Misfit continued, "and He shouldn't have done it. He thrown everything off balance. If He did what He said, then it's nothing for you to do but thow away everything and follow Him, and if He didn't, then it's nothing for you to do but enjoy the few minutes you got left the best way you can—by killing somebody or burning down his house or doing some other meanness to him. No pleasure but meanness," he said and his voice had become almost a snarl.

"Maybe He didn't raise the dead," the old lady mumbled, not knowing what she was saying and feeling so dizzy that she sank down in the ditch with her legs twisted under her.

"I wasn't there so I can't say He didn't," The Misfit said. "I wisht I had of been there," he said, hitting the ground with his fist. "It ain't right I wasn't there because if I had of been there I would of known. Listen lady," he said in a high voice, "if I had of been there I would of known and I wouldn't be like I am now." His voice seemed about to crack and the grandmother's head cleared for an instant. She saw the man's face twisted close to her own as if he were going to cry and she murmured, "Why you're one of my babies. You're one of my own children!" She reached out and touched him on the shoulder. The Misfit sprang back as if a snake had bitten him and shot her three times through the chest. Then he put his gun down on the ground and took off his glasses and began to clean them.

Hiram and Bobby Lee returned from the woods and stood over the ditch, looking down at the grandmother who half sat and half lay in a puddle of blood with her legs crossed under her like a child's and her face smiling up at the cloudless sky.

Without his glasses, The Misfit's eyes were red-rimmed and pale and de-fenceless-looking. "Take her off and thow her where you thown the others," he said, picking up the cat that was rubbing itself against his leg.

"She was a talker, wasn't she?" Bobby Lee said, sliding down the ditch with a yodel.

"She would of been a good woman," The Misfit said, "if it had been some-body there to shoot her every minute of her life."

"Some fun!" Bobby Lee said.

"Shut up, Bobby Lee," The Misfit said. "It's no real pleasure in life."

—1953

Ursula K. Le Guin
1929–2018

Few writers have done more to elevate the standing of science fiction as a recognized literary genre than Ursula K. Le Guin. Together with fellow American authors Philip K. Dick and Samuel R. Delany, Le Guin was instrumental in the emergence of New Wave science fiction, a movement that distinguished itself from the genre's so-called Golden Age of the 1940s and 1950s by a greater attention to style, increasingly nuanced characterization, a mounting interest in experimental narrative, and a more forthright engagement with political and gender issues. Le Guin's finest works—amongst them the Hugo and Nebula Award-winning novels *The Left Hand of Darkness* (1969) and *The Dispossessed* (1974)—are remarkable not only for the fluent evenness of their prose and the conceptual seriousness of their subject matter but also for their political astuteness and the minutely observed social and cultural details of the worlds they imagine into being.

The daughter of a noted anthropologist and psychologist, Le Guin was educated at Radcliffe College and Columbia. Her early interest in cultural anthropology, Jungian psychology, and Taoist philosophy would eventually come to provide a unifying conceptual framework for her writing. In the tradition of J.R.R. Tolkien's world-building, many of Le Guin's novels and stories dramatize a conflict between vividly realized alien cultures that the protagonist—frequently a traveller—observes and participates in as a quasi anthropologist. Archetypal figures and settings such as psychologist Carl Jung believed to symbolize humanity's shared psychic heritage also figure prominently in her work, which often has a richly allegorical dimension. Taoism, a third key element in Le Guin's intellectual framework, is likewise central to many of her texts, particularly the doctrine of inaction, which urges passivity over aggression, and the principle of the relativity of opposites, which posits the interdependence of light and darkness, good and evil, and male and female.

More than a master storyteller, Le Guin did much to advance the place of science fiction as a literature of ideas. In affirming the importance of imagination to human experience, her work demonstrates that science fiction can reflect the world more faithfully than what conventionally passes for realism.

The Ones Who Walk Away from Omelas

With a clamour of bells that set the swallows soaring, the Festival of Summer came to the city. Omelas, bright-towered by the sea. The rigging of the boats in harbour sparkled with flags. In the streets between houses with red roofs and painted walls, between old moss-grown gardens and under avenues of trees, past great parks and public buildings, processions moved. Some were decorous: old people in long stiff robes of mauve and grey, grave master work-men, quiet, merry women carrying their babies and chatting as they walked. In other streets the music beat faster, a shimmering of gong and tambourine, and the people went dancing, the procession was a dance. Children dodged in and out, their high calls rising like the swallows' crossing flights over the music and the singing. All the processions wound towards the north side of the city, where on the great water-meadow called the Green Fields boys and girls, naked in the bright air, with mud-stained feet and ankles and long, lithe arms, exercised their restive horses before the race. The horses wore no gear at all but a halter without bit. Their manes were braided with streamers of silver, gold, and green. They flared their nostrils and pranced and boasted to one another; they were vastly excited, the horse being the only animal who has adopted our ceremonies as his own. Far off to the north and west the mountains stood up half encircling Omelas on her bay. The air of morning was so clear that the snow still crowning the Eighteen Peaks burned with white-gold fire across the miles of sunlit air, under the dark blue of the sky. There was just enough wind to make the banners that marked the racecourse snap and flutter now and then. In the silence of the broad green meadows one could hear the music winding through the city streets, farther and nearer and ever approaching, a cheerful faint sweetness of the air that from time to time trembled and gathered together and broke out into the great joyous clanging of the bells.

Joyous! How is one to tell about joy? How describe the citizens of Omelas?

They were not simple folk, you see, though they were happy. But we do not say the words of cheer much any more. All smiles have become archaic.[1] Given a description such as this one tends to make certain assumptions. Given a description such as this one tends to look next for the King, mounted on a splendid stallion and surrounded by his noble knights, or perhaps in a golden litter borne by great-muscled slaves. But there was no king. They did not use swords, or keep slaves. They were not barbarians. I do not know the rules and laws of their society, but I suspect that they were singularly few.

---

1   *All smiles ... archaic* Reference to the "archaic smile," an expression found on the faces of many sculpted figures from Ancient Greece.

As they did without monarchy and slavery, so they also got on without the stock exchange, the advertisement, the secret police, and the bomb. Yet I repeat that these were not simple folk, not dulcet shepherds, noble savages, bland utopians. They were not less complex than us. The trouble is that we have a bad habit, encouraged by pedants and sophisticates, of considering happiness as something rather stupid. Only pain is intellectual, only evil interesting. This is the treason of the artist: a refusal to admit the banality of evil and the terrible boredom of pain. If you can't lick 'em, join 'em. If it hurts, repeat it. But to praise despair is to condemn delight, to embrace violence is to lose hold of everything else. We have almost lost hold; we can no longer describe a happy man, nor make any celebration of joy. How can I tell you about the people of Omelas? They were not naive and happy children—though their children were, in fact, happy. They were mature, intelligent, passionate adults whose lives were not wretched. O miracle! but I wish I could describe it better. I wish I could convince you. Omelas sounds in my words like a city in a fairy tale, long ago and far away, once upon a time. Perhaps it would be best if you imagined it as your own fancy bids, assuming it will rise to the occasion, for certainly I cannot suit you all. For instance, how about technology? I think that there would be no cars or helicopters in and above the streets; this follows from the fact that the people of Omelas are happy people. Happiness is based on a just discrimination of what is necessary, what is neither necessary nor destructive, and what is destructive. In the middle category, however—that of the unnecessary but undestructive, that of comfort, luxury, exuberance, etc.—they could perfectly well have central heating, subway trains, washing machines, and all kinds of marvellous devices not yet invented here, floating light-sources, fuelless power, a cure for the common cold. Or they could have none of that: it doesn't matter. As you like it. I incline to think that people from towns up and down the coast have been coming in to Omelas during the last days before the Festival on very fast little trains and double-decked trains and that the train station of Omelas is actually the handsomest building in town, though plainer than the magnificent Farmers' Market. But even granted trains, I fear that Omelas so far strikes some of you as goody-goody. Smiles, bells, parades, horses, bleh. If so, please add an orgy. If an orgy would help, don't hesitate. Let us not, however, have temples from which issue beautiful nude priests and priestesses already half in ecstasy and ready to copulate with any man or woman, lover or stranger, who desires union with the deep godhead of the blood, although that was my first idea. But really it would be better not to have any temples in Omelas—at least, not manned temples. Religion yes, clergy no. Surely the beautiful nudes can just wander about, offering themselves like divine soufflés to the hunger of the needy and the rapture of the flesh. Let them join the processions. Let tambourines be struck above the copulations, and the glory of desire be proclaimed upon the gongs, and (a not unimportant point) let the offspring of these delightful rituals be beloved and looked after by all. One thing I know there is none of in Omelas is guilt. But what else should there be? I thought at first there were no drugs, but that is puritanical. For those who like it, the faint insistent sweetness of *drooz* may perfume the ways of the city, *drooz* which first brings a great lightness and brilliance to the mind and limbs, and then after some hours a dreamy languor, and wonderful visions at last of the very arcana and inmost secrets of the Universe, as well as exciting the pleasure of sex beyond all belief; and it is not habit-forming. For more modest tastes I think there ought to be beer. What else, what else belongs in the joyous city? The sense of victory, surely, the celebration of courage. But as we did without clergy, let us do without soldiers. The joy built upon successful slaughter is not the right kind of joy; it will not do; it is fearful and it is trivial. A boundless and generous contentment, a magnanimous triumph felt not against some outer enemy but in communion with the finest and fairest in the souls of all men everywhere and the splendour of the world's summer: this is what swells the hearts of the people of Omelas, and the victory they celebrate is that of life. I really don't think many of them need to take *drooz*.

Most of the processions have reached the Green Fields by now. A marvellous smell of cooking goes forth from the red and blue tents of the provisioners. The faces of small children are amiably sticky; in the benign grey beard of a man a couple of crumbs of rich pastry are entangled. The youths and girls have mounted their horses and are beginning to group around the starting line of the course. An old woman, small, fat, and laughing, is passing out flowers from a basket, and tall young men wear her flowers in their shining hair. A child of nine or ten sits at the edge of the crowd, alone, playing on a wooden flute. People pause to listen, and they smile, but they do not speak to him, for he never ceases playing and never sees them, his dark eyes wholly rapt in the sweet, thin magic of the tune.

He finishes, and slowly lowers his hands holding the wooden flute.

As if that little private silence were the signal, all at once a trumpet sounds from the pavilion near the starting line: imperious, melancholy, piercing. The horses rear on their slender legs, and some of them neigh in answer. Soberfaced, the young riders stroke the horses' necks and soothe them, whispering, "Quiet, quiet, there my beauty, my hope...." They begin to form in rank along the starting line. The crowds along the racecourse are like a field of grass and flowers in the wind. The Festival of Summer has begun.

Do you believe? Do you accept the festival, the city, the joy? No? Then let me describe one more thing.

In a basement under one of the beautiful public buildings of Omelas, or perhaps in the cellar of one of its spacious private homes, there is a room. It has one locked door, and no window. A little light seeps in dustily between cracks in the boards, secondhand from a cobwebbed window somewhere across the cellar. In one corner of the little room a couple of mops, with stiff, clotted, foul-smelling heads, stand near a rusty bucket. The floor is dirt, a little damp to the touch, as cellar dirt usually is. The room is about three paces long and two wide: a mere broom closet or disused tool room. In the room a child is sitting. It could be a boy or a girl. It looks about six, but actually is nearly ten. It is feeble-minded. Perhaps it was born defective, or perhaps it has become imbecile through fear, malnutrition, and neglect. It picks its nose and occasionally fumbles vaguely with its toes or genitals, as it sits hunched in the corner farthest from the bucket and the two mops. It is afraid of the mops. It finds them horrible. It shuts its eyes, but it knows the mops are still standing there; and the door is locked; and nobody will come. The door is always locked; and nobody ever comes, except that sometimes—the child has no understanding of time or interval—sometimes the door rattles terribly and opens, and a person, or several people, are there. One of them may come in and kick the child to make it stand up. The others never come close, but peer in at it with frightened, disgusted eyes. The food bowl and the water jug are hastily filled, the door is locked, the eyes disappear. The people at the door never say anything, but the child, who has not always lived in the tool room, and can remember sunlight and its mother's voice, sometimes speaks. "I will be good," it says. "Please let me out. I will be good!" They never answer. The child used to scream for help at night, and cry a good deal, but now it only makes a kind of whining, "eh-haa, eh-haa," and it speaks less and less often. It is so thin there are no calves to its legs; its belly protrudes; it lives on a half-bowl of corn meal and grease a day. It is naked. Its buttocks and thighs are a mass of festered sores, as it sits in its own excrement continually.

They all know it is there, all the people of Omelas. Some of them have come to see it, others are content merely to know it is there. They all know that it has to be there. Some of them understand why, and some do not, but they all understand that their happiness, the beauty of their city, the tenderness of their friendships, the health of their children, the wisdom of their scholars, the skill of their makers, even the abundance of their harvest and the kindly weathers of their skies, depend wholly on this child's abominable misery.

This is usually explained to children when they are between eight and twelve, whenever they seem capable of understanding; and most of those who come to see the child are young people, though often enough an adult comes, or comes back, to see the child. No matter how well the matter has been explained to them, these young spectators are always shocked and sickened at the sight. They feel disgust, which they had thought themselves superior to. They feel anger, outrage, impotence, despite all the explanations. They would like to do something for the child. But there is nothing they can do. If the child were brought up into the sunlight out of that vile place, if it were cleaned and fed and comforted, that would be a good thing, indeed; but if it were done, in that day and hour all the prosperity and beauty and delight of Omelas would wither and be destroyed. Those are the terms. To exchange all the goodness and grace of every life in Omelas for that single, small improvement: to throw away the happiness of thousands for the chance of the happiness of one: that would be to let guilt within the walls indeed.

The terms are strict and absolute; there may not even be a kind word spoken to the child.

Often the young people go home in tears, or in a tearless rage, when they have seen the child and faced this terrible paradox. They may brood over it for weeks or years. But as time goes on they begin to realize that even if the child could be released, it would not get much good of its freedom: a little vague pleasure of warmth and food, no doubt, but little more. It is too degraded and imbecile to know any real joy. It has been afraid too long ever to be free of fear. Its habits are too uncouth for it to respond to humane treatment. Indeed, after so long it would probably be wretched without walls about it to protect it, and darkness for its eyes, and its own excrement to sit in. Their tears at the bitter injustice dry when they begin to perceive the terrible justice of reality and to accept it. Yet it is their tears and anger, the trying of their generosity and the acceptance of their helplessness, which are perhaps the true source of the splendour of their lives. Theirs is no vapid, irresponsible happiness. They know that they, like the child, are not free. They know compassion. It is the existence of the child, and their knowledge of its existence, that makes possible the nobility of their architecture, the poignancy of their music, the profundity of their science. It is because of the child that they are so gentle with children. They know that if the wretched one were not there snivelling in the dark, the other one, the flute-player, could make no joyful music as the young riders line up in their beauty for the race in the sunlight of the first morning of summer.

Now do you believe in them? Are they not more credible? But there is one more thing to tell, and this is quite incredible.

At times one of the adolescent girls or boys who go to see the child does not go home to weep or rage, does not, in fact, go home at all. Sometimes also a man or woman much older falls silent for a day or two, and then leaves home. These people go out into the street, and walk down the street alone. They keep walking, and walk straight out of the city of Omelas, through the beautiful gates. They keep walking across the farmlands of Omelas. Each one goes alone, youth or girl, man or woman. Night falls; the traveller must pass down village streets, between the houses with yellow-lit windows, and on out into the darkness of the fields. Each alone, they go west or north, towards the mountains. They go on. They leave Omelas, they walk ahead into the darkness, and they do not come back. The place they go towards is a place even less imaginable to most of us than the city of happiness. I cannot describe it at all. It is possible that it does not exist. But they seem to know where they are going, the ones who walk away from Omelas.

—1973

Chinua Achebe

1930–2013

Chinua Achebe was born in Nigeria when the country was still a colonial territory of the British Empire. He established his place as an important figure in world literature with the publication of his first novel, *Things Fall Apart*, in 1958. It remains, perhaps, the work for which he is best known, but Achebe was a prolific and wide-ranging writer who steadily published novels, short stories, poetry, essays, and children's books until his death in 2013.

While still a student, Achebe read literary accounts of Africa written by Europeans, many of which he found "appalling." This experience taught him that more African voices should represent Africans; Achebe writes that he "decided that the story we had to tell could not be told by anyone else no matter how gifted or well intentioned." For Achebe, telling such stories accurately was of political as well as artistic importance because his writing was "concerned with universal human communication across racial and cultural boundaries as a means of fostering respect for all people" and, he believed, "such respect can only issue from understanding." This aim of understanding across racial and cultural boundaries is one of the reasons he chose to write in English.

As in the selection here, as well as in novels such as *No Longer at Ease* (1960) and *Arrow of God* (1964), Achebe's protagonists are often flawed individuals, recalling the characters of the classical tragedies. He resisted simple tales of good and evil, attempting instead to represent the complexity and uncertainty of the human experience.

Dead Men's Path

Michael Obi's hopes were fulfilled much earlier than he had expected. He was appointed headmaster of Ndume Central School in January 1949. It had always been an unprogressive school, so the Mission authorities[1] decided to send a young and energetic man to run it. Obi accepted this responsibility with enthusiasm. He had many wonderful ideas and this was an opportunity to put them into practice. He had had sound secondary school education which designated him a "pivotal teacher" in the official records and set him apart from the other headmasters in the mission field. He was outspoken in his condemnation of the narrow views of these older and often less-educated ones.

---

1   *Mission authorities* Many schools in African countries colonized by the British were run by Christian missionary organizations.

"We shall make a good job of it, shan't we?" he asked his young wife when they first heard the joyful news of his promotion.

"We shall do our best," she replied. "We shall have such beautiful gardens and everything will be just *modern* and delightful...." In their two years of married life she had become completely infected by his passion for "modern methods" and his denigration of "these old and superannuated people in the teaching field who would be better employed as traders in the Onitsha[1] market." She began to see herself already as the admired wife of the young headmaster, the queen of the school.

The wives of the other teachers would envy her position. She would set the fashion in everything.... Then, suddenly, it occurred to her that there might not be other wives. Wavering between hope and fear, she asked her husband, looking anxiously at him.

"All our colleagues are young and unmarried," he said with enthusiasm which for once she did not share. "Which is a good thing," he continued.

"Why?"

"Why? They will give all their time and energy to the school."

Nancy was downcast. For a few minutes she became skeptical about the new school; but it was only for a few minutes. Her little personal misfortune could not blind her to her husband's happy prospects. She looked at him as he sat folded up in a chair. He was stoop-shouldered and looked frail. But he sometimes surprised people with sudden bursts of physical energy. In his present posture, however, all his bodily strength seemed to have retired behind his deep-set eyes, giving them an extraordinary power of penetration. He was only twenty-six, but looked thirty or more. On the whole, he was not unhandsome.

"A penny for your thoughts, Mike," said Nancy after a while, imitating the woman's magazine she read.

"I was thinking what a grand opportunity we've got at last to show these people how a school should be run."

Ndume School was backward in every sense of the word. Mr. Obi put his whole life into the work, and his wife hers too. He had two aims. A high standard of teaching was insisted upon, and the school compound was to be turned into a place of beauty. Nancy's dream-gardens came to life with the coming of the rains, and blossomed. Beautiful hibiscus and allamanda hedges in brilliant red and yellow marked out the carefully tended school compound from the rank neighbourhood bushes.

---

1   *Onitsha* City in southeastern Nigeria; the Onitsha market is one of the largest in West Africa.

One evening as Obi was admiring his work he was scandalized to see an old woman from the village hobble right across the compound, through a marigold flower-bed and the hedges. On going up there he found faint signs of an almost disused path from the village across the school compound to the bush on the other side.

"It amazes me," said Obi to one of his teachers who had been three years in the school, "that you people allowed the villagers to make use of this footpath. It is simply incredible." He shook his head.

"The path," said the teacher apologetically, "appears to be very important to them. Although it is hardly used, it connects the village shrine with their place of burial."

"And what has that got to do with the school?" asked the headmaster.

"Well, I don't know," replied the other with a shrug of the shoulders. "But I remember there was a big row some time ago when we attempted to close it."

"That was some time ago. But it will not be used now," said Obi as he walked away. "What will the Government Education Officer think of this when he comes to inspect the school next week? The villagers might, for all I know, decide to use the schoolroom for a pagan ritual during the inspection."

Heavy sticks were planted closely across the path at the two places where it entered and left the school premises. These were further strengthened with barbed wire.

Three days later the village priest of *Ani*[1] called on the headmaster. He was an old man and walked with a slight stoop. He carried a stout walking-stick which he usually tapped on the floor, by way of emphasis, each time he made a new point in his argument.

"I have heard," he said after the usual exchange of cordialities, "that our ancestral footpath has recently been closed...."

"Yes," replied Mr. Obi. "We cannot allow people to make a highway of our school compound."

"Look here, my son," said the priest bringing down his walking-stick, "this path was here before you were born and before your father was born. The whole life of this village depends on it. Our dead relatives depart by it and our ancestors visit us by it. But most important, it is the path of children coming in to be born...."

Mr. Obi listened with a satisfied smile on his face.

"The whole purpose of our school," he said finally, "is to eradicate just such beliefs as that. Dead men do not require footpaths. The whole idea is just fantastic. Our duty is to teach your children to laugh at such ideas."

---

1   *Ani* Traditional belief system of the Igbo people of Nigeria, often called Odinani.

"What you say may be true," replied the priest, "but we follow the practices of our fathers. If you reopen the path we shall have nothing to quarrel about. What I always say is: let the hawk perch and let the eagle perch." He rose to go.

"I am sorry," said the young headmaster. "But the school compound cannot be a thoroughfare. It is against our regulations. I would suggest your constructing another path, skirting our premises. We can even get our boys to help in building it. I don't suppose the ancestors will find the little detour too burdensome."

"I have no more words to say," said the old priest, already outside.

Two days later a young woman in the village died in childbed. A diviner was immediately consulted and he prescribed heavy sacrifices to propitiate ancestors insulted by the fence.

Obi woke up next morning among the ruins of his work. The beautiful hedges were torn up not just near the path but right round the school, the flowers trampled to death and one of the school buildings pulled down ... That day, the white Supervisor came to inspect the school and wrote a nasty report on the state of the premises but more seriously about the "tribal-war situation developing between the school and the village, arising in part from the misguided zeal of the new headmaster."

—1953

Alice Munro
b. 1931

Alice Munro is acclaimed as a writer with a keen eye for detail and a fine sense of emotional nuance. In 2009, when she received the Man Booker International Prize, the award panel commented that "she brings as much depth, wisdom, and precision to every story as most novelists bring to a lifetime of novels." On October 10, 2013 Munro was awarded the 2013 Nobel Prize in Literature.

Alice Laidlaw was born into a farming community in Wingham, Ontario. After graduating from high school, she won a partial scholarship to attend the University of Western Ontario. She completed two years towards a degree in English, but she was unable to continue her studies due to strained finances. In 1951, she married James Munro; they moved to Vancouver and then to Victoria, British Columbia, where the couple opened a bookstore. They eventually had three daughters; Munro has often commented that the genre of the short story is well-suited to a working mother whose time for writing is limited.

Munro's work began to receive wide attention with the 1971 publication of *The Lives of Girls and Women*, a collection of interlinked stories (described later by the author as "autobiographical in form but not in fact") that traces the development of Del Jordan as she grows up in the constricting atmosphere of the small town of Jubilee. Everyday concerns over money and class and love and sex are recurrent themes in Munro's stories. Sensational events do happen in her fiction, but, as Alison Lurie has observed, "they usually take place offstage"; the focus of a Munro story is typically on emotion, not on incident.

Friend of My Youth

With Thanks to R.J.T.

I used to dream about my mother, and though the details in the dream varied, the surprise in it was always the same. The dream stopped, I suppose because it was too transparent in its hopefulness, too easy in its forgiveness.

In the dream I would be the age I really was, living the life I was really living, and I would discover that my mother was still alive. (The fact is, she died when I was in my early twenties and she in her early fifties.) Sometimes I would find myself in our old kitchen, where my mother would be rolling out piecrust on the table, or washing the dishes in the battered cream-coloured dish-pan with the red rim. But other times I would run into her on the street, in places where I would never have expected to see her. She might be walking through a handsome hotel lobby, or lining up in an airport. She would be looking quite well—not exactly youthful, not entirely untouched by the paralyzing disease that held her in its grip for a decade or more before her death, but so much better than I remembered that I would be astonished. Oh, I just have this little tremor in my arm, she would say, and a little stiffness up this side of my face. It is a nuisance but I get around.

I recovered then what in waking life I had lost—my mother's liveliness of face and voice before her throat muscles stiffened and a woeful, impersonal mask fastened itself over her features. How could I have forgotten this, I would think in the dream—the casual humour she had, not ironic but merry, the lightness and impatience and confidence? I would say that I was sorry I hadn't been to see her in such a long time—meaning not that I felt guilty but that I was sorry I had kept a bugbear in my mind, instead of this reality—and the strangest, kindest thing of all to me was her matter-of-fact reply.

Oh, well, she said, better late than never. I was sure I'd see you someday.

When my mother was a young woman with a soft, mischievous face and shiny, opaque silk stockings on her plump legs (I have seen a photograph of her, with her pupils), she went to teach at a one-room school, called Grieves School, in the Ottawa Valley. The school was on a corner of the farm that belonged to the Grieves family—a very good farm for that country. Well-drained fields with none of the Precambrian rock[1] shouldering through the soil, a little willow-edged river running alongside, a sugar bush, log barns, and a large, unornamented house whose wooden walls had never been painted but had been left to weather. And when wood weathers in the Ottawa Valley, my mother said, I do not know why this is, but it never turns grey, it turns black. There must be something in the air, she said. She often spoke of the Ottawa Valley, which was her home—she had grown up about twenty miles away from Grieves School—in a dogmatic, mystified way, emphasizing things about it that distinguished it from any other place on earth. Houses turn black, maple syrup has a taste no maple syrup produced elsewhere can equal, bears amble within sight of farmhouses. Of course I was disappointed when I finally got to see this place. It was not a valley at all, if by that you mean a cleft between hills; it was a mixture of flat fields and low rocks and heavy bush and little lakes—a scrambled, disarranged sort of country with no easy harmony about it, not yielding readily to any description.

The log barns and unpainted house, common enough on poor farms, were not in the Grieveses' case a sign of poverty but of policy. They had the

---

1   *Precambrian rock* I.e., the rock of the Canadian Shield, a plateau spanning a large portion of Eastern and Central Canada.

money but they did not spend it. That was what people told my mother. The Grieveses worked hard and they were far from ignorant, but they were very backward. They didn't have a car or electricity or a telephone or a tractor. Some people thought this was because they were Cameronians—they were the only people in the school district who were of that religion—but in fact their church (which they themselves always called the Reformed Presbyterian) did not forbid engines or electricity or any inventions of that sort, just card playing, dancing, movies, and, on Sundays, any activity at all that was not religious or unavoidable.

My mother could not say who the Cameronians were or why they were called that. Some freak religion from Scotland, she said from the perch of her obedient and lighthearted Anglicanism. The teacher always boarded with the Grieveses, and my mother was a little daunted at the thought of going to live in that black board house with its paralytic Sundays and coal-oil lamps and primitive notions. But she was engaged by that time, she wanted to work on her trousseau[1] instead of running around the country having a good time, and she figured she could get home one Sunday out of three. (On Sundays at the Grieveses' house, you could light a fire for heat but not for cooking, you could not even boil the kettle to make tea, and you were not supposed to write a letter or swat a fly. But it turned out that my mother was exempt from these rules. "No, no," said Flora Grieves, laughing at her. "That doesn't mean you. You must just go on as you're used to doing." And after a while my mother had made friends with Flora to such an extent that she wasn't even going home on the Sundays when she'd planned to.)

Flora and Ellie Grieves were the two sisters left of the family. Ellie was married, to a man called Robert Deal, who lived there and worked the farm but had not changed its name to Deal's in anyone's mind. By the way people spoke, my mother expected the Grieves sisters and Robert Deal to be middle-aged at least, but Ellie, the younger sister, was only about thirty, and Flora seven or eight years older. Robert Deal might be in between.

The house was divided in an unexpected way. The married couple didn't live with Flora. At the time of their marriage, she had given them the parlour and the dining room, the front bedrooms and staircase, the winter kitchen. There was no need to decide about the bathroom, because there wasn't one. Flora had the summer kitchen, with its open rafters and uncovered brick walls, the old pantry made into a narrow dining room and sitting room, and the two back bedrooms, one of which was my mother's. The teacher was housed with Flora, in the poorer part of the house. But my mother didn't mind. She

---

1   *trousseau* Collection of clothing and household items assembled by a bride in preparation for her wedding.

immediately preferred Flora, and Flora's cheerfulness, to the silence and sick-room atmosphere of the front rooms. In Flora's domain it was not even true that all amusements were forbidden. She had a crokinole[1] board—she taught my mother how to play.

The division had been made, of course, in the expectation that Robert and Ellie would have a family, and that they would need the room. This hadn't happened. They had been married for more than a dozen years and there had not been a live child. Time and again Ellie had been pregnant, but two babies had been stillborn, and the rest she had miscarried. During my mother's first year, Ellie seemed to be staying in bed more and more of the time, and my mother thought that she must be pregnant again, but there was no mention of it. Such people would not mention it. You could not tell from the look of Ellie, when she got up and walked around, because she showed a stretched and ruined though slack-chested shape. She carried a sickbed odour, and she fretted in a childish way about everything. Flora took care of her and did all the work. She washed the clothes and tidied up the rooms and cooked the meals served in both sides of the house, as well as helping Robert with the milking and separating. She was up before daylight and never seemed to tire. During the first spring my mother was there, a great housecleaning was embarked upon, during which Flora climbed the ladders herself and carried down the storm windows, washed and stacked them away, carried all the furniture out of one room after another so that she could scrub the woodwork and varnish the floors. She washed every dish and glass that was sitting in the cupboards sup-posedly clean already. She scalded every pot and spoon. Such need and energy possessed her that she could hardly sleep—my mother would wake up to the sound of stovepipes being taken down, or the broom, draped in a dish towel, whacking at the smoky cobwebs. Through the washed uncurtained windows came a torrent of unmerciful light. The cleanliness was devastating. My mother slept now on sheets that had been bleached and starched and that gave her a rash. Sick Ellie complained daily of the smell of varnish and cleansing powders. Flora's hands were raw. But her disposition remained topnotch. Her kerchief and apron and Robert's baggy overalls that she donned for the climbing jobs gave her the air of a comedian—sportive, unpredictable.

My mother called her a whirling dervish.[2]

"You're a regular whirling dervish, Flora," she said, and Flora halted. She wanted to know what was meant. My mother went ahead and explained, though she was a little afraid lest piety should be offended. (Not piety ex-

---

1   *crokinole* Tabletop game played by flicking small disks toward a target at the centre of the board.

2   *whirling dervish* Islamic mystic whose spiritual practice includes an ecstatic, spinning dance; figuratively, "whirling dervish" refers to an extremely energetic person.

actly—you could not call it that. Religious strictness.) Of course it wasn't.
There was not a trace of nastiness or smug vigilance in Flora's observance of
her religion. She had no fear of heathens—she had always lived in the midst
of them. She liked the idea of being a dervish, and went to tell her sister.

"Do you know what the teacher says I am?"

Flora and Ellie were both dark-haired, dark-eyed women, tall and narrow-
shouldered and long-legged. Ellie was a wreck, of course, but Flora was still
superbly straight and graceful. She could look like a queen, my mother said—
even riding into town in that cart they had. For church they used a buggy or
a cutter,[1] but when they went to town they often had to transport sacks of
wool—they kept a few sheep—or of produce, to sell, and they had to bring
provisions home. The trip of a few miles was not made often. Robert rode in
front, to drive the horse—Flora could drive a horse perfectly well, but it must
always be the man who drove. Flora would be standing behind holding on to
the sacks. She rode to town and back standing up, keeping an easy balance,
wearing her black hat. Almost ridiculous but not quite. A gypsy queen, my
mother thought she looked like, with her black hair and her skin that always
looked slightly tanned, and her lithe and bold serenity. Of course she lacked
the gold bangles and the bright clothes. My mother envied her her slenderness,
and her cheekbones.

Returning in the fall for her second year, my mother learned what was the
matter with Ellie.

"My sister has a growth," Flora said. Nobody then spoke of cancer.

My mother had heard that before. People suspected it. My mother knew
many people in the district by that time. She had made particular friends with
a young woman who worked in the post office; this woman was going to be
one of my mother's bridesmaids. The story of Flora and Ellie and Robert had
been told—or all that people knew of it—in various versions. My mother did
not feel that she was listening to gossip, because she was always on the alert
for any disparaging remarks about Flora—she would not put up with that.
But indeed nobody offered any. Everybody said that Flora had behaved like
a saint. Even when she went to extremes, as in dividing up the house—that
was like a saint.

Robert came to work at Grieveses' some months before the girls' father
died. They knew him already, from church. (Oh, that church, my mother
said, having attended it once, out of curiosity—that drear building miles on
the other side of town, no organ or piano and plain glass in the windows and
a doddery old minister with his hours-long sermon, a man hitting a tuning

---

1　*cutter* Sleigh.

fork for the singing.) Robert had come out from Scotland and was on his way west. He had stopped with relatives or people he knew, members of the scanty congregation. To earn some money, probably, he came to Grieveses'. Soon he and Flora were engaged. They could not go to dances or to card parties like other couples, but they went for long walks. The chaperone—unofficially— was Ellie. Ellie was then a wild tease, a long-haired, impudent, childish girl full of lolloping energy. She would run up hills and smite the mullein stalks with a stick, shouting and prancing and pretending to be a warrior on horseback. That, or the horse itself. This when she was fifteen, sixteen years old. Nobody but Flora could control her, and generally Flora just laughed at her, being too used to her to wonder if she was quite right in the head. They were wonderfully fond of each other. Ellie, with her long skinny body, her long pale face, was like a copy of Flora—the kind of copy you often see in families, in which because of some carelessness or exaggeration of features or colouring, the handsomeness of one person passes into the plainness—or almost plainness—of the other. But Ellie had no jealousy about this. She loved to comb out Flora's hair and pin it up. They had great times, washing each other's hair. Ellie would press her face into Flora's throat, like a colt nuzzling its mother. So when Robert laid claim to Flora, or Flora to him—nobody knew how it was—Ellie had to be included. She didn't show any spite toward Robert, but she pursued and waylaid them on their walks; she sprung on them out of the bushes or sneaked up behind them so softly that she could blow on their necks. People saw her do it. And they heard of her jokes. She had always been terrible for jokes and sometimes it had got her into trouble with her father, but Flora had protected her. Now she put thistles in Robert's bed. She set his place at the table with the knife and fork the wrong way around. She switched the milk pails to give him the old one with the hole in it. For Flora's sake, maybe, Robert humoured her.

The father had made Flora and Robert set the wedding day a year ahead, and after he died they did not move it any closer. Robert went on living in the house. Nobody knew how to speak to Flora about this being scandal- ous, or looking scandalous. Flora would just ask why. Instead of putting the wedding ahead, she put it back—from next spring to early fall, so that there should be a full year between it and her father's death. A year from wedding to funeral—that seemed proper to her. She trusted fully in Robert's patience and in her own purity.

So she might. But in the winter a commotion started. There was Ellie, vomiting, weeping, running off and hiding in the haymow, howling when they found her and pulled her out, jumping to the barn floor, running around in circles, rolling in the snow. Ellie was deranged. Flora had to call the doctor. She told him that her sister's periods had stopped—could the backup of blood be driving her wild? Robert had had to catch her and tie her up, and together he and Flora had put her to bed. She would not take food, just whipped her head from side to side, howling. It looked as if she would die speechless. But somehow the truth came out. Not from the doctor, who could not get close enough to examine her, with all her thrashing about. Probably, Robert confessed. Flora finally got wind of the truth, through all her high-mindedness. Now there had to be a wedding, though not the one that had been planned.

No cake, no new clothes, no wedding trip, no congratulations. Just a shameful hurry-up visit to the manse.[1] Some people, seeing the names in the paper, thought the editor must have got the sisters mixed up. They thought it must be Flora. A hurry-up wedding for Flora! But no—it was Flora who pressed Robert's suit—it must have been—and got Ellie out of bed and washed her and made her presentable. It would have been Flora who picked one geranium from the window plant and pinned it to her sister's dress. And Ellie hadn't torn it out. Ellie was meek now, no longer flailing or crying. She let Flora fix her up, she let herself be married, she was never wild from that day on.

Flora had the house divided. She herself helped Robert build the necessary partitions. The baby was carried full term—nobody even pretended that it was early—but it was born dead after a long, tearing labour. Perhaps Ellie had damaged it when she jumped from the barn beam and rolled in the snow and beat on herself. Even if she hadn't done that, people would have expected something to go wrong, with that child or maybe one that came later. God dealt out punishment for hurry-up marriages—not just Presbyterians but almost everybody else believed that. God rewarded lust with dead babies, idiots, harelips and withered limbs and clubfeet.

In this case the punishment continued. Ellie had one miscarriage after another, then another stillbirth and more miscarriages. She was constantly pregnant, and the pregnancies were full of vomiting fits that lasted for days, headaches, cramps, dizzy spells. The miscarriages were as agonizing as full-term births. Ellie could not do her own work. She walked around holding on to chairs. Her numb silence passed off, and she became a complainer. If anybody came to visit, she would talk about the peculiarities of her headaches or describe her latest fainting fit, or even—in front of men, in front of unmarried girls or children—go into bloody detail about what Flora called her "disappointments." When people changed the subject or dragged the children away, she turned sullen. She demanded new medicine, reviled the doctor, nagged Flora. She accused Flora of washing the dishes with a great clang and clatter, out of spite, of pulling her—Ellie's—hair when she combed it out, of stingily substituting water-and-molasses for her real medicine. No matter what she said, Flora soothed her. Everybody who came into the house had some story

---

1   *manse* Minister's house.

of that kind to tell. Flora said, "Where's my little girl, then? Where's my Ellie? This isn't my Ellie, this is some crosspatch[1] got in here in place of her!"

In the winter evenings after she came in from helping Robert with the barn chores, Flora would wash and change her clothes and go next door to read Ellie to sleep. My mother might invite herself along, taking whatever sewing she was doing, on some item of her trousseau. Ellie's bed was set up in the big dining room, where there was a gas lamp over the table. My mother sat on one side of the table, sewing, and Flora sat on the other side, reading aloud. Sometimes Ellie said, "I can't hear you." Or if Flora paused for a little rest Ellie said, "I'm not asleep yet."

What did Flora read? Stories about Scottish life—not classics. Stories about urchins and comic grandmothers. The only title my mother could remember was *Wee Macgregor*.[2] She could not follow the stories very well, or laugh when Flora laughed and Ellie gave a whimper, because so much was in Scots dialect or read with that thick accent. She was surprised that Flora could do it—it wasn't the way Flora ordinarily talked, at all.

(But wouldn't it be the way Robert talked? Perhaps that is why my mother never reports anything that Robert said, never has him contributing to the scene. He must have been there, he must have been sitting there in the room. They would only heat the main room of the house. I see him black-haired, heavy-shouldered, with the strength of a plow horse, and the same kind of sombre, shackled beauty.)

Then Flora would say, "That's all of that for tonight." She would pick up another book, an old book written by some preacher of their faith. There was in it such stuff as my mother had never heard. What stuff? She couldn't say. All the stuff that was in their monstrous old religion. That put Ellie to sleep, or made her pretend she was asleep, after a couple of pages.

All that configuration of the elect and the damned, my mother must have meant—all the arguments about the illusion and necessity of free will. Doom and slippery redemption. The torturing, defeating, but for some minds irresistible pileup of interlocking and contradictory notions. My mother could resist it. Her faith was easy, her spirits at that time robust. Ideas were not what she was curious about, ever.

But what sort of thing was that, she asked (silently), to read to a dying woman? This was the nearest she got to criticizing Flora.

The answer—that it was the only thing, if you believed it—never seemed to have occurred to her.

---

1   *crosspatch* Grump.
2   *Wee Macgregor* Comic short story collection by John Joy Bell (1902).

By spring a nurse had arrived. That was the way things were done then. People died at home, and a nurse came in to manage it.

The nurse's name was Audrey Atkinson. She was a stout woman with corsets as stiff as barrel hoops, marcelled[1] hair the colour of brass candlesticks, a mouth shaped by lipstick beyond its own stingy outlines. She drove a car into the yard—her own car, a dark-green coupé, shiny and smart. News of Audrey Atkinson and her car spread quickly. Questions were asked. Where did she get the money? Had some rich fool altered his will on her behalf? Had she exercised influence? Or simply helped herself to a stash of bills under the mattress? How was she to be trusted?

Hers was the first car ever to sit in the Grieveses' yard overnight.

Audrey Atkinson said that she had never been called out to tend a case in so primitive a house. It was beyond her, she said, how people could live in such a way.

"It's not that they're poor, even," she said to my mother. "It isn't, is it? That I could understand. Or it's not even their religion. So what is it? They do not care!"

She tried at first to cozy up to my mother, as if they would be natural allies in this benighted place. She spoke as if they were around the same age—both stylish, intelligent women who liked a good time and had modern ideas. She offered to teach my mother to drive the car. She offered her cigarettes. My mother was more tempted by the idea of learning to drive than she was by the cigarettes. But she said no, she would wait for her husband to teach her. Audrey Atkinson raised her pinkish-orange eyebrows at my mother behind Flora's back, and my mother was furious. She disliked the nurse far more than Flora did.

"I knew what she was like and Flora didn't," my mother said. She meant that she caught a whiff of a cheap life, maybe even of drinking establishments and unsavory men, of hard bargains, which Flora was too unworldly to notice.

Flora started into the great housecleaning again. She had the curtains spread out on stretchers, she beat the rugs on the line, she leapt up on the stepladder to attack the dust on the moulding. But she was impeded all the time by Nurse Atkinson's complaining.

"I wondered if we could have a little less of the running and clattering?" said Nurse Atkinson with offensive politeness. "I only ask for my patient's sake." She always spoke of Ellie as "my patient" and pretended that she was the only one to protect her and compel respect. But she was not so respectful of Ellie herself. "Allee-oop," she would say, dragging the poor creature up on her pillows. And she told Ellie she was not going to stand for fretting and whimpering. "You don't do yourself any good that way," she said. "And you

---

1   *marcelled* Artificially wavy.

certainly don't make me come any quicker. What you just as well might do is learn to control yourself." She exclaimed at Ellie's bedsores in a scolding way, as if they were a further disgrace of the house. She demanded lotions, ointments, expensive soap—most of them, no doubt, to protect her own skin, which she claimed suffered from the hard water. (How could it be hard, my mother asked her—sticking up for the household when nobody else would—how could it be hard when it came straight from the rain barrel?)

Nurse Atkinson wanted cream, too—she said that they should hold some back, not sell it all to the creamery. She wanted to make nourishing soups and puddings for her patient. She did make puddings, and jellies, from packaged mixes such as had never before entered this house. My mother was convinced that she ate them all herself.

Flora still read to Ellie, but now it was only short bits from the Bible. When she finished and stood up, Ellie tried to cling to her. Ellie wept, sometimes she made ridiculous complaints. She said there was a horned cow outside, trying to get into the room and kill her.

"They often get some kind of idea like that," Nurse Atkinson said. "You mustn't give in to her or she won't let you go day or night. That's what they're like, they only think about themselves. Now, when I'm here alone with her, she behaves herself quite nice. I don't have any trouble at all. But after you been in here I have trouble all over again because she sees you and she gets upset. You don't want to make my job harder for me, do you? I mean, you brought me here to take charge, didn't you?"

"Ellie, now, Ellie dear, I must go," said Flora, and to the nurse she said, "I understand. I do understand that you have to be in charge and I admire you, I admire you for your work. In your work you have to have so much patience and kindness."

My mother wondered at this—was Flora really so blinded, or did she hope by this undeserved praise to exhort Nurse Atkinson to the patience and kindness that she didn't have? Nurse Atkinson was too thick-skinned and self-approving for any trick like that to work.

"It is a hard job, all right, and not many can do it," she said. "It's not like those nurses in the hospital, where they got everything laid out for them." She had no time for more conversation—she was trying to bring in "Make-Believe Ballroom"[1] on her battery radio.

My mother was busy with the final exams and the June exercises at the school. She was getting ready for her wedding in July. Friends came in cars and whisked her off to the dressmaker's, to parties, to choose the invitations

---

1   *"Make-Believe Ballroom"* Radio program (1930s–1950s) that broadcast recordings of popular music.

and order the cake. The lilacs came out, the evenings lengthened, the birds were back and nesting, my mother bloomed in everybody's attention, about to set out on the deliciously solemn adventure of marriage. Her dress was to be appliquéd with silk roses, her veil held by a cap of seed pearls. She belonged to the first generation of young women who saved their money and paid for their own weddings—far fancier than their parents could have afforded.

On her last evening, the friend from the post office came to drive her away, with her clothes and her books and the things she had made for her trousseau and the gifts her pupils and others had given her. There was great fuss and laughter about getting everything loaded into the car. Flora came out and helped. This getting married is even more of a nuisance than I thought, said Flora, laughing. She gave my mother a dresser scarf, which she had crocheted in secret. Nurse Atkinson could not be shut out of an important occasion—she presented a spray bottle of cologne. Flora stood on the slope at the side of the house to wave good-bye. She had been invited to the wedding, but of course she had said she could not come, she could not "go out" at such a time. The last my mother ever saw of her was this solitary, energetically waving figure in her housecleaning apron and bandanna, on the green slope by the black-walled house, in the evening light.

"Well, maybe now she'll get what she should've got the first time round," the friend from the post office said. "Maybe now they'll be able to get married. Is she too old to start a family? How old is she, anyway?"

My mother thought that this was a crude way of talking about Flora and replied that she didn't know. But she had to admit to herself that she had been thinking the very same thing.

When she was married and settled in her own home, three hundred miles away, my mother got a letter from Flora. Ellie was dead. She had died firm in her faith, Flora said, and grateful for her release. Nurse Atkinson was staying on for a little while, until it was time for her to go off to her next case. This was late in the summer.

News of what happened next did not come from Flora. When she wrote at Christmas, she seemed to take for granted that information would have gone ahead of her.

"You have in all probability heard," wrote Flora, "that Robert and Nurse Atkinson have been married. They are living on here, in Robert's part of the house. They are fixing it up to suit themselves. It is very impolite of me to call her Nurse Atkinson, as I see I have done. I ought to have called her Audrey."

Of course the post-office friend had written, and so had others. It was a great shock and scandal and a matter that excited the district—the wedding as secret and surprising as Robert's first one had been (though surely not for the same reason), Nurse Atkinson permanently installed in the community, Flora losing out for the second time. Nobody had been aware of any courtship, and they asked how the woman could have enticed him. Did she promise children, lying about her age?

The surprises were not to stop with the wedding. The bride got down to business immediately with the "fixing up" that Flora mentioned. In came the electricity and then the telephone. Now Nurse Atkinson—she would always be called Nurse Atkinson—was heard on the party line lambasting painters and paperhangers and delivery services. She was having everything done over. She was buying an electric stove and putting in a bathroom, and who knew where the money was coming from? Was it all hers, got in her deathbed dealings, in shady bequests? Was it Robert's, was he claiming his share? Ellie's share, left to him and Nurse Atkinson to enjoy themselves with, the shameless pair?

All these improvements took place on one side of the house only. Flora's side remained just as it was. No electric lights there, no fresh wallpaper or new venetian blinds. When the house was painted on the outside—cream with dark-green trim—Flora's side was left bare. This strange open statement was greeted at first with pity and disapproval, then with less sympathy, as a sign of Flora's stubbornness and eccentricity (she could have bought her own paint and made it look decent), and finally as a joke. People drove out of their way to see it.

There was always a dance given in the schoolhouse for a newly married couple. A cash collection—called "a purse of money"—was presented to them. Nurse Atkinson sent out word that she would not mind seeing this custom followed, even though it happened that the family she had married into was opposed to dancing. Some people thought it would be a disgrace to gratify her, a slap in the face to Flora. Others were too curious to hold back. They wanted to see how the newlyweds would behave. Would Robert dance? What sort of outfit would the bride show up in? They delayed a while, but finally the dance was held, and my mother got her report.

The bride wore the dress she had worn at her wedding, or so she said. But who would wear such a dress for a wedding at the manse? More than likely it was bought specially for her appearance at the dance. Pure-white satin with a sweetheart neckline, idiotically youthful. The groom was got up in a new dark-blue suit, and she had stuck a flower in his buttonhole. They were a sight. Her hair was freshly done to blind the eye with brassy reflections, and her face looked as if it would come off on a man's jacket, should she lay it against his shoulder in the dancing. Of course she did dance. She danced with every man present except the groom, who sat scrunched into one of the school desks along the wall. She danced with every man present—they all claimed they had to do it, it was the custom—and then she dragged Robert out to receive the money and to thank everybody for their best wishes. To the ladies in the cloakroom she even hinted that she was feeling unwell, for the usual newlywed reason. Nobody believed her, and indeed nothing ever came of this hope, if she really had it. Some of the women thought that she was lying to them out of malice, insulting them, making them out to be so credulous. But nobody challenged her, nobody was rude to her—maybe because it was plain that she could summon a rudeness of her own to knock anybody flat.

Flora was not present at the dance.

"My sister-in-law is not a dancer," said Nurse Atkinson. "She is stuck in the olden times." She invited them to laugh at Flora, whom she always called her sister-in-law, though she had no right to do so.

My mother wrote a letter to Flora after hearing about all these things. Being removed from the scene, and perhaps in a flurry of importance due to her own newly married state, she may have lost sight of the kind of person she was writing to. She offered sympathy and showed outrage, and said blunt disparaging things about the woman who had—as my mother saw it—dealt Flora such a blow. Back came a letter from Flora saying that she did not know where my mother had been getting her information, but that it seemed she had misunderstood, or listened to malicious people, or jumped to unjustified conclusions. What happened in Flora's family was nobody else's business, and certainly nobody needed to feel sorry for her or angry on her behalf. Flora said that she was happy and satisfied in her life, as she always had been, and she did not interfere with what others did or wanted, because such things did not concern her. She wished my mother all happiness in her marriage and hoped that she would soon be too busy with her own responsibilities to worry about the lives of people that she used to know.

This well-written letter cut my mother, as she said, to the quick. She and Flora stopped corresponding. My mother did become busy with her own life and finally a prisoner in it.

But she thought about Flora. In later years, when she sometimes talked about the things she might have been, or done, she would say, "If I could have been a writer—I do think I could have been; I could have been a writer—then I would have written the story of Flora's life. And do you know what I would have called it? 'The Maiden Lady.'"

The Maiden Lady. She said these words in a solemn and sentimental tone of voice that I had no use for. I knew, or thought I knew, exactly the value she found in them. The stateliness and mystery. The hint of derision turning to reverence. I was fifteen or sixteen years old by that time, and I believed that I could see into my mother's mind. I could see what she would do with Flora, what she had already done. She would make her into a noble figure, one who accepts defection, treachery, who forgives and stands aside, not once but twice. Never a moment of complaint. Flora goes about her cheerful labours, she cleans the house and shovels out the cow byre, she removes some bloody mess from her sister's bed, and when at last the future seems to open up for her—Ellie will die and Robert will beg forgiveness and Flora will silence him with the proud gift of herself—it is time for Audrey Atkinson to drive into the yard and shut Flora out again, more inexplicably and thoroughly the second time than the first. She must endure the painting of the house, the electric lights, all the prosperous activity next door. "Make-Believe Ballroom," "Amos 'n' Andy."[1] No more Scottish comedies or ancient sermons. She must see them drive off to the dance—her old lover and that coldhearted, stupid, by no means beautiful woman in the white satin wedding dress. She is mocked. (And of course she has made over the farm to Ellie and Robert, of course he has inherited it, and now everything belongs to Audrey Atkinson.) The wicked flourish. But it is all right. It is all right—the elect are veiled in patience and humility and lighted by a certainty that events cannot disturb.

That was what I believed my mother would make of things. In her own plight her notions had turned mystical, and there was sometimes a hush, a solemn thrill in her voice that grated on me, alerted me to what seemed a personal danger. I felt a great fog of platitudes and pieties lurking, an incontestable crippled-mother power, which could capture and choke me. There would be no end to it. I had to keep myself sharp-tongued and cynical, arguing and deflating. Eventually I gave up even that recognition and opposed her in silence.

This is a fancy way of saying that I was no comfort and poor company to her when she had almost nowhere else to turn.

I had my own ideas about Flora's story. I didn't think that I could have written a novel but that I would write one. I would take a different tack. I saw through my mother's story and put in what she left out. My Flora would be as black as hers was white. Rejoicing in the bad turns done to her and in her own forgiveness, spying on the shambles of her sister's life. A Presbyterian witch, reading out of her poisonous book. It takes a rival ruthlessness, the comparatively innocent brutality of the thick-skinned nurse, to drive her back, to flourish in her shade. But she is driven back; the power of sex and ordinary greed drive her back and shut her up in her own part of the house with the coal-oil lamps. She shrinks, she caves in, her bones harden and her joints thicken, and—oh, this is it, this is it, I see the bare beauty of the ending I will contrive!—she becomes crippled herself, with arthritis, hardly able to move. Now Audrey Atkinson comes into her full power—she demands the whole house. She wants those partitions knocked out that Robert put up with Flora's help when he married Ellie. She will provide Flora with a room, she will take

1   "Amos 'n' Andy" Comedy radio program (1928–58).

care of her. (Audrey Atkinson does not wish to be seen as a monster, and perhaps she really isn't one.) So one day Robert carries Flora—for the first and last time he carries her in his arms—to the room that his wife Audrey has prepared for her. And once Flora is settled in her well-lit, well-heated corner Audrey Atkinson undertakes to clean out the newly vacated rooms, Flora's rooms. She carries a heap of old books out into the yard. It's spring again, housecleaning time, the season when Flora herself performed such feats, and now the pale face of Flora appears behind the new net curtains. She has dragged herself from her corner, she sees the light-blue sky with its high skidding clouds over the watery fields, the contending crows, the flooded creeks, the reddening tree branches. She sees the smoke rise out of the incinerator in the yard, where her books are burning. Those smelly old books, as Audrey has called them. Words and pages, the ominous dark spines. The elect, the damned, the slim hopes, the mighty torments—up in smoke. There was the ending.

To me the really mysterious person in the story, as my mother told it, was Robert. He never has a word to say. He gets engaged to Flora. He is walking beside her along the river when Ellie leaps out at them. He finds Ellie's thistles in his bed. He does the carpentry made necessary by his and Ellie's marriage. He listens or does not listen while Flora reads. Finally he sits scrunched up in the school desk while his flashy bride dances by with all the men.

So much for his public acts and appearances. But he was the one who started everything, in secret. He *did it to* Ellie. He did it to that skinny wild girl at a time when he was engaged to her sister, and he did it to her again and again when she was nothing but a poor botched body, a failed childbearer, lying in bed.

He must have done it to Audrey Atkinson, too, but with less disastrous results.

Those words, *did it to*—the words my mother, no more than Flora, would never bring herself to speak—were simply exciting to me. I didn't feel any decent revulsion or reasonable indignation. I refused the warning. Not even the fate of Ellie could put me off. Not when I thought of that first encounter—the desperation of it, the ripping and striving. I used to sneak longing looks at men in those days. I admired their wrists and their necks and any bit of their chests a loose button let show, and even their ears and their feet in shoes. I expected nothing reasonable of them, only to be engulfed by their passion. I had similar thoughts about Robert.

What made Flora evil in my story was just what made her admirable in my mother's—her turning away from sex. I fought against everything my mother wanted to tell me on this subject; I despised even the drop in her voice, the gloomy caution, with which she approached it. My mother had grown up in a time and in a place where sex was a dark undertaking for women. She knew that you could die of it. So she honoured the decency, the prudery, the frigidity, that might protect you. And I grew up in horror of that very protection, the dainty tyranny that seemed to me to extend to all areas of life, to enforce tea parties and white gloves and all other sorts of tinkling inanities. I favoured bad words and a breakthrough, I teased myself with the thought of a man's recklessness and domination. The odd thing is that my mother's ideas were in line with some progressive notions of her times, and mine echoed the notions that were favoured in my time. This in spite of the fact that we both believed ourselves independent, and lived in backwaters that did not register such changes. It's as if tendencies that seem most deeply rooted in our minds, most private and singular, have come in as spores on the prevailing wind, looking for any likely place to land, any welcome.

Not long before she died, but when I was still at home, my mother got a letter from the real Flora. It came from that town near the farm, the town that Flora used to ride to, with Robert, in the cart, holding on to the sacks of wool or potatoes.

Flora wrote that she was no longer living on the farm.

"Robert and Audrey are still there," she wrote. "Robert has some trouble with his back but otherwise he is very well. Audrey has poor circulation and is often short of breath. The doctor says she must lose weight but none of the diets seem to work. The farm has been doing very well. They are out of sheep entirely and into dairy cattle. As you may have heard, the chief thing nowadays is to get your milk quota from the government and then you are set. The old stable is all fixed up with milking machines and the latest modern equipment, it is quite a marvel. When I go out there to visit I hardly know where I am."

She went on to say that she had been living in town for some years now, and that she had a job clerking in a store. She must have said what kind of a store this was, but I cannot now remember. She said nothing, of course, about what had led her to this decision—whether she had in fact been put off her own farm, or had sold out her share, apparently not to much advantage. She stressed the fact of her friendliness with Robert and Audrey. She said her health was good.

"I hear that you have not been so lucky in that way," she wrote. "I ran into Cleta Barnes who used to be Cleta Stapleton at the post office out at home, and she told me that there is some problem with your muscles and she said your speech is affected too. This is sad to hear but they can do such wonderful things nowadays so I am hoping that the doctors may be able to help you."

An unsettling letter, leaving so many things out. Nothing in it about God's will or His role in our afflictions. No mention of whether Flora still went to that church. I don't think my mother ever answered. Her fine legible handwriting, her schoolteacher's writing, had deteriorated, and she had difficulty holding a pen. She was always beginning letters and not finishing them. I would find them lying around the house. *My dearest Mary*, they began. *My darling Ruth, My dear little Joanne (though I realize you are not little anymore), My dear old friend Cleta, My lovely Margaret.* These women were friends from her teaching days, her Normal School days, and from high school. A few were former pupils. I have friends all over the country, she would say defiantly. I have dear, dear friends.

I remember seeing one letter that started out: *Friend of my Youth.* I don't know whom it was to. They were all friends of her youth. I don't recall one that began with *My dear and most admired Flora.* I would always look at them, try to read the salutation and the few sentences she had written, and because I could not bear to feel sadness I would feel an impatience with the flowery language, the direct appeal for love and pity. She would get more of that, I thought (more from myself, I meant), if she could manage to withdraw with dignity, instead of reaching out all the time to cast her stricken shadow.

I had lost interest in Flora by then. I was always thinking of stories, and by this time I probably had a new one on my mind.

But I have thought of her since. I have wondered what kind of a store. A hardware store or a five-and-ten, where she has to wear a coverall, or a drugstore, where she is uniformed like a nurse, or a Ladies' Wear, where she is expected to be genteelly fashionable? She might have had to learn about food blenders or chain saws, negligees, cosmetics, even condoms. She would have to work all day under electric lights, and operate a cash register. Would she get a permanent, paint her nails, put on lipstick? She must have found a place to live—a little apartment with a kitchenette, overlooking the main street, or a room in a boarding house. How could she go on being a Cameronian? How could she get to that out-of-the-way church unless she managed to buy a car and learned to drive it? And if she did that she might drive not only to church but to other places. She might go on holidays. She might rent a cottage on a lake for a week, learn to swim, visit a city. She might eat meals in a restaurant, possibly in a restaurant where drinks were served. She might make friends with women who were divorced.

She might meet a man. A friend's widowed brother, perhaps. A man who did not know that she was a Cameronian or what Cameronians were. Who knew nothing of her story. A man who had never heard about the partial painting of the house or the two betrayals, or that it took all her dignity and innocence to keep her from being a joke. He might want to take her dancing, and she would have to explain that she could not go. He would be surprised but not put off—all that Cameronian business might seem quaint to him, almost charming. So it would to everybody. She was brought up in some weird religion, people would say. She lived a long time out on some godforsaken farm. She is a little bit strange but really quite nice. Nice-looking, too. Especially since she went and got her hair done.

I might go into a store and find her.

No, no. She would be dead a long time now.

But suppose I had gone into a store—perhaps a department store. I see a place with the brisk atmosphere, the straightforward displays, the old-fashioned modern look of the fifties. Suppose a tall, handsome woman, nicely turned out, had come to wait on me, and I had known, somehow, in spite of the sprayed and puffed hair and the pink or coral lips and fingernails—I had known that this was Flora. I would have wanted to tell her that I knew, I knew her story, though we had never met. I imagine myself trying to tell her. (This is a dream now, I understand it as a dream.) I imagine her listening, with a pleasant composure. But she shakes her head. She smiles at me, and in her smile there is a degree of mockery, a faint, self-assured malice. Weariness, as well. She is not surprised that I am telling her this, but she is weary of it, of me and my idea of her, my information, my notion that I can know anything about her.

Of course it's my mother I'm thinking of, my mother as she was in those dreams, saying, It's nothing, just this little tremor; saying with such astonishing lighthearted forgiveness, Oh, I knew you'd come someday. My mother surprising me, and doing it almost indifferently. Her mask, her fate, and most of her affliction taken away. How relieved I was, and happy. But I now recall that I was disconcerted as well. I would have to say that I felt slightly cheated. Yes. Offended, tricked, cheated, by this welcome turnaround, this reprieve. My mother moving rather carelessly out of her old prison, showing options and powers I never dreamed she had, changes more than herself. She changes the bitter lump of love I have carried all this time into a phantom—something useless and uncalled for, like a phantom pregnancy.

The Cameronians, I have discovered, are or were an uncompromising remnant of the Covenanters—those Scots who in the seventeenth century bound themselves, with God, to resist prayer books, bishops, any taint of popery or interference by the King. Their name comes from Richard Cameron, an outlawed, or "field," preacher, soon cut down. The Cameronians—for a long time they have preferred to be called the Reformed Presbyterians—went into battle singing the seventy-fourth and the seventy-eighth Psalms. They hacked the haughty Bishop of St. Andrews to death on the highway and rode their horses over his body. One of their ministers, in a mood of firm rejoicing at his own hanging, excommunicated all the other preachers in the world.

—1990

Alistair MacLeod
1936–2014

Alistair MacLeod was a Canadian short story writer and novelist. Born in North Battleford, Saskatchewan, to Nova Scotian parents, he was raised in Cape Breton, Nova Scotia, from the age of ten. MacLeod began publishing short stories in journals in the 1960s and 1970s, and attracted international recognition following the publication of "The Boat" in the *Massachusetts Review* in 1968. This story was republished in the annual volume of *The Best American Short Stories* of 1969. His first collection, *The Lost Salt Gift of Blood*, was published to critical acclaim in 1976. His novel *No Great Mischief* (1999) made him the first Canadian to win the International IMPAC Dublin Literary Award in 2001.

Much of MacLeod's fiction depicts the psychological, physical, and emotional experience of the mining and fishing communities of Nova Scotia, set against the natural cycles of the seasons, of the sea, and of life and death. He often uses first-person present-tense narration, which lends immediacy to his subjects and themes and foregrounds the experience of memory. Joyce Carol Oates writes that the "single underlying motive" for the stories "is the urge to memorialize, the urge to sanctify." This elegiac tone is reminiscent of the Scottish and English traditions of oral literature, and the lyrical power of MacLeod's prose underscores this association, as does the natural ease of the storytelling.

MacLeod accepted a post at the University of Windsor in 1969, where he taught literature and creative writing. Each summer, he and his family returned to Inverness in Cape Breton, where he wrote his stories. He retired in 2000.

As Birds Bring Forth the Sun

Once there was a family with a highland name who lived beside the sea. And the man had a dog of which he was very fond. She was large and grey, a sort of staghound from another time. And if she jumped up to lick his face, which she loved to do, her paws would jolt against his shoulders with such force that she would come close to knocking him down and he would be forced to take two or three backward steps before he could regain his balance. And he himself was not a small man, being slightly over six feet and perhaps one hundred and eighty pounds.

She had been left, when a pup, at the family's gate in a small handmade box and no one knew where she had come from or that she would eventually grow to such a size. Once, while still a small pup, she had been run over by the steel wheel of a horse-drawn cart which was hauling kelp from the shore to be used as fertilizer. It was in October and the rain had been falling for some weeks and the ground was soft. When the wheel of the cart passed over her, it sunk her body into the wet earth as well as crushing some of her ribs; and apparently the silhouette of her small crushed body was visible in the earth after the man lifted her to his chest while she yelped and screamed. He ran his fingers along her broken bones, ignoring the blood and urine which fell upon his shirt, trying to soothe her bulging eyes and her scrabbling front paws and her desperately licking tongue.

The more practical members of his family, who had seen run-over dogs before, suggested that her neck be broken by his strong hands or that he grasp her by the hind legs and swing her head against a rock, thus putting an end to her misery, but he would not do it.

Instead, he fashioned a small box and lined it with woollen remnants from a sheep's fleece and one of his old and frayed shirts. He placed her within the box and placed the box behind the stove and then he warmed some milk in a small saucepan and sweetened it with sugar. And he held open her small and trembling jaws with his left hand while spooning the sweetened milk with his right, ignoring the needle-like sharpness of her small teeth. She lay in the box most of the remaining fall and into the early winter, watching everything with her large brown eyes.

Although some members of the family complained about her presence and the odour from the box and the waste of time she involved, they gradually adjusted to her; and as the weeks passed by, it became evident that her ribs were knitting together in some form or other and that she was recovering with the resilience of the young. It also became evident that she would grow to a tremendous size, as she outgrew one box and then another and the grey hair began to feather from her huge front paws. In the spring she was outside almost all of the time and followed the man everywhere; and when she came inside during the following months, she had grown so large that she would no longer fit into her accustomed place behind the stove and was forced to lie beside it. She was never given a name but was referred to in Gaelic as *cù mòr glas*, the big grey dog.

By the time she came into her first heat, she had grown to a tremendous height, and although her signs and her odour attracted many panting and highly aroused suitors, none was big enough to mount her and the frenzy of their disappointment and the longing of her unfulfilment were more than the man could stand. He went, so the story goes, to a place where he knew there was a big dog. A dog not as big as she was, but still a big dog, and he brought him home with him. And at the proper time he took the *cù mòr glas* and the big dog down to the sea where he knew there was a hollow in the rock which appeared only at low tide. He took some sacking to provide footing for the male dog and he placed the *cù mòr glas* in the hollow of the rock and knelt beside her and steadied her with his left arm under her throat and helped position the male dog above her and guided his blood-engorged penis. He was a man used to working with the breeding of animals, with the guiding of rams and bulls and stallions and often with the funky smell of animal semen heavy on his large and gentle hands.

The winter that followed was a cold one and ice formed on the sea and frequent squalls and blizzards obliterated the offshore islands and caused the people to stay near their fires much of the time, mending clothes and nets and harness and waiting for the change in season. The *cù mòr glas* grew heavier and even more large until there was hardly room for her around the stove or even under the table. And then one morning, when it seemed that spring was about to break, she was gone.

The man and even his family, who had become more involved than they cared to admit, waited for her but she did not come. And as the frenzy of spring wore on, they busied themselves with readying their land and their fishing gear and all of the things that so desperately required their attention. And then they were into summer and fall and winter and another spring which saw the birth of the man and his wife's twelfth child. And then it was summer again.

That summer the man and two of his teenaged sons were pulling their herring nets about two miles offshore when the wind began to blow off the land and the water began to roughen. They became afraid that they could not make it safely back to shore, so they pulled in behind one of the offshore islands, knowing that they would be sheltered there and planning to outwait the storm. As the prow of their boat approached the gravelly shore they heard a sound above them, and looking up they saw the *cù mòr glas* silhouetted on the brow of the hill which was the small island's highest point.

"*M'eudal cù mòr glas*" shouted the man in his happiness—*m'eudal* meaning something like dear or darling; and as he shouted, he jumped over the side of his boat into the waist-deep water, struggling for footing on the rolling gravel as he waded eagerly and awkwardly towards her and the shore. At the same time, the *cù mòr glas* came hurtling down towards him in a shower of small rocks dislodged by her feet; and just as he was emerging from the water, she met him as she used to, rearing up on her hind legs and placing her huge front paws on his shoulders while extending her eager tongue.

The weight and speed of her momentum met him as he tried to hold his balance on the sloping angle and the water rolling gravel beneath his feet, and he staggered backwards and lost his footing and fell beneath her force. And in that instant again, as the story goes, there appeared over the brow of the hill six more huge grey dogs hurtling down towards the gravelled strand. They had never seen him before; and seeing him stretched prone beneath their mother, they misunderstood, like so many armies, the intention of their leader.

They fell upon him in a fury, slashing his face and tearing aside his lower jaw and ripping out his throat, crazed with blood-lust or duty or perhaps starvation. The *cù mòr glas* turned on them in her own savagery, slashing and snarling and, it seemed, crazed by their mistake; driving them bloodied and yelping before her, back over the brow of the hill where they vanished from sight but could still be heard screaming in the distance. It all took perhaps little more than a minute.

The man's two sons, who were still in the boat and had witnessed it all, ran sobbing through the salt water to where their mauled and mangled father lay; but there was little they could do other than hold his warm and bloodied hands for a few brief moments. Although his eyes "lived" for a small fraction of time, he could not speak to them because his face and throat had been torn away, and of course there was nothing they could do except to hold and be held tightly until that too slipped away and his eyes glazed over and they could no longer feel his hands holding theirs. The storm increased and they could not get home and so they were forced to spend the night huddled beside their father's body. They were afraid to try to carry the body to the rocking boat because he was so heavy and they were afraid that they might lose even what little of him remained and they were afraid also, huddled on the rocks, that the dogs might return. But they did not return at all and there was no sound from them, no sound at all, only the moaning of the wind and the washing of the water on the rocks.

In the morning they debated whether they should try to take his body with them or whether they should leave it and return in the company of older and wiser men. But they were afraid to leave it unattended and felt that the time needed to cover it with protective rocks would be better spent in trying to get across to their home shore. For a while they debated as to whether one should go in the boat and the other remain on the island, but each was afraid to be alone and so in the end they managed to drag and carry and almost float him towards the bobbing boat. They lay him face-down and covered him with what clothes there were and set off across the still-rolling sea. Those who waited on the shore missed the large presence of the man within the boat and some of them waded into the water and others rowed out in skiffs, attempting to hear the tearful messages called out across the rolling waves.

The *cù mòr glas* and her six young dogs were never seen again, or perhaps I should say they were never seen again in the same way. After some weeks, a group of men circled the island tentatively in their boats but they saw no sign. They went again and then again but found nothing. A year later, and grown much braver, they beached their boats and walked the island carefully, looking into the small sea caves and the hollows at the base of the wind-ripped trees, thinking perhaps that if they did not find the dogs, they might at least find their whitened bones; but again they discovered nothing.

The *cù mòr glas*, though, was supposed to be sighted here and there for a number of years. Seen on a hill in one region or silhouetted on a ridge in another or loping across the valleys or glens in the early morning or the shadowy evening. Always in the area of the half perceived. For a while she became rather like the Loch Ness Monster or the Sasquatch on a smaller scale. Seen but not recorded. Seen when there were no cameras. Seen but never taken.

The mystery of where she went became entangled with the mystery of whence she came. There was increased speculation about the handmade box in which she had been found and much theorizing as to the individual or individuals who might have left it. People went to look for the box but could not find it. It was felt she might have been part of a *buidseachd* or evil spell cast on the man by some mysterious enemy. But no one could go much farther than that. All of his caring for her was recounted over and over again and nobody missed any of the ironies.

What seemed literally known was that she had crossed the winter ice to have her pups and had been unable to get back. No one could remember ever seeing her swim; and in the early months at least, she could not have taken her young pups with her.

The large and gentle man with the smell of animal semen often heavy on his hands was my great-great-great-grandfather, and it may be argued that he died because he was too good at breeding animals or that he cared too much about their fulfillment and well-being. He was no longer there for his own child of the spring who, in turn, became my great-great-grandfather, and he was perhaps too much there in the memory of his older sons who saw him fall beneath the ambiguous force of the *cù mòr glas*. The youngest boy in the boat was haunted and tormented by the awfulness of what he had seen. He would wake at night screaming that he had seen the *cù mòr glas a'bhàis*, the big grey dog of death, and his screams filled the house and the ears and minds of the listeners, bringing home again and again the consequences of their loss. One morning, after a night in which he saw the *cù mòr glas a'bhàis* so vividly that his sheets were drenched with sweat, he walked to the high cliff which faced the island and there he cut his throat with a fish knife and fell into the sea.

The other brother lived to be forty, but, again so the story goes, he found himself in a Glasgow pub one night, perhaps looking for answers, deep and sodden with the whiskey which had become his anaesthetic. In the half darkness he saw a large, grey-haired man sitting by himself against the wall and mumbled something to him. Some say he saw the *cù mòr glas a'bhàis* or uttered the name. And perhaps the man heard the phrase through ears equally affected by drink and felt he was being called a dog or a son of a bitch or something of that nature. They rose to meet one another and struggled outside into the cobble-stoned passageway behind the pub where, most improbably, there were supposed to be six other large, grey-haired men who beat him to death on the cobblestones, smashing his bloodied head into the stone again and again before vanishing and leaving him to die with his face turned to the sky. The *cù mòr glas a'bhàis* had come again, said his family, as they tried to piece the tale together.

This is how the *cù mòr glas a'bhàis* came into our lives, and it is obvious that all of this happened a long, long time ago. Yet with succeeding generations it seemed the spectre had somehow come to stay and that it had become *ours*—not in the manner of an unwanted skeleton in the closet from a family's ancient past but more in the manner of something close to a genetic possibility. In the deaths of each generation, the grey dog was seen by some—by women who were to die in childbirth; by soldiers who went forth to the many wars but did not return; by those who went forth to feuds or dangerous love affairs; by those who answered mysterious midnight messages; by those who swerved on the highway to avoid the real or imagined grey dog and ended in masses of crumpled steel. And by one professional athlete who, in addition to his ritualized athletic superstitions, carried another fear or belief as well. Many of the man's descendants moved like careful hemophiliacs, fearing that they carried unwanted possibilities deep within them. And others, while they laughed, were like members of families in which there is a recurrence over the generations of repeated cancer or the diabetes which comes to those beyond middle age. The feeling of those who may say little to others but who may say often and quietly to themselves, "It has not happened to me," while adding always the cautionary "*yet.*"

I am thinking all of this now as the October rain falls on the city of Toronto and the pleasant, white-clad nurses pad confidently in and out of my father's room. He lies quietly amidst the whiteness, his head and shoulders elevated so that he is in that hospital position of being neither quite prone nor yet sitting. His hair is white upon his pillow and he breathes softly and sometimes unevenly, although it is difficult ever to be sure.

My five grey-haired brothers and I take turns beside his bedside, holding his heavy hands in ours and feeling their response, hoping ambiguously that he will speak to us, although we know that it may tire him. And trying to read his life and ours into his eyes when they are open. He has been with us for a long time, well into our middle age. Unlike those boys in that boat of so long ago, we did not see him taken from us in our youth. And unlike their youngest brother who, in turn, became our great-great-grandfather, we did not grow into a world in which there was no father's touch. We have been lucky to have this large and gentle man so deep into our lives.

No one in this hospital has mentioned the *cù mòr glas a'bhàis*. Yet as my mother said ten years ago, before slipping into her own death as quietly as a grownup child who leaves or enters her parents' house in the early hours, "It is hard to *not* know what you do know."

Even those who are most skeptical, like my oldest brother who has driven here from Montreal, betray themselves by their nervous actions. "I avoided the Greyhound bus stations in both Montreal and Toronto," he smiled upon his arrival, and then added, "Just in case."

He did not realize how ill our father was and has smiled little since then. I watch him turning the diamond ring upon his finger, knowing that he hopes he will not hear the Gaelic he knows too well. Not having the luxury, as he once said, of some who live in Montreal and are able to pretend they do not understand the "other" language. You cannot *not* know what you do know.

Sitting here, taking turns holding the hands of the man who gave us life, we are afraid for him and for ourselves. We are afraid of what he may see and we are afraid to hear the phrase born of the vision. We are aware that it may become confused with what the doctors call "the will to live" and we are aware that some beliefs are what others would dismiss as "garbage." We are aware that there are men who believe the earth is flat and that the birds bring forth the sun.

Bound here in our own peculiar mortality, we do not wish to see or see others see that which signifies life's demise. We do not want to hear the voice of our father, as did those other sons, calling down his own particular death upon him.

We would shut our eyes and plug our ears, even as we know such actions to be of no avail. Open still and fearful to the grey hair rising on our necks if and when we hear the scrabble of the paws and the scratching at the door.

—1985

Margaret Atwood

b. 1939

Aptly described as "a nationalist who rankles nationalists, a feminist who rankles feminists," and "a political satirist who resists political solutions," Margaret Atwood is a writer who defies traditional categories. Her internationally renowned novels, short stories, and poems span and splice together a multitude of genres and have established her as a germinal figure in Canadian literature.

Atwood was born in Ottawa but spent much of her childhood in the Canadian bush. Educated at the University of Toronto and Radcliffe College, Atwood is a self-consciously Canadian writer, working in a tradition that she characterized in *Survival* (1972), her thematic survey of Canadian literature, as uniquely preoccupied with victimhood.

Although it was the stark, terse, eerily detached poetry in collections like *The Journals of Susanna Moodie* (1970) that made her reputation, Atwood's fiction is astonishing for its variety of tone, mingling seriousness, playful irony, sardonic humour, and even Gothic terror across a similarly diverse range of genres, from the dystopian "speculative fiction" of *The Handmaid's Tale* (1985) and *The Year of the Flood* (2009) to historical novels like *Alias Grace* (1996).

For Atwood, every art form is enclosed by a "set of brackets," conventions that check "the deviousness[,] inventiveness[,] audacity[,] and perversity of the creative spirit." In her work she aims to "expand the brackets," rewriting traditions to deliver the creative spirit from restraint. Though she has written a good deal of realist fiction, her fascination with storytelling has also led her to experiment widely with metafictional techniques, as in the at once open-ended and inexorable plots of "Happy Endings."

Of all the labels critics have applied to her, perhaps "trickster" suits Atwood best, for she is a master fabricator of great wit and imagination whose work refashions the rules to prove that, in the end, "art is what you can get away with."

Happy Endings

John and Mary meet.
What happens next?
If you want a happy ending, try A.

A

John and Mary fall in love and get married. They both have worthwhile and remunerative jobs which they find stimulating and challenging. They buy a charming house. Real estate values go up. Eventually, when they can afford live-in help, they have two children, to whom they are devoted. The children turn out well. John and Mary have a stimulating and challenging sex life and worthwhile friends. They go on fun vacations together. They retire. They both have hobbies which they find stimulating and challenging. Eventually they die. This is the end of the story.

B

Mary falls in love with John but John doesn't fall in love with Mary. He merely uses her body for selfish pleasure and ego gratification of a tepid kind. He comes to her apartment twice a week and she cooks him dinner, you'll notice that he doesn't even consider her worth the price of a dinner out, and after he's eaten the dinner he fucks her and after that he falls asleep, while she does the dishes so he won't think she's untidy, having all those dirty dishes lying around, and puts on fresh lipstick so she'll look good when he wakes up, but when he wakes up he doesn't even notice, he puts on his socks and his shorts and his pants and his shirt and his tie and his shoes, the reverse order from the one in which he took them off. He doesn't take off Mary's clothes, she takes them off herself, she acts as if she's dying for it every time, not because she likes sex exactly, she doesn't, but she wants John to think she does because if they do it often enough surely he'll get used to her, he'll come to depend on her and they will get married, but John goes out the door with hardly so much as a goodnight and three days later he turns up at six o'clock and they do the whole thing over again.

Mary gets run-down. Crying is bad for your face, everyone knows that and so does Mary but she can't stop. People at work notice. Her friends tell her John is a rat, a pig, a dog, he isn't good enough for her, but she can't believe it. Inside John, she thinks, is another John, who is much nicer. This other John will emerge like a butterfly from a cocoon, a Jack from a box, a pit from a prune, if the first John is only squeezed enough.

One evening John complains about the food. He has never complained about the food before. Mary is hurt.

Her friends tell her they've seen him in a restaurant with another woman, whose name is Madge. It's not even Madge that finally gets to Mary: it's the restaurant. John has never taken Mary to a restaurant. Mary collects all the sleeping pills and aspirins she can find, and takes them and a half a bottle of sherry. You can see what kind of a woman she is by the fact that it's not even whiskey. She leaves a note for John. She hopes he'll discover her and get her to the hospital in time and repent and then they can get married, but this fails to happen and she dies.

John marries Madge and everything continues as in A.

C

John, who is an older man, falls in love with Mary, and Mary, who is only twenty-two, feels sorry for him because he's worried about his hair falling out. She sleeps with him even though she's not in love with him. She met him at work. She's in love with someone called James, who is twenty-two also and not yet ready to settle down.

John on the contrary settled down long ago: this is what is bothering him. John has a steady, respectable job and is getting ahead in his field, but Mary isn't impressed by him, she's impressed by James, who has a motorcycle and a fabulous record collection. But James is often away on his motorcycle, being free. Freedom isn't the same for girls, so in the meantime Mary spends Thursday evenings with John. Thursdays are the only days John can get away.

John is married to a woman called Madge and they have two children, a charming house which they bought just before the real estate values went up, and hobbies which they find stimulating and challenging, when they have the time. John tells Mary how important she is to him, but of course he can't leave his wife because a commitment is a commitment. He goes on about this more than is necessary and Mary finds it boring, but older men can keep it up longer so on the whole she has a fairly good time.

One day James breezes in on his motorcycle with some top-grade California hybrid and James and Mary get higher than you'd believe possible and they climb into bed. Everything becomes very underwater, but along comes John, who has a key to Mary's apartment. He finds them stoned and entwined. He's hardly in any position to be jealous, considering Madge, but nevertheless he's overcome with despair. Finally he's middle-aged, in two years he'll be bald as an egg and he can't stand it. He purchases a handgun, saying he needs it for target practice—this is the thin part of the plot, but it can be dealt with later—and shoots the two of them and himself.

Madge, after a suitable period of mourning, marries an understanding man called Fred and everything continues as in A, but under different names.

D

Fred and Madge have no problems. They get along exceptionally well and are good at working out any little difficulties that may arise. But their charming house is by the seashore and one day a giant tidal wave approaches. Real estate values go down. The rest of the story is about what caused the tidal wave and how they escape from it. They do, though thousands drown, but Fred and

Madge are virtuous and lucky. Finally on high ground they clasp each other, wet and dripping and grateful, and continue as in A.

E

Yes, but Fred has a bad heart. The rest of the story is about how kind they both are until Fred dies. Then Madge devotes herself to charity work until the end of A. If you like, it can be "Madge," "cancer," "guilty and confused," and "bird watching."

F

If you think this is all too bourgeois, make John a revolutionary and Mary a counterespionage agent and see how far that gets you. Remember, this is Canada. You'll still end up with A, though in between you may get a lustful brawling saga of passionate involvement, a chronicle of our times, sort of.

You'll have to face it, the endings are the same however you slice it. Don't be deluded by any other endings, they're all fake, either deliberately fake, with malicious intent to deceive, or just motivated by excessive optimism if not by downright sentimentality.

The only authentic ending is the one provided here:

John and Mary die. John and Mary die. John and Mary die.

So much for endings. Beginnings are always more fun. True connoisseurs, however, are known to favour the stretch in between, since it's the hardest to do anything with.

That's about all that can be said for plots, which anyway are just one thing after another, a what and a what and a what.

Now try How and Why.

—1983

Thomas King
b. 1943

One of the first Native writers to gain a significant popular and critical following in Canada and the United States, Thomas King has explored Indigenous identities and experiences in a wide range of forms, genres, and mediums. Though often identified as a comic writer, King considers himself a satirist who uses comedy to deal with serious subjects—the exploitation of cultures, the loss of a way of life, the struggle for self-definition, and the question of authenticity—without descending into polemical denunciations. As King explains, "Tragedy is my topic. Comedy is my strategy."

In novels like *Green Grass, Running Water* (1993) and the stories collected in *A Short History of Indians in Canada* (2005), King often confronts head-on the traumatic legacy of colonization. His characters are not woebegone "solitary figures poised on the brink of extinction" but many-sided individuals bound by a nourishing sense of community. For King, the term *postcolonial* misleadingly implies that European contact was the primary generative impetus of Native literature. As he argues in "Godzilla vs. Post-Colonial" (1990), "the idea of post-colonial writing effectively cuts us off from our traditions, traditions that were in place before colonialism ever became a question, traditions which have come down to us through our cultures in spite of colonialism."

King takes up and carries forward many of these traditions, often fusing the conventions of oral storytelling with those of written narratives. Certain stories, including "A Short History of Indians in Canada," were written as oral performance pieces. In all his work, King aims not only to reclaim Native culture from reductive stereotypical representations but to reinforce "the notion that, in addition to the useable past that the concurrence of oral literature and traditional history provides us with, we also have an active present marked by cultural tenacity and a viable future."

A Short History of Indians in Canada

Can't sleep, Bob Haynie tells the doorman at the King Eddie. Can't sleep, can't sleep.

First time in Toronto? says the doorman.

Yes, says Bob.

Businessman?

Yes.

Looking for some excitement?

Yes.

Bay Street,[1] sir, says the doorman.

Bob Haynie catches a cab to Bay Street at three in the morning. He loves the smell of concrete. He loves the look of city lights. He loves the sound of skyscrapers.

Bay Street.

Smack!

Bob looks up just in time to see a flock of Indians fly into the side of the building.

Smack! Smack!

Bob looks up just in time to get out of the way.

Whup!

An Indian hits the pavement in front of him.

Whup! Whup!

Two Indians hit the pavement behind him.

Holy Cow! shouts Bob, and he leaps out of the way of the falling Indians.

Whup! Whup! Whup!

Bob throws his hands over his head and dashes into the street. And is almost hit by a city truck.

Honk!

Two men jump out of the truck. Hi, I'm Bill. Hi, I'm Rudy.

Hi, I'm Bob.

Businessman? says Bill.

Yes.

First time in Toronto? says Rudy.

Yes.

Whup! Whup! Whup!

Look out! Bob shouts. There are Indians flying into the skyscrapers and falling on the sidewalk.

Whup!

Mohawk, says Bill.

Whup! Whup!

Couple of Cree over here, says Rudy.

Amazing, says Bob. How can you tell?

By the feathers, says Bill. We got a book.

It's our job, says Rudy.

Whup!

Bob looks around. What's this one? he says.

Holy! says Bill. Holy! says Rudy.

Check the book, says Bill. Just to be sure.

Flip, flip, flip.

---

1   *Bay Street* Major street in Toronto's financial district.

Navajo!

Bill and Rudy put their arms around Bob. A Navajo! Don't normally see Navajos this far north. Don't normally see Navajos this far east.

Is she dead? says Bob.

Nope, says Bill. Just stunned.

Most of them are just stunned, says Rudy.

Some people never see this, says Bill. One of nature's mysteries. A natural phenomenon.

They're nomadic you know, says Rudy. And migratory.

Toronto's in the middle of the flyway, says Bill. The lights attract them.

Bob counts the bodies. Seventy-three. No. Seventy-four. What can I do to help?

Not much that anyone can do, says Bill. We tried turning off the lights in the buildings.

We tried broadcasting loud music from the roofs, says Rudy.

Rubber owls? asks Bob.

It's a real problem this time of the year, says Bill.

Whup! Whup! Whup!

Bill and Rudy pull green plastic bags out of their pockets and try to find the open ends.

The dead ones we bag, says Rudy.

The lives ones we tag, says Bill. Take them to the shelter. Nurse them back to health. Release them in the wild.

Amazing, says Bob.

A few wander off dazed and injured. If we don't find them right away, they don't stand a chance.

Amazing, says Bob.

You're one lucky guy, says Bill. In another couple of weeks, they'll be gone.

A family from Alberta came through last week and didn't even see an Ojibway, says Rudy.

Your first time in Toronto? says Bill.

It's a great town, says Bob. You're doing a great job.

Whup!

Don't worry, says Rudy. By the time the commuters show up, you'll never even know the Indians were here.

Bob catches a cab back to the King Eddie and shakes the doorman's hand. I saw the Indians, he says.

Thought you'd enjoy that, sir, says the doorman.

Thank you, says Bob. It was spectacular.

Not like the old days. The doorman sighs and looks up into the night. In the old days, when they came through, they would black out the entire sky.

—2005

Octavia Butler

1947–2006

Octavia Butler was an American author best known for psychologically realistic science fiction that examines racial, sexual, and environmental politics. A leading figure of the Afrofuturism movement, Butler addressed the history, present concerns, and possible futures of Black Americans through her fiction. A creator of complex speculative worlds, Butler was, in her own words, "a pessimist, a feminist always, a Black, a quiet egoist, a former Baptist, and an oil-and-water combination of ambition, laziness, insecurity, certainty, and drive."

Born in Pasadena, California, Butler was raised by her mother and grandmother. At the age of ten, she decided that writing was her vocation. After graduating from Pasadena Community College, Butler enrolled in a screenwriting workshop, where her talent was noticed by the established science-fiction writer Harlan Ellison, who would become her mentor. Butler's first novel, *Patternmaster* (1976), was well-received by critics, with Orson Scott Card describing the text as a "vibrant [study] of the ethics of power and submission." The novel became the first in a series employing concepts such as human selective breeding, genetic mutation, and social control though telepathy. As she worked on this series, Butler also published *Kindred* (1979), one of her most widely read novels, about a Black woman who is transported back in time to the era of slavery.

In the 1980s, as she published follow-ups to *Patternmaster* as well as other novels and short stories, Butler met with increasing critical and commercial success, winning two Hugo Awards and a Nebula Award. In the 1990s, she became the first science-fiction writer to receive a prestigious MacArthur "Genius Grant." Her last major works were the highly influential Earthseed books—*Parable of the Sower* (1993) and *Parable of the Talents* (1998)—in which she envisioned American society disintegrating as a result of extreme inequality and environmental degradation.

Through her penetrating engagement with racial, sexual, and social power structures, Butler challenged science fiction's domination by white men. "When I began writing science fiction ... I wasn't in any of this stuff I read," Butler once remarked in an interview with *The New York Times*. "I wrote myself in."

Speech Sounds

There was trouble aboard the Washington Boulevard bus. Rye had expected trouble sooner or later in her journey. She had put off going until loneliness and hopelessness drove her out. She believed she might have one group of relatives left alive—a brother and his two children twenty miles away in Pasadena. That was a day's journey one-way, if she were lucky. The unexpected arrival of the bus as she left her Virginia Road home had seemed to be a piece of luck—until the trouble began.

Two young men were involved in a disagreement of some kind, or, more likely, a misunderstanding. They stood in the aisle, grunting and gesturing at each other, each in his own uncertain T stance as the bus lurched over the potholes. The driver seemed to be putting some effort into keeping them off balance. Still, their gestures stopped just short of contact—mock punches, hand games of intimidation to replace lost curses.

People watched the pair, then looked at one another and made small anxious sounds. Two children whimpered.

Rye sat a few feet behind the disputants and across from the back door. She watched the two carefully, knowing the fight would begin when someone's nerve broke or someone's hand slipped or someone came to the end of his limited ability to communicate. These things could happen anytime.

One of them happened as the bus hit an especially large pothole and one man, tall, thin, and sneering, was thrown into his shorter opponent.

Instantly, the shorter man drove his left fist into the disintegrating sneer. He hammered his larger opponent as though he neither had nor needed any weapon other than his left fist. He hit quickly enough, hard enough to batter his opponent down before the taller man could regain his balance or hit back even once.

People screamed or squawked in fear. Those nearby scrambled to get out of the way. Three more young men roared in excitement and gestured wildly. Then, somehow, a second dispute broke out between two of these three—probably because one inadvertently touched or hit the other.

As the second fight scattered frightened passengers, a woman shook the driver's shoulder and grunted as she gestured toward the fighting.

The driver grunted back through bared teeth. Frightened, the woman drew away.

Rye, knowing the methods of bus drivers, braced herself and held on to the crossbar of the seat in front of her. When the driver hit the brakes, she was ready and the combatants were not. They fell over seats and onto screaming passengers, creating even more confusion. At least one more fight started.

The instant the bus came to a full stop, Rye was on her feet, pushing the back door. At the second push, it opened and she jumped out, holding her pack in one arm. Several other passengers followed, but some stayed on the bus. Buses were rare and irregular now, people rode when they could, no matter what. There might not be another bus today—or tomorrow. People started walking, and if they saw a bus they flagged it down. People making intercity trips like Rye's from Los Angeles to Pasadena made plans to camp out, or risked seeking shelter with locals who might rob or murder them.

The bus did not move, but Rye moved away from it. She intended to wait until the trouble was over and get on again, but if there was shooting, she wanted the protection of a tree. Thus, she was near the curb when a battered blue Ford on the other side of the street made a U-turn and pulled up in front of the bus. Cars were rare these days—as rare as a severe shortage of fuel and of relatively unimpaired mechanics could make them. Cars that still ran were as likely to be used as weapons as they were to serve as transportation. Thus, when the driver of the Ford beckoned to Rye, she moved away warily. The driver got out—a big man, young, neatly bearded with dark, thick hair. He wore a long overcoat and a look of wariness that matched Rye's. She stood several feet from him, waiting to see what he would do. He looked at the bus, now rocking with the combat inside, then at the small cluster of passengers who had gotten off. Finally he looked at Rye again.

She returned his gaze, very much aware of the old forty-five automatic her jacket concealed. She watched his hands.

He pointed with his left hand toward the bus. The dark tinted windows prevented him from seeing what was happening inside.

His use of the left hand interested Rye more than his obvious question. Left-handed people tended to be less impaired, more reasonable and comprehending, less driven by frustration, confusion, and anger.

She imitated his gesture, pointing toward the bus with her own left hand, then punching the air with both fists.

The man took off his coat revealing a Los Angeles Police Department uniform complete with baton and service revolver.

Rye took another step back from him. There was no more LAPD, no more *any* large organization, governmental or private. There were neighbourhood patrols and armed individuals. That was all.

The man took something from his coat pocket, then threw the coat into the car. Then he gestured Rye back, back toward the rear of the bus. He had something made of plastic in his hand. Rye did not understand what he wanted until he went to the rear door of the bus and beckoned her to stand there. She obeyed mainly out of curiosity. Cop or not, maybe he could do something to stop the stupid fighting.

He walked around the front of the bus, to the street side where the driver's window was open. There, she thought she saw him throw something into the bus. She was still trying to peer through the tinted glass when people began stumbling out the rear door, choking and weeping. Gas.

Rye caught an old woman who would have fallen, lifted two little children down when they were in danger of being knocked down and trampled. She could see the bearded man helping people at the front door. She caught a thin old man shoved out by one of the combatants. Staggered by the old man's weight, she was barely able to get out of the way as the last of the young men pushed his way out. This one, bleeding from nose and mouth, stumbled into another, and they grappled blindly, still sobbing from the gas.

The bearded man helped the bus driver out through the front door, though the driver did not seem to appreciate his help. For a moment, Rye thought there would be another fight. The bearded man stepped back and watched the driver gesture threateningly, watched him shout in wordless anger.

The bearded man stood still, made no sound, refused to respond to clearly obscene gestures. The least impaired people tended to do this—stand back unless they were physically threatened and let those with less control scream and jump around. It was as though they felt it beneath them to be as touchy as the less comprehending. This was an attitude of superiority, and that was the way people like the bus driver perceived it. Such "superiority" was frequently punished by beatings, even by death. Rye had had close calls of her own. As a result, she never went unarmed. And in this world where the only likely common language was body language, being armed was often enough. She had rarely had to draw her gun or even display it.

The bearded man's revolver was on constant display. Apparently that was enough for the bus driver. The driver spat in disgust, glared at the bearded man for a moment longer, then strode back to his gas-filled bus. He stared at it for a moment, dearly wanting to get in, but the gas was still too strong. Of the windows, only his tiny driver's window actually opened. The front door was open, but the rear door would not stay open unless someone held it. Of course, the air conditioning had failed long ago. The bus would take some time to clear. It was the driver's property, his livelihood. He had pasted old magazine pictures of items he would accept as fare on its sides. Then he would use what he collected to feed his family or to trade. If his bus did not run, he did not eat. On the other hand, if the inside of his bus was torn apart by senseless fighting, he would not eat very well either. He was apparently unable to perceive this. All he could see was that it would be some time before he could use his bus again. He shook his fist at the bearded man and shouted. There seemed to be words in his shout, but Rye could not understand them. She did not know whether this was his fault or hers. She had heard so little coherent human speech for the past three years, she was no longer certain how well she recognized it, no longer certain of the degree of her own impairment.

The bearded man sighed. He glanced toward his car, then beckoned to Rye. He was ready to leave, but he wanted something from her first. No. No, he wanted her to leave with him. Risk getting into his car when, in spite of his uniform, law and order were nothing—not even words any longer.

She shook her head in a universally understood negative, but the man continued to beckon.

She waved him away. He was doing what the less impaired rarely did—drawing potentially negative attention to another of his kind. People from the bus had begun to look at her.

One of the men who had been fighting tapped another on the arm, then pointed from the bearded man to Rye, and finally held up the first two fingers of his right hand as though giving two-thirds of a Boy Scout salute. The gesture was very quick, its meaning obvious even at a distance. She had been grouped with the bearded man. Now what?

The man who had made the gesture started toward her.

She had no idea what he intended, but she stood her ground. The man was half a foot taller than she was and perhaps ten years younger. She did not imagine she could outrun him. Nor did she expect anyone to help her if she needed help. The people around her were all strangers.

She gestured once—a clear indication to the man to stop. She did not intend to repeat the gesture. Fortunately, the man obeyed. He gestured obscenely and several other men laughed. Loss of verbal language had spawned a whole new set of obscene gestures. The man, with stark simplicity, had accused her of sex with the bearded man and had suggested she accommodate the other men present—beginning with him.

Rye watched him wearily. People might very well stand by and watch if he tried to rape her. They would also stand and watch her shoot him. Would he push things that far?

He did not. After a series of obscene gestures that brought him no closer to her, he turned contemptuously and walked away.

And the bearded man still waited. He had removed his service revolver, holster and all. He beckoned again, both hands empty. No doubt his gun was in the car and within easy reach, but his taking it off impressed her. Maybe he was all right. Maybe he was just alone. She had been alone herself for three years. The illness had stripped her, killing her children one by one, killing her husband, her sister, her parents ...

The illness, if it was an illness, had cut even the living off from one another. As it swept over the country, people hardly had time to lay blame on the Soviets[1] (though they were falling silent along with the rest of the world), on a new virus, a new pollutant, radiation, divine retribution ... The illness was stroke-swift in the way it cut people down and strokelike in some of its effects.

---

1   *blame on the Soviets* The second half of the twentieth century was characterized by political tensions between the United States and the Soviet Union, with continual threat of a nuclear war between the two nations. In 1991 the Soviet Union collapsed into Russia and other independent states.

But it was highly specific. Language was always lost or severely impaired. It was never regained. Often there was also paralysis, intellectual impairment, death.

Rye walked toward the bearded man, ignoring the whistling and applauding of two of the young men and their thumbs-up signs to the bearded man. If he had smiled at them or acknowledged them in any way, she would almost certainly have changed her mind. If she had let herself think of the possible deadly consequences of getting into a stranger's car, she would have changed her mind. Instead, she thought of the man who lived across the street from her. He rarely washed since his bout with the illness. And he had gotten into the habit of urinating wherever he happened to be. He had two women already—one tending each of his large gardens. They put up with him in exchange for his protection. He had made it clear that he wanted Rye to become his third woman.

She got into the car and the bearded man shut the door. She watched as he walked around to the driver's door—watched for his sake because his gun was on the seat beside her. And the bus driver and a pair of young men had come a few steps closer. They did nothing, though, until the bearded man was in the car. Then one of them threw a rock. Others followed his example, and as the car drove away, several rocks bounced off harmlessly.

When the bus was some distance behind them, Rye wiped sweat from her forehead and longed to relax. The bus would have taken her more than halfway to Pasadena. She would have had only ten miles to walk. She wondered how far she would have to walk now—and wondered if walking a long distance would be her only problem.

At Figueroa and Washington where the bus normally made a left turn, the bearded man stopped, looked at her, and indicated that she should choose a direction. When she directed him left and he actually turned left, she began to relax. If he was willing to go where she directed, perhaps he was safe.

As they passed blocks of burned, abandoned buildings, empty lots, and wrecked or stripped cars, he slipped a gold chain over his head and handed it to her. The pendant attached to it was a smooth, glassy, black rock. Obsidian. His name might be Rock or Peter[1] or Black, but she decided to think of him as Obsidian. Even her sometimes useless memory would retain a name like Obsidian.

She handed him her own name symbol—a pin in the shape of a large golden stalk of wheat. She had bought it long before the illness and the silence began. Now she wore it, thinking it was as close as she was likely to come to Rye. People like Obsidian who had not known her before probably thought

---

1   *Peter*   The name Peter is derived from the Greek word for "stone."

of her as Wheat. Not that it mattered. She would never hear her name spoken again.

Obsidian handed her pin back to her. He caught her hand as she reached for it and rubbed his thumb over her calluses.

He stopped at First Street and asked which way again. Then, after turning right as she had indicated, he parked near the Music Center. There, he took a folded paper from the dashboard and unfolded it. Rye recognized it as a street map, though the writing on it meant nothing to her. He flattened the map, took her hand again, and put her index finger on one spot. He touched her, touched himself, pointed toward the floor. In effect, "We are here." She knew he wanted to know where she was going. She wanted to tell him, but she shook her head sadly. She had lost reading and writing. That was her most serious impairment and her most painful. She had taught history at UCLA. She had done freelance writing. Now she could not even read her own manuscripts. She had a houseful of books that she could neither read nor bring herself to use as fuel. And she had a memory that would not bring back to her much of what she had read before.

She stared at the map, trying to calculate. She had been born in Pasadena, had lived for fifteen years in Los Angeles. Now she was near L.A. Civic Center. She knew the relative positions of the two cities, knew streets, directions, even knew to stay away from freeways, which might be blocked by wrecked cars and destroyed overpasses. She ought to know how to point out Pasadena even though she could not recognize the word.

Hesitantly, she placed her hand over a pale orange patch in the upper right corner of the map. That should be right. Pasadena.

Obsidian lifted her hand and looked under it, then folded the map and put it back on the dashboard. He could read, she realized belatedly. He could probably write, too. Abruptly, she hated him—deep, bitter hatred. What did literacy mean to him—a grown man who played cops and robbers? But he was literate and she was not. She never would be. She felt sick to her stomach with hatred, frustration, and jealousy. And only a few inches from her hand was a loaded gun.

She held herself still, staring at him, almost seeing his blood. But her rage crested and ebbed and she did nothing.

Obsidian reached for her hand with hesitant familiarity. She looked at him. Her face had already revealed too much. No person still living in what was left of human society could fail to recognize that expression, that jealousy.

She closed her eyes wearily, drew a deep breath. She had experienced longing for the past, hatred of the present, growing hopelessness, purposelessness, but she had never experienced such a powerful urge to kill another person. She had left her home, finally, because she had come near to killing herself.

She had found no reason to stay alive. Perhaps that was why she had gotten into Obsidian's car. She had never before done such a thing.

He touched her mouth and made chatter motions with thumb and fingers. Could she speak?

She nodded and watched his milder envy come and go. Now both had admitted what it was not safe to admit, and there had been no violence. He tapped his mouth and forehead and shook his head. He did not speak or comprehend spoken language. The illness had played with them, taking away, she suspected, what each valued most.

She plucked at his sleeve, wondering why he had decided on his own to keep the LAPD alive with what he had left. He was sane enough otherwise. Why wasn't he at home raising corn, rabbits, and children? But she did not know how to ask. Then he put his hand on her thigh and she had another question to deal with.

She shook her head. Disease, pregnancy, helpless, solitary agony ... no.

He massaged her thigh gently and smiled in obvious disbelief.

No one had touched her for three years. She had not wanted anyone to touch her. What kind of world was this to chance bringing a child into even if the father were willing to stay and help raise it? It was too bad, though. Obsidian could not know how attractive he was to her—young, probably younger than she was, clean, asking for what he wanted rather than demanding it. But none of that mattered. What were a few moments of pleasure measured against a lifetime of consequences?

He pulled her closer to him and for a moment she let herself enjoy the closeness. He smelled good—male and good. She pulled away reluctantly.

He sighed, reached toward the glove compartment. She stiffened, not knowing what to expect, but all he took out was a small box. The writing on it meant nothing to her. She did not understand until he broke the seal, opened the box, and took out a condom. He looked at her, and she first looked away in surprise. Then she giggled. She could not remember when she had last giggled.

He grinned, gestured toward the backseat, and she laughed aloud. Even in her teens, she had disliked backseats of cars. But she looked around at the empty streets and ruined buildings, then she got out and into the backseat. He let her put the condom on him, then seemed surprised at her eagerness.

Sometime later, they sat together, covered by his coat, unwilling to become clothed near strangers again just yet. He made rock-the-baby gestures and looked questioningly at her.

She swallowed, shook her head. She did not know how to tell him her children were dead.

He took her hand and drew a cross in it with his index finger, then made his baby-rocking gesture again.

She nodded, held up three fingers, then turned away, trying to shut out a sudden flood of memories. She had told herself that the children growing up now were to be pitied. They would run through the downtown canyons with no real memory of what the buildings had been or even how they had come to be. Today's children gathered books as well as wood to be burned as fuel. They ran through the streets chasing one another and hooting like chimpanzees. They had no future. They were now all they would ever be.

He put his hand on her shoulder, and she turned suddenly, fumbling for his small box, then urging him to make love to her again. He could give her forgetfulness and pleasure. Until now, nothing had been able to do that. Until now, every day had brought her closer to the time when she would do what she had left home to avoid doing: putting her gun in her mouth and pulling the trigger.

She asked Obsidian if he would come home with her, stay with her.

He looked surprised and pleased once he understood. But he did not answer at once. Finally, he shook his head as she had feared he might. He was probably having too much fun playing cops and robbers and picking up women.

She dressed in silent disappointment, unable to feel any anger toward him. Perhaps he already had a wife and a home. That was likely. The illness had been harder on men than on women—had killed more men, had left male survivors more severely impaired. Men like Obsidian were rare. Women either settled for less or stayed alone. If they found an Obsidian, they did what they could to keep him. Rye suspected he had someone younger, prettier keeping him.

He touched her while she was strapping her gun on and asked with a complicated series of gestures whether it was loaded.

She nodded grimly.

He patted her arm.

She asked once more if he would come home with her, this time using a different series of gestures. He had seemed hesitant. Perhaps he could be courted.

He got out and into the front seat without responding.

She took her place in front again, watching him. Now he plucked at his uniform and looked at her. She thought she was being asked something but did not know what it was.

He took off his badge, tapped it with one finger, then tapped his chest. Of course.

She took the badge from his hand and pinned her wheat stalk to it. If playing cops and robbers was his only insanity, let him play. She would take him, uniform and all. It occurred to her that she might eventually lose him to someone he would meet as he had met her. But she would have him for a while.

He took the street map down again, tapped it, pointed vaguely northeast toward Pasadena, then looked at her.

She shrugged, tapped his shoulder, then her own, and held up her index and second fingers tight together, just to be sure.

He grasped the two fingers and nodded. He was with her.

She took the map from him and threw it onto the dashboard. She pointed back southwest—back toward home. Now he did not have to go to Pasadena. Now she could go on having a brother there and two nephews—three right-handed males. Now she did not have to find out for certain whether she was as alone as she feared. Now she was not alone.

Obsidian took Hill Street south, then Washington west, and she leaned back, wondering what it would be like to have someone again. With what she had scavenged, what she had preserved, and what she grew, there was easily enough food for them. There was certainly room enough in a four-bedroom house. He could move his possessions in. Best of all, the animal across the street would pull back and possibly not force her to kill him.

Obsidian had drawn her closer to him, and she had put her head on his shoulder when suddenly he braked hard, almost throwing her off the seat. Out of the corner of her eye, she saw that someone had run across the street in front of the car. One car on the street and someone had to run in front of it.

Straightening up, Rye saw that the runner was a woman, fleeing from an old frame house to a boarded-up storefront. She ran silently, but the man who followed her a moment later shouted what sounded like garbled words as he ran. He had something in his hand. Not a gun. A knife, perhaps.

The woman tried a door, found it locked, looked around desperately, finally snatched up a fragment of glass broken from the storefront window. With this she turned to face her pursuer. Rye thought she would be more likely to cut her own hand than to hurt anyone else with the glass.

Obsidian jumped from the car, shouting. It was the first time Rye had heard his voice—deep and hoarse from disuse. He made the same sound over and over the way some speechless people did, "Da, da, da!"

Rye got out of the car as Obsidian ran toward the couple. He had drawn his gun. Fearful, she drew her own and released the safety. She looked around to see who else might be attracted to the scene. She saw the man glance at Obsidian, then suddenly lunge at the woman. The woman jabbed his face with her glass, but he caught her arm and managed to stab her twice before Obsidian shot him.

The man doubled, then toppled, clutching his abdomen. Obsidian shouted, then gestured Rye over to help the woman.

Rye moved to the woman's side, remembering that she had little more than bandages and antiseptic in her pack. But the woman was beyond help. She had been stabbed with a long, slender boning knife.

She touched Obsidian to let him know the woman was dead. He had bent to check the wounded man who lay still and also seemed dead. But as Obsidian looked around to see what Rye wanted, the man opened his eyes. Face contorted, he seized Obsidian's just-holstered revolver and fired. The bullet caught Obsidian in the temple and he collapsed.

It happened just that simply, just that fast. An instant later, Rye shot the wounded man as he was turning the gun on her.

And Rye was alone—with three corpses.

She knelt beside Obsidian, dry-eyed, frowning, trying to understand why everything had suddenly changed. Obsidian was gone. He had died and left her—like everyone else.

Two very small children came out of the house from which the man and woman had run—a boy and girl perhaps three years old. Holding hands, they crossed the street toward Rye. They stared at her, then edged past her and went to the dead woman. The girl shook the woman's arm as though trying to wake her.

This was too much. Rye got up, feeling sick to her stomach with grief and anger. If the children began to cry, she thought she would vomit.

They were on their own, those two kids. They were old enough to scavenge. She did not need any more grief. She did not need a stranger's children who would grow up to be hairless chimps.

She went back to the car. She could drive home, at least. She remembered how to drive.

The thought that Obsidian should be buried occurred to her before she reached the car, and she did vomit.

She had found and lost the man so quickly. It was as though she had been snatched from comfort and security and given a sudden, inexplicable beating. Her head would not clear. She could not think.

Somehow, she made herself go back to him, look at him. She found herself on her knees beside him with no memory of having knelt. She stroked his face, his beard. One of the children made a noise and she looked at them, at the woman who was probably their mother. The children looked back at her, obviously frightened. Perhaps it was their fear that reached her finally.

She had been about to drive away and leave them. She had almost done it, almost left two toddlers to die. Surely there had been enough dying. She would have to take the children home with her. She would not be able to live with any other decision. She looked around for a place to bury three bodies. Or two. She wondered if the murderer were the children's father. Before the silence, the police had always said some of the most dangerous calls they went out on were domestic disturbance calls. Obsidian should have known that—not that the knowledge would have kept him in the car. It would not have held her back either. She could not have watched the woman murdered and done nothing.

She dragged Obsidian toward the car. She had nothing to dig with her, and no one to guard for her while she dug. Better to take the bodies with her and bury them next to her husband and her children. Obsidian would come home with her after all.

When she had gotten him onto the floor in the back, she returned for the woman. The little girl, thin, dirty, solemn, stood up and unknowingly gave Rye a gift. As Rye began to drag the woman by her arms, the little girl screamed, "No!"

Rye dropped the woman and stared at the girl.

"No!" the girl repeated. She came to stand beside the woman. "Go away!" she told Rye.

"Don't talk," the little boy said to her. There was no blurring or confusing of sounds. Both children had spoken and Rye had understood. The boy looked at the dead murderer and moved further from him. He took the girl's hand. "Be quiet," he whispered.

Fluent speech! Had the woman died because she could talk and had taught her children to talk? Had she been killed by a husband's festering anger or by a stranger's jealous rage?

And the children ... they must have been born after the silence. Had the disease run its course, then? Or were these children simply immune? Certainly they had had time to fall sick and silent. Rye's mind leaped ahead. What if children of three or fewer years were safe and able to learn language? What if all they needed were teachers? Teachers and protectors.

Rye glanced at the dead murderer. To her shame, she thought she could understand some of the passions that must have driven him, whomever he was. Anger, frustration, hopelessness, insane jealousy ... how many more of him were there—people willing to destroy what they could not have?

Obsidian had been the protector, had chosen that role for who knew what reason. Perhaps putting on an obsolete uniform and patrolling the empty streets had been what he did instead of putting a gun into his mouth. And now that there was something worth protecting, he was gone.

She had been a teacher. A good one. She had been a protector, too, though only of herself. She had kept herself alive when she had no reason to live. If the illness let these children alone, she could keep them alive.

Somehow she lifted the dead woman into her arms and placed her on the backseat of the car. The children began to cry, but she knelt on the broken pavement and whispered to them, fearful of frightening them with the harshness of her long unused voice.

"It's all right," she told them. "You're going with us, too. Come on." She lifted them both, one in each arm. They were so light. Had they been getting enough to eat?

The boy covered her mouth with his hand, but she moved her face away. "It's all right for me to talk," she told him. "As long as no one's around, it's all right." She put the boy down on the front seat of the car and he moved over without being told to, to make room for the girl. When they were both in the car, Rye leaned against the window, looking at them, seeing that they were less afraid now, that they watched her with at least as much curiosity as fear.

"I'm Valerie Rye," she said, savoring the words. "It's all right for you to talk to me."

—1983

Haruki Murakami
b. 1949

Though he was born in Kyoto to two professors of Japanese literature, Haruki Murakami didn't consider a career in writing until the age of 29. In the introduction to *Wind/Pinball*, the first English release of his two earliest novels, Murakami claims that he decided to become a writer, "for no reason and on no grounds whatsoever," during a baseball game in 1978. Over the following decades, Murakami has become probably the most widely read Japanese author outside Japan, as well as a literary celebrity in his native country—though his continual rejection of Japanese influences has rankled critics at home.

As a youth, Murakami immersed himself in Western culture, especially through jazz music and American crime novels. His first novel, *Hear the Wind Sing*, was written during evenings after work at the jazz café he ran in Tokyo with his wife. *Norwegian Wood* (1987), named after the Beatles song beloved by one of the novel's characters, was Murakami's first truly popular success. It is also, somewhat unusually for him, written in the realist style: most of Murakami's other novels possess a surreal element that contrasts with the almost blandly ordinary characters his narratives tend to follow, resulting in what Sam Anderson of *The New York Times* has described as "a strange broth of ennui and exoticism."

Since the 1970s Murakami has published more than a dozen novels, several collections of short stories, and some works of nonfiction. Increasingly, with novels such as *The Wind-Up Bird Chronicle* (1995), his writing has also touched on the dark and violent aspects of Japan's recent history, including its role in World War II, of which he is very critical. While John Wray of *The Paris Review* has described Murakami as the "voice of his generation" in Japan, Murakami's own literary influences range far beyond his home country, including Raymond Chandler, Franz Kafka, Fyodor Dostoevsky, and Leo Tolstoy. His work has been recognized by many awards including the World Fantasy Award and the prestigious Japanese Yomiuri Prize.

On Seeing the 100% Perfect Girl One Beautiful April Morning[1]

One beautiful April morning, on a narrow side street in Tokyo's fashionable Harajuku neighbourhood, I walk past the 100% perfect girl.

Tell you the truth, she's not that good-looking. She doesn't stand out in any way. Her clothes are nothing special. The back of her hair is still bent out

---

1   *On Seeing ... Morning* Translated by Jay Rubin.

of shape from sleep. She isn't young, either—must be near thirty, not even close to a "girl," properly speaking. But still, I know from fifty yards away: She's the 100% perfect girl for me. The moment I see her, there's a rumbling in my chest, and my mouth is as dry as a desert.

Maybe you have your own particular favourite type of girl—one with slim ankles, say, or big eyes, or graceful fingers, or you're drawn for no good reason to girls who take their time with every meal. I have my own preferences, of course. Sometimes in a restaurant I'll catch myself staring at the girl at the table next to mine because I like the shape of her nose.

But no one can insist that his 100% perfect girl correspond to some preconceived type. Much as I like noses, I can't recall the shape of hers—or even if she had one. All I can remember for sure is that she was no great beauty. It's weird.

"Yesterday on the street I passed the 100% perfect girl," I tell someone.

"Yeah?" he says. "Good-looking?"

"Not really."

"Your favourite type, then?"

"I don't know. I can't seem to remember anything about her—the shape of her eyes or the size of her breasts."

"Strange."

"Yeah. Strange."

"So anyhow," he says, already bored, "what did you do? Talk to her? Follow her?"

"Nah. Just passed her on the street."

She's walking east to west, and I west to east. It's a really nice April morning.

Wish I could talk to her. Half an hour would be plenty: just ask her about herself, tell her about myself, and—what I'd really like to do—explain to her the complexities of fate that have led to our passing each other on a side street in Harajuku on a beautiful April morning in 1981. This was something sure to be crammed full of warm secrets, like an antique clock built when peace filled the world.

After talking, we'd have lunch somewhere, maybe see a Woody Allen[1] movie, stop by a hotel bar for cocktails. With any kind of luck, we might end up in bed.

Potentiality knocks on the door of my heart.

Now the distance between us has narrowed to fifteen yards.

How can I approach her? What should I say?

---

1   *Woody Allen* American film director (b. 1935).

"Good morning, miss. Do you think you could spare half an hour for a little conversation?"

Ridiculous. I'd sound like an insurance salesman.

"Pardon me, but would you happen to know if there is an all-night cleaners in the neighbourhood?"

No, this is just as ridiculous. I'm not carrying any laundry, for one thing. Who's going to buy a line like that?

Maybe the simple truth would do. "Good morning. You are the 100% perfect girl for me."

No, she wouldn't believe it. Or even if she did, she might not want to talk to me. Sorry, she could say, I might be the 100% perfect girl for you, but you're not the 100% perfect boy for me. It could happen. And if I found myself in that situation, I'd probably go to pieces. I'd never recover from the shock. I'm thirty-two, and that's what growing older is all about.

We pass in front of a flower shop. A small, warm air mass touches my skin. The asphalt is damp, and I catch the scent of roses. I can't bring myself to speak to her. She wears a white sweater, and in her right hand she holds a crisp white envelope lacking only a stamp. So: She's written somebody a letter, maybe spent the whole night writing, to judge from the sleepy look in her eyes. The envelope could contain every secret she's ever had.

I take a few more strides and turn: She's lost in the crowd.

Now, of course, I know exactly what I should have said to her. It would have been a long speech, though, far too long for me to have delivered it properly. The ideas I come up with are never very practical.

Oh, well. It would have started "Once upon a time" and ended "A sad story, don't you think?"

Once upon a time, there lived a boy and a girl. The boy was eighteen and the girl sixteen. He was not unusually handsome, and she was not especially beautiful. They were just an ordinary lonely boy and an ordinary lonely girl, like all the others. But they believed with their whole hearts that somewhere in the world there lived the 100% perfect boy and the 100% perfect girl for them. Yes, they believed in a miracle. And that miracle actually happened.

One day the two came upon each other on the corner of a street.

"This is amazing," he said. "I've been looking for you all my life. You may not believe this, but you're the 100% perfect girl for me."

"And you," she said to him, "are the 100% perfect boy for me, exactly as I'd pictured you in every detail. It's like a dream."

They sat on a park bench, held hands, and told each other their stories hour after hour. They were not lonely anymore. They had found and been found by their 100% perfect other. What a wonderful thing it is to find and be found by your 100% perfect other. It's a miracle, a cosmic miracle.

As they sat and talked, however, a tiny, tiny sliver of doubt took root in their hearts: Was it really all right for one's dreams to come true so easily?

And so, when there came a momentary lull in their conversation, the boy said to the girl, "Let's test ourselves—just once. If we really are each other's 100% perfect lovers, then sometime, somewhere, we will meet again without fail. And when that happens, and we know that we are the 100% perfect ones, we'll marry then and there. What do you think?"

"Yes," she said, "that is exactly what we should do."

And so they parted, she to the east, and he to the west.

The test they had agreed upon, however, was utterly unnecessary. They should never have undertaken it, because they really and truly were each other's 100% perfect lovers, and it was a miracle that they had ever met. But it was impossible for them to know this, young as they were. The cold, indifferent waves of fate proceeded to toss them unmercifully.

One winter, both the boy and the girl came down with the season's terrible influenza; and after drifting for weeks between life and death they lost all memory of their earlier years. When they awoke, their heads were as empty as the young D.H. Lawrence's piggy bank.[1]

They were two bright, determined young people, however, and through their unremitting efforts they were able to acquire once again the knowledge and feeling that qualified them to return as full-fledged members of society. Heaven be praised, they became truly upstanding citizens who knew how to transfer from one subway line to another, who were fully capable of sending a special-delivery letter at the post office. Indeed, they even experienced love again, sometimes as much as 75% or even 85% love.

Time passed with shocking swiftness, and soon the boy was thirty-two, the girl thirty.

One beautiful April morning, in search of a cup of coffee to start the day, the boy was walking from west to east, while the girl, intending to send a special-delivery letter, was walking from east to west, both along the same narrow street in the Harajuku neighbourhood of Tokyo. They passed each other in the very centre of the street. The faintest gleam of their lost memories glimmered for the briefest moment in their hearts. Each felt a rumbling in the chest. And they knew:

She is the 100% perfect girl for me.

He is the 100% perfect boy for me.

---

1   *as empty ... piggy bank* This reference has puzzled critics, but may simply refer to the childhood poverty of the novelist D.H. Lawrence (1885–1930).

But the glow of their memories was far too weak, and their thoughts no longer had the clarity of fourteen years earlier. Without a word, they passed each other, disappearing into the crowd. Forever.

A sad story, don't you think?

Yes, that's it, that is what I should have said to her.

—1993

Barbara Gowdy
b. 1950

Barbara Gowdy is one of Canada's most original and acclaimed writers. Born in Windsor, Ontario, Gowdy was trained as a pianist, but gave up music in her twenties when she decided that her abilities were "mediocre." She began writing fiction while working as an editor at a Toronto publishing house. Her second novel, *Falling Angels* (1989), was the first of her works to garner serious critical attention, and contains the same threads of violence and deadpan humour that run through her later works. The novel *Mister Sandman* (1995) was a finalist for the Trillium Award, the Governor General's Award for Fiction, and the Giller Prize. A later finalist for the same prizes was *The White Bone* (1999), a novel about a clan of African elephants told from the elephants' perspectives (Gowdy is a longtime vegan, and has spoken publicly about the treatment of non-human animals). Gowdy's most recent novels are *The Romantic* (2003), which was a nominee for the Man Booker Prize and a finalist for the Trillium Award, and *Helpless* (2007), which tells the story of a child abduction in Toronto; the latter novel's subject matter led to complaints from listeners when it was adapted for a BBC Radio 4 broadcast.

The protagonists of the stories in Gowdy's only collection, *We So Seldom Look on Love* (1992), include a woman with a conjoined twin, a two-headed man, and a woman drawn into exhibitionism by her voyeuristic neighbour. Though the stories avoid sensationalism, they can be unsparingly graphic. Perhaps most notorious is the title story, which was adapted into a 1996 film, *Kissed,* directed by Lynne Stopkewich. "We So Seldom Look on Love" is characteristic of Gowdy's work in both its "lyrical use of ordinary language" (in the words of the novelist Katherine Dunn) and its compassionate portrayal of aberrant desire.

We So Seldom Look on Love

When you die, and your earthly self begins turning into your disintegrated self, you radiate an intense current of energy. There is always energy given off when a thing turns into its opposite, when love, for instance, turns into hate. There are always sparks at those extreme points. But life turning into death is the most extreme of extreme points. So just after you die, the sparks are really stupendous. Really magical and explosive.

I've seen cadavers shining like stars. I'm the only person I've ever heard of who has. Almost everyone senses something, though, some vitality. That's why you get resistance to the idea of cremation or organ donation. "I want to be in one piece," people say. Even Matt, who claimed there was no soul and no afterlife, wrote a P.S. in his suicide note that he be buried intact.

As if it would have made any difference to his energy emission. No matter what you do—slice open the flesh, dissect everything, burn everything—you're in the path of a power way beyond your little interferences.

I grew up in a nice, normal, happy family outside a small town in New Jersey. My parents and my brothers are still living there. My dad owned a flower store. Now my brother owns it. My brother is three years older than I am, a serious, remote man. But loyal. When I made the headlines he phoned to say that if I needed money for a lawyer, he would give it to me. I was really touched. Especially as he was standing up to Carol, his wife. She got on the extension and screamed, "You're sick! You should be put away!"

She'd been wanting to tell me that since we were thirteen years old.

I had an animal cemetery back then. Our house was beside a woods and we had three outdoor cats, great hunters who tended to leave their kills in one piece. Whenever I found a body, usually a mouse or a bird, I took it into my bedroom and hid it until midnight. I didn't know anything about the ritual significance of the midnight hour. My burials took place then because that's when I woke up. It no longer happens, but I was such a sensitive child that I think I must have been aroused by the energy given off as day clicked over into the dead of night and, simultaneously, as the dead of night clicked over into the next day.

In any case, I'd be wide awake. I'd get up and go to the bathroom to wrap the body in toilet paper. I felt compelled to be so careful, so respectful. I whispered a chant. At each step of the burial I chanted. "I shroud the body, shroud the body, shroud little sparrow with broken wing." Or "I lower the body, lower the body ..." And so on.

Climbing out the bathroom window was accompanied by: "I enter the night, enter the night ..." At my cemetery I set the body down on a special flat rock and took my pyjamas off. I was behaving out of pure inclination. I dug up four or five graves and unwrapped the animals from their shrouds. The rotting smell was crucial. So was the cool air. Normally I'd be so keyed up at this point that I'd burst into a dance.

I used to dance for dead men, too. Before I climbed on top of them, I'd dance all around the prep room. When I told Matt about this he said that I was shaking my personality out of my body so that the sensation of participating in the cadaver's energy eruption would be intensified. "You're trying to imitate the disintegration process," he said.

Maybe—on an unconscious level. But what I was aware of was the heat, the heat of my danced-out body, which I cooled by lying on top of the cadaver. As a child I'd gently wipe my skin with two of the animal's I'd just unwrapped. When I was covered all over with their scent, I put them aside, unwrapped the new corpse and did the same with it. I called this the Anointment. I can't describe how it felt. The high, high rapture. The electricity that shot through me.

The rest, wrapping the bodies back up and burying them, was pretty much what you'd expect.

It astonishes me now to think how naive I was. I thought I had discovered something that certain other people, if they weren't afraid to give it a try, would find just as fantastic as I did. It was a dark and forbidden thing, yes, but so was sex. I really had no idea I was jumping across a vast behavioural gulf. In fact, I couldn't see that I was doing anything wrong. I still can't, and I'm including what happened with Matt. Carol said I should have been put away, but I'm not bad-looking, so if offering my body to dead men is a crime, I'd like to know who the victim is.

Carol has always been jealous of me. She's fat and has a wandering eye. Her eye gives her a dreamy, distracted quality that I fell for (as I suppose my brother would eventually do) one day at a friend's thirteenth birthday party. It was the beginning of the summer holidays, and I was yearning for a kindred spirit, someone to share my secret life with. I saw Carol standing alone, looking everywhere at once, and I chose her.

I knew to take it easy, though. I knew not to push anything. We'd search for dead animals and birds, we'd chant and swaddle the bodies, dig graves, make popsicle-stick crosses. All by daylight. At midnight I'd go out and dig up the grave and conduct a proper burial.

There must have been some chipmunk sickness that summer. Carol and I found an incredible number of chipmunks, and a lot of them had no blood on them, no sign of cat. One day we found a chipmunk that evacuated a string of fetuses when I picked it up. The fetuses were still alive, but there was no saving them, so I took them into the house and flushed them down the toilet.

A mighty force was coming from the mother chipmunk. It was as if, along with her own energy, she was discharging all the energy of her dead brood. When Carol and I began to dance for her, we both went a little crazy. We stripped down to our underwear, screamed, spun in circles, threw dirt up into the air. Carol has always denied it, but she took off her bra and began whipping trees with it. I'm sure the sight of her doing this is what inspired me to take off my undershirt and underpants and to perform the Anointment.

Carol stopped dancing. I looked at her, and the expression on her face stopped me dancing, too. I looked down at the chipmunk in my hand. It was bloody. There were streaks of blood all over my body. I was horrified. I thought I'd squeezed the chipmunk too hard.

But what had happened was, I'd begun my period. I figured this out a few minutes after Carol ran off. I wrapped the chipmunk in its shroud and buried it. Then I got dressed and lay down on the grass. A little while later my mother appeared over me.

"Carol's mother phoned," she said. "Carol is very upset. She says you made her perform some disgusting witchcraft dance. You made her take her clothes off, and you attacked her with a bloody chipmunk."

"That's a lie," I said. "I'm menstruating."

After my mother had fixed me up with a sanitary napkin, she told me she didn't think I should play with Carol any more. "There's a screw loose in there somewhere," she said.

I had no intention of playing with Carol any more, but I cried at what seemed like a cruel loss. I think I knew that it was all loneliness from that moment on. Even though I was only thirteen, I was cutting any lines that still drifted out toward normal eroticism. Bosom friends, crushes, pyjama-party intimacy, I was cutting all those lines off.

A month or so after becoming a woman I developed a craving to perform autopsies. I resisted doing it for almost a year, though. I was frightened. Violating the intactness of the animal seemed sacrilegious and dangerous. Also unimaginable—I couldn't imagine what would happen.

Nothing. Nothing would happen, as I found out. I've read that necrophiles are frightened of getting hurt by normal sexual relationships, and maybe there's some truth in that (although my heart's been broken plenty of times by cadavers, and not once by a live man), but I think that my attraction to cadavers isn't driven by fear, it's driven by excitement, and that one of the most exciting things about a cadaver is how dedicated it is to dying. Its will is all directed to a single intention, like a huge wave heading for shore, and you can ride along on the wave if you want to, because no matter what you do, because with you or without you, that wave is going to hit the beach.

I felt this impetus the first time I worked up enough nerve to cut open a mouse. Like anyone else, I balked a little at slicing into the flesh, and I was repelled for a few seconds when I saw the insides. But something drove me to go through these compunctions. It was as if I were acting solely on instinct and curiosity, and anything I did was all right, provided it didn't kill me.

After the first few times, I started sticking my tongue into the incision. I don't know why. I thought about it, I did it, and I kept on doing it. One day I removed the organs and cleaned them with water, then put them back in, and I kept on doing that, too. Again, I couldn't tell you why except to say that any provocative thought, if you act upon it, seems to set you on a trajectory.

By the time I was sixteen I wanted human corpses. Men. (That way I'm straight.) I got my chauffeur's licence, but I had to wait until I was finished high school before Mr. Wallis would hire me as a hearse driver at the funeral home.

Mr. Wallis knew me because he bought bereavement flowers at my father's store. Now *there* was a weird man. He would take a trocar, which is the big needle you use to draw out a cadaver's fluids, and he would push it up the penises of dead men to make them look semi-erect, and then he'd sodomize them. I caught him at it once, and he tried to tell me that he'd been urinating in the hopper. I pretended to believe him. I was upset though, because I knew that dead men were just dead flesh to him. One minute he'd be locked up with a young male corpse, having his way with him, and the next minute he'd be embalming him as if nothing had happened, and making sick jokes about him, pretending to find evidence of rampant homosexuality—colons stalagmited with dried semen, and so on.

None of this joking ever happened in front of me. I heard about it from the crazy old man who did the mopping up. He was also a necrophile, I'm almost certain, but no longer active. He called dead women Madonnas. He rhapsodized about the beautiful Madonnas he'd had the privilege of seeing in the 1940s, about how much more womanly and feminine the Madonnas were twenty years before.

I just listened. I never let on what I was feeling, and I don't think anyone suspected. Necrophiles aren't supposed to be blond and pretty, let alone female. When I'd been working at the funeral home for about a year, a committee from the town council tried to get me to enter the Milk Marketer's Beauty Pageant. They knew about my job, and they knew I was studying embalming at night, but I had told people I was preparing myself for medical school, and I guess the council believed me.

For fifteen years, ever since Matt died, people have been asking me how a woman makes love to a corpse.

Matt was the only person who figured it out. He was a medical student, so he knew that if you apply pressure to the chest of certain fresh corpses, they purge blood out of their mouths.

Matt was smart. I wish I could have loved him with more than sisterly love. He was tall and thin. My type. We met at the doughnut shop across from the medical library, got to talking, and liked each other immediately, an unusual experience for both of us. After about an hour I knew that he loved me and that his love was unconditional. When I told him where I worked and what I was studying, he asked why.

"Because I'm a necrophile," I said.

He lifted his head and stared at me. He had eyes like high-resolution monitors. Almost too vivid. Normally I don't like looking people in the eye, but I found myself staring back. I could see that he believed me.

"I've never told anyone else," I said.

"With men or women?" he asked.

"Men. Young men."

"How?"

"Cunnilingus."

"Fresh corpses?"

"If I can get them."

"What do you do, climb on top of them?"

"Yes."

"You're turned on by blood."

"It's a lubricant." I said. "It's colourful. Stimulating. It's the ultimate bodily fluid."

"Yes," he said, nodding. "When you think about it. Sperm propagates life. But blood sustains it. Blood is primary."

He kept asking questions, and I answered them as truthfully as I could. Having confessed what I was, I felt myself driven to testing his intellectual rigour and the strength of his love at first sight. Throwing rocks at him without any expectation that he'd stay standing. He did, though. He caught the whole arsenal and asked for more. It began to excite me.

We went back to his place. He had a basement apartment in an old run-down building. There were books in orange-crate shelves, in piles on the floor, all over the bed. On the wall above his desk was a poster of Doris Day in the movie *Tea for Two*. Matt said she looked like me.

"Do you want to dance first?" he asked, heading for his record player. I'd told him about how I danced before climbing on corpses.

"No."

He swept the books off the bed. Then he undressed me. He had an erection until I told him I was a virgin. "Don't worry," he said, sliding his head down my stomach. "Lie still."

The next morning he phoned me at work. I was hungover and blue from the night before. After leaving his place I'd gone straight to the funeral home and made love to an autopsy case. Then I'd got drunk in a seedy country-and-western bar and debated going back to the funeral home and suctioning out my own blood until I lost consciousness.

It had finally hit me that I was incapable of falling in love with a man who wasn't dead. I kept thinking, "I'm not normal." I'd never faced this before. Obviously, making love to corpses isn't normal, but while I was still a virgin I must have been assuming that I could give it up any time I liked. Get married, have babies. I must have been banking on a future that I didn't even want, let alone have access to.

Matt was phoning to get me to come around again after work.

"I don't know," I said.

"You had a good time. Didn't you?"

"Sure, I guess."

"I think you're fascinating," he said.

I sighed.

"Please," he said. "Please."

A few nights later I went to his apartment. From then on we started to meet every Tuesday and Thursday evening after my embalming class, and as soon as I left his place, if I knew there was a corpse at the mortuary—any male corpse, young or old—I went straight there and climbed in a basement window.

Entering the prep room, especially at night when there was nobody else around, was like diving into a lake. Sudden cold and silence, and the sensation of penetrating a new element where the rules of other elements don't apply. Being with Matt was like lying on the beach of the lake. Matt had warm, dry skin. His apartment was overheated and noisy. I lay on Matt's bed and soaked him up, but only to make the moment when I entered the prep room even more overpowering.

If the cadaver was freshly embalmed, I could usually smell him from the basement. The smell is like a hospital and old cheese. For me, it's the smell of danger and permission, it used to key me up like amphetamine, so that by the time I reached the prep room, tremors were running up and down my legs. I locked the door behind me and broke into a wild dance, tearing my clothes off, spinning around, pulling at my hair. I'm not sure what this was all about, whether or not I was trying to take part in the chaos of the corpse's disintegration, as Matt suggested. Maybe I was prostrating myself, I don't know.

Once the dancing was over I was always very calm, almost entranced. I drew back the sheet. This was the most exquisite moment. I felt as if I were being blasted by white light. Almost blinded, I climbed onto the table and straddled the corpse. I ran my hands over his skin. My hands and the insides of my thighs burned as if I were touching dry ice. After a few minutes I lay down and pulled the sheet up over my head. I began to kiss his mouth. By now he might be drooling blood. A corpse's blood is thick, cool and sweet. My head roared.

I was no longer depressed. Far from it, I felt better, more confident, than I had ever felt in my life. I had discovered myself to be irredeemably abnormal. I could either slit my throat or surrender—wholeheartedly now—to my obsession. I surrendered. And what happened was that obsession began to storm through me, as if I were a tunnel. I became the medium of obsession as well as both ends of it. With Matt, when we made love, I was the receiving end, I was the cadaver. When I left him and went to the funeral home, I was the lover. Through me Matt's love poured into the cadavers at the funeral home, and through me the cadavers filled Matt with explosive energy.

He quickly got addicted to this energy. The minute I arrived at his apartment, he had to hear every detail about the last corpse I'd been with. For a month or so I had him pegged as a latent homosexual necrophile voyeur, but then I began to see that it wasn't the corpses themselves that excited him, it was my passion for them. It was the power that went into that passion and that came back, doubled, for his pleasure. He kept asking. "How did you feel? Why do you think you felt that way?" And then, because the source of all this power disturbed him, he'd try to prove that my feelings were delusory.

"A corpse shows simultaneous extremes of character," I told him. "Wisdom and innocence, happiness and grief, and so on."

"Therefore all corpses are alike," he said. "Once you've had one you've had them all."

"No, no. They're all different. Each corpse contains his own extremes. Each corpse is only as wise and as innocent as the living person could have been."

He said, "You're drafting personalities onto corpses in order to have power over them."

"In that case," I said, "I'm pretty imaginative, since I've never met two corpses who were alike."

"You *could* be that imaginative," he argued. "Schizophrenics are capable of manufacturing dozens of complex personalities."

I didn't mind these attacks. There was no malice in them, and there was no way they could touch me, either. It was as if I were luxuriously pouring my heart out to a very clever, very concerned, very tormented analyst. I felt sorry for him. I understood his twisted desire to turn me into somebody else (somebody who might love him). I used to fall madly in love with cadavers and then cry because they were dead. The difference between Matt and me was that I had become philosophical. I was all right.

I thought that he was, too. He was in pain, yes, but he seemed confident that what he was going through was temporary and not unnatural. "I am excessively curious," he said. "My fascination is any curious man's fascination with the unusual." He said that by feeding his lust through mine, he would eventually saturate it, then turn it to disgust.

I told him to go ahead, give it a try. So he began to scour the newspapers for my cadavers' obituaries and to go to their funerals and memorial services. He made charts of my preferences and the frequency of my morgue encounters. He followed me to the morgue at night and waited outside so that he could get a replay while I was still in an erotic haze. He sniffed my skin. He pulled me over to streetlights and examined the blood on my face and hands.

I suppose I shouldn't have encouraged him. I can't really say why I did except that in the beginning I saw his obsession as the outer edge of my own obsession, a place I didn't have to visit as long as he was there. And then later, and despite his increasingly erratic behaviour, I started to have doubts about an obsession that could come on so suddenly and that could come through me.

One night he announced that he might as well face it, he was going to have to make love to corpses, male corpses. The idea nauseated him, he said, but he said that secretly, deep down, unknown even to himself, making love to male corpses was clearly the target of his desire. I blew up. I told him that necrophilia wasn't something you forced yourself to do. You longed to do it, you needed to do it. You were born to do it.

He wasn't listening. He was glued to the dresser mirror. In the last weeks of his life he stared at himself in the mirror without the least self-consciousness. He focused on his face, even though what was going on from the neck down was the arresting part. He had begun to wear incredibly weird outfits. Velvet capes, pantaloons, high-heeled red boots. When we made love, he kept these outfits on. He stared into my eyes, riveted (it later occurred to me) by his own reflection.

Matt committed suicide, there was never any doubt about that. As for the necrophilia, it wasn't a crime, not fifteen years ago. So even though I was caught in the act, naked and straddling an unmistakably dead body, even though the newspapers found out about it and made it front-page news, there was nothing the police could charge me with.

In spite of which I made a full confession. It was crucial to me that the official report contain more than the detective's bleak observations. I wanted two things on record: one, that Matt was ravished by a reverential expert; two, that his cadaver blasted the energy of a star.

"Did this energy blast happen before or after he died?" the detective asked.

"After," I said, adding quickly that I couldn't have foreseen such a blast. The one tricky area was why I hadn't stopped the suicide. Why I hadn't talked, or cut, Matt down.

I lied. I said that as soon as I entered Matt's room, he kicked away the ladder. Nobody could prove otherwise. But I've often wondered how much time actually passed between when I opened the door and when his neck broke. In crises, a minute isn't a minute. There's the same chaos you get at the instant of death, with time and form breaking free, and everything magnifying and coming apart.

Matt must have been in a state of crisis for days, maybe weeks before he died. All that staring in mirrors, thinking, "Is this my face?" Watching as his face separated into its infinitesimal particles and reassembled into a strange new face. The night before he died, he had a mask on. A Dracula mask, but he wasn't joking. He wanted to wear the mask while I made love to him as if he were a cadaver. No way, I said. The whole point, I reminded him, was that *I* played the cadaver. He begged me, and I laughed because of the mask and with relief. If he wanted to turn the game around, then it was over between us, and I was suddenly aware of how much I liked that idea.

The next night he phoned me at my parents' and said, "I love you," then hung up.

I don't know how I knew, but I did. A gun, I thought. Men always use guns. And then I thought, no, poison, cyanide. He was a medical student and had access to drugs. When I arrived at his apartment, the door was open. Across from the door, taped to the wall, was a note: "DEAD PERSON IN BED-ROOM."

But he wasn't dead. He was standing on a stepladder. He was naked. An impressively knotted noose, attached to a pipe that ran across the ceiling, was looped around his neck.

He smiled tenderly. "I knew you'd come," he said.

"So why the note?" I demanded.

"Pull away the ladder," he crooned. "My beloved."

"Come on. This is stupid. Get down." I went up to him and punched his leg.

"All you have to do," he said, "is pull away the ladder."

His eyes were even darker and more expressive than usual. His cheekbones appeared to be highlighted. (I discovered minutes later he had makeup on.) I glanced around the room for a chair or a table that I could bring over and stand on. I was going to take the noose off him myself.

"If you leave," he said, "if you take a step back, if you do anything other than pull away the ladder, I'll kick it away."

"I love you," I said. "Okay?"

"No, you don't," he said.

"I do!" To sound like I meant it I stared at his legs and imagined them lifeless. "I do!"

"No, you don't," he said softly. "But," he said, "you will."

I was gripping the ladder. I remember thinking that if I held tight to the ladder, he wouldn't be able to kick it away. I was gripping the ladder, and then it was by the wall, tipped over. I have no memory of transition between these two events. There was a loud crack, and gushing of water. Matt dropped gracefully, like a girl fainting. Water poured on him from the broken pipe. There was a smell of excrement. I dragged him by the noose.

In the living room I pulled him onto the green shag carpet. I took my clothes off. I knelt over him. I kissed the blood at the corner of his mouth.

True obsession depends on the object's absolute unresponsiveness. When I used to fall for a particular cadaver, I would feel as if I were a hollow instrument, a bell or a flute. I'd empty out. I would clear out (it was involuntary) until I was an instrument for the cadaver to swell into and be amplified. As the object of Matt's obsession how could I be, other than impassive, while he was alive?

He was playing with fire, playing with me. Not just because I couldn't love him, but because I was irradiated. The whole time that I was involved with Matt, I was making love to corpses, absorbing their energy, blazing it back out. Since that energy came from the act of life alchemizing into death, there's a possibility that it was alchemical itself. Even if it wasn't, I'm sure it gave Matt the impression that I had the power to change him in some huge and dangerous way.

I now believe that his addiction to my energy was really a craving for such a transformation. In fact, I think that all desire is desire for transformation, and that all transformation—all movement, all process—happens because life turns into death.

I am still a necrophile, occasionally and recklessly. I have found no replacement for the torrid serenity of a cadaver.

—1992

Rohinton Mistry

b. 1952

Rohinton Mistry is a Mumbai-born Canadian novelist and short story writer. In a review in *The New Yorker*, literary critic and fellow novelist John Updike wrote that he "harks back to the nineteenth-century novelists, for whom every detail, every urban alley, every character however lowly added a vital piece to the full social picture, and for whom every incident illustrated the eventually crushing weight of the world."

At 23, Mistry emigrated with his wife to Canada and settled in Toronto. He worked as a bank clerk but studied English literature at the University of Toronto, earning his BA in 1983. In 1987, he published *Tales from Firozsha Baag*, a collection of short stories set in both the writer's own minority Parsi community in Bombay (now Mumbai) and abroad. Each story deals with topics that would recur in Mistry's writing: community, identity, diaspora, poverty, dreams, and human conflict.

His first novel, *Such a Long Journey* (1991), set in Bombay during the Indian-Pakistan War of 1971, won the Governor General's Award and the Commonwealth Writers Prize. Mistry's second novel, *A Fine Balance* (1995), set in India during The Emergency imposed by Indira Gandhi, 1975–77, won a host of awards, including the Giller Prize. *Family Matters* (2002), set in mid-1990s Bombay, was another critical success, garnering the Kiriyama Pacific Rim Book Prize, a third straight Commonwealth Writers Prize, and a third straight appearance on the prestigious Man Booker Prize shortlist. In 2012, Mistry was awarded the Neustadt International Prize in recognition of his contributions to world literature.

Squatter[1]

Whenever Nariman Hansotia returned in the evening from the Cawasji Framji Memorial Library in a good mood the signs were plainly evident.

First, he parked his 1932 Mercedes-Benz (he called it the apple of his eye) outside A Block, directly in front of his ground-floor veranda window, and beeped the horn three long times. It annoyed Rustomji who also had a ground-floor flat in A Block. Ever since he had defied Nariman in the matter of painting the exterior of the building, Rustomji was convinced that nothing

---

1   *Squatter* This story appeared in Mistry's *Tales from Firozsha Baag*, in which all of the short stories are linked to an apartment block in Mumbai, India. Most of the inhabitants of the block are Parsis, members of a Zoroastrian religious minority with Persian roots that has lived in India for the past thousand years.

the old coot did was untainted by the thought of vengeance and harassment, his retirement pastime.

But the beeping was merely Nariman's signal to let Hirabai inside know that though he was back he would not step indoors for a while. Then he raised the hood, whistling "Rose Marie,"[1] and leaned his tall frame over the engine. He checked the oil, wiped here and there with a rag, tightened the radiator cap, and lowered the hood. Finally, he polished the Mercedes star and let the whistling modulate into the march from *The Bridge on the River Kwai*.[2] The boys playing in the compound knew that Nariman was ready now to tell a story. They started to gather round.

"*Sahibji*,[3] Nariman Uncle," someone said tentatively and Nariman nodded, careful not to lose his whistle, his bulbous nose flaring slightly. The pursed lips had temporarily raised and reshaped his Clark Gable[4] moustache. More boys walked up. One called out, "How about a story, Nariman Uncle?" at which point Nariman's eyes began to twinkle, and he imparted increased energy to the polishing. The cry was taken up by others, "Yes, yes, Nariman Uncle, a story!" He swung into a final verse of the march. Then the lips relinquished the whistle, the Clark Gable moustache descended. The rag was put away, and he began.

"You boys know the great cricketers: Contractor, Polly Umrigar, and recently, the young chap, Farokh Engineer.[5] Cricket *aficionados*, that's what you all are." Nariman liked to use new words, especially big ones, in the stories he told, believing it was his duty to expose young minds to as shimmering and varied a vocabulary as possible; if they could not spend their days at the Cawasji Framji Memorial Library then he, at least, could carry bits of the library out to them.

The boys nodded; the names of the cricketers were familiar.

"But does any one know about Savukshaw, the greatest of them all?" They shook their heads in unison.

"This, then, is the story about Savukshaw, how he saved the Indian team from a humiliating defeat when they were touring in England." Nariman sat on the steps of A Block. The few diehards who had continued with their games could not resist any longer when they saw the gathering circle, and ran up to

---

1   "*Rose Marie*" Popular theme song from a 1924 Broadway musical set in the Rocky Mountains of Canada, remade several times into Hollywood films.

2   *The Bridge … Kwai* 1957 film about a group of Allied soldiers imprisoned in a Japanese prisoner-of-war camp in World War II.

3   *Sahibji* Plural of *sahib*, a respectful honorific often associated with colonial India.

4   *Clark Gable* American actor, most famous for his performance in the 1939 film *Gone with the Wind*.

5   *great cricketers … Engineer* Cricket is a bat-and-ball sport popular in the United Kingdom and its past colonies, including India. The cricketers mentioned were all Parsi members of India's national team.

listen. They asked their neighbours in whispers what the story was about, and were told: Savukshaw the greatest cricketer. The whispering died down and Nariman began.

"The Indian team was to play the indomitable MCC as part of its tour of England. Contractor was our captain. Now the MCC being the strongest team they had to face, Contractor was almost certain of defeat. To add to Contractor's troubles, one of his star batsmen, Nadkarni, had caught influenza early in the tour, and would definitely not be well enough to play against the MCC. By the way, does anyone know what those letters stand for? You, Kersi, you wanted to be a cricketer once."

Kersi shook his head. None of the boys knew, even though they had heard the MCC mentioned in radio commentaries, because the full name was hardly ever used.

Then Jehangir Bulsara spoke up, or Bulsara Bookworm, as the boys called him. The name given by Pesi *paadmaroo*[1] had stuck even though it was now more than four years since Pesi had been sent away to boarding-school, and over two years since the death of Dr. Mody. Jehangir was still unliked by the boys in the Baag, though they had come to accept his aloofness and respect his knowledge and intellect. They were not surprised that he knew the answer to Nariman's question: "Marylebone Cricket Club."[2]

"Absolutely correct," said Nariman, and continued with the story. "The MCC won the toss and elected to bat. They scored four hundred and ninety-seven runs in the first inning before our spinners[3] could get them out. Early in the second day's play our team was dismissed for one hundred and nine runs, and the extra who had taken Nadkarni's place was injured by a vicious bumper[4] that opened a gash on his forehead." Nariman indicated the spot and the length of the gash on his furrowed brow. "Contractor's worst fears were coming true. The MCC waived their own second inning and gave the Indian team a follow-on,[5] wanting to inflict an inning's defeat. And this time he had to use the second extra. The second extra was a certain Savukshaw."

The younger boys listened attentively; some of them, like the two sons of the chartered accountant in B Block, had only recently been deemed old

---

1   *paadmaroo* Pesi is given this punning nickname in another story in *Tales from Firozsha Baag*; it is a reference to his pungent flatulence.

2   *Marylebone Cricket Club* Based in London, the MCC is the most famous cricket club in the world. The governing body of international cricket until 1993, the MCC holds the copyright to the sport's official laws.

3   *spinners* Cricket bowlers who use trickery to oust opposing batters, roughly equivalent to changeup pitchers in baseball.

4   *bumper* Ball pitched fast and bounced toward the batter's head.

5   *follow-on* Inning in which the team that has just batted is required to bat again because their score from the first inning is less than half the other team's.

enough by their parents to come out and play in the compound, and had not received any exposure to Nariman's stories. But the others like Jehangir, Kersi, and Viraf were familiar with Nariman's technique.

Once, Jehangir had overheard them discussing Nariman's stories, and he could not help expressing his opinion: that unpredictability was the brush he used to paint his tales with, and ambiguity the palette he mixed his colours in. The others looked at him with admiration. Then Viraf asked what exactly he meant by that. Jehangir said that Nariman sometimes told a funny incident in a very serious way, or expressed a significant matter in a light and playful manner. And these were only two rough divisions, in between were lots of subtle gradations of tone and texture. Which, then, was the funny story and which the serious? Their opinions were divided, but ultimately, said Jehangir, it was up to the listener to decide.

"So," continued Nariman, "Contractor first sent out his two regular openers, convinced that it was all hopeless. But after five wickets were lost[1] for just another thirty-eight runs, out came Savukshaw the extra. Nothing mattered any more."

The street lights outside the compound came on, illuminating the iron gate where the watchman stood. It was a load off the watchman's mind when Nariman told a story. It meant an early end to the hectic vigil during which he had to ensure that none of the children ran out on the main road, or tried to jump over the wall. For although keeping out riff-raff was his duty, keeping in the boys was as important if he wanted to retain the job.

"The first ball Savukshaw faced was wide outside the off stump.[2] He just lifted his bat and ignored it. But with what style! What panache! As if to say, come on, you blighters, play some polished cricket. The next ball was also wide, but not as much as the first. It missed the off stump narrowly. Again Savukshaw lifted his bat, boredom written all over him. Everyone was now watching closely. The bowler was annoyed by Savukshaw's arrogance, and the third delivery was a vicious fast pitch, right down on the middle stump.

"Savukshaw was ready, quick as lightning. No one even saw the stroke of his bat, but the ball went like a bullet towards the square leg.[3]

"Fielding at square leg was a giant of a fellow, about six feet seven, weighing two hundred and fifty pounds, a veritable Brobdingnagian,[4] with arms like branches and hands like a pair of huge *sapaat*, the kind that Dr. Mody

---

1   *five ... lost* I.e., five players were out.

2   *stump* One of the three standing wooden sticks that comprise a wicket. The batter stands in front of the wicket to protect it from the pitcher, who attempts to hit it; if the pitch knocks one of the stumps out of the ground, the player is out.

3   *square leg* Fielder positioned to the side of the batter.

4   *Brobdingnagian* Giant. See Jonathan Swift's *Gulliver's Travels* (1726).

used to wear, you remember what big feet Dr. Mody had." Jehangir was the only one who did; he nodded. "Just to see him standing there was scary. Not one ball had got past him, and he had taken some great catches. Savukshaw purposely aimed his shot right at him. But he was as quick as Savukshaw, and stuck out his huge *sapaat* of a hand to stop the ball. What do you think happened then, boys?"

The older boys knew what Nariman wanted to hear at this point. They asked, "What happened, Nariman Uncle, what happened?" Satisfied, Nariman continued.

"A howl is what happened. A howl from the giant fielder, a howl that rang through the entire stadium, that soared like the cry of a banshee[1] right up to the cheapest seats in the furthest, highest corners, a howl that echoed from the scoreboard and into the pavilion, into the kitchen, startling the chap inside who was preparing tea and scones for after the match, who spilled boiling water all over himself and was severely hurt. But not nearly as bad as the giant fielder at square leg. Never at any English stadium was a howl heard like that one, not in the whole history of cricket. And why do you think he was howling, boys?"

The chorus asked, "Why, Nariman Uncle, why?"

"Because of Savukshaw's bullet-like shot, of course. The hand he had reached out to stop it, he now held up for all to see, and *dhur-dhur, dhur-dhur* the blood was gushing like a fountain in an Italian piazza, like a burst watermain from the Vihar-Powai reservoir, dripping onto his shirt and his white pants, and sprinkling the green grass, and only because he was such a giant of a fellow could he suffer so much blood loss and not faint. But even he could not last forever; eventually, he felt dizzy, and was helped off the field. And where do you think the ball was, boys, that Savukshaw had smacked so hard?"

And the chorus rang out again on the now dark steps of A Block: "Where, Nariman Uncle, where?"

"Past the boundary line, of course. Lying near the fence. Rent asunder. Into two perfect leather hemispheres. All the stitches had ripped, and some of the insides had spilled out. So the umpires sent for a new one, and the game resumed. Now none of the fielders dared to touch any ball that Savukshaw hit. Every shot went to the boundary, all the way for four runs. Single-handedly, Savukshaw wiped out the deficit, and had it not been for loss of time due to rain, he would have taken the Indian team to a thumping victory against the MCC. As it was, the match ended in a draw."

Nariman was pleased with the awed faces of the youngest ones around him. Kersi and Viraf were grinning away and whispering something. From

---

1   *banshee* Fairy woman in Irish folklore whose wail foretells death.

one of the flats the smell of frying fish swam out to explore the night air, and tickled Nariman's nostrils. He sniffed appreciatively, aware that it was in his good wife Hirabai's pan that the frying was taking place. This morning, he had seen the pomfret[1] she had purchased at the door, waiting to be cleaned, its mouth open and eyes wide, like the eyes of some of these youngsters. It was time to wind up the story.

"The MCC will not forget the number of new balls they had to produce that day because of Savukshaw's deadly strokes. Their annual ball budget was thrown badly out of balance. Any other bat would have cracked under the strain, but Savukshaw's was seasoned with a special combination of oils, a secret formula given to him by a *sadhu*[2] who had seen him one day playing cricket when he was a small boy. But Savukshaw used to say his real secret was practice, lots of practice, that was the advice he gave to any young lad who wanted to play cricket."

The story was now clearly finished, but none of the boys showed any sign of dispersing. "Tell us about more matches that Savukshaw played in," they said.

"More nothing. This was his greatest match. Anyway, he did not play cricket for long because soon after the match against the MCC he became a champion bicyclist, the fastest human on two wheels. And later, a pole-vaulter—when he glided over on his pole, so graceful, it was like watching a bird in flight. But he gave that up, too, and became a hunter, the mightiest hunter ever known, absolutely fearless, and so skilful, with a gun he could have, from the third floor of A Block, shaved the whisker of a cat in the backyard of C Block."

"Tell us about that," they said, "about Savukshaw the hunter!"

The fat ayah,[3] Jaakaylee, arrived to take the chartered accountant's two children home. But they refused to go without hearing about Savukshaw the hunter. When she scolded them and things became a little hysterical, some other boys tried to resurrect the ghost she had once seen: "Ayah *bhoot*![4] Ayah *bhoot*!" Nariman raised a finger in warning—that subject was still taboo in Firozsha Baag; none of the adults was in a hurry to relive the wild and rampageous days that Pesi *paadmaroo* had ushered in, once upon a time, with the *bhoot* games.

Jaakaylee sat down, unwilling to return without the children, and whispered to Nariman to make it short. The smell of frying fish which had tickled Nariman's nostrils ventured into and awakened his stomach. But the story of Savukshaw the hunter was one he had wanted to tell for a long time.

---

1   *pomfret* Fish common in southern Asia.
2   *sadhu* Gujarati: monk.
3   *ayah* Nanny.
4   *bhoot* Gujarati: ghost.

"Savukshaw always went hunting alone, he preferred it that way. There are many incidents in the life of Savukshaw the hunter, but the one I am telling you about involves a terrifying situation. Terrifying for us, of course; Savukshaw was never terrified of anything. What happened was, one night he set up camp, started a fire and warmed up his bowl of chicken-*dhansaak*."

The frying fish had precipitated famishment upon Nariman, and the subject of chicken-*dhansaak* suited him well. His own mouth watering, he elaborated: "Mrs. Savukshaw was as famous for her *dhansaak* as Mr. was for hunting. She used to put in tamarind and brinjal, coriander and cumin, cloves and cinnamon, and dozens of other spices no one knows about. Women used to come from miles around to stand outside her window while she cooked it, to enjoy the fragrance and try to penetrate her secret, hoping to identify the ingredients as the aroma floated out, layer by layer, growing more complex and delicious. But always, the delectable fragrance enveloped the women and they just surrendered to the ecstasy, forgetting what they had come for. Mrs. Savukshaw's secret was safe."

Jaakaylee motioned to Nariman to hurry up, it was past the children's dinner-time. He continued: "The aroma of savoury spices soon filled the night air in the jungle, and when the *dhansaak* was piping hot he started to eat, his rifle beside him. But as soon as he lifted the first morsel to his lips, a tiger's eyes flashed in the bushes! Not twelve feet from him! He emerged licking his chops! What do you think happened then, boys?"

"What, what, Nariman Uncle?"

Before he could tell them, the door of his flat opened. Hirabai put her head out and said, "*Chaalo ni*,[1] Nariman, it's time. Then if it gets cold you won't like it."

That decided the matter. To let Hirabai's fried fish, crisp on the outside, yet tender and juicy inside, marinated in turmeric and cayenne—to let that get cold would be something that *Khoedaiji*[2] above would not easily forgive. "Sorry boys, have to go. Next time about Savukshaw and the tiger."

There were some groans of disappointment. They hoped Nariman's good spirits would extend into the morrow when he returned from the Memorial Library, or the story would get cold.

But a whole week elapsed before Nariman again parked the apple of his eye outside his ground-floor flat and beeped the horn three times. When he had raised the hood, checked the oil, polished the star and swung into the "Colonel Bogie March,"[3] the boys began drifting towards A Block.

1   *Chaalo ni* Gujarati: Come along now.
2   *Khoedaiji* Gujarati: God.
3   *"Colonel Bogie March"* Marching song of the imprisoned soldiers in *Bridge on the River Kwai*.

Some of them recalled the incomplete story of Savukshaw and the tiger, but they knew better than to remind him. It was never wise to prompt Nariman until he had dropped the first hint himself, or things would turn out badly.

Nariman inspected the faces: the two who stood at the back, always looking superior and wise, were missing. So was the quiet Bulsara boy, the intelligent one. "Call Kersi, Viraf, and Jehangir," he said. "I want them to listen to today's story."

Jehangir was sitting alone on the stone steps of C Block. The others were chatting by the compound gate with the watchman. Someone went to fetch them.

"Sorry to disturb your conference, boys, and your meditation, Jehangir," Nariman said facetiously, "but I thought you would like to hear this story. Especially since some of you are planning to go abroad."

This was not strictly accurate, but Kersi and Viraf did talk a lot about America and Canada. Kersi had started writing to universities there since his final high-school year, and had also sent letters of inquiry to the Canadian High Commission in New Delhi and to the US Consulate at Breach Candy. But so far he had not made any progress. He and Viraf replied with as much sarcasm as their unripe years allowed, "Oh yes, next week, just have to pack our bags."

"Riiiight," drawled Nariman. Although he spoke perfect English, this was the one word with which he allowed himself to take liberties, indulging in a broadness of vowel more American than anything else. "But before we go on with today's story, what did you learn about Savukshaw, from last week's story?"

"That he was a very talented man," said someone.

"What else?"

"He was also a very lucky man, to have so many talents," said Viraf.

"Yes, but what else?"

There was silence for a few moments. Then Jehangir said, timidly: "He was a man searching for happiness, by trying all kinds of different things."

"Exactly! And he never found it. He kept looking for new experiences, and though he was very successful at everything he attempted, it did not bring him happiness. Remember this, success alone does not bring happiness. Nor does failure have to bring unhappiness. Keep it in mind when you listen to today's story."

A chant started somewhere in the back: "We-want-a-story! We-want-a-story!"

"Riiiight," said Nariman. "Now, everyone remembers Vera and Dolly, daughters of Najamai from C Block." There were whistles and hoots; Viraf nudged Kersi with his elbow, who was smiling wistfully. Nariman held up his hand: "Now now, boys, behave yourselves. Those two girls went abroad for studies many years ago, and never came back. They settled there happily.

"And like them, a fellow called Sarosh also went abroad, to Toronto, but did not find happiness there. This story is about him. You probably don't know him, he does not live in Firozsha Baag, though he is related to someone who does."

"Who? Who?"

"Curiosity killed the cat," said Nariman, running a finger over each branch of his moustache, "and what's important is the tale. So let us continue. This Sarosh began calling himself Sid after living in Toronto for a few months, but in our story he will be Sarosh and nothing but Sarosh, for that is his proper Parsi name. Besides, that was his own stipulation when he entrusted me with the sad but instructive chronicle of his recent life." Nariman polished his glasses with his handkerchief, put them on again, and began.

"At the point where our story commences, Sarosh had been living in Toronto for ten years. We find him depressed and miserable, perched on top of the toilet, crouching on his haunches, feet planted firmly for balance upon the white plastic oval of the toilet seat.

"Daily for a decade had Sarosh suffered this position. Morning after morning, he had no choice but to climb up and simulate the squat of our Indian latrines. If he sat down, no amount of exertion could produce success.

"At first, this inability was not more than mildly incommodious. As time went by, however, the frustrated attempts caused him grave anxiety. And when the failure stretched unbroken over ten years, it began to torment and haunt all his waking hours."

Some of the boys struggled hard to keep straight faces. They suspected that Nariman was not telling just a funny story, because if he intended them to laugh there was always some unmistakable way to let them know. Only the thought of displeasing Nariman and prematurely terminating the story kept their paroxysms of mirth from bursting forth unchecked.

Nariman continued: "You see, ten years was the time Sarosh had set himself to achieve complete adaptation to the new country. But how could he claim adaptation with any honesty if the acceptable catharsis[1] continually failed to favour him? Obtaining his new citizenship had not helped either. He remained dependent on the old way, and this unalterable fact, strengthened afresh every morning of his life in the new country, suffocated him.

"The ten-year time limit was more an accident than anything else. But it hung over him with the awesome presence and sharpness of a guillotine.

---

1   *catharsis* Purgation; usually refers to emotional release, but can also refer to defecation.

Careless words, boys, careless words in a moment of lightheartedness, as is so often the case with us all, had led to it.

"Ten years before, Sarosh had returned triumphantly to Bombay after fulfilling the immigration requirements of the Canadian High Commission in New Delhi. News of his imminent departure spread amongst relatives and friends. A farewell party was organized. In fact, it was given by his relatives in Firozsha Baag. Most of you will be too young to remember it, but it was a very loud party, went on till late in the night. Very lengthy and heated arguments took place, which is not the thing to do at a party. It started like this: Sarosh was told by some what a smart decision he had made, that his whole life would change for the better; others said he was making a mistake, emigration was all wrong, but if he wanted to be unhappy that was his business, they wished him well.

"By and by, after substantial amounts of Scotch and soda and rum and Coke had disappeared, a fierce debate started between the two groups. To this day Sarosh does not know what made him raise his glass and announce: 'My dear family, my dear friends, if I do not become completely Canadian in exactly ten years from the time I land there, then I will come back. I promise. So please, no more arguments. Enjoy the party.' His words were greeted with cheers and shouts of hear! hear! They told him never to fear embarrassment; there was no shame if he decided to return to the country of his birth.

"But shortly, his poor worried mother pulled him aside. She led him to the back room and withdrew her worn and aged prayer book from her purse, saying, 'I want you to place your hand upon the *Avesta*[1] and swear that you will keep that promise.'

"He told her not to be silly, that it was just a joke. But she insisted. '*Kassum khà*[2]—on the *Avesta*. One last thing for your mother. Who knows when you will see me again?' and her voice grew tremulous as it always did when she turned deeply emotional. Sarosh complied, and the prayer book was returned to her purse.

"His mother continued: 'It is better to live in want among your family and your friends, who love you and care for you, than to be unhappy surrounded by vacuum cleaners and dishwashers and big shiny motor cars.' She hugged him. Then they joined the celebration in progress.

"And Sarosh's careless words spoken at the party gradually forged themselves into a commitment as much to himself as to his mother and the others. It stayed with him all his years in the new land, reminding him every morning

---

1   *Avesta*   Sacred text of Zoroastrianism.
2   *Kassum khà*   Gujarati: Swear.

of what must happen at the end of the tenth, as it reminded him now while he descended from his perch."

Jehangir wished the titters and chortles around him would settle down, he found them annoying. When Nariman structured his sentences so carefully and chose his words with extreme care as he was doing now, Jehangir found it most pleasurable to listen. Sometimes, he remembered certain words Nariman had used, or combinations of words, and repeated them to himself, enjoying again the beauty of their sounds when he went for his walks to the Hanging Gardens[1] or was sitting alone on the stone steps of C Block. Mumbling to himself did nothing to mitigate the isolation which the other boys in the Baag had dropped around him like a heavy cloak, but he had grown used to all that by now.

Nariman continued: "In his own apartment Sarosh squatted barefoot. Elsewhere, if he had to go with his shoes on, he would carefully cover the seat with toilet paper before climbing up. He learnt to do this after the first time, when his shoes had left telltale footprints on the seat. He had had to clean it with a wet paper towel. Luckily, no one had seen him.

"But there was not much he could keep secret about his ways. The world of washrooms is private and at the same time very public. The absence of his feet below the stall door, the smell of faeces, the rustle of paper, glimpses caught through the narrow crack between stall door and jamb—all these added up to only one thing: a foreign presence in the stall, not doing things in the conventional way. And if the one outside could receive the fetor of Sarosh's business wafting through the door, poor unhappy Sarosh too could detect something malodorous in the air: the presence of xenophobia and hostility."

What a feast, thought Jehangir, what a feast of words! This would be the finest story Nariman had ever told, he just knew it.

"But Sarosh did not give up trying. Each morning he seated himself to push and grunt, grunt and push, squirming and writhing unavailingly on the white plastic oval. Exhausted, he then hopped up, expert at balancing now, and completed the movement quite effortlessly.

"The long morning hours in the washroom created new difficulties. He was late going to work on several occasions, and one such day, the supervisor called him in: 'Here's your time-sheet for this month. You've been late eleven times. What's the problem?'"

Here, Nariman stopped because his neighbour Rustomji's door creaked open. Rustomji peered out, scowling and muttered, "*Saala*[2] loafers, sitting all

---

1   *Hanging Gardens* Terraced gardens in Bombay (Mumbai) featuring hedges sculpted into animal shapes.

2   *Saala* Hindi swear word.

evening outside people's houses, making a nuisance, and being encouraged by grownups at that."

He stood there a moment longer, fingering the greying chest hair that was easily accessible through his *sudra*, then went inside. The boys immediately took up a soft and low chant: "Rustomji-the-curmudgeon! Rustomji-the-curmudgeon!"

Nariman held up his hand disapprovingly. But secretly, he was pleased that the name was still popular, the name he had given Rustomji when the latter had refused to pay his share for painting the building. "Quiet, quiet!" said he. "Do you want me to continue or not?"

"Yes, yes!" The chanting died away, and Nariman resumed the story.

"So Sarosh was told by his supervisor that he was coming late to work too often. What could poor Sarosh say?"

"What, Nariman Uncle?" rose the refrain.

"Nothing, of course. The supervisor, noting his silence, continued: 'If it keeps up, the consequences could be serious as far as your career is concerned.'

"Sarosh decided to speak. He said embarrassedly, 'It's a different kind of problem. I ... I don't know how to explain ... it's an immigration-related problem.'

"Now this supervisor must have had experience with other immigrants, because right away he told Sarosh, 'No problem. Just contact your Immigrant Aid Society. They should be able to help you. Every ethnic group has one: Vietnamese, Chinese—I'm certain that one exists for Indians. If you need time off to go there, no problem. That can be arranged, no problem. As long as you do something about your lateness, there's no problem.' That's the way they talk over there, nothing is ever a problem.

"So Sarosh thanked him and went to his desk. For the umpteenth time he bitterly rued his oversight. Could fate have plotted it, concealing the western toilet behind a shroud of anxieties which had appeared out of nowhere to beset him just before he left India? After all, he had readied himself meticulously for the new life. Even for the great, merciless Canadian cold he had heard so much about. How could he have overlooked preparation for the western toilet with its matutinal[1] demands unless fate had conspired? In Bombay, you know that offices of foreign businesses offer both options in their bathrooms. So do all hotels with three stars or more. By practising in familiar surroundings, Sarosh was convinced he could have mastered a seated evacuation before departure.

"But perhaps there was something in what the supervisor said. Sarosh found a telephone number for the Indian Immigrant Aid Society and made

---

1   *matutinal* Early-morning.

an appointment. That afternoon, he met Mrs. Maha-Lepate[1] at the Society's office."

Kersi and Viraf looked at each other and smiled. Nariman Uncle had a nerve, there was more *lepate* in his own stories than anywhere else.

"Mrs. Maha-Lepate was very understanding, and made Sarosh feel at ease despite the very personal nature of his problem. She said, 'Yes, we get many referrals. There was a man here last month who couldn't eat Wonder Bread—it made him throw up.'

"By the way, boys, Wonder Bread is a Canadian bread which all happy families eat to be happy in the same way; the unhappy families are unhappy in their own fashion[2] by eating other brands." Jehangir was the only one who understood, and murmured, "Tolstoy," at Nariman's little joke. Nariman noticed it, pleased. He continued.

"Mrs. Maha-Lepate told Sarosh about that case: 'Our immigrant specialist, Dr. No-Ilaaz, recommended that the patient eat cake instead.[3] He explained that Wonder Bread caused vomiting because the digestive system was used to Indian bread only, made with Indian flour in the village he came from. However, since his system was unfamiliar with cake, Canadian or otherwise, it did not react but was digested as a newfound food. In this way he got used to Canadian flour first in cake form. Just yesterday we received a report from Dr. No-Ilaaz. The patient successfully ate his first slice of whole-wheat Wonder Bread with no ill effects. The ultimate goal is pure white Wonder Bread.'

"Like a polite Parsi boy, Sarosh said, 'That's very interesting.' The garrulous Mrs. Maha-Lepate was about to continue, and he tried to interject: 'But I—' but Mrs. Maha-Lepate was too quick for him: 'Oh, there are so many interesting cases I could tell you about. Like the woman from Sri Lanka—referred to us because they don't have their own Society—who could not drink the water here. Dr. No-Ilaaz said it was due to the different mineral content. So he started her on Coca-Cola and then began diluting it with water, bit by bit. Six weeks later she took her first sip of unadulterated Canadian water and managed to keep it down.'

"Sarosh could not halt Mrs. Maha-Lepate as she launched from one case history into another: 'Right now, Dr. No-Ilaaz is working on a very unusual case. Involves a whole Pakistani family. Ever since immigrating to Canada,

1   *Maha-Lepate* Hindi: Great Yarn-Teller.

2   *the unhappy ... own fashion* See the opening sentence of Leo Tolstoy's classic Russian novel *Anna Karenina* (1873–77): "Happy families are all alike; every unhappy family is unhappy in its own way."

3   *No-Ilaaz* Hindi: No-Cure; *eat cake instead* Reference to a quotation attributed to Marie Antoinette (1755–93), Queen of France. When told that the peasants had no bread to eat, she supposedly declared, "let them eat cake."

none of them can swallow. They choke on their own saliva, and have to spit constantly. But we are confident that Dr. No-Ilaaz will find a remedy. He has never been stumped by any immigrant problems. Besides, we have an information network with other third-world Immigrant Aid Societies. We all seem to share a history of similar maladies, and regularly compare notes. Some of us thought these problems were linked to retention of original citizenship. But this was a false lead.'

"Sarosh, out of his own experience, vigorously nodded agreement. By now he was truly fascinated by Mrs. Maha-Lepate's wealth of information. Reluctantly, he interrupted: 'But will Dr. No-Ilaaz be able to solve my problem?'

"'I have every confidence that he will,' replied Mrs. Maha-Lepate in great earnest. 'And if he has no remedy for you right away, he will be delighted to start working on one. He loves to take up new projects.'"

Nariman halted to blow his nose, and a clear shrill voice travelled the night air of the Firozsha Baag compound from C Block to where the boys had collected around Nariman in A Block: "Jehangoo! O Jehangoo! Eight o'clock! Upstairs now!"

Jehangir stared at his feet in embarrassment. Nariman looked at his watch and said, "Yes, it's eight." But Jehangir did not move, so he continued.

"Mrs. Maha-Lepate was able to arrange an appointment while Sarosh waited, and he went directly to the doctor's office. What he had heard so far sounded quite promising. Then he cautioned himself not to get overly optimistic, that was the worst mistake he could make. But along the way to the doctor's, he could not help thinking what a lovely city Toronto was. It was the same way he had felt when he first saw it ten years ago, before all the joy had dissolved in the acid of his anxieties."

Once again that shrill voice travelled through the clear night: "*Arré* Jehangoo! *Muà*, do I have to come down and drag you upstairs!"

Jehangir's mortification was now complete. Nariman made it easy for him, though: "The first part of the story is over. Second part continues tomorrow. Same time, same place." The boys were surprised, Nariman did not make such commitments. But never before had he told such a long story. They began drifting back to their homes.

As Jehangir strode hurriedly to C Block, falsettos and piercing shrieks followed him in the darkness: "*Arré* Jehangoo! *Muà*, Jehangoo! Bulsara Bookworm! Eight o'clock Jehangoo!" Shaking his head, Nariman went indoors to Hirabai.

Next evening the story punctually resumed when Nariman took his place on the topmost step of A Block: "You remember that we left Sarosh on his way to see the Immigrant Aid Society's doctor. Well, Dr. No-Ilaaz listened patiently to Sarosh's concerns, then said, 'As a matter of fact, there is a remedy which is so new even the IAS does not know about it. Not even that Mrs. Maha-Lepate who knows it all,' he added drolly, twirling his stethoscope like a stunted lasso. He slipped it on around his neck before continuing: 'It involves a minor operation which was developed with financial assistance from the Multicultural Department. A small device, *Crappus Non Interruptus*, or CNI as we call it, is implanted in the bowel. The device is controlled by an external handheld transmitter similar to the ones used for automatic garage door-openers—you may have seen them in hardware stores."

Nariman noticed that most of the boys wore puzzled looks and realized he had to make some things clearer. "The Multicultural Department is a Canadian invention. It is supposed to ensure that ethnic cultures are able to flourish, so that Canadian society will consist of a mosaic of cultures—that's their favourite word, mosaic—instead of one uniform mix, like the American melting pot. If you ask me, mosaic and melting pot are both nonsense, and ethnic is a polite way of saying bloody foreigner. But anyway, you understand Multicultural Department? Good. So Sarosh nodded, and Dr. No-Ilaaz went on: 'You can encode the hand-held transmitter with a personal ten-digit code. Then all you do is position yourself on the toilet seat and activate your transmitter. Just like a garage door, your bowel will open without pushing or grunting.'"

There was some snickering in the audience, and Nariman raised his eyebrows, whereupon they covered up their mouths with their hands. "The doctor asked Sarosh if he had any questions. Sarosh thought for a moment, then asked if it required any maintenance.

"Dr. No-Ilaaz replied: 'CNI is semi-permanent and operates on solar energy. Which means you would have to make it a point to get some sun periodically, or it would cease and lead to constipation. However, you don't have to strip for a tan. Exposing ten percent of your skin surface once a week during summer will let the device store sufficient energy for year-round operation.'

"Sarosh's next question was: 'Is there any hope that someday the bowels can work on their own, without operating the device?' at which Dr. No-Ilaaz grimly shook his head: 'I'm afraid not. You must think very, very carefully before making a decision. Once CNI is implanted, you can never pass a motion in the natural way—neither sitting nor squatting.'

"He stopped to allow Sarosh time to think it over, then continued: 'And you must understand what that means. You will never be able to live a normal life again. You will be permanently different from your family and friends because of this basic internal modification. In fact, in this country or that, it will set you apart from your fellow countrymen. So you must consider the whole thing most carefully.'

"Dr. No-Ilaaz paused, toyed with his stethoscope, shuffled some papers on his desk, then resumed: 'There are other dangers you should know about.

Just as a garage door can be accidentally opened by a neighbour's transmitter on the same frequency, CNI can also be activated by someone with similar apparatus.' To ease the tension he attempted a quick laugh and said, 'Very embarrassing, eh, if it happened at the wrong place and time. Mind you, the risk is not so great at present, because the chances of finding yourself within a fifty-foot radius of another transmitter on the same frequency are infinitesimal. But what about the future? What if CNI becomes very popular? Sufficient permutations may not be available for transmitter frequencies and you could be sharing the code with others. Then the risk of accidents becomes greater.'"

Something landed with a loud thud in the yard behind A Block, making Nariman startle. Immediately, a yowling and screeching and caterwauling went up from the stray cats there, and the *kuchrawalli*'s[1] dog started barking. Some of the boys went around the side of A Block to peer over the fence into the backyard. But the commotion soon died down of its own accord. The boys returned and, once again, Nariman's voice was the only sound to be heard.

"By now, Sarosh was on the verge of deciding against the operation. Dr. No-Ilaaz observed this and was pleased. He took pride in being able to dissuade his patients from following the very remedies which he first so painstakingly described. True to his name, Dr. No-Ilaaz believed no remedy is the best remedy, rather than prescribing this-mycin and that-mycin for every little ailment. So he continued: 'And what about our sons and daughters? And the quality of their lives? We still don't know about the long-term effects of CNI. Some researchers speculate that it could generate a genetic deficiency, that the offspring of a CNI parent would also require CNI. On the other hand, they could be perfectly healthy toilet seat-users, without any congenital defects. We just don't know at this stage.'

"Sarosh rose from his chair: 'Thank you very much for your time, Dr. No-Ilaaz. But I don't think I want to take such a drastic step. As you suggest, I will think it over carefully.'

"'Good, good,' said Dr. No-Ilaaz, 'I was hoping you would say that. There is one more thing. The operation is extremely expensive, and is not covered by the province's Health Insurance Plan. Many immigrant groups are lobbying to obtain coverage for special immigration-related health problems. If they succeed, then good for you.'

"Sarosh left Dr. No-Ilaaz's office with his mind made up. Time was running out. There had been a time when it was perfectly natural to squat. Now it seemed a grotesquely aberrant thing to do. Wherever he went he was reminded of the ignominy of his way. If he could not be westernized in all respects, he was nothing but a failure in this land—a failure not just in the washrooms

---

1   *kuchrawalli* Garbage collector.

of the nation but everywhere. He knew what he must do if he was to be true to himself and to the decade-old commitment. So what do you think Sarosh did next?"

"What, Nariman Uncle?"

"He went to the travel agent specializing in tickets to India. He bought a fully refundable ticket to Bombay for the day when he would complete exactly ten immigrant years—if he succeeded even once before that day dawned, he would cancel the booking.

"The travel agent asked sympathetically, 'Trouble at home?' His name was Mr. Rawaana, and he was from Bombay too.

"'No,' said Sarosh, 'trouble in Toronto.'

"'That's a shame,' said Mr. Rawaana. 'I don't want to poke my nose into your business, but in my line of work I meet so many people who are going back to their homeland because of their problems here. Sometimes I forget I'm a travel agent, that my interest is to convince them to travel. Instead, I tell them: don't give up, God is great, stay and try again. It's bad for my profits but gives me a different, a spiritual kind of satisfaction when I succeed. And I succeed about half the time. Which means,' he added with a wry laugh, 'I could double my profits if I minded my own business.'

"After the lengthy sessions with Mrs. Maha-Lepate and Dr. No-Ilaaz, Sarosh felt he had listened to enough advice and kind words. Much as he disliked doing it, he had to hurt Mr. Rawaana's feelings and leave his predicament undiscussed: 'I'm sorry, but I'm in a hurry. Will you be able to look after the booking?'

"'Well, okay,' said Mr. Rawaana, a trifle crestfallen; he did not relish the travel business as much as he did counselling immigrants. 'Hope you solve your problem. I will be happy to refund your fare, believe me.'

"Sarosh hurried home. With only four weeks to departure, every spare minute, every possible method had to be concentrated on a final attempt at adaptation.

"He tried laxatives, crunching down the tablets with a prayer that these would assist the sitting position. Changing brands did not help, and neither did various types of suppositories. He spent long stretches on the toilet seat each morning. The supervisor continued to reprimand him for tardiness. To make matters worse, Sarosh left his desk every time he felt the slightest urge, hoping: maybe this time.

"The working hours expended in the washroom were noted with unflagging vigilance by the supervisor. More counselling sessions followed. Sarosh refused to extinguish his last hope, and the supervisor punctiliously recorded 'No Improvement' in his daily log. Finally, Sarosh was fired. It would soon have been time to resign in any case, and he could not care less.

"Now whole days went by seated on the toilet, and he stubbornly refused to relieve himself the other way. The doorbell would ring only to be ignored. The telephone went unanswered. Sometimes, he would awake suddenly in the dark hours before dawn and rush to the washroom like a madman."

Without warning, Rustomji flung open his door and stormed: "Ridiculous nonsense this is becoming! Two days in a row, whole Firozsha Baag gathers here! This is not Chaupatty beach,[1] this is not a squatters' colony, this is a building, people want to live here in peace and quiet!" Then just as suddenly, he stamped inside and slammed the door. Right on cue, Nariman continued, before the boys could say anything.

"Time for meals was the only time Sarosh allowed himself off the seat. Even in his desperation he remembered that if he did not eat well, he was doomed—the downward pressure on his gut was essential if there was to be any chance of success.

"But the ineluctable day of departure dawned, with grey skies and the scent of rain, while success remained out of sight. At the airport Sarosh checked in and went to the dreary lounge. Out of sheer habit he started towards the washroom. Then he realized the hopelessness of it and returned to the cold, clammy plastic of the lounge seats. Airport seats are the same almost anywhere in the world.

"The boarding announcement was made, and Sarosh was the first to step onto the plane. The skies were darker now. Out of the window he saw a flash of lightning fork through the clouds. For some reason, everything he'd learned years ago in St. Xavier's about sheet lightning and forked lightning went through his mind. He wished it would change to sheet, there was something sinister and unpropitious about forked lightning."

Kersi, absorbedly listening, began cracking his knuckles quite unconsciously. His childhood habit still persisted. Jehangir frowned at the disturbance, and Viraf nudged Kersi to stop it.

"Sarosh fastened his seat-belt and attempted to turn his thoughts towards the long journey home: to the questions he would be expected to answer, the sympathy and criticism that would be thrust upon him. But what remained uppermost in his mind was the present moment—him in the plane, dark skies lowering, lightning on the horizon—irrevocably spelling out: defeat.

"But wait. Something else was happening now. A tiny rumble. Inside him. Or was it his imagination? Was it really thunder outside which, in his present disoriented state, he was internalizing? No, there it was again. He had to go.

"He reached the washroom, and almost immediately the sign flashed to 'Please return to seat and fasten seat-belts.' Sarosh debated whether to squat

---

1   *Chaupatty beach* Public beach in Bombay (Mumbai).

and finish the business quickly, abandoning the perfunctory seated attempt. But the plane started to move and that decided him; it would be difficult now to balance while squatting.

"He pushed. The plane continued to move. He pushed again, trembling with the effort. The seat-belt sign flashed quicker and brighter now. The plane moved faster and faster. And Sarosh pushed hard, harder than he had ever pushed before, harder than in all his ten years of trying in the new land. And the memories of Bombay, the immigration interview in New Delhi, the farewell party, his mother's tattered prayer book, all these, of their own accord, emerged from beyond the region of the ten years to push with him and give him newfound strength."

Nariman paused and cleared his throat. Dusk was falling, and the frequency of B.E.S.T. buses plying the main road outside Firozsha Baag had dropped. Bats began to fly madly from one end of the compound to the other, silent shadows engaged in endless laps over the buildings.

"With a thunderous clap the rain started to fall. Sarosh felt a splash under him. Could it really be? He glanced down to make certain. Yes, it was. He had succeeded!

"But was it already too late? The plane waited at its assigned position on the runway, jet engines at full thrust. Rain was falling in torrents and takeoff could be delayed. Perhaps even now they would allow him to cancel his flight, to disembark. He lurched out of the constricting cubicle.

"A stewardess hurried towards him: 'Excuse me, sir, but you must return to your seat immediately and fasten your belt.'

"'You don't understand!' Sarosh shouted excitedly. 'I must get off the plane! Everything is all right. I don't have to go anymore ...'

"'That's impossible, sir!' said the stewardess, aghast. 'No one can leave now. Takeoff procedures are in progress!' The wild look in his sleepless eyes, and the dark rings around them scared her. She beckoned for help.

"Sarosh continued to argue, and a steward and the chief stewardess hurried over: 'What seems to be the problem, sir? You *must* resume your seat. We are authorized, if necessary, to forcibly restrain you, sir.'

"The plane began to move again, and suddenly Sarosh felt all the urgency leaving him. His feverish mind, the product of nightmarish days and tortuous nights, was filled again with the calm which had fled a decade ago, and he spoke softly now: 'That ... that will not be necessary ... it's okay, I understand.' He readily returned to his seat.

"As the aircraft sped down the runway, Sarosh's first reaction was one of joy. The process of adaptation was complete. But later, he could not help wondering if success came before or after the ten-year limit had expired. And since he had already passed through the customs and security check, was he really an immigrant in every sense of the word at the moment of achievement?

"But such questions were merely academic. Or were they? He could not decide. If he returned, what would it be like? Ten years ago, the immigration officer who had stamped his passport had said, 'Welcome to Canada.' It was one of Sarosh's dearest memories, and thinking of it, he fell asleep.

"The plane was flying above the rainclouds. Sunshine streamed into the cabin. A few raindrops were still clinging miraculously to the windows, reminders of what was happening below. They sparkled as the sunlight caught them."

Some of the boys made as if to leave, thinking the story was finally over. Clearly, they had not found this one as interesting as the others Nariman had told. What dolts, thought Jehangir, they cannot recognize a masterpiece when they hear one. Nariman motioned with his hand for silence.

"But our story does not end there. There was a welcome-home party for Sarosh a few days after he arrived in Bombay. It was not in Firozsha Baag this time because his relatives in the Baag had a serious sickness in the house. But I was invited to it anyway. Sarosh's family and friends were considerate enough to wait till the jet lag had worked its way out of his system. They wanted him to really enjoy this one.

"Drinks began to flow freely again in his honour: Scotch and soda, rum and Coke, brandy. Sarosh noticed that during his absence all the brand names had changed—the labels were different and unfamiliar. Even for the mixes. Instead of Coke there was Thums-Up, and he remembered reading in the papers about Coca-Cola being kicked out by the Indian Government for refusing to reveal their secret formula.

"People slapped him on the back and shook his hand vigorously, over and over, right through the evening. They said: 'Telling the truth, you made the right decision, look how happy your mother is to live to see this day'; or they asked: 'Well, bossy, what changed your mind?' Sarosh smiled and nodded his way through it all, passing around Canadian currency at the insistence of some of the curious ones who, egged on by his mother, also pestered him to display his Canadian passport and citizenship card. She had been badgering him since his arrival to tell her the real reason: 'Saachoo kahé,[1] what brought you back?' and was hoping that tonight, among his friends, he might raise his glass and reveal something. But she remained disappointed.

"Weeks went by and Sarosh found himself desperately searching for his old place in the pattern of life he had vacated ten years ago. Friends who had organized the welcome-home party gradually disappeared. He went walking

---

1   *Saachoo kahé* Gujarati: Tell the truth.

in the evenings along Marine Drive, by the sea-wall, where the old crowd used to congregate. But the people who sat on the parapet while waves crashed behind their backs were strangers. The tetrapods[1] were still there, staunchly protecting the reclaimed land from the fury of the sea. He had watched as a kid when cranes had lowered these cement and concrete hulks of respectable grey into the water. They were grimy black now, and from their angularities rose the distinct stench of human excrement. The old pattern was never found by Sarosh; he searched in vain. Patterns of life are selfish and unforgiving.

"Then one day, as I was driving past Marine Drive, I saw someone sitting alone. He looked familiar, so I stopped. For a moment I did not recognize Sarosh, so forlorn and woebegone was his countenance. I parked the apple of my eye and went to him, saying, 'Hullo, Sid, what are you doing here on your lonesome?' And he said, 'No, no! No more Sid, please, that name reminds me of all my troubles.' Then, on the parapet at Marine Drive, he told me his unhappy and wretched tale, with the waves battering away at the tetrapods, and around us the hawkers screaming about coconut-water and sugar-cane juice and *paan*.[2]

"When he finished, he said that he had related to me the whole sad saga because he knew how I told stories to boys in the Baag, and he wanted me to tell this one, especially to those who were planning to go abroad. 'Tell them,' said Sarosh, 'that the world can be a bewildering place, and dreams and ambitions are often paths to the most pernicious of traps.' As he spoke, I could see that Sarosh was somewhere far away, perhaps in New Delhi at his immigration interview, seeing himself as he was then, with what he thought was a life of hope and promise stretching endlessly before him. Poor Sarosh. Then he was back beside me on the parapet.

"'I pray you, in your stories,' said Sarosh, his old sense of humour returning as he deepened his voice for his favourite *Othello* lines"—and here, Nariman produced a basso profundo of his own—"'when you shall these unlucky deeds relate, speak of me as I am; nothing extenuate, nor set down aught in malice: tell them that in Toronto once there lived a Parsi boy as best as he could. Set you down this; and say, besides, that for some it was good and for some it was bad, but for me life in the land of milk and honey was just a pain in the posterior.'"[3]

And now, Nariman allowed his low-pitched rumbles to turn into chuckles. The boys broke into cheers and loud applause and cries of "Encore!"

---

1   *tetrapods* Four-pointed concrete shapes placed on the shoreline to prevent erosion.

2   *paan* Preparation of betel leaves, a natural stimulant.

3   *"I pray you ... the posterior"* Parody of Othello's last words in Shakespeare's *Othello*.

and "More!" Finally, Nariman had to silence them by pointing warningly at Rustomji-the-curmudgeon's door.

While Kersi and Viraf were joking and wondering what to make of it all, Jehangir edged forward and told Nariman this was the best story he had ever told. Nariman patted his shoulder and smiled. Jehangir left, wondering if Nariman would have been as popular if Dr. Mody was still alive. Probably, since the two were liked for different reasons: Dr. Mody used to be constantly jovial, whereas Nariman had his periodic story-telling urges.

Now the group of boys who had really enjoyed the Savukshaw story during the previous week spoke up. Capitalizing on Nariman's extraordinarily good mood, they began clamouring for more Savukshaw: "Nariman Uncle, tell the one about Savukshaw the hunter, the one you had started that day."

"What hunter? I don't know which one you mean." He refused to be reminded of it, and got up to leave. But there was a loud protest, and the boys started chanting, "We-want-Savukshaw! We-want-Savukshaw!"

Nariman looked fearfully towards Rustomji's door and held up his hands placatingly: "All right, all right! Next time it will be Savukshaw again. Savukshaw the artist. The story of Parsi Picasso."[1]

—1987

---

1   *Parsi Picasso* Pun on the name of Spanish artist Pablo Picasso (1881–1973).

Kazuo Ishiguro
b. 1954

Kazuo Ishiguro was born in Nagasaki, Japan. He and his family moved to England in 1960, when his father accepted a two-year research post at the National Institute of Oceanography. The family considered their life in England a temporary situation. Ishiguro has said that his parents "didn't have the mentality of immigrants because they always thought they would go home at some stage." The confluence of Ishiguro's memory of Japan—"a few hazy images"—his family's continued observance of Japanese culture in the home, and his growth to maturity in England informs his work, which often speaks of regret, unresolved emotion, and a yearning to recapture the past.

Before the age of 35, Ishiguro wrote three novels that established his credentials as a serious author: *A Pale View of Hills* (1982), which was awarded the Winifred Holtby Memorial Prize; *An Artist of the Floating World* (1986), which was awarded the Whitbread Book of the Year award and was short-listed for the Man Booker Prize for Fiction; and *The Remains of the Day* (1989), which was awarded the Man Booker Prize for Fiction and was made into a full-length feature film. Ishiguro won the 2017 Nobel Prize in Literature.

Ishiguro's fourth novel, *The Unconsoled* (1995), revealed a change in his artistic direction, previously mischaracterized, he believes, as realist. The novel received mixed reviews and baffled many readers, including the critic James Wood, who said that it "invented its own category of badness." Nevertheless, *The Unconsoled* won the Cheltenham Prize, which is awarded yearly to a book of considerable merit that is overlooked by critics. Since *The Unconsoled*, Ishiguro has continued to produce works that challenge and interrogate the novel's conventions, including *Never Let Me Go* (2005), the second of his novels to be made into a feature film. He has also written two original screenplays, *The Saddest Music in the World* (2003) and *The White Countess* (2005).

A Family Supper

Fugu is a fish caught off the Pacific shores of Japan. The fish has held a special significance for me ever since my mother died through eating one. The poison resides in the sexual glands of the fish, inside two fragile bags. When preparing the fish, these bags must be removed with caution, for any clumsiness will result in the poison leaking into the veins. Regrettably, it is not easy to tell whether or not this operation has been carried out successfully. The proof is, as it were, in the eating.

Fugu poisoning is hideously painful and almost always fatal. If the fish has been eaten during the evening, the victim is usually overtaken by pain during his sleep. He rolls about in agony for a few hours and is dead by morning. The fish became extremely popular in Japan after the war. Until stricter regulations were imposed, it was all the rage to perform the hazardous gutting operation in one's own kitchen, then to invite neighbours and friends round for the feast.

At the time of my mother's death, I was living in California. My relationship with my parents had become somewhat strained around that period, and consequently I did not learn of the circumstances surrounding her death until I returned to Tokyo two years later. Apparently, my mother had always refused to eat fugu, but on this particular occasion she had made an exception, having been invited by an old schoolfriend whom she was anxious not to offend. It was my father who supplied me with the details as we drove from the airport to his house in the Kamakura district. When we finally arrived, it was nearing the end of a sunny autumn day.

"Did you eat on the plane?" my father asked. We were sitting on the tatami[1] floor of his tea-room.

"They gave me a light snack."

"You must be hungry. We'll eat as soon as Kikuko arrives."

My father was a formidable-looking man with a large stony jaw and furious black eyebrows. I think now in retrospect that he much resembled Chou En-lai,[2] although he would not have cherished such a comparison, being particularly proud of the pure samurai blood that ran in the family. His general presence was not one which encouraged relaxed conversation; neither were things helped much by his odd way of stating each remark as if it were the concluding one. In fact, as I sat opposite him that afternoon, a boyhood memory came back to me of the time he had struck me several times around the head for "chattering like an old woman." Inevitably, our conversation since my arrival at the airport had been punctuated by long pauses.

"I'm sorry to hear about the firm," I said when neither of us had spoken for some time. He nodded gravely.

"In fact the story didn't end there," he said. "After the firm's collapse, Watanabe killed himself. He didn't wish to live with the disgrace."

"I see."

"We were partners for seventeen years. A man of principle and honour. I respected him very much."

"Will you go into business again?" I asked.

---

1   *tatami* Straw mat traditionally used as floor covering in Japanese homes.
2   *Chou En-lai* Chinese communist politician (1898–1976).

"I am—in retirement. I'm too old to involve myself in new ventures now. Business these days has become so different. Dealing with foreigners. Doing things their way. I don't understand how we've come to this. Neither did Watanabe." He sighed. "A fine man. A man of principle."

The tea-room looked out over the garden. From where I sat I could make out the ancient well which as a child I had believed haunted. It was just visible now through the thick foliage. The sun had sunk low and much of the garden had fallen into shadow.

"I'm glad in any case that you've decided to come back," my father said. "More than a short visit, I hope."

"I'm not sure what my plans will be."

"I for one am prepared to forget the past. Your mother too was always ready to welcome you back—upset as she was by your behaviour."

"I appreciate your sympathy. As I say, I'm not sure what my plans are."

"I've come to believe now that there were no evil intentions in your mind," my father continued. "You were swayed by certain—influences. Like so many others."

"Perhaps we should forget it, as you suggest."

"As you will. More tea?"

Just then a girl's voice came echoing through the house.

"At last." My father rose to his feet. "Kikuko has arrived."

Despite our difference in years, my sister and I had always been close. Seeing me again seemed to make her excessively excited and for a while she did nothing but giggle nervously. But she calmed down somewhat when my father started to question her about Osaka and her university. She answered him with short formal replies. She in turn asked me a few questions, but she seemed inhibited by the fear that her questions might lead to awkward topics. After a while, the conversation had become even sparser than prior to Kikuko's arrival. Then my father stood up, saying: "I must attend to the supper. Please excuse me for being burdened down by such matters. Kikuko will look after you."

My sister relaxed quite visibly once he had left the room. Within a few minutes, she was chatting freely about her friends in Osaka and about her classes at university. Then quite suddenly she decided we should walk in the garden and went striding out onto the veranda. We put on some straw sandals that had been left along the veranda rail and stepped out into the garden. The daylight had almost gone.

"I've been dying for a smoke for the last half-hour," she said, lighting a cigarette.

"Then why didn't you smoke?"

She made a furtive gesture back towards the house, then grinned mischievously.

"Oh I see," I said.

"Guess what? I've got a boyfriend now."

"Oh yes?"

"Except I'm wondering what to do. I haven't made up my mind yet."

"Quite understandable."

"You see, he's making plans to go to America. He wants me to go with him as soon as I finish studying."

"I see. And you want to go to America?"

"If we go, we're going to hitch-hike." Kikuko waved a thumb in front of my face. "People say it's dangerous, but I've done it in Osaka and it's fine."

"I see. So what is it you're unsure about?"

We were following a narrow path that wound through the shrubs and finished by the old well. As we walked, Kikuko persisted in taking unnecessarily theatrical puffs on her cigarette.

"Well. I've got lots of friends now in Osaka. I like it there. I'm not sure I want to leave them all behind just yet. And Suichi—I like him, but I'm not sure I want to spend so much time with him. Do you understand?"

"Oh perfectly."

She grinned again, then skipped on ahead of me until she had reached the well. "Do you remember," she said, as I came walking up to her, "how you used to say this well was haunted?"

"Yes, I remember."

We both peered over the side.

"Mother always told me it was the old woman from the vegetable store you'd seen that night," she said. "But I never believed her and never came out here alone."

"Mother used to tell me that too. She even told me once the old woman had confessed to being the ghost. Apparently she'd been taking a short cut through our garden. I imagine she had some trouble clambering over these walls."

Kikuko gave a giggle. She then turned her back to the well, casting her gaze about the garden.

"Mother never really blamed you, you know," she said, in a new voice. I remained silent. "She always used to say to me how it was their fault, hers and Father's, for not bringing you up correctly. She used to tell me how much more careful they'd been with me, and that's why I was so good." She looked up and the mischievous grin had returned to her face. "Poor Mother," she said.

"Yes. Poor Mother."

"Are you going back to California?"

"I don't know. I'll have to see."

"What happened to—to her? To Vicki?"

"That's all finished with," I said. "There's nothing much left for me now in California."

"Do you think I ought to go there?"

"Why not? I don't know. You'll probably like it." I glanced towards the house. "Perhaps we'd better go in soon. Father might need a hand with the supper."

But my sister was once more peering down into the well. "I can't see any ghosts," she said. Her voice echoed a little.

"Is Father very upset about his firm collapsing?"

"Don't know. You can never tell with Father." Then suddenly she straightened up and turned to me. "Did he tell you about old Watanabe? What he did?"

"I heard he committed suicide."

"Well, that wasn't all. He took his whole family with him. His wife and his two little girls."

"Oh yes?"

"Those two beautiful little girls. He turned on the gas while they were all asleep. Then he cut his stomach with a meat knife."

"Yes, Father was just telling me how Watanabe was a man of principle."

"Sick." My sister turned back to the well.

"Careful. You'll fall right in."

"I can't see any ghost," she said. "You were lying to me all that time."

"But I never said it lived down the well."

"Where is it, then?"

We both looked around at the trees and shrubs. The light in the garden had grown very dim. Eventually I pointed to a small clearing some ten yards away.

"Just there I saw it. Just there."

We stared at the spot.

"What did it look like?"

"I couldn't see very well. It was dark."

"But you must have seen something."

"It was an old woman. She was just standing there, watching me."

We kept staring at the spot as if mesmerized.

"She was wearing a white kimono," I said. "Some of her hair had come undone. It was blowing around a little."

Kikuko pushed her elbow against my arm. "Oh be quiet. You're trying to frighten me all over again." She trod on the remains of her cigarette, then for a brief moment stood regarding it with a perplexed expression. She kicked some pine needles over it, then once more displayed her grin. "Let's see if supper's ready," she said.

We found my father in the kitchen. He gave us a quick glance, then carried on with what he was doing.

"Father's become quite a chef since he's had to manage on his own," Kikuko said with a laugh. He turned and looked at my sister coldly.

"Hardly a skill I'm proud of," he said. "Kikuko, come here and help."

For some moments my sister did not move. Then she stepped forward and took an apron hanging from a drawer.

"Just these vegetables need cooking now," he said to her. "The rest just needs watching." Then he looked up and regarded me strangely for some seconds. "I expect you want to look around the house," he said eventually. He put down the chopsticks he had been holding. "It's a long time since you've seen it."

As we left the kitchen I glanced back towards Kikuko, but her back was turned.

"She's a good girl," my father said quietly.

I followed my father from room to room. I had forgotten how large the house was. A panel would slide open and another room would appear. But the rooms were all startlingly empty. In one of the rooms the lights did not come on, and we stared at the stark walls and tatami in the pale light that came from the windows.

"This house is too large for a man to live in alone," my father said. "I don't have much use for most of these rooms now."

But eventually my father opened the door to a room packed full of books and papers. There were flowers in vases and pictures on the walls. Then I noticed something on a low table in the corner of the room. I came nearer and saw it was a plastic model of a battleship, the kind constructed by children. It had been placed on some newspaper; scattered around it were assorted pieces of grey plastic.

My father gave a laugh. He came up to the table and picked up the model.

"Since the firm folded," he said, "I have a little more time on my hands." He laughed again, rather strangely. For a moment his face looked almost gentle. "A little more time."

"That seems odd," I said. "You were always so busy."

"Too busy perhaps." He looked at me with a small smile. "Perhaps I should have been a more attentive father."

I laughed. He went on contemplating his battleship. Then he looked up. "I hadn't meant to tell you this, but perhaps it's best that I do. It's my belief that your mother's death was no accident. She had many worries. And some disappointments."

We both gazed at the plastic battleship.

"Surely," I said eventually, "my mother didn't expect me to live here forever."

"Obviously you don't see. You don't see how it is for some parents. Not only must they lose their children, they must lose them to things they don't understand." He spun the battleship in his fingers. "These little gunboats here could have been better glued, don't you think?"

"Perhaps. I think it looks fine."

"During the war I spent some time on a ship rather like this. But my ambition was always the air force. I figured it like this. If your ship was struck by the enemy, all you could do was struggle in the water hoping for a lifeline. But in an aeroplane—well—there was always the final weapon." He put the model back onto the table. "I don't suppose you believe in war."

"Not particularly."

He cast an eye around the room. "Supper should be ready by now," he said. "You must be hungry."

Supper was waiting in a dimly lit room next to the kitchen. The only source of light was a big lantern that hung over the table, casting the rest of the room into shadow. We bowed to each other before starting the meal.

There was little conversation. When I made some polite comment about the food, Kikuko giggled a little. Her earlier nervousness seemed to have returned to her. My father did not speak for several minutes. Finally he said:

"It must feel strange for you, being back in Japan."

"Yes, it is a little strange."

"Already, perhaps, you regret leaving America."

"A little. Not so much. I didn't leave behind much. Just some empty rooms."

"I see."

I glanced across the table. My father's face looked stony and forbidding in the half-light. We ate on in silence.

Then my eye caught something at the back of the room. At first I continued eating, then my hands became still. The others noticed and looked at me. I went on gazing into the darkness past my father's shoulder.

"Who is that? In that photograph there?"

"Which photograph?" My father turned slightly, trying to follow my gaze.

"The lowest one. The old woman in the white kimono."

My father put down his chopsticks. He looked first at the photograph, then at me.

"Your mother." His voice had become very hard. "Can't you recognize your own mother?"

"My mother. You see, it's dark. I can't see it very well."

No one spoke for a few seconds, then Kikuko rose to her feet. She took the photograph down from the wall, came back to the table and gave it to me.

"She looks a lot older," I said.

"It was taken shortly before her death," said my father.

"It was the dark. I couldn't see very well."

I looked up and noticed my father holding out a hand. I gave him the photograph. He looked at it intently, then held it towards Kikuko. Obediently, my sister rose to her feet once more and returned the picture to the wall.

There was a large pot left unopened at the centre of the table. When Kikuko had seated herself again, my father reached forward and lifted the lid. A cloud of steam rose up and curled towards the lantern. He pushed the pot a little towards me.

"You must be hungry," he said. One side of his face had fallen into shadow.

"Thank you." I reached forward with my chopsticks. The steam was almost scalding. "What is it?"

"Fish."

"It smells very good."

In amidst soup were strips of fish that had curled almost into balls. I picked one out and brought it to my bowl.

"Help yourself. There's plenty."

"Thank you." I took a little more, then pushed the pot towards my father. I watched him take several pieces to his bowl. Then we both watched as Kikuko served herself.

My father bowed slightly. "You must be hungry," he said again. He took some fish to his mouth and started to eat. Then I too chose a piece and put it in my mouth. It felt soft, quite fleshy against my tongue.

"Very good," I said. "What is it?"

"Just fish."

"It's very good."

The three of us ate on in silence. Several minutes went by.

"Some more?"

"Is there enough?"

"There's plenty for all of us." My father lifted the lid and once more steam rose up. We all reached forward and helped ourselves.

"Here," I said to my father, "you have this last piece."

"Thank you."

When we had finished the meal, my father stretched out his arms and yawned with an air of satisfaction. "Kikuko," he said. "Prepare a pot of tea, please."

My sister looked at him, then left the room without comment. My father stood up.

"Let's retire to the other room. It's rather warm in here."

I got to my feet and followed him into the tea-room. The large sliding windows had been left open, bringing in a breeze from the garden. For a while we sat in silence.

"Father," I said, finally.

"Yes?"

"Kikuko tells me Watanabe-San took his whole family with him."

My father lowered his eyes and nodded. For some moments he seemed deep in thought. "Watanabe was very devoted to his work," he said at last. "The collapse of the firm was a great blow to him. I fear it must have weakened his judgment."

"You think what he did—it was a mistake?"

"Why, of course. Do you see it otherwise?"

"No, no. Of course not."

"There are other things besides work."

"Yes."

We fell silent again. The sound of locusts came in from the garden. I looked out into the darkness. The well was no longer visible.

"What do you think you will do now?" my father asked. "Will you stay in Japan for a while?"

"To be honest, I hadn't thought that far ahead."

"If you wish to stay here, I mean here in this house, you would be very welcome. That is, if you don't mind living with an old man."

"Thank you. I'll have to think about it."

I gazed out once more into the darkness.

"But of course," said my father, "this house is so dreary now. You'll no doubt return to America before long."

"Perhaps. I don't know yet."

"No doubt you will."

For some time my father seemed to be studying the back of his hands. Then he looked up and sighed.

"Kikuko is due to complete her studies next spring," he said. "Perhaps she will want to come home then. She's a good girl."

"Perhaps she will."

"Things will improve then."

"Yes, I'm sure they will."

We fell silent once more, waiting for Kikuko to bring the tea.

—1982

Eden Robinson
b. 1968

Eden Robinson, the author of some of the most startling and macabre fiction in contemporary Canadian literature, counts among her major influences Edgar Allan Poe, Stephen King, and filmmaker David Cronenberg. In many of her best-known stories, notably those in her first collection, *Traplines* (1996), extremes of physical and psychological violence are not disruptions of a peaceful norm but rather part of everyday, less to be wondered at than endured as a matter of course.

Much, though not all, of Robinson's work engages with the lives of First Nations people today, and Robinson herself was born to a Heiltsuk mother and a Haisla father on a reserve in northern British Columbia. However, Robinson, like so many writers, is suspicious of labels, including the label of "Native writer." As she has observed: "Once you've been put in the box of being a native writer, then it's hard to get out."

It is difficult to fashion any sort of box to hold Robinson's fiction: it is dark, disturbing, traversed by characters she describes as "flamboyant psychopaths," and yet full of humour. While Robinson gained much acclaim for *Traplines*, her first novel, *Monkey Beach* (2000), became a national bestseller and was nominated for both the Scotiabank Giller Prize and the Governor General's Award. A story that follows the journey of a young Haisla woman as she seeks to unravel the mystery of her missing brother, it is both stylistically bold and intensely readable. Robinson's latest novel is *Son of a Trickster* (2017), which was shortlisted for the Scotiabank Giller Prize.

Terminal Avenue

His brother once held a peeled orange slice up against the sun. When the light shone through it, the slice became a brilliant amber: the setting sun is this colour, ripe orange. The uniforms of the five advancing Peace Officers are robin's egg blue, but the slanting light catches their visors and sets their faces aflame.

∞

In his memory, the water of the Douglas Channel[1] is a hard blue, baked to a glassy translucence by the August sun. The mountains in the distance form a crown; *Gabiswa*, the mountain in the centre, is the same shade of blue as his lover's veins.

She raises her arms to sweep her hair from her face. Her breasts lift. In the cool morning air, her nipples harden to knobby raspberries. Her eyes are widening in indignation: he once saw that shade of blue in a dragonfly's wing, but this is another thing he will keep secret.

ଓ

Say nothing, his mother said, without moving her lips, careful not to attract attention. They waited in their car in silence after that. His father and mother were in the front seat, stiff.

Blood plastered his father's hair to his skull; blood leaked down his father's blank face. In the flashing lights of the patrol car, the blood looked black and moved like honey.

ଓ

A rocket has entered the event horizon[2] of a black hole. To an observer who is watching this from a safe distance, the rocket trapped here, in the black hole's inescapable halo of gravity, will appear to stop.

To an astronaut in the rocket, however, gravity is a rack that stretches his body like taffy, thinner and thinner, until there is nothing left but x-rays.

ଓ

In full body-armour, the five Peace Officers are sexless and anonymous. With their visors down, they look like old-fashioned astronauts. The landscape they move across is the rapid transit line, the Surreycentral Skytrain station, but if they remove their body-armour, it may as well be the moon.

The Peace Officers begin to match strides until they move like a machine. This is an intimidation tactic that works, is working on him even though he knows what it is. He finds himself frozen. He can't move, even as they roll towards him, a train on invisible tracks.

ଓ

---

1   *Douglas Channel* Inlet on the coast of northern British Columbia. At the end of the inlet is Kitamaat Village, the site of a Haisla First Nations community.
2   *event horizon* Boundary at the edge of a black hole where the force of gravity becomes so strong that no light can escape.

Once, when his brother dared him, he jumped off the high diving tower. He wasn't really scared until he stepped away from the platform. In that moment, he realized he couldn't change his mind.

You stupid shit, his brother said when he surfaced.

In his dreams, everything is the same, except there is no water in the swimming pool and he crashes into the concrete like a dropped pumpkin.

꙾

He thinks of his brother, who is so perfect he wasn't born, but chiselled from stone. There is nothing he can do against that brown Apollo's face, nothing he can say that will justify his inaction. Kevin would know what to do, with doom coming towards him in formation.

But Kevin is dead. He walked through their mother's door one day, wearing the robin's egg blue uniform of the great enemy, and his mother struck him down. She summoned the ghost of their father and put him in the room, sat him beside her, bloody and stunned. Against this Kevin said, I can stop it, Mom. I have the power to change things now.

She turned away, then the family turned away. Kevin looked at him, pleading, before he left her house and never came back, disappeared. Wil closed his eyes, a dark, secret joy welling in him, to watch his brother fall: Kevin never made the little mistakes in his life, never so much as sprouted a pimple. He made up for it though by doing the unforgivable.

Wil wonders if his brother knows what is happening. If, in fact, he isn't one of the Peace Officers, filled himself with secret joy.

꙾

His lover will wait for him tonight. Ironically, she will be wearing a complete Peace Officer's uniform, bought at great expense on the black market, and very, very illegal. She will wait at the door of her club, Terminal Avenue, and she will frisk clients that she knows will enjoy it. She will have the playroom ready, with its great wooden beams stuck through with hook and cages, with its expensive equipment built for the exclusive purpose of causing pain. On a steel cart, her toys will be spread out as neatly as surgical instruments.

When he walks through the door, she likes to have her bouncers, also dressed as Peace Officers, hurl him against the wall. They let him struggle before they handcuff him. Their uniforms are slippery as rubber. He can't get a grip on them. The uniforms are padded with the latest in wonderfabric so no matter how hard he punches them, he can't hurt them. They will drag him into the back and strip-search him in front of clients who pay for the privilege of watching. He stands under a spotlight that shines an impersonal cone of light from the ceiling. The rest of the room is darkened. He can see reflections of glasses, red-eyed cigarettes, the glint of ice clinking against glass, shadows shifting. He can hear zippers coming undone, low moans; he can smell the cum when he's beaten into passivity.

Once, he wanted to cut his hair, but she wouldn't let him, said she'd never speak to him again if he did. She likes it when the bouncers grab him by his hair and drag him to the exploratory table in the centre of the room. She says she likes the way it veils his face when he's kneeling.

In the playroom though, she changes. He can't hurt her the way she wants him to; she is tiring of him. He whips her half-heartedly until she tells the bouncer to do it properly.

A man walked in one day, in a robin's egg blue uniform, and Wil froze. When he could breathe again, when he could think, he found her watching him, thoughtful.

She borrowed the man's uniform and lay on the table, her face blank and smooth and round as a basketball under the visor. He put a painstick against the left nipple. It darkened and bruised. Her screams were muffled by the helmet. Her bouncers whispered things to her as they pinned her to the table, and he hurt her. When she begged him to stop, he moved the painstick to her right nipple.

He kept going until he was shaking so hard he had to stop.

That's enough for tonight, she said, breathless, wrapping her arms around him, telling the bouncers to leave when he started to cry. My poor virgin. It's not pain so much as it is a cleansing.

Is it, he asked her, one of those whiteguilt things?

She laughed, kissed him. Rocked him and forgave him, on the evening he discovered that it wasn't just easy to do terrible things to another person: it could give pleasure. It could give power.

She said she'd kill him if he told anyone what happened in the play-room. She has a reputation and is vaguely ashamed of her secret weakness. He wouldn't tell, not ever. He is addicted to her pain.

To distinguish it from real uniforms, hers has an inverted black triangle[1] on the left side, just over her heart: asocialism, she says with a laugh, and he doesn't get it. She won't explain it, her blue eyes black with desire as her pupils widened suddenly like a cat's.

The uniforms advancing on him, however, are clean and pure and real.

&

---

1   *inverted black triangle* Badge given to Nazi concentration camp inmates to mark them as "asocial"—a broad category that included prostitutes, lesbians, and homeless people.

Wil wanted to be an astronaut. He bought the books, he watched the movies and he dreamed. He did well in Physics, Math, and Sciences, and his mother bragged, He's got my brains.

He was so dedicated, he would test himself, just like the astronauts on TV. He locked himself in his closet once with nothing but a bag of potato chips and a bottle of pop. He wanted to see if he could spend time in a small space, alone and deprived. It was July and they had no air conditioning. He fainted in the heat, dreamed that he was floating over the Earth on his way to Mars, weightless.

Kevin found him, dragged him from the closet, and laughed at him.

You stupid shit, he said. Don't you know anything?

When his father slid off the hood leaving a snail's trail of blood, Kevin ran out of the car.

Stop it! Kevin screamed, his face contorted in the headlight's beam. Shadows loomed over him, but he was undaunted. Stop it!

Kevin threw himself on their dad and saved his life.

Wil stayed with their father in the hospital, never left his side. He was there when the Peace Officers came and took their father's statement. When they closed the door in his face and he heard his father screaming. The nurses took him away and he let them. Wil watched his father withdraw into himself after that, never quite healing.

He knew the names of all the constellations, the distances of the stars, the equations that would launch a ship to reach them. He knew how to stay alive in any conditions, except when someone didn't want to stay alive.

No one was surprised when his father shot himself.

At the funeral potlatch, his mother split his father's ceremonial regalia between Wil and Kevin. She gave Kevin his father's frontlet.[1] He placed it immediately on his head and danced. The room became still, the family shocked at his lack of tact. When Kevin stopped dancing, she gave Wil his father's button blanket.[2] The dark wool held his smell. Wil knew then that he would never be an astronaut. He didn't have a backup dream and drifted through school, coasting on a reputation of Brain he'd stopped trying to earn.

Kevin, on the other hand, ran away and joined the Mohawk Warriors.[3] He was at Oka[4] on August 16 when the bombs rained down and the last Canadian reserve was Adjusted.

---

1   *frontlet* Headdress worn on the forehead, used in Haisla regalia.
2   *button blanket* Ceremonial wool blanket decorated with abalone buttons.
3   *Mohawk Warriors* Native activist group.
4   *Oka* Quebec town and site of the 1990 Oka Crisis, a Mohawk protest over disputed land that developed into a violent conflict with government military and police forces. The government used guns and tear gas, but did not bomb the activists.

Wil expected him to come back broken. He was ready with patience, with forgiveness. Kevin came back a Peace Officer.

Why? his aunts, his uncles, cousins, and friends asked.

How could you? his mother asked.

Wil said nothing. When his brother looked up, Wil knew the truth, even if Kevin didn't. There were things that adjusted to rapid change—pigeons, dogs, rats, cockroaches. Then there were things that didn't—panda bears, whales, flamingos, Atlantic cod, salmon, owls.

Kevin would survive the Adjustment. Kevin had found a way to come through it and be better for it. He instinctively felt the changes coming and adapted. I, on the other hand, he thought, am going the way of the dodo bird.

∞

There are rumours in the neighbourhood. No one from the Vancouver Urban Reserve #2 can get into Terminal Avenue. They don't have the money or the connections. Whispers follow him, anyway, but no one will ask him to his face. He suspects that his mother suspects. He has been careful, but he sees the questions in her eyes when he leaves for work. Someday she'll ask him what he really does and he'll lie to her.

To allay suspicion, he smuggles cigarettes and sweetgrass[1] from the downtown core to Surreycentral. This is useful, makes him friends, adds a kick to his evening train ride. He finds that he needs these kicks. Has a morbid fear of becoming dead like his father, talking and breathing and eating, but frightened into vacancy, a living blankness.

His identity card that gets him to the downtown core says *Occupation: Waiter*. He pins it to his jacket so that no one will mistake him for a terrorist and shoot him.

He is not really alive until he steps past the industrial black doors of his lover's club. Until that moment, he is living inside his head, lost in memories. He knows that he is a novelty item, a real living Indian: that is why his prices are so inflated. He knows there will come a time when he is yesterday's condom.

He walks past the club's façade, the elegant dining rooms filled with the glittering people who watch the screens or dance across the dimly-lit ballroom-sized floor. He descends the stairs where his lover waits for him with her games and her toys, where they do things that aren't sanctioned by the Purity laws, where he gets hurt and gives hurt.

---

1   *sweetgrass* Marijuana; also refers to a herb used in First Nations spiritual ceremonies.

He is greeted by his high priestess. He enters her temple of discipline and submits. When the pain becomes too much, he hallucinates. There is no preparing for that moment when reality shifts and he is free.

∞

They have formed a circle around him. Another standard intimidation tactic. The Peace Officer facing him is waiting for him to talk. He stares up at it. This will be different from the club. He is about to become an example.

Wilson Wilson? the Officer says. The voice sounds male but is altered by computers so it won't be recognizable.

He smiles. The name is one of his mother's little jokes, a little defiance. He has hated her for it all his life, but now he doesn't mind. He is in a forgiving mood. *Yes, that's me.*

In the silence that stretches, Wil realizes that he always believed this moment would come. That he has been preparing himself for it. The smiling-faced lies from the TV haven't fooled him, or anyone else. After the Uprisings, it was only a matter of time before someone decided to solve the Indian problem once and for all.

The Peace Officer raises his club and brings it down.

∞

His father held a potlatch before they left Kitamaat, before they came to Vancouver to earn a living, after the aluminum smelter closed.

They had to hold it in secret, so they hired three large seiners[1] for the family and rode to Monkey Beach. They left in their old beat-up speedboat, early in the morning, when the Douglas Channel was calm and flat, before the winds blew in from the ocean, turning the water choppy. The seine boats fell far behind them, heavy with people. Kevin begged and begged to steer and his father laughingly gave in.

Wil knelt on the bow and held his arms open, wishing he could take off his lifejacket. In four hours they will land on Monkey Beach and will set up for the potlatch where they will dance and sing and say goodbye. His father will cook salmon around fires, roasted the old-fashioned way: split down the centre and splayed open like butterflies, thin sticks of cedar woven through the skin to hold the fish open, the sticks planted in the sand; as the flesh darkens, the juice runs down and hisses on the fire. The smell will permeate the beach. Camouflage nets will be set up all over the beach so they won't be spotted by planes. Family will lounge under them as if they were beach umbrellas. The

---

1   *seiners* Fishing boats.

more daring of the family will dash into the water, which is still glacier-cold and shocking.

This will happen when they land in four hours, but Wil chooses to remember the boat ride with his mother resting in his father's arm when Wil comes back from the bow and sits beside them. She is wearing a blue scarf and black sunglasses and red lipstick. She can't stop smiling even though they are going to leave home soon. She looks like a movie star. His father has his hair slicked back, and it makes him look like an otter. He kisses her, and she kisses him back.

Kevin is so excited that he raises one arm and makes the Mohawk salute they see on TV all the time. He loses control of the boat, and they swerve violently. His father cuffs Kevin and takes the wheel.

The sun rises as they pass Costi Island, and the water sparkles and shifts. The sky hardens into a deep summer blue.

The wind and the noise of the engine prevent them from talking. His father begins to sing. Wil doesn't understand the words, couldn't pronounce them if he tried. He can see that his father is happy. Maybe he's drunk on the excitement of the day, on the way that his wife touches him, tenderly. He gives Wil the wheel.

His father puts on his button blanket, rests it solemnly on his shoulders. He balances on the boat with the ease of someone who's spent all his life on the water. He does a twirl, when he reaches the bow of the speedboat and the button blanket opens, a navy lotus. The abalone buttons sparkle when they catch the light. She's laughing as he poses. He dances, suddenly inspired, exuberant.

Later he will understand what his father is doing, the rules he is breaking, the risks he is taking, and the price he will pay on a deserted road, when the siren goes off and the lights flash and they are pulled over.

At the time, though, Wil is white-knuckled, afraid to move the boat in a wrong way and toss his father overboard. He is also embarrassed, wishing his father were more reserved. Wishing he was being normal instead of dancing, a whirling shadow against the sun, blocking his view of the Channel.

This is the moment he chooses to be in, the place he goes to when the club flattens him to the Surreycentral tiles. He holds himself there, in the boat with his brother, his father, his mother. The sun on the water makes pale northern lights flicker against everyone's faces, and the smell of the water is clean and salty, and the boat's spray is cool against his skin.

—1996

Lynn Coady

b. 1970

Canadian novelist and journalist Lynn Coady's work has been praised for its honesty and its "shrewd examination of the underexplored byways of human psychology." "I'm trying to get at something a little transcendent between humans," she said in an interview with the *National Post*. "But at the same time, there's all that baggage: What's beautiful about humans is what's balanced by what's kind of ugly and petty and depressing."

Born in Port Hawkesbury, Nova Scotia, Coady began making up stories at a young age. She began to write in earnest when, as a young adult, she briefly worked for her hometown's social services and investigated cases of abused or neglected children. "[I]t was kind of like a Flannery O'Connor story," Coady explains, and she found the resemblance inspiring: "I wrote about a family of little girls, the kind of family that social services would be concerned about." Though Coady left Nova Scotia at 18 to attend Carleton University, she is still considered an important Atlantic Canadian writer; she edited the collection *Victory Meat: New Fiction from Atlantic Canada* in 2003.

In 1996, Coady earned an MFA in creative writing from the University of British Columbia. Her work has received much critical recognition: her first book, *Strange Heaven* (1998), was shortlisted for the Governor-General's Award; her third novel, *The Antagonist* (2011), about a hockey enforcer learning to define himself, was nominated for the Giller Prize; and two years later, Coady won the Giller for *Hellgoing* (2013), a collection whose titular story is included here. A regular contributor to *The Globe and Mail* (often writing on relationships), Coady has also published work in *Chatelaine* and *This Magazine*, and she is the founding editor of the literary magazine *Eighteen Bridges*.

Hellgoing

Once she got back Theresa told her friends about how her father said she was overweight not even an hour into the visit. Just—boom, *you're fat*, he lays this on her. "Not, you know," said Theresa, "you look well, or you look healthy or, you know, maybe: however you might look, it's good to see you." Her friends held their faces and smiled in pain, the same way her brother had when he was sitting across the kitchen table from her with their father hunched and slurping tea between them.

Her brother had been her enemy once. Even though it was just the two of them, and only a year's difference in their age, they had never been the kind of siblings who were each other's greatest ally and defender. They weren't really each other's greatest enemy either—just petty rivals, but the rivalry was immediate and ongoing. The longer Theresa had been away as an adult, however, the nicer and better-adjusted Ricky seemed to get.

She had expected the worst when he decided to move in with their father after their mother's death and Ricky's divorce. She had expected the two men, who were so alike already, to simply merge into one horrific masculine amalgam. And end up one of those bachelor pairs of fathers and sons that she knew so well from back home, finishing each other's sentences, eating the same thing every day—cereal, cheddar, toast, bologna with ketchup—pissing in the kitchen sink because the bathroom was too far away, wiping their hands on the arms of their chairs after finishing up a meal of cereal and cheese. Served on a TV tray. A TV tray never folded and put away, never scrubbed free of solidified ketchup puddles, never not stationed in front of the chair.

But Ricky got better instead of worse—he'd refused to merge into the two-headed, tea-slurping father-thing that haunted Theresa. Maybe it had haunted Ricky too, that bogeyman—perhaps he'd steeled himself against it. He had taken to wearing ironed, button-front shirts, for example, clean ones, even around the house, instead of T-shirts and sweats. He didn't wear a ball cap anymore, which was astounding because Theresa had never seen him out of one since seventh grade—he'd spent adolescent eternities in front of the hallway mirror attempting to get the curve of the brim just right.

Theresa arrived in their childhood home to find things neat, dust-free and zero TV trays in sight. Their father was expected to come to the table when his tea was ready—he didn't get it brought to him, like their mother would have done. "I'm not here to wait on ya, buddy," Ricky would call into the living room. "Get your arse to the table." He somehow had made it a new ritual from what it was when their mother was alive—something tougher, less domestic. Just a couple of dudes drinking tea. As if coming to the table was now a minor challenge thrown down from son to father, like their dad would be sort of a pussy if he didn't rise to the occasion. She wanted to applaud at that first sight of the old man heaving himself to his feet without so much as an irritated grunt. She wanted to take her brother aside and congratulate him on it.

She told a potted version of all this to her girlfriends as they sat around drinking vodka gimlets—they were on a gimlet kick—in Dana's living room. To set them up for the climax of the story, the big outrage: *Put on a few pounds, didn't ya?* She used the pissing in the sink line to make them smile, but also to ensure they had a solid sense of where Theresa and her father stood. Ruth's father, by way of contrast, was a provincial supreme court justice, long divorced, and he and Ruth went on cruises together to a different part of the world every year, where they had pictures taken of themselves holding hands.

Theresa had packed off her girls to their dad's house and flown home for the Thanksgiving long weekend. It was a long way to come for three days, but Ricky called her and asked her.

"Jeez, Ricky," she'd said on the phone, "I'd love to, but we're into mid-terms now. I'd planned on spending the whole time marking."

"With Mom gone," Ricky interrupted—it didn't feel like an interruption so much as an ambush, a bludgeoning. He silenced her by breaking the rules of their brother-sister interactions as she'd understood them up to this point. Theresa had been busy making her breezy, half-assed excuse and out of no-where Ricky hits her with the grotesque reality of *with Mom gone*.

"With Mom gone," said Ricky, "I feel like we all have to make an extra effort here."

For years, she and Ricky were not in touch. They weren't estranged, it just never occurred to them to call each other. They sent Christmas cards, some Christmases. It took Ricky forever to get the hang of email, but once he was on email, they emailed. Ricky "wasn't much for typing," though. So they didn't email very often. Point being, Theresa knew what Ricky was saying in evoking their lack of mother—he was acknowledging that they had for years depended on their mother to give a shit on everybody else's behalf. Their mother giving a shit was the only thing that kept the family together. It was their mother who, at Christmas, made sure everyone had a present for everyone else. It was their mother who always passed the phone to Ricky when Theresa called on Christ-mas Eve. Their mother gave Theresa Ricky's news throughout the year (the divorce, the knee operation) and gave Ricky Theresa's (the divorce, tenure).

"The women of our mothers' generation," Theresa said to her friends. "That's what they do, right? That's their job—to give a shit so the rest of us don't have to bother—"

Jenn was sprawled on the loveseat shaking her head tightly as she spat an olive pit into her palm. "I get so mad, I get so mad," she interrupted. "My mom hauling out the address book every year and writing Christmas cards to everyone she's ever met in her life. I mean it takes her *days*. Then she carries them all over to Dad's chair for him to sign. It just—it infuriates me! Like he's had to put any effort into it whatsoever. Gavin—he doesn't get why it pisses me off so much when I'm sending a present to his mom or someone. He al-ways goes, Hey, can we go in on that together? And I'm like, No, we fucking can't! I went *shopping* for your *mother*. I put actual *thought* into it. It took me an *afternoon* of my own *free time*! And I bought her a *card* and I *wrapped* the present and I'm going to drop it off at the *post office*. Do you know why you didn't do any of that? Because it's a pain in the ass! It's *effort*! But now you wanna get in on it? No! Go and get your mother a present *yourself* if you want to send her a present."

Everybody laughed. Jenn was playing up her anger for effect, because who among them hadn't tried to get in on someone else's present, piggybacking on another, better person's kindness? Her friends were being angry in solidarity with Theresa, dredging up their own slights and outrages and laying them neatly down like place settings—napkins, knives and forks.

"So what happens when women stop giving a shit?" asked Ruth then, trying to turn things into a seminar all of a sudden. You could always hear the 'y' when Ruth said "women"—*womyn*. Just like she wrote it. They all loved Ruth, but she never "punched the clock," as Dana liked to say. Her students all adored her, because she was like them—what her friends referred to, in private, as a "true believer."

Theresa spoke next in order to shut Ruth down—to avoid the classroom discussion her question was meant to provoke and get back to her story. "The real question is," she said, "what happens when they all die off, our mothers?"

It was not the nicest way to get things back on track. Everyone else's mother but Theresa's was still alive, so every brow but her own was pinched in existential dread. But at least the attention was back on Theresa. This was her particular gift, she knew, after years of running seminars and sitting on panels. She knew how to manipulate the attention of others—to get it where she needed it to be. She knew how to be ruthless when she had to and she knew this was a trait she had inherited.

"What happens, I guess," said Theresa, "sometimes at least, is that people, sons, step up, the way Ricky has."

Ricky saw what a motherless future might hold and, by God, he took the helm. Yes, he moved in with a parent, but at least he didn't wear a ball cap anymore. (He must have looked in the mirror one day and thought: This is ridiculous. The hair is gone and everyone knows it.) And he hired a house-keeper to come in once a week—a masterstroke. And the housekeeper, she laundered the flowered armchair covers Theresa's mother had sewn years ago precisely in response to her husband's habit of wiping his food-smeared hands on the arms of the chair. It all meant that clean, orderly adulthood continued apace on Ricky's watch, with or without a mother on hand. Theresa had been fully braced for everything in her childhood home, including the dregs of her family (because what was her mother if not the best of their family, the cream, and what were Ricky, her father and Theresa herself if not the grounds at the bottom of the cup), to have gone completely to hell. But things had not gone to hell.

"Ahem," said Ricky, as they walked together down the dirt road to check the mailbox. "You don't have to sound, you know, quite so astounded."

She didn't tell this part to her friends—what she did to Ricky after what her father did to her. They walked down the road together, Theresa still vibrating. She'd been mugged, once, in Miami while taking a smoke break outside the hotel where her conference was being held, and she'd vibrated like this, exactly like this, after having her bag wrenched out of her hands by a scabbed meth-head who'd called her cunt box. "Cunt box?" Theresa had repeated in disbelief, trying to catch the meth-head's eye as they struggled—and that's when she lost her bag, because she'd been more focused on trying to prompt the scabbed man to elaborate than on maintaining her grip.

She was forty-four. *I am forty-four!* she'd sputtered at her father. She had had babies. *I have had babies! Put on some pounds? I've put on some pounds?*

Theresa had jumped out of her chair so fast it fell over. Goosed by insult—the shock of the insult, the unexpectedness of the attack. Her father sat there looking affrontedly at the overturned chair as Ricky ran a hand over his bristled head, maybe wishing for his ball cap, wishing for a brim with which to fiddle. The truth is, Theresa wanted to run across the yard into the wall of pines at the edge of her father's property, there to hide and cry.

She was the Assistant Chair of her department. She had a paper coming out in *Hypatia*.[1] She was flying to Innsbruck, Austria, in the spring to deliver that very paper. There would be another conference in Santa Cruz a few months later where she was the keynote motherfucking speaker. She was being flown down there. *I am being flown down*, she'd hacked, asphyxiating on the rest of the sentence.

"However," Theresa narrated to her friends, "who gives a shit about any of that, right? The important thing I need to know is I'm a fat piece of crap."

"Don't say that," pleaded Ruth. "Don't say 'I'm fat,' because then it's like you're agreeing with him, you're affirming it on some level."

Dana leaned forward. "Did you have an eating disorder when you were a kid?"

"*Of course* I had an eating disorder," yelled Theresa. "Who didn't have an eating disorder?"

"They push our buttons," said Jenn. "The buttons are installed at puberty and they can push them whenever they want."

"I didn't think I had the buttons anymore," said Theresa.

"We always have the buttons," said Dana.

"*They fuck you up, your mom and dad*,"[2] quoted Jenn.

It was an obvious quote, there was no other quote in the world more appropriate to quote at that moment, but Ruth jerked around, frowning. Disappointed at Jenn, because feminists weren't supposed to quote the likes of

---

1   *Hypatia* Prominent academic journal of feminist philosophy.
2   *They ... dad* Opening line of Philip Larkin's 1971 poem "This Be the Verse."

Philip Larkin.[1] Theresa and Dana fired a secret *true-believer* grin at each other. Theresa was finally feeling like herself again.

She didn't tell her friends about anything else—the climax of the story had been told: *Put on a few pounds, didn't ya?* Ba dum *bump*. Punchline! She didn't tell them how she tried to offload her feelings onto Ricky as they walked the dirt road. He was only trying to make her feel better with the walk. But she kept jawing on about how great the house looked, how well their father seemed ("Same old Dad!"), how monumental it was that Ricky made him get up from in front of the TV and come to the table. And hiring a house-keeper—how had he known where to look? Then it just seemed natural that she move on to Ricky himself—he was looking great! He'd stopped smoking, she noticed. He seemed so fit, so together. She was getting personal now. Was he running? Going to the gym? He was dressing better, wasn't he—had that been, like, a conscious decision at some point? When had he ditched the ball cap—she had to be honest, that was a good call. Just shave the head, rock the bald-guy thing. Everyone was doing it these days. He was looking, she told him—forty-four-year-old divorcee sister to forty-three-year-old divorcee brother—very grown up.

Which was when he told her she did not have to sound quite so astounded by it all.

She used to do this to her mother, she remembered abruptly. Because she didn't have the nerve to retaliate against her father, she would torment her mother instead. Ricky had never done that, she was sure. He protected their mother. He absorbed things like a sponge, whereas Theresa had always needed someone to pay.

"Sorry," said Theresa.

"I was married for many years," said Ricky.

"Sure, I know," said Theresa.

"So I know how to run a home, is what I'm saying."

She realized she knew nothing about her brother's married life. The wom-an's name was June, they had eloped to Vegas (according to Theresa's mother, who'd told her over the phone) and so there wasn't even a wedding to attend, no in-laws to meet. June was a cashier at Ricky's pharmacy. Theresa had to admit she hadn't taken a huge interest in June. The last she heard about their activities as a couple, just before she heard about the divorce, was that they'd bought a speedboat.

"June," said Ricky, "struggled with depression."

He said it like an ad, a PSA. Like he had read many pamphlets, posters on a doctor's wall.

---

1   *feminists weren't ... Larkin* Some critics have condemned Larkin as a misogynist.

"Oh," said Theresa.

"Sometimes she would go to bed for weeks."

"Whoa," said Theresa. "Jeez."

"So that was shitty," he sighed.

And now you live with Dad? Theresa wanted to say. Now you reward yourself by moving in with Dad?

"It just made me see how easy it is for people to give up," said Ricky. "You have to be vigilant."

"Yeah," said Theresa. "Well—" She had nothing insightful to say to her brother. She'd spent her life being vigilant about other things. You can only be vigilant, she thought, about a few things at a time. Otherwise it's not vigilance anymore. It starts to be more like panic.

"Well, I just think it's great, Ricky. I mean—good for you. Really."

Ricky sighed again. They had arrived at the mailbox. As they were approaching it, Theresa could see the flag wasn't up. But they walked the rest of the distance anyway and Ricky rested his hand on the box like it was the head of a faithful dog.

"You wanna check?" he said.

This was sudden childhood. The walk to the mailbox. The peek inside for mail-treasure. Because sometimes, Theresa remembered, the postman just forgot to put the flag up. Or it fell down on its own, but the mail remained within. That was the earliest lesson, when it came to vigilance, the giddiest lesson. You flew to the end of the road no matter what the flag was doing, you didn't hesitate, you stood up on your toes and had a look either way. You could never trust the flag.

—2013

Leanne Betasamosake Simpson
b. 1971

"When I think about my life as an Indigenous woman, one of the things that I circle back to is this feeling of being lost or fragmented which, I think, comes from the experience of the violence of colonialism," says Leanne Betasamosake Simpson, a Michi Saagiig Nishnaabeg[1] writer, scholar, and musician. Simpson addresses Canadian colonialism not only in her nonfiction writing, teaching, and activism, but also in her fiction, music, and poetry. The power of the land, including urban landscapes, is a recurring motif in her work; Simpson has written on the importance of land as a form of pedagogy in Nishnaabeg education and epistemology. She positions her work in opposition to the racist narrative that justifies colonialism by suggesting that Indigenous thought "lack[s] theory, analysis, and intellect.... Naming our intelligence is important," she says, "because it is intervention, resistance and resurgence."

Simpson is a Distinguished Visiting Professor of Sociology at Ryerson University and has taught at the Dechinta Centre for Research and Learning, though she has conducted much of her academic work as an independent scholar. In *Dancing on Our Turtle's Back: Stories of Nishnaabeg Re-Creation, Resurgence, and a New Emergence* (2011), she examines how Nishnaabeg people "can re-establish the processes by which we live who we are within the current context," which she sees as "the first step in transforming our relationship with the state." In *As We Have Always Done: Indigenous Freedom through Radical Resistance* (2017), she goes further, envisioning possibilities for cultural and political resurgence that are not based on seeking recognition from the colonizing state but are instead founded in rebuilding Indigenous intellectual traditions and relationship to place.

Simpson published her first short story collection, *Islands of Decolonial Love*, in 2013. A major influence on her creative work is traditional Indigenous fiction;[2] its importance to her work is reflected in *The Gift Is in the Making* (2013), a collection of her retellings of Anishaabeg stories. In her next fiction book, *This Accident of Being Lost* (2017), songs appear alongside tightly constructed short stories, most only a few pages long; reviewer Melanie Lefebvre has praised these stories as "incredibly economical, with each word seemingly measured and weighed with great care, producing just the right balance of sarcasm and the sacred." Simpson is also a musician; her second album, *f(l)ight*, was released in 2016.

---

1   The Michi Saagiig Nishnaabeg are a traditionally Anishinaabe-speaking First Nations people whose territory, in southern Ontario, incorporates Toronto and Peterborough.
2   "Big Water," for example, references an Earth Diver origin story. See the first chapter of Thomas King's *The Truth about Stories*, in which he tells and discusses one version of this origin story.

Big Water

I'm lying in bed with my legs entangled in Kwe's. My chest is against the precious thin skin on her back and my arms hold her warm brown. I'm imagining us lying in smoky calm on cedar boughs instead of in this damp on Oakwood Avenue. I wish I could fall asleep like this, with her so close, but I'm too nervous when nice happens; I get more anxious than normal. I'm shallow breathing at her atlas and I'm worrying that my breath is too moist on the back of her neck and that it feels gross for her, maybe so gross that it will wake her up. So I roll over and check my phone, just in case.

There are eight new notifications from Signal, all from Niibish. She just made me switch from imessage to threema to Signal because Edward Snowden[1] tweeted that Signal is the safest texting app, mostly because the code is open source and has been independently verified. I wonder if she knows what "code" and "open source" mean, but if anyone can be trusted about these things my money's on Snowden. Also I have no idea why she cares about internet security, but she clearly does. I have to look at my iphone every four minutes so I don't miss anything because I can't get the sound notifications to work on this app even though I've googled it. To be honest, this isn't actually that big of a problem because I look at my beloved screen every four minutes, whether or not the sound notifications are on anyway. We all do and we all lie about it.

Niibish wants to know where I am, why I'm not up yet, why I'm not texting her back, and she'd like my opinion on the stories in the *Toronto Star* and *Vice* this morning about the flood. "ARE THEY GETTING IT?" is the second-last text. The last text is another "Where are you? ffs."

Niibish is mad at me for making her text me instead of doing things the old way and she's right and I promised it's just a tool and that we'll still do things the right way once this crisis is over. She typed in "PROMISE" in all caps like she was yelling. I texted back "of course," like she was insane for thinking otherwise. Kwe texts me "of course" when she wants to think I'm insane for thinking otherwise too.

I get dressed, take the bus and then the subway to headquarters. Headquarters is high up, like Nishnaabeg Mount Olympus,[2] so we can see Lake Ontario out of the window. Only I call it headquarters—really it's just a condo at Yonge and Dundas.

---

1   *Edward Snowden* American activist (b. 1983) who, when working for the CIA, copied a large number of classified government documents and released them to journalists in order to expose secret mass surveillance being conducted by the National Security Agency.

2   *Mount Olympus* The home of the gods in Greek mythology.

We call the lake Chi'Niibish, which means big water, and we share this brilliant peacemaker with the Mohawks. I call her Niibish for short and I'm the one that got her the iphone and taught her how to text. I look out the south-facing window of the condo and see her dense blue. She is full, too full, and she's tipsy from the birth control pills, the plastics, the sewage, and the contraband that washes into her no matter what. She is too full and overflowing and no one saw this coming like no one saw Calgary flooding, even though every single one of us should have.

Five days ago she spilled over the boardwalk and flooded the Power Plant and Queens Quay, and we all got into twitter fights about the waterfront. Six days ago, she crept over the Lakeshore and drank up Union Station,[1] and we called New York City because remember the hurricane. We found new places to charge our devices. She smothered the beach. She bathed the train tracks and Oshawa[2] carpooled. She's not angry even though she looks angry. She is full. She is full of sad. She wants us to see her, to see what we're doing to her, and change. That's the same thing that Kwe wants, so I know both the problem and the solution, and I know how much brave solutions like these require.

Niibish is just sitting and thinking and sporadically texting. They call it a crest, but not confidently because she should be receding by now. The math says receding and math is always confident, even when it's dead wrong. The weather is also confident when it is happening, and the predictors are being fed a string of variables in which they can only predict unpredictability. The public is not happy.

Niibish is reflecting and no one knows how long reflecting takes or what the outcome will be. She is wondering if this is enough for us to stay woke. She is wondering what will happen if she recedes—*Will they just build a big wall? Will they just breathe relief? Will they reflect on things?*

Should this be a Braxton Hicks warning[3] or creation?

While she's sitting and thinking she's also talking to Binesiwag. Those guys, hey. Only around in the summer, bringing big rains and big thunder and sometimes careless lightning and the fog that lets them do the things that need to get done and no one else wants to do. There's the crucial decision,

---

1   *Power Plant* Toronto art gallery on the shore of Lake Ontario; *Queens Quay* Road immediately adjacent to Toronto's lakefront; *Union Station* Toronto's train and bus transportation hub, less than a kilometre inland. All the locations named are in downtown Toronto.

2   *Oshawa* City about 60 kilometres east of Toronto.

3   *Braxton Hicks warning* Braxton Hicks contractions, sometimes called "false labour," are contractions felt during pregnancy that can be mistaken for actual labour.

which is always the same no matter what the question: Do we make the crisis bigger or smaller or keep it just the same?

I'm getting the log ready just in case. I've gathered my crew together and we're meeting where the nude beach used to be at Hanlan's Point[1] to practise holding our breath and diving. Everyone sat on a log during the last big flood, until we came up with a plan to create a new world. Muskrat got a handful of earth from the bottom of the lake like a rock star because everyone had already tried and failed. I breathed. Turtle shared her back, and we put her name on the place in return. We all danced a new world into reality. We made Turtle Island and it wasn't so bad for a while. For a while we all got lost in the beauty of things, and the intelligence of hopeless romantics won the day. We're not so confident in our making powers this time around though. Our false consciousness is large, our anxiety set to panic, our depression waiting just around the corner. We're in a mid-life crisis, out of shape and overcompensating because it's too late to change any of that. Beaver's doing push-ups on the soggy grass. Bear's doing power squats and bragging about his seven-minute workout app and the option of having a hippie with a whistle call out the next exercise. Muskrat is in his new wetsuit doing sit-ups, and not very good ones either. I'm wandering around the island instagramming pictures of big logs, deciding which one will be ours. And I'm texting Kwe, telling her that I love her, because she likes that, telling her to just stay in bed because I'll be back soon and we almost always survive.

—2017

---

1   *Hanlan's Point* Traditionally clothing-optional beach on an island near downtown Toronto.

David Bezmozgis
b. 1973

David Bezmozgis was born in Riga, Latvia; in 1980, at the age of six, he emigrated with his family to Canada. Writing was not considered a proper profession by Bezmozgis's Russian-Jewish parents, who thought that their son's interest in filmmaking would result in a more suitable career. Bezmozgis has since pursued both activities, but in 2010, he was named to *The New Yorker*'s "20 Under 40" list of top young writers of contemporary fiction. His fiction is informed by his family's relocation from Europe to Toronto and, in his own words, describes "the experience of arriving and assimilating."

"Tapka" illustrates this focus. It first appeared in a 2003 issue of *The New Yorker* and later became the opening piece in *Natasha and Other Stories* (2004), a collection of seven linked short stories that span the life of their narrator, Mark Berman, from his childhood to early adulthood. Like Bezmozgis, Mark is a Jewish immigrant who grows up in Toronto. Describing his approach to autobiographical fiction, Bezmozgis says, "It's the game that the author plays and the purpose of the game is to establish a compelling intimacy between the story contained in the narrative and the reader's own life experiences and sensibility." This collection won the Commonwealth Writers Prize for First Book and was also nominated for a Governor General's Award. *The Calgary Herald*'s Meghan O'Rourke notes that Bezmozgis's strength is his "covert subtlety" and likens his immigrant stories to those of Jhumpa Lahiri, Nathan Englander, and Aleksandar Hemon.

Since *Natasha and Other Stories*, Bezmozgis has written his first novel, *The Free World* (2011), the story of a family fleeing the Soviet Union to Rome in 1978 to escape the Iron Curtain. His most recent novel is *The Betrayers* (2014).

Tapka

Goldfinch was flapping clotheslines, a tenement delirious with striving. 6030 Bathurst: insomniac, scheming Odessa. Cedarcroft:[1] reeking borscht in the hallways. My parents, Soviet refugees but Baltic aristocrats,[2] took an apartment at 715 Finch, fronting a ravine and across from an elementary school—one respectable block away from the Russian swarm. We lived on the fifth floor, my cousin, aunt, and uncle directly below us on the fourth. Except for the Nahu-

---

1   *Goldfinch ... Cedarcroft* Streets in the Bathurst-Finch area of northern Toronto, the site of Toronto's largest community of Russian immigrants.

2   *Soviet ... aristocrats* The Soviet Union forcibly occupied the Baltic states—Estonia, Latvia, and Lithuania—from the 1940s until 1991.

movskys, a couple in their fifties, there were no other Russians in the building. For this privilege, my parents paid twenty extra dollars a month in rent.

In March of 1980, near the end of the school year but only three weeks after our arrival in Toronto, I was enrolled in Charles H. Best Elementary. Each morning, with our house key hanging from a brown shoelace around my neck, I kissed my parents goodbye and, along with my cousin Jana, tramped across the ravine—I to the first grade, she to the second. At three o'clock, bearing the germs of a new vocabulary, we tramped back home. Together, we then waited until six for our parents to return from George Brown City College, where they were taking an obligatory six-month course in English—a course that provided them with the rudiments of communication along with a modest government stipend.

In the evenings, we assembled and compiled our linguistic bounty.

Hello, havaryew?
Red, yellow, green, blue.
May I please go to the washroom?
Seventeen, eighteen, nineteen, twenny.

Joining us most nights were the Nahumovskys. They attended the same English classes and travelled with my parents on the same bus. Rita Nahumovsky was a beautician who wore layers of makeup, and Misha Nahumovsky was a tool-and-die maker.[1] They came from Minsk and didn't know a soul in Canada. With abounding enthusiasm, they incorporated themselves into our family. My parents were glad to have them. Our life was tough, we had it hard—but the Nahumovskys had it harder. They were alone, they were older, they were stupefied by the demands of language. Being essentially helpless themselves, my parents found it gratifying to help the more helpless Nahumovskys.

After dinner, with everyone gathered on cheap stools around our table, my mother repeated the day's lessons for the benefit of the Nahumovskys and, to a slightly lesser degree, for the benefit of my father. My mother had always been an exceptional and dedicated student, and she extended this dedication to George Brown City College. My father and the Nahumovskys came to rely on her detailed notes and her understanding of the curriculum. For as long as they could, they listened attentively and groped desperately toward comprehension. When this became too frustrating, my father put on the kettle, Rita painted my mother's nails, and Misha told Soviet *anekdoti*.[2]

---

1   *tool-and-die maker* Machinist who makes tools and moulds for use in manufacturing.
2   *anekdoti* Russian: anecdotes.

In a first-grade classroom a teacher calls on her students and inquires after their nationalities. "Sasha," she says. Sasha says, "Russian." "Very good," says the teacher. "Arnan," she says. Arnan says, "Armenian." "Very good," says the teacher. "Lyubka," she says. Lyubka says, "Ukrainian." "Very good," says the teacher. And then she asks Dima. Dima says, "Jewish." "What a shame," says the teacher. "So young and already a Jew."

The Nahumovskys had no children, only a white Lhasa Apso named Tapka. The dog had lived with them for years before they emigrated and then travelled with them from Minsk to Vienna, from Vienna to Rome, and from Rome to Toronto. During our first month in the building, Tapka was in quarantine, and I saw her only in photographs. Rita had dedicated an entire album to the dog, and, to dampen the pangs of separation, she consulted the album daily. There were shots of Tapka in the Nahumovskys' old Minsk apartment, seated on the cushions of faux-Louis XIV furniture; there was Tapka on the steps of a famous Viennese palace; Tapka at the Vatican, in front of the Colosseum, at the Sistine Chapel, and under the Leaning Tower of Pisa. My mother—despite having grown up with goats and chickens in her yard—didn't like animals and found it impossible to feign interest in Rita's dog. Shown a picture of Tapka, my mother wrinkled her nose and said, "Phoo." My father also couldn't be bothered. With no English, no money, no job, and only a murky conception of what the future held, he wasn't equipped to admire Tapka on the Italian Riviera. Only I cared. Through the photographs, I became attached to Tapka and projected upon her the ideal traits of the dog I did not have. Like Rita, I counted the days until Tapka's liberation.

The day Tapka was to be released from quarantine, Rita prepared an elaborate dinner. My family was invited to celebrate the dog's arrival. While Rita cooked, Misha was banished from their apartment. For distraction, he seated himself at our table with a deck of cards. As my mother reviewed sentence construction, Misha played hand after hand of *durak*[1] with me.

"The woman loves this dog more than me. A taxi to the customs facility is going to cost us ten, maybe fifteen dollars. But what can I do? The dog is truly a sweet little dog."

When it came time to collect the dog, my mother went with Misha and Rita to act as their interpreter. With my nose to the window, I watched the taxi take them away. Every few minutes, I reapplied my nose to the window. Three hours later, the taxi pulled into our parking lot, and Rita emerged from the back seat cradling animated fur. She set the fur down on the pavement where it assumed the shape of a dog. The length of its coat concealed its legs, and, as it hovered around Rita's ankles, it appeared to have either a thousand

---

1   *durak* A popular Russian card game.

tiny legs or none at all. My head ringing "Tapka, Tapka, Tapka," I raced into the hallway to meet the elevator.

That evening, Misha toasted the dog: "This last month, for the first time in years, I have enjoyed my wife's undivided attention. But I believe no man, not even one as perfect as me, can survive so much attention from his wife. So I say, with all my heart, thank God our Tapka is back home with us. Another day and I fear I may have requested a divorce."

Before he drank, Misha dipped his pinkie finger into his vodka glass and offered it to the dog. Obediently, Tapka gave Misha's finger a thorough licking. Impressed, my uncle declared her a good Russian dog. He also gave her a lick of his vodka. I gave her a piece of my chicken. Jana rolled her a pellet of bread. Misha taught us how to dangle food just out of Tapka's reach and thereby induce her to perform a charming little dance. Rita also produced Clonchik, a red-and-yellow rag clown. She tossed Clonchik under the table, onto the couch, down the hallway, and into the kitchen; over and over, Rita called, "Tapka, get Clonchik," and, without fail, Tapka got Clonchik. Everyone delighted in Tapka's antics except my mother, who sat stiffly in her chair, her feet slightly off the floor, as though preparing herself for a mild electric shock.

After the dinner, when we returned home, my mother announced that she would no longer set foot in the Nahumovskys' apartment. She liked Rita, she liked Misha, but she couldn't sympathize with their attachment to the dog. She understood that the attachment was a consequence of their lack of sophistication and also their childlessness. They were simple people. Rita had never attended university. She could derive contentment from talking to a dog, brushing its coat, putting ribbons in its hair, and repeatedly throwing a rag clown across the apartment. And Misha, although very lively and a genius with his hands, was also not an intellectual. They were good people, but a dog ruled their lives.

Rita and Misha were sensitive to my mother's attitude toward Tapka. As a result, and to the detriment of her progress with English, Rita stopped visiting our apartment. Nightly, Misha would arrive alone while Rita attended to the dog. Tapka never set foot in our home. This meant that, in order to see her, I spent more and more time at the Nahumovskys'. Each evening, after I had finished my homework, I went to play with Tapka. My heart soared every time Rita opened the door and Tapka raced to greet me. The dog knew no hierarchy of affection. Her excitement was infectious. In Tapka's presence, I resonated with doglike glee.

Because of my devotion to the dog, and their lack of an alternative, Misha and Rita added their house key to the shoelace hanging around my neck. During our lunch break and again after school, Jana and I were charged with caring for Tapka. Our task was simple: put Tapka on her leash, walk her to the ravine, release her to chase Clonchik, and then bring her home.

Every day, sitting in my classroom, understanding little, effectively friendless, I counted down the minutes to lunchtime. When the bell rang, I met Jana on the playground and we sprinted across the grass toward our building. In the hall, our approaching footsteps elicited panting and scratching. When I inserted the key into the lock, I felt emanations of love through the door. And once the door was open Tapka hurled herself at us, her entire body consumed with an ecstasy of wagging. Jana and I took turns embracing her, petting her, covertly vying for her favour. Free of Rita's scrutiny, we also satisfied certain anatomical curiosities. We examined Tapka's ears, her paws, her teeth, the roots of her fur, and her doggy genitals. We poked and prodded her, we threw her up in the air, rolled her over and over, and swung her by her front legs. I felt such overwhelming love for Tapka that sometimes, when hugging her, I had to restrain myself from squeezing too hard and crushing her little bones.

It was April when we began to care for Tapka. Snow melted in the ravine; sometimes it rained. April became May. Grass absorbed the thaw, turned green; dandelions and wildflowers sprouted yellow and blue; birds and insects flew, crawled, and made their characteristic noises. Faithfully and reliably, Jana and I attended to Tapka. We walked her across the parking lot and down into the ravine. We threw Clonchik and said, "Tapka, get Clonchik." Tapka always got Clonchik. Everyone was proud of us. My mother and my aunt wiped tears from their eyes while talking about how responsible we were. Rita and Misha rewarded us with praise and chocolates. Jana was seven and I was six; much had been asked of us, but we had risen to the challenge.

Inspired by everyone's confidence, we grew confident. Whereas at first we made sure to walk thirty paces into the ravine before releasing Tapka, we gradually reduced that requirement to ten paces, then five paces, until finally we released her at the grassy border between the parking lot and the ravine. We did this not because of laziness or intentional recklessness but because we wanted proof of Tapka's love. That she came when we called was evidence of her love, that she didn't piss in the elevator was evidence of her love, that she offered up her belly for scratching was evidence of her love, that she licked our faces was evidence of her love. All of this was evidence, but it wasn't proof. Proof could come in only one form. We had intuited an elemental truth: love needs no leash.

That first spring, even though most of what was said around me remained a mystery, a thin rivulet of meaning trickled into my cerebral catch basin and collected into a little pool of knowledge. By the end of May, I could sing the ABC song. Television taught me to say "What's up, Doc?" and "super-duper."

The playground introduced me to "shithead," "mental case," and "gaylord." I seized upon every opportunity to apply my new knowledge.

One afternoon, after spending nearly an hour in the ravine throwing Clonchik in a thousand different directions, Jana and I lolled in sunlit pollen. I called her shithead, mental case, and gaylord, and she responded by calling me gaylord, shithead, and mental case.

"Shithead."

"Gaylord."

"Mental case."

"Tapka, get Clonchik."

"Shithead."

"Gaylord."

"Come, Tapka-lapka."

"Mental case."

We went on like this, over and over, until Jana threw the clown and said, "Shithead, get Clonchik." Initially, I couldn't tell if she had said this on purpose or if it had merely been a blip in her rhythm. But when I looked at Jana her smile was triumphant.

"Mental case, get Clonchik."

For the first time, as I watched Tapka bounding happily after Clonchik, the profanity sounded profane.

"Don't say that to the dog."

"Why not?"

"It's not right."

"But she doesn't understand."

"You shouldn't say it."

"Don't be a baby. Come, shithead, come my dear one."

Her tail wagging with accomplishment, Tapka dropped Clonchik at my feet.

"You see, she likes it."

I held Clonchik as Tapka pawed frantically at my shins.

"Call her shithead. Throw the clown."

"I'm not calling her shithead."

"What are you afraid of, shithead?"

I aimed the clown at Jana's head and missed.

"Shithead, get Clonchik."

As the clown left my hand, Tapka, a white shining blur, oblivious to insult, was already cutting through the grass. I wanted to believe that I had intended the "shithead" exclusively for Jana, but I knew it wasn't true.

"I told you, gaylord, she doesn't care."

I couldn't help thinking, Poor Tapka. I felt moral residue and looked around for some sign of recrimination. The day, however, persisted in unimpeachable brilliance: sparrows winged overhead; bumblebees levitated above flowers; beside a lilac shrub, Tapka clamped down on Clonchik. I was amazed at the absence of consequences.

Jana said, "I'm going home."

As she started for home, I saw that she was still holding Tapka's leash. It swung insouciantly from her hand. I called after her just as, once again, Tapka deposited Clonchik at my feet.

"I need the leash."

"Why?"

"Don't be stupid. I need the leash."

"No, you don't. She comes when we call her. Even shithead. She won't run away."

Jana turned her back on me and proceeded toward our building. I called her again, but she refused to turn around. Her receding back was a blatant provocation. Guided more by anger than by logic, I decided that if Tapka was closer to Jana then the onus of responsibility would be on her. I picked up the doll and threw it as far as I could into the parking lot.

"Tapka, get Clonchik."

Clonchik tumbled through the air. I had put everything in my six-year-old arm behind the throw, which still meant that the doll wasn't going very far. Its trajectory promised a drop no more than twenty feet from the edge of the ravine. Running, her head arched to the sky, Tapka tracked the flying clown. As the doll reached its apex, it crossed paths with a sparrow. The bird veered off toward Finch Avenue, and the clown plummeted to the asphalt. When the doll hit the ground, Tapka raced past it after the bird.

A thousand times we had thrown Clonchik and a thousand times Tapka had retrieved him. But who knows what passes for a thought in the mind of a dog? One moment a Clonchik is a Clonchik, and the next moment a sparrow is a Clonchik.

I shouted at Jana to catch Tapka and then watched in abject horror as the dog, her attention fixed on the sparrow, skirted past Jana and directly into traffic. From my vantage point on the slope of the ravine, I couldn't see what happened. I saw only that Jana broke into a sprint and I heard the caterwauling of tires, followed by Tapka's shrill fractured yip.

By the time I reached the street, a line of cars already stretched a block beyond Goldfinch. At the front of the line were a brown station wagon and a pale-blue sedan blistered with rust. As I neared, I noted the chrome letters on the back of the sedan: D-U-S-T-E-R. In front of the sedan, Jana knelt in a tight semicircle with a pimply young man and an older woman with very large sunglasses. Tapka lay on her side at the centre of their circle. She panted in quick shallow bursts. She stared impassively at me, at Jana. Except for a hind leg twitching at the sky at an impossible angle, she seemed completely unharmed. She looked much as she did when she rested on the rug at the Nahumovskys' apartment after a vigorous romp in the ravine.

Seeing her this way, barely mangled, I felt a sense of relief. I started to convince myself that things weren't as bad as I had feared, and I tentatively edged forward to pet her. The woman in the sunglasses said something in a restrictive tone that I neither understood nor heeded. I placed my hand on Tapka's head, and she responded by opening her mouth and allowing a trickle of blood to escape onto the asphalt. This was the first time I had ever seen dog blood, and I was struck by the depth of its colour. I hadn't expected it to be red, although I also hadn't expected it to be not-red. Set against the grey asphalt and her white coat, Tapka's blood was the red I envisioned when I closed my eyes and thought: red.

I sat with Tapka until several dozen car horns demanded that we clear the way. The woman with the large sunglasses ran to her station wagon, returned with a blanket, and scooped Tapka off the street. The pimply young man stammered a few sentences, of which I understood nothing except the word "sorry." Then we were in the back seat of the station wagon with Tapka in Jana's lap. The woman kept talking until she finally realized that we couldn't understand her at all. As we started to drive off, Jana remembered something. I motioned for the woman to stop the car and scrambled out. Above the atonal chorus of car horns, I heard: "Mark, get Clonchik."

I ran and got Clonchik.

For two hours, Jana and I sat in the reception area of a small veterinary clinic in an unfamiliar part of town. In another room, with a menagerie of afflicted creatures, Tapka lay in traction, connected to a blinking machine by a series of tubes. Jana and I had been allowed to see her once but were rushed out when we both burst into tears. Tapka's doctor, a woman wearing a white coat and furry slippers resembling bear paws, tried to calm us down. Again, we could neither explain ourselves nor understand what she was saying. We managed only to establish that Tapka was not our dog. The doctor gave us colouring books, stickers, and access to the phone. Every fifteen minutes, we called home. Between phone calls, we absently flipped pages and sniffled for Tapka and for ourselves. We had no idea what would happen to Tapka; all we knew was that she wasn't dead. As for ourselves, we already felt punished and knew only that more punishment was to come.

"Why did you throw Clonchik?"

"Why didn't you give me the leash?"

"You could have held on to her collar."

"You shouldn't have called her shithead."

At six-thirty, my mother picked up the phone. I could hear the agitation in her voice. The ten minutes she had spent at home not knowing where I was had taken their toll. For ten minutes, she had been the mother of a dead child. I explained to her about the dog and felt a twinge of resentment when she said, "So it's only the dog?" Behind her I heard other voices. It sounded as though everyone were speaking at once, pursuing personal agendas, translating the phone conversation from Russian to Russian until one anguished voice separated itself: "My God, what happened?" Rita.

After getting the address from the veterinarian, my mother hung up and ordered another expensive taxi. Within a half hour, my parents, my aunt, and Misha and Rita pulled up at the clinic. Jana and I waited for them on the sidewalk. As soon as the taxi doors opened, we began to sob uncontrollably, partly out of relief but mainly in the hope of engendering sympathy. I ran to my mother and caught sight of Rita's face. Her face made me regret that I also hadn't been hit by a car.

As we clung to our mothers, Rita descended upon us.

"Children, what, oh, what have you done?"

She pinched compulsively at the loose skin of her neck, raising a cluster of pink marks.

While Misha methodically counted individual bills for the taxi-driver, we swore on our lives that Tapka had simply got away from us. That we had minded her as always but, inexplicably, she had seen a bird and bolted from the ravine and into the road. We had done everything in our power to catch her, but she had surprised us, eluded us, been too fast.

Rita considered our story.

"You are liars. Liars!"

She uttered the words with such hatred that we again burst into sobs.

My father spoke in our defence.

"Rita Borisovna, how can you say this? They are children."

"They are liars. I know my Tapka. Tapka never chased birds. Tapka never ran from the ravine."

"Maybe today she did?"

"Liars."

Having delivered her verdict, she had nothing more to say. She waited anxiously for Misha to finish paying the driver.

"Misha, enough already. Count it a hundred times, it will still be the same."

Inside the clinic, there was no longer anyone at the reception desk. During our time there, Jana and I had watched a procession of dyspeptic cats and lethargic parakeets disappear into the back rooms for examination and diagnosis. One after another they had come and gone until, by the time of our parents' arrival, the waiting area was entirely empty and the clinic officially closed. The only people remaining were a night nurse and the doctor in the bear-paw slippers, who had stayed expressly for our sake.

Looking desperately around the room, Rita screamed, "Doctor! Doctor!" But when the doctor appeared she was incapable of making herself understood. Haltingly, with my mother's help, it was communicated to the doctor that Rita wanted to see her dog. Pointing vigorously at herself, Rita asserted, "Tapka. Mine dog."

The doctor led Rita and Misha into the veterinary version of an intensive-care ward. Tapka lay on her little bed, Clonchik resting directly beside her. At the sight of Rita and Misha, Tapka weakly wagged her tail. Little more than an hour had elapsed since I had seen her last, but somehow over the course of that time Tapka had shrunk considerably. She had always been a small dog, but now she looked desiccated. She was the embodiment of defeat. Rita started to cry, grotesquely smearing her mascara. With trembling hands, and with sublime tenderness, she stroked Tapka's head.

"My God, my God, what has happened to you, my Tapkochka?"

Through my mother, and with the aid of pen and paper, the doctor provided the answer. Tapka required two operations. One for her leg. Another to stop internal bleeding. An organ had been damaged. For now, a machine was helping her, but without the machine she would die. On the paper, the doctor drew a picture of a scalpel, of a dog, of a leg, of an organ. She made an arrow pointing at the organ and drew a teardrop and coloured it in to represent blood. She also wrote down a number preceded by a dollar sign. The number was fifteen hundred.

At the sight of the number, Rita let out a low animal moan and steadied herself against Tapka's little bed. My parents exchanged a glance. I looked at the floor. Misha said, "My dear God." The Nahumovskys and my parents each took in less than five hundred dollars a month. We had arrived in Canada with almost nothing, a few hundred dollars, which had all but disappeared on furniture. There were no savings. Fifteen hundred dollars. The doctor could just as well have written a million.

In the middle of the intensive-care ward, Rita slid down to the floor and wailed. Her head thrown back, she appealed to the fluorescent lights: "*Nu*, Tapkochka, what is going to become of us?"

I looked up from my feet and saw horror and bewilderment on the doctor's face. She tried to put a hand on Rita's shoulder, but Rita violently shrugged it off.

My father attempted to intercede.

"Rita Borisovna, I understand that it is painful, but it is not the end of the world."

"And what do you know about it?"

"I know that it must be hard, but soon you will see.... Even tomorrow we could go and help you find a new one."

My father looked to my mother for approval, to insure that he had not promised too much. He needn't have worried.

"A new one? What do you mean, a new one? I don't want a new one. Why don't you get yourself a new son? A new little liar? How about that? New. Everything we have now is new. New everything."

On the linoleum floor, Rita keened, rocking back and forth. She hiccupped, as though hyperventilating. Pausing for a moment, she looked up at my mother and told her to translate for the doctor. To tell her that she would not let Tapka die.

"I will sit here on this floor forever. And if the police come to drag me out I will bite them."

"Ritochka, this is crazy."

"Why is it crazy? My Tapka's life is worth more than a thousand dollars. Because we don't have the money, she should die here? It's not her fault."

Seeking rationality, my mother turned to Misha—Misha who had said nothing all this time except "My dear God."

"Misha, do you want me to tell the doctor what Rita said?"

Misha shrugged philosophically.

"Tell her or don't tell her, you see my wife has made up her mind. The doctor will figure it out soon enough."

"And you think this is reasonable?"

"Sure. Why not? I'll sit on the floor, too. The police can take us both to jail. Besides Tapka, what else do we have?"

Misha sat on the floor beside his wife.

I watched as my mother struggled to explain to the doctor what was happening. With a mixture of words and gesticulations, she got the point across. The doctor, after considering her options, sat down on the floor beside Rita and Misha. Once again, she tried to put her hand on Rita's shoulder. This time, Rita, who was still rocking back and forth, allowed it. Misha rocked in time to his wife's rhythm. So did the doctor. The three of them sat in a line, swaying together, like campers at a campfire. Nobody said anything. We looked at each other. I watched Rita, Misha, and the doctor swaying and swaying. I became mesmerized by the swaying. I wanted to know what would happen to Tapka; the swaying answered me.

The swaying said: Listen, shithead, Tapka will live. The doctor will perform the operation. Either money will be found or money will not be necessary.

I said to the swaying: This is very good. I love Tapka. I meant her no harm. I want to be forgiven.

The swaying replied: There is reality and then there is truth. The reality is that Tapka will live. But, let's be honest, the truth is you killed Tapka. Look at Rita; look at Misha. You see, who are you kidding? You killed Tapka and you will never be forgiven.

—2003

Hassan Blasim

b. 1973

Born in Iraq, Hassan Blasim is a filmmaker and the author of two acclaimed—and provocative—collections of Arabic short stories. While he tells the stories of Iraqis both in Iraq and abroad, Blasim's focus is not, he says, "the big events that lots of writers and journalists talk about; I'm more interested in the marginal events that don't get talked about." The resulting fiction is, in the words of the critic Boyd Tonkin, "[o]ften surreal in style and savage in detail, but always planted in heart-breaking reality."

Blasim studied filmmaking at the Academy of Cinematic Arts in Baghdad. After his politically subversive films began to draw the attention of government informants, he was urged by his instructors to leave the city. He lived for a period in Iraqi Kurdistan, where he shot the drama *Wounded Camera* (2004) under a pseudonym, but ultimately fled to Europe, settling in Finland. His first collection of short fiction, written in Arabic but published first in English as *The Madman of Freedom Square* (2009), offers dark, macabre, and surreal stories addressing matters of cultural integration, personal identity, trauma, refugee life, and madness. Blasim's second collection, *The Iraqi Christ* (2014), which won the Independent Foreign Fiction Prize, maintains his violently surreal style.

Though he still writes in his native Arabic, Blasim's taboo-breaking stories have been met with criticism and censorship in Arabic countries; his first collection, for example, was not published in the original language until 2012, with some of the most controversial content altered, and it was banned in Jordan upon its publication. English translations of his work, however, continue to be celebrated. The *Guardian* critic Robin Yassin-Kassab has described Blasim's writing as "tight, intelligent, urgent in each word," calling him "perhaps the best writer of Arabic fiction alive."

The Nightmare of Carlos Fuentes[1]

In Iraq his name was Salim Abdul Husain and he worked for the municipality in the cleaning department, part of a group assigned by the manager to clear up in the aftermath of explosions.[2] He died in Holland in 2009 under another name: Carlos Fuentes.

---

1   *The Nightmare of Carlos Fuentes* Translated by Jonathan Wright; *Carlos Fuentes* Prominent Mexican author and political figure (1928–2012).

2   *aftermath of explosions* Iraq was invaded in 2003 by a group of countries led by the United States; the resulting war led to years of violence and political instability in the country.

Bored and disgusted as on every miserable day, Salim and his colleagues were sweeping a street market after a petrol tanker had exploded nearby, incinerating chickens, fruit and vegetables, and some people. They were sweeping the market slowly and cautiously for fear they might sweep up with the debris any human body parts left over. But they were always looking for an intact wallet or perhaps a gold chain, a ring or a watch which could still tell the time. Salim was not as lucky as his colleagues in finding the valuables left over from death. He needed money to buy a visa to go to Holland and escape this hell of fire and death. His only lucky find was a man's finger with a valuable silver ring of great beauty. Salim put his foot over the finger, bent down carefully, and with disgust pulled the silver ring off. He picked up the finger and put it in a black bag where they collected all the body parts. The ring ended up on Salim's finger and he would contemplate the gemstone in surprise and wonder, and in the end he abandoned the idea of selling it. Might one say that he felt a secret spiritual relationship with the ring?

When he applied for asylum in Holland he also applied to change his name: from Salim Abdul Husain to Carlos Fuentes. He explained his request to the official in the immigration department on the grounds that he was frightened of the fanatical Islamist groups, because his request for asylum was based on his work as a translator for the U.S. forces and his fear that someone might assassinate him as a traitor to his country. Salim had consulted his cousin who lived in France about changing his name. He called him on his mobile from the immigration department because Salim had no clear idea of a new foreign name that would suit him. In his flat in France his cousin was taking a deep drag on a joint when Salim called. Suppressing a laugh, his cousin said: "You're quite right. It's a hundred times better to be from Senegal or China than it is to have an Arab name in Europe. But you couldn't possibly have a name like Jack or Stephen, I mean a European name. Perhaps you should choose a brown name—a Cuban or Argentine name would suit your complexion, which is the colour of burnt barley bread." His cousin was looking through a pile of newspapers in the kitchen as he continued the conversation on the phone, and he remembered that two days earlier he had read a name, perhaps a Spanish name, in a literary article of which he did not understand much. Salim thanked his cousin warmly for the help he had given him and wished him a happy life in the great country of France.

Carlos Fuentes was very happy with his new name and the beauty of Amsterdam made him happy too. Fuentes wasted no time. He joined classes to learn Dutch and promised himself he would not speak Arabic from then on, or mix with Arabs or Iraqis, whatever happened in life. "Had enough of misery, backwardness, death, shit, piss, and camels," he said to himself. In the first year of his new life Fuentes let nothing pass without comparing it with the state of affairs in his original country, sometimes in the form of a question, sometimes as an exclamation. He would walk down the street muttering to himself sulkily and enviously: "Look how clean the streets are! Look at the toilet seat, it's sparkling clean! Why can't we eat like them? We gobble down our food as though it's about to disappear. If this girl wearing a short skirt and showing her legs were now walking across Eastern Gate Square,[1] she would disappear in an instant. She would only have to walk ten yards and the ground would swallow her up. Why are the trees so green and beautiful, as though they're washed with water every day? Why can't we be peaceful like them? We live in houses like pig sties while their houses are warm, safe, and colourful. Why do they respect dogs as much as humans? Why do we masturbate twenty-four hours a day? How can we get a decent government like theirs?" Everything Carlos Fuentes saw amazed him and humiliated him at the same time, from the softness of the toilet paper in Holland to the parliament building protected only by security cameras.

Carlos Fuentes's life went on as he had planned it. Every day he made progress in burying his identity and his past. He always scoffed at the immigrants and other foreigners who did not respect the rules of Dutch life and who complained all the time. He called them "retarded gerbils." They work in restaurants illegally, they don't pay taxes, and they don't respect any law. They are Stone Age savages. They hate the Dutch, who have fed and housed them. He felt he was the only one who deserved to be adopted by this compassionate and tolerant country, and that the Dutch government should expel all those who did not learn the language properly and anyone who committed the slightest misdemeanor, even crossing the street in violation of the safety code. Let them go shit there in their shitty countries.

After learning Dutch in record time, to the surprise of everyone who knew him, Carlos Fuentes worked non-stop, paid his taxes, and refused to live on welfare. The highlight of his efforts to integrate his mind and spirit into Dutch society came when he acquired a goodhearted Dutch girlfriend who loved and respected him. She weighed 90 kilos and had childlike features, like a cartoon character. Fuentes tried hard to treat her as a sensitive and liberated man would, like a Western man, in fact a little more so. Of course he always introduced himself as someone of Mexican origin whose father had left his country and settled in Iraq to work as an engineer with the oil companies. Carlos liked to describe the Iraqi people as an uncivilized and backward people who did not know what humanity means. "They are just savage clans," he would say.

Because of his marriage to a Dutch woman, his proficiency in Dutch, his enrolment in numerous courses on Dutch culture and history, and the fact

---

1   *Eastern Gate Square* Area in central Baghdad.

that he had no legal problems or criminal record in his file, he was able to obtain Dutch citizenship sooner than other immigrants could even dream of, and Carlos Fuentes decided to celebrate every year the anniversary of the day he became a Dutch national. Fuentes felt that his skin and blood had changed forever and that his lungs were now breathing real life. To strengthen his determination he would always repeat: "Yes, give me a country that treats me with respect, so that I can worship it all my life and pray for it." That's how things were until the dream problem began and everything fell to pieces, or as they say, proverbs and old adages do not wear out; it's only man that wears out. The wind did not blow fair for Fuentes. The first of the dreams was grim and distressing. In the dream he was unable to speak Dutch. He was standing in front of his Dutch boss and speaking to him in an Iraqi dialect, which caused him great concern and a horrible pain in his head. He would wake up soaked in sweat, then burst into tears. At first he thought they were just fleeting dreams that would inevitably pass. But the dreams continued to assail him without mercy. In his dreams he saw a group of children in the poor district where he was born, running after him and making fun of his new name. They were shouting after him and clapping: "Carlos the coward, Carlos the sissy, Carlos the silly billy." These irritating dreams evolved night after night into terrifying nightmares. One night he dreamt that he had planted a car bomb in the centre of Amsterdam. He was standing in the courtroom, ashamed and embarrassed. The judges were strict and would not let him speak Dutch, with the intent to humiliate and degrade him. They fetched him an Iraqi translator, who asked him not to speak in his incomprehensible rustic accent, which added to his agony and distress.

Fuentes began to sit in the library for hours looking through books about dreams. On his first visit he came across a book called *The Forgotten Language*, by Erich Fromm.[1] He did not understand much of it and he did not like the opinions of the writer, which he could not fully grasp because he had not even graduated from middle school. "This is pure bullshit," Fuentes said as he read Fromm's book: "We are free when we are asleep, in fact freer than we are when awake.... We may resemble angels in that we are not subject to the laws of reality. During sleep the realm of necessity recedes and gives way to the realm of freedom. The existence of the ego becomes the only reference point for thoughts and feelings."

Feeling a headache, Fuentes put the book back. How can we be free when we cannot control our dreams? What nonsense! Fuentes asked the librarian if

---

1   *Erich Fromm* German psychoanalyst and philosopher whose book *The Forgotten Language: An Introduction to the Understanding of Dreams, Fairytales, and Myths* (1951) argues that dreams and myths employ a universal language of symbols.

there were any simple books on dreams. The librarian did not understand his question properly, or else she wanted to show off how cultured and well-read she was on the subject. She told him of a book about the connection between dreams and food and how one sleeps, then she started to give him more information and advice. She also directed him to a library that had specialist magazines on the mysteries of the world of dreams.

Fuentes's wife had noticed her husband's strange behaviour, as well as the changes in his eating and sleeping habits and in when he went into and came out of the bathroom. Fuentes no longer, for example, ate sweet potato, having previously liked it in all its forms. He was always buying poultry meat, which was usually expensive. Of course his wife did not know he had read that eating any root vegetable would probably be the cause of dreams related to a person's past and roots. Eating the roots of plants has an effect different from that of eating fish, which live in water, or eating the fruits of trees. Fuentes would sit at the table chewing each piece of food like a camel, because he had read that chewing it well helps to get rid of nightmares. He had read nothing about poultry meat, for example, but he just guessed that eating the fowls of the air might bring about dreams that were happier and more liberated.

In all his attempts to better integrate his dreams with his new life, he would veer between what he imagined and the information he found in books. In the end he came to this idea: his ambition went beyond getting rid of troublesome dreams; he had to control the dreams, to modify them, purge them of all their foul air, and integrate them with the salubrious rules of life in Holland. The dreams must learn the new language of the country so that they could incorporate new images and ideas. All the old gloomy and miserable faces had to go. So Fuentes read more and more books and magazines about the mysteries of sleep and dreams according to a variety of approaches and philosophies. Fuentes also gave up sleeping naked and touching his wife's naked skin. In bed he began to wear a thick woolen overcoat, which gave rise to arguments with his wife, and so he had to go to the sitting room and sleep on the sofa. Nakedness attracts the sleeper to the zone of childhood, that's what he read too. Every day at 12:05 exactly he would go and have a bath and after coming out of the bathroom he would sit at the kitchen table and take some drops of jasmine oil. Before going to bed at night he would write down on a piece of paper the main calmative foodstuffs which he would buy the following day. This state of affairs went on for more than a month and Fuentes did not achieve good results. But he was patient and his will was invincible. As the days passed he started to perform mysterious secret rituals: He would dye his hair and his toenails green and sleep on his stomach repeating obscure words. One night he painted his face like an American Indian, slept wearing diaphanous orange pyjamas, and put under his pillow three feathers taken from various birds.

Fuentes's dignity did not permit him to tell his wife what was happening to him. He believed it was his problem and he could overcome it, since in the past he had survived the most trying and miserable conditions. In return his wife was more indulgent of his eccentric behaviour, because she had not forgotten how kind and generous he was. She decided to give him another chance before intervening and putting an end to what was happening. On one beautiful summer night Carlos Fuentes was sleeping in a military uniform with a toy plastic rifle by his side. As soon as he began to dream, a wish he had long awaited came true for the first time: he realized in his dream that he was dreaming. This was exactly what he had been seeking, to activate his conscious mind inside the dream so that he could sweep out all the rubbish of the unconscious. In the dream he was standing in front of the door to an old building that looked as though it had been ravaged by fire in its previous life. The building was in central Baghdad. What annoyed him was seeing things through the telescopic sights of the rifle he was holding in his hands. Fuentes broke through the door of the building and went into one flat after another, mercilessly wiping out everyone inside. Even the children did not survive the bursts of bullets. There was screaming, panic and chaos. But Fuentes had strong nerves and picked off his victims with skill and precision. He was worried he might wake up before he had completed his mission, and he thought, "If I had some hand grenades I could very soon finish the job in this building and move on to somewhere else." But on the sixth floor a surprise hit him when he stormed the first flat and found himself face to face with Salim Abdul Husain! Salim was standing naked next to the window, holding a broom stained with blood. With a trembling hand Fuentes aimed his rifle at Salim's head. Salim began to smile and repeated in derision: "Salim the Dutchman, Salim the Mexican, Salim the Iraqi, Salim the Frenchman, Salim the Indian, Salim the Pakistani, Salim the Nigerian ..."

Fuentes's nerves snapped and he panicked. He let out a resounding scream and started to spray Salim Abdul Husain with bullets, but Salim jumped out the window and not a single bullet hit him.

When Fuentes's wife woke up to the scream and stuck her head out the window, Carlos Fuentes was dead on the pavement and a pool of blood was spreading slowly under his head. Perhaps Fuentes would have forgiven the Dutch newspapers, which wrote that an Iraqi man had committed suicide at night by jumping from a sixth floor window, instead of writing that a Dutch national had committed suicide. But he will never forgive his brothers, who had his body taken back to Iraq and buried in the cemetery in Najaf. The most beautiful part of the Carlos Fuentes story, however, is the image captured by an amateur photographer who lived close to the scene of the incident. The young man took the picture from a low angle. The police had covered the body and the only part that protruded from under the blue sheet was his outstretched right hand. The picture was in black and white, but the stone in the ring on Carlos Fuentes's finger glowed red in the foreground, like a sun in hell.

—2009

Anders Nilsen
b. 1973

American author and artist Anders Nilsen is known for comics that confront what he calls "big, complicated things"—the major philosophical issues underlying human existence. *Big Questions* (1999–2011) is the title of one of his most ambitious and acclaimed books: a 600-page illustrated fable that follows a community of birds and their interactions with a stranded pilot in the aftermath of a plane crash. Many of Nilsen's works, like *Big Questions*, adopt the tone of a parable set in bleak, abstracted landscapes reminiscent of absurdist theatre, and some draw their inspiration from religious or mythological figures. In other books, he has explored questions of life and death in a more directly personal way: *Don't Go Where I Can't Follow* (2006) recounts the death by cancer of his fiancée, Cheryl Weaver, and *The End* (2007–13) details his subsequent grief.

Nilsen was raised in Minneapolis and New Hampshire by "hippie" parents—his father was an artist and his mother, a librarian, gave him some of his first underground comics. He studied fine arts at the University of New Mexico and the Art Institute of Chicago, but cites as his main influences the cartoonist Chester Brown and Hergé, the creator of Tintin. In his own art style, Nilsen is best known for meticulous line drawing, though he has used a range of approaches to suit specific works; his "stream of consciousness" collection *Monologues for the Coming Plague* (2006), for example, employs a scribbling style, while *Don't Go Where I Can't Follow* makes use of collage materials from his life with Weaver.

Big Questions won the Lynd Ward Graphic Novel Prize and was a *New York Times* Notable Book for 2011, and Nilsen has also received three Ignatz Awards, which recognize excellence in comics or cartoons. In addition to his eight books, Nilsen has published shorter pieces in *Poetry* magazine, *Pitchfork Media*, *Medium*, and elsewhere. "Towards a Conceptual Framework ..." first appeared in the *New York Times*'s Opinionator section in 2014, as part of the paper's series of commissioned memoir comics. Nilsen classifies the piece as a "universal memoir," calling it "a slightly absurdist attempt to put one's own life into the largest of all possible contexts without losing sight of its deep personal meaning and importance."

TOWARD A CONCEPTUAL FRAMEWORK FOR UNDERSTANDING YOUR INDIVIDUAL RELATIONSHIP TO THE TOTALITY OF THE UNIVERSE IN FOUR SIMPLE DIAGRAMS

1. THE PAST (COSMIC, NOT TO SCALE)

BEFORE THE BEGINNING OF THE UNIVERSE YOU DID NOT EXIST. IT WAS A LONG TIME AGO, BUT SCIENTISTS ARE PRETTY SURE.

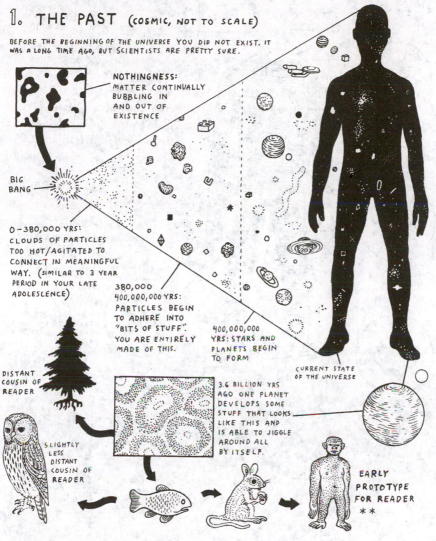

NOTHINGNESS: MATTER CONTINUALLY BUBBLING IN AND OUT OF EXISTENCE

BIG BANG

0 – 380,000 YRS: CLOUDS OF PARTICLES TOO HOT/AGITATED TO CONNECT IN MEANINGFUL WAY. (SIMILAR TO 3 YEAR PERIOD IN YOUR LATE ADOLESCENCE)

380,000 – 400,000,000 YRS: PARTICLES BEGIN TO ADHERE INTO "BITS OF STUFF". YOU ARE ENTIRELY MADE OF THIS.

400,000,000 YRS: STARS AND PLANETS BEGIN TO FORM

CURRENT STATE OF THE UNIVERSE

DISTANT COUSIN OF READER

SLIGHTLY LESS DISTANT COUSIN OF READER

3.6 BILLION YRS AGO ONE PLANET DEVELOPS SOME STUFF THAT LOOKS LIKE THIS AND IS ABLE TO JIGGLE AROUND ALL BY ITSELF.

EARLY PROTOTYPE FOR READER **

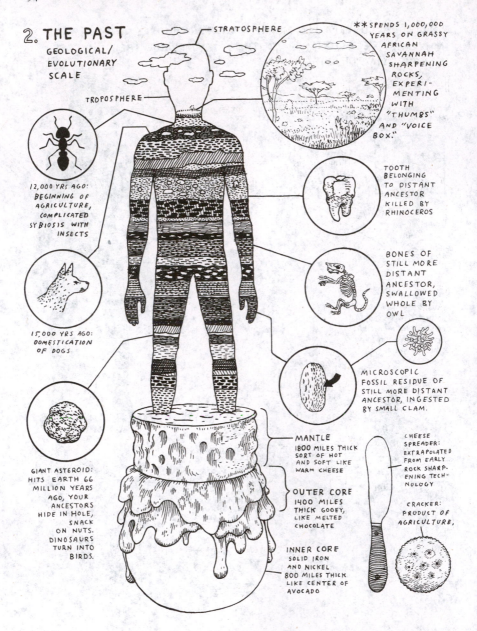

2. THE PAST

GEOLOGICAL/
EVOLUTIONARY
SCALE

STRATOSPHERE

TROPOSPHERE

**SPENDS 1,000,000 YEARS ON GRASSY AFRICAN SAVANNAH SHARPENING ROCKS, EXPERIMENTING WITH "THUMBS" AND "VOICE BOX."

12,000 YRS AGO: BEGINNING OF AGRICULTURE, COMPLICATED SYBIOSIS WITH INSECTS

TOOTH BELONGING TO DISTANT ANCESTOR KILLED BY RHINOCEROS

BONES OF STILL MORE DISTANT ANCESTOR, SWALLOWED WHOLE BY OWL

15,000 YRS AGO: DOMESTICATION OF DOGS

MICROSCOPIC FOSSIL RESIDUE OF STILL MORE DISTANT ANCESTOR, INGESTED BY SMALL CLAM.

GIANT ASTEROID: HITS EARTH 66 MILLION YEARS AGO, YOUR ANCESTORS HIDE IN HOLE, SNACK ON NUTS. DINOSAURS TURN INTO BIRDS.

MANTLE
1800 MILES THICK SORT OF HOT AND SOFT LIKE WARM CHEESE

OUTER CORE
1400 MILES THICK GOOEY, LIKE MELTED CHOCOLATE

INNER CORE
SOLID IRON AND NICKEL 800 MILES THICK LIKE CENTER OF AVOCADO

CHEESE SPREADER: EXTRAPOLATED FROM EARLY ROCK SHARPENING TECHNOLOGY

CRACKER: PRODUCT OF AGRICULTURE,

3. THE PRESENT (MORE OR LESS)

1903 - ANNA BREKHUS, AGE 16, RECEIVES LETTER IN NORWAY FROM AMERICAN COUSIN: "MY HUSBAND HAS A BROTHER."

BECOMES YOUR GREAT-GRANDMOTHER.

1906 - ANNA NILSEN EXPELLED FROM CANADA FOR ASSAULTING POLICE OFFICER DURING STRIKE.

BECOMES YOUR OTHER GREAT-GRANDMOTHER.

1972 - EN ROUTE FROM SAN FRANCISCO TO ERIE, PENNSYLVANIA YOUR MOTHER TO YOUR FATHER: "I DON'T WANT TO BE IN THE COMMUNE ANYMORE."

1973 - YOU ARE CONCEIVED ON LONG, COLD WINTER NIGHT DURING SNOW STORM. CELLS BEGIN DIVIDING ACCORDING TO ANCIENT PATTERN.

1973 YOU ARE BORN.

U.S. PULLS OUT OF VIETNAM.

1977-1979 YOU GRADUALLY BECOME SELF-AWARE.

PUNK ROCK INVENTED.

GENOCIDE IN CAMBODIA.

1981 YOU PRACTICE DRAWING SPACESHIPS, DINOSAURS, GIANT DIAGRAMMATIC BATTLE SCENES.

RONALD REAGAN SHOT.

1983 YOU ARE CAUGHT SHOP LIFTING LEGOS AT TARGET.

1984 CLASSMATE PUNCHES YOU IN STOMACH FOLLOWING COMMENT RE: HIS MOTHER.

YOU GO THROUGH BRIEF CRIMINAL PHASE:

1986 STEAL FIRST HOOD ORNAMENT.

1987 STEAL SUNGLASSES, CANDY, CASSETTE TAPES, UMBRELLA. ALMOST CAUGHT STEALING EXPENSIVE CHOCOLATE, GIVE FALSE NAME TO MALL SECURITY WHEREUPON CRIMINAL PHASE MOSTLY ABATES UNTIL 2010 WHEN YOU FAIL TO FILE STATE INCOME TAX.

1987 YOU EXPERIENCE MUTABILITY OF BRAIN CHEMISTRY VIA COMBUSTION/INHALATION OF THC: STARE AT DOORKNOB FOR 138 MINUTES.

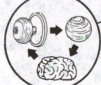

1990 YOU HAVE SEX FOR THE FIRST TIME AFTER WATCHING MOVIE: THE ADVENTURES OF BARON MUNCHAUSEN.

SOVIET UNION COLLAPSES, COLD WAR ENDS.

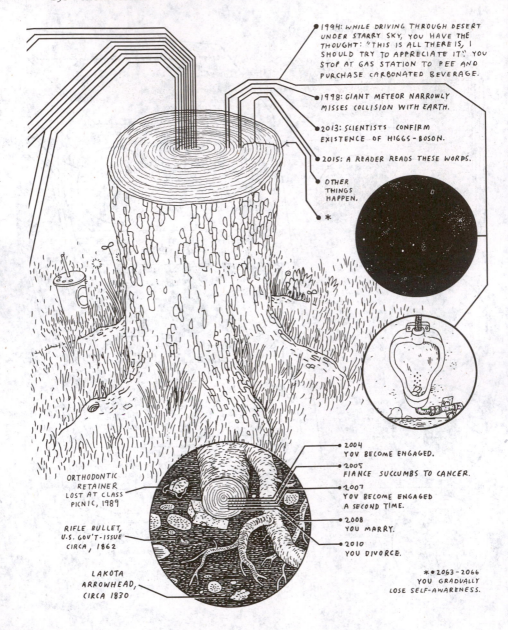

1994: WHILE DRIVING THROUGH DESERT UNDER STARRY SKY, YOU HAVE THE THOUGHT: "THIS IS ALL THERE IS, I SHOULD TRY TO APPRECIATE IT." YOU STOP AT GAS STATION TO PEE AND PURCHASE CARBONATED BEVERAGE.

1998: GIANT METEOR NARROWLY MISSES COLLISION WITH EARTH.

2013: SCIENTISTS CONFIRM EXISTENCE OF HIGGS-BOSON.

2015: A READER READS THESE WORDS.

OTHER THINGS HAPPEN.

*

2004 YOU BECOME ENGAGED.

2005 FIANCE SUCCUMBS TO CANCER.

2007 YOU BECOME ENGAGED A SECOND TIME.

2008 YOU MARRY.

2010 YOU DIVORCE.

ORTHODONTIC RETAINER LOST AT CLASS PICNIC, 1989

RIFLE BULLET, U.S. GOV'T-ISSUE CIRCA, 1862

LAKOTA ARROWHEAD, CIRCA 1830

*2063-2066 YOU GRADUALLY LOSE SELF-AWARENESS.

3. THE FUTURE (NOT TO SCALE)

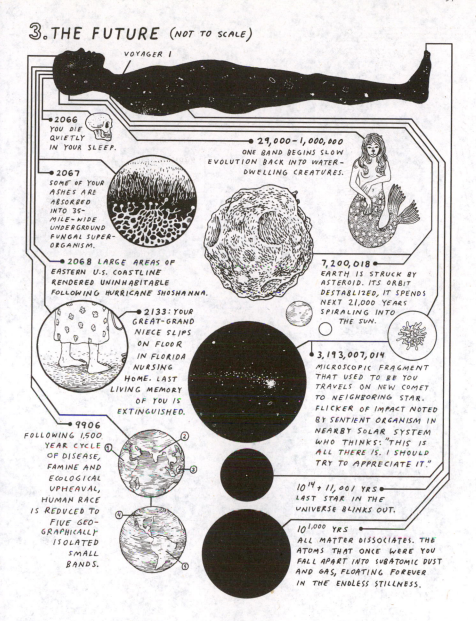

VOYAGER I

2066 YOU DIE QUIETLY IN YOUR SLEEP.

2067 SOME OF YOUR ASHES ARE ABSORBED INTO 35-MILE-WIDE UNDERGROUND FUNGAL SUPER-ORGANISM.

2068 LARGE AREAS OF EASTERN U.S. COASTLINE RENDERED UNINHABITABLE FOLLOWING HURRICANE SHOSHANNA.

2133: YOUR GREAT-GRAND NIECE SLIPS ON FLOOR IN FLORIDA NURSING HOME. LAST LIVING MEMORY OF YOU IS EXTINGUISHED.

9906 FOLLOWING 1,500 YEAR CYCLE OF DISEASE, FAMINE AND ECOLOGICAL UPHEAVAL, HUMAN RACE IS REDUCED TO FIVE GEO-GRAPHICALLY ISOLATED SMALL BANDS.

29,000–1,000,000 ONE BAND BEGINS SLOW EVOLUTION BACK INTO WATER-DWELLING CREATURES.

7,200,018 EARTH IS STRUCK BY ASTEROID. ITS ORBIT DESTABILIZED, IT SPENDS NEXT 21,000 YEARS SPIRALING INTO THE SUN.

3,193,007,014 MICROSCOPIC FRAGMENT THAT USED TO BE YOU TRAVELS ON NEW COMET TO NEIGHBORING STAR. FLICKER OF IMPACT NOTED BY SENTIENT ORGANISM IN NEARBY SOLAR SYSTEM WHO THINKS: "THIS IS ALL THERE IS. I SHOULD TRY TO APPRECIATE IT."

$10^{14} + 11,001$ YRS LAST STAR IN THE UNIVERSE BLINKS OUT.

$10^{1,000}$ YRS ALL MATTER DISSOCIATES. THE ATOMS THAT ONCE WERE YOU FALL APART INTO SUBATOMIC DUST AND GAS, FLOATING FOREVER IN THE ENDLESS STILLNESS.

—2014, revised 2016

Drama

In Tom Stoppard's *Rosencrantz and Guildenstern Are Dead*, the character of The Player contemplates the peculiarity of what it means to be a stage actor: "There we are—demented children mincing about in clothes that no one ever wore, speaking as no man ever spoke, swearing love in wigs and rhymed couplets, killing each other with wooden swords ... Don't you see?! We're actors—we're the opposite of people!" While it is true that texts belonging to other generic categories might more or less explicitly refer to their own status as fictions—think, for example, of Margaret Atwood's short story "Happy Endings"—dramatic texts must foreground the matter of the conventions that go along with fictionality, at least in terms of form. (In referring to "fiction" here, the issue is not genre or "drama" versus "fiction" versus "poetry," but rather that the dramatic text tells a fictitious story, that it is a product of the imagination.) Consider the act of going to see a play: you and several or several hundred other people gather together in a specific place and, at a specific time, quiet down and focus your attention at a specific location. In that location, for a certain length of time, other people say and do things, all the while pretending to be other people and pretending that they have no idea they are being watched by several or several hundred others. For your part, you pretend that the people pretending to be other people are in fact those other people, and that you, and several or several hundred others, are completely invisible. In what other context would such bizarre conduct seem not only reasonable, but absolutely necessary? Daniel MacIvor's play *House Humans* describes an instance when this strange balancing act of reciprocal pretending is threatened: "Harold is an old man who goes to the theatre ... He always sits at the front and claps in all the wrong places and yells out Marxist slogans during the tender moments and calls the actors by their real names. (Once he went to see a play where at one point a watermelon would roll out and surprise the audience, and he went back several times so that just before the watermelon would roll out he could yell: 'Here comes the watermelon!')" No other literary genre is at risk for this type of sabotage. In considering some of the basic conventions of drama, then, it is helpful to think about how they flow from both its central principle and its central constraint: the drama is built around the potentially fragile concept of the willing suspension of disbelief.

The Drama and the Performance

The expression "willing suspension of disbelief" was coined by the poet Samuel Taylor Coleridge in his 1817 autobiography, *Biographia Literaria*. Coleridge explained that, in order for readers to appreciate some of his more fantastical narratives—for example, his ballad "The Rime of the Ancient Mariner," with its ghostly figures and supernatural events—they would have to temporarily set aside—or suspend—any inclination towards skepticism about the truthfulness of such a tale. Willing suspension of disbelief is a crucial component of what makes the dramatic performance work. In the eighteenth century, Denis Diderot asserted that actors should perform as if the spectator did not exist, as if a "large wall" separated the stage from the audience, and as if "the curtain did not rise."

Diderot's treatise on acting technique followed the development of the **proscenium stage**, as his mention of a "curtain" makes clear; proscenium stages, introduced in Europe during the seventeenth century, make use of an archway or large frame to separate the stage area from the audience area and thus provide for the possibility of hanging a curtain and marking more easily, for example, the beginnings and endings of acts. Before the advent of the proscenium stage, dramatists often wrote plays meant to be performed on a **thrust stage**, a raised platform encircled by the audience on three sides; thus, a play such as Shakespeare's *Twelfth Night* was written before it was possible to use a curtain, and one might consider the different techniques employed to indicate the breaks between scenes and acts. Other popular stage formats are the **arena** or **theatre-in-the-round stage**, in which the audience, sitting in sloped seating, completely (or almost completely) encircles the stage area, or the **found space**, in which the stage area and audience area might be configured in any number of ways. In the contemporary era, directors and stage designers have the opportunity to stage plays along various designs, though unless a found space or a specially built space is being used, they must take into account an existing physical structure, be it an arena, proscenium stage, or otherwise.

What becomes interesting to consider is the way dramatists sometimes make explicit reference to the idea of the willing suspension of disbelief, not only in terms of a clear addressing of the audience—as in Viola's asides in *Twelfth Night*—but also in terms of a thematic concern with the operation of illusion that is so easily observable in drama. Though the **realism** of Henrik Ibsen and Tennessee Williams, whereby everything on stage is meant to register as a potential, everyday activity, has not been entirely abandoned in recent years (witness Hannah Moscovitch's *Essay*), interest in **metafictional** theatre, or plays that call attention to their own fictionality in their content, has also exploded. Dramatists have made use of the inherent strangeness at the heart of playgoing to raise such questions as: "how do we believe what we believe?," "why are humans so engrossed by illusion-making and art?," and "how can our perceptions be produced and undermined by mere words?"

This notion of a reader or audience member's temporary willingness to simply believe things that are patently untrue is a crucial factor in the success of the drama, especially the success of the drama's performance. For the critical analysis of this genre, it is important to distinguish between the notion of the drama or play, that is, the written version of the work, and theatre, which is the live enactment of mutual pretending described above. In his critical work *The Semiotics of Performance*, Marco De Marinis helpfully refines this distinction, referring to the **dramatic text** vs. the **performance text**. The dramatic text—the written play—consists of dialogue and **stage directions**, which are the instructions contained in the written play that specify how characters are supposed to move on, off, and about the stage, and sometimes how they are meant to behave. While the stage directions in some plays, especially older ones, are basically limited to such instructions as "*Enter*" and "*Exit*," they may also provide detailed, evocative information on the mood of the play, as in Sharon Pollock's stage directions for *Blood Relations*, or about the arrangement of stage décor, as in those for Henrik Ibsen's *A Doll's House*. The performance text, on the other hand, consists of the intended or implicit acting out of the written play. Thus, the performance text is not quite the same thing as a specific theatrical production of a given play on a given evening; rather, it is the *potential* of theatrical production that is embedded in the written play, a potential that readers of the dramatic text must somehow imagine in their mind's eye, and that to a large extent limits the type of action that can be portrayed. While it is true that some authors—for example, Mary Sidney and Percy Shelley—have written what are called **closet dramas**, or plays not meant to be performed, most plays are predicated on the idea of being acted out and of requiring a temporary agreement between actors and audience to accept all manner of imitation, impersonation, and active use of the imagination.

Constructing the Drama: Plot, Character, Space, and Speech

In the earliest surviving work of dramatic theory, *The Poetics*, Aristotle compares tragic drama to epic poetry, asserting that, while both genres should be concerned with heroic action, the events portrayed in a tragic drama must "fall within a single revolution of the sun, or slightly exceed this," while the epic is "unlimited in point of time." Later in the work, Aristotle adds that tragic drama should present "an action that is heroic and complete and of a certain magnitude." During the sixteenth and seventeenth centuries, Italian, French, and English neoclassicists expanded upon and refined these remarks, claiming that, ideally, all dramas should adhere to what were termed the **three classical unities**. Italian critic Lodovico Castelvetro explained that a play must have a **unity of action** (a focus on a single incident or two interrelated incidents), a **unity of time**, and a **unity of space**, with the dramatized events taking place within a 24-hour time frame and in a single locale. Later critics noted that exceptions might be made; for example, Pierre Corneille argued that the restricted timeframe of Aeschylus's *Agamemnon* was absurd and that the periods of time represented in a play should not strain verisimilitude (except in the final act, when the audience is more interested in finding out what happens than they are in the likelihood that it might all happen very quickly). In *Of Dramatic Poesy: An Essay*, John Dryden noted that while Ben Jonson "has given us the most correct plays," in which the adherence to the three unities provides "profitable rules for perfecting the stage," Shakespeare's ignorance of such rules might be forgiven because of his great wit.

By the beginning of the nineteenth century, most drama critics and theorists had abandoned the notion of the three unities, at least as a prescriptive set of rules. That said, these foundational conventions are still worth keeping in mind for the student of literature who is attuned to how the drama is built. It may be helpful to consider how the notion of unity of action is associated with the **plotting** of drama. The terms associated with **Freytag's pyramid**, such as **exposition**, **rising action**, **climax**, **falling action**, and **dénouement/resolution**, are often used to discuss prose narratives, though Gustav Freytag himself was concerned only with the five-act plot structure of classical and Renaissance plays. While few contemporary plays retain the five-act structure, the student of literature should consider how the plotting of dramas tends to retain a sense of tightness, chronological simplicity, and forward momentum, likely because the implied audience of the performance text will experience the performance in real time. Other important plotting techniques associated with drama include **suspense**—or the anticipation about how things will turn out—and suspense's customary partner, **foreshadowing**—or how anticipation is created via hints. In thinking about suspense, one might consider whether the play leaves the audience in the dark as to what might occur in the end, thus leading up to a feeling of surprise, or whether foreshadowing makes it seem as if the resolution to the plot is inevitable.

Moreover, it is often important to think about how the dramatist negotiates breaking the action down into chunks that can be performed, i.e., into

acts and **scenes**. Whereas a prose narrative can suggest a change in action, space, or time using mere words, the convention of the embedded performance text necessitates that the dramatist consider how each unit of action will be made evident, whether by the closing and opening of a curtain, by the dimming of lights, or by some other means. The implicit performance text within a drama also complicates the way one thinks of **characterization**: while all fictional narrative texts might contain characters—that is, represented individuals who have particular personality traits—in a drama the process of defining and indicating those traits cannot be achieved through direct authorial exposition, whereby the author simply tells the reader what the character is like via narration. In a drama, the characters reveal themselves through speech and action, though it is sometimes the case that dramatists "cheat," as in moments where characters describe one another or when a character describes—sometimes at length—himself or herself. Some characters will go so far as to articulate their **motivations**, the reasons for particular actions or desires, though it is often left to the student of literature to glean a character's motivations based on what that character says and does. And, just as with first-person narrators, it is sometimes the case that the motivations characters give to us, or the way a character might describe himself or herself, is inaccurate; it is the task of the audience member to evaluate the information that is given. Usually, if a character's motivations can be assessed and analyzed, one is dealing with what is called a **round character**, one that is fully developed and whose actions are credible. At the other end of the spectrum is the **flat character**, one defined by a small number of traits, or that functions as a **stock character**, which is a familiar stereotype—for example, the young, naïve female lover, the scheming revenge-seeker, or the bumbling father figure. A character may be thought of as a **foil** if his or her main function is to reflect something important about a main character.

Castelvetro made his case for the unity of space by drawing attention to "the limitation of the space in which [the play] is acted"; in other words, the theoretical concept and literary convention derive from a practical concern: how many places can one reasonably include in a drama, given the implicit performance text embedded in every play and the necessity of representing those places, live? And what, then, is the significance of the place or places a dramatist chooses to include, especially given that the selections must be limited? Ibsen's *A Doll's House* is set entirely in one room, the living room of the Helmers' apartment, though various other rooms are gestured toward as characters move off stage. Why does Ibsen choose this space—which is both domestic, and yet somehow public—for his exploration of the Helmers' marriage?

The term dramatists and literary critics use to refer to the location of represented action is **setting**, a term also associated with prose narratives, but used in a very specific way for discussions of dramas. The French term **mise en scène** is perhaps a more helpful way to refer to a drama's setting, as it encompasses the scenery, the properties or moveable set pieces, the way everything on stage is arranged, and even the way lighting and sound effects are to be used throughout a performance. The issue of properties (usually called props) is especially interesting, as it is often the case that such items take on **symbolic** meaning, which is not surprising given—again—that there are only so many items a dramatist can reasonably have cluttering up the performance area. Any item that is important enough to be lugged onto a stage thus has the potential to transcend its function as décor—even in a play such as *A Doll's House*, the setting of which is meant to register as a real living room. For example, in Act III, the stage directions inform the reader that, while preparing to open his letter-box, *"Helmer takes his bunch of keys from his pocket and goes into the hall."* It is perfectly realistic that a man wishing to unlock his letter-box would fish keys out of his pocket. Yet Ibsen's choice to represent this action on the stage—which requires that a fake set of keys be made up and carried by the actor playing Torvald Helmer—leads one to ask whether the keys might have any additional or symbolic significance. Might they indicate, for example, the sort of control Helmer holds over his wife?

Another distinguishing convention of the drama is that, unlike a prose or poetry narrative, in which an omniscient narrator or speaker might describe what is happening, in a drama the action must be expressed through what can be physically represented on stage and what the characters in a play say to one another, or to themselves. The term **dialogue**, which comes from the Greek words meaning "through" (dia) and "to speak" (legein), refers to the way conversations between two or more persons on stage work to reveal character and to advance the plot. The drama's formal dependence on dialogue—as opposed to expository or descriptive or figurative writing, such as is used regularly and to great effect in other genres—is often accompanied by explorations within the drama of the power of language. Consider, for example, Moscovitch's play *Essay*, in which the characters deal with the way a footnote in a history textbook becomes the source of a complex power struggle. It is sometimes the case in a drama that only one person is speaking, either in a **monologue** or in a **soliloquy**. Monologues occur when one person is speaking aloud, for an extended length of time, to one or more listeners, while soliloquies are meant to represent a circumstance in which a character talks to himself or herself. In a prose narrative, such internal musing is common and, arguably, most lyric poems represent this same contemplative activity.

In a drama, however, the audience must accept the convention that people do their internal musing aloud, as when, in Act II of *Twelfth Night*, Viola meditates (aloud, in iambic pentameter) on the frailty of women. Another convention of speech used in drama, one that seems to oppose so many of the genre's other conventions, is the **aside**. This is a moment when the spell of mutual pretending is broken and a character directly addresses the audience, with the implicit understanding that the character's words to the audience cannot be heard by anyone else on stage. After Viola swears to Orsino that she—in the guise of Cesario—will help him court Olivia, for example, she then makes an aside to the audience asserting that she wishes Orsino would have her as a wife.

The aside is an example of what is known as "breaking the fourth wall," an expression that references Diderot's assertion about "the large wall." Asides draw attention to the idea that, when an audience is watching a play, they are peeking into a room—a room with one invisible wall—where people are simply going about their business. Other examples of breaking the fourth wall in dramas include the use of prologues or epilogues; the use of a **chorus**, when a group of characters offer commentary on the action; and the inclusion of a song, or even a dance in the middle of the play. In much historical drama, for example Renaissance and Restoration drama, the aside is meant to register as "truth," whereby the character looks through the invisible wall and confesses something genuine to the audience. Contemporary playwrights have often experimented with the convention of character-audience interaction. A kind of opposition to the aside is the notion of **dramatic irony**, a type of irony in which the audience knows more about a particular situation than the characters themselves (an archetypal instance occurs in Shakespeare's *Romeo and Juliet*, when the audience knows that Juliet is not really dead but only drugged, but can only watch helplessly as Romeo poisons himself out of grief).

Drama and Mode

Another important effect of the dramatic text being linked with its implicit performance text is that clues about the play's **mode**—whether the play fits into the subgenre of tragedy, comedy, or something else—can be given very efficiently. As with a film, the drama can make use of both words and aspects of the mise en scène, lighting, and music to set up expectations about the treatment of the subject matter. The idea of mode as a defining trait of a subgenre such as the tragic or comedic play derives from the notion that the same subject can be handled in a variety of ways, and that choices made in the handling will produce different expectations. If, in the first five minutes of a film set in a high school, the audience is faced with grainy images of unhappy teens loitering about the back door and exhausted teachers trying to bring order to unruly classrooms, the audience may reasonably expect a gritty and possibly tragic film about youth. On the other hand, if the opening shots of the high school reveal brightly dressed, laughing teens engaging in back-to-school chatter and hijinks, the audience may reasonably expect a lighthearted and comedic film about youth. The drama has often been crudely considered as being an either/or affair when it comes to mode. Lord Byron summarized it this way: "All tragedies are finished by death, / All comedies are ended by marriage." Aristotle, for his part, saw tragedies as intended to inspire "pity and fear," and comedies as intended to entertain via wit and humour.

Such simplistic divisions do not always make sense. Even the exemplary tragic hero Oedipus doesn't die at the end of Sophocles' play, and some of Shakespeare's romantic comedies, in particular *Measure for Measure* and *The Merchant of Venice*, are not exactly lighthearted (though they do both end with a focus on marriage). Playwrights often make use of the expectations associated with the modes of tragedy or comedy to explore the grey area between the two. For example, in seventeenth- and eighteenth-century France, the idea of tragedy was associated with plays about history or public matters. Such subject matter was considered important enough to warrant serious treatment; the issue of death was not mandatory. In some contemporary tragedies the conventional focus on a hero is set aside, or explicitly challenged. In Arthur Miller's *Death of a Salesman*, Willy Loman is just an ordinary businessman who has a fraught relationship with his sons, and ends up committing suicide. A play such as Ibsen's *A Doll's House* also fits into the mode of tragedy, though it is unclear if the audience is meant to fear or be inspired by Nora's escape from her marriage. Likewise, the comedic mode is made use of in many plays that have nothing to do with marriage. Throughout the Elizabethan and Jacobean periods, both the comedy of humours and the city comedy were popular alternatives to the romantic comedy; both of these subgenres take a satiric view of human behaviour, showing how ordinary humans let the faults in their own nature get the better of them. (Ben Jonson's city comedy *Volpone*, for example, focuses on the greed of various men and the foolish behaviour that greed generates.) In the Restoration period and through the eighteenth century, the **comedy of manners** (exemplified by Sheridan's *The School for Scandal*) was likewise focused on human folly, especially in terms of the way particular characteristics were associated with social class. The **farce** may be defined as a comedy that depicts broadly humourous situations, in which plot devices such as mistaken identities, plans gone awry, and surprise endings take precedent over the subtleties of characterization or thematic development. Farce has a very long history, from the Roman comedies of Plautus—which featured all manner of clever servants, braggart warriors, and disguised lovers—to Michael Frayn's 1982 play *Noises Off*, a somewhat metafictional farce about a theatre company's rehearsals and performance of *Nothing On*, a fictional play chiefly about people trying to get in and out of each others' bedrooms.

One of the most interesting grey areas between tragedy and comedy is the subgenre of the **tragicomedy**. In the classical period, the term was used by Plautus to describe the mixing of low- and high-born characters in a single play. Many of Shakespeare's so-called problem plays might also be thought to fit into the idea of tragicomedy as a catch-all category, whereby the marriages at the end of *A Winter's Tale* don't quite make up for the cruelty of Leontes and the suffering of Hermione. In the more contemporary period, playwrights such as Ibsen, Anton Chekhov, and Sean O'Casey experimented with the idea that everyday existence could be both funny and unhappy, often because a character—for example Chekhov's Uncle Vanya—mistakenly perceives himself or herself to be living a noble life. Many plays associated with the **Theatre of the Absurd** might be considered tragicomedies. A metafictional play such as Pollock's *Blood Relations* is similarly mixed in terms of the expectations it seems to raise, as the playwright uses wit to explore dark or complex themes.

[N.G.]

Henrik Ibsen
1828–1906

Henrik Ibsen's plays, which sought to be true to life and tackled serious moral issues, shocked audiences far more used to the light, diverting works of drama that were common during his era. His influence reached far beyond his native Norway, helping to shape such major English-language playwrights as Bernard Shaw and Arthur Miller.

Ibsen was born to prosperous parents, but the dissolution of his father's business led to the family's exile from the bourgeois circles they had comfortably moved within. After some time working as a director and theatre manager in Norway, Ibsen exiled himself in 1864; thereafter he lived in Italy and then in Germany, where he composed many of his most famous plays. These plays—among them *A Doll's House* (1879), *Ghosts* (1881), and *Hedda Gabler* (1890)—present unflattering portraits of the hypocrisies and expectations of late nineteenth-century society. Ibsen's work from this period often concerns a central character placed under pressure by societal forces such as religion, marriage, or middle-class norms; moreover, we frequently see these characters brought to a moment of crisis by the burden of their own dark secrets or moral failings. Toward the end of his career, Ibsen's emphasis gradually shifted from the examination of social problems to the exploration of psychological complexity in his characters.

Ibsen returned to Norway in 1891, by which time his international reputation as an important, if controversial, playwright was firmly established; Shaw would publish an essay expounding the concept of "Ibsenism" that same year. Writing in 1905, the British theatre critic William Archer observed that "Ibsen sees one side of a case intensely at one moment, and the other side at another moment, with no less intensity." That intensity, whether focused on social or on psychological forces, continues to engage audiences more than a century after Ibsen's death.

A Doll's House[1]

CHARACTERS

Torvald Helmer
Nora, his wife
Dr. Rank
Mrs. Linden[2]
Nils Krogstad
Anna[3]   } *Servants*
Ellen
Ivar   } *The Helmers' children*
Emmy
Bob
A porter.

Scene: Sitting-room in Helmer's house (a flat) in Christiania.[4]
Time: The present day;[5] *Christmastime.*
The action takes place on three consecutive days.

ACT 1

A room furnished comfortably and tastefully, but not expensively. In the background, on the right, a door leads to the hall; to the left another door leads to Helmer's study. Between the two doors a piano. In the middle of the left wall, a door, and nearer the front a window. Near the window a round table with armchairs and a small sofa. In the right wall, somewhat to the back, a door; and against the same wall, further forward, a porcelain stove; in front of it a couple of armchairs and a rocking chair. Between the stove and the side door a small table. Engravings on the walls. A display cabinet with china and small decorative items. A small bookcase filled with showily bound books. Carpet. A fire in the stove. A winter day.

---

1   *A Doll's House* Translated by William Archer, from the Walter H. Baker edition prepared by Edmund Gosse. The translation has been lightly modernized for this anthology by Broadview Press.

2   *Mrs. Linden* Called Linde in Ibsen's original.

3   *Anna* Called Anne-Marie in Ibsen's original.

4   *Christiania* Former name of Oslo, Norway.

5   *present day* I.e., around 1879.

A bell rings in the hall outside. Presently the outer door is heard to open. Then Nora enters, humming contentedly. She is wearing outdoor clothes, and carries several parcels, which she lays on the right-hand table. She leaves the door into the hall open behind her, and a porter is seen outside, carrying a Christmas tree and a basket, which he gives to the maidservant who has opened the door.

NORA. Hide the Christmas tree carefully, Ellen; the children mustn't see it before this evening, when it's lit up. (*To the porter, taking out her purse.*) How much?

PORTER. Fifty øre.[1]

5   NORA. There's a crown. No, keep the change.

(*The porter thanks her and goes. Nora shuts the door. She continues smiling in quiet glee as she takes off her cloak and hat. Then she takes from her pocket a bag of macaroons, and eats one or two. As she does so, she goes on tip-toe to her husband's door and listens.*)

NORA. Yes; he is at home. (*She begins humming again, going to the table on the right.*)

HELMER. (*In his room.*) Is that my lark twittering there?

NORA. (*Busy opening some of her parcels.*) Yes, it is.

HELMER. Is it the squirrel skipping about?

10   NORA. Yes!

HELMER. When did the squirrel get home?

NORA. Just this minute. (*Hides the bag of macaroons in her pocket and wipes her mouth.*) Come here, Torvald, and see what I've bought.

HELMER. Don't disturb me. (*A little later he opens the door and looks in, pen
15   in hand.*) "Bought," did you say? What! All that? Has my little spendthrift been making the money fly again?

NORA. Why, Torvald, surely we can afford to launch out a little now! It's the first Christmas we haven't had to pinch.

HELMER. Come, come; we can't afford to squander money.

20   NORA. Oh yes, Torvald, do let us squander a little—just the least little bit, won't you? You know you'll soon be earning heaps of money.

HELMER. Yes, from New Year's Day. But there's a whole quarter before my first salary is due.

NORA. Never mind; we can borrow in the meantime.

25   HELMER. Nora! (*He goes up to her and takes her playfully by the ear.*) Thoughtless as ever! Supposing I borrowed a thousand crowns today, and you spent

---

1   øre Norwegian currency; one hundred øre equals one *krone* (crown).

it during Christmas week, and that on New Year's Eve a tile blew off the roof and knocked my brains out—

NORA. (*Laying her hand on his mouth.*) Hush! How can you talk so horridly?

HELMER. But supposing it were to happen—what then?

NORA. If anything so dreadful happened, I shouldn't care whether I was in debt or not.

HELMER. But what about the creditors?

NORA. They! Who cares for them? They're only strangers.

HELMER. Nora, Nora! What a woman you are! But seriously, Nora, you know my ideas on these points. No debts! No credit! Home life ceases to be free and beautiful as soon as it is founded on borrowing and debt. We two have held out bravely till now, and we won't give in at the last.

NORA. (*Going to the fireplace.*) Very well—as you like, Torvald.

HELMER. (*Following her.*) Come come; my little lark mustn't let her wings droop like that. What? Is the squirrel pouting there? (*Takes out his purse.*) Nora, what do you think I've got here?

NORA. (*Turning round quickly.*) Money!

HELMER. There! (*Gives her some notes.*) Of course I know all sorts of things are wanted at Christmas.

NORA. (*Counting.*) Ten, twenty, thirty, forty. Oh! Thank you, thank you, Torvald. This will go a long way.

HELMER. I should hope so.

NORA. Yes, indeed, a long way! But come here, and see all I've been buying. And so cheap! Look, here is a new suit for Ivar, and a little sword. Here are a horse and a trumpet for Bob. And here are a doll and a cradle for Emmy. They're only simple; but she'll soon pull them all to pieces. And dresses and neckties for the servants; only I should have got something better for dear old Anna.

HELMER. And what's in that other parcel?

NORA. (*Crying out.*) No, Torvald, you're not to see that until this evening.

HELMER. Oh! Ah! But now tell me, you little rogue, what have you got for yourself?

NORA. For myself? Oh, I don't want anything.

HELMER. Nonsense. Just tell me something sensible you would like to have.

NORA. No. Really I want nothing … Well, listen, Torvald—

HELMER. Well?

NORA. (*Playing with his coat buttons, without looking him in the face.*) If you really want to give me something, you might, you know, you might—

HELMER. Well, well? Out with it!

NORA. (*Quickly.*) You might give me money, Torvald. Only just what you think you can spare; then I can buy something with it later.

HELMER. But, Nora—

NORA. Oh, please do, dear Torvald, please do! Then I would hang the money
70 in lovely gilt paper on the Christmas tree. Wouldn't that be fun?

HELMER. What do they call the birds that are always making the money fly?

NORA. Yes, I know—spendthrifts, of course. But please do as I say, Torvald.
Then I shall have time to think what I want most. Isn't that very sensible,
now?

75 HELMER. (*Smiling.*) Certainly; that is to say, if you really kept the money
I gave you, and really bought yourself something with it. But it all goes
toward housekeeping, and for all sorts of useless things, and then I have
to find more.

NORA. But, Torvald—

80 HELMER. Can you deny it, Nora dear? (*He puts his arm round her.*) It's a sweet
little lark; but it gets through a lot of money. No one would believe how
much it costs a man to keep such a little bird as you.

NORA. For shame! How can you say so? Why, I really save as much as I can.

HELMER. (*Laughing.*) Very true—as much as you can—but you can't.

85 NORA. (*Hums and smiles in quiet satisfaction.*) H'm! You should just know,
Torvald, what expenses we larks and squirrels have.

HELMER. You're a strange little being! Just like your father—always eager
to get hold of money; but the moment you have it, it seems to slip
through your fingers; you never know what becomes of it. Well, one
90 must take you as you are. It's in the blood. Yes, Nora, that sort of thing
is inherited.

NORA. I wish I had inherited many of my father's qualities.

HELMER. And I don't wish you to be anything but just what you are—my
own, sweet little songbird. But I say—it strikes me you look so—so—what
95 can I call it? So suspicious today—

NORA. Do I?

HELMER. You do, indeed. Look me full in the face.

NORA. (*Looking at him.*) Well?

HELMER. (*Threatening with his finger.*) Hasn't the little sweet-tooth been
100 breaking the rules today?

NORA. No! How can you think of such a thing!

HELMER. Didn't she just look in at the confectioner's?

NORA. No, Torvald, really—

HELMER. Not to sip a little jelly?

105 NORA. No, certainly not.

HELMER. Hasn't she even nibbled a macaroon or two?

NORA. No, Torvald, indeed, indeed!

HELMER. Well, well, well; of course I'm only joking.

NORA. (*Goes to the table on the right.*) I shouldn't think of doing what you disapprove of.   110

HELMER. No, I'm sure of that; and, besides, you've given me your word. (*Going towards her.*) Well, keep your little Christmas secrets to yourself, Nora darling. The Christmas tree will bring them all to light, I daresay.

NORA. Have you remembered to ask Doctor Rank?

HELMER. No. But it's not necessary; he'll come as a matter of course. Besides,   115
I shall invite him when he looks in today. I've ordered some fine wine. Nora, you can't think how I look forward to this evening.

NORA. And I too. How the children will enjoy themselves, Torvald!

HELMER. Ah! It's glorious to feel that one has an assured position and ample means. Isn't it delightful to think of?   120

NORA. Oh, it's wonderful!

HELMER. Do you remember last Christmas? For three whole weeks beforehand you shut yourself up every evening till long past midnight to make flowers for the Christmas tree, and all sorts of other marvels that were to have astonished us. I was never so bored in my life.   125

NORA. I did not bore myself at all.

HELMER. (*Smiling.*) And it came to so little after all, Nora.

NORA. Oh! Are you going to tease me about that again? How could I help the cat getting in and spoiling it all?

HELMER. To be sure you couldn't, my poor little Nora. You did your best to   130
amuse us all, and that's the main thing. But, all the same, it's a good thing the hard times are over.

NORA. Oh, isn't it wonderful?

HELMER. Now I needn't sit here boring myself all alone; and you needn't tire your dear eyes and your delicate little fingers—   135

NORA. (*Clapping her hands.*) No, I needn't, need I, Torvald? Oh! It's wonderful to think of! (*Takes his arm.*) And now I'll tell you how I think we ought to manage, Torvald. As soon as Christmas is over—(*The hall doorbell rings.*) Oh, there's a ring! (*Arranging the room.*) That's somebody come to call. How vexing!   140

HELMER. I am not at home to callers; remember that.

ELLEN. (*In the doorway.*) A lady to see you, ma'am.

NORA. Show her in.

ELLEN. (*To Helmer.*) And the doctor is just come, sir.

HELMER. Has he gone into my study?   145

ELLEN. Yes, sir.

(*Helmer goes into his study. Ellen ushers in Mrs. Linden, in travelling clothes, and shuts the door behind her.*)

MRS. LINDEN. (*Timidly and with hesitation.*) How do you do, Nora?

NORA. (*Doubtfully.*) How do you do?

MRS. LINDEN. I daresay you don't recognize me?

150 NORA. No, I don't think—oh yes!—I believe—(*Effusively.*) What! Christina! Is it really you?

MRS. LINDEN. Yes, really I!

NORA. Christina! And to think I didn't know you! But how could I—(*More softly.*) How changed you are, Christina!

155 MRS. LINDEN. Yes, no doubt. In nine or ten years—

NORA. Is it really so long since we met? Yes, so it is. Oh! The last eight years have been a happy time, I can tell you. And now you have come to town? All that long journey in midwinter! How brave of you!

MRS. LINDEN. I arrived by this morning's steamer.

160 NORA. To keep Christmas, of course. Oh, how delightful! What fun we shall have! Take your things off. Aren't you frozen? (*Helping her.*) There, now we'll sit down here cosily by the fire. No, you take the armchair; I'll sit in this rocking chair. (*Seizes her hand.*) Yes, now I can see your dear old face again. It was only at first glance—But you're a little paler, Christina, and 165 perhaps a little thinner.

MRS. LINDEN. And much, much older, Nora.

NORA. Yes, perhaps a little older—not much—ever so little. (*She suddenly stops; seriously.*) Oh! What a thoughtless wretch I am! Here I sit chattering on, and—Dear, dear Christina, can you forgive me!

170 MRS. LINDEN. What do you mean, Nora?

NORA. (*Softly.*) Poor Christina! I forgot, you are a widow?

MRS. LINDEN. Yes, my husband died three years ago.

NORA. I know, I know, I saw it in the papers. Oh! Believe me, Christina, I did mean to write to you; but I kept putting it off, and something always 175 came in the way.

MRS. LINDEN. I can quite understand that, Nora dear.

NORA. No, Christina; it was horrid of me. Oh, you poor darling! How much you must have gone through! And he left you nothing?

MRS. LINDEN. Nothing.

180 NORA. And no children?

MRS. LINDEN. None.

NORA. Nothing, nothing at all?

MRS. LINDEN. Not even a sorrow or a longing to dwell upon.

NORA. (*Looking at her incredulously.*) My dear Christina, how is that possible?

185 MRS. LINDEN. (*Smiling sadly and stroking her hair.*) Oh, it happens so sometimes, Nora.

NORA. So utterly alone. How dreadful that must be! I have three of the loveliest children. I can't show them to you just now; they're out with their nurse. But now you must tell me everything.

MRS. LINDEN. No, no, I want you to tell me— 190

NORA. No, you must begin; I won't be egotistical today. Today, I will think of you only. Oh! I must tell you one thing; but perhaps you've heard of our great stroke of fortune?

MRS. LINDEN. No. What is it?

NORA. Only think! My husband has been made manager of the Joint Stock 195 Bank.

MRS. LINDEN. Your husband! Oh, how fortunate!

NORA. Yes, isn't it? A lawyer's position is so uncertain, you see, especially when he won't touch any business that's the least bit … shady, as of course Torvald won't; and in that I quite agree with him. Oh! You can imagine 200 how glad we are. He is to enter on his new position at the New Year, and then he will have a large salary, and percentages. In future we shall be able to live quite differently—just as we please, in fact. Oh, Christina, I feel so light and happy! It's splendid to have lots of money, and no need to worry about things, isn't it? 205

MRS. LINDEN. Yes, it must be delightful to have what you need.

NORA. No, not only what you need, but heaps of money—heaps!

MRS. LINDEN. (*Smiling.*) Nora, Nora, haven't you learnt reason yet? In our school days you were a shocking little spendthrift!

NORA. (*Quietly smiling.*) Yes, Torvald says I am still. (*Threatens with her fin-* 210 *ger.*) But "Nora, Nora," is not so silly as you all think. Oh! I haven't had the chance to be much of a spendthrift. We have both had to work.

MRS. LINDEN. You too?

NORA. Yes, light needlework—crochet, and embroidery, and things of that sort, (*significantly*) and other work too. You know, of course, that Torvald 215 left the Government service when we were married. He had little chance of promotion, and of course he needed to make more money. But in the first year of our marriage he overworked himself terribly. He had to undertake all sorts of odd jobs, you know, and to work early and late. He couldn't stand it, and fell dangerously ill. Then the doctors declared he must go to 220 the South.

MRS. LINDEN. Yes, you spent a whole year in Italy, didn't you?

NORA. We did. It wasn't easy to manage, I can tell you. It was just after Ivar's birth. But of course we had to go. Oh, it was a delicious journey! And it saved Torvald's life. But it cost a frightful lot of money, Christina. 225

MRS. LINDEN. So I should think.

NORA. Twelve hundred dollars! Four thousand eight hundred crowns! Isn't that a lot of money?

MRS. LINDEN. How lucky you had the money to spend!

230 NORA. I must tell you we got it from father.

MRS. LINDEN. Ah, I see. He died just about that time, didn't he?

NORA. Yes, Christina, just then. And only think! I couldn't go and nurse him! I was expecting little Ivar's birth daily. And then I had my Torvald to attend to. Dear, kind old father! I never saw him again, Christina. Oh! That's

235 the hardest thing I have had to bear since my marriage.

MRS. LINDEN. I know how fond you were of him. And then you went to Italy?

NORA. Yes; we had the money, and the doctors insisted. We started a month later.

240 MRS. LINDEN. And your husband returned completely cured?

NORA. Sound as a bell.

MRS. LINDEN. But—the doctor?

NORA. What about him?

MRS. LINDEN. I thought as I came in your servant announced the doctor—

245 NORA. Oh, yes, Doctor Rank. But he doesn't come as a doctor. He's our best friend, and never lets a day pass without looking in. No, Torvald hasn't had an hour's illness since that time. And the children are so healthy and well, and so am I. (*Jumps up and claps her hands.*) Oh, Christina, Christina, it's so lovely to live and to be happy! Oh! But it's really too horrid of me!

250 Here am I talking about nothing but my own concerns. (*Sits down upon a footstool close to her and lays her arms on Christina's lap.*) Oh! Don't be angry with me! Now just tell me, is it really true that you didn't love your husband? What made you take him?

MRS. LINDEN. My mother was alive then, bedridden and helpless; and I had

255 my two younger brothers to think of. I thought it my duty to accept him.

NORA. Perhaps it was. I suppose he was rich then?

MRS. LINDEN. Very well off, I believe. But his business was uncertain. It fell to pieces at his death, and there was nothing left.

NORA. And then—?

260 MRS. LINDEN. Then I had to fight my way by keeping a shop, a little school, anything I could turn my hand to. The last three years have been one long struggle for me. But now it's over, Nora. My poor mother no longer needs me; she is at rest. And the boys are in business, and can look after themselves.

265 NORA. How free your life must feel!

MRS. LINDEN. No, Nora, only inexpressibly empty. No one to live for. (*Stands up restlessly.*) That is why I couldn't bear to stay any longer in that out-of-

the-way corner. Here it must be easier to find something really worth doing—something to occupy one's thoughts. If I could only get some settled
employment—some office work.   270

NORA. But, Christina, that's so tiring, and you look worn out already. You
should rather go to some health resort and rest.

MRS. LINDEN. (*Going to the window.*) I have no father to give me the money,
Nora.

NORA. (*Rising.*) Oh! Don't be angry with me.   275

MRS. LINDEN. (*Going toward her.*) My dear Nora, don't you be angry with
me. The worst of a position like mine is that it makes one bitter. You have
no one to work for, yet you have to strain yourself constantly. You must
live; and so you become selfish. When I heard of the happy change in your
circumstances—can you believe it?—I rejoiced more on my own account   280
than on yours.

NORA. How do you mean? Ah! I see. You mean Torvald could perhaps do
something for you.

MRS. LINDEN. Yes, I thought so.

NORA. And so he shall, Christina. Just you leave it all to me. I shall lead up   285
to it beautifully, and think of something pleasant to put him in a good
humour! Oh! I should so love to do something for you.

MRS. LINDEN. How good of you, Nora! And doubly good in you, who know
so little of the troubles of life.

NORA. I? I know so little of—?   290

MRS. LINDEN. (*Smiling.*) Ah, well! A little needlework, and so forth. You're
a mere child, Nora.

NORA. (*Tosses her head and paces the room.*) Oh, come, you mustn't be so
patronizing!

MRS. LINDEN. No?   295

NORA. You're like the rest. You all think I'm fit for nothing really serious—

MRS. LINDEN. Well—

NORA. You think I've had no troubles in this weary world.

MRS. LINDEN. My dear Nora, you've just told me all your troubles.

NORA. Pooh—these trifles! (*Softly.*) I haven't told you the great thing.   300

MRS. LINDEN. The great thing? What do you mean?

NORA. I know you look down upon me, Christina; but you've no right to.
You are proud of having worked so hard and so long for your mother?

MRS. LINDEN. I'm sure I don't look down upon anyone, but it's true I'm both
proud and glad when I remember that I was able to make my mother's last   305
days free from care.

NORA. And you're proud to think of what you have done for your brothers,
too.

MRS. LINDEN. Don't I have the right to be?

310 NORA. Yes, surely. But now let me tell you, Christina—I, too, have something to be proud and glad of.

MRS. LINDEN. I don't doubt it. But what do you mean?

NORA. Hush! Not so loud. Only think, if Torvald were to hear! He mustn't—not for anything in the world! No one must know about it, Christina—no

315 one but you.

MRS. LINDEN. What can it be?

NORA. Come over here. (*Draws her beside her on the sofa.*) Yes—I, too, have something to be proud and glad of. *I* saved Torvald's life.

MRS. LINDEN. Saved his life? How?

320 NORA. I told you about our going to Italy. Torvald would have died but for that.

MRS. LINDEN. Yes—and your father gave you the money.

NORA. (*Smiling.*) Yes, so Torvald and everyone believes, but—

MRS. LINDEN. But—?

NORA. Father didn't give us one penny. *I* found the money.

325 MRS. LINDEN. You? All that money?

NORA. Twelve hundred dollars. Four thousand eight hundred crowns. What do you say to that?

MRS. LINDEN. My dear Nora, how did you manage it? Did you win it in the lottery?

330 NORA. (*Contemptuously.*) In the lottery? Pooh! Any fool could have done that!

MRS. LINDEN. Then wherever did you get it from?

NORA. (*Hums and smiles mysteriously.*) H'm; tra-la-la-la!

MRS. LINDEN. Of course you couldn't borrow it.

335 NORA. No? Why not?

MRS. LINDEN. Why, a wife can't borrow without her husband's consent.

NORA. (*Tossing her head.*) Oh! When the wife knows a little of business, and how to set about things, then—

MRS. LINDEN. But, Nora, I don't understand—

340 NORA. Well you needn't. I never said I borrowed the money. Perhaps I got it another way. (*Throws herself back on the sofa.*) I may have got it from some admirer. When one is so—attractive as I am—

MRS. LINDEN. You're too silly, Nora.

NORA. Now I'm sure you're dying of curiosity, Christina—

345 MRS. LINDEN. Listen to me, Nora dear. Haven't you been a little rash?

NORA. (*Sitting upright again.*) Is it rash to save one's husband's life?

MRS. LINDEN. I think it was rash of you, without his knowledge—

NORA. But it would have been fatal for him to know! Can't you understand that? He was never to suspect how ill he was. The doctors came to me

privately and told me that his life was in danger—that nothing could save 350
him but a trip to the South. Do you think I didn't try diplomacy first? I
told him how I longed to have a trip abroad, like other young wives; I wept
and prayed; I said he ought to think of my condition, and indulge me;
and then I hinted that he could borrow the money. But then, Christina,
he almost got angry. He said I was frivolous, and that it was his duty as a 355
husband not to yield to my whims and fancies—so he called them. Very
well, I thought, but saved you must be; and then I found the way to do it.

MRS. LINDEN. And did your husband never learn from your father that the
money was not from him?

NORA. No, never. Father died at that very time. I meant to have told him all 360
about it, and begged him to say nothing. But he was so ill—sadly, it was
not necessary.

MRS. LINDEN. And you have never confessed to your husband?

NORA. Good heavens! What can you be thinking? Tell him, when he has such
a loathing of debt? And besides—how painful and humiliating it would be 365
for Torvald, with his manly self-reliance, to know that he owed anything
to me! It would utterly upset the relation between us; our beautiful, happy
home would never again be what it is.

MRS. LINDEN. Will you never tell him?

NORA. (*Thoughtfully, half-smiling.*) Yes, sometime perhaps—after many years, 370
when I'm—not so pretty. You mustn't laugh at me. Of course I mean when
Torvald is not so much in love with me as he is now; when it doesn't amuse
him any longer to see me skipping about, and dressing up and acting. Then
it might be good to have something in reserve. (*Breaking off.*) Nonsense!
Nonsense! That time will never come. Now, what do you say to my grand 375
secret, Christina? Am I fit for nothing now? You may believe it has cost me
a lot of anxiety. It has not been easy to meet my commitments on time.
You must know, Christina, that in business there are things called install-
ments, and quarterly interest, that are terribly hard to meet. So I had to
pinch a little here and there, wherever I could. I could not save anything 380
out of the housekeeping, for of course Torvald had to live well. And I
couldn't let the children go about badly dressed; all I got for them, I spent
on them, the darlings.

MRS. LINDEN. Poor Nora! So it had to come out of your own necessities.

NORA. Yes, of course. After all, the whole thing was my doing. When Torvald 385
gave me money for clothes, and so on, I never spent more than half of it; I
always bought the simplest things. It's a mercy everything suits me so well;
Torvald never noticed anything. But it was often very hard, Christina dear.
For it's nice to be beautifully dressed. Now, isn't it?

MRS. LINDEN. Indeed it is.
                                                                              390

NORA. Well, and besides that, I made money in other ways. Last winter I was so lucky—I got a heap of copying to do. I shut myself up every evening and wrote far on into the night. Oh, sometimes I was so tired, so tired. And yet it was splendid to work like that and earn money. I almost felt as
395 if I was a man.

MRS. LINDEN. Then how much have you been able to pay off?

NORA. Well, I can't precisely say. It's difficult to keep that sort of business clear. I only know that I paid everything I could scrape together. Sometimes I really didn't know where to turn. (*Smiles.*) Then I used to imagine
400 that a rich old gentleman was in love with me—

MRS. LINDEN. What! What gentleman?

NORA. Oh! Nobody—that he was now dead, and that when his will was opened, there stood in large letters: Pay over at once everything I possess to that charming person, Mrs. Nora Helmer.

405 MRS. LINDEN. But, dear Nora, what gentleman do you mean?

NORA. Dear, dear, can't you understand? There wasn't any old gentleman: it was only what I used to dream and dream when I was at my wits' end for money. But it's all over now—the tiresome old creature may stay where he is for me; I care nothing for him or his will; for now my troubles are over.
410 (*Springing up.*) Oh, Christina, how glorious it is to think of! Free from all cares! Free, quite free. To be able to play and romp about with the children; to have things tasteful and pretty in the house, exactly as Torvald likes it! And then the spring is coming, with the great blue sky. Perhaps then we shall have a short holiday. Perhaps I shall see the sea again. Oh,
415 what a wonderful thing it is to live and to be happy! (*The hall doorbell rings.*)

MRS. LINDEN. (*Rising.*) There's a ring. Perhaps I had better go.

NORA. No, do stay. No one will come here. It's sure to be someone for Torvald.

ELLEN. (*In the doorway.*) If you please, ma'am, there's a gentleman to speak
420 to Mr. Helmer.

NORA. Who is the gentleman?

KROGSTAD. (*In the doorway.*) It is I, Mrs. Helmer. (*Ellen goes. Mrs. Linden starts and turns away to the window.*)

NORA. (*Goes a step towards him, anxiously, half aloud.*) You? What is it? What do you want with my husband?

425 KROGSTAD. Bank business—in a way. I hold a small post in the Joint Stock Bank, and your husband is to be our new chief, I hear.

NORA. Then it is—?

KROGSTAD. Only tiresome business, Mrs. Helmer; nothing more.

NORA. Then will you please go to his study. (*Krogstad goes. She bows indifferently while she closes the door into the hall. Then she goes to the stove and looks to the fire.*)

MRS. LINDEN. Nora—who was that man?   430

NORA. A Mr. Krogstad. Do you know him?

MRS. LINDEN. I used to know him—many years ago. He was in a lawyer's office in our town.

NORA. Yes, so he was.

MRS. LINDEN. How he has changed!   435

NORA. I believe his marriage was unhappy.

MRS. LINDEN. And he is a widower now?

NORA. With a lot of children. There! Now it'll burn up. (*She closes the stove, and pushes the rocking chair a little aside.*)

MRS. LINDEN. His business is not of the most creditable, they say?

NORA. Isn't it? I daresay not. I don't know—But don't let us think of business—it's so tiresome.   440

(*Dr. Rank comes out of Helmer's room.*)

RANK. (*Still in the doorway.*) No, no, I won't keep you. I'll just go and have a chat with your wife. (*Shuts the door and sees Mrs. Linden.*) Oh, I beg your pardon. I am in the way here too.

NORA. No, not in the least. (*Introduces them.*) Doctor Rank—Mrs. Linden.   445

RANK. Oh, indeed; I've often heard Mrs. Linden's name; I think I passed you on the stairs as we came up.

MRS. LINDEN. Yes, I go so very slowly. Stairs try me so much.

RANK. You're not very strong?

MRS. LINDEN. Only overworked.   450

RANK. Ah! Then you have come to town to find rest in recreation.

MRS. LINDEN. I have come to look for employment.

RANK. Is that an approved remedy for overwork?

MRS. LINDEN. One must live, Doctor Rank.

RANK. Yes, that seems to be the general opinion.   455

NORA. Come, Doctor Rank, you know you want to live yourself.

RANK. To be sure I do. However wretched I may be, I want to drag on as long as possible. And my patients all have the same mania. And it's the same with people whose complaint is moral. At this very moment Helmer is talking to such a wreck as I mean.   460

MRS. LINDEN. (*Softly.*) Ah!

NORA. Whom do you mean?

RANK. Oh, a fellow named Krogstad, a man you know nothing about—corrupt to the very core of his character. But even he began by announcing solemnly that he must live.   465

NORA. Indeed? And what did he want with Torvald?

RANK. I have no idea; I only gathered that it was some bank business.

NORA. I didn't know that Krog—that this Mr. Krogstad had anything to do with the bank?

470 RANK. He has some sort of place there. (*To Mrs. Linden.*) I don't know whether, in your part of the country, you have people who go wriggling and snuffing around in search of moral rottenness—whose policy it is to fill good places with men of tainted character whom they can keep under their eye and in their power? The honest men they leave out in the cold.

475 MRS. LINDEN. Well, I suppose the—delicate characters require most care.

RANK. (*Shrugs his shoulders.*) There we have it! It's that notion that makes society a hospital. (*Nora, deep in her own thoughts, breaks into half-stifled laughter and claps her hands.*) What are you laughing at? Have you any idea what society is?

480 NORA. What do I care for your tiresome society. I was laughing at something else—something awfully amusing. Tell me, Doctor Rank, are all the employees at the bank dependent on Torvald now?

RANK. Is that what strikes you as awfully amusing?

NORA. (*Smiles and hums.*) Never mind, never mind! (*Walks about the room.*)

485 Yes, it *is* amusing to think that we—that Torvald has such power over so many people. (*Takes the bag from her pocket.*) Doctor Rank, will you have a macaroon?

RANK. Oh dear, dear—macaroons! I thought they were contraband here.

NORA. Yes, but Christina brought me these.

490 MRS. LINDEN. What! I?

NORA. Oh, well! Don't be frightened. You couldn't possibly know that Torvald had forbidden them. The fact is, he is afraid of me spoiling my teeth. But, oh bother, just for once! That's for you, Doctor Rank! (*Puts a macaroon into his mouth.*) And you, too, Christina. And I will have one at the

495 same time—only a tiny one, or at most two. (*Walks about again.*) Oh dear, I *am* happy! There is only one thing in the world I really want.

RANK. Well; what's that?

NORA. There's something I should so like to say—in Torvald's hearing.

RANK. Then why don't you say it?

500 NORA. Because I daren't, it's so ugly.

MRS. LINDEN. Ugly?

RANK. In that case you'd better not. But to us you might. What is it you would so like to say in Helmer's hearing?

NORA. I should so love to say—"Damn!"[1]

---

1   [Archer's note] "Död og pine," literally "death and torture"; but by usage a comparatively mild oath.

RANK. Are you out of your mind?   505

MRS. LINDEN. Good gracious, Nora!

RANK. Say it. There he is!

NORA. (*Hides the macaroons.*) Hush, hush, hush!

(*Helmer comes out of his room, hat in hand, with his overcoat on his arm.*)

NORA. (*Going toward him.*) Well, Torvald, dear, have you got rid of him?

HELMER. Yes, he's just gone.   510

NORA. May I introduce you? This is Christina, who has come to town—

HELMER. Christina? Pardon me, but I don't know—

NORA. Mrs. Linden, Torvald dear—Christina Linden.

HELMER. (*To Mrs. Linden.*) A school-friend of my wife's, no doubt?

MRS. LINDEN. Yes, we knew each other as girls.   515

NORA. And only think! She has taken this long journey to speak to you.

HELMER. To speak to me!

MRS. LINDEN. Well, not quite—

NORA. You see Christina is tremendously clever at accounts, and she is so
anxious to work under a first-rate man of business in order to learn still   520
more—

HELMER. (*To Mrs. Linden.*) Very sensible indeed.

NORA. And when she heard you were appointed manager—it was tele-
graphed, you know—she started off at once, and—Torvald dear, for my
sake, you must do something for Christina. Now can't you?   525

HELMER. It's not impossible. I presume Mrs. Linden is a widow?

MRS. LINDEN. Yes.

HELMER. And you have already had some experience in office work?

MRS. LINDEN. A good deal.

HELMER. Well then, it is very likely I may be able to find a place for you.   530

NORA. (*Clapping her hands.*) There now! There now!

HELMER. You have come at a lucky moment, Mrs. Linden.

MRS. LINDEN. Oh! How can I thank you—?

HELMER. (*Smiling.*) There's no need. (*Puts his overcoat on.*) But for the present
you must excuse me.   535

RANK. Wait; I'll go with you. (*Fetches his fur coat from the hall and warms it
at the fire.*)

NORA. Don't be long, dear Torvald.

HELMER. Only an hour; not more.

NORA. Are you going too, Christina?

MRS. LINDEN. (*Putting on her cloak and hat.*) Yes, I must start looking for   540
lodgings.

HELMER. Then perhaps we can go together?

NORA. (*Helping her.*) What a pity we haven't a spare room for you, but I'm afraid—

545 MRS. LINDEN. I shouldn't think of troubling you. Goodbye, dear Nora, and thank you for all your kindness.

NORA. Goodbye for a little while. Of course you'll come back this evening. And you, too, Doctor Rank. What! If you're well enough? Of course you'll be well enough. Only wrap up warmly. (*They go out into the hall, talking.*

550 *Outside on the stairs are heard children's voices.*) There they are! There they are! (*She runs to the door and opens it. The nurse Anna enters with the children.*) Come in! Come in! (*Bends down and kisses the children.*) Oh! my sweet darlings! Do you see them, Christina? Aren't they lovely?

RANK. Don't let's stand here chattering in the draught.

555 HELMER. Come, Mrs. Linden; only mothers can stand such a temperature. (*Dr. Rank, Helmer, and Mrs. Linden go down the stairs; Anna enters the room with the children; Nora also, shutting the door.*)

NORA. How fresh and bright you look! And what red cheeks you have! Like apples and roses. (*The children talk low to her during the following.*) Have you had great fun? That's splendid! Oh, really! You've been giving Emmy and Bob a ride on your sledge! Both at once, only think! Why you're quite

560 a man, Ivar. Oh, give her to me a little, Anna. My sweet little dolly! (*Takes the smallest from the nurse and dances with her.*) Yes, yes, mother will dance with Bob too. What! Did you have a game of snowballs? Oh! I wish I'd been there. No, leave them, Anna; I'll take their things off. Oh, yes, let me do it; it's such fun. Go to the nursery; you look frozen. You'll find some hot

565 coffee on the stove. (*The nurse goes into the room on the left. Nora takes off the children's things, and throws them down anywhere, while the children talk to each other and to her.*) Really! A big dog ran after you all the way home? But he didn't bite you? No, dogs don't bite dear little dolly children. Don't peep into those parcels, Ivar. What is it? Wouldn't you like to know? Take care—it'll bite! What! Shall we have a game? What shall we play at? Hide-

570 and-seek? Yes, let's play hide-and-seek. Bob shall hide first. Should I? Yes, let me hide first. (*She and the children play, with laughter and shouting, in the room and the adjacent one to the right. At last Nora hides under the table; the children come rushing in, look for her, but cannot find her, hear her half-choked laughter, rush to the table, lift up the cover and see her. Loud shouts. She creeps out, as though to frighten them. Fresh shouts. Meanwhile there has been a knock at the door leading into the hall. No one has heard it. Now the door is half opened and Krogstad is seen. He waits a little; the game is renewed.*)

KROGSTAD. I beg your pardon, Mrs. Helmer—

NORA. (*With a suppressed cry, turns round and half jumps up.*) Ah! What do you want?

KROGSTAD. Excuse me; the outer door was ajar—somebody must have for- 575
gotten to shut it—

NORA. (*Standing up.*) My husband is not at home, Mr. Krogstad.

KROGSTAD. I know it.

NORA. Then—what do you want here?

KROGSTAD. To say a few words to you. 580

NORA. To me? (*To the children, softly.*) Go in to Anna. What? No, the strange
man won't hurt mamma. When he's gone we'll go on playing. (*She leads
the children into the left-hand room, and shuts the door behind them. Uneasy,
with suspense.*) It's with me you wish to speak?

KROGSTAD. Yes.

NORA. Today? But it's not the first yet— 585

KROGSTAD. No, today is Christmas Eve. It will depend upon yourself whether you have a merry Christmas.

NORA. What do you want? I certainly can't today—

KROGSTAD. Never mind that just now. It's about another matter. You have a
minute to spare? 590

NORA. Oh, yes, I suppose so, although—

KROGSTAD. Good. I was sitting in the restaurant opposite, and I saw your
husband go down the street.

NORA. Well!

KROGSTAD. With a lady. 595

NORA. What then?

KROGSTAD. May I ask if the lady was a Mrs. Linden?

NORA. Yes.

KROGSTAD. Who has just come to town?

NORA. Yes. Today. 600

KROGSTAD. I believe she's an intimate friend of yours?

NORA. Certainly. But I don't understand—

KROGSTAD. I used to know her too.

NORA. I know you did.

KROGSTAD. Ah! You know all about it. I thought as much. Now, frankly, is 605
Mrs. Linden to have a place at the bank?

NORA. How dare you interrogate me in this way, Mr. Krogstad, you, a sub-
ordinate of my husband's? But since you ask you shall know. Yes, Mrs.
Linden is to be employed. And it's I who recommended her, Mr. Krogstad.
Now you know. 610

KROGSTAD. Then my guess was right.

NORA. (*Walking up and down.*) You see one has a little wee bit of influence. It
doesn't follow because one's only a woman that—When one is in a subordinate position, Mr. Krogstad, one ought really to take care not to offend
anybody who—h'm— 615

KROGSTAD. Who has influence?

NORA. Exactly!

KROGSTAD. (*Taking another tone.*) Mrs. Helmer, will you have the kindness to employ your influence on my behalf?

620 NORA. What? How do you mean?

KROGSTAD. Will you be so good as to see that I retain my subordinate position at the bank?

NORA. What do you mean? Who wants to take it from you?

KROGSTAD. Oh, you needn't pretend ignorance. I can very well understand
625   that it cannot be pleasant for your friend to meet me; and I can also understand now for whose sake I am to be hounded out.

NORA. But I assure you—

KROGSTAD. Come now, once for all: there is time yet, and I advise you to use your influence to prevent it.

630 NORA. But, Mr. Krogstad, I have absolutely no influence.

KROGSTAD. None? I thought you just said—

NORA. Of course not in that sense! I! How should I have such influence over my husband?

KROGSTAD. Oh! I know your husband from our college days. I don't think
635   he's firmer than other husbands.

NORA. If you talk disrespectfully of my husband, I must ask you to go.

KROGSTAD. You are bold, madam.

NORA. I am afraid of you no longer. When New Year's Day is over, I shall soon be out of the whole business.

640 KROGSTAD. (*Controlling himself.*) Listen to me, Mrs. Helmer. If need be, I shall fight as though for my life to keep my little place at the bank.

NORA. Yes, so it seems.

KROGSTAD. It's not only for the money; that matters least to me. It's something else. Well, I'd better make a clean breast of it. Of course you know,
645   like everyone else, that some years ago I—got into trouble.

NORA. I think I've heard something of the sort.

KROGSTAD. The matter never came into court, but from that moment all paths were barred to me. Then I took up the business you know about. I was obliged to grasp at something, and I don't think I've been one of the
650   worst. But now I must clear out of it all. My sons are growing up; for their sake I must try to win back as much respectability as I can. This place in the bank was the first step, and now your husband wants to kick me off the ladder, back into the mire.

NORA. But I assure you, Mr. Krogstad, I haven't the power to help you.

655 KROGSTAD. You have not the will; but I can compel you.

NORA. You won't tell my husband that I owe you money!

KROGSTAD. H'm; suppose I were to?

NORA. It would be shameful of you! (*With tears in her voice.*) This secret which is my joy and my pride—that he should learn it in such an ugly, coarse way—and from you! It would involve me in all sorts of unpleasant- ness. 660

KROGSTAD. Only unpleasantness?

NORA. (*Hotly.*) But just do it. It will be worst for you, for then my husband will see what a bad man you are, and then you certainly won't keep your place. 665

KROGSTAD. I asked if it was only domestic unpleasantness you feared?

NORA. If my husband gets to know about it, he will of course pay you off at once, and then we'll have nothing more to do with you.

KROGSTAD. (*Stepping a pace nearer.*) Listen, Mrs. Helmer. Either you have a weak memory, or you don't know much about business. I must make your 670 position clearer to you.

NORA. How so?

KROGSTAD. When your husband was ill, you came to me to borrow twelve hundred dollars.

NORA. I knew nobody else. 675

KROGSTAD. I promised to find you the money—

NORA. And you did find it.

KROGSTAD. I promised to find you the money under certain conditions. You were then so much taken up with your husband's illness, and so eager to have the money for your journey, that you probably did not give much 680 thought to the details. Let me to remind you of them. I promised to find you the amount in exchange for a promissory note which I drew up.

NORA. Yes, and I signed it.

KROGSTAD. Quite right. But then I added a few lines, making your father a security for the debt. Your father was to sign this. 685

NORA. Was to? He did sign it!

KROGSTAD. I had left the date blank. That is to say, your father was himself to date his signature. Do you recollect that?

NORA. Yes, I believe—

KROGSTAD. Then I gave you the paper to send to your father. Is not that so? 690

NORA. Yes.

KROGSTAD. And of course you did so at once? For within five or six days you brought me back the paper, signed by your father, and I gave you the money.

NORA. Well! Haven't I made my payments punctually? 695

KROGSTAD. Fairly—yes. But to return to the point. You were in great trouble at the time, Mrs. Helmer.

NORA. I was indeed!

KROGSTAD. Your father was very ill, I believe?

700 NORA. He was on his deathbed.

KROGSTAD. And died soon after?

NORA. Yes.

KROGSTAD. Tell me, Mrs. Helmer, do you happen to recollect the day of his death? The day of the month, I mean?

705 NORA. Father died on the 29th of September.

KROGSTAD. Quite correct. I have made inquiries, and here comes in the remarkable point—(*produces a paper*) which I cannot explain.

NORA. What remarkable point? I don't know—

KROGSTAD. The remarkable point, madam, that your father signed this paper
710   three days after his death!

NORA. What! I don't understand—

KROGSTAD. Your father died on the 29th of September. But look here, he has dated his signature October 2nd! Isn't that remarkable, Mrs. Helmer? (*Nora is silent.*) Can you explain it? (*Nora continues to be silent.*) It is note-
715   worthy too that the words "October 2nd" and the year are not in your father's handwriting, but in one which I believe I know. Well, this may be explained; your father may have forgotten to date his signature, and some-body may have added the date at random before the fact of your father's death was known. There is nothing wrong in that. Everything depends
720   on the signature. Of course it is genuine, Mrs. Helmer? It was really your father who with his own hand wrote his name here?

NORA. (*After a short silence throws her head back and looks defiantly at him.*) No. I wrote father's name there.

KROGSTAD. Ah! Are you aware, madam, that that is a dangerous admission?

NORA. Why? You'll soon get your money.

725 KROGSTAD. May I ask you one more question? Why did you not send the paper to your father?

NORA. It was impossible. Father was ill. If I had asked him for his signature, I should have had to tell him why I wanted the money; but he was so ill I really could not tell him that my husband's life was in danger. It was
730   impossible.

KROGSTAD. Then it would have been better to have given up your tour.

NORA. No, I couldn't do that; my husband's life depended on that journey. I couldn't give it up.

KROGSTAD. And did you not consider that you were playing me false?

735 NORA. That was nothing to me. I didn't care in the least about you. I couldn't endure you for all the cruel difficulties you made, although you knew how ill my husband was.

KROGSTAD. Mrs. Helmer, you have evidently no clear idea what you have really done. But I can assure you it was nothing more and nothing worse that made me an outcast from society.   740

NORA. You! You want me to believe that you did a brave thing to save your wife's life?

KROGSTAD. The law takes no account of motives.

NORA. Then it must be a very bad law.

KROGSTAD. Bad or not, if I lay this document before a court of law you will   745 be condemned according to law.

NORA. I don't believe that. Do you mean to tell me that a daughter has no right to spare her dying father anxiety? That a wife has no right to save her husband's life? I don't know much about the law, but I'm sure that, somewhere or another, *that* is allowed. And you don't know that—you, a lawyer!   750 You must be a bad one, Mr. Krogstad.

KROGSTAD. Possibly. But business—such business as ours—I do understand. You believe that? Very well; now do as you please. But this I can tell you, that if I am flung into the gutter a second time, you shall keep me company. (*Bows and goes out through hall.*)   755

NORA. (*Stands a while thinking, then throws her head back.*) Never! He wants to frighten me. I'm not so foolish as that. (*Begins folding the children's clothes. Pauses.*) But—? No, it's impossible. I did it for love!

CHILDREN. (*At the door, left.*) Mamma, the strange man is gone now.

NORA. Yes, yes, I know. But don't tell anyone about the strange man. Do you   760 hear? Not even papa!

CHILDREN. No, mamma; and now will you play with us again?

NORA. No, no, not now.

CHILDREN. Oh, do, mamma; you know you promised.

NORA. Yes, but I can't just now. Run to the nursery; I've so much to do. Run   765 along, run along, and be good, my darlings! (*She pushes them gently into the inner room, and closes the door behind them. Sits on the sofa, embroiders a few stitches, but soon pauses.*) No! (*Throws down the work, rises, goes to the hall door and calls out.*) Ellen, bring in the Christmas tree! (*Goes to table, left, and opens the drawer; again pauses.*) No, it's quite impossible!

ELLEN. (*With Christmas tree.*) Where shall I stand it, ma'am?   770

NORA. There, in the middle of the room.

ELLEN. Shall I bring in anything else?

NORA. No, thank you, I have all I want.

(*Ellen, having put down the tree, goes out.*)

NORA. (*Busy dressing the tree.*) There must be a candle here, and flowers there.—The horrid man! Nonsense, nonsense! There's nothing in it. The   775

Christmas tree shall be beautiful. I will do everything to please you, Torvald; I'll sing and dance, and—

(*Enter Helmer by the hall door, with bundle of documents.*)

NORA. Oh! You're back already?

HELMER. Yes. Has anybody been here?

780 NORA. Here? No.

HELMER. Curious! I saw Krogstad come out of the house.

NORA. Did you? Oh, yes, by the bye, he was here for a minute.

HELMER. Nora, I can see by your manner that he has been asking you to put in a good word for him.

785 NORA. Yes.

HELMER. And you were to do it as if of your own accord? You were to say nothing to me of his having been here! Didn't he suggest that too?

NORA. Yes, Torvald, but—

HELMER. Nora, Nora! And you could condescend to that! To speak to such
790   a man, to make him a promise! And then to tell me an untruth about it!

NORA. An untruth!

HELMER. Didn't you say nobody had been here? (*Threatens with his finger.*) My little bird must never do that again. A songbird must never sing false notes. (*Puts his arm round her.*) That's so, isn't it? Yes, I was sure of it. (*Lets
795   her go.*) And now we'll say no more about it. (*Sits down before the fire.*) Oh, how cosy and quiet it is here. (*Glances into his documents.*)

NORA. (*Busy with the tree, after a short silence.*) Torvald.

HELMER. Yes.

NORA. I'm looking forward so much to the Stenborgs' fancy ball the day after
800   tomorrow.

HELMER. And I'm incredibly curious to see what surprise you have in store for me.

NORA. Oh, it's too tiresome!

HELMER. What is?

805 NORA. I can't think of anything good. Everything seems so foolish and meaningless.

HELMER. Has little Nora made that discovery?

NORA. (*Behind his chair, with her arms on the back.*) Are you very busy, Torvald?

810 HELMER. Well—

NORA. What papers are those?

HELMER. Bank business.

NORA. Already?

HELMER. I got the retiring manager to let me make some necessary changes

in the staff, and so forth. This will occupy Christmas week. Everything will   815
be straight by the New Year.

NORA. Then that's why that poor Krogstad—

HELMER. H'm.

NORA. (*Still leaning over the chair back, and slowly stroking his hair.*) If you
hadn't been so very busy I should have asked you a great, great favour,   820
Torvald.

HELMER. What can it be? Let's hear it.

NORA. Nobody has such exquisite taste as you. Now, I should so love to look
nice at the fancy ball. Torvald dear, couldn't you take me in hand, and
settle what I'm to be, and arrange my costume for me?   825

HELMER. Aha! So my wilful little woman's at a loss, and making signals of
distress.

NORA. Yes *please*, Torvald. I can't get on without you.

HELMER. Well, well, I'll think it over, and we'll soon hit upon something.

NORA. Oh, how good that is of you! (*Goes to the tree again; pause.*) How well   830
the red flowers show. Tell me, was it anything so very dreadful this Krogstad got into trouble about?

HELMER. Forgery, that's all. Don't you know what that means?

NORA. Mayn't he have been driven to it by need?

HELMER. Yes, or like so many others, done it out of heedlessness. I'm not so   835
hard-hearted as to condemn a man absolutely for a single fault.

NORA. No, surely not, Torvald!

HELMER. Many a man can retrieve his character if he owns his crime and
takes the punishment.

NORA. Crime?   840

HELMER. But Krogstad didn't do that; he resorted to tricks and dodges; and
it's that that has corrupted him.

NORA. Do you think that—?

HELMER. Just think how a man with that on his conscience must be always
lying and shamming. Think of the mask he must wear even toward his own   845
wife and children. It's worst for the children, Nora!

NORA. Why?

HELMER. Because such a dust cloud of lies poisons and contaminates the whole
air of a home. Every breath the children draw contains some germ of evil.

NORA. (*Closer behind him.*) Are you sure of that!   850

HELMER. As a lawyer, my dear, I've seen it often enough. Nearly all cases of
early corruption may be traced to lying mothers.

NORA. Why—mothers?

HELMER. It generally comes from the mother's side, but of course the father's
influence may act in the same way. And this Krogstad has been poison-   855

ing his own children for years with his life of lies and hypocrisy—that's why I say he is morally ruined. (*Stretches out his hands toward her.*) So my sweet little Nora must promise not to plead his cause. Shake hands upon it. Come, come, what's this? Give me your hand. That's right. Then it's a bargain. I assure you it would have been impossible for me to work with him. It gives me a positive sense of physical discomfort to come in contact with such people. (*Nora snatches her hand away, and moves to the other side of the Christmas tree.*)

NORA. How warm it is here; and I have so much to do.

HELMER. Yes, and I must try to get some of these papers looked through before dinner; and I'll think over your costume, too. And perhaps I may even find something to hang in gilt paper on the Christmas tree! (*Lays his hand on her head.*) My precious little songbird. (*He goes into his room and shuts the door behind him.*)

NORA. (*Softly, after a pause.*) It can't be—It's impossible. It must be impossible!

ANNA. (*At the door, left.*) The little ones are begging so prettily to come to mamma.

NORA. No, no, don't let them come to me! Keep them with you, Anna.

ANNA. Very well, ma'am. (*Shuts the door.*)

NORA. (*Pale with terror.*) Corrupt my children! Poison my home! (*Short pause. She raises her head.*) It's not true. It can never, never be true.

ACT 2

The same room. In the corner, beside the piano, stands the Christmas tree, stripped, and the candles burnt out. Nora's cloak and hat lie on the sofa. Nora discovered walking about restlessly. She stops by the sofa, and takes up cloak, then lays it down again.

NORA. There's somebody coming. (*Goes to hall door; listens.*) Nobody; nobody is likely to come today, Christmas day; nor tomorrow either. But perhaps—(*Opens the door and looks out.*) No, nothing in the letter box; quite empty. (*Comes forward.*) Stuff and nonsense! Of course he only meant to frighten me. There's no fear of any such thing. It's impossible! Why, I have three little children.

(*Enter Anna, from the left with a large cardboard box.*)

ANNA. At last I've found the box with the fancy dress.

NORA. Thanks; put it down on the table.

ANNA. (*Does so.*) But I'm afraid it's in terrible disarray.

NORA. Oh, I wish I could tear it into a hundred thousand pieces.

ANNA. Oh, no. It can easily be put to rights—just a little patience.

NORA. I'll go and get Mrs. Linden to help me.

ANNA. Going out again! In such weather as this! You'll catch cold, ma'am, and be ill.

NORA. Worse things might happen—What are the children doing?   15

ANNA. They're playing with their Christmas presents, poor little dears; but—

NORA. Do they often ask for me?

ANNA. You see they've been so used to having their mamma with them.

NORA. Yes, but, Anna, in future I can't have them so much with me.

ANNA. Well, little children get used to anything.   20

NORA. Do you think they do? Do you believe they would forget their mother if she went quite away?

ANNA. Gracious me! Quite away?

NORA. Tell me, Anna—I've so often wondered about it—how could you bring yourself to give your child up to strangers?   25

ANNA. I had to when I came as nurse to my little Miss Nora.

NORA. But how could you make up your mind to it?

ANNA. When I had the chance of such a good place? A poor girl who's been in trouble must take what comes. That wicked man did nothing for me.

NORA. But your daughter must have forgotten you.   30

ANNA. Oh, no, ma'am, that she hasn't. She wrote to me both when she was confirmed[1] and when she was married.

NORA. (*Embracing her.*) Dear old Anna—you were a good mother to me when I was little.

ANNA. My poor little Nora had no mother but me.   35

NORA. And if my little ones had nobody else, I'm sure you would—nonsense, nonsense! (*Opens the box.*) Go in to the children. Now I must—Tomorrow you shall see how beautiful I'll be.

ANNA. I'm sure there will be no one at the ball so beautiful as my Miss Nora. (*She goes into the room on the left.*)

NORA. (*Takes the costume out of the box, but soon throws it down again.*) Oh,   40 if I dared go out. If only nobody would come. If only nothing would happen here in the meantime. Rubbish; nobody will come. Only not to think. What a delicious muff! Beautiful gloves, beautiful gloves! Away with it all—away with it all! One, two, three, four, five, six—(*With a scream.*) Ah, there they come—(*Goes toward the door, then stands undecidedly.*)   45

(*Mrs. Linden enters from hall where she has taken off her things.*)

---

1   *confirmed* Fully admitted into the Christian church after affirming religious faith; confirmation ceremonies are most often held for older children or teenagers.

NORA. Oh, it's you, Christina. There's nobody else there? How delightful of
you to come.

MRS. LINDEN. I hear you called at my lodgings.

NORA. Yes, I was just passing. I do so want you to help me. Let us sit here on
50   the sofa—like so. Tomorrow evening there's to be a fancy ball at Consul
Stenborg's, who lives upstairs, and Torvald wants me to appear as a Nea-
politan fisher girl, and dance the tarantella; I learnt it at Capri.[1]

MRS. LINDEN. I see—quite a performance!

NORA. Yes, Torvald wishes me to. Look, this is the costume; Torvald had it
55   made for me in Italy. But now it is all so torn, I don't know—

MRS. LINDEN. Oh! We'll soon set that to rights. It's only the trimming that's
got loose here and there. Have you a needle and thread? Ah! Here's the
very thing.

NORA. Oh, how kind of you.

60   MRS. LINDEN. So you're to be in costume tomorrow, Nora? I'll tell you
what—I shall come in for a moment to see you in all your glory. But I've
quite forgotten to thank you for the pleasant evening yesterday.

NORA. (*Rises and walks across the room.*) Oh! Yesterday, it didn't seem so
pleasant as usual. You should have come a little sooner, Christina. Torvald
65   certainly has the art of making a home bright and beautiful.

MRS. LINDEN. You, too, I should think, or you wouldn't be your father's
daughter. But tell me—is Doctor Rank always as depressed as he was yesterday?

NORA. No, yesterday it was particularly striking. You see he has a terrible ill-
70   ness. He has spinal consumption,[2] poor fellow. They say his father led a
terrible life—kept mistresses and all sorts of things—so the son has been
sickly from his childhood, you understand.

MRS. LINDEN. (*Lets her sewing fall into her lap.*) Why, my darling Nora, how
do you learn such things?

75   NORA. (*Walking.*) Oh! When one has three children one has visits from wom-
en who know something about medicine—and they talk of this and that.

MRS. LINDEN. (*Goes on sewing—a short pause.*) Does Doctor Rank come here
every day?

NORA. Every day. He's been Torvald's friend from boyhood, and he's a good
80   friend of mine too. Doctor Rank is quite one of the family.

---

1   *tarantella* Italian folkdance. It was thought that the bite of a tarantula caused "tarantism,"
an irrepressible urge to dance, which an afflicted person could supposedly cure by dancing the tarantella until he or she was too tired to continue; *Capri* Italian island near
Naples.

2   *spinal consumption* Pott's disease, a form of tuberculosis that can cause severe curvature of
the spine and other health problems.

MRS. LINDEN.   But tell me—is he quite sincere? I mean, doesn't he like to say
    flattering things to people?

NORA.   On the contrary. Why should you think so?

MRS. LINDEN.   When you introduced us yesterday he declared he had often
    heard my name, but I noticed your husband had no notion who I was.   85
    How could Doctor Rank—?

NORA.   Yes, he was quite right, Christina. You see, Torvald loves me so in-
    describably, he wants to have me all to himself, as he says. When we were
    first married he was almost jealous if I even mentioned one of the people
    at home, so naturally I let it alone. But I often talk to Doctor Rank about   90
    the old times, for he likes to hear about them.

MRS. LINDEN.   Listen to me, Nora! You're still a child in many ways. I am
    older than you, and have had more experience. I'll tell you something: you
    ought to get clear of all the whole affair with Dr. Rank.

NORA.   What affair?   95

MRS. LINDEN.   You were talking yesterday of a rich admirer who was to find
    you money—

NORA.   Yes, one who never existed, worse luck. What then?

MRS. LINDEN.   Has Doctor Rank money?

NORA.   Yes, he has.   100

MRS. LINDEN.   And nobody to provide for?

NORA.   Nobody. But—?

MRS. LINDEN.   And he comes here every day?

NORA.   Yes, every day.

MRS. LINDEN.   I should have thought he'd have acted in better taste.   105

NORA.   I don't understand you.

MRS. LINDEN.   Don't pretend, Nora. Do you suppose I don't guess who lent
    you the twelve hundred dollars?

NORA.   Are you out of your senses? You think *that*! A friend who comes here
    every day! How painful that would be!   110

MRS. LINDEN.   Then it really is not him?

NORA.   No, I assure you. It never for a moment occurred to me. Besides, at
    that time he had nothing to lend; he came into his property afterward.

MRS. LINDEN.   Well, I believe that was lucky for you, Nora dear.

NORA.   No, really, it would never have struck me to ask Dr. Rank. But I'm   115
    certain that if I did—

MRS. LINDEN.   But of course you never would?

NORA.   Of course not. It's inconceivable that it should ever be necessary. But
    I'm quite sure that if I spoke to Doctor Rank—

MRS. LINDEN.   Behind your husband's back?   120

NORA.   I must get out of the other thing; that's behind his back too. I must
    get out of that.

MRS. LINDEN. Yes, yes, I told you so yesterday; but—

NORA. (*Walking up and down.*) A man can manage these things much better than a woman.

MRS. LINDEN. One's own husband, yes.

NORA. Nonsense. (*Stands still.*) When everything is paid, one gets back the paper?

MRS. LINDEN. Of course.

NORA. And can tear it into a hundred thousand pieces, and burn it, the nasty, filthy thing!

MRS. LINDEN. (*Looks at her fixedly, lays down her work, and rises slowly.*) Nora, you're hiding something from me.

NORA. Can you see that in my face?

MRS. LINDEN. Something has happened since yesterday morning. Nora, what is it?

NORA. (*Going toward her.*) Christina (*listens*)—Hush! There's Torvald coming home. Here, go into the nursery. Torvald cannot bear to see dressmaking. Let Anna help you.

MRS. LINDEN. (*Gathers some of the things together.*) Very well, but I shan't go away until you've told me all about it. (*She goes out to the left as Helmer enters from the hall.*)

NORA. (*Runs to meet him.*) Oh! How I've been longing for you to come, Torvald dear.

HELMER. Was the dressmaker here?

NORA. No, Christina. She is helping me with my costume. You'll see how nice I shall look.

HELMER. Yes, wasn't that a lucky thought of mine?

NORA. Splendid. But isn't it good of me, too, to have given in to you?

HELMER. (*Takes her under the chin.*) Good of you! To give in to your own husband? Well, well, you little madcap, I know you don't mean it. But I won't disturb you. I daresay you want to try on your dress.

NORA. And you are going to work, I suppose?

HELMER. Yes. (*Shows her bundle of papers.*) Look here. (*Goes toward his room.*) I've just come from the bank.

NORA. Torvald.

HELMER. (*Stopping.*) Yes?

NORA. If your little squirrel were to beg you for something so prettily—

HELMER. Well?

NORA. Would you do it?

HELMER. I must know first what it is.

NORA. The squirrel would jump about and play all sorts of tricks if you would only be nice and kind.

HELMER. Come, then, out with it.

NORA. Your lark would twitter from morning till night—

HELMER. Oh, that she does in any case. 165

NORA. I'll be an elf and dance in the moonlight for you, Torvald.

HELMER. Nora—you can't mean what you were hinting at this morning?

NORA. (*Coming nearer.*) Yes, Torvald, I beg and implore you.

HELMER. Have you really the courage to begin that again?

NORA. Yes, yes, for my sake, you must let Krogstad keep his place at the bank. 170

HELMER. My dear Nora, it's his place I intend for Mrs. Linden.

NORA. Yes, that's so good of you. But instead of Krogstad, you could dismiss some other clerk.

HELMER. Why, this is incredible obstinacy! Because you thoughtlessly prom- ised to put in a word for him, I am to— 175

NORA. It's not that, Torvald. It's for your own sake. This man writes for the most slanderous newspapers; you said so yourself. He can do you such a lot of harm. I'm terribly afraid of him.

HELMER. Oh, I understand; it's old recollections that are frightening you.

NORA. What do you mean? 180

HELMER. Of course you're thinking of your father.

NORA. Yes, of course. Only think of the shameful things wicked people used to write about father. I believe they'd have got him dismissed if you hadn't been sent to look into the thing and been kind to him and helped him.

HELMER. My dear Nora, between your father and me there is all the differ- 185 ence in the world. Your father was not altogether unimpeachable. I am; and I hope to remain so.

NORA. Oh, no one knows what wicked men can hit upon. We could live so happily now, in our cosy, quiet home, you and I and the children, Torvald! That's why I beg and implore you— 190

HELMER. And it's just by pleading his cause that you make it impossible for me to keep him. It's already known at the bank that I intend to dismiss Krogstad. If it were now reported that the new manager let himself be turned round his wife's little finger—

NORA. What then? 195

HELMER. Oh, nothing! So long as a wilful woman can have her way I am to make myself the laughingstock of everyone, and make people think I de- pend on all kinds of outside influence? Take my word for it, I should soon feel the consequences. And besides, there's one thing that makes Krogstad impossible for me to work with. 200

NORA. What thing?

HELMER. I could perhaps have overlooked his shady character in a pinch—

NORA. Yes, couldn't you, Torvald?

HELMER. And I hear he is good at his work. But the fact is, he was a college
chum of mine—there was one of those rash friendships between us that
one so often repents of later. I don't mind confessing it—he calls me by
my first name, and he insists on doing it even when others are present. He
delights in putting on airs of familiarity—Torvald here, Torvald there! I assure you it's most painful to me. He would make my position at the bank
perfectly unendurable.

NORA. Torvald, you're not serious?

HELMER. No? Why not?

NORA. That's such a petty reason.

HELMER. What! Petty! Do you consider me petty?

NORA. No, on the contrary, Torvald dear and that's just why—

HELMER. Never mind; you call my motives petty; then I must be petty too.
Petty! Very well. Now we'll put an end to this once for all. (*Goes to the door
into the hall and calls.*) Ellen!

NORA. What do you want?

HELMER. (*Searching among his papers.*) To settle the thing. (*Ellen enters.*)
There, take this letter, give it to a messenger. See that he takes it at once.
The address is on it. Here is the money.

ELLEN. Very well. (*Goes with the letter.*)

HELMER. (*Arranging papers.*) There, Madam Obstinacy!

NORA. (*Breathless.*) Torvald—what was in that letter?

HELMER. Krogstad's dismissal.

NORA. Call it back again, Torvald! There is still time. Oh, Torvald, get it back
again! For my sake, for your own, for the children's sake! Do you hear,
Torvald? Do it. You don't know what that letter may bring upon us all.

HELMER. Too late.

NORA. Yes, too late.

HELMER. My dear Nora, I forgive your anxiety, though it's anything but
flattering to me. Why should I be afraid of a lowlife scribbler's spite? But
I forgive you all the same, for it's a proof of your great love for me. (*Takes
her in his arms.*) That's how it should be, my own dear Nora. Let what
will happen—when the time comes, I shall have strength and courage
enough. You shall see, my shoulders are broad enough to bear the whole
burden.

NORA. (*Terror-struck.*) What do you mean by that?

HELMER. The whole burden, I say.

NORA. (*With decision.*) That you shall never, never do.

HELMER. Very well, then we'll share it, Nora, as man and wife. (*Petting her.*)
Are you satisfied now? Come, come, come, don't look like a scared dove. It
is all nothing—just fancy. Now you must play the tarantella through, and

practise the tambourine. I shall sit in my inner room and shut both doors,   245
so that I shall hear nothing. You can make as much noise as you please.
(*Turns round in doorway.*) And when Rank comes, just tell him where I'm
to be found. (*He nods to her, and goes with his papers into his room, closing
the door.*)

NORA. (*Bewildered with terror, stands as though rooted to the ground, and whispers.*) He would do it. Yes, he would do it. He would do it, in spite of all
the world. No, never that, never, never! Anything rather than that! Oh, for   250
some way of escape! What to do! (*Hall bell rings.*) Anything rather than
that—anything, anything! (*Nora draws her hands over her face, pulls herself
together, goes to the door and opens it. Rank stands outside hanging up his
overcoat. During the following, it grows dark.*)

NORA. Good afternoon, Doctor Rank, I knew you by your ring. But you
mustn't go to Torvald now. I believe he's busy.

RANK. And you?   255

NORA. Oh, you know very well I've always time for you.

RANK. Thank you. I shall avail myself of your kindness as long as I can!

NORA. What do you mean? As long as you can?

RANK. Yes. Does that frighten you?

NORA. I think it's an odd expression. Do you expect anything to happen?   260

RANK. Something I've long been prepared for, but I didn't think it would
come so soon.

NORA. (*Seizing his arm.*) What is it, Doctor Rank? You must tell me.

RANK. (*Sitting down by the stove.*) I am running downhill. There's no help
for it.   265

NORA. (*Draws a long breath of relief.*) It's *you*?

RANK. Who else should it be? Why lie to oneself? I'm the most wretched
of all my patients, Mrs. Helmer. I have been auditing my life-account—
bankrupt! Before a month is over I shall lie rotting in the churchyard.

NORA. Oh! What an ugly way to talk.   270

RANK. The thing itself is so confoundedly ugly, you see. But the worst of it is,
so many other ugly things have to be gone through first. There is only one
last investigation to be made, and when that is over I shall know exactly
when the breakdown will begin. There's one thing I want to say to you:
Helmer's delicate nature shrinks with such disgust from all that is horrible;   275
I will not have him in my sickroom.

NORA. But, Doctor Rank—

RANK. I won't have him, I say—not on any account! I shall lock my door
against him. As soon as I have ascertained the worst, I shall send you my
visiting card with a black cross on it, and then you will know that the final   280
horror has begun.

NORA. Why, you're perfectly unreasonable today. And I did so want you to be in a really good humour.

RANK. With death staring me in the face? And to suffer thus for another's sin! Where's the justice of it? And in every family you can see some such inexorable retribution—

NORA. (*Stopping her ears.*) Nonsense, nonsense; now cheer up.

RANK. Well, after all, the whole thing's only worth laughing at. My poor innocent spine must do penance for my father's wild oats.

NORA. (*At table, left.*) I suppose he was too fond of asparagus and Strasbourg paté, wasn't he?

RANK. Yes; and truffles.

NORA. Yes, truffles, to be sure. And oysters,[1] I believe?

RANK. Yes, oysters; oysters, of course.

NORA. And then all the port and champagne. It's sad that all these good things should attack the spine.

RANK. Especially when the luckless spine attacked never had the good of them.

NORA. Yes, that's the worst of it.

RANK. (*Looks at her searchingly.*) H'm—

NORA. (*A moment later.*) Why did you smile?

RANK. No; it was you that laughed.

NORA. No; it was you that smiled, Doctor Rank.

RANK. (*Standing up.*) You're more of a rogue than I thought.

NORA. I'm in such a crazy mood today.

RANK. So it seems.

NORA. (*With her hands on his shoulders.*) Dear, dear Doctor Rank, death shall not take you away from Torvald and me.

RANK. Oh, you'll easily get over the loss. The absent are soon forgotten.

NORA. (*Looks at him anxiously.*) Do you think so?

RANK. People make fresh ties, and then—

NORA. Who will make fresh ties?

RANK. You and Helmer will, when I'm gone. You yourself are already on your way to it, it seems to me. What was that Mrs. Linden doing here yesterday?

NORA. Oh! You're surely not jealous of Christina?

RANK. Yes, I am. She will be my successor in this house. When I'm gone, this woman will perhaps—

NORA. Hush! Not so loud; she is in there.

RANK. Today as well? You see!

---

1 *I suppose ... oysters* Asparagus, Strasbourg paté, truffles, and oysters are all foods commonly thought to be aphrodisiacs.

NORA. Only to put my costume in order—how unreasonable you are! (*Sits* 320
on *sofa.*) Now do be good, Doctor Rank. Tomorrow you shall see how
beautifully I dance; and then you may fancy that I am doing it all to please
you—and of course Torvald as well. (*Takes various things out of box.*) Doctor Rank, sit here, and I'll show you something.

RANK. (*Sitting.*) What is it? 325

NORA. Look here. Look!

RANK. Silk stockings.

NORA. Flesh-coloured. Aren't they lovely? Oh, it's so dark here now, but tomorrow—No, no, no, you must only look at the feet. Oh, well, I suppose
you may look at the rest too. 330

RANK. H'm—

NORA. What are you looking so critical about? Do you think they won't fit me?

RANK. I can't possibly have any valid opinion on that point.

NORA. (*Looking at him a moment.*) For shame! (*Hits him lightly on the ear
with the stockings.*) Take that. (*Rolls them up again.*) 335

RANK. And what other wonders am I to see?

NORA. You shan't see any more, for you don't behave nicely. (*She hums a little
and searches among the things.*)

RANK. (*After a short silence.*) When I sit here gossiping with you, I simply
can't imagine what would have become of me if I had never entered this
house. 340

NORA. (*Smiling.*) Yes, I think you do feel at home with us.

RANK. (*More softly—looking straight before him.*) And now to have to leave
it all—

NORA. Nonsense. You shan't leave us.

RANK. (*In the same tone.*) And not to be able to leave behind the slightest 345
token of gratitude; scarcely even a passing regret—nothing but an empty
place, that can be filled by the first comer.

NORA. And if I were to ask for—? No—

RANK. For what?

NORA. For a great proof of your friendship. 350

RANK. Yes? Yes?

NORA. No, I mean—for a very, very great service.

RANK. Would you really for once make me so happy?

NORA. Oh! You don't know what it is.

RANK. Then tell me. 355

NORA. No, I really can't; it's far, far too much—not only a service, but help
and advice besides—

RANK. So much the better. I can't think what you can mean. But go on. Don't
you trust me?

360 NORA. As I trust no one else. I know you are my best and truest friend. So I will tell you. Well then, Doctor Rank, you must help me to prevent something. You know how deeply, how wonderfully Torvald loves me; he would not hesitate a moment to give his very life for my sake.

RANK. (*Bending towards her.*) Nora, do you think he is the only one who—

365 NORA. (*With a slight start.*) Who—?

RANK. Who would gladly give his life for you?

NORA. (*Sadly.*) Oh!

RANK. I have sworn that you shall know it before I—go. I should never find a better opportunity—Yes, Nora, now you know it; and now you know too

370 that you can trust me as you can no one else.

NORA. (*Standing up, simply and calmly.*) Let me pass, please.

RANK. (*Makes way for her, but remains sitting.*) Nora—

NORA. (*In the doorway.*) Ellen, bring the lamp. (*Crosses to the stove.*) Oh, dear, Doctor Rank, that was too bad of you.

375 RANK. (*Rising.*) That I have loved you as deeply as—anyone else? Was that too bad of me?

NORA. No, but that you should tell me so. It was so unnecessary—

RANK. What do you mean? Did you know—?

(*Ellen enters with the lamp; sets it on the table and goes out again.*)

RANK. Nora—Mrs. Helmer—I ask you, did you know?

380 NORA. Oh, how can I tell what I knew or didn't know. I really can't say— How could you be so clumsy, Doctor Rank? It was all so nice!

RANK. Well, at any rate, you know now that I am at your service, soul and body. And now, go on.

NORA. (*Looking at him.*) Go on—now?

385 RANK. I beg you to tell me what you want.

NORA. I can tell you nothing now.

RANK. Yes, yes! You mustn't punish me in that way. Let me do for you whatever a man can.

NORA. You can really do nothing for me now. Besides, I really want no help.

390 You'll see it was only my fancy. Yes, it must be so. Of course! (*Sits in the rocking chair smiling at him.*) You're a nice person, Doctor Rank. Aren't you ashamed of yourself now that the lamp's on the table?

RANK. No, not exactly. But perhaps I ought to go—forever.

NORA. No, indeed you mustn't. Of course you must come and go as you've

395 always done. You know very well that Torvald can't do without you.

RANK. Yes, but you?

NORA. Oh, you know I always like to have you here.

RANK. That's just what led me astray. You're a riddle to me. It has often seemed to me as if you liked being with me almost as much as being with Helmer.   400

NORA. Yes, don't you see? There are people one loves, and others one likes to talk to.

RANK. Yes—there's something in that.

NORA. When I was a girl I naturally loved papa best. But it always delighted me to steal into the servants' room. In the first place they never lectured   405 me, and in the second it was such fun to hear them talk.

RANK. Oh, I see; then it's their place I have taken?

NORA. (*Jumps up and hurries towards him.*) Oh, my dear Doctor Rank, I don't mean that. But you understand, with Torvald it's the same as with papa—

(*Ellen enters from the hall.*)

ELLEN. Please, ma'am—(*Whispers to Nora, and gives her a card.*)   410

NORA. (*Glances at the card.*) Ah! (*Puts it in her pocket.*)

RANK. Anything wrong?

NORA. No, not in the least. It's only—it's my new costume—

RANK. Why, it's there.

NORA. Oh, that one, yes. But it's another that—I ordered it—Torvald   415 mustn't know—

RANK. Aha! So that's the great secret.

NORA. Yes, of course. Do just go to him; he's in the inner room; do keep him as long as you can.

RANK. Make yourself easy; he shan't escape. (*Goes into Helmer's room.*)   420

NORA. (*To Ellen.*) Is he waiting in the kitchen?

ELLEN. Yes, he came up the back stair—

NORA. Didn't you tell him I was engaged?

ELLEN. Yes, but it was no use.

NORA. He won't go away?   425

ELLEN. No, ma'am, not until he has spoken to you.

NORA. Then let him come in, but quietly. And, Ellen—say nothing about it; it's a surprise for my husband.

ELLEN. Oh, yes, ma'am, I understand—(*She goes out.*)

NORA. It's coming! It's coming after all. No, no, no, it can never be; it shall   430 not! (*She goes to Helmer's door and slips the bolt. Ellen opens the hall door for Krogstad, and shuts it after him. He wears a travelling coat, high boots, and a fur cap.*)

NORA. Speak quietly; my husband is at home.

KROGSTAD. All right. I don't care.

NORA. What do you want.

KROGSTAD. A little information.   435

NORA. Be quick, then. What is it?

KROGSTAD. You know I've got my dismissal.

NORA. I could not prevent it, Mr. Krogstad. I fought for you to the last, but it was no good.

440 KROGSTAD. Does your husband care for you so little? He knows what I can bring upon you, and yet he dares—

NORA. How can you think I would tell him?

KROGSTAD. I knew very well you hadn't. It wasn't like my friend Torvald Helmer to show so much courage—

445 NORA. Mr. Krogstad, be good enough to speak respectfully of my husband.

KROGSTAD. Certainly, with all due respect. But since you're so anxious to keep the matter secret, I suppose you're a little clearer than yesterday as to what you have done.

NORA. Clearer than you could ever make me.

450 KROGSTAD. Yes, such a bad lawyer as I—

NORA. What is it you want?

KROGSTAD. Only to see how you're getting on, Mrs. Helmer. I've been thinking about you all day. Even a mere moneylender, a newspaper hack, a—in short, a creature like me—has a little bit of what people call "heart."

455 NORA. Then show it; think of my little children.

KROGSTAD. Did you and your husband think of mine? But enough of that. I only wanted to tell you that you needn't take this matter too seriously. I shall not prosecute you for the present.

NORA. No, surely not. I knew you would not.

460 KROGSTAD. The whole thing can be settled quite quietly. Nobody need know. It can remain among us three.

NORA. My husband must never know.

KROGSTAD. How can you prevent it? Can you pay off the debt?

NORA. No, not at once.

465 KROGSTAD. Or have you any means of raising the money in the next few days?

NORA. None that I will make use of.

KROGSTAD. And if you had it would be no good to you now. If you offered me ever so much ready money, you should not get back your IOU.

470 NORA. Tell me what you want to do with it.

KROGSTAD. I only want to keep it, to have it in my possession. No outsider shall hear anything of it. So, if you've got any desperate scheme in your head—

NORA. What if I have?

475 KROGSTAD. If you should think of leaving your husband and children—

NORA. What if I do?

KROGSTAD. Or if you should think of—something worse—

NORA. How do you know that?

KROGSTAD. Put all that out of your head.

NORA. How did you know what I had in my mind? 480

KROGSTAD. Most of us think of *that* at first. I thought of it, too; but I had not the courage—

NORA. (*Voicelessly.*) Nor I.

KROGSTAD. (*Relieved.*) No, you don't, you haven't the courage either, have you? 485

NORA. I haven't, I haven't.

KROGSTAD. Besides, it would be very silly—once the first storm is over—I have a letter in my pocket for your husband—

NORA. Telling him everything?

KROGSTAD. Sparing you as much as possible. 490

NORA. (*Quickly.*) He must never have that letter. Tear it up. I will get the money somehow.

KROGSTAD. Pardon me, Mrs. Helmer, but I believe I told you—

NORA. Oh, I'm not talking about the money I owe you. Tell me how much you demand from my husband—I'll get it. 495

KROGSTAD. I demand no money from your husband.

NORA. What *do* you demand then?

KROGSTAD. I'll tell you. I want to regain my footing in the world. I want to rise, and your husband shall help me to do it. For the last eighteen months my record has been spotless; I've been in bitter need all the time, but I was 500 content to fight my way up, step by step. Now, I've been thrust down, and I won't be satisfied with merely being allowed to sneak back again. I want to rise, I tell you. I must get into the bank again, in a higher position than before. Your husband shall create a place for me—

NORA. He will never do that! 505

KROGSTAD. He will do it; I know him—he won't dare to refuse! And when I'm in, you'll soon see! I shall be the manager's right hand. It won't be Torvald Helmer, but Nils Krogstad, that manages the Joint Stock Bank.

NORA. That will never be.

KROGSTAD. Perhaps you'll—? 510

NORA. *Now* I have the courage for it.

KROGSTAD. Oh, you don't frighten me! A sensitive, petted creature like you—

NORA. You shall see, you shall see!

KROGSTAD. Under the ice, perhaps? Down in the cold, black water? And next spring to come up again, ugly, hairless, unrecognizable— 515

NORA. You can't frighten me.

KROGSTAD. Nor you me. People don't do that sort of thing, Mrs. Helmer. And, after all, what good would it be? I have your husband in my pocket all the same.

520 NORA. Afterward? When I am no longer—

KROGSTAD. You forget, your reputation remains in my hands! (*Nora stands speechless and looks at him.*) Well, now you are prepared. Do nothing foolish. As soon as Helmer has received my letter I shall expect to hear from him. And remember that it is your husband himself who has forced me

525 back again onto such paths. That I will never forgive him. Goodbye, Mrs. Helmer. (*Goes through hall. Nora hurries to the door, opens it a little, and listens.*)

NORA. He's going. He is not putting the letter into the box. No, no, it would be impossible. (*Opens the door farther and farther.*) What's that? He's standing still, not going downstairs. Is he changing his mind? Is he—? (*A letter falls into the box. Krogstad's footsteps are heard gradually receding down the

530 stair. Nora utters a suppressed shriek; pause.*) In the letterbox! (*Slips shrinkingly up to the hall door.*) There it lies—Torvald, Torvald—now we are lost!

(*Mrs. Linden enters from the left with the costume.*)

MRS. LINDEN. There, I think it's all right now. Shall we just try it on?

NORA. (*Hoarsely and softly.*) Christina, come here.

MRS. LINDEN. (*Throws dress on sofa.*) What's the matter? You look quite

535 aghast.

NORA. Come here. Do you see that letter? There, see—through the glass of the letterbox.

MRS. LINDEN. Yes, yes, I see it.

NORA. That letter is from Krogstad—

540 MRS. LINDEN. Nora—it was Krogstad who lent you the money!

NORA. Yes, and now Torvald will know everything.

MRS. LINDEN. Believe me, Nora, it's the best thing for both of you.

NORA. You don't know all yet. I have forged a name—

MRS. LINDEN. Good heavens!

545 NORA. Now, listen to me, Christina; you shall bear me witness.

MRS. LINDEN. What do you mean? Witness? What am I to—?

NORA. If I should go out of my mind—it might easily happen—

MRS. LINDEN. Nora!

NORA. Or if anything else should happen to me—so that I couldn't be here

550 myself—!

MRS. LINDEN. Now, Nora, you're quite beside yourself!

NORA. In case anyone wanted to take it all upon himself—the whole blame—you understand—

MRS. LINDEN. Yes, but how can you think—

NORA. You shall bear witness that it's not true, Christina. I'm not out of my   555
mind at all; I know quite well what I'm saying; and I tell you nobody else
knew anything about it; I did the whole thing, I myself. Don't forget that.

MRS. LINDEN. I won't forget. But I don't understand what you mean—

NORA. Oh, how should you? It's the miracle coming to pass.

MRS. LINDEN. The miracle?   560

NORA. Yes, the miracle. But it's so terrible, Christina; it mustn't happen for
anything in the world.

MRS. LINDEN. I will go straight to Krogstad and talk to him.

NORA. Don't; he will do you some harm.

MRS. LINDEN. Once he would have done anything for me.   565

NORA. He?

MRS. LINDEN. Where does he live?

NORA. Oh, how should I know—? Yes; (*feels in her pocket*) here's his card. But
the letter, the letter!

HELMER. (*Knocking outside.*) Nora!   570

NORA. (*Shrieks in terror.*) What is it? What do you want?

HELMER. Don't be frightened, we're not coming in; you've bolted the door.
Are you trying on your dress?

NORA. Yes, yes, I'm trying it on. It suits me so well, Torvald.

MRS. LINDEN. (*Who has read the card.*) Then he lives close by here?   575

NORA. Yes, but it's no use now. The letter is actually in the box.

MRS. LINDEN. And your husband has the key?

NORA. Always.

MRS. LINDEN. Krogstad must demand his letter back, unread. He must make
some excuse—   580

NORA. But this is the very time when Torvald generally—

MRS. LINDEN. Prevent him. Keep him occupied. I'll come back as quickly as
I can. (*She goes out quickly through the hall door.*)

NORA. (*Opens Helmer's door and peeps in.*) Torvald!

HELMER. Well, now may one come back into one's own room? Come, Rank,   585
we'll have a look—(*In the doorway.*) But how's this?

NORA. What, Torvald dear?

HELMER. Rank led me to expect a grand dressing-up.

RANK. (*In the doorway.*) So I understood. I suppose I was mistaken.

NORA. No, no one shall see me in my glory till tomorrow evening.   590

HELMER. Why, Nora dear, you look so tired. Have you been practising too
hard?

NORA. No, I haven't practised at all yet.

HELMER. But you'll have to—

595   NORA. Yes, it's absolutely necessary. But, Torvald, I can't get on without your help. I've forgotten everything.

HELMER. Oh, we shall soon freshen it up again.

NORA. Yes, do help me, Torvald. You must promise me—Oh, I'm so nervous about it. Before so many people—this evening you must give yourself up

600   entirely to me. You mustn't do a stroke of work! Now promise, Torvald dear!

HELMER. I promise. All this evening I will be your slave. Little helpless thing! But, by the bye, I must first—(*Going to hall door.*)

NORA. What do you want there?

605   HELMER. Only to see if there are any letters.

NORA. No, no, don't do that, Torvald.

HELMER. Why not?

NORA. Torvald, I beg you not to. There are none there.

HELMER. Let me just see. (*Is going. Nora, at the piano, plays the first bars of the tarantella.*)

610   HELMER. (*At the door, stops.*) Aha!

NORA. I can't dance tomorrow if I don't rehearse with you first.

HELMER. (*Going to her.*) Are you really so nervous, dear Nora?

NORA. Yes, dreadfully! Let me rehearse at once. We have time before dinner. Oh! Do sit down and accompany me, Torvald dear; direct me, as you usu-

615   ally do.

HELMER. With all the pleasure in life, if you wish it. (*Sits at piano. Nora snatches the tambourine out of the box, and hurriedly drapes herself in a long multi-coloured shawl; then, with a bound, stands in the middle of the floor.*)

NORA. Now play for me! Now I'll dance! (*Helmer plays and Nora dances. Rank stands at the piano behind Helmer and looks on.*)

HELMER. (*Playing.*) Slower! Slower!

NORA. Can't do it slower.

620   HELMER. Not so violently, Nora.

NORA. I must! I must!

HELMER. (*Stops.*) Nora—that'll never do.

NORA. (*Laughs and swings her tambourine.*) Didn't I tell you so?

RANK. Let me accompany her.

625   HELMER. (*Rising.*) Yes, do—then I can direct her better. (*Rank sits down to the piano and plays. Nora dances more and more wildly. Helmer stands by the stove and addresses frequent corrections to her. She seems not to hear. Her hair breaks loose, and falls over her shoulders. She does not notice it, but goes on dancing. Mrs. Linden enters and stands spellbound in the doorway.*)

MRS. LINDEN. Ah!

NORA. (*Dancing.*) We're having such fun here, Christina!

HELMER. Why, Nora dear, you're dancing as if it were a matter of life and
   death.

NORA. So it is.   630

HELMER. Rank, stop! This is absolute madness. Stop, I say! (*Rank stops playing, and Nora comes to a sudden standstill. Helmer going toward her.*) I
   couldn't have believed it. You've positively forgotten all I taught you.

NORA. (*Throws tambourine away.*) You see for yourself.

HELMER. You really do need teaching.   635

NORA. Yes, you see how much I need it. You must practise with me up to the
   last moment. Will you promise me, Torvald?

HELMER. Certainly, certainly.

NORA. Neither today nor tomorrow must you think of anything but me. You
   mustn't open a single letter—mustn't look at the letterbox!   640

HELMER. Ah, you're still afraid of that man—

NORA. Oh yes, yes, I am.

HELMER. Nora, I can see it in your face—there's a letter from him in the box.

NORA. I don't know, I believe so. But you're not to read anything now; nothing ugly must come between us until it's all over.   645

RANK. (*Softly to Helmer.*) You mustn't contradict her.

HELMER. (*Putting his arm around her.*) The child shall have her own way. But
   tomorrow night, when the dance is over—

NORA. Then you will be free.

   (*Ellen appears in doorway, right.*)

ELLEN. Dinner is ready, ma'am.   650

NORA. We'll have some champagne, Ellen!

ELLEN. Yes, ma'am. (*Goes out.*)

HELMER. Dear me! Quite a feast.

NORA. Yes, and we'll keep it up till morning. (*Calling out.*) And macaroons,
   Ellen—plenty—just this once.   655

HELMER. (*Seizing her hands.*) Come, come, don't let us have this wild excitement! Be my own little lark again.

NORA. Oh, yes I will. But now go into the dining room; and you too, Doctor
   Rank. Christina, you must help me to do up my hair.

RANK. (*Softly, as they go.*) There is nothing going on? Nothing—I mean— 660

HELMER. Oh no, nothing of the kind. It's merely this babyish anxiety I was
   telling you about. (*They go out to the right.*)

NORA. Well?

MRS. LINDEN. He's gone out of town.

NORA. I saw it in your face.   665

MRS. LINDEN. He comes back tomorrow evening. I left a note for him.

NORA. You shouldn't have done that. Things must take their course. After all, there's something glorious in waiting for the miracle.

MRS. LINDEN. What are you waiting for?

670 NORA. Oh, you can't understand. Go to them in the dining room; I'll come in a moment. (*Mrs. Linden goes into the dining room; Nora stands for a moment as though collecting her thoughts; then looks at her watch.*) Five. Seven hours till midnight. Then twenty-four hours till the next midnight. Then the tarantella will be over. Twenty-four and seven? Thirty-one hours to

675 live.

(*Helmer appears at the door, right.*)

HELMER. What's become of my little lark?

NORA. (*Runs to him with open arms.*) Here she is!

ACT 3

The same room. The table with the chairs around it is in the middle. A lamp lit on the table. The door to the hall stands open. Dance music is heard from the floor above. Mrs. Linden sits by the table, and turns the pages of a book absently. She tries to read, but seems unable to fix her attention; she frequently listens and looks anxiously toward the hall door.

MRS. LINDEN. (*Looks at her watch.*) Still not here; and the time's nearly up. If only he hasn't—(*Listens again.*) Ah, there he is—(*She goes into the hall and opens the outer door; soft footsteps are heard on the stairs; she whispers:*) Come in; there's no one here.

5 KROGSTAD. (*In the doorway.*) I found a note from you at my house. What does it mean?

MRS. LINDEN. I must speak with you.

KROGSTAD. Indeed? And in this house?

MRS. LINDEN. I could not see you at my rooms. They have no separate en-

10 trance. Come in; we are quite alone. The servants are asleep and the Helmers are at the ball upstairs.

KROGSTAD. (*Coming into room.*) Ah! So the Helmers are dancing this evening? Really?

MRS. LINDEN. Yes. Why not?

15 KROGSTAD. Quite right. Why not?

MRS. LINDEN. And now let us talk a little.

KROGSTAD. Have we anything to say to each other?

MRS. LINDEN. A great deal.

KROGSTAD. I should not have thought so.

20 MRS. LINDEN. Because you have never really understood me.

KROGSTAD. What was there to understand? The most natural thing in the world—a heartless woman throws a man over when a better match offers itself.

MRS. LINDEN. Do you really think me so heartless? Do you think I broke with you lightly?

KROGSTAD. Did you not?

MRS. LINDEN. Do you really think so?

KROGSTAD. If not, why did you write me that letter?

MRS. LINDEN. Was it not best? Since I had to break with you, was it not right that I should try to put an end to your love for me?

KROGSTAD. (*Pressing his hands together.*) So that was it? And all this—for the sake of money!

MRS. LINDEN. You ought not to forget that I had a helpless mother and two little brothers. We could not wait for you, Nils, as your prospects then stood.

KROGSTAD. Did that give you the right to discard me for another?

MRS. LINDEN. I don't know. I've often asked myself whether I did right.

KROGSTAD. (*More softly.*) When I had lost you the very ground seemed to sink from under my feet. Look at me now. I am a shipwrecked man clinging to a wreck.

MRS. LINDEN. Rescue may be at hand.

KROGSTAD. It was at hand, but then you stood in the way.

MRS. LINDEN. Without my knowledge, Nils. I did not know till today that it was you I was to replace at the bank.

KROGSTAD. Well, I take your word for it. But now you do know, do you mean to give way?

MRS. LINDEN. No, for that would not help you.

KROGSTAD. Oh, help, help! I should do it whether it helped or not.

MRS. LINDEN. I have learnt prudence. Life and bitter necessity have schooled me.

KROGSTAD. And life has taught me not to trust fine speeches.

MRS. LINDEN. Then life has taught you a very sensible thing. But deeds you will trust?

KROGSTAD. What do you mean?

MRS. LINDEN. You said you were a shipwrecked man, clinging to a wreck.

KROGSTAD. I have good reason to say so.

MRS. LINDEN. I am a shipwrecked woman clinging to a wreck. I have no one to care for.

KROGSTAD. You made your own choice.

MRS. LINDEN. I had no choice.

KROGSTAD. Well, what then?

MRS. LINDEN. Nils, what if we two shipwrecked people could join hands?

KROGSTAD. What!

MRS. LINDEN. Suppose we lashed the wrecks together?

65 KROGSTAD. Christina!

MRS. LINDEN. What do you think brought me to town?

KROGSTAD. Had you any thought of me?

MRS. LINDEN. I must have work, or I can't live. All my life, as long as I can remember, I have worked; work has been my one great joy. Now I stand 70 quite alone in the world, so terribly aimless and forsaken. There is no happiness in working for oneself. Nils, give me somebody and something to work for.

KROGSTAD. No, no, that can never be. It's simply a woman's romantic notion of self-sacrifice.

75 MRS. LINDEN. Have you ever found me romantic?

KROGSTAD. Would you really—? Tell me, do you know my past?

MRS. LINDEN. Yes.

KROGSTAD. And do you know what people say of me?

MRS. LINDEN. Did you not say just now that with me you would have been 80 another man?

KROGSTAD. I am sure of it.

MRS. LINDEN. Is it too late?

KROGSTAD. Christina, do you know what you are doing? Yes, you do; I see it in your face. Have you the courage?

85 MRS. LINDEN. I need someone to tend, and your children need a mother. You need me, and I—I need you. Nils, I believe in your better self. With you I fear nothing.

KROGSTAD. (*Seizing her hands.*) Thank you—thank you, Christina. Now I shall make others see me as you do. Ah, I forgot—

90 MRS. LINDEN. (*Listening.*) Hush! The tarantella! Go, go!

KROGSTAD. Why? What is it?

MRS. LINDEN. Don't you hear the dancing overhead? As soon as that is over they will be here.

KROGSTAD. Oh yes, I'll go. But it's too late now. Of course you don't know 95 the step I have taken against the Helmers?

MRS. LINDEN. Yes, Nils, I do know.

KROGSTAD. And yet you have the courage to—

MRS. LINDEN. I know what lengths despair can drive a man to.

KROGSTAD. Oh, if I could only undo it!

100 MRS. LINDEN. You can. Your letter is still in the box.

KROGSTAD. Are you sure?

MRS. LINDEN. Yes, but—

KROGSTAD. (*Looking to her searchingly.*) Ah, now I understand. You want to save your friend at any price. Say it outright—is that your idea?

MRS. LINDEN. Nils, a woman who has once sold herself for the sake of others does not do so again. 105

KROGSTAD. I will demand my letter back again.

MRS. LINDEN. No, no.

KROGSTAD. Yes, of course. I'll wait till Helmer comes; I'll tell him to give it back to me—that it's only about my dismissal—that I don't want it read. 110

MRS. LINDEN. No, Nils, you must not recall the letter.

KROGSTAD. But tell me, wasn't that just why you got me to come here?

MRS. LINDEN. Yes, in my first terror. But a day has passed since then, and in that day I have seen incredible things in this house. Helmer must know everything; there must be an end to this unhappy secret. These two must 115 come to a full understanding. They can't possibly go on with all these shifts and concealments.

KROGSTAD. Very well, if you want to risk it. But one thing I can do, and at once—

MRS. LINDEN. (*Listening.*) Make haste! Go, go! The dance is over; we are not 120 safe another moment.

KROGSTAD. I'll wait for you in the street.

MRS. LINDEN. Yes, do; you must see me home.

KROGSTAD. I never was so happy in all my life! (*Krogstad goes, by the outer door. The door between the room and the hall remains open.*)

MRS. LINDEN. (*Setting furniture straight and getting her outdoor things together.*) What a change! What a change! To have someone to work for; a 125 home to make happy. I shall have to set to work in earnest. I wish they would come. (*Listens.*) Ah, here they are! I must get my things on. (*Takes bonnet and cloak. Helmer's and Nora's voices are heard outside; a key is turned in the lock, and Helmer drags Nora almost by force into the hall. She wears the Italian costume with a large black shawl over it. He is in evening dress and wears a black domino.[1]*)

NORA. (*Still struggling with him in the doorway.*) No, no, no; I won't go in! I want to go upstairs again; I don't want to leave so early!

HELMER. But, my dearest girl— 130

NORA. Oh, please, please, Torvald, only one hour more.

HELMER. Not one minute more, Nora dear; you know what we agreed! Come, come in; you are catching cold here. (*He leads her gently into the room in spite of her resistance.*)

MRS. LINDEN. Good evening.

---

1   *domino* Hooded cloak worn with a mask during masquerades.

135 NORA. Christina!

HELMER. What, Mrs. Linden, you here so late!

MRS. LINDEN. Yes, pardon me! I did so want to see Nora in her costume!

NORA. Have you been sitting here waiting for me?

MRS. LINDEN. Yes; unfortunately I came too late. You had already gone up-
140   stairs, and I couldn't go away without seeing you.

HELMER. (*Taking Nora's shawl off.*) Well then, just look at her! I think she's
    worth looking at. Isn't she lovely, Mrs. Linden?

MRS. LINDEN. Yes, I must say—

HELMER. Isn't she exquisite? Everyone said so. But she is dreadfully obstinate,
145   dear little creature. What's to be done with her? Just think, I almost had
    to force her away.

NORA. Oh, Torvald, you'll be sorry someday you didn't let me stay, if only
    for one half hour.

HELMER. There! You hear her, Mrs. Linden? She dances her tarantella with
150   wild applause, and well she deserved it, I must say—though there was,
    perhaps, a little too much nature in her rendering of the idea—more than
    was, strictly speaking, artistic. But never mind—she was a great success,
    and that's the main thing. Ought I to let her stay after that—to weaken the
    impression? Not in the least. I took my sweet little Capri girl—my capri-
155   cious little Capri girl, I might say—under my arm; a rapid turn round the
    room, a curtsey to all sides, and—as they say in novels—the lovely appari-
    tion vanished! An exit should always be effective, Mrs. Linden, but I can't
    get Nora to see it. By Jove, it's warm here. (*Throws his domino on a chair
    and opens the door to his room.*) What! No light here? Oh, of course. Excuse
160   me—(*Goes in and lights candles.*)

NORA. (*Whispers breathlessly.*) Well?

MRS. LINDEN. (*Softly.*) I have spoken to him.

NORA. And—?

MRS. LINDEN. Nora—you must tell your husband everything—

165 NORA. (*Almost voiceless.*) I knew it!

MRS. LINDEN. You have nothing to fear from Krogstad, but you must speak
    out.

NORA. I shall not speak!

MRS. LINDEN. Then the letter will.

170 NORA. Thank you, Christina. Now I know what I have to do. Hush!

HELMER. (*Coming back.*) Well, Mrs. Linden, have you admired her?

MRS. LINDEN. Yes, and now I'll say goodnight.

HELMER. What, already? Does this knitting belong to you?

MRS. LINDEN. (*Takes it.*) Yes, thanks; I was nearly forgetting it.

175 HELMER. Then you do knit?

MRS. LINDEN. Yes.

HELMER. Do you know, you ought to embroider instead?

MRS. LINDEN. Indeed! Why?

HELMER. Because it's so much prettier. Look now! You hold the embroidery
in the left hand so, and then work the needle with the right hand, in a   180
long, easy curve, don't you?

MRS. LINDEN. Yes, I suppose so.

HELMER. But knitting is always ugly. Look now, your arms close to your
sides, and the needles going up and down—there's something Chinese
about it—They really gave us splendid champagne tonight.   185

MRS. LINDEN. Well, goodnight, Nora, and don't be obstinate any more.

HELMER. Well said, Mrs. Linden!

MRS. LINDEN. Goodnight, Mr. Helmer.

HELMER. (*Going with her to the door.*) Goodnight, goodnight; I hope you'll
get safely home. I should be glad to—but really you haven't far to go.   190
Goodnight, goodnight! (*She goes; Helmer shuts the door after her and comes
down again.*) At last we've got rid of her: she's an awful bore.

NORA. Aren't you very tired, Torvald?

HELMER. No, not in the least.

NORA. Nor sleepy?   195

HELMER. Not a bit. I feel particularly lively. But you? You do look tired and
sleepy.

NORA. Yes, very tired. I shall soon sleep now.

HELMER. There, you see. I was right after all not to let you stay longer.

NORA. Oh, everything you do is right.   200

HELMER. (*Kissing her forehead.*) Now my lark is speaking like a reasonable
being. Did you notice how jolly Rank was this evening?

NORA. Was he? I had no chance to speak to him.

HELMER. Nor I, much; but, I haven't seen him in such good spirits for a long
time. (*Looks at Nora a little, then comes nearer to her.*) It's splendid to be   205
back in our own home, to be quite alone together! Oh, you enchanting
creature!

NORA. Don't look at me that way, Torvald.

HELMER. I am not to look at my dearest treasure? At the loveliness that is
mine, mine only, wholly and entirely mine?   210

NORA. (*Goes to the other side of the table.*) You mustn't say these things to me
this evening.

HELMER. (*Following.*) I see you have the tarantella still in your blood—and
that makes you all the more enticing. Listen! the other people are going
now. (*More softly.*) Nora—soon the whole house will be still.   215

NORA. I hope so.

HELMER. Yes, don't you, Nora darling? When we're among strangers do you know why I speak so little to you, and keep so far away, and only steal a glance at you now and then—do you know why I do it? Because I am fan-
220 cying that we love each other in secret, that I am secretly betrothed to you, and that no one dreams there is anything between us.

NORA. Yes, yes, yes. I know all your thoughts are with me.

HELMER. And then, when we have to go, and I put the shawl about your smooth, soft shoulders, and this glorious neck of yours, I imagine you are
225 my bride, that our wedding is just over, that I am bringing you for the first time to my home, and that I am alone with you for the first time, quite alone with you, in your quivering loveliness! All this evening I was longing for you, and you only. When I watched you swaying and whirling in the tarantella—my blood boiled—I could endure it no longer, and that's why
230 I made you come home with me so early.

NORA. Go now, Torvald. Go away from me. I won't have all this.

HELMER. What do you mean? Ah! I see you're teasing me! "Won't! Won't!" Am I not your husband? (*A knock at the outer door.*)

NORA. (*Starts.*) Did you hear?

235 HELMER. (*Going toward the hall.*) Who's there?

RANK. (*Outside.*) It's I; may I come in for a moment?

HELMER. (*In a low tone, annoyed.*) Oh! What can he want? (*Aloud.*) Wait a moment. (*Opens door.*) Come, it's nice of you to give us a look in.

RANK. I thought I heard your voice, and that put it into my head. (*Looks
240 round.*) Ah! This dear old place! How cosy you two are here!

HELMER. You seemed to find it pleasant enough upstairs, too.

RANK. Exceedingly. Why not? Why shouldn't one get all one can out of the world? All one can for as long as one can. The wine was splendid—

HELMER. Especially the champagne.

245 RANK. Did you notice it? It's incredible the quantity I managed to get down.

NORA. Torvald drank plenty of champagne too.

RANK. Did he?

NORA. Yes, and it always puts him in such spirits.

RANK. Well, why shouldn't one have a jolly evening after a well-spent day?

250 HELMER. Well-spent! Well, I haven't much to boast of.

RANK. (*Slapping him on the shoulder.*) But I have, don't you see?

NORA. I suppose you have been engaged in a scientific investigation, Doctor Rank?

RANK. Quite right.

255 HELMER. Bless me! Little Nora talking about scientific investigations!

NORA. Am I to congratulate you on the result?

RANK. By all means.

NORA. It was good then?

RANK. The best possible, both for doctor and patient—certainty.

NORA. (*Quickly and searchingly.*) Certainty?   260

RANK. Absolute certainty. Wasn't I right to enjoy myself after it?

NORA. Yes, quite right, Doctor Rank.

HELMER. And so say I, provided you don't have to pay for it tomorrow.

RANK. Well, in this life nothing's to be had for nothing.

NORA. Doctor Rank, aren't you very fond of masquerades?   265

RANK. Yes, when there are plenty of comical disguises.

NORA. Tell me, what shall we two be at our next masquerade?

HELMER. Little insatiable! Thinking of your next already!

RANK. We two? I'll tell you. You must go as a good fairy.

HELMER. Oh, but what costume would indicate that?   270

RANK. She has simply to wear her everyday dress.

HELMER. Splendid! But don't you know what you yourself will be?

RANK. Yes, my dear friend, I am perfectly clear upon that point.

HELMER. Well?

RANK. At the next masquerade I shall be invisible.   275

HELMER. What a comical idea!

RANK. There's a big black hat—haven't you heard of the invisible hat? It comes down all over you, and then no one can see you.

HELMER. (*With a suppressed smile.*) No, you're right there.

RANK. But I'm quite forgetting what I came for. Helmer, give me a cigar, one   280
of the dark Havanas.

HELMER. With the greatest pleasure. (*Hands case.*)

RANK. (*Takes one and cuts the end off.*) Thanks.

NORA. (*Striking a wax match.*) Let me give you a light.

RANK. A thousand thanks. (*She holds match. He lights his cigar at it.*) And   285
now, goodbye.

HELMER. Goodbye, goodbye, my dear fellow.

NORA. Sleep well, Doctor Rank.

RANK. Thanks for the wish.

NORA. Wish me the same.   290

RANK. You? Very well, since you ask me—Sleep well. And thanks for the light. (*He nods to them both and goes out.*)

HELMER. (*In an undertone.*) He's been drinking a good deal.

NORA. (*Absently.*) I daresay. (*Helmer takes his bunch of keys from his pocket and goes into the hall.*) Torvald, what are you doing there?   295

HELMER. I must empty the letterbox, it's quite full; there will be no room for the newspapers tomorrow morning.

NORA. Are you going to work tonight?

HELMER. Not very likely! Why, what's this? Someone has been at the lock.

300 NORA. The lock—?

HELMER. I'm sure of it. What does it mean? I can't think that the servants—? Here's a broken hairpin. Nora, it's one of yours.

NORA. (*Quickly.*) It must have been the children.

HELMER. Then you must break them of such tricks. H'm, h'm! There! At
305 last I've got it open. (*Takes contents out and calls into the kitchen.*) Ellen! Ellen, just put the hall door lamp out. (*He returns with letters in his hand, and shuts the inner door.*) Just see how they've accumulated. (*Turning them over.*) Why, what's this?

NORA. (*At the window.*) The letter! Oh, no, no, Torvald!

310 HELMER. Two visiting cards—from Rank.

NORA. From Doctor Rank?

HELMER. (*Looking at them.*) Doctor Rank. They were on the top. He must just have put them in.

NORA. Is there anything on them?

315 HELMER. There's a black cross over the name. Look at it. What a horrid idea! It looks just as if he were announcing his own death.

NORA. So he is.

HELMER. What! Do you know anything? Has he told you anything?

NORA. Yes. These cards mean that he has taken his last leave of us. He intends
320 to shut himself up and die.

HELMER. Poor fellow! Of course I knew we couldn't hope to keep him long. But so soon—and to go and creep into his lair like a wounded animal—

NORA. What must be, must be, and the fewer words the better. Don't you think so, Torvald?

325 HELMER. (*Walking up and down.*) He had so grown into our lives, I can't realize that he's gone. He and his sufferings and his loneliness formed a sort of cloudy background to the sunshine of our happiness. Well, perhaps it's best so—at any rate for him. (*Stands still.*) And perhaps for us, too, Nora. Now we two are thrown entirely upon each other. (*Puts his arm round her.*)
330 My darling wife! I feel as if I could never hold you close enough. Do you know, Nora, I often wish some danger might threaten you, that I might risk body and soul, and everything, everything, for your dear sake.

NORA. (*Tears herself from him and says firmly.*) Now you shall read your letters, Torvald.

335 HELMER. No, no, not tonight. I want to be with you, sweet wife.

NORA. With the thought of your dying friend?

HELMER. You are right. This has shaken us both. Unloveliness has come between us—thoughts of death and decay. We must seek to cast them off. Till then we will remain apart.

NORA. (*Her arms round his neck.*) Torvald! Goodnight, goodnight.   340

HELMER. (*Kissing her forehead.*) Goodnight, my little songbird. Sleep well, Nora. Now I'll go and read my letters. (*He goes into his room and shuts the door.*)

NORA. (*With wild eyes, gropes about her, seizes Helmer's domino, throws it round her, and whispers quickly, hoarsely, and brokenly.*) Never to see him again. Never, never, never. (*Throws her shawl over her head.*) Never to see the children again. Never, never. Oh that black, icy water! Oh that bot-   345
tomless—If it were only over! Now he has it; he's reading it. Oh, no, no, no, not yet. Torvald, goodbye. Goodbye, my little ones! (*She is rushing out by the hall; at the same moment Helmer tears his door open, and stands with an open letter in his hand.*)

HELMER. Nora!

NORA. (*Shrieking.*) Ah—!

HELMER. What is this? Do you know what is in this letter?   350

NORA. Yes, I know. Let me go! Let me pass!

HELMER. (*Holds her back.*) Where do you want to go?

NORA. (*Tries to get free.*) You shan't save me, Torvald.

HELMER. (*Falling back.*) True! Is it true what he writes? No, no, it cannot be.

NORA. It is true. I have loved you beyond all else in the world.   355

HELMER. Pshaw—no silly evasions.

NORA. (*A step nearer him.*) Torvald—

HELMER. Wretched woman! What have you done?

NORA. Let me go—you shall not save me. You shall not take my guilt upon yourself.   360

HELMER. I don't want any melodramatic games. (*Locks the door.*) Here you shall stay and give an account of yourself. Do you understand what you have done? Answer. Do you understand it?

NORA. (*Looks at him fixedly, and says with a stiffening expression.*) Yes, now I begin fully to understand it.   365

HELMER. (*Walking up and down.*) Oh, what an awful awakening! During all these eight years—she who was my pride and my joy—a hypocrite, a liar—worse, worse—a criminal. Oh! The hideousness of it! Ugh! Ugh! (*Nora is silent, and continues to look fixedly at him.*) I ought to have foreseen something of the kind. All your father's dishonesty—be silent! I say all   370
your father's dishonesty you have inherited—no religion, no morality, no sense of duty. How I am punished for shielding him! I did it for your sake, and you reward me like this.

NORA. Yes—like this!

HELMER. You have destroyed my whole happiness. You have ruined my fu-   375
ture. Oh! It's frightful to think of! I am in the power of a scoundrel; he

can do whatever he pleases with me, demand whatever he chooses, and I must submit. And all this disaster is brought upon me by an unprincipled woman!

380 NORA. When I am gone, you will be free.

HELMER. Oh, no fine phrases. Your father, too, was always ready with them. What good would it do to me, if you were "gone," as you say? No good in the world! He can publish the story all the same; I might even be suspected of collusion. People will think I was at the bottom of it all and egged you 385 on. And for all this I have you to thank—you whom I have done nothing but pet and spoil during our whole married life. Do you understand now what you have done to me?

NORA. (*With cold calmness.*) Yes.

HELMER. It's incredible. I can't grasp it. But we must come to an under- 390 standing. Take that shawl off. Take it off, I say. I must try to pacify him in one way or another—the secret must be kept, cost what it may. As for ourselves, we must live as we have always done, but of course only in the eyes of the world. Of course you will continue to live here. But the children cannot be left in your care. I dare not trust them to you—Oh, to 395 have to say this to one I have loved so tenderly—whom I still—but that must be a thing of the past. Henceforward there can be no question of happiness, but merely of saving the ruins, the shreds, the show of it. (*A ring; Helmer starts.*) What's that? So late! Can it be the worst? Can he—? Hide yourself, Nora; say you are ill. (*Nora stands motionless. Helmer goes to the door and opens it.*)

400 ELLEN. (*Half dressed, in the hall.*) Here is a letter for you, ma'am.

HELMER. Give it to me. (*Seizes the letter and shuts the door.*) Yes, from him. You shall not have it. I shall read it.

NORA. Read it!

HELMER. (*By the lamp.*) I have hardly the courage to. We may be lost, both 405 you and I. Ah! I must know. (*Tears the letter hastily open; reads a few lines, looks at an enclosure; a cry of joy.*) Nora! (*Nora looks interrogatively at him.*) Nora! Oh! I must read it again. Yes, yes, it is so. I am saved! Nora, I am saved!

NORA. And I?

410 HELMER. You too, of course; we are both saved, both of us. Look here, he sends you back your promissory note. He writes that he regrets and apologizes—that a happy turn in his life—Oh, what matter what he writes. We are saved, Nora! No one can harm you. Oh! Nora, Nora—No, first to get rid of this hateful thing. I'll just see—(*Glances at the IOU*) No, I won't 415 look at it; the whole thing shall be nothing but a dream to me. (*Tears the IOU and both letters in pieces. Throws them into the fire and watches*

them burn.) There, it's gone. He wrote that ever since Christmas Eve—Oh, Nora, they must have been three awful days for you!

NORA.   I have fought a hard fight for the last three days.

HELMER.   And in your agony you saw no other outlet but—no; we won't think of that horror. We will only rejoice and repeat—it's over, all over.   420
Don't you hear, Nora? You don't seem able to grasp it. Yes, it's over. What is this set look on your face? Oh, my poor Nora, I understand; you can't believe that I have forgiven you. But I have, Nora; I swear it. I have forgiven everything. I know that what you did was all for love of me.

NORA.   That's true.   425

HELMER.   You loved me as a wife should love her husband. It was only the means you misjudged. But do you think I love you the less for your helplessness? No, no. Only lean on me. I will counsel and guide you. I should be no true man if this very womanly helplessness did not make you doubly dear in my eyes. You mustn't think of the hard things I said in my first   430
moment of terror, when the world seemed to be tumbling about my ears. I have forgiven you, Nora—I swear I have forgiven you.

NORA.   I thank you for your forgiveness. (*Goes out, right.*)

HELMER.   No, stay. (*Looks in.*) What are you going to do?

NORA.   (*Inside.*) To take off my doll's dress.   435

HELMER.   (*In doorway.*) Yes, do, dear. Try to calm down, and recover your balance, my scared little songbird. You may rest secure. I have broad wings to shield you. (*Walking up and down near the door.*) Oh, how lovely—how cosy our home is, Nora. Here you are safe; here I can shelter you like a hunted dove, whom I have saved from the claws of the hawk. I shall soon   440
bring your poor beating heart to rest; believe me, Nora, I will. Tomorrow all this will seem quite different—everything will be as before. I shall not need to tell you again that I forgive you; you will feel for yourself that it is true. How could you think I could find it in my heart to drive you away, or even so much as to reproach you? Oh, you don't know a true man's heart,   445
Nora. There is something indescribably sweet and soothing to a man in having forgiven his wife—honestly forgiven her from the bottom of his heart. She becomes his property in a double sense. She is as though born again; she has become, so to speak, at once his wife and his child. That is what you shall henceforth be to me, my bewildered, helpless darling.   450
Don't be troubled about anything, Nora; only open your heart to me, and I will be both will and conscience to you. (*Nora enters, crossing to table in everyday dress.*) Why, what's this? Not gone to bed? You have changed your dress.

NORA.   Yes, Torvald; now I have changed my dress.   455

HELMER.   But why now so late?

NORA. I shall not sleep tonight.

HELMER. But, Nora dear—

NORA. (*Looking at her watch.*) It's not so late yet. Sit down, Torvald; you and I have much to say to each other. (*She sits on one side of the table.*)

HELMER. Nora, what does this mean? Your cold, set face—

NORA. Sit down. It will take some time; I have much to talk over with you. (*Helmer sits at the other side of the table.*)

HELMER. You alarm me; I don't understand you.

NORA. No, that's just it. You don't understand me; and I have never understood you—till tonight. No, don't interrupt. Only listen to what I say. We must come to a final settlement, Torvald!

HELMER. How do you mean?

NORA. (*After a short silence.*) Does not one thing strike you as we sit here?

HELMER. What should strike me?

NORA. We have been married eight years. Does it not strike you that this is the first time we two, you and I, man and wife, have talked together seriously?

HELMER. Seriously! Well, what do you call seriously?

NORA. During eight whole years, and more—ever since the day we first met—we have never exchanged one serious word about serious things.

HELMER. Was I always to trouble you with the cares you could not help me to bear?

NORA. I am not talking of cares. I say that we have never yet set ourselves seriously to get to the bottom of anything.

HELMER. Why, my dear Nora, what have you to do with serious things?

NORA. There we have it! You have never understood me. I have had great injustice done me, Torvald; first by my father and then by you.

HELMER. What! By your father and me? By us who have loved you more than all the world?

NORA. (*Shaking her head.*) You have never loved me. You only thought it amusing to be in love with me.

HELMER. Why, Nora, what a thing to say!

NORA. Yes, it is so, Torvald. While I was at home with father, he used to tell me all his opinions, and I held the same opinions. If I had others I concealed them, because he would not have liked it. He used to call me his doll child, and play with me as I played with my dolls. Then I came to live in your house—

HELMER. What an expression to use about our marriage!

NORA. (*Undisturbed.*) I mean I passed from father's hands into yours. You settled everything according to your taste; and I got the same tastes as you; or I pretended to—I don't know which—both ways, perhaps. When I look back on it now, I seem to have been living here like a beggar, from hand to mouth. I lived by performing tricks for you, Torvald. But you would have it so. You and father have done me a great wrong. It's your fault that my life has been wasted.   500

HELMER. Why, Nora, how unreasonable and ungrateful you are. Haven't you been happy here?

NORA. No, never; I thought I was, but I never was.

HELMER. Not—not happy?

NORA. No; only merry. And you have always been so kind to me. But our   505 house has been nothing but a playroom. Here I have been your doll-wife, just as at home I used to be papa's doll-child. And the children in their turn have been my dolls. I thought it fun when you played with me, just as the children did when I played with them. That has been our marriage, Torvald.   510

HELMER. There is some truth in what you say, exaggerated and overstrained though it is. But henceforth it shall be different. Playtime is over; now comes the time for education.

NORA. Whose education? Mine, or the children's.

HELMER. Both, my dear Nora.   515

NORA. Oh, Torvald, you are not the man to teach me to be a fit wife for you.

HELMER. And you say that?

NORA. And I—am I fit to educate the children?

HELMER. Nora!

NORA. Did you not say yourself a few minutes ago you dared not trust them   520 to me?

HELMER. In the excitement of the moment! Why should you dwell upon that?

NORA. No—you are perfectly right. That problem is beyond me. There's another to be solved first—I must try to educate myself. You are not the   525 man to help me in that. I must set about it alone. And that is why I am leaving you!

HELMER. (*Jumping up.*) What—do you mean to say—?

NORA. I must stand quite alone to know myself and my surroundings; so I cannot stay with you.   530

HELMER. Nora! Nora!

NORA. I am going at once. Christina will take me in for tonight—

HELMER. You are mad. I shall not allow it. I forbid it.

NORA. It's no use your forbidding me anything now. I shall take with me what belongs to me. From you I will accept nothing, either now or after-   535 ward.

HELMER. What madness!

NORA. Tomorrow I shall go home.

HELMER. Home!

540 NORA. I mean to what was my home. It will be easier for me to find some opening there.

HELMER. Oh, in your blind inexperience—

NORA. I must try to gain experience, Torvald.

HELMER. To forsake your home, your husband, and your children! You don't 545 consider what the world will say.

NORA. I can pay no heed to that! I only know that I must do it.

HELMER. It's exasperating! Can you forsake your holiest duties in this way?

NORA. What do you call my holiest duties?

HELMER. Do you ask me that? Your duties to your husband and your chil-550 dren.

NORA. I have other duties equally sacred.

HELMER. Impossible! What duties do you mean?

NORA. My duties toward myself.

HELMER. Before all else you are a wife and a mother.

555 NORA. That I no longer believe. I believe that before all else I am a human being, just as much as you are—or at least that I will try to become one. I know that most people agree with you, Torvald, and that they say so in books. But henceforth I can't be satisfied with what most people say, and what is in books. I must think things out for myself, and try to get clear 560 about them.

HELMER. Are you not clear about your place in your own home? Have you not an infallible guide in questions like these? Have you not religion?

NORA. Oh, Torvald, I don't know properly what religion is.

HELMER. What do you mean?

565 NORA. I know nothing but what our clergyman told me when I was con-firmed. He explained that religion was this and that. When I get away from here and stand alone I will look into that matter too. I will see whether what he taught me is true, or, at any rate, whether it is true for me.

HELMER. Oh, this is unheard of! But if religion cannot keep you right, let me 570 appeal to your conscience—I suppose you have some moral feeling? Or, answer me, perhaps you have none?

NORA. Well, Torvald, it's not easy to say. I really don't know—I am all at sea about these things. I only know that I think quite differently from you about them. I hear, too, that the laws are different from what I thought; 575 but I can't believe that they are right. It appears that a woman has no right to spare her dying father, or to save her husband's life. I don't believe that.

HELMER. You talk like a child. You don't understand the society in which you live.

NORA. No, I don't. But now I shall try to. I must make up my mind which
is right—society or I.   580

HELMER. Nora, you are ill, you are feverish. I almost think you are out of
your senses.

NORA. I have never felt so much clearness and certainty as tonight.

HELMER. You are clear and certain enough to forsake husband and children?

NORA. Yes, I am.   585

HELMER. Then there is only one explanation possible.

NORA. What is that?

HELMER. You no longer love me.

NORA. No, that is just it.

HELMER. Nora! Can you say so!   590

NORA. Oh, I'm so sorry, Torvald, for you've always been so kind to me. But
I can't help it. I do not love you any longer.

HELMER. (*Keeping his composure with difficulty*.) Are you clear and certain on
this point too?

NORA. Yes, quite. That is why I won't stay here any longer.   595

HELMER. And can you also make clear to me, how I have forfeited your love?

NORA. Yes, I can. It was this evening, when the miracle did not happen. For
then I saw you were not the man I had taken you for.

HELMER. Explain yourself more clearly; I don't understand.

NORA. I have waited so patiently all these eight years, for, of course, I saw   600
clearly enough that miracles do not happen every day. When this crushing
blow threatened me, I said to myself, confidently, "Now comes the miracle!" When Krogstad's letter lay in the box, it never for a moment occurred
to me that you would think of submitting to that man's conditions. I was
convinced that you would say to him, "Make it known to all the world,"   605
and that then—

HELMER. Well? When I had given my own wife's name up to disgrace and
shame?

NORA. Then I firmly believed that you would come forward, take everything
upon yourself, and say, "I am the guilty one."   610

HELMER. Nora!

NORA. You mean I would never have accepted such a sacrifice? No, certainly not. But what would my assertions have been worth in opposition
to yours? That was the miracle that I hoped for and dreaded. And it was to
hinder that that I wanted to die.   615

HELMER. I would gladly work for you day and night, Nora—bear sorrow
and want for your sake—but no man sacrifices his honour, even for one
he loves.

NORA. Millions of women have done so.

620 HELMER. Oh, you think and talk like a silly child.

NORA. Very likely. But you neither think nor talk like the man I can share my life with. When your terror was over—not for me, but for yourself—when there was nothing more to fear—then it was to you as though nothing had happened. I was your lark again, your doll—whom you would take twice

625 as much care of in future, because she was so weak and fragile. (*Stands up.*) Torvald, in that moment it burst upon me that I had been living here these eight years with a strange man, and had borne him three children—Oh, I can't bear to think of it—I could tear myself to pieces!

HELMER. (*Sadly.*) I see it, I see it; an abyss has opened between us—But,

630 Nora, can it never be filled up?

NORA. As I now am, I am no wife for you.

HELMER. I have strength to become another man.

NORA. Perhaps—when your doll is taken away from you.

HELMER. To part—to part from you! No, Nora, no; I can't grasp the thought.

635 NORA. (*Going into room, right.*) The more reason for the thing to happen. (*She comes back with a cloak, hat, and small travelling bag, which she puts on a chair.*)

HELMER. Nora, Nora, not now! Wait till tomorrow.

NORA. (*Putting on cloak.*) I can't spend the night in a strange man's house.

HELMER. But can't we live here as brother and sister?

NORA. (*Fastening her hat.*) You know very well that would not last long.

640 Goodbye, Torvald. No, I won't go to the children. I know they are in better hands than mine. As I now am, I can be nothing to them.

HELMER. But some time, Nora—some time—

NORA. How can I tell? I have no idea what will become of me.

HELMER. But you are my wife, now and always!

645 NORA. Listen, Torvald—when a wife leaves her husband's house, as I am doing, I have heard that in the eyes of the law he is free from all duties toward her. At any rate I release you from all duties. You must not feel yourself bound any more than I shall. There must be perfect freedom on both sides. There, there is your ring back. Give me mine.

650 HELMER. That too?

NORA. That too.

HELMER. Here it is.

NORA. Very well. Now it is all over. Here are the keys. The servants know about everything in the house, better than I do. Tomorrow, when I have

655 started, Christina will come to pack up my things. I will have them sent after me.

HELMER. All over! All over! Nora, will you never think of me again?

NORA. Oh, I shall often think of you, and the children—and this house.

HELMER. May I write to you, Nora?

NORA. No, never. You must not.   660

HELMER. But I must send you—

NORA. Nothing, nothing.

HELMER. I must help you if you need it.

NORA. No, I say. I take nothing from strangers.

HELMER. Nora, can I never be more than a stranger to you?   665

NORA. (*Taking her travelling bag.*) Oh, Torvald, then the miracle of miracles would have to happen.

HELMER. What is the miracle of miracles?

NORA. Both of us would have to change so that—Oh, Torvald, I no longer believe in miracles.   670

HELMER. But I will believe. We must so change that—?

NORA. That our lives together could be a marriage. Goodbye. (*She goes out.*)

HELMER. (*Sinks in a chair by the door with his face in his hands.*) Nora! Nora! (*He looks around and stands up.*) Empty. She's gone! (*A hope inspires him.*) Ah! The miracle of miracles—?! (*From below is heard the reverberation of a*   675 *heavy door closing.*)

—1879[1]

---

1   *1879* Shortly after the play's first performance, Ibsen wrote an alternative ending to *A Doll's House* in an attempt to prevent unauthorized, less controversial adaptations from appearing in Germany. In the alternative ending, after Nora says goodbye, Helmer takes her by the arm and leads her to the room where their children are sleeping. Unable to leave her children, Nora is overcome and falls to the floor. Ibsen made the change in an attempt to maintain control of his play, but publicly stated his dislike of the altered ending, and said that whoever performed it did so against his wishes.

Betty Hennings in the role of Nora, 1880. A Doll's House *was first performed at the Royal Danish Theatre in Copenhagen, Denmark; Hennings originated the role in this production.*

Oscar Wilde
1854–1900

Notorious for his flamboyance and wit before he had ever published a word, the Irish writer Oscar Wilde established himself in the literary world with his sole novel, *The Picture of Dorian Gray*, and even more with such sparkling social comedies as *An Ideal Husband* and *The Importance of Being Earnest*. He was a vocal advocate of aestheticism; Wilde saw in art the possibility for a life beyond the day-to-day monotony of ordinary existence.

Born into a family of accomplished writers, Wilde grew up in the colourful environment of his mother's famous salon, where she hosted leading Dublin artists and writers. Once when Wilde returned from college, he invited a friend to Lady Wilde's weekly "conversazione," saying: "I want to introduce you to my mother. We have founded a society for the suppression of virtue." Wilde was a brilliant student at Trinity College, Dublin, and at Oxford's Magdalen College, where he was celebrated for his wit, decadence, and ostentatious appearance. By the time he published a book of poems in 1881, Wilde had already become the butt of many caricatures in *Punch* magazine; he had taken to modelling his look on the character of Bunthorne in Gilbert and Sullivan's satirical comic opera *Patience*. For the next few years Wilde delivered lectures in which he gave voice to his ideas about art and life: "The supreme object of life is to live. Few people live. It is true life only to realize one's own perfection, to make one's every dream a reality. Even this is possible." In 1884 Wilde married Constance Lloyd, with whom he would have two sons, Cyril and Vyvyan. From 1887 to 1889 he edited *Woman's World*, a popular magazine.

Wilde was at his very best in the early 1890s. In addition to *Dorian Gray*, Wilde penned a string of brilliant social comedies, including *Lady Windermere's Fan* (1892), *A Woman of No Importance* (1893), and *An Ideal Husband* (1895). His final comedy was his masterpiece of farce, *The Importance of Being Earnest*; it first played in 1895 to wildly enthusiastic crowds at the St. James Theatre in London. Success came to an end only through Wilde's ill-fated affair with a young aristocrat, Lord Alfred Douglas ("Bosie"). Homosexuality was a criminal offence: Wilde was found guilty of "gross indecency" and sentenced to two years of imprisonment with hard labour. Upon his release he composed "The Ballad of Reading Gaol" (1898), a heartfelt indictment of the prison system and capital punishment, as well as a meditation on the universal characteristics of human nature. Wilde never recovered fully from his prison experience; he died in 1900, aged 46.

The Importance of Being Earnest

A Trivial Comedy for Serious People

THE PERSONS IN THE PLAY

John Worthing, J.P.[1]
Algernon Moncrieff
Rev. Canon Chasuble, D.D.[2]
Merriman, *Butler*
Lane, *Manservant*
Lady Bracknell
Hon.[3] Gwendolen Fairfax
Cecily Cardew
Miss Prism, *Governess*

THE SCENES IN THE PLAY

ACT 1. Algernon Moncrieff's Flat in Half-Moon Street,[4] W.
ACT 2. The Garden at the Manor House, Woolton.[5]
ACT 3. Drawing-Room at the Manor House, Woolton.

TIME: The Present.

ACT 1

SCENE

Morning-room in Algernon's flat in Half-Moon Street. The room is luxuriously and artistically furnished. The sound of a piano is heard in the adjoining room.

(Lane is arranging afternoon tea on the table, and after the music has ceased, Algernon enters.)

ALGERNON. Did you hear what I was playing, Lane?

---

1   *J.P.*   Justice of the Peace.
2   *D.D.*   Doctor of Divinity.
3   *Hon.*   I.e., The Honourable. The honorific in this case designates the daughter of a peer below the rank of Earl.
4   *Half-Moon Street*   Street located in a fashionable area of London.
5   *Woolton*   Fictional location.

LANE. I didn't think it polite to listen, sir.

ALGERNON. I'm sorry for that, for your sake. I don't play accurately—any one can play accurately—but I play with wonderful expression. As far as the piano is concerned, sentiment is my forte. I keep science for Life.

LANE. Yes, sir.

ALGERNON. And, speaking of the science of Life, have you got the cucumber sandwiches[1] cut for Lady Bracknell?

LANE. Yes, sir. (*Hands them on a salver.*[2])

ALGERNON. (*Inspects them, takes two, and sits down on the sofa.*) Oh! ... by the way, Lane, I see from your book that on Thursday night, when Lord Shoreman and Mr. Worthing were dining with me, eight bottles of champagne are entered as having been consumed.

LANE. Yes, sir; eight bottles and a pint.

ALGERNON. Why is it that at a bachelor's establishment the servants invariably drink the champagne? I ask merely for information.

LANE. I attribute it to the superior quality of the wine, sir. I have often observed that in married households the champagne is rarely of a first-rate brand.

ALGERNON. Good heavens! Is marriage so demoralizing as that?

LANE. I believe it is a very pleasant state, sir. I have had very little experience of it myself up to the present. I have only been married once. That was in consequence of a misunderstanding between myself and a young person.

ALGERNON. (*Languidly.*) I don't know that I am much interested in your family life, Lane.

LANE. No, sir; it is not a very interesting subject. I never think of it myself.

ALGERNON. Very natural, I am sure. That will do, Lane, thank you.

LANE. Thank you, sir. (*Lane goes out.*)

ALGERNON. Lane's views on marriage seem somewhat lax. Really, if the lower orders don't set us a good example, what on earth is the use of them? They seem, as a class, to have absolutely no sense of moral responsibility.

    (*Enter Lane.*)

LANE. Mr. Ernest Worthing.

    (*Enter Jack. Lane goes out.*)

ALGERNON. How are you, my dear Ernest? What brings you up to town?

JACK. Oh, pleasure, pleasure! What else should bring one anywhere? Eating as usual, I see, Algy!

---

1   *cucumber sandwiches* Small sandwiches of cucumber on thinly sliced bread, a staple of afternoon tea in polite English society.

2   *salver* Serving tray, typically silver.

ALGERNON. (*Stiffly.*) I believe it is customary in good society to take some slight refreshment at five o'clock. Where have you been since last Thursday?

JACK. (*Sitting down on the sofa.*) In the country.

40 ALGERNON. What on earth do you do there?

JACK. (*Pulling off his gloves.*) When one is in town[1] one amuses oneself. When one is in the country one amuses other people. It is excessively boring.

ALGERNON. And who are the people you amuse?

JACK. (*Airily.*) Oh, neighbours, neighbours.

45 ALGERNON. Got nice neighbours in your part of Shropshire?

JACK. Perfectly horrid! Never speak to one of them.

ALGERNON. How immensely you must amuse them! (*Goes over and takes sandwich.*) By the way, Shropshire is your county, is it not?

JACK. Eh? Shropshire? Yes, of course. Hallo! Why all these cups? Why cucum-
50 ber sandwiches? Why such reckless extravagance in one so young? Who is coming to tea?

ALGERNON. Oh! merely Aunt Augusta and Gwendolen.

JACK. How perfectly delightful!

ALGERNON. Yes, that is all very well; but I am afraid Aunt Augusta won't
55 quite approve of your being here.

JACK. May I ask why?

ALGERNON. My dear fellow, the way you flirt with Gwendolen is perfectly disgraceful. It is almost as bad as the way Gwendolen flirts with you.

JACK. I am in love with Gwendolen. I have come up to town expressly to
60 propose to her.

ALGERNON. I thought you had come up for pleasure? … I call that business.

JACK. How utterly unromantic you are!

ALGERNON. I really don't see anything romantic in proposing. It is very romantic to be in love. But there is nothing romantic about a definite
65 proposal. Why, one may be accepted. One usually is, I believe. Then the excitement is all over. The very essence of romance is uncertainty. If ever I get married, I'll certainly try to forget the fact.

JACK. I have no doubt about that, dear Algy. The Divorce Court was specially invented for people whose memories are so curiously constituted.

70 ALGERNON. Oh! there is no use speculating on that subject. Divorces are made in Heaven—(*Jack puts out his hand to take a sandwich. Algernon at once interferes.*) Please don't touch the cucumber sandwiches. They are ordered specially for Aunt Augusta. (*Takes one and eats it.*)

JACK. Well, you have been eating them all the time.

---

1   *in town*   I.e., in London.

ALGERNON. That is quite a different matter. She is my aunt. (*Takes plate from* 75
below.) Have some bread and butter. The bread and butter is for Gwendolen. Gwendolen is devoted to bread and butter.

JACK. (*Advancing to table and helping himself.*) And very good bread and butter it is too.

ALGERNON. Well, my dear fellow, you need not eat as if you were going to eat 80
it all. You behave as if you were married to her already. You are not married
to her already, and I don't think you ever will be.

JACK. Why on earth do you say that?

ALGERNON. Well, in the first place girls never marry the men they flirt with.
Girls don't think it right. 85

JACK. Oh, that is nonsense!

ALGERNON. It isn't. It is a great truth. It accounts for the extraordinary number of bachelors that one sees all over the place. In the second place, I don't
give my consent.

JACK. Your consent! 90

ALGERNON. My dear fellow, Gwendolen is my first cousin. And before I
allow you to marry her, you will have to clear up the whole question of
Cecily. (*Rings bell.*)

JACK. Cecily! What on earth do you mean? What do you mean, Algy, by Cecily! I don't know any one of the name of Cecily. 95

(*Enter Lane.*)

ALGERNON. Bring me that cigarette case Mr. Worthing left in the smoking-
room the last time he dined here.

LANE. Yes, sir.

(*Lane goes out.*)

JACK. Do you mean to say you have had my cigarette case all this time? I wish
to goodness you had let me know. I have been writing frantic letters to 100
Scotland Yard about it. I was very nearly offering a large reward.

ALGERNON. Well, I wish you would offer one. I happen to be more than
usually hard up.

JACK. There is no good offering a large reward now that the thing is found.

(*Enter Lane with the cigarette case on a salver. Algernon takes it at once.
Lane goes out.*)

ALGERNON. I think that is rather mean of you, Ernest, I must say. (*Opens case* 105
and examines it.) However, it makes no matter, for, now that I look at the
inscription inside, I find that the thing isn't yours after all.

JACK. Of course it's mine. (*Moving to him.*) You have seen me with it a hundred times, and you have no right whatsoever to read what is written inside. It is a very ungentlemanly thing to read a private cigarette case.

ALGERNON. Oh! it is absurd to have a hard and fast rule about what one should read and what one shouldn't. More than half of modern culture depends on what one shouldn't read.

JACK. I am quite aware of the fact, and I don't propose to discuss modern culture. It isn't the sort of thing one should talk of in private. I simply want my cigarette case back.

ALGERNON. Yes; but this isn't your cigarette case. This cigarette case is a present from some one of the name of Cecily, and you said you didn't know any one of that name.

JACK. Well, if you want to know, Cecily happens to be my aunt.

ALGERNON. Your aunt!

JACK. Yes. Charming old lady she is, too. Lives at Tunbridge Wells. Just give it back to me, Algy.

ALGERNON. (*Retreating to back of sofa.*) But why does she call herself little Cecily if she is your aunt and lives at Tunbridge Wells? (*Reading.*) "From little Cecily with her fondest love."

JACK. (*Moving to sofa and kneeling upon it.*) My dear fellow, what on earth is there in that? Some aunts are tall, some aunts are not tall. That is a matter that surely an aunt may be allowed to decide for herself. You seem to think that every aunt should be exactly like your aunt! That is absurd! For Heaven's sake give me back my cigarette case. (*Follows Algernon round the room.*)

ALGERNON. Yes. But why does your aunt call you her uncle? "From little Cecily, with her fondest love to her dear Uncle Jack." There is no objection, I admit, to an aunt being a small aunt, but why an aunt, no matter what her size may be, should call her own nephew her uncle, I can't quite make out. Besides, your name isn't Jack at all; it is Ernest.

JACK. It isn't Ernest; it's Jack.

ALGERNON. You have always told me it was Ernest. I have introduced you to every one as Ernest. You answer to the name of Ernest. You look as if your name was Ernest. You are the most earnest-looking person I ever saw in my life. It is perfectly absurd your saying that your name isn't Ernest. It's on your cards. Here is one of them. (*Taking it from case.*) "Mr. Ernest Worthing, B. 4, The Albany."[1] I'll keep this as a proof that your name is Ernest if ever you attempt to deny it to me, or to Gwendolen, or to any one else. (*Puts the card in his pocket.*)

---

1 *The Albany* Fashionable men's club in London.

JACK. Well, my name is Ernest in town and Jack in the country, and the ciga-   145
rette case was given to me in the country.

ALGERNON. Yes, but that does not account for the fact that your small Aunt
Cecily, who lives at Tunbridge Wells, calls you her dear uncle. Come, old
boy, you had much better have the thing out at once.

JACK. My dear Algy, you talk exactly as if you were a dentist. It is very vulgar   150
to talk like a dentist when one isn't a dentist. It produces a false impression.

ALGERNON. Well, that is exactly what dentists always do. Now, go on! Tell me
the whole thing. I may mention that I have always suspected you of being
a confirmed and secret Bunburyist; and I am quite sure of it now.

JACK. Bunburyist? What on earth do you mean by a Bunburyist?   155

ALGERNON. I'll reveal to you the meaning of that incomparable expression
as soon as you are kind enough to inform me why you are Ernest in town
and Jack in the country.

JACK. Well, produce my cigarette case first.

ALGERNON. Here it is. (*Hands cigarette case.*) Now produce your explanation,   160
and pray make it improbable. (*Sits on sofa.*)

JACK. My dear fellow, there is nothing improbable about my explanation at
all. In fact it's perfectly ordinary. Old Mr. Thomas Cardew, who adopted
me when I was a little boy, made me in his will guardian to his grand-
daughter, Miss Cecily Cardew. Cecily, who addresses me as her uncle from   165
motives of respect that you could not possibly appreciate, lives at my place
in the country under the charge of her admirable governess, Miss Prism.

ALGERNON. Where is that place in the country, by the way?

JACK. That is nothing to you, dear boy. You are not going to be invited ... I
may tell you candidly that the place is not in Shropshire.   170

ALGERNON. I suspected that, my dear fellow! I have Bunburyed all over
Shropshire on two separate occasions. Now, go on. Why are you Ernest in
town and Jack in the country?

JACK. My dear Algy, I don't know whether you will be able to understand
my real motives. You are hardly serious enough. When one is placed in the   175
position of guardian, one has to adopt a very high moral tone on all subjects. It's one's duty to do so. And as a high moral tone can hardly be said
to conduce very much to either one's health or one's happiness, in order to
get up to town I have always pretended to have a younger brother of the
name of Ernest, who lives in the Albany, and gets into the most dreadful   180
scrapes. That, my dear Algy, is the whole truth pure and simple.

ALGERNON. The truth is rarely pure and never simple. Modern life would
be very tedious if it were either, and modern literature a complete impossibility!

JACK. That wouldn't be at all a bad thing.   185

ALGERNON. Literary criticism is not your forte, my dear fellow. Don't try it. You should leave that to people who haven't been at a University. They do it so well in the daily papers. What you really are is a Bunburyist. I was quite right in saying you were a Bunburyist. You are one of the most ad-
190   vanced Bunburyists I know.

JACK. What on earth do you mean?

ALGERNON. You have invented a very useful younger brother called Ernest, in order that you may be able to come up to town as often as you like. I have invented an invaluable permanent invalid called Bunbury, in order that I
195   may be able to go down into the country whenever I choose. Bunbury is perfectly invaluable. If it wasn't for Bunbury's extraordinary bad health, for instance, I wouldn't be able to dine with you at Willis's tonight, for I have been really engaged to Aunt Augusta for more than a week.

JACK. I haven't asked you to dine with me anywhere tonight.

200 ALGERNON. I know. You are absurdly careless about sending out invitations. It is very foolish of you. Nothing annoys people so much as not receiving invitations.

JACK. You had much better dine with your Aunt Augusta.

ALGERNON. I haven't the smallest intention of doing anything of the kind.
205   To begin with, I dined there on Monday, and once a week is quite enough to dine with one's own relations. In the second place, whenever I do dine there I am always treated as a member of the family, and sent down[1] with either no woman at all, or two. In the third place, I know perfectly well whom she will place me next to, tonight. She will place me next Mary
210   Farquhar, who always flirts with her own husband across the dinner-table. That is not very pleasant. Indeed, it is not even decent … and that sort of thing is enormously on the increase. The amount of women in London who flirt with their own husbands is perfectly scandalous. It looks so bad. It is simply washing one's clean linen in public. Besides, now that I know
215   you to be a confirmed Bunburyist I naturally want to talk to you about Bunburying. I want to tell you the rules.

JACK. I'm not a Bunburyist at all. If Gwendolen accepts me, I am going to kill my brother, indeed I think I'll kill him in any case. Cecily is a little too much interested in him. It is rather a bore. So I am going to get rid of
220   Ernest. And I strongly advise you to do the same with Mr. … with your invalid friend who has the absurd name.

ALGERNON. Nothing will induce me to part with Bunbury, and if you ever get married, which seems to me extremely problematic, you will be very

---

1   *sent down*   I.e., sent from the drawing room (typically upstairs) down to the dining room (typically on a lower floor).

glad to know Bunbury. A man who marries without knowing Bunbury has a very tedious time of it.

JACK. That is nonsense. If I marry a charming girl like Gwendolen, and she is the only girl I ever saw in my life that I would marry, I certainly won't want to know Bunbury.

ALGERNON. Then your wife will. You don't seem to realize, that in married life three is company and two is none.

JACK. (*Sententiously.*) That, my dear young friend, is the theory that the corrupt French Drama has been propounding for the last fifty years.

ALGERNON. Yes; and that the happy English home has proved in half the time.

JACK. For heaven's sake, don't try to be cynical. It's perfectly easy to be cynical.

ALGERNON. My dear fellow, it isn't easy to be anything nowadays. There's such a lot of beastly competition about. (*The sound of an electric bell is heard.*) Ah! that must be Aunt Augusta. Only relatives, or creditors, ever ring in that Wagnerian[1] manner. Now, if I get her out of the way for ten minutes, so that you can have an opportunity for proposing to Gwendolen, may I dine with you tonight at Willis's?

JACK. I suppose so, if you want to.

ALGERNON. Yes, but you must be serious about it. I hate people who are not serious about meals. It is so shallow of them.

(*Enter Lane.*)

Lady Bracknell and Miss Fairfax.

(*Algernon goes forward to meet them. Enter Lady Bracknell and Gwendolen.*)

LADY BRACKNELL. Good afternoon, dear Algernon, I hope you are behaving very well.

ALGERNON. I'm feeling very well, Aunt Augusta.

LADY BRACKNELL. That's not quite the same thing. In fact the two things rarely go together. (*Sees Jack and bows to him with icy coldness.*)

ALGERNON. (*To Gwendolen.*) Dear me, you are smart!

GWENDOLEN. I am always smart! Am I not, Mr. Worthing?

JACK. You're quite perfect, Miss Fairfax.

GWENDOLEN. Oh! I hope I am not that. It would leave no room for developments, and I intend to develop in many directions.

(*Gwendolen and Jack sit down together in the corner.*)

---

1   *Wagnerian* Intense and theatrical; characteristic of the German composer Richard Wagner (1813–83).

LADY BRACKNELL. I'm sorry if we are a little late, Algernon, but I was obliged to call on dear Lady Harbury. I hadn't been there since her poor husband's death. I never saw a woman so altered; she looks quite twenty years younger. And now I'll have a cup of tea, and one of those nice cucumber
260   sandwiches you promised me.

ALGERNON. Certainly, Aunt Augusta. (*Goes over to tea-table.*)

LADY BRACKNELL. Won't you come and sit here, Gwendolen?

GWENDOLEN. Thanks, mamma, I'm quite comfortable where I am.

ALGERNON. (*Picking up empty plate in horror.*) Good heavens! Lane! Why are
265   there no cucumber sandwiches? I ordered them specially.

LANE. (*Gravely.*) There were no cucumbers in the market this morning, sir. I went down twice.

ALGERNON. No cucumbers!

LANE. No, sir. Not even for ready money.

270 ALGERNON. That will do, Lane, thank you.

LANE. Thank you, sir. (*Goes out.*)

ALGERNON. I am greatly distressed, Aunt Augusta, about there being no cucumbers, not even for ready money.

LADY BRACKNELL. It really makes no matter, Algernon. I had some crumpets
275   with Lady Harbury, who seems to me to be living entirely for pleasure now.

ALGERNON. I hear her hair has turned quite gold from grief.

LADY BRACKNELL. It certainly has changed its colour. From what cause I, of course, cannot say. (*Algernon crosses and hands tea.*) Thank you. I've quite a treat for you tonight, Algernon. I am going to send you down with Mary
280   Farquhar. She is such a nice woman, and so attentive to her husband. It's delightful to watch them.

ALGERNON. I am afraid, Aunt Augusta, I shall have to give up the pleasure of dining with you tonight after all.

LADY BRACKNELL. (*Frowning.*) I hope not, Algernon. It would put my table
285   completely out. Your uncle would have to dine upstairs. Fortunately he is accustomed to that.

ALGERNON. It is a great bore, and, I need hardly say, a terrible disappointment to me, but the fact is I have just had a telegram to say that my poor friend Bunbury is very ill again. (*Exchanges glances with Jack.*) They seem
290   to think I should be with him.

LADY BRACKNELL. It is very strange. This Mr. Bunbury seems to suffer from curiously bad health.

ALGERNON. Yes; poor Bunbury is a dreadful invalid.

LADY BRACKNELL. Well, I must say, Algernon, that I think it is high time that
295   Mr. Bunbury made up his mind whether he was going to live or to die. This shilly-shallying with the question is absurd. Nor do I in any way ap-

prove of the modern sympathy with invalids. I consider it morbid. Illness of any kind is hardly a thing to be encouraged in others. Health is the primary duty of life. I am always telling that to your poor uncle, but he never seems to take much notice … as far as any improvement in his ailment goes. I should be much obliged if you would ask Mr. Bunbury, from me, to be kind enough not to have a relapse on Saturday, for I rely on you to arrange my music for me. It is my last reception, and one wants something that will encourage conversation, particularly at the end of the season[1] when every one has practically said whatever they had to say, which, in most cases, was probably not much.

ALGERNON. I'll speak to Bunbury, Aunt Augusta, if he is still conscious, and I think I can promise you he'll be all right by Saturday. Of course the music is a great difficulty. You see, if one plays good music, people don't listen, and if one plays bad music people don't talk. But I'll run over the program I've drawn out, if you will kindly come into the next room for a moment.

LADY BRACKNELL. Thank you, Algernon. It is very thoughtful of you. (*Rising, and following Algernon.*) I'm sure the program will be delightful, after a few expurgations. French songs I cannot possibly allow. People always seem to think that they are improper, and either look shocked, which is vulgar, or laugh, which is worse. But German sounds a thoroughly respectable language, and indeed, I believe is so. Gwendolen, you will accompany me.

GWENDOLEN. Certainly, mamma.

(*Lady Bracknell and Algernon go into the music-room, Gwendolen remains behind.*)

JACK. Charming day it has been, Miss Fairfax.

GWENDOLEN. Pray don't talk to me about the weather, Mr. Worthing. Whenever people talk to me about the weather, I always feel quite certain that they mean something else. And that makes me so nervous.

JACK. I do mean something else.

GWENDOLEN. I thought so. In fact, I am never wrong.

JACK. And I would like to be allowed to take advantage of Lady Bracknell's temporary absence …

GWENDOLEN. I would certainly advise you to do so. Mamma has a way of coming back suddenly into a room that I have often had to speak to her about.

---

1   *the season*   The London social season, which ran while Parliament was sitting. Many wealthy families spent the rest of the year at their country homes.

JACK. (*Nervously.*) Miss Fairfax, ever since I met you I have admired you more than any girl ... I have ever met since ... I met you.

GWENDOLEN. Yes, I am quite well aware of the fact. And I often wish that in public, at any rate, you had been more demonstrative. For me you have always had an irresistible fascination. Even before I met you I was far from indifferent to you. (*Jack looks at her in amazement.*) We live, as I hope you know, Mr. Worthing, in an age of ideals. The fact is constantly mentioned in the more expensive monthly magazines, and has reached the provincial[1] pulpits, I am told; and my ideal has always been to love some one of the name of Ernest. There is something in that name that inspires absolute confidence. The moment Algernon first mentioned to me that he had a friend called Ernest, I knew I was destined to love you.

JACK. You really love me, Gwendolen?

GWENDOLEN. Passionately!

JACK. Darling! You don't know how happy you've made me.

GWENDOLEN. My own Ernest!

JACK. But you don't really mean to say that you couldn't love me if my name wasn't Ernest?

GWENDOLEN. But your name is Ernest.

JACK. Yes, I know it is. But supposing it was something else? Do you mean to say you couldn't love me then?

GWENDOLEN. (*Glibly.*) Ah! that is clearly a metaphysical speculation, and like most metaphysical speculations has very little reference at all to the actual facts of real life, as we know them.

JACK. Personally, darling, to speak quite candidly, I don't much care about the name of Ernest ... I don't think the name suits me at all.

GWENDOLEN. It suits you perfectly. It is a divine name. It has a music of its own. It produces vibrations.

JACK. Well, really, Gwendolen, I must say that I think there are lots of other much nicer names. I think Jack, for instance, a charming name.

GWENDOLEN. Jack? ... No, there is very little music in the name Jack, if any at all, indeed. It does not thrill. It produces absolutely no vibrations ... I have known several Jacks, and they all, without exception, were more than usually plain. Besides, Jack is a notorious domesticity for John! And I pity any woman who is married to a man called John. She would probably never be allowed to know the entrancing pleasure of a single moment's solitude. The only really safe name is Ernest.

---

1   *provincial*   "Province" does not indicate a formal British jurisdiction; "the provinces" is a colloquial term for all areas of the country that are some distance from London.

JACK. Gwendolen, I must get christened at once—I mean we must get married at once. There is no time to be lost.   370

GWENDOLEN. Married, Mr. Worthing?

JACK. (*Astounded.*) Well … surely. You know that I love you, and you led me to believe, Miss Fairfax, that you were not absolutely indifferent to me.

GWENDOLEN. I adore you. But you haven't proposed to me yet. Nothing has been said at all about marriage. The subject has not even been touched on. 375

JACK. Well … may I propose to you now?

GWENDOLEN. I think it would be an admirable opportunity. And to spare you any possible disappointment, Mr. Worthing, I think it only fair to tell you quite frankly before-hand that I am fully determined to accept you.

JACK. Gwendolen!   380

GWENDOLEN. Yes, Mr. Worthing, what have you got to say to me?

JACK. You know what I have got to say to you.

GWENDOLEN. Yes, but you don't say it.

JACK. Gwendolen, will you marry me? (*Goes on his knees.*)

GWENDOLEN. Of course I will, darling. How long you have been about it! I 385
am afraid you have had very little experience in how to propose.

JACK. My own one, I have never loved any one in the world but you.

GWENDOLEN. Yes, but men often propose for practice. I know my brother Gerald does. All my girl-friends tell me so. What wonderfully blue eyes you have, Ernest! They are quite, quite, blue. I hope you will always look 390
at me just like that, especially when there are other people present. (*Enter Lady Bracknell.*)

LADY BRACKNELL. Mr. Worthing! Rise, sir, from this semi-recumbent posture. It is most indecorous.

GWENDOLEN. Mamma! (*He tries to rise; she restrains him.*) I must beg you to retire. This is no place for you. Besides, Mr. Worthing has not quite 395
finished yet.

LADY BRACKNELL. Finished what, may I ask?

GWENDOLEN. I am engaged to Mr. Worthing, mamma.

(*They rise together.*)

LADY BRACKNELL. Pardon me, you are not engaged to any one. When you do become engaged to some one, I, or your father, should his health permit 400
him, will inform you of the fact. An engagement should come on a young girl as a surprise, pleasant or unpleasant, as the case may be. It is hardly a matter that she could be allowed to arrange for herself … And now I have a few questions to put to you, Mr. Worthing. While I am making these inquiries, you, Gwendolen, will wait for me below in the carriage. 405

GWENDOLEN. (*Reproachfully.*) Mamma!

LADY BRACKNELL. In the carriage, Gwendolen!

(*Gwendolen goes to the door. She and Jack blow kisses to each other behind Lady Bracknell's back. Lady Bracknell looks vaguely about as if she could not understand what the noise was. Finally turns round.*)

Gwendolen, the carriage!

GWENDOLEN. Yes, mamma. (*Goes out, looking back at Jack.*)

410 LADY BRACKNELL. (*Sitting down.*) You can take a seat, Mr. Worthing. (*Looks in her pocket for note-book and pencil.*)

JACK. Thank you, Lady Bracknell, I prefer standing.

LADY BRACKNELL. (*Pencil and note-book in hand.*) I feel bound to tell you that you are not down on my list of eligible young men, although I have the same list as the dear Duchess of Bolton has. We work together, in fact.

415 However, I am quite ready to enter your name, should your answers be what a really affectionate mother requires. Do you smoke?

JACK. Well, yes, I must admit I smoke.

LADY BRACKNELL. I am glad to hear it. A man should always have an occupation of some kind. There are far too many idle men in London as it is.

420 How old are you?

JACK. Twenty-nine.

LADY BRACKNELL. A very good age to be married at. I have always been of opinion that a man who desires to get married should know either everything or nothing. Which do you know?

425 JACK. (*After some hesitation.*) I know nothing, Lady Bracknell.

LADY BRACKNELL. I am pleased to hear it. I do not approve of anything that tampers with natural ignorance. Ignorance is like a delicate exotic fruit; touch it and the bloom is gone. The whole theory of modern education is radically unsound. Fortunately in England, at any rate, education pro-

430 duces no effect whatsoever. If it did, it would prove a serious danger to the upper classes, and probably lead to acts of violence in Grosvenor Square.[1] What is your income?

JACK. Between seven and eight thousand a year.

LADY BRACKNELL. (*Makes a note in her book.*) In land, or in investments?

435 JACK. In investments, chiefly.

LADY BRACKNELL. That is satisfactory. What between the duties[2] expected of one during one's lifetime, and the duties exacted from one after one's death, land has ceased to be either a profit or a pleasure. It gives one position, and prevents one from keeping it up. That's all that can be said about land.

---

1 *Grosvenor Square* Located in a fashionable part of central London.
2 *duties* Taxes.

JACK. I have a country house with some land, of course, attached to it, about   440
fifteen hundred acres, I believe; but I don't depend on that for my real
income. In fact, as far as I can make out, the poachers are the only people
who make anything out of it.

LADY BRACKNELL. A country house! How many bedrooms? Well, that point
can be cleared up afterwards. You have a town house, I hope? A girl with   445
a simple, unspoiled nature, like Gwendolen, could hardly be expected to
reside in the country.

JACK. Well, I own a house in Belgrave Square, but it is let by the year to
Lady Bloxham. Of course, I can get it back whenever I like, at six months'
notice.   450

LADY BRACKNELL. Lady Bloxham? I don't know her.

JACK. Oh, she goes about very little. She is a lady considerably advanced in years.

LADY BRACKNELL. Ah, nowadays that is no guarantee of respectability of
character. What number in Belgrave Square?

JACK. 149.   455

LADY BRACKNELL. (*Shaking her head.*) The unfashionable side. I thought
there was something. However, that could easily be altered.

JACK. Do you mean the fashion, or the side?

LADY BRACKNELL. (*Sternly.*) Both, if necessary, I presume. What are your
politics?   460

JACK. Well, I am afraid I really have none. I am a Liberal Unionist.[1]

LADY BRACKNELL. Oh, they count as Tories.[2] They dine with us. Or come in
the evening, at any rate. Now to minor matters. Are your parents living?

JACK. I have lost both my parents.

LADY BRACKNELL. To lose one parent, Mr. Worthing, may be regarded as   465
a misfortune; to lose both looks like carelessness. Who was your father?
He was evidently a man of some wealth. Was he born in what the Radical
papers call the purple of commerce,[3] or did he rise from the ranks of the
aristocracy?

JACK. I am afraid I really don't know. The fact is, Lady Bracknell, I said I had   470
lost my parents. It would be nearer the truth to say that my parents seem
to have lost me ... I don't actually know who I am by birth. I was ... well,
I was found.

---

1   *Liberal Unionist*   The Liberal Unionists, who in 1886 had broken away from the Lib-
eral party in reaction to Prime Minister William Gladstone's support for Irish Home
Rule, occupied the political centre between the two large parties, the Liberals and the
Conservatives.

2   *Tories*   Conservatives.

3   *Was he born ... of commerce*   I.e., was he born into a wealthy merchant or trading family. (The colour purple is traditionally associated with royalty.)

LADY BRACKNELL. Found!

475 JACK. The late Mr. Thomas Cardew, an old gentleman of a very charitable and kindly disposition, found me, and gave me the name of Worthing, because he happened to have a first-class ticket for Worthing in his pocket at the time. Worthing is a place in Sussex. It is a seaside resort.

LADY BRACKNELL. Where did the charitable gentleman who had a first-class
480   ticket for this seaside resort find you?

JACK. (*Gravely.*) In a hand-bag.

LADY BRACKNELL. A hand-bag?

JACK. (*Very seriously.*) Yes, Lady Bracknell. I was in a hand-bag—a somewhat large, black leather hand-bag, with handles to it—an ordinary hand-bag
485   in fact.

LADY BRACKNELL. In what locality did this Mr. James, or Thomas, Cardew come across this ordinary hand-bag?

JACK. In the cloak-room at Victoria Station. It was given to him in mistake for his own.

490 LADY BRACKNELL. The cloak-room at Victoria Station?

JACK. Yes. The Brighton line.

LADY BRACKNELL. The line is immaterial. Mr. Worthing, I confess I feel somewhat bewildered by what you have just told me. To be born, or at any rate bred, in a hand-bag, whether it had handles or not, seems to me to dis-
495   play a contempt for the ordinary decencies of family life that reminds one of the worst excesses of the French Revolution. And I presume you know what that unfortunate movement led to? As for the particular locality in which the hand-bag was found, a cloak-room at a railway station might serve to conceal a social indiscretion—has probably, indeed, been used for
500   that purpose before now—but it could hardly be regarded as an assured basis for a recognized position in good society.

JACK. May I ask you then what you would advise me to do? I need hardly say I would do anything in the world to ensure Gwendolen's happiness.

LADY BRACKNELL. I would strongly advise you, Mr. Worthing, to try and
505   acquire some relations as soon as possible, and to make a definite effort to produce at any rate one parent, of either sex, before the season is quite over.

JACK. Well, I don't see how I could possibly manage to do that. I can produce the hand-bag at any moment. It is in my dressing-room at home. I really
510   think that should satisfy you, Lady Bracknell.

LADY BRACKNELL. Me, sir! What has it to do with me? You can hardly imagine that I and Lord Bracknell would dream of allowing our only daughter—a girl brought up with the utmost care—to marry into a cloak-room, and form an alliance with a parcel? Good morning, Mr. Worthing!

(Lady Bracknell sweeps out in majestic indignation.)

JACK. Good morning! *(Algernon, from the other room, strikes up the Wedding* 515
March. Jack looks perfectly furious, and goes to the door.) For goodness' sake
don't play that ghastly tune, Algy. How idiotic you are!

(The music stops and Algernon enters cheerily.)

ALGERNON. Didn't it go off all right, old boy? You don't mean to say Gwendolen refused you? I know it is a way she has. She is always refusing people.
I think it is most ill-natured of her.   520

JACK. Oh, Gwendolen is as right as a trivet.[1] As far as she is concerned, we
are engaged. Her mother is perfectly unbearable. Never met such a Gorgon[2] ... I don't really know what a Gorgon is like, but I am quite sure that
Lady Bracknell is one. In any case, she is a monster, without being a myth,
which is rather unfair ... I beg your pardon, Algy, I suppose I shouldn't 525
talk about your own aunt in that way before you.

ALGERNON. My dear boy, I love hearing my relations abused. It is the only
thing that makes me put up with them at all. Relations are simply a tedious
pack of people, who haven't got the remotest knowledge of how to live, nor
the smallest instinct about when to die.   530

JACK. Oh, that is nonsense!

ALGERNON. It isn't!

JACK. Well, I won't argue about the matter. You always want to argue about
things.

ALGERNON. That is exactly what things were originally made for.   535

JACK. Upon my word, if I thought that, I'd shoot myself ... *(A pause.)* You
don't think there is any chance of Gwendolen becoming like her mother in
about a hundred and fifty years, do you, Algy?

ALGERNON. All women become like their mothers. That is their tragedy. No
man does. That's his.   540

JACK. Is that clever?

ALGERNON. It is perfectly phrased! and quite as true as any observation in
civilized life should be.

JACK. I am sick to death of cleverness. Everybody is clever nowadays. You
can't go anywhere without meeting clever people. The thing has become 545
an absolute public nuisance. I wish to goodness we had a few fools left.

---

1   *as right as a trivet* Proverbial expression indicating stability (a trivet is a three-footed
     stand or support).
2   *Gorgon* In Greek mythology the three Gorgons are sisters who have repulsive features
     (including snakes growing out of their heads instead of hair); anyone who looks at them
     turns into stone.

ALGERNON. We have.

JACK. I should extremely like to meet them. What do they talk about?

ALGERNON. The fools? Oh! about the clever people, of course.

550 JACK. What fools!

ALGERNON. By the way, did you tell Gwendolen the truth about your being
Ernest in town, and Jack in the country?

JACK. (*In a very patronizing manner.*) My dear fellow, the truth isn't quite the
sort of thing one tells to a nice, sweet, refined girl. What extraordinary
555   ideas you have about the way to behave to a woman!

ALGERNON. The only way to behave to a woman is to make love to[1] her, if she
is pretty, and to some one else, if she is plain.

JACK. Oh, that is nonsense.

ALGERNON. What about your brother? What about the profligate Ernest?

560 JACK. Oh, before the end of the week I shall have got rid of him. I'll say he
died in Paris of apoplexy.[2] Lots of people die of apoplexy, quite suddenly,
don't they?

ALGERNON. Yes, but it's hereditary, my dear fellow. It's a sort of thing that
runs in families. You had much better say a severe chill.

565 JACK. You are sure a severe chill isn't hereditary, or anything of that kind?

ALGERNON. Of course it isn't!

JACK. Very well, then. My poor brother Ernest is carried off suddenly, in
Paris, by a severe chill. That gets rid of him.

ALGERNON. But I thought you said that … Miss Cardew was a little too
570   much interested in your poor brother Ernest? Won't she feel his loss a
good deal?

JACK. Oh, that is all right. Cecily is not a silly romantic girl, I am glad to
say. She has got a capital appetite, goes on long walks, and pays no attention at all to her lessons.

575 ALGERNON. I would rather like to see Cecily.

JACK. I will take very good care you never do. She is excessively pretty, and
she is only just eighteen.

ALGERNON. Have you told Gwendolen yet that you have an excessively pretty
ward who is only just eighteen?

580 JACK. Oh! one doesn't blurt these things out to people. Cecily and Gwendolen are perfectly certain to be extremely great friends. I'll bet you anything
you like that half an hour after they have met, they will be calling each
other sister.

---

1   *make love to* I.e., court or flirt with.
2   *apoplexy* Stroke.

ALGERNON. Women only do that when they have called each other a lot of
    other things first. Now, my dear boy, if we want to get a good table at Wil-   585
    lis's, we really must go and dress. Do you know it is nearly seven?

JACK. (*Irritably.*) Oh! It always is nearly seven.

ALGERNON. Well, I'm hungry.

JACK. I never knew you when you weren't …

ALGERNON. What shall we do after dinner? Go to a theatre?   590

JACK. Oh no! I loathe listening.

ALGERNON. Well, let us go to the Club?

JACK. Oh, no! I hate talking.

ALGERNON. Well, we might trot round to the Empire[1] at ten?

JACK. Oh, no! I can't bear looking at things. It is so silly.   595

ALGERNON. Well, what shall we do?

JACK. Nothing!

ALGERNON. It is awfully hard work doing nothing. However, I don't mind
    hard work where there is no definite object of any kind.

    (*Enter Lane.*)

LANE. Miss Fairfax.   600

    (*Enter Gwendolen. Lane goes out.*)

ALGERNON. Gwendolen, upon my word!

GWENDOLEN. Algy, kindly turn your back. I have something very particular
    to say to Mr. Worthing.

ALGERNON. Really, Gwendolen, I don't think I can allow this at all.

GWENDOLEN. Algy, you always adopt a strictly immoral attitude towards life.   605
    You are not quite old enough to do that. (*Algernon retires to the fireplace.*)

JACK. My own darling!

GWENDOLEN. Ernest, we may never be married. From the expression on
    mamma's face I fear we never shall. Few parents nowadays pay any re-
    gard to what their children say to them. The old-fashioned respect for the   610
    young is fast dying out. Whatever influence I ever had over mamma, I lost
    at the age of three. But although she may prevent us from becoming man
    and wife, and I may marry some one else, and marry often, nothing that
    she can possibly do can alter my eternal devotion to you.

JACK. Dear Gwendolen!   615

GWENDOLEN. The story of your romantic origin, as related to me by mamma,
    with unpleasing comments, has naturally stirred the deeper fibres of my
    nature. Your Christian name has an irresistible fascination. The simplic-

---

1   *the Empire* Theatre that often featured risqué variety shows.

ity of your character makes you exquisitely incomprehensible to me. Your town address at the Albany I have. What is your address in the country?

620

JACK. The Manor House, Woolton, Hertfordshire.

(Algernon, who has been carefully listening, smiles to himself, and writes the address on his shirt-cuff. Then picks up the Railway Guide.)

GWENDOLEN. There is a good postal service, I suppose? It may be necessary to do something desperate. That of course will require serious consideration. I will communicate with you daily.

625

JACK. My own one!

GWENDOLEN. How long do you remain in town?

JACK. Till Monday.

GWENDOLEN. Good! Algy, you may turn round now.

ALGERNON. Thanks, I've turned round already.

630

GWENDOLEN. You may also ring the bell.

JACK. You will let me see you to your carriage, my own darling?

GWENDOLEN. Certainly.

JACK. *(To Lane, who now enters.)* I will see Miss Fairfax out.

LANE. Yes, sir. *(Jack and Gwendolen go off.)*

(Lane presents several letters on a salver to Algernon. It is to be surmised that they are bills, as Algernon, after looking at the envelopes, tears them up.)

635

ALGERNON. A glass of sherry, Lane.

LANE. Yes, sir.

ALGERNON. Tomorrow, Lane, I'm going Bunburying.

LANE. Yes, sir.

ALGERNON. I shall probably not be back till Monday. You can put up my

640

dress clothes, my smoking jacket, and all the Bunbury suits …

LANE. Yes, sir. *(Handing sherry.)*

ALGERNON. I hope tomorrow will be a fine day, Lane.

LANE. It never is, sir.

ALGERNON. Lane, you're a perfect pessimist.

645

LANE. I do my best to give satisfaction, sir.

(Enter Jack. Lane goes off.)

JACK. There's a sensible, intellectual girl! the only girl I ever cared for in my life. *(Algernon is laughing immoderately.)* What on earth are you so amused at?

ALGERNON. Oh, I'm a little anxious about poor Bunbury, that is all.

650

JACK. If you don't take care, your friend Bunbury will get you into a serious scrape some day.

ALGERNON. I love scrapes. They are the only things that are never serious.

JACK. Oh, that's nonsense, Algy. You never talk anything but nonsense.

ALGERNON. Nobody ever does.

(*Jack looks indignantly at him, and leaves the room. Algernon lights a cigarette, reads his shirt-cuff, and smiles.*)

ACT DROP

ACT 2

SCENE

Garden at the Manor House. A flight of grey stone steps leads up to the house. The garden, an old-fashioned one, full of roses. Time of year, July. Basket chairs, and a table covered with books, are set under a large yew-tree. Miss Prism discovered seated at the table. Cecily is at the back watering flowers.

MISS PRISM. (*Calling.*) Cecily, Cecily! Surely such a utilitarian occupation as the watering of flowers is rather Moulton's duty than yours? Especially at a moment when intellectual pleasures await you. Your German grammar is on the table. Pray open it at page fifteen. We will repeat yesterday's lesson.

CECILY. (*Coming over very slowly.*) But I don't like German. It isn't at all a   5
becoming language. I know perfectly well that I look quite plain after my German lesson.

MISS PRISM. Child, you know how anxious your guardian is that you should improve yourself in every way. He laid particular stress on your German, as he was leaving for town yesterday. Indeed, he always lays stress on your   10
German when he is leaving for town.

CECILY. Dear Uncle Jack is so very serious! Sometimes he is so serious that I think he cannot be quite well.

MISS PRISM. (*Drawing herself up.*) Your guardian enjoys the best of health, and his gravity of demeanour is especially to be commended in one so   15
comparatively young as he is. I know no one who has a higher sense of duty and responsibility.

CECILY. I suppose that is why he often looks a little bored when we three are together.

MISS PRISM. Cecily! I am surprised at you. Mr. Worthing has many troubles   20
in his life. Idle merriment and triviality would be out of place in his conversation. You must remember his constant anxiety about that unfortunate young man his brother.

CECILY. I wish Uncle Jack would allow that unfortunate young man, his
25 brother, to come down here sometimes. We might have a good influence
over him, Miss Prism. I am sure you certainly would. You know German,
and geology, and things of that kind influence a man very much. (*Cecily
begins to write in her diary.*)

MISS PRISM. (*Shaking her head.*) I do not think that even I could produce
any effect on a character that according to his own brother's admission is
30 irretrievably weak and vacillating. Indeed I am not sure that I would desire
to reclaim him. I am not in favour of this modern mania for turning bad
people into good people at a moment's notice. As a man sows so let him
reap.[1] You must put away your diary, Cecily. I really don't see why you
should keep a diary at all.

35 CECILY. I keep a diary in order to enter the wonderful secrets of my life. If I
didn't write them down, I should probably forget all about them.

MISS PRISM. Memory, my dear Cecily, is the diary that we all carry about
with us.

CECILY. Yes, but it usually chronicles the things that have never happened,
40 and couldn't possibly have happened. I believe that Memory is responsible
for nearly all the three-volume novels that Mudie sends us.[2]

MISS PRISM. Do not speak slightingly of the three-volume novel, Cecily. I
wrote one myself in earlier days.

CECILY. Did you really, Miss Prism? How wonderfully clever you are! I hope
45 it did not end happily? I don't like novels that end happily. They depress
me so much.

MISS PRISM. The good ended happily, and the bad unhappily. That is what
Fiction means.

CECILY. I suppose so. But it seems very unfair. And was your novel ever
50 published?

MISS PRISM. Alas! no. The manuscript unfortunately was abandoned. (*Cecily
starts.*) I use the word in the sense of lost or mislaid. To your work, child,
these speculations are profitless.

CECILY. (*Smiling.*) But I see dear Dr. Chasuble coming up through the gar-
55 den.

MISS PRISM. (*Rising and advancing.*) Dr. Chasuble! This is indeed a pleasure.

(*Enter Canon Chasuble.*)

CHASUBLE. And how are we this morning? Miss Prism, you are, I trust, well?

---

1   *As a man ... him reap* Galatians 6.7: "whatsoever a man soweth, that shall he also
reap."
2   *nearly all ... Mudie sends us* Commercial lending libraries of the time, such as Mudie's, specialized in lending novels that were published in three volumes.

CECILY. Miss Prism has just been complaining of a slight headache. I think it would do her so much good to have a short stroll with you in the Park, Dr. Chasuble. 60

MISS PRISM. Cecily, I have not mentioned anything about a headache.

CECILY. No, dear Miss Prism, I know that, but I felt instinctively that you had a headache. Indeed I was thinking about that, and not about my German lesson, when the Rector came in.

CHASUBLE. I hope, Cecily, you are not inattentive. 65

CECILY. Oh, I am afraid I am.

CHASUBLE. That is strange. Were I fortunate enough to be Miss Prism's pupil, I would hang upon her lips. (*Miss Prism glares.*) I spoke metaphorically.— My metaphor was drawn from bees. Ahem! Mr. Worthing, I suppose, has not returned from town yet? 70

MISS PRISM. We do not expect him till Monday afternoon.

CHASUBLE. Ah yes, he usually likes to spend his Sunday in London. He is not one of those whose sole aim is enjoyment, as, by all accounts, that unfortunate young man his brother seems to be. But I must not disturb Egeria[1] and her pupil any longer. 75

MISS PRISM. Egeria? My name is Lætitia, Doctor.

CHASUBLE. (*Bowing.*) A classical allusion merely, drawn from the Pagan authors. I shall see you both no doubt at Evensong?[2]

MISS PRISM. I think, dear Doctor, I will have a stroll with you. I find I have a headache after all, and a walk might do it good. 80

CHASUBLE. With pleasure, Miss Prism, with pleasure. We might go as far as the schools and back.

MISS PRISM. That would be delightful. Cecily, you will read your Political Economy in my absence. The chapter on the Fall of the Rupee[3] you may omit. It is somewhat too sensational. Even these metallic problems have 85 their melodramatic side.

(*Goes down the garden with Dr. Chasuble.*)

CECILY. (*Picks up books and throws them back on table.*) Horrid Political Economy! Horrid Geography! Horrid, horrid German!

(*Enter Merriman with a card on a salver.*)

---

1   *Egeria*   In Roman mythology, the nymph Egeria taught Numa, the second King of Rome, the lessons of wisdom and law which he then used to found the institutions of Rome.

2   *Evensong*   The evening service in the Anglican Church (and various other Christian denominations).

3   *Fall of the Rupee*   The rupee (India's currency) declined dramatically in the early 1890s as a result of a variety of disasters, including an outbreak of plague.

MERRIMAN. Mr. Ernest Worthing has just driven over from the station. He
has brought his luggage with him.

CECILY. (*Takes the card and reads it.*) "Mr. Ernest Worthing, B. 4, The Albany,
W." Uncle Jack's brother! Did you tell him Mr. Worthing was in town?

MERRIMAN. Yes, Miss. He seemed very much disappointed. I mentioned that
you and Miss Prism were in the garden. He said he was anxious to speak to
you privately for a moment.

CECILY. Ask Mr. Ernest Worthing to come here. I suppose you had better
talk to the housekeeper about a room for him.

MERRIMAN. Yes, Miss.

(Merriman goes off.)

CECILY. I have never met any really wicked person before. I feel rather frightened. I am so afraid he will look just like every one else. (*Enter Algernon,
very gay and debonair.*) He does!

ALGERNON. (*Raising his hat.*) You are my little cousin Cecily, I'm sure.

CECILY. You are under some strange mistake. I am not little. In fact, I believe
I am more than usually tall for my age. (*Algernon is rather taken aback.*)
But I am your cousin Cecily. You, I see from your card, are Uncle Jack's
brother, my cousin Ernest, my wicked cousin Ernest.

ALGERNON. Oh! I am not really wicked at all, cousin Cecily. You mustn't
think that I am wicked.

CECILY. If you are not, then you have certainly been deceiving us all in a
very inexcusable manner. I hope you have not been leading a double life,
pretending to be wicked and being really good all the time. That would be
hypocrisy.

ALGERNON. (*Looks at her in amazement.*) Oh! Of course I have been rather
reckless.

CECILY. I am glad to hear it.

ALGERNON. In fact, now you mention the subject, I have been very bad in
my own small way.

CECILY. I don't think you should be so proud of that, though I am sure it
must have been very pleasant.

ALGERNON. It is much pleasanter being here with you.

CECILY. I can't understand how you are here at all. Uncle Jack won't be back
till Monday afternoon.

ALGERNON. That is a great disappointment. I am obliged to go up by the
first train on Monday morning. I have a business appointment that I am
anxious … to miss!

CECILY. Couldn't you miss it anywhere but in London?

ALGERNON. No: the appointment is in London.

CECILY. Well, I know, of course, how important it is not to keep a business
     engagement, if one wants to retain any sense of the beauty of life, but still I
     think you had better wait till Uncle Jack arrives. I know he wants to speak   130
     to you about your emigrating.
ALGERNON. About my what?
CECILY. Your emigrating. He has gone up to buy your outfit.
ALGERNON. I certainly wouldn't let Jack buy my outfit. He has no taste in
     neckties at all.   135
CECILY. I don't think you will require neckties. Uncle Jack is sending you to
     Australia.[1]
ALGERNON. Australia! I'd sooner die.
CECILY. Well, he said at dinner on Wednesday night, that you would have to
     choose between this world, the next world, and Australia.   140
ALGERNON. Oh, well! The accounts I have received of Australia and the next
     world are not particularly encouraging. This world is good enough for me,
     cousin Cecily.
CECILY. Yes, but are you good enough for it?
ALGERNON. I'm afraid I'm not that. That is why I want you to reform me.   145
     You might make that your mission, if you don't mind, cousin Cecily.
CECILY. I'm afraid I've no time, this afternoon.
ALGERNON. Well, would you mind my reforming myself this afternoon?
CECILY. It is rather Quixotic of you. But I think you should try.
ALGERNON. I will. I feel better already.   150
CECILY. You are looking a little worse.
ALGERNON. That is because I am hungry.
CECILY. How thoughtless of me. I should have remembered that when one
     is going to lead an entirely new life, one requires regular and wholesome
     meals. Won't you come in?   155
ALGERNON. Thank you. Might I have a buttonhole[2] first? I never have any
     appetite unless I have a buttonhole first.
CECILY. A Maréchal Niel?[3] (*Picks up scissors.*)
ALGERNON. No, I'd sooner have a pink rose.
CECILY. Why? (*Cuts a flower.*)   160
ALGERNON. Because you are like a pink rose, Cousin Cecily.
CECILY. I don't think it can be right for you to talk to me like that. Miss
     Prism never says such things to me.

---

1   *Australia*   A former penal colony, at the time still considered to be largely composed
     of wilderness.
2   *buttonhole*   Boutonniere, flower for one's lapel.
3   *Maréchal Niel*   Variety of yellow rose.

ALGERNON. Then Miss Prism is a short-sighted old lady. (*Cecily puts the rose*
165   *in his buttonhole.*) You are the prettiest girl I ever saw.

CECILY. Miss Prism says that all good looks are a snare.

ALGERNON. They are a snare that every sensible man would like to be caught in.

CECILY. Oh, I don't think I would care to catch a sensible man. I shouldn't
   know what to talk to him about.

     (*They pass into the house. Miss Prism and Dr. Chasuble return.*)

170 MISS PRISM. You are too much alone, dear Dr. Chasuble. You should get
   married. A misanthrope I can understand—a womanthrope,[1] never!

CHASUBLE. (*With a scholar's shudder.*) Believe me, I do not deserve so neologistic[2] a phrase. The precept as well as the practice of the Primitive Church[3]
   was distinctly against matrimony.

175 MISS PRISM. (*Sententiously.*) That is obviously the reason why the Primitive
   Church has not lasted up to the present day. And you do not seem to realize, dear Doctor, that by persistently remaining single, a man converts
   himself into a permanent public temptation. Men should be more careful;
   this very celibacy leads weaker vessels astray.

180 CHASUBLE. But is a man not equally attractive when married?

MISS PRISM. No married man is ever attractive except to his wife.

CHASUBLE. And often, I've been told, not even to her.

MISS PRISM. That depends on the intellectual sympathies of the woman. Maturity can always be depended on. Ripeness can be trusted. Young women
185   are green. (*Dr. Chasuble starts.*) I spoke horticulturally. My metaphor was
   drawn from fruits. But where is Cecily?

CHASUBLE. Perhaps she followed us to the schools.

     (*Enter Jack slowly from the back of the garden. He is dressed in the deepest
     mourning, with crepe hatband and black gloves.*)

MISS PRISM. Mr. Worthing!

CHASUBLE. Mr. Worthing?

190 MISS PRISM. This is indeed a surprise. We did not look for you till Monday
   afternoon.

JACK. (*Shakes Miss Prism's hand in a tragic manner.*) I have returned sooner
   than I expected. Dr. Chasuble, I hope you are well?

CHASUBLE. Dear Mr. Worthing, I trust this garb of woe does not betoken
195   some terrible calamity?

---

1   *misanthrope … womanthrope* The correct word for someone who hates women is a
   "misogynist"; a "misanthrope" is someone who hates all humanity.

2   *neologistic* A "neologism" is a newly invented word.

3   *Primitive Church* Early Christian Church.

JACK. My brother.

MISS PRISM. More shameful debts and extravagance?

CHASUBLE. Still leading his life of pleasure?

JACK. (*Shaking his head.*) Dead!

CHASUBLE. Your brother Ernest dead?   200

JACK. Quite dead.

MISS PRISM. What a lesson for him! I trust he will profit by it.

CHASUBLE. Mr. Worthing, I offer you my sincere condolence. You have at
    least the consolation of knowing that you were always the most generous
    and forgiving of brothers.   205

JACK. Poor Ernest! He had many faults, but it is a sad, sad blow.

CHASUBLE. Very sad indeed. Were you with him at the end?

JACK. No. He died abroad; in Paris, in fact. I had a telegram last night from
    the manager of the Grand Hotel.

CHASUBLE. Was the cause of death mentioned?   210

JACK. A severe chill, it seems.

MISS PRISM. As a man sows, so shall he reap.

CHASUBLE. (*Raising his hand.*) Charity, dear Miss Prism, charity! None of us
    are perfect. I myself am peculiarly susceptible to draughts. Will the inter-
    ment take place here?   215

JACK. No. He seems to have expressed a desire to be buried in Paris.

CHASUBLE. In Paris! (*Shakes his head.*) I fear that hardly points to any very
    serious state of mind at the last. You would no doubt wish me to make
    some slight allusion to this tragic domestic affliction next Sunday. (*Jack
    presses his hand convulsively.*) My sermon on the meaning of the manna in   220
    the wilderness[1] can be adapted to almost any occasion, joyful, or, as in the
    present case, distressing. (*All sigh.*) I have preached it at harvest celebra-
    tions, christenings, confirmations,[2] on days of humiliation and festal days.
    The last time I delivered it was in the Cathedral, as a charity sermon on
    behalf of the Society for the Prevention of Discontent among the Upper   225
    Orders. The Bishop, who was present, was much struck by some of the
    analogies I drew.

JACK. Ah! that reminds me, you mentioned christenings I think, Dr. Cha-
    suble? I suppose you know how to christen all right? (*Dr. Chasuble looks
    astounded.*) I mean, of course, you are continually christening, aren't you?   230

---

1   *manna in the wilderness* See Exodus 16.
2   *christenings, confirmations* Whereas a christening formally admits a person to the
     Christian Church through baptism (usually in infancy), in many Christian denomina-
     tions a person's standing as a full member of the Church must be confirmed at a later
     ceremony (typically in young adulthood).

MISS PRISM. It is, I regret to say, one of the Rector's most constant duties in this parish. I have often spoken to the poorer classes on the subject. But they don't seem to know what thrift is.

CHASUBLE. But is there any particular infant in whom you are interested, Mr.
235   Worthing? Your brother was, I believe, unmarried, was he not?

JACK. Oh yes.

MISS PRISM. (*Bitterly.*) People who live entirely for pleasure usually are.

JACK. But it is not for any child, dear Doctor. I am very fond of children. No! the fact is, I would like to be christened myself, this afternoon, if you have
240   nothing better to do.

CHASUBLE. But surely, Mr. Worthing, you have been christened already?

JACK. I don't remember anything about it.

CHASUBLE. But have you any grave doubts on the subject?

JACK. I certainly intend to have. Of course I don't know if the thing would
245   bother you in any way, or if you think I am a little too old now.

CHASUBLE. Not at all. The sprinkling, and, indeed, the immersion of adults is a perfectly canonical practice.

JACK. Immersion!

CHASUBLE. You need have no apprehensions. Sprinkling is all that is neces-
250   sary, or indeed I think advisable. Our weather is so changeable. At what hour would you wish the ceremony performed?

JACK. Oh, I might trot round about five if that would suit you.

CHASUBLE. Perfectly, perfectly! In fact I have two similar ceremonies to perform at that time. A case of twins that occurred recently in one of the out-
255   lying cottages on your own estate. Poor Jenkins the carter,[1] a most hard-working man.

JACK. Oh! I don't see much fun in being christened along with other babies. It would be childish. Would half-past five do?

CHASUBLE. Admirably! Admirably! (*Takes out watch.*) And now, dear Mr.
260   Worthing, I will not intrude any longer into a house of sorrow. I would merely beg you not to be too much bowed down by grief. What seem to us bitter trials are often blessings in disguise.

MISS PRISM. This seems to me a blessing of an extremely obvious kind.

(*Enter Cecily from the house.*)

CECILY. Uncle Jack! Oh, I am pleased to see you back. But what horrid
265   clothes you have got on! Do go and change them.

MISS PRISM. Cecily!

CHASUBLE. My child! my child!

---

1   *carter* Cart driver.

(Cecily goes towards Jack; he kisses her brow in a melancholy manner.)

CECILY. What is the matter, Uncle Jack? Do look happy! You look as if you had toothache, and I have got such a surprise for you. Who do you think is in the dining-room? Your brother! 270

JACK. Who?

CECILY. Your brother Ernest. He arrived about half an hour ago.

JACK. What nonsense! I haven't got a brother.

CECILY. Oh, don't say that. However badly he may have behaved to you in the past he is still your brother. You couldn't be so heartless as to disown 275 him. I'll tell him to come out. And you will shake hands with him, won't you, Uncle Jack? *(Runs back into the house.)*

CHASUBLE. These are very joyful tidings.

MISS PRISM. After we had all been resigned to his loss, his sudden return seems to me peculiarly distressing. 280

JACK. My brother is in the dining-room? I don't know what it all means. I think it is perfectly absurd.

(Enter Algernon and Cecily hand in hand. They come slowly up to Jack.)

JACK. Good heavens! *(Motions Algernon away.)*

ALGERNON. Brother John, I have come down from town to tell you that I am very sorry for all the trouble I have given you, and that I intend to lead 285 a better life in the future. *(Jack glares at him and does not take his hand.)*

CECILY. Uncle Jack, you are not going to refuse your own brother's hand?

JACK. Nothing will induce me to take his hand. I think his coming down here disgraceful. He knows perfectly well why.

CECILY. Uncle Jack, do be nice. There is some good in every one. Ernest has 290 just been telling me about his poor invalid friend Mr. Bunbury whom he goes to visit so often. And surely there must be much good in one who is kind to an invalid, and leaves the pleasures of London to sit by a bed of pain.

JACK. Oh! he has been talking about Bunbury, has he? 295

CECILY. Yes, he has told me all about poor Mr. Bunbury, and his terrible state of health.

JACK. Bunbury! Well, I won't have him talk to you about Bunbury or about anything else. It is enough to drive one perfectly frantic.

ALGERNON. Of course I admit that the faults were all on my side. But I must 300 say that I think that Brother John's coldness to me is peculiarly painful. I expected a more enthusiastic welcome, especially considering it is the first time I have come here.

CECILY. Uncle Jack, if you don't shake hands with Ernest I will never forgive you. 305

JACK. Never forgive me?

CECILY. Never, never, never!

JACK. Well, this is the last time I shall ever do it. (*Shakes hands with Algernon and glares.*)

CHASUBLE. It's pleasant, is it not, to see so perfect a reconciliation? I think we might leave the two brothers together.

MISS PRISM. Cecily, you will come with us.

CECILY. Certainly, Miss Prism. My little task of reconciliation is over.

CHASUBLE. You have done a beautiful action today, dear child.

MISS PRISM. We must not be premature in our judgments.

CECILY. I feel very happy.

(*They all go off except Jack and Algernon.*)

JACK. You young scoundrel, Algy, you must get out of this place as soon as possible. I don't allow any Bunburying here.

(*Enter Merriman.*)

MERRIMAN. I have put Mr. Ernest's things in the room next to yours, sir. I suppose that is all right?

JACK. What?

MERRIMAN. Mr. Ernest's luggage, sir. I have unpacked it and put it in the room next to your own.

JACK. His luggage?

MERRIMAN. Yes, sir. Three portmanteaus, a dressing-case, two hat-boxes, and a large luncheon-basket.

ALGERNON. I am afraid I can't stay more than a week this time.

JACK. Merriman, order the dog-cart[1] at once. Mr. Ernest has been suddenly called back to town.

MERRIMAN. Yes, sir. (*Goes back into the house.*)

ALGERNON. What a fearful liar you are, Jack. I have not been called back to town at all.

JACK. Yes, you have.

ALGERNON. I haven't heard any one call me.

JACK. Your duty as a gentleman calls you back.

ALGERNON. My duty as a gentleman has never interfered with my pleasures in the smallest degree.

JACK. I can quite understand that.

ALGERNON. Well, Cecily is a darling.

---

1   *dog-cart*   Small horse-drawn carriage in which the occupants would sit back-to-back; a box for conveying hunting dogs was also typically part of the contraption.

JACK. You are not to talk of Miss Cardew like that. I don't like it.

ALGERNON. Well, I don't like your clothes. You look perfectly ridiculous in   340
them. Why on earth don't you go up and change? It is perfectly childish to
be in deep mourning for a man who is actually staying for a whole week
with you in your house as a guest. I call it grotesque.

JACK. You are certainly not staying with me for a whole week as a guest or
anything else. You have got to leave … by the four-five train.   345

ALGERNON. I certainly won't leave you so long as you are in mourning. It
would be most unfriendly. If I were in mourning you would stay with me,
I suppose. I should think it very unkind if you didn't.

JACK. Well, will you go if I change my clothes?

ALGERNON. Yes, if you are not too long. I never saw anybody take so long to   350
dress, and with such little result.

JACK. Well, at any rate, that is better than being always over-dressed as you
are.

ALGERNON. If I am occasionally a little over-dressed, I make up for it by being always immensely over-educated.   355

JACK. Your vanity is ridiculous, your conduct an outrage, and your presence
in my garden utterly absurd. However, you have got to catch the four-five,
and I hope you will have a pleasant journey back to town. This Bunburying, as you call it, has not been a great success for you. (*Goes into the house.*)

ALGERNON. I think it has been a great success. I'm in love with Cecily, and   360
that is everything.

*(Enter Cecily at the back of the garden. She picks up the can and begins to
water the flowers.)*

But I must see her before I go, and make arrangements for another Bunbury. Ah, there she is.

CECILY. Oh, I merely came back to water the roses. I thought you were with
Uncle Jack.   365

ALGERNON. He's gone to order the dog-cart for me.

CECILY. Oh, is he going to take you for a nice drive?

ALGERNON. He's going to send me away.

CECILY. Then have we got to part?

ALGERNON. I am afraid so. It's a very painful parting.   370

CECILY. It is always painful to part from people whom one has known for a
very brief space of time. The absence of old friends one can endure with
equanimity. But even a momentary separation from anyone to whom one
has just been introduced is almost unbearable.

ALGERNON. Thank you.   375

(Enter Merriman.)

MERRIMAN. The dog-cart is at the door, sir.

(Algernon looks appealingly at Cecily.)

CECILY. It can wait, Merriman for … five minutes.

MERRIMAN. Yes, Miss.

(Exit Merriman.)

ALGERNON. I hope, Cecily, I shall not offend you if I state quite frankly and
380 openly that you seem to me to be in every way the visible personification
of absolute perfection.

CECILY. I think your frankness does you great credit, Ernest. If you will allow
me, I will copy your remarks into my diary. (Goes over to table and begins
writing in diary.)

385 ALGERNON. Do you really keep a diary? I'd give anything to look at it. May I?

CECILY. Oh no. (Puts her hand over it.) You see, it is simply a very young girl's
record of her own thoughts and impressions, and consequently meant for
publication. When it appears in volume form I hope you will order a copy.
But pray, Ernest, don't stop. I delight in taking down from dictation. I
390 have reached "absolute perfection." You can go on. I am quite ready for
more.

ALGERNON. (Somewhat taken aback.) Ahem! Ahem!

CECILY. Oh, don't cough, Ernest. When one is dictating one should speak
fluently and not cough. Besides, I don't know how to spell a cough. (Writes
as Algernon speaks.)

395 ALGERNON. (Speaking very rapidly.) Cecily, ever since I first looked upon your
wonderful and incomparable beauty, I have dared to love you wildly, passionately, devotedly, hopelessly.

CECILY. I don't think that you should tell me that you love me wildly, passionately, devotedly, hopelessly. Hopelessly doesn't seem to make much
400 sense, does it?

ALGERNON. Cecily!

(Enter Merriman.)

MERRIMAN. The dog-cart is waiting, sir.

ALGERNON. Tell it to come round next week, at the same hour.

MERRIMAN. (Looks at Cecily, who makes no sign.) Yes, sir.

(Merriman retires.)

405 CECILY. Uncle Jack would be very much annoyed if he knew you were staying on till next week, at the same hour.

ALGERNON. Oh, I don't care about Jack. I don't care for anybody in the whole
world but you. I love you, Cecily. You will marry me, won't you?

CECILY. You silly boy! Of course. Why, we have been engaged for the last three months. 410

ALGERNON. For the last three months?

CECILY. Yes, it will be exactly three months on Thursday.

ALGERNON. But how did we become engaged?

CECILY. Well, ever since dear Uncle Jack first confessed to us that he had a younger brother who was very wicked and bad, you of course have formed 415 the chief topic of conversation between myself and Miss Prism. And of course a man who is much talked about is always very attractive. One feels there must be something in him, after all. I daresay it was foolish of me, but I fell in love with you, Ernest.

ALGERNON. Darling! And when was the engagement actually settled? 420

CECILY. On the 14th of February last. Worn out by your entire ignorance of my existence, I determined to end the matter one way or the other, and after a long struggle with myself I accepted you under this dear old tree here. The next day I bought this little ring in your name, and this is the little bangle with the true lover's knot I promised you always to wear. 425

ALGERNON. Did I give you this? It's very pretty, isn't it?

CECILY. Yes, you've wonderfully good taste, Ernest. It's the excuse I've always given for your leading such a bad life. And this is the box in which I keep all your dear letters. (*Kneels at table, opens box, and produces letters tied up with blue ribbon.*)

ALGERNON. My letters! But, my own sweet Cecily, I have never written you 430 any letters.

CECILY. You need hardly remind me of that, Ernest. I remember only too well that I was forced to write your letters for you. I wrote always three times a week, and sometimes oftener.

ALGERNON. Oh, do let me read them, Cecily? 435

CECILY. Oh, I couldn't possibly. They would make you far too conceited. (*Replaces box.*) The three you wrote me after I had broken off the engagement are so beautiful, and so badly spelled, that even now I can hardly read them without crying a little.

ALGERNON. But was our engagement ever broken off? 440

CECILY. Of course it was. On the 22nd of last March. You can see the entry if you like. (*Shows diary.*) "Today I broke off my engagement with Ernest. I feel it is better to do so. The weather still continues charming."

ALGERNON. But why on earth did you break it off? What had I done? I had done nothing at all. Cecily, I am very much hurt indeed to hear you broke 445 it off. Particularly when the weather was so charming.

CECILY. It would hardly have been a really serious engagement if it hadn't been broken off at least once. But I forgave you before the week was out.

ALGERNON. (*Crossing to her, and kneeling.*) What a perfect angel you are,
450   Cecily.

CECILY. You dear romantic boy. (*He kisses her, she puts her fingers through his hair.*) I hope your hair curls naturally, does it?

ALGERNON. Yes, darling, with a little help from others.

CECILY. I am so glad.

455 ALGERNON. You'll never break off our engagement again, Cecily?

CECILY. I don't think I could break it off now that I have actually met you. Besides, of course, there is the question of your name.

ALGERNON. Yes, of course. (*Nervously.*)

CECILY. You must not laugh at me, darling, but it had always been a girlish
460   dream of mine to love some one whose name was Ernest. (*Algernon rises, Cecily also.*) There is something in that name that seems to inspire absolute confidence. I pity any poor married woman whose husband is not called Ernest.

ALGERNON. But, my dear child, do you mean to say you could not love me
465   if I had some other name?

CECILY. But what name?

ALGERNON. Oh, any name you like—Algernon—for instance …

CECILY. But I don't like the name of Algernon.

ALGERNON. Well, my own dear, sweet, loving little darling, I really can't see
470   why you should object to the name of Algernon. It is not at all a bad name. In fact, it is rather an aristocratic name. Half of the chaps who get into the Bankruptcy Court are called Algernon. But seriously, Cecily … (*Moving to her*) … if my name was Algy, couldn't you love me?

CECILY. (*Rising.*) I might respect you, Ernest, I might admire your character,
475   but I fear that I should not be able to give you my undivided attention.

ALGERNON. Ahem! Cecily! (*Picking up hat.*) Your Rector here is, I suppose, thoroughly experienced in the practice of all the rites and ceremonials of the Church?

CECILY. Oh, yes. Dr. Chasuble is a most learned man. He has never written
480   a single book, so you can imagine how much he knows.

ALGERNON. I must see him at once on a most important christening—I mean on most important business.

CECILY. Oh!

ALGERNON. I shan't be away more than half an hour.

485 CECILY. Considering that we have been engaged since February the 14th, and that I only met you today for the first time, I think it is rather hard that you should leave me for so long a period as half an hour. Couldn't you make it twenty minutes?

ALGERNON. I'll be back in no time.

(Kisses her and rushes down the garden.)

CECILY. What an impetuous boy he is! I like his hair so much. I must enter   490
his proposal in my diary.

(Enter Merriman.)

MERRIMAN. A Miss Fairfax has just called to see Mr. Worthing. On very
important business, Miss Fairfax states.

CECILY. Isn't Mr. Worthing in his library?

MERRIMAN. Mr. Worthing went over in the direction of the Rectory some   495
time ago.

CECILY. Pray ask the lady to come out here; Mr. Worthing is sure to be back
soon. And you can bring tea.

MERRIMAN. Yes, Miss. *(Goes out.)*

CECILY. Miss Fairfax! I suppose one of the many good elderly women who   500
are associated with Uncle Jack in some of his philanthropic work in London. I don't quite like women who are interested in philanthropic work. I
think it is so forward of them.

(Enter Merriman.)

MERRIMAN. Miss Fairfax.

(Enter Gwendolen. Exit Merriman.)

CECILY. *(Advancing to meet her.)* Pray let me introduce myself to you. My   505
name is Cecily Cardew.

GWENDOLEN. Cecily Cardew? *(Moving to her and shaking hands.)* What a
very sweet name! Something tells me that we are going to be great friends.
I like you already more than I can say. My first impressions of people are
never wrong.   510

CECILY. How nice of you to like me so much after we have known each other
such a comparatively short time. Pray sit down.

GWENDOLEN. *(Still standing up.)* I may call you Cecily, may I not?

CECILY. With pleasure!

GWENDOLEN. And you will always call me Gwendolen, won't you?   515

CECILY. If you wish.

GWENDOLEN. Then that is all quite settled, is it not?

CECILY. I hope so. *(A pause. They both sit down together.)*

GWENDOLEN. Perhaps this might be a favourable opportunity for my men-
tioning who I am. My father is Lord Bracknell. You have never heard of   520
Papa, I suppose?

CECILY. I don't think so.

GWENDOLEN. Outside the family circle, Papa, I am glad to say, is entirely unknown. I think that is quite as it should be. The home seems to me to be the proper sphere for the man. And certainly once a man begins to neglect his domestic duties he becomes painfully effeminate, does he not? And I don't like that. It makes men so very attractive. Cecily, Mamma, whose views on education are remarkably strict, has brought me up to be extremely short-sighted; it is part of her system; so do you mind my looking at you through my glasses?

CECILY. Oh! not at all, Gwendolen. I am very fond of being looked at.

GWENDOLEN. (*After examining Cecily carefully through a lorgnette.*[1]) You are here on a short visit, I suppose.

CECILY. Oh no! I live here.

GWENDOLEN. (*Severely.*) Really? Your mother, no doubt, or some female relative of advanced years, resides here also?

CECILY. Oh no! I have no mother, nor, in fact, any relations.

GWENDOLEN. Indeed?

CECILY. My dear guardian, with the assistance of Miss Prism, has the arduous task of looking after me.

GWENDOLEN. Your guardian?

CECILY. Yes, I am Mr. Worthing's ward.

GWENDOLEN. Oh! It is strange he never mentioned to me that he had a ward. How secretive of him! He grows more interesting hourly. I am not sure, however, that the news inspires me with feelings of unmixed delight. (*Rising and going to her.*) I am very fond of you, Cecily; I have liked you ever since I met you! But I am bound to state that now that I know that you are Mr. Worthing's ward, I cannot help expressing a wish you were—well, just a little older than you seem to be—and not quite so very alluring in appearance. In fact, if I may speak candidly—

CECILY. Pray do! I think that whenever one has anything unpleasant to say, one should always be quite candid.

GWENDOLEN. Well, to speak with perfect candour, Cecily, I wish that you were fully forty-two, and more than usually plain for your age. Ernest has a strong upright nature. He is the very soul of truth and honour. Disloyalty would be as impossible to him as deception. But even men of the noblest possible moral character are extremely susceptible to the influence of the physical charms of others. Modern, no less than Ancient History, supplies us with many most painful examples of what I refer to. If it were not so, indeed, History would be quite unreadable.

CECILY. I beg your pardon, Gwendolen, did you say Ernest?

---

1   *lorgnette*   Pair of glasses held up to the eyes with a handle.

GWENDOLEN. Yes.

CECILY. Oh, but it is not Mr. Ernest Worthing who is my guardian. It is his brother—his elder brother.

GWENDOLEN. (*Sitting down again.*) Ernest never mentioned to me that he 565 had a brother.

CECILY. I am sorry to say they have not been on good terms for a long time.

GWENDOLEN. Ah! that accounts for it. And now that I think of it I have never heard any man mention his brother. The subject seems distasteful to most men. Cecily, you have lifted a load from my mind. I was growing almost 570 anxious. It would have been terrible if any cloud had come across a friendship like ours, would it not? Of course you are quite, quite sure that it is not Mr. Ernest Worthing who is your guardian?

CECILY. Quite sure. (*A pause.*) In fact, I am going to be his.

GWENDOLEN. (*Inquiringly.*) I beg your pardon? 575

CECILY. (*Rather shy and confidingly.*) Dearest Gwendolen, there is no reason why I should make a secret of it to you. Our little county newspaper is sure to chronicle the fact next week. Mr. Ernest Worthing and I are engaged to be married.

GWENDOLEN. (*Quite politely, rising.*) My darling Cecily, I think there must be 580 some slight error. Mr. Ernest Worthing is engaged to me. The announcement will appear in the *Morning Post* on Saturday at the latest.

CECILY. (*Very politely, rising.*) I am afraid you must be under some misconception. Ernest proposed to me exactly ten minutes ago. (*Shows diary.*)

GWENDOLEN. (*Examines diary through her lorgnette carefully.*) It is certainly 585 very curious, for he asked me to be his wife yesterday afternoon at 5:30. If you would care to verify the incident, pray do so. (*Produces diary of her own.*) I never travel without my diary. One should always have something sensational to read in the train. I am so sorry, dear Cecily, if it is any disappointment to you, but I am afraid I have the prior claim. 590

CECILY. It would distress me more than I can tell you, dear Gwendolen, if it caused you any mental or physical anguish, but I feel bound to point out that since Ernest proposed to you he clearly has changed his mind.

GWENDOLEN. (*Meditatively.*) If the poor fellow has been entrapped into any foolish promise I shall consider it my duty to rescue him at once, and with 595 a firm hand.

CECILY. (*Thoughtfully and sadly.*) Whatever unfortunate entanglement my dear boy may have got into, I will never reproach him with it after we are married.

GWENDOLEN. Do you allude to me, Miss Cardew, as an entanglement? You 600 are presumptuous. On an occasion of this kind it becomes more than a moral duty to speak one's mind. It becomes a pleasure.

CECILY. Do you suggest, Miss Fairfax, that I entrapped Ernest into an engagement? How dare you? This is no time for wearing the shallow mask of manners. When I see a spade I call it a spade.

605

GWENDOLEN. (*Satirically.*) I am glad to say that I have never seen a spade. It is obvious that our social spheres have been widely different.

(*Enter Merriman, followed by the footman. He carries a salver, table cloth, and plate stand. Cecily is about to retort. The presence of the servants exercises a restraining influence, under which both girls chafe.*)

MERRIMAN. Shall I lay tea here as usual, Miss?

CECILY. (*Sternly, in a calm voice.*) Yes, as usual.

(*Merriman begins to clear table and lay cloth. A long pause. Cecily and Gwendolen glare at each other.*)

610

GWENDOLEN. Are there many interesting walks in the vicinity, Miss Cardew?

CECILY. Oh! yes! a great many. From the top of one of the hills quite close one can see five counties.

GWENDOLEN. Five counties! I don't think I should like that; I hate crowds.

CECILY. (*Sweetly.*) I suppose that is why you live in town?

(*Gwendolen bites her lip, and beats her foot nervously with her parasol.*)

615

GWENDOLEN. (*Looking round.*) Quite a well-kept garden this is, Miss Cardew.

CECILY. So glad you like it, Miss Fairfax.

GWENDOLEN. I had no idea there were any flowers in the country.

CECILY. Oh, flowers are as common here, Miss Fairfax, as people are in London.

620

GWENDOLEN. Personally I cannot understand how anybody manages to exist in the country, if anybody who is anybody does. The country always bores me to death.

CECILY. Ah! This is what the newspapers call agricultural depression,[1] is it not? I believe the aristocracy are suffering very much from it just at present. It is almost an epidemic amongst them, I have been told. May I offer you some tea, Miss Fairfax?

625

GWENDOLEN. (*With elaborate politeness.*) Thank you. (*Aside.*) Detestable girl! But I require tea!

CECILY. (*Sweetly.*) Sugar?

---

1   *agricultural depression*   The British economy in general was in depression from 1873 until the mid-1890s; the agricultural sector was depressed from 1875 until the mid-1890s.

GWENDOLEN. (*Superciliously.*) No, thank you. Sugar is not fashionable any 630
more. (*Cecily looks angrily at her, takes up the tongs and puts four lumps of
sugar into the cup.*)

CECILY. (*Severely.*) Cake or bread and butter?

GWENDOLEN. (*In a bored manner.*) Bread and butter, please. Cake is rarely
seen at the best houses nowadays.

CECILY. (*Cuts a very large slice of cake, and puts it on the tray.*) Hand that to 635
Miss Fairfax.

(*Merriman does so, and goes out with footman. Gwendolen drinks the tea
and makes a grimace. Puts down cup at once, reaches out her hand to the
bread and butter, looks at it, and finds it is cake. Rises in indignation.*)

GWENDOLEN. You have filled my tea with lumps of sugar, and though I asked
most distinctly for bread and butter, you have given me cake. I am known
for the gentleness of my disposition, and the extraordinary sweetness of my
nature, but I warn you, Miss Cardew, you may go too far. 640

CECILY. (*Rising.*) To save my poor, innocent, trusting boy from the machinations of any other girl there are no lengths to which I would not go.

GWENDOLEN. From the moment I saw you I distrusted you. I felt that you
were false and deceitful. I am never deceived in such matters. My first impressions of people are invariably right. 645

CECILY. It seems to me, Miss Fairfax, that I am trespassing on your valuable
time. No doubt you have many other calls of a similar character to make
in the neighbourhood.

(*Enter Jack.*)

GWENDOLEN. (*Catching sight of him.*) Ernest! My own Ernest!

JACK. Gwendolen! Darling! (*Offers to kiss her.*) 650

GWENDOLEN. (*Draws back.*) A moment! May I ask if you are engaged to be
married to this young lady? (*Points to Cecily.*)

JACK. (*Laughing.*) To dear little Cecily! Of course not! What could have put
such an idea into your pretty little head?

GWENDOLEN. Thank you. You may! (*Offers her cheek.*) 655

CECILY. (*Very sweetly.*) I knew there must be some misunderstanding, Miss
Fairfax. The gentleman whose arm is at present round your waist is my
guardian, Mr. John Worthing.

GWENDOLEN. I beg your pardon?

CECILY. This is Uncle Jack.

GWENDOLEN. (*Receding.*) Jack! Oh! 660

(*Enter Algernon.*)

CECILY. Here is Ernest.

ALGERNON. (*Goes straight over to Cecily without noticing any one else.*) My own love! (*Offers to kiss her.*)

665 CECILY. (*Drawing back.*) A moment, Ernest! May I ask you—are you engaged to be married to this young lady?

ALGERNON. (*Looking round.*) To what young lady? Good heavens! Gwendolen!

CECILY. Yes! to good heavens, Gwendolen, I mean to Gwendolen.

670 ALGERNON. (*Laughing.*) Of course not! What could have put such an idea into your pretty little head?

CECILY. Thank you. (*Presenting her cheek to be kissed.*) You may.

(*Algernon kisses her.*)

GWENDOLEN. I felt there was some slight error, Miss Cardew. The gentleman who is now embracing you is my cousin, Mr. Algernon Moncrieff.

675 CECILY. (*Breaking away from Algernon.*) Algernon Moncrieff! Oh!

(*The two girls move towards each other and put their arms round each other's waists as if for protection.*)

CECILY. Are you called Algernon?

ALGERNON. I cannot deny it.

CECILY. Oh!

GWENDOLEN. Is your name really John?

680 JACK. (*Standing rather proudly.*) I could deny it if I liked. I could deny anything if I liked. But my name certainly is John. It has been John for years.

CECILY. (*To Gwendolen.*) A gross deception has been practised on both of us.

GWENDOLEN. My poor wounded Cecily!

CECILY. My sweet wronged Gwendolen!

685 GWENDOLEN. (*Slowly and seriously.*) You will call me sister, will you not? (*They embrace. Jack and Algernon groan and walk up and down.*)

CECILY. (*Rather brightly.*) There is just one question I would like to be allowed to ask my guardian.

GWENDOLEN. An admirable idea! Mr. Worthing, there is just one question 690 I would like to be permitted to put to you. Where is your brother Ernest? We are both engaged to be married to your brother Ernest, so it is a matter of some importance to us to know where your brother Ernest is at present.

JACK. (*Slowly and hesitatingly.*) Gwendolen—Cecily—it is very painful for me to be forced to speak the truth. It is the first time in my life that I 695 have ever been reduced to such a painful position, and I am really quite inexperienced in doing anything of the kind. However, I will tell you quite frankly that I have no brother Ernest. I have no brother at all. I never had a brother in my life, and I certainly have not the smallest intention of ever having one in the future.

CECILY.   (*Surprised.*) No brother at all? 700

JACK.   (*Cheerily.*) None!

GWENDOLEN.   (*Severely.*) Had you never a brother of any kind?

JACK.   (*Pleasantly.*) Never. Not even of any kind.

GWENDOLEN.   I am afraid it is quite clear, Cecily, that neither of us is engaged to be married to any one. 705

CECILY.   It is not a very pleasant position for a young girl suddenly to find herself in. Is it?

GWENDOLEN.   Let us go into the house. They will hardly venture to come after us there.

CECILY.   No, men are so cowardly, aren't they? 710

(*They retire into the house with scornful looks.*)

JACK.   This ghastly state of things is what you call Bunburying, I suppose?

ALGERNON.   Yes, and a perfectly wonderful Bunbury it is. The most wonderful Bunbury I have ever had in my life.

JACK.   Well, you've no right whatsoever to Bunbury here.

ALGERNON.   That is absurd. One has a right to Bunbury anywhere one chooses. Every serious Bunburyist knows that. 715

JACK.   Serious Bunburyist! Good heavens!

ALGERNON.   Well, one must be serious about something, if one wants to have any amusement in life. I happen to be serious about Bunburying. What on earth you are serious about I haven't got the remotest idea. About everything, I should fancy. You have such an absolutely trivial nature. 720

JACK.   Well, the only small satisfaction I have in the whole of this wretched business is that your friend Bunbury is quite exploded. You won't be able to run down to the country quite so often as you used to do, dear Algy. And a very good thing too. 725

ALGERNON.   Your brother is a little off colour, isn't he, dear Jack? You won't be able to disappear to London quite so frequently as your wicked custom was. And not a bad thing either.

JACK.   As for your conduct towards Miss Cardew, I must say that your taking in a sweet, simple, innocent girl like that is quite inexcusable. To say nothing of the fact that she is my ward. 730

ALGERNON.   I can see no possible defence at all for your deceiving a brilliant, clever, thoroughly experienced young lady like Miss Fairfax. To say nothing of the fact that she is my cousin.

JACK.   I wanted to be engaged to Gwendolen, that is all. I love her. 735

ALGERNON.   Well, I simply wanted to be engaged to Cecily. I adore her.

JACK. There is certainly no chance of your marrying Miss Cardew.

ALGERNON. I don't think there is much likelihood, Jack, of you and Miss Fairfax being united.

740 JACK. Well, that is no business of yours.

ALGERNON. If it was my business, I wouldn't talk about it. (*Begins to eat muffins.*) It is very vulgar to talk about one's business. Only people like stockbrokers do that, and then merely at dinner parties.

JACK. How can you sit there, calmly eating muffins when we are in this hor-
745 rible trouble, I can't make out. You seem to me to be perfectly heartless.

ALGERNON. Well, I can't eat muffins in an agitated manner. The butter would probably get on my cuffs. One should always eat muffins quite calmly. It is the only way to eat them.

JACK. I say it's perfectly heartless your eating muffins at all, under the cir-
750 cumstances.

ALGERNON. When I am in trouble, eating is the only thing that consoles me. Indeed, when I am in really great trouble, as any one who knows me intimately will tell you, I refuse everything except food and drink. At the present moment I am eating muffins because I am unhappy. Besides, I am
755 particularly fond of muffins. (*Rising.*)

JACK. (*Rising.*) Well, that is no reason why you should eat them all in that greedy way. (*Takes muffins from Algernon.*)

ALGERNON. (*Offering tea-cake.*) I wish you would have tea-cake instead. I don't like tea-cake.

760 JACK. Good heavens! I suppose a man may eat his own muffins in his own garden.

ALGERNON. But you have just said it was perfectly heartless to eat muffins.

JACK. I said it was perfectly heartless of you, under the circumstances. That is a very different thing.

765 ALGERNON. That may be. But the muffins are the same.

(*He seizes the muffin-dish from Jack.*)

JACK. Algy, I wish to goodness you would go.

ALGERNON. You can't possibly ask me to go without having some dinner. It's absurd. I never go without my dinner. No one ever does, except vegetarians and people like that. Besides I have just made arrangements with Dr.
770 Chasuble to be christened at a quarter to six under the name of Ernest.

JACK. My dear fellow, the sooner you give up that nonsense the better. I made arrangements this morning with Dr. Chasuble to be christened myself at 5:30, and I naturally will take the name of Ernest. Gwendolen would wish it. We can't both be christened Ernest. It's absurd. Besides, I have a perfect
775 right to be christened if I like. There is no evidence at all that I have ever

been christened by anybody. I should think it extremely probable I never was, and so does Dr. Chasuble. It is entirely different in your case. You have been christened already.

ALGERNON. Yes, but I have not been christened for years.

JACK. Yes, but you have been christened. That is the important thing.   780

ALGERNON. Quite so. So I know my constitution can stand it. If you are not quite sure about your ever having been christened, I must say I think it rather dangerous your venturing on it now. It might make you very unwell. You can hardly have forgotten that some one very closely connected with you was very nearly carried off this week in Paris by a severe chill.   785

JACK. Yes, but you said yourself that a severe chill was not hereditary.

ALGERNON. It usen't to be, I know—but I daresay it is now. Science is always making wonderful improvements in things.

JACK. (*Picking up the muffin-dish.*) Oh, that is nonsense; you are always talking nonsense.   790

ALGERNON. Jack, you are at the muffins again! I wish you wouldn't. There are only two left. (*Takes them.*) I told you I was particularly fond of muffins.

JACK. But I hate tea-cake.

ALGERNON. Why on earth then do you allow tea-cake to be served up for your guests? What ideas you have of hospitality!   795

JACK. Algernon! I have already told you to go. I don't want you here. Why don't you go!

ALGERNON. I haven't quite finished my tea yet! and there is still one muffin left. (*Jack groans, and sinks into a chair. Algernon still continues eating.*)

ACT DROP

ACT 3

SCENE

Morning-room at the Manor House. Gwendolen and Cecily are at the window, looking out into the garden.

GWENDOLEN. The fact that they did not follow us at once into the house, as any one else would have done, seems to me to show that they have some sense of shame left.

CECILY. They have been eating muffins. That looks like repentance.

GWENDOLEN. (*After a pause.*) They don't seem to notice us at all. Couldn't you cough?   5

CECILY. But I haven't got a cough.

GWENDOLEN. They're looking at us. What effrontery!

CECILY. They're approaching. That's very forward of them.

10 GWENDOLEN. Let us preserve a dignified silence.

CECILY. Certainly. It's the only thing to do now.

> (*Enter Jack followed by Algernon. They whistle some dreadful popular air from a British Opera.*)

GWENDOLEN. This dignified silence seems to produce an unpleasant effect.

CECILY. A most distasteful one.

GWENDOLEN. But we will not be the first to speak.

15 CECILY. Certainly not.

GWENDOLEN. Mr. Worthing, I have something very particular to ask you. Much depends on your reply.

CECILY. Gwendolen, your common sense is invaluable. Mr. Moncrieff, kindly answer me the following question. Why did you pretend to be my
20 guardian's brother?

ALGERNON. In order that I might have an opportunity of meeting you.

CECILY. (*To Gwendolen.*) That certainly seems a satisfactory explanation, does it not?

GWENDOLEN. Yes, dear, if you can believe him.

25 CECILY. I don't. But that does not affect the wonderful beauty of his answer.

GWENDOLEN. True. In matters of grave importance, style, not sincerity is the vital thing. Mr. Worthing, what explanation can you offer to me for pretending to have a brother? Was it in order that you might have an opportunity of coming up to town to see me as often as possible?

30 JACK. Can you doubt it, Miss Fairfax?

GWENDOLEN. I have the gravest doubts upon the subject. But I intend to crush them. This is not the moment for German skepticism.[1] (*Moving to Cecily.*) Their explanations appear to be quite satisfactory, especially Mr. Worthing's. That seems to me to have the stamp of truth upon it.

35 CECILY. I am more than content with what Mr. Moncrieff said. His voice alone inspires one with absolute credulity.

GWENDOLEN. Then you think we should forgive them?

CECILY. Yes. I mean no.

GWENDOLEN. True! I had forgotten. There are principles at stake that one
40 cannot surrender. Which of us should tell them? The task is not a pleasant one.

---

1   *German skepticism*   Probably a reference to the German philosopher Immanuel Kant (1724–1804), who is not usually considered a skeptic but argued that we cannot directly perceive the true state of things-in-themselves.

CECILY. Could we not both speak at the same time?

GWENDOLEN. An excellent idea! I nearly always speak at the same time as other people. Will you take the time from me?

CECILY. Certainly.   45

(Gwendolen beats time with uplifted finger.)

GWENDOLEN and CECILY. (*Speaking together.*) Your Christian names are still an insuperable barrier. That is all!

JACK and ALGERNON. (*Speaking together.*) Our Christian names! Is that all? But we are going to be christened this afternoon.

GWENDOLEN. (*To Jack.*) For my sake you are prepared to do this terrible   50 thing?

JACK. I am.

CECILY. (*To Algernon.*) To please me you are ready to face this fearful ordeal?

ALGERNON. I am!

GWENDOLEN. How absurd to talk of the equality of the sexes! Where ques-   55 tions of self-sacrifice are concerned, men are infinitely beyond us.

JACK. We are. (*Clasps hands with Algernon.*)

CECILY. They have moments of physical courage of which we women know absolutely nothing.

GWENDOLEN. (*To Jack.*) Darling!   60

ALGERNON. (*To Cecily.*) Darling! (*They fall into each other's arms.*)

(Enter Merriman. When he enters he coughs loudly, seeing the situation.)

MERRIMAN. Ahem! Ahem! Lady Bracknell!

JACK. Good heavens!

(Enter Lady Bracknell. The couples separate in alarm. Exit Merriman.)

LADY BRACKNELL. Gwendolen! What does this mean?

GWENDOLEN. Merely that I am engaged to be married to Mr. Worthing,   65 Mamma.

LADY BRACKNELL. Come here. Sit down. Sit down immediately. Hesitation of any kind is a sign of mental decay in the young, of physical weakness in the old. (*Turns to Jack.*) Apprised, sir, of my daughter's sudden flight by her trusty maid, whose confidence I purchased by means of a small coin, I   70 followed her at once by a luggage train. Her unhappy father is, I am glad to say, under the impression that she is attending a more than usually lengthy lecture by the University Extension Scheme on the Influence of a perma- nent income on Thought. I do not propose to undeceive him. Indeed I have never undeceived him on any question. I would consider it wrong.   75 But of course, you will clearly understand that all communication between yourself and my daughter must cease immediately from this moment. On this point, as indeed on all points, I am firm.

JACK. I am engaged to be married to Gwendolen, Lady Bracknell!

80 LADY BRACKNELL. You are nothing of the kind, sir. And now, as regards Algernon! … Algernon!

ALGERNON. Yes, Aunt Augusta.

LADY BRACKNELL. May I ask if it is in this house that your invalid friend Mr. Bunbury resides?

85 ALGERNON. (*Stammering.*) Oh! No! Bunbury doesn't live here. Bunbury is somewhere else at present. In fact, Bunbury is dead.

LADY BRACKNELL. Dead! When did Mr. Bunbury die? His death must have been extremely sudden.

ALGERNON. (*Airily.*) Oh! I killed Bunbury this afternoon. I mean poor Bun-90 bury died this afternoon.

LADY BRACKNELL. What did he die of?

ALGERNON. Bunbury? Oh, he was quite exploded.

LADY BRACKNELL. Exploded! Was he the victim of a revolutionary outrage? I was not aware that Mr. Bunbury was interested in social legislation. If so, 95 he is well punished for his morbidity.

ALGERNON. My dear Aunt Augusta, I mean he was found out! The doctors found out that Bunbury could not live, that is what I mean—so Bunbury died.

LADY BRACKNELL. He seems to have had great confidence in the opinion of 100 his physicians. I am glad, however, that he made up his mind at the last to some definite course of action, and acted under proper medical advice. And now that we have finally got rid of this Mr. Bunbury, may I ask, Mr. Worthing, who is that young person whose hand my nephew Algernon is now holding in what seems to me a peculiarly unnecessary manner?

105 JACK. That lady is Miss Cecily Cardew, my ward.

(Lady Bracknell bows coldly to Cecily.)

ALGERNON. I am engaged to be married to Cecily, Aunt Augusta.

LADY BRACKNELL. I beg your pardon?

CECILY. Mr. Moncrieff and I are engaged to be married, Lady Bracknell.

LADY BRACKNELL. (*With a shiver, crossing to the sofa and sitting down.*) I do 110 not know whether there is anything peculiarly exciting in the air of this particular part of Hertfordshire, but the number of engagements that go on seems to me considerably above the proper average that statistics have laid down for our guidance. I think some preliminary inquiry on my part would not be out of place. Mr. Worthing, is Miss Cardew at all connected 115 with any of the larger railway stations in London? I merely desire information. Until yesterday I had no idea that there were any families or persons whose origin was a Terminus.

(Jack looks perfectly furious, but restrains himself.)

JACK. (*In a clear, cold voice.*) Miss Cardew is the grand-daughter of the late Mr. Thomas Cardew of 149 Belgrave Square, S.W.; Gervase Park, Dorking, Surrey; and the Sporran, Fifeshire, N.B.   120

LADY BRACKNELL. That sounds not unsatisfactory. Three addresses always inspire confidence, even in tradesmen. But what proof have I of their authenticity?

JACK. I have carefully preserved the Court Guides[1] of the period. They are open to your inspection, Lady Bracknell.   125

LADY BRACKNELL. (*Grimly.*) I have known strange errors in that publication.

JACK. Miss Cardew's family solicitors are Messrs. Markby, Markby, and Markby.

LADY BRACKNELL. Markby, Markby, and Markby? A firm of the very highest position in their profession. Indeed I am told that one of the Mr. Markbys   130
is occasionally to be seen at dinner parties. So far I am satisfied.

JACK. (*Very irritably.*) How extremely kind of you, Lady Bracknell! I have also in my possession, you will be pleased to hear, certificates of Miss Cardew's birth, baptism, whooping cough, registration, vaccination, confirmation, and the measles; both the German and the English variety.   135

LADY BRACKNELL. Ah! A life crowded with incident, I see; though perhaps somewhat too exciting for a young girl. I am not myself in favour of premature experiences. (*Rises, looks at her watch.*) Gwendolen! the time approaches for our departure. We have not a moment to lose. As a matter of form, Mr. Worthing, I had better ask you if Miss Cardew has any little   140
fortune?

JACK. Oh! about a hundred and thirty thousand pounds in the Funds. That is all. Goodbye, Lady Bracknell. So pleased to have seen you.

LADY BRACKNELL. (*Sitting down again.*) A moment, Mr. Worthing. A hundred and thirty thousand pounds! And in the Funds! Miss Cardew seems   145
to me a most attractive young lady, now that I look at her. Few girls of the present day have any really solid qualities, any of the qualities that last, and improve with time. We live, I regret to say, in an age of surfaces. (*To Cecily.*) Come over here, dear. (*Cecily goes across.*) Pretty child! your dress is sadly simple, and your hair seems almost as Nature might have left it. But   150
we can soon alter all that. A thoroughly experienced French maid produces

---

1   *Court Guides*   Directories containing the names and addresses of those members of the nobility, gentry, and society who have been presented at court.

a really marvellous result in a very brief space of time. I remember recommending one to young Lady Lancing, and after three months her own husband did not know her.

155 JACK. And after six months nobody knew her.

LADY BRACKNELL. (*Glares at Jack for a few moments. Then bends, with a practised smile, to Cecily.*) Kindly turn round, sweet child. (*Cecily turns completely round.*) No, the side view is what I want. (*Cecily presents her profile.*) Yes, quite as I expected. There are distinct social possibilities in
160 your profile. The two weak points in our age are its want of principle and its want of profile. The chin a little higher, dear. Style largely depends on the way the chin is worn. They are worn very high, just at present. Algernon!

ALGERNON. Yes, Aunt Augusta!

165 LADY BRACKNELL. There are distinct social possibilities in Miss Cardew's profile.

ALGERNON. Cecily is the sweetest, dearest, prettiest girl in the whole world. And I don't care twopence about social possibilities.

LADY BRACKNELL. Never speak disrespectfully of Society, Algernon. Only
170 people who can't get into it do that. (*To Cecily.*) Dear child, of course you know that Algernon has nothing but his debts to depend upon. But I do not approve of mercenary marriages. When I married Lord Bracknell I had no fortune of any kind. But I never dreamed for a moment of allowing that to stand in my way. Well, I suppose I must give my consent.

175 ALGERNON. Thank you, Aunt Augusta.

LADY BRACKNELL. Cecily, you may kiss me!

CECILY. (*Kisses her.*) Thank you, Lady Bracknell.

LADY BRACKNELL. You may also address me as Aunt Augusta for the future.

CECILY. Thank you, Aunt Augusta.

180 LADY BRACKNELL. The marriage, I think, had better take place quite soon.

ALGERNON. Thank you, Aunt Augusta.

CECILY. Thank you, Aunt Augusta.

LADY BRACKNELL. To speak frankly, I am not in favour of long engagements. They give people the opportunity of finding out each other's character
185 before marriage, which I think is never advisable.

JACK. I beg your pardon for interrupting you, Lady Bracknell, but this engagement is quite out of the question. I am Miss Cardew's guardian, and she cannot marry without my consent until she comes of age. That consent I absolutely decline to give.

190 LADY BRACKNELL. Upon what grounds may I ask? Algernon is an extremely, I may almost say an ostentatiously, eligible young man. He has nothing, but he looks everything. What more can one desire?

JACK. It pains me very much to have to speak frankly to you, Lady Bracknell, about your nephew, but the fact is that I do not approve at all of his moral character. I suspect him of being untruthful.   195

(Algernon and Cecily look at him in indignant amazement.)

LADY BRACKNELL. Untruthful! My nephew Algernon? Impossible! He is an Oxonian.[1]

JACK. I fear there can be no possible doubt about the matter. This afternoon during my temporary absence in London on an important question of romance, he obtained admission to my house by means of the false pretence   200 of being my brother. Under an assumed name he drank, I've just been informed by my butler, an entire pint bottle of my Perrier-Jouet, Brut, '89; wine I was specially reserving for myself. Continuing his disgraceful deception, he succeeded in the course of the afternoon in alienating the affections of my only ward. He subsequently stayed to tea, and devoured   205 every single muffin. And what makes his conduct all the more heartless is, that he was perfectly well aware from the first that I have no brother, that I never had a brother, and that I don't intend to have a brother, not even of any kind. I distinctly told him so myself yesterday afternoon.

LADY BRACKNELL. Ahem! Mr. Worthing, after careful consideration I have   210 decided entirely to overlook my nephew's conduct to you.

JACK. That is very generous of you, Lady Bracknell. My own decision, however, is unalterable. I decline to give my consent.

LADY BRACKNELL. (*To Cecily.*) Come here, sweet child. (*Cecily goes over.*) How old are you, dear?   215

CECILY. Well, I am really only eighteen, but I always admit to twenty when I go to evening parties.

LADY BRACKNELL. You are perfectly right in making some slight alteration. Indeed, no woman should ever be quite accurate about her age. It looks so calculating ... (*In a meditative manner.*) Eighteen, but admitting to twenty   220 at evening parties. Well, it will not be very long before you are of age and free from the restraints of tutelage. So I don't think your guardian's consent is, after all, a matter of any importance.

JACK. Pray excuse me, Lady Bracknell, for interrupting you again, but it is only fair to tell you that according to the terms of her grandfather's will   225 Miss Cardew does not come legally of age till she is thirty-five.

LADY BRACKNELL. That does not seem to me to be a grave objection. Thirty-five is a very attractive age. London society is full of women of the very highest birth who have, of their own free choice, remained thirty-five for

---

1   *Oxonian*   One who has attended Oxford University.

230 years. Lady Dumbleton is an instance in point. To my own knowledge she has been thirty-five ever since she arrived at the age of forty, which was many years ago now. I see no reason why our dear Cecily should not be even still more attractive at the age you mention than she is at present. There will be a large accumulation of property.

235 CECILY. Algy, could you wait for me till I was thirty-five?

ALGERNON. Of course I could, Cecily. You know I could.

CECILY. Yes, I felt it instinctively, but I couldn't wait all that time. I hate waiting even five minutes for anybody. It always makes me rather cross. I am not punctual myself, I know, but I do like punctuality in others, and

240 waiting, even to be married, is quite out of the question.

ALGERNON. Then what is to be done, Cecily?

CECILY. I don't know, Mr. Moncrieff.

LADY BRACKNELL. My dear Mr. Worthing, as Miss Cardew states positively that she cannot wait till she is thirty-five—a remark which I am bound to

245 say seems to me to show a somewhat impatient nature—I would beg of you to reconsider your decision.

JACK. But my dear Lady Bracknell, the matter is entirely in your own hands. The moment you consent to my marriage with Gwendolen, I will most gladly allow your nephew to form an alliance with my ward.

250 LADY BRACKNELL. (*Rising and drawing herself up.*) You must be quite aware that what you propose is out of the question.

JACK. Then a passionate celibacy is all that any of us can look forward to.

LADY BRACKNELL. That is not the destiny I propose for Gwendolen. Algernon, of course, can choose for himself. (*Pulls out her watch.*) Come, dear,

255 (*Gwendolen rises*) we have already missed five, if not six, trains. To miss any more might expose us to comment on the platform.

(*Enter Dr. Chasuble.*)

CHASUBLE. Everything is quite ready for the christenings.

LADY BRACKNELL. The christenings, sir! Is not that somewhat premature?

CHASUBLE. (*Looking rather puzzled, and pointing to Jack and Algernon.*)

260 Both these gentlemen have expressed a desire for immediate baptism.

LADY BRACKNELL. At their age? The idea is grotesque and irreligious! Algernon, I forbid you to be baptized. I will not hear of such excesses. Lord Bracknell would be highly displeased if he learned that that was the way in which you wasted your time and money.

265 CHASUBLE. Am I to understand then that there are to be no christenings at all this afternoon?

JACK. I don't think that, as things are now, it would be of much practical value to either of us, Dr. Chasuble.

CHASUBLE. I am grieved to hear such sentiments from you, Mr. Worthing. They savour of the heretical views of the Anabaptists,[1] views that I   270
have completely refuted in four of my unpublished sermons. However,
as your present mood seems to be one peculiarly secular, I will return to
the church at once. Indeed, I have just been informed by the pew-opener[2]
that for the last hour and a half, Miss Prism has been waiting for me in
the vestry.   275

LADY BRACKNELL. (*Starting.*) Miss Prism! Did I hear you mention a Miss
Prism?

CHASUBLE. Yes, Lady Bracknell. I am on my way to join her.

LADY BRACKNELL. Pray allow me to detain you for a moment. This matter
may prove to be one of vital importance to Lord Bracknell and myself.   280
Is this Miss Prism a female of repellent aspect, remotely connected with
education?

CHASUBLE. (*Somewhat indignantly.*) She is the most cultivated of ladies, and
the very picture of respectability.

LADY BRACKNELL. It is obviously the same person. May I ask what position   285
she holds in your household?

CHASUBLE. (*Severely.*) I am a celibate, madam.

JACK. (*Interposing.*) Miss Prism, Lady Bracknell, has been for the last three
years Miss Cardew's esteemed governess and valued companion.

LADY BRACKNELL. In spite of what I hear of her, I must see her at once. Let   290
her be sent for.

CHASUBLE. (*Looking off.*) She approaches; she is nigh.

(*Enter Miss Prism hurriedly.*)

MISS PRISM. I was told you expected me in the vestry, dear Canon. I have
been waiting for you there for an hour and three-quarters.

(*Catches sight of Lady Bracknell, who has fixed her with a stony glare. Miss
Prism grows pale and quails. She looks anxiously round as if desirous to
escape.*)

LADY BRACKNELL. (*In a severe, judicial voice.*) Prism! (*Miss Prism bows her*   295
head in shame.) Come here, Prism! (*Miss Prism approaches in a humble*
manner.) Prism! Where is that baby? (*General consternation. The Canon*
starts back in horror. Algernon and Jack pretend to be anxious to shield Ce-

---

1   *Anabaptists*   Although Anabaptists, members of a Protestant sect that rejects Anglican
doctrine, believe in baptism, they reject the Anglican custom of baptizing infants. Dr.
Chasuble is suggesting that Jack is heretical in denying the value of baptism in the
Anglican Church.

2   *pew-opener*   Person assigned to open the doors of pews for privileged churchgoers.

cily and Gwendolen from hearing the details of a terrible public scandal.) Twenty-eight years ago, Prism, you left Lord Bracknell's house, Number 104, Upper Grosvenor Street, in charge of a perambulator that contained a baby of the male sex. You never returned. A few weeks later, through the elaborate investigations of the Metropolitan police, the perambulator was discovered at midnight, standing by itself in a remote corner of Bayswater. It contained the manuscript of a three-volume novel of more than usually revolting sentimentality. (*Miss Prism starts in involuntary indignation.*) But the baby was not there! (*Every one looks at Miss Prism.*) Prism! Where is that baby? (*A pause.*)

MISS PRISM. Lady Bracknell, I admit with shame that I do not know. I only wish I did. The plain facts of the case are these. On the morning of the day you mention, a day that is for ever branded on my memory, I prepared as usual to take the baby out in its perambulator. I had also with me a somewhat old, but capacious hand-bag in which I had intended to place the manuscript of a work of fiction that I had written during my few unoccupied hours. In a moment of mental abstraction, for which I never can forgive myself, I deposited the manuscript in the bassinette, and placed the baby in the hand-bag.

JACK. (*Who has been listening attentively.*) But where did you deposit the hand-bag?

MISS PRISM. Do not ask me, Mr. Worthing.

JACK. Miss Prism, this is a matter of no small importance to me. I insist on knowing where you deposited the hand-bag that contained that infant.

MISS PRISM. I left it in the cloak-room of one of the larger railway stations in London.

JACK. What railway station?

MISS PRISM. (*Quite crushed.*) Victoria. The Brighton line. (*Sinks into a chair.*)

JACK. I must retire to my room for a moment. Gwendolen, wait here for me.

GWENDOLEN. If you are not too long, I will wait here for you all my life.

(*Exit Jack in great excitement.*)

CHASUBLE. What do you think this means, Lady Bracknell?

LADY BRACKNELL. I dare not even suspect, Dr. Chasuble. I need hardly tell you that in families of high position strange coincidences are not supposed to occur. They are hardly considered the thing.

(*Noises heard overhead as if some one was throwing trunks about. Every one looks up.*)

CECILY. Uncle Jack seems strangely agitated.

CHASUBLE. Your guardian has a very emotional nature.

LADY BRACKNELL. This noise is extremely unpleasant. It sounds as if he was having an argument. I dislike arguments of any kind. They are always vulgar, and often convincing.   335

CHASUBLE. (*Looking up.*) It has stopped now. (*The noise is redoubled.*)

LADY BRACKNELL. I wish he would arrive at some conclusion.

GWENDOLEN. This suspense is terrible. I hope it will last.

(*Enter Jack with a hand-bag of black leather in his hand.*)

JACK. (*Rushing over to Miss Prism.*) Is this the handbag, Miss Prism? Examine it carefully before you speak. The happiness of more than one life depends   340 on your answer.

MISS PRISM. (*Calmly.*) It seems to be mine. Yes, here is the injury it received through the upsetting of a Gower Street omnibus[1] in younger and happier days. Here is the stain on the lining caused by the explosion of a temperance beverage,[2] an incident that occurred at Leamington. And here, on   345 the lock, are my initials. I had forgotten that in an extravagant mood I had had them placed there. The bag is undoubtedly mine. I am delighted to have it so unexpectedly restored to me. It has been a great inconvenience being without it all these years.

JACK. (*In a pathetic voice.*) Miss Prism, more is restored to you than this   350 hand-bag. I was the baby you placed in it.

MISS PRISM. (*Amazed.*) You?

JACK. (*Embracing her.*) Yes … mother!

MISS PRISM. (*Recoiling in indignant astonishment.*) Mr. Worthing! I am unmarried!   355

JACK. Unmarried! I do not deny that is a serious blow. But after all, who has the right to cast a stone against one who has suffered? Cannot repentance wipe out an act of folly? Why should there be one law for men, and another for women? Mother, I forgive you. (*Tries to embrace her again.*)

MISS PRISM. (*Still more indignant.*) Mr. Worthing, there is some error.   360 (*Pointing to Lady Bracknell.*) There is the lady who can tell you who you really are.

JACK. (*After a pause.*) Lady Bracknell, I hate to seem inquisitive, but would you kindly inform me who I am?

LADY BRACKNELL. I am afraid that the news I have to give you will not   365 altogether please you. You are the son of my poor sister, Mrs. Moncrieff, and consequently Algernon's elder brother.

---

1   *Gower Street omnibus*   Public horse-drawn bus on a route in central London.

2   *temperance beverage*   Non-alcoholic drink. (The temperance movement aimed to prohibit all alcoholic beverages.)

JACK. Algy's elder brother! Then I have a brother after all. I knew I had a brother! I always said I had a brother! Cecily, how could you have ever doubted that I had a brother? (*Seizes hold of Algernon.*) Dr. Chasuble, my unfortunate brother. Miss Prism, my unfortunate brother. Gwendolen, my unfortunate brother. Algy, you young scoundrel, you will have to treat me with more respect in the future. You have never behaved to me like a brother in all your life.

ALGERNON. Well, not till today, old boy, I admit. I did my best, however, though I was out of practice. (*Shakes hands.*)

GWENDOLEN. (*To Jack.*) My own! But what own are you? What is your Christian name, now that you have become some one else?

JACK. Good heavens! … I had quite forgotten that point. Your decision on the subject of my name is irrevocable, I suppose?

GWENDOLEN. I never change, except in my affections.

CECILY. What a noble nature you have, Gwendolen!

JACK. Then the question had better be cleared up at once. Aunt Augusta, a moment. At the time when Miss Prism left me in the hand-bag, had I been christened already?

LADY BRACKNELL. Every luxury that money could buy, including christening, had been lavished on you by your fond and doting parents.

JACK. Then I was christened! That is settled. Now, what name was I given? Let me know the worst.

LADY BRACKNELL. Being the eldest son you were naturally christened after your father.

JACK. (*Irritably.*) Yes, but what was my father's Christian name?

LADY BRACKNELL. (*Meditatively.*) I cannot at the present moment recall what the General's Christian name was. But I have no doubt he had one. He was eccentric, I admit. But only in later years. And that was the result of the Indian climate, and marriage, and indigestion, and other things of that kind.

JACK. Algy! Can't you recollect what our father's Christian name was?

ALGERNON. My dear boy, we were never even on speaking terms. He died before I was a year old.

JACK. His name would appear in the Army Lists[1] of the period, I suppose, Aunt Augusta?

LADY BRACKNELL. The General was essentially a man of peace, except in his domestic life. But I have no doubt his name would appear in any military directory.

JACK. The Army Lists of the last forty years are here. These delightful records should have been my constant study. (*Rushes to bookcase and tears the books*

---

1   *Army Lists* Directories of officers.

out.) M. Generals … Mallam, Maxbohm, Magley, what ghastly names they have—Markby, Migsby, Mobbs, Moncrieff! Lieutenant 1840, Captain, Lieutenant-Colonel, Colonel, General 1869, Christian names, Ernest John. (*Puts book very quietly down and speaks quite calmly.*) I always told   410
you, Gwendolen, my name was Ernest, didn't I? Well, it is Ernest after all. I mean it naturally is Ernest.

LADY BRACKNELL. Yes, I remember now that the General was called Ernest, I knew I had some particular reason for disliking the name.

GWENDOLEN. Ernest! My own Ernest! I felt from the first that you could   415
have no other name!

JACK. Gwendolen, it is a terrible thing for a man to find out suddenly that all his life he has been speaking nothing but the truth. Can you forgive me?

GWENDOLEN. I can. For I feel that you are sure to change.

JACK. My own one!   420

CHASUBLE. (*To Miss Prism.*) Lætitia! (*Embraces her.*)

MISS PRISM. (*Enthusiastically.*) Frederick! At last!

ALGERNON. Cecily! (*Embraces her.*) At last!

JACK. Gwendolen! (*Embraces her.*) At last!

LADY BRACKNELL. My nephew, you seem to be displaying signs of triviality.   425

JACK. On the contrary, Aunt Augusta, I've now realized for the first time in my life the vital Importance of Being Earnest.

TABLEAU

—1895

Sharon Pollock
b. 1936

Sharon Pollock is known for stage and radio plays with politically charged ideas at their centre. Her daring choice of subject matter is matched by an experimental approach to playwriting; as critic Anne Nothof observes, in Pollock's work "scenes intersect or blend, time inhabits a simultaneous present and past, [and] characters are divided into multiple selves who interact with and observe each other."

Pollock was born in New Brunswick in 1936. Her young adult life was marked by a series of personal hardships, including her mother's suicide and an abusive marriage. Pollock moved to Calgary in 1966, and a few years later she won the Alberta Culture playwriting competition with her first work, *A Compulsory Option* (1972).

Especially in her early plays, Pollock often incorporates events from Canadian history; *Walsh* (1973), for example, addresses the relationship between a Mounted Police superintendent and the Sioux chief Sitting Bull, while *The Komagata Maru Incident* (1976) is based on a 1914 confrontation that resulted from Canada's racist immigration policies. Such plays use the past to comment on present-day issues while also correcting, Pollock says, Canadians' false "view of themselves as nice civilized people who have never participated in historical crimes and atrocities."

With works such as *Generations* (1981) and the semi-autobiographical *Doc* (1986), Pollock shifted her focus from major events to the ways in which family dynamics and individual psychology are shaped by political or historical circumstances. Her sources range from the Lizzie Borden murder trial in 1890s Massachusetts—the subject of *Blood Relations* (1980)—to the treatment of suspected terrorists held by the American military in *Man Out of Joint* (2007).

As well as a prolific playwright, Pollock is an award-winning actor and has been artistic director at several theatres. She received Governor General's Awards for *Doc* and for *Blood Relations*, and in 2012 she was awarded the Order of Canada.

Blood Relations

CHARACTERS

Miss Lizzie, *who will play* Bridget, *the Irish maid*
The Actress, *who will play* Lizzie Borden[1]
Harry, *Mrs. Borden's brother*
Emma, *Lizzie's older sister*
Andrew, *Lizzie's father*
Abigail, *Lizzie's step-mother*
Dr. Patrick, *the Irish doctor; sometimes* The Defence

SETTING

The time proper is late Sunday afternoon and evening, late fall, in Fall River, 1902; the year of the "dream thesis," if one might call it that, is 1892.

The playing areas include (a) within the Borden house: the dining room from which there is an exit to the kitchen; the parlour; a flight of stairs leading to the second floor; and (b) in the Borden yard: the walk outside the house; the area in which the birds are kept.

PRODUCTION NOTE

Action must be free-flowing. There can be no division of the script into scenes by blackout, movement of furniture, or sets. There may be freezes of some characters while other scenes are being played. There is no necessity to "get people off" and "on" again for, with the exception of The Actress and Miss Lizzie (and Emma in the final scene), all characters are imaginary, and all action in reality would be taking place between Miss Lizzie and The Actress in the dining room and parlour of her home.

The defence may actually be seen, may be a shadow, or a figure behind a scrim.[2]

While Miss Lizzie exits and enters with her Bridget business, she is a presence, often observing unobtrusively when as Bridget she takes no part in the action.

---

1   *Lizzie Borden* American murder suspect (1860–1927) who in 1892 allegedly killed her father and stepmother with a hatchet. She was tried for the crime but acquitted, and she continued to live in her hometown of Fall River, Massachusetts, until her death. The case was never solved, and many remained convinced that she was guilty.

2   *scrim* Screen that is opaque when lit from the front and translucent when lit from behind.

ACT 1

Lights up on the figure of a woman standing centre stage. It is a somewhat formal pose. A pause. She speaks:

"Since what I am about to say must be but that
Which contradicts my accusation, and
The testimony on my part no other
But what comes from myself, it shall scarce boot me
5   To say 'Not Guilty.'
But, if Powers Divine
Behold our human action as they do,
I doubt not then but innocence shall make
False accusation blush and tyranny
10   Tremble at ... at ..."[1]

   (*She wriggles the fingers of an outstretched hand searching for the word.*)

"Aaaat" ... Bollocks!!

   (*She raises her script, takes a bite of chocolate.*)

"Tremble at Patience," patience patience! ...

   (*Miss Lizzie enters from the kitchen with tea service. The actress's attention drifts to Miss Lizzie. The actress watches Miss Lizzie sit in the parlour and proceed to pour two cups of tea. The actress sucks her teeth a bit to clear the chocolate as she speaks:*)

THE ACTRESS. Which ... is proper, Lizzie?

MISS LIZZIE. Proper?

15   THE ACTRESS. To pour first the cream, and add the tea—or first tea and add cream. One is proper. Is the way you do the proper way, the way it's done in circles where it counts?

MISS LIZZIE. Sugar?

THE ACTRESS. Well, is it?

20   MISS LIZZIE. I don't know, sugar?

THE ACTRESS. Mmmn. (*Miss Lizzie adds sugar.*) I suppose if we had Mrs. Beeton's *Book of Etiquette*,[2] we could look it up.

MISS LIZZIE. I do have it, shall I get it?

---

1   *Since what ... at ...* See Shakespeare's *The Winter's Tale* 3.2.22–32; the actress is rehearsing Hermione's speech, delivered when the character is falsely accused of adultery and attempted poisoning; *boot* Benefit.

2   *Mrs. Beeton's ... Etiquette* First published in 1861, *Mrs. Beeton's Book of Household Management*, a wide-ranging book of recipes and domestic advice, remained popular until well into the twentieth century.

THE ACTRESS. No.... You could ask your sister, she might know.

MISS LIZZIE. Do you want this tea or not?   25

THE ACTRESS. I hate tea.

MISS LIZZIE. You drink it every Sunday.

THE ACTRESS. I drink it because you like to serve it.

MISS LIZZIE. Pppu.

THE ACTRESS. It's true. You've no idea how I suffer from this toast and tea   30
ritual. I really do. The tea upsets my stomach and the toast makes me fat
because I eat so much of it.

MISS LIZZIE. Practice some restraint then.

THE ACTRESS. Mmmm ... Why don't we ask your sister which is proper?

MISS LIZZIE. You ask her.   35

THE ACTRESS. How can I? She doesn't speak to me. I don't think she even
sees me. She gives no indication of it. (*She looks up the stairs.*) What do you
suppose she does up there every Sunday afternoon?

MISS LIZZIE. She sulks.

THE ACTRESS. And reads the Bible I suppose, and Mrs. Beeton's *Book of Eti-*   40
quette. Oh Lizzie.... What a long day. The absolutely longest day.... When
does that come anyway, the longest day?

MISS LIZZIE. June.

THE ACTRESS. Ah yes, June. (*She looks at Miss Lizzie.*) June?

MISS LIZZIE. June.   45

THE ACTRESS. Mmmmmm....

MISS LIZZIE. I know what you're thinking.

THE ACTRESS. Of course you do.... I'm thinking ... shall I pour the sherry—
or will you.

MISS LIZZIE. No.   50

THE ACTRESS. I'm thinking ... June ... in Fall River.

MISS LIZZIE. No.

THE ACTRESS. August in Fall River? (*She smiles. Pause.*)

MISS LIZZIE. We could have met in Boston.

THE ACTRESS. I prefer it here.   55

MISS LIZZIE. You don't find it ... a trifle boring?

THE ACTRESS. Au contraire.

(*Miss Lizzie gives a small laugh at the affectation.*)

THE ACTRESS. What?

MISS LIZZIE. I find it a trifle boring ... I know what you're doing. You're soak-
ing up the ambience.   60

THE ACTRESS. Nonsense, Lizzie. I come to see you.

MISS LIZZIE. Why?

THE ACTRESS. Because ... of us. (*Pause.*)

MISS LIZZIE. You were a late arrival last night. Later than usual.

65 THE ACTRESS. Don't be silly.

MISS LIZZIE. I wonder why.

THE ACTRESS. The show was late, late starting, late coming down.

MISS LIZZIE. And?

THE ACTRESS. And—then we all went out for drinks.

70 MISS LIZZIE. We?

THE ACTRESS. The other members of the cast.

MISS LIZZIE. Oh yes.

THE ACTRESS. And then I caught a cab ... all the way from Boston.... Do you know what it cost?

75 MISS LIZZIE. I should. I paid the bill, remember?

THE ACTRESS. (*Laughs.*) Of course. What a jumble all my thoughts are. There're too many words running round inside my head today. It's terrible.

MISS LIZZIE. It sounds it.

(*Pause.*)

THE ACTRESS. ... You know ... you do this thing ... you stare at me ... You look
80 directly at my eyes. I think ... you think ... that if I'm lying ... it will come up, like lemons on a slot machine. (*She makes a gesture at her eyes.*) Tick. Tick ... (*Pause.*) In the alley, behind the theatre the other day, there were some kids. You know what they were doing?

MISS LIZZIE. How could I?

85 THE ACTRESS. They were playing skip rope, and you know what they were singing? (*She sings, and claps her hands arhythmically to:*)

> "Lizzie Borden took an ax,
> Gave her Mother forty whacks,
> When the job was nicely done,
90 > She gave her father forty-one."

MISS LIZZIE. Did you stop them?

THE ACTRESS. No.

MISS LIZZIE. Did you tell them I was acquitted?

THE ACTRESS. No.

95 MISS LIZZIE. What did you do?

THE ACTRESS. I shut the window.

MISS LIZZIE. A noble gesture on my behalf.

THE ACTRESS. We were doing lines—the noise they make is dreadful. Some-times they play ball, ka-thunk, ka-thunk, ka-thunk against the wall. Once
100 I saw them with a cat and—

MISS LIZZIE. And you didn't stop them?

THE ACTRESS. That time I stopped them.

(*The actress crosses to table where there is a gramophone. She prepares to play a record. She stops.*)

THE ACTRESS. Should I?

MISS LIZZIE. Why not?

THE ACTRESS. Your sister, the noise upsets her.   105

MISS LIZZIE. And she upsets me. On numerous occasions.

THE ACTRESS. You're incorrigible, Lizzie.

(*The actress holds out her arms to Miss Lizzie. They dance the latest "in" dance, a Scott Joplin[1] composition. It requires some concentration, but they chat while dancing rather formally in contrast to the music.*)

THE ACTRESS. ... Do you think your jawline's heavy?

MISS LIZZIE. Why do you ask?

THE ACTRESS. They said you had jowls.   110

MISS LIZZIE. Did they.

THE ACTRESS. The reports of the day said you were definitely jowly.

MISS LIZZIE. That was ten years ago.

THE ACTRESS. Imagine. You were only thirty-four.

MISS LIZZIE. Yes.   115

THE ACTRESS. It happened here, this house.

MISS LIZZIE. You're leading.

THE ACTRESS. I know.

MISS LIZZIE. ... I don't think I'm jowly. Then or now. Do you?

THE ACTRESS. Lizzie? Lizzie.   120

MISS LIZZIE. What?

THE ACTRESS. ... did you?

MISS LIZZIE. Did I what?

(*Pause.*)

THE ACTRESS. You never tell *me* anything. (*She turns off the music.*)

MISS LIZZIE. I tell you everything.   125

THE ACTRESS. No you don't!

MISS LIZZIE. Oh yes, I tell you the most personal things about myself, my thoughts, my dreams, my—

THE ACTRESS. But never that one thing.... (*She lights a cigarette.*)

MISS LIZZIE. And don't smoke those—they stink.   130

(*The actress ignores her, inhales, exhales a volume of smoke in Miss Lizzie's direction.*)

---

1   *Scott Joplin* Ragtime composer and pianist (1868–1917).

MISS LIZZIE. Do you suppose ... people buy you drinks ... or cast you even ... because you have a "liaison" with Lizzie Borden? Do you suppose they do that?

THE ACTRESS. They cast me because I'm good at what I do.

135 MISS LIZZIE. They never pry? They never ask? What's she really like? Is she really jowly? Did she? Didn't she?

THE ACTRESS. What could I tell them? You never tell me anything.

MISS LIZZIE. I tell you everything.

THE ACTRESS. But that! (*Pause.*) You think everybody talks about you—they
140 don't.

MISS LIZZIE. Here they do.

THE ACTRESS. You think they talk about you.

MISS LIZZIE. But never to me.

THE ACTRESS. Well ... you give them lots to talk about.

145 MISS LIZZIE. You know you're right, your mind is a jumble.

THE ACTRESS. I told you so.

(*Pause.*)

MISS LIZZIE. You remind me of my sister.

THE ACTRESS. Oh God, in what way?

MISS LIZZIE. Day in, day out, ten years now, sometimes at breakfast as she
150 rolls little crumbs of bread in little balls, sometimes at noon, or late at night ... "Did you, Lizzie?" "Lizzie, did you?"

THE ACTRESS. Ten years, day in, day out?

MISS LIZZIE. Oh yes. She sits there where Papa used to sit and I sit there, where I have always sat. She looks at me and at her plate, then at me, and
155 at her plate, then at me and then she says "Did you Lizzie?" "Lizzie, did you?"

THE ACTRESS. (*A nasal imitation of Emma's voice.*) "Did-you-Lizzie—Lizzie-did-you." (*Laughs.*)

MISS LIZZIE. Did I what?

160 THE ACTRESS. (*Continues her imitation of Emma.*) "You know."

MISS LIZZIE. Well, what do you think?

THE ACTRESS. "Oh, I believe you didn't, in fact I know you didn't, what a thought! After all, you were acquitted."

MISS LIZZIE. Yes, I was.

165 THE ACTRESS. "But sometimes when I'm on the street ... or shopping ... or at the church even, I catch somebody's eye, they look away ... and I think to myself 'Did-you-Lizzie—Lizzie-did-you.'"

MISS LIZZIE. (*Laughs.*) Ah, poor Emma.

THE ACTRESS. (*Dropping her Emma imitation.*) Well, did you?

MISS LIZZIE. Is it important? 170

THE ACTRESS. Yes.

MISS LIZZIE. Why?

THE ACTRESS. I have ... a compulsion to know the truth.

MISS LIZZIE. The truth?

THE ACTRESS. Yes. 175

MISS LIZZIE. ... Sometimes I think you look like me, and you're not jowly.

THE ACTRESS. No.

MISS LIZZIE. You look like me, or how I think I look, or how I ought to look ... sometimes you think like me ... do you feel that?

THE ACTRESS. Sometimes. 180

MISS LIZZIE. (*Triumphant.*) You shouldn't have to ask then. You should know. "Did I, didn't I." You tell me.

THE ACTRESS. I'll tell you what I think.... I think ... that you're aware there is a certain fascination in the ambiguity.... You always paint the background but leave the rest to my imagination. Did Lizzie Borden take an axe? ... If 185 you didn't I should be disappointed ... and if you did I should be horrified.

MISS LIZZIE. And which is worse?

THE ACTRESS. To have murdered one's parents, or to be a pretentious small-town spinster? I don't know.

MISS LIZZIE. Why're you so cruel to me? 190

THE ACTRESS. I'm teasing, Lizzie, I'm only teasing. Come on, paint the background again.

MISS LIZZIE. Why?

THE ACTRESS. Perhaps you'll give something away.

MISS LIZZIE. Which you'll dine out on. 195

THE ACTRESS. Of course. (*Laughs.*) Come on, Lizzie. Come on.

MISS LIZZIE. A game.

THE ACTRESS. What?

MISS LIZZIE. A game? ... And you'll play me.

THE ACTRESS. Oh— 200

MISS LIZZIE. It's your stock in trade, my love.

THE ACTRESS. Alright.... A game!

MISS LIZZIE. Let me think ... Bridget ... Brrridget. We had a maid then. And her name was Bridget. Oh, she was a great one for stories, stood like this, very straight back, and her hair ... and there she was in the courtroom in 205 her new dress on the stand. "Do you swear to tell the truth, the whole truth, and nothing but the truth, so help you God?" (*Imitates Irish accent.*)
"I do sir," she said.
"Would you give the court your name."
"Bridget O'Sullivan, sir." 210

(*Very faint echo of the voice of the defence under Miss Lizzie's next line.*)

"And occupation."

"I'm like what you'd call a maid, sir. I do a bit of everything, cleanin' and cookin'."

(*The actual voice of the defence is heard alone; he may also be seen.*)

THE DEFENCE. You've been in Fall River how long?

215 MISS LIZZIE. (*Who continues as Bridget, while the actress [who will play Lizzie] observes.*) Well now, about five years sir, ever since I came over. I worked up on the hill for a while but it didn't—well, you could say, suit me, too lah-de-dah—so I—

THE DEFENCE. Your employer in June of 1892 was?

220 BRIDGET. Yes sir. Mr. Borden, sir. Well, more rightly, Mrs. Borden for she was the one who—

THE DEFENCE. Your impression of the household?

BRIDGET. Well ... the man of the house, Mr. Borden, was a bit of a ... tight-wad, and Mrs. B. could nag you into the grave, still she helped with the

225 dishes and things which not everyone does when they hire a maid. (*Harry appears on the stairs; approaches Bridget stealthily. She is unaware of him.*) Then there was the daughters, Miss Emma and Lizzie, and that day, Mr. Wingate, Mrs. B.'s brother who'd stayed for the night and was—(*He grabs her ass with both hands. She screams.*)

BRIDGET. Get off with you!

230 HARRY. Come on, Bridget, give me a kiss!

BRIDGET. I'll give you a good poke in the nose if you don't keep your hands to yourself.

HARRY. Ohhh-hh-hh Bridget!

BRIDGET. Get away you old sod!

235 HARRY. Haven't you missed me?

BRIDGET. I have not! I was pinched black and blue last time—and I'll be suf-ferin' the same before I see the end of you this time.

HARRY. (*Tilts his ass at her.*) You want to see my end?

BRIDGET. You're a dirty old man.

240 HARRY. If Mr. Borden hears that, you'll be out on the street. (*Grabs her.*) Where's my kiss!

BRIDGET. (*Dumps glass of water on his head.*) There! (*Harry splutters.*) Would you like another? You silly thing you—and leave me towels alone!

HARRY. You've soaked my shirt.

245 BRIDGET. Shut up and pour yourself a cup of coffee.

HARRY. You got no sense of fun, Bridget.

BRIDGET. Well now, if you tried actin' like the gentleman farmer you're supposed to be, Mr. Wingate—

HARRY. I'm tellin' you you can't take a joke.

BRIDGET. If Mr. Borden sees you jokin', it's not his maid he'll be throwin' out   250
on the street, but his brother-in-law, and that's the truth.

HARRY. What's between you and me's between you and me, eh?

BRIDGET. There ain't nothin' between you and me.

HARRY. ... Finest cup of coffee in Fall River.

BRIDGET. There's no gettin' on the good side of me now, it's too late for   255
that.

HARRY. ... Bridget? ... You know what tickles my fancy?

BRIDGET. No and I don't want to hear.

HARRY. It's your Irish temper.

BRIDGET. It is, is it? ... Can I ask you something?   260

HARRY. Ooohhh—anything.

BRIDGET. (*Innocently.*) Does Miss Lizzie know you're here? ... I say does Miss Lizzie—

HARRY. Why do you bring her up?

BRIDGET. She don't then, eh? (*Teasing.*) It's a surprise visit?   265

HARRY. No surprise to her father.

BRIDGET. Oh?

HARRY. We got business.

BRIDGET. I'd of thought the last bit of business was enough.

HARRY. It's not for—[*you to say*]   270

BRIDGET. You don't learn a thing, from me or Lizzie, do you?

HARRY. Listen here—

BRIDGET. You mean you've forgotten how mad she was when you got her father to sign the rent from the mill house over to your sister? Oh my.

HARRY. She's his wife, isn't she?   275

BRIDGET. (*Lightly.*) Second wife.

HARRY. She's still got her rights.

BRIDGET. Who am I to say who's got a right? But I can tell you this—Miss Lizzie don't see it that way.

HARRY. It don't matter how Miss Lizzie sees it.   280

BRIDGET. Oh it matters enough—she had you thrown out last time, didn't she? By jasus that was a laugh!

HARRY. You mind your tongue.

BRIDGET. And after you left, you know what happened?

HARRY. Get away.   285

BRIDGET. She and sister Emma got her father's rent money from the other mill house to make it all even-steven—and now, here you are back again?

What kind of business you up to this time? (*Whispers in his ear.*) Mind Lizzie doesn't catch you.

290 HARRY. Get away!

BRIDGET. (*Laughs.*) Ohhhh—would you like some more coffee, sir? It's the finest coffee in all Fall River! (*She pours it.*) Thank you sir. You're welcome, sir. (*She exits to the kitchen.*)

HARRY. There'll be no trouble this time!! Do you hear me!

295 BRIDGET. (*Off.*) Yes sir.

HARRY. There'll be no trouble. (*Sees a basket of crusts.*) What the hell's this? I said is this for breakfast!

BRIDGET. (*Entering.*) Is what for—oh no—Mr. Borden's not economizin' to that degree yet, it's the crusts for Miss Lizzie's birds.

300 HARRY. What birds?

BRIDGET. Some kind of pet pigeons she's raisin' out in the shed. Miss Lizzie loves her pigeons.

HARRY. Miss Lizzie loves kittens and cats and horses and dogs. What Miss Lizzie doesn't love is people.

305 BRIDGET. Some people. (*She looks past Harry to the actress/Lizzie. Harry turns to follow Bridget's gaze. Bridget speaks, encouraging an invitation for the actress to join her.*) Good mornin' Lizzie.

THE ACTRESS. (*She is a trifle tentative in the role of Lizzie.*) Is the coffee on?

BRIDGET. Yes ma'am.

310 LIZZIE. I'll have some then.

BRIDGET. Yes ma'am. (*She makes no move to get it, but watches as Lizzie stares at Harry.*)

HARRY. Well ... I think ... maybe I'll ... just split a bit of that kindling out back. (*He exits. Lizzie turns to Bridget.*)

LIZZIE. Silly ass.

315 BRIDGET. Oh Lizzie. (*She laughs. She enjoys the actress/Lizzie's comments as she guides her into her role by "painting the background."*)

LIZZIE. Well, he is. He's a silly ass.

BRIDGET. Can you remember him last time with your Papa? Oh, I can still hear him: "Now Andrew, I've spent my life raisin' horses and I'm gonna tell you somethin'—a *woman* is just like a *horse!* You keep her on a tight rein,

320 or she'll take the bit in her teeth and next thing you know, road, destination, and purpose is all behind you, and you'll be damn lucky if she don't pitch you right in a sewer ditch!"

LIZZIE. Stupid bugger.

BRIDGET. Oh Lizzie, what language! What would your father say if he heard

325 you?

LIZZIE. Well ... I've never used a word I didn't hear from him first.

BRIDGET. Do you think he'd be congratulatin' you?

LIZZIE. Possibly. (*Bridget gives a subtle shake of her head.*) Not.

BRIDGET. Possibly not is right.... And what if *Mrs.* B. should hear you?

LIZZIE. I hope and pray that she does.... Do you know what I think, Bridget?   330
I think there's nothing wrong with Mrs. B.... that losing 80 pounds and
tripling her intellect wouldn't cure.

BRIDGET. (*Loving it.*) You ought to be ashamed.

LIZZIE. It's the truth, isn't it?

BRIDGET. Still, what a way to talk of your Mother.   335

LIZZIE. Step-mother.

BRIDGET. Still you don't mean it, do you?

LIZZIE. Don't I? (*Louder.*) She's a *silly ass* too!

BRIDGET. Shhhh.

LIZZIE. It's alright, she's deaf as a picket fence when she wants to be.... What's   340
he here for?

BRIDGET. Never said.

LIZZIE. He's come to worm more money out of Papa I bet.

BRIDGET. Lizzie.

LIZZIE. What.   345

BRIDGET. Your sister, Lizzie. (*Bridget indicates Emma, Lizzie turns to see her
on the stairs.*)

EMMA. You want to be quiet, Lizzie, a body can't sleep for the racket upstairs.

LIZZIE. Oh?

EMMA. You've been makin' too much noise.

LIZZIE. It must have been Bridget, she dropped a pot, didn't you, Bridget.   350

EMMA. A number of pots from the sound of it.

BRIDGET. I'm all thumbs this mornin', ma'am.

EMMA. You know it didn't sound like pots.

LIZZIE. Oh.

EMMA. Sounded more like voices.   355

LIZZIE. Oh?

EMMA. Sounded like your voice, Lizzie.

LIZZIE. Maybe you dreamt it.

EMMA. I wish I had, for someone was using words no lady would use.

LIZZIE. When Bridget dropped the pot, she did say "pshaw!" didn't you,   360
Bridget.

BRIDGET. Pshaw! That's what I said.

EMMA. That's not what I heard.

(*Bridget will withdraw.*)

LIZZIE. Pshaw?

365 EMMA. If Mother heard you, you know what she'd say.

LIZZIE. She's not my mother or yours.

EMMA. Well she married our father twenty-seven years ago, if that doesn't make her our mother—

LIZZIE. It doesn't.

370 EMMA. Don't talk like that.

LIZZIE. I'll talk as I like.

EMMA. We're not going to fight, Lizzie. We're going to be quiet and have our breakfast!

LIZZIE. Is that what we're going to do?

375 EMMA. Yes.

LIZZIE. Oh.

EMMA. At least—that's what I'm going to do.

LIZZIE. Bridget, Emma wants her breakfast!

EMMA. I could have yelled myself.

380 LIZZIE. You could, but you never do.

(*Bridget serves Emma, Emma is reluctant to argue in front of Bridget.*)

EMMA. Thank you, Bridget.

LIZZIE. Did you know Harry Wingate's back for a visit? ... He must have snuck in late last night so I wouldn't hear him. Did you?

(*Emma shakes her head. Lizzie studies her.*)

LIZZIE. Did you know he was coming?

385 EMMA. No.

LIZZIE. No?

EMMA. But I do know he wouldn't be here unless Papa asked him.

LIZZIE. That's not the point. You know what happened last time he was here. Papa was signing property over to her.

390 EMMA. Oh Lizzie.

LIZZIE. Oh Lizzie nothing. It's bad enough Papa's worth thousands of dollars, and here we are, stuck in this tiny bit of a house on Second Street, when we should be up on the hill—and that's her doing. Or hers and Harry's.

EMMA. Shush.

395 LIZZIE. I won't shush. They cater to Papa's worst instincts.

EMMA. They'll hear you.

LIZZIE. I don't care if they do. It's true, isn't it? Papa tends to be miserly, he probably has the first penny he ever earned—or more likely *she* has it.

EMMA. You talk rubbish.

400 LIZZIE. Papa *can* be very warm-hearted and generous *but he needs encouragement.*

EMMA. If Papa didn't save his money, Papa wouldn't have any money.

LIZZIE. And neither will we if he keeps signing things over to her.

EMMA. I'm not going to listen.

LIZZIE. Well try thinking.   405

EMMA. Stop it.

LIZZIE. (*Not a threat, a simple statement of fact.*) Someday Papa will die—

EMMA. Don't say that.

LIZZIE. Someday Papa will die. And I don't intend to spend the rest of my life
licking Harry Wingate's boots, or toadying to his sister.   410

MRS. BORDEN. (*From the stairs.*) What's that?

LIZZIE. Nothing.

MRS. BORDEN. (*Making her way downstairs.*) Eh?

LIZZIE. I said, nothing!

BRIDGET. (*Holds out basket of crusts. Lizzie looks at it.*) For your birds, Miss 415
Lizzie.

LIZZIE. (*She takes the basket.*) You want to know what I think? I think she's a
fat cow and I hate her. (*She exits.*)

EMMA. ... Morning, Mother.

MRS. BORDEN. Morning Emma.   420

EMMA. ... Did you have a good sleep?

(*Bridget will serve breakfast.*)

MRS. BORDEN. So so.... It's the heat you know. It never cools off proper at
night. It's too hot for a good sleep.

EMMA. ... Is Papa up?

MRS. BORDEN. He'll be down in a minute ... sooo.... What's wrong with 425
Lizzie this morning?

EMMA. Nothing.

MRS. BORDEN. ... Has Harry come down?

EMMA. I'm not sure.

MRS. BORDEN. Bridget. Has Harry come down?

BRIDGET. Yes ma'am.   430

MRS. BORDEN. And?

BRIDGET. And he's gone out back for a bit.

MRS. BORDEN. Lizzie see him?

BRIDGET. Yes ma'am. (*Beats it back to the kitchen.*)   435

(*Emma concentrates on her plate.*)

MRS. BORDEN. ... You should have said so.... She have words with him?

EMMA. Lizzie has more manners than that.

MRS. BORDEN. She's incapable of disciplining herself like a lady and we all know it.

440 EMMA. Well she doesn't make a habit of picking fights with people.

MRS. BORDEN. That's just it. She does.

EMMA. Well—she may—

MRS. BORDEN. And you can't deny that.

EMMA. (*Louder.*) Well this morning she may have been a bit upset because no one told her he was coming and when she came down he was here. But that's all there was to it.

MRS. BORDEN. If your father wants my brother in for a stay, he's to ask Lizzie's permission I suppose.

EMMA. No.

450 MRS. BORDEN. You know, Emma—

EMMA. She didn't argue with him or anything like that.

MRS. BORDEN. You spoiled her. You may have had the best of intentions, but you spoiled her.

(*Miss Lizzie/Bridget is speaking to Actress/Lizzie.*)

MISS LIZZIE/BRIDGET. I was thirty-four years old, and I still daydreamed....

455 I did ... I daydreamed ... I dreamt that my name was Lisbeth ... and I lived up on the hill in a corner house ... and my hair wasn't red. I hate red hair. When I was little, everyone teased me.... When I was little, we never stayed in this house for the summer, we'd go to the farm.... I remember ... my knees were always covered with scabs, god knows how I got them, but you

460 know what I'd do? I'd sit in the field, and haul up my skirts, and my petticoat and my bloomers and roll down my stockings and I'd *pick* the scabs on my knees! And Emma would catch me! You know what she'd say? "Nice little girls don't have scabs on their knees!"

(*They laugh.*)

LIZZIE. Poor Emma.

465 MISS LIZZIE/BRIDGET. I dreamt ... someday I'm going to live ... in a corner house on the hill.... I'll have parties, grand parties. I'll be ... witty, not biting, but witty. Everyone will be witty. Everyone who is *any*one will want to come to my parties ... and if ... I can't ... live in a corner house on the hill ... I'll live on the farm, all by myself on the farm! There was a barn there, with

470 barn cats and barn kittens and two horses and barn swallows that lived in the eaves.... The birds I kept here were pigeons, not swallows.... They were grey, a dull grey ... but ... when the sun struck their feathers, I'd see blue, a steel blue with a sheen, and when they'd move in the sun they were bright blue and maroon and over it all, an odd sparkle as if you'd ... grated a new

silver dollar and the gratings caught in their feathers.... Most of the time   475
they were dull ... and stupid perhaps ... but they weren't really. They were
... hiding I think.... They knew me.... They liked me.... The truth ... is ...

ACTRESS/LIZZIE. The truth is ... thirty-four is too old to daydream....

MRS. BORDEN. The truth is she's spoilt rotten. (*Mr. Borden will come down
stairs and take his place at the table. Mrs. Borden continues for his benefit.*   480
*Mr. Borden ignores her. He has learned the fine art of tuning her out. He is not
intimidated or henpecked.*) And we're paying the piper for that. In most of
the places I've been the people who pay the piper call the tune. Of course I
haven't had the advantage of a trip to Europe with a bunch of lady friends
like our Lizzie had three years ago, all expenses paid by her father.   485

EMMA. Morning Papa.

MR. BORDEN. Mornin'.

MRS. BORDEN. I haven't had the benefit of that experience.... Did you know
Lizzie's seen Harry?

MR. BORDEN. Has she.   490

MRS. BORDEN. You should have met him down town. You should never have
asked him to stay over.

MR. BORDEN. Why not?

MRS. BORDEN. You know as well as I do why not. I don't want a repeat of last
time. She didn't speak civil for months.   495

MR. BORDEN. There's no reason for Harry to pay for a room when we've got
a spare one.... Where's Lizzie?

EMMA. Out back feeding the birds.

MR. BORDEN. She's always out at those birds.

EMMA. Yes Papa.   500

MR. BORDEN. And tell her to get a new lock for the shed. There's been someone in it again.

EMMA. Alright.

MR. BORDEN. It's those little hellions from next door. We had no trouble with
them playin' in that shed before, they always played in their own yard before.   505

EMMA. ... Papa?

MR. BORDEN. It's those damn birds, that's what brings them into the yard.

EMMA. ... About Harry ...

MR. BORDEN. What about Harry?

EMMA. Well ... I was just wondering why ... [*he's here*]   510

MR. BORDEN. You never mind Harry—did you speak to Lizzie about Johnny
MacLeod?

EMMA. I ah—

MR. BORDEN. Eh?

EMMA. I said I tried to—   515

MR. BORDEN. What do you mean, you tried to.

EMMA. Well, I was working my way round to it but—

MR. BORDEN. What's so difficult about telling Lizzie Johnny MacLeod wants to call?

520 EMMA. Then why don't you tell her? I'm always the one that has to go running to Lizzie telling her this and telling her that, and taking the abuse for it!

MRS. BORDEN. We all know why that is, she can wrap her father round her little finger, always has, always could. If everything else fails, she throws a
525 tantrum and her father buys her off, trip to Europe, rent to the mill house, it's all the same.

EMMA. Papa, what's Harry here for?

MR. BORDEN. None of your business.

MRS. BORDEN. And don't you go runnin' to Lizzie stirring things up.

530 EMMA. You know I've never done that!

MR. BORDEN. What she means—

EMMA. (*With anger but little fatigue.*) I'm tired, do you hear? Tired! (*She gets up from the table and leaves for upstairs.*)

MR. BORDEN. Emma!

EMMA. You ask Harry here, you know there'll be trouble, and when I try to
535 find out what's going on, so once again good old Emma can stand between you and Lizzie, all you've got to say is "none of your business"! Well then, it's *your* business, you look after it, because I'm not! (*She exits.*)

MRS. BORDEN. ... She's right.

MR. BORDEN. That's enough. I've had enough. I don't want to hear from you
540 too.

MRS. BORDEN. I'm only saying she's right. You have to talk straight and plain to Lizzie and tell her things she don't want to hear.

MR. BORDEN. About the farm?

MRS. BORDEN. About Johnny MacLeod! Keep your mouth shut about the
545 farm and she won't know the difference.

MR. BORDEN. Alright.

MRS. BORDEN. Speak to her about Johnny MacLeod.

MR. BORDEN. Alright!

MRS. BORDEN. You know what they're sayin' in town. About her and that
550 doctor.

(*Miss Lizzie/Bridget is speaking to the actress/Lizzie.*)

MISS LIZZIE/BRIDGET. They're saying if you live on Second Street and you need a house call, and you don't mind the Irish, call Dr. Patrick. Dr. Patrick is very prompt with his Second Street house calls.

ACTRESS/LIZZIE. Do they really say that?

MISS LIZZIE/BRIDGET. No they don't. I'm telling a lie. But he is very prompt   555
with a Second Street call, do you know why that is?

ACTRESS/LIZZIE. Why?

MISS LIZZIE/BRIDGET. Well—he's hoping to see someone who lives on Second Street—someone who's yanking up her skirt and showing her ankle—
so she can take a decent-sized step—and forgetting everything she was ever   560
taught in Miss Cornelia's School for Girls, and talking to the Irish as if she
never heard of the Pope! Oh yes, he's very prompt getting to Second Street
... getting away is something else....

DR. PATRICK. Good morning, Miss Borden!

LIZZIE. I haven't decided ... if it is ... or it isn't ...   565

DR. PATRICK. No, you've got it all wrong. The proper phrase is "good morning, Dr. Patrick," and then you smile, discreetly of course, and lower the
eyes just a titch, twirl the parasol—

LIZZIE. The parasol?

DR. PATRICK. The parasol, but not too fast; and then you murmur in a voice   570
that was ever sweet and low, "And how are you doin' this morning, Dr.
Patrick?" Your education's been sadly neglected, Miss Borden.

LIZZIE. You're forgetting something. You're married—and Irish besides—I'm
supposed to ignore you.

DR. PATRICK. No.   575

LIZZIE. Yes. Don't you realize Papa and Emma have fits every time we engage
in "illicit conversation." They're having fits right now.

DR. PATRICK. Well, does Mrs. Borden approve?

LIZZIE. Ahhh. She's the real reason I keep stopping and talking. Mrs. Borden
is easily shocked. I'm hoping she dies from the shock.   580

DR. PATRICK. (*Laughs.*) Why don't you ... run away from home, Lizzie?

LIZZIE. Why don't you "run away" with me?

DR. PATRICK. Where'll we go?

LIZZIE. Boston.

DR. PATRICK. Boston?   585

LIZZIE. For a start.

DR. PATRICK. And when will we go?

LIZZIE. Tonight.

DR. PATRICK. But you don't really mean it, you're havin' me on.

LIZZIE. I do mean it.   590

DR. PATRICK. How can you joke—and look so serious?

LIZZIE. It's a gift.

DR. PATRICK. (*Laughs.*) Oh Lizzie—

LIZZIE. Look!

595   DR. PATRICK. What is it?

LIZZIE. It's those little beggars next door. Hey! Hey get away! Get away there!
... They break into the shed to get at my birds and Papa gets angry.

DR. PATRICK. It's a natural thing.

LIZZIE. Well, Papa doesn't like it.

600   DR. PATRICK. They just want to look at them.

LIZZIE. Papa says what's his is his own—you need a formal invitation to get
into our yard.... (*Pause.*) How's your wife?

DR. PATRICK. My wife.

LIZZIE. Shouldn't I ask that? I thought nice polite ladies always inquired after
605   the wives of their friends or acquaintances or ... whatever.

(*Harry observes them.*)

DR. PATRICK. You've met my wife, my wife is always the same.

LIZZIE. How boring for you.

DR. PATRICK. Uh-huh.

LIZZIE. And for her—

610   DR. PATRICK. Yes indeed.

LIZZIE. And for me.

DR. PATRICK. Do you know what they say, Lizzie? They say if you live on
Second Street, and you need a house call, and you don't mind the Irish, call
Dr. Patrick. Dr. Patrick is very prompt with his Second Street house calls.

615   LIZZIE. I'll tell you what I've heard them say—Second Street is a nice place to
visit, but you wouldn't want to live there. I certainly don't.

HARRY. Lizzie.

LIZZIE. Well, look who's here. Have you had the pleasure of meeting my
uncle, Mr. Wingate.

620   DR. PATRICK. No, Miss Borden, that pleasure has never been mine.

LIZZIE. That's exactly how I feel.

DR. PATRICK. Mr. Wingate, sir.

HARRY. Dr.... Patrick is it?

DR. PATRICK. Yes it is, sir.

625   HARRY. Who's sick? (*In other words, "What the hell are you doing here?"*)

LIZZIE. No one. He just dropped by for a visit; you see Dr. Patrick and I are
very old, very dear friends, isn't that so?

(*Harry stares at Dr. Patrick.*)

DR. PATRICK. Well ... (*Lizzie jabs him in the ribs.*) Ouch! ... It's her sense of
humour, sir ... a rare trait in a woman....

630   HARRY. You best get in, Lizzie, it's gettin' on for lunch.

LIZZIE. Don't be silly, we just had breakfast.

HARRY. You best get in!

LIZZIE. ... Would you give me your arm, Dr. Patrick? (*She moves away with Dr. Patrick, ignoring Harry.*)

DR. PATRICK. Now see what you've done?

LIZZIE. What?   635

DR. PATRICK. You've broken two of my ribs and ruined my reputation all in one blow.

LIZZIE. It's impossible to ruin an Irishman's reputation.

DR. PATRICK. (*Smiles.*) ... I'll be seeing you, Lizzie....

MISS LIZZIE/BRIDGET. They're sayin' it's time you were married.   640

LIZZIE. What time is that?

MISS LIZZIE/BRIDGET. You need a place of your own.

LIZZIE. How would getting married get me that?

MISS LIZZIE/BRIDGET. Though I don't know what man would put up with your moods!   645

LIZZIE. What about me putting up with his!

MISS LIZZIE/BRIDGET. Oh Lizzie!

LIZZIE. What's the matter, don't men have moods?

HARRY. I'm tellin' you, as God is my witness, she's out in the walk talkin' to that Irish doctor, and he's fallin' all over her.   650

MRS. BORDEN. What's the matter with you? For her own sake you should speak to her.

MR. BORDEN. I will.

HARRY. The talk around town can't be doin' you any good.

MRS. BORDEN. Harry's right.   655

HARRY. Yes sir.

MRS. BORDEN. He's tellin' you what you should know.

HARRY. If a man can't manage his own daughter, how the hell can he manage a business—that's what people say, and it don't matter a damn whether there's any sense in it or not.   660

MR. BORDEN. I know that.

MRS. BORDEN. Knowin' is one thing, doin' something about it is another. What're you goin' to do about it?

MR. BORDEN. God damn it! I said I was goin' to speak to her and I am!

MRS. BORDEN. Well speak good and plain this time!   665

MR. BORDEN. Jesus christ woman!

MRS. BORDEN. Your "speakin' to Lizzie" is a ritual around here.

MR. BORDEN. Abbie—

MRS. BORDEN. She talks, you listen, and nothin' changes!

MR. BORDEN. That's enough!   670

MRS. BORDEN. Emma isn't the only one that's fed to the teeth!

MR. BORDEN. Shut up!

MRS. BORDEN. You're gettin' old, Andrew! You're gettin' old! (*She exits.*)

(*An air of embarrassment from Mr. Borden at having words in front of Harry. Mr. Borden fumbles with his pipe.*)

HARRY. (*Offers his pouch of tobacco.*) Here ... have some of mine.

675 MR. BORDEN. Don't mind if I do.... Nice mix.

HARRY. It is.

MR. BORDEN. ... I used to think ... by my seventies ... I'd be bouncin' a grandson on my knee....

HARRY. Not too late for that.

680 MR. BORDEN. Nope ... never had any boys ... and girls ... don't seem to have the same sense of family.... You know it's all well and good to talk about speakin' plain to Lizzie, but the truth of the matter is, if Lizzie puts her mind to a thing, she does it, and if she don't, she don't.

HARRY. It's up to you to see she does.

685 MR. BORDEN. It's like Abigail says, knowin' is one thing, doin' is another.... You're lucky you never brought any children into the world, Harry, you don't have to deal with them.

HARRY. Now that's no way to be talkin'.

MR. BORDEN. There's Emma ... Emma's a good girl ... when Abbie and I get

690 on, there'll always be Emma.... Well! You're not sittin' here to listen to me and my girls, are you, you didn't come here for that. Business, eh, Harry?

(*Harry whips out a sheet of figures.*)

MISS LIZZIE/BRIDGET. I can remember distinctly ... that moment I was undressing for bed, and I looked at my knees—and there were no scabs! At last! I thought I'm the nice little girl Emma wants me to be! ... But it wasn't

695 that at all. I was just growing up. I didn't fall down so often.... (*She smiles.*) Do you suppose ... do you suppose there's a formula, a magic formula for being "a woman"? Do you suppose every girl baby receives it at birth, it's the last thing that happens just before birth, the magic formula is stamped indelibly on the brain—Ka Thud!! (*Her mood of amusement changes.*) ...

700 and ... through some terrible oversight ... perhaps the death of my Mother ... I didn't get that Ka Thud!! I was born ... defective.... (*She looks at the actress.*)

LIZZIE. (*Low.*) No.

MISS LIZZIE/BRIDGET. Not defective?

LIZZIE. Just ... born.

705 THE DEFENCE. Gentlemen of the Jury!! I ask you to look at the defendant, Miss Lizzie Borden. I ask you to recall the nature of the crime of which

she is accused. I ask you—do you believe Miss Lizzie Borden, the youngest daughter of a scion of our community, a recipient of the fullest amenities our society can bestow upon its most fortunate members, do you believe Miss Lizzie Borden capable of wielding the murder weapon—thirty-two blows, gentlemen, thirty-two blows—fracturing Abigail Borden's skull, leaving her bloody and broken body in an upstairs bedroom, then, Miss Borden, with no hint of frenzy, hysteria, or trace of blood upon her person, engages in casual conversation with the maid, Bridget O'Sullivan, while awaiting her father's return home, upon which, after sending Bridget to her attic room, Miss Borden deals thirteen blows to the head of her father, and minutes later—in a state utterly compatible with that of a loving daughter upon discovery of murder most foul—Miss Borden calls for aid! Is this the aid we give her? Accusation of the most heinous and infamous of crimes? Do you believe Miss Lizzie Borden capable of these acts? I can tell you I do not!! I can tell you these acts of violence are acts of madness!! Gentlemen! If this gentlewoman is capable of such an act—I say to you—look to your daughters—if this gentlewoman is capable of such an act, which of us can lie abed at night, hear a step upon the stairs, a rustle in the hall, a creak outside the door.... Which of you can plump your pillow, nudge your wife, close your eyes, and sleep? Gentlemen, Lizzie Borden is not mad. Gentlemen, Lizzie Borden is not guilty.

MR. BORDEN. Lizzie?

LIZZIE. Papa ... have you and Harry got business?

HARRY. 'lo Lizzie. I'll ah ... finish up later. (*He exits with the figures. Lizzie watches him go.*)

MR. BORDEN. Lizzie?

LIZZIE. What?

MR. BORDEN. Could you sit down a minute?

LIZZIE. If it's about Dr. Patrick again, I—

MR. BORDEN. It isn't.

LIZZIE. Good.

MR. BORDEN. But we could start there.

LIZZIE. Oh Papa.

MR. BORDEN. Sit down Lizzie.

LIZZIE. But I've heard it all before, another chat for a wayward girl.

MR. BORDEN. (*Gently.*) Bite your tongue, Lizzie.

(*She smiles at him, there is affection between them. She has the qualities he would like in a son but deplores in a daughter.*)

MR. BORDEN. Now ... first off ... I want you to know that I ... understand about you and the doctor.

LIZZIE. What do you understand?

745 MR. BORDEN. I understand ... that it's a natural thing.

LIZZIE. What is?

MR. BORDEN. I'm saying there's nothing unnatural about an attraction between a man and a woman. That's a natural thing.

LIZZIE. I find Dr. Patrick ... amusing and entertaining ... if that's what you
755   mean ... is that what you mean?

MR. BORDEN. This attraction ... points something up—you're a woman of thirty-four years—

LIZZIE. I know that.

MR. BORDEN. Just listen to me, Lizzie.... I'm choosing my words, and I want
760   you to listen. Now ... in most circumstances ... a woman of your age would be married, eh? have children, be running her own house, that's the natural thing, eh? (*Pause.*) Eh, Lizzie?

LIZZIE. I don't know.

MR. BORDEN. Of course you know.

765 LIZZIE. You're saying I'm unnatural ... am I supposed to agree, is that what you want?

MR. BORDEN. No, I'm not saying that! I'm saying the opposite to that! ... I'm saying the feelings you have towards Dr. Patrick—

LIZZIE. What feelings?

770 MR. BORDEN. What's ... what's happening there, I can understand, but what you have to understand is that he's a married man, and there's nothing for you there.

LIZZIE. If he weren't married, Papa, I wouldn't be bothered talking to him! It's just a game, Papa, it's a game.

775 MR. BORDEN. A game.

LIZZIE. You have no idea how boring it is looking eligible, interested, and alluring, when I feel none of the three. So I play games. And it's a blessed relief to talk to a married man.

MR. BORDEN. What're his feelings for you?

780 LIZZIE. I don't know, I don't care. Can I go now?

MR. BORDEN. I'm not finished yet! ... You know Mr. MacLeod, Johnny MacLeod?

LIZZIE. I know his three little monsters.

MR. BORDEN. He's trying to raise three boys with no mother!

785 LIZZIE. That's not my problem! I'm going.

MR. BORDEN. Lizzie!

LIZZIE. What!

MR. BORDEN. Mr. MacLeod's asked to come over next Tuesday.

LIZZIE. I'll be out that night.

MR. BORDEN. No you won't!   790

LIZZIE. Yes I will! ... Whose idea was this?

MR. BORDEN. No one's.

LIZZIE. That's a lie. She wants to get rid of me.

MR. BORDEN. I want what's best for you!

LIZZIE. No you don't! 'Cause you don't care what I want!   795

MR. BORDEN. You don't know what you want!

LIZZIE. But I know what you want! You want me living my life by the Farmers' Almanac; having everyone over for Christmas dinner; waiting up for
  my husband; and *serving at socials!*

MR. BORDEN. It's good enough for your mother!   800

LIZZIE. She is *not* my *mother!*

MR. BORDEN. ... John MacLeod is looking for a wife.

LIZZIE. No, god damn it, he isn't!

MR. BORDEN. Lizzie!

LIZZIE. He's looking for a housekeeper and it isn't going to be me!   805

MR. BORDEN. You've a filthy mouth!

LIZZIE. Is that why you hate me?

MR. BORDEN. You don't make sense.

LIZZIE. Why is it when I pretend things I don't feel, that's when you like me?

MR. BORDEN. You talk foolish.   810

LIZZIE. I'm supposed to be a mirror. I'm supposed to reflect what you want to
  see, but everyone wants something different. If no one looks in the mirror,
  I'm not even there, I don't exist!

MR. BORDEN. Lizzie, you talk foolish!

LIZZIE. No, I don't, that isn't true.   815

MR. BORDEN. About Mr. MacLeod—

LIZZIE. You can't make me get married!

MR. BORDEN. Lizzie, do you want to spend the rest of your life in this house?

LIZZIE. No ... No ... I want out of it, but I won't get married to do it.

MRS. BORDEN. (*On her way through to the kitchen.*) You've never been asked. 820

LIZZIE. Oh listen to her! I must be some sort of failure, then, eh? You had no
  son and a daughter that failed! What does that make you, Papa!

MR. BORDEN. I want you to think about Johnny MacLeod!

LIZZIE. To hell with him!!!

   (*Mr. Borden appears defeated. After a moment, Lizzie goes to him, she holds
   his hand, strokes his hair.*)

LIZZIE. Papa? ... Papa, I love you, I try to be what you want, really I do try, I   825
  try ... but ... I don't want to get married. I wouldn't be a good mother, I—

MR. BORDEN. How do you know—

LIZZIE. I know it! ... I want out of all this ... I hate this house, I hate ... I want
out. Try to understand how I feel ... Why can't I do something? ... Eh? I
830 mean ... I could ... I could go into your office ... I could ... learn how to
keep books?

MR. BORDEN. Lizzie.

LIZZIE. Why can't I do something like that?

MR. BORDEN. For god's sake, talk sensible.

835 LIZZIE. Alright then! Why can't we move up on the hill to a house where we
aren't in each other's laps!

MRS. BORDEN. (*Returning from kitchen.*) Why don't you move out!

LIZZIE. Give me the money and I'll go!

MRS. BORDEN. Money.

840 LIZZIE. And give me enough that I won't ever have to come back!

MRS. BORDEN. She always gets round to money!

LIZZIE. You drive me to it!

MRS. BORDEN. She's crazy!

LIZZIE. You drive me to it!

845 MRS. BORDEN. She should be locked up!

LIZZIE. (*Begins to smash the plates in the dining room.*) There!! There!!

MR. BORDEN. Lizzie!

MRS. BORDEN. Stop her!

LIZZIE. There!

(*Mr. Borden attempts to restrain her.*)

850 MRS. BORDEN. For god's sake, Andrew!

LIZZIE. Lock me up! Lock me up!

MR. BORDEN. Stop it! Lizzie!

(*She collapses against him, crying.*)

LIZZIE. Oh, Papa, I can't stand it.

MR. BORDEN. There, there, come on now, it's alright, listen to me, Lizzie, it's
855 alright.

MRS. BORDEN. You may as well get down on your knees.

LIZZIE. Look at her. She's jealous of me. She can't stand it whenever you're
nice to me.

MR. BORDEN. There now.

860 MRS. BORDEN. Ask her about Dr. Patrick.

MR. BORDEN. I'll handle this my way.

LIZZIE. He's an entertaining person, there're very few around!

MRS. BORDEN. Fall River ain't Paris and ain't that a shame for our Lizzie!

LIZZIE. One trip three years ago and you're still harping on it; it's true, Papa, an elephant never forgets!   865

MR. BORDEN. Show some respect!

LIZZIE. She's a fat cow and I hate her!

(*Mr. Borden slaps Lizzie. There is a pause as he regains control of himself.*)

MR. BORDEN. Now ... now ... you'll see Mr. MacLeod Tuesday night.

LIZZIE. No.

MR. BORDEN. God damn it!! I said you'll see Johnny MacLeod Tuesday   870
night!!

LIZZIE. No.

MR. BORDEN. Get the hell upstairs to your room!

LIZZIE. No.

MR. BORDEN. I'm telling you to go upstairs to your room!!   875

LIZZIE. I'll go when I'm ready.

MR. BORDEN. I said, Go!

(*He grabs her arm to move her forcibly, she hits his arm away.*)

LIZZIE. No! ... There's something you don't understand, Papa. You can't make me do one thing that I don't want to do. I'm going to keep on doing just what I want just when I want—like always!   880

MR. BORDEN. (*Shoves her to the floor to gain a clear exit from the room. He stops on the stairs, looks back to her on the floor.*) ... I'm ... (*He continues off.*)

MRS. BORDEN. (*Without animosity.*) You know, Lizzie, your father keeps you. You know you got nothing but what he gives you. And that's a fact of life. You got to come to deal with facts. I did.   885

LIZZIE. And married Papa.

MRS. BORDEN. And married your father. You never made it easy for me. I took on a man with two little ones, and Emma was your mother.

LIZZIE. You got stuck so I should too, is that it?

MRS. BORDEN. What?   890

LIZZIE. The reason I should marry Johnny MacLeod.

MRS. BORDEN. I just know, this time, in the end, you'll do what your Papa says, you'll see.

LIZZIE. No, I won't. I have a right. A right that frees me from all that.

MRS. BORDEN. No, Lizzie, you got no rights.   895

LIZZIE. I've a legal right to one-third because I am his flesh and blood.

MRS. BORDEN. What you don't understand is your father's not dead yet, your father's got many good years ahead of him, and when his time comes, well, we'll see what his will says then.... Your father's no fool, Lizzie.... Only a fool would leave money to you. (*She exits.*)   900

(*After a moment, Bridget enters from the kitchen.*)

BRIDGET.   Ah Lizzie ... you outdid yourself that time. (*She is comforting Lizzie.*) ... Yes you did ... an elephant never forgets!

LIZZIE.   Oh Bridget.

BRIDGET.   Come on now.

905 LIZZIE.   I can't help it.

BRIDGET.   Sure you can ... sure you can ... stop your cryin' and come and sit down ... you want me to tell you a story?

LIZZIE.   No.

BRIDGET.   Sure, a story. I'll tell you a story. Come on now ... now ... before I
910   worked here I worked up on the hill and the lady of the house ... are you listenin'? Well, she swore by her cook, finest cook in creation, yes, always bowin' and scrapin' and smilin' and givin' up her day off if company arrived. Oh the lady of the house she loved that cook—and I'll tell you her name! It was Mary! Now listen! Do you know what Mary was doin'?
915   (*Lizzie shakes her head.*) Before eatin' the master'd serve drinks in the parlour—and out in the kitchen, Mary'd be spittin' in the soup!

LIZZIE.   What?

BRIDGET.   She'd spit in the soup! And she'd smile when they served it!

LIZZIE.   No.

920 BRIDGET.   Yes. I've seen her cut up hair for an omelette.

LIZZIE.   You're lying.

BRIDGET.   Cross me heart.... They thought it was pepper!

LIZZIE.   Oh, Bridget!

BRIDGET.   These two eyes have seen her season up mutton stew when it's off
925   and gone bad.

LIZZIE.   Gone bad?

BRIDGET.   Oh and they et it, every bit, and the next day they was hit with ... *stomach flu!* So cook called it. By jasus Lizzie, I daren't tell you what she served up in their food, for fear you'd be sick!

930 LIZZIE.   That's funny.... (*A fact—Lizzie does not appear amused.*)

BRIDGET.   (*Starts to clear up the dishes.*) Yes, well, I'm tellin' you I kept on the good side of cook.

(*Lizzie watches her for a moment.*)

LIZZIE.   ... Do you ... like me?

BRIDGET.   Sure I do ... You should try bein' more like cook, Lizzie. Smile and
935   get round them. You can do it.

LIZZIE.   It's not ... *fair* that I have to.

BRIDGET.   There ain't nothin' fair in this world.

LIZZIE. Well then ... well then, I don't want to!

BRIDGET. You dream, Lizzie ... you dream dreams ... Work. Be sensible. What could you do? 940

LIZZIE. I could ...

MISS LIZZIE/BRIDGET. No.

LIZZIE. I could ...

MISS LIZZIE/BRIDGET. No.

LIZZIE. I could ... 945

MISS LIZZIE/BRIDGET. No!

LIZZIE. I ... dream.

MISS LIZZIE/BRIDGET. You dream ... of a carousel ... you see a carousel ... you see lights that go on and go off ... you see yourself on a carousel horse, a red-painted horse with its head in the air, and green staring eyes, and a 950 white flowing mane, it looks wild! ... It goes up and comes down, and the carousel whirls round with the music and lights, on and off ... and you watch ... watch yourself on the horse. You're wearing a mask, a white mask like the mane of the horse, it looks like your face except that it's rigid and white ... and it changes! With each flick of the lights, the expression, it 955 changes, but always so rigid and hard, like the flesh of the horse that is red that you ride. You ride with no hands! No hands on this petrified horse, its head flung in the air, its wide staring eyes like those of a doe run down by the dogs! ... And each time you go round, your hands rise a fraction nearer the mask ... and the music and the carousel and the horse ... they 960 all three slow down, and they stop.... You can reach out and touch ... you ... you on the horse ... with your hands so at the eyes.... You look into the eyes! (*A sound from Lizzie, she is horrified and frightened. She covers her eyes.*) There are none! None! Just black holes in a white mask.... (*Pause.*) Only a dream.... The eyes of your birds ... are round ... and bright ... a light shines 965 from inside ... they ... can see into your heart ... they're pretty ... they love you....

MR. BORDEN. I want this settled, Harry, I want it settled while Lizzie's out back.

(*Miss Lizzie/Bridget draws Lizzie's attention to the Mr. Borden/Harry scene. Lizzie listens, will move closer.*)

HARRY. You know I'm for that. 970

MR. BORDEN. I want it all done but the signin' of the papers tomorrow, that's if I decide to—

HARRY. You can't lose, Andrew. That farm's just lyin' fallow.

MR. BORDEN. Well, let's see what you got.

975   HARRY. (*Gets out his papers.*) Look at this ... I'll run horse auctions and a
      buggy rental—now I'll pay no rent for the house or pasturage but you get
      twenty percent, eh? That figure there—

  MR. BORDEN. Mmmn.

  HARRY. From my horse auctions last year, it'll go up on the farm and you'll
980   get twenty percent off the top.... My buggy rental won't do so well ... that's
      that figure there, approximate ... but it all adds up, eh? Adds up for you.

  MR. BORDEN. It's a good deal, Harry, but ...

  HARRY. Now I know why you're worried—but the farm will still be in the
      family, 'cause aren't I family? and whenever you or the girls want to come
985   over for a visit, why I'll send a buggy from the rental, no need for you to
      have the expense of a horse, eh?

  MR. BORDEN. It looks good on paper.

  HARRY. There's ... ah ... something else, it's a bit awkward but I got to men-
      tion it; I'll be severin' a lot of my present connections, and what I figure
990   I've a right to, is some kind of guarantee....

  MR. BORDEN. You mean a renewable lease for the farm?

  HARRY. Well—what I'm wondering is ... No offence, but you're an older
      man, Andrew ... now if something should happen to you, where would the
      farm stand in regards to your will? That's what I'm wondering.

995   MR. BORDEN. I've not made a will.

  HARRY. You know best—but I wouldn't want to be in a position where Lizzie
      would be havin' anything to do with that farm. The less she knows now
      the better, but she's bound to find out—I don't feel I'm steppin' out of line
      by bringin' this up.

     (*Lizzie is within earshot. She is staring at Harry and Mr. Borden. They do
     not see her.*)

1000   MR. BORDEN. No.

  HARRY. If you mind you come right out and say so.

  MR. BORDEN. That's alright.

  HARRY. Now ... if you ... put the farm—in Abbie's name, what do you think?

  MR. BORDEN. I don't know, Harry.

1005   HARRY. I don't want to push.

  MR. BORDEN. ... I should make a will ... I want the girls looked after, it don't
      seem like they'll marry ... and Abbie, she's younger than me, I know Emma
      will see to her, still ... money-wise I got to consider these things ... it makes
      a difference no men in the family.

1010   HARRY. You know you can count on me for whatever.

  MR. BORDEN. If ... *If* I changed title to the farm, Abbie'd have to come down
      to the bank, I wouldn't want Lizzie to know.

HARRY. You can send a note for her when you get to the bank; she can say it's a note from a friend, and come down and meet you. Simple as that.

MR. BORDEN. I'll give it some thought.   1015

HARRY. You see, Abbie owns the farm, it's no difference to you, but it gives me protection.

MR. BORDEN. Who's there?

HARRY. It's Lizzie.

MR. BORDEN. What do you want? ... Did you lock the shed? ... Is the shed 1020 locked? (*Lizzie makes a slow motion which Mr. Borden takes for assent.*) Well you make sure it stays locked! I don't want any more of those god damned.... I ... ah ... I think we about covered everything, Harry, we'll ... ah ... we'll let it go till tomorrow.

HARRY. Good enough ... well ... I'll just finish choppin' that kindlin', give a 1025 shout when it's lunchtime. (*He exits.*)

   (*Lizzie and Mr. Borden stare at each other for a moment.*)

LIZZIE. (*Very low.*) What are you doing with the farm?

   (*Mr. Borden slowly picks up the papers, places them in his pocket.*)

LIZZIE. Papa! ... Papa. I want you to show me what you put in your pocket.

MR. BORDEN. It's none of your business.

LIZZIE. The farm is my business.   1030

MR. BORDEN. It's nothing.

LIZZIE. Show me!

MR. BORDEN. I said it's nothing!

   (*Lizzie makes a quick move towards her father to seize the paper from his pocket. Even more quickly and smartly he slaps her face. It is all very quick and clean. A pause as they stand frozen.*)

HARRY. (*Off.*) Andrew, there's a bunch of kids broken into the shed!

MR. BORDEN. Jesus christ.   1035

LIZZIE. (*Whispers.*) What about the farm.

MR. BORDEN. You! You and those god damn birds! I've told you! I've told you time and again!

LIZZIE. What about the farm!

MR. BORDEN. Jesus christ ... You never listen! Never!   1040

HARRY. (*Enters carrying the hand hatchet.*) Andrew!!

MR. BORDEN. (*Grabs the hand hatchet from Harry, turns to Lizzie.*) There'll be no more of your god damn birds in this yard!!

LIZZIE. No!

   (*Mr. Borden raises the hatchet and smashes it into the table as Lizzie screams.*)

1045   LIZZIE. No Papa!! Nooo!!

(*The hatchet is embedded in the table. Mr. Borden and Harry assume a soft freeze as the actress/Lizzie whirls to see Miss Lizzie/Bridget observing the scene.*)

LIZZIE. Nooo!
MISS LIZZIE. I loved them.

(*Blackout.*)

ACT 2

Lights come up on the actress/Lizzie sitting at the dining-room table. She is very still, her hands clasped in her lap. Miss Lizzie/Bridget is near her. She too is very still. A pause.

ACTRESS/LIZZIE. (*Very low.*) Talk to me.
MISS LIZZIE/BRIDGET. I remember ...
ACTRESS/LIZZIE. (*Very low.*) No.
MISS LIZZIE/BRIDGET. On the farm, Papa's farm, Harry's farm, when I was
5   little and thought it was my farm and I loved it, we had some puppies, the farm dog had puppies, brown soft little puppies with brown ey ... (*She does not complete the word "eyes."*) And one of the puppies got sick. I didn't know it was sick, it seemed like the others, but the mother, she knew. It would lie at the back of the box, she would lie in front of it while she
10   nursed all the others. They ignored it, that puppy didn't exist for the others.... I think inside it was different, and the mother thought the difference she sensed was a sickness ... and after a while ... anyone could tell it was sick. It had nothing to eat! ... And Papa took it and drowned it. That's what you do on a farm with things that are different.
15   ACTRESS/LIZZIE. Am I different?
MISS LIZZIE/BRIDGET. You kill them.

(*Actress/Lizzie looks at Miss Lizzie/Bridget. Miss Lizzie/Bridget looks towards the top of the stairs. Bridget gets up and exits to the kitchen. Emma appears at the top of the stairs. She is dressed for travel and carries a small suitcase and her gloves. She stares down at Lizzie still sitting at the table. After several moments Lizzie becomes aware of that gaze and turns to look at Emma. Emma then descends the stairs. She puts down her suitcase. She is not overjoyed at seeing Lizzie, having hoped to get away before Lizzie arose, nevertheless she begins with an excess of enthusiasm to cover the implications of her departure.*)

EMMA. Well! You're up early ... Bridget down? ... did you put the coffee on? (*She puts her gloves on the table.*) My goodness, Lizzie, cat got your tongue? (*She exits to the kitchen. Lizzie picks up the gloves. Emma returns.*) Bridget's down, she's in the kitchen.... Well ... looks like a real scorcher today, doesn't it? ...

LIZZIE. What's the bag for?

EMMA. I ... decided I might go for a little trip, a day or two, get away from the heat.... The girls've rented a place out beach way and I thought ... with the weather and all ...

LIZZIE. How can you do that?

EMMA. Do what? ... Anyway, I thought I might stay with them a few days.... Why don't you come with me?

LIZZIE. No.

EMMA. Just for a few days, come with me.

LIZZIE. No.

EMMA. You know you like the water.

LIZZIE. I said no!

EMMA. Oh, Lizzie.

(*Pause.*)

LIZZIE. I don't see how you can leave me like this.

EMMA. I asked you to come with me.

LIZZIE. You know I can't do that.

EMMA. Why not?

LIZZIE. Someone has to *do* something, you just run away from things.

(*Pause.*)

EMMA. ... Lizzie ... I'm sorry about the—[*birds*]

LIZZIE. No!

EMMA. Papa was angry.

LIZZIE. I don't want to talk about it.

EMMA. He's sorry now.

LIZZIE. Nobody *listens* to me, can't you hear me? I said *don't* talk about it. I don't want to talk about it. Stop talking about it!!

(*Bridget enters with the coffee.*)

EMMA. Thank you, Bridget.

(*Bridget withdraws.*)

EMMA. Well! ... I certainly can use this this morning.... Your coffee's there.

LIZZIE. I don't want it.

50   EMMA. You're going to ruin those gloves.

      LIZZIE. I don't care.

      EMMA. Since they're not yours.

(Lizzie bangs the gloves down on the table. A pause. Then Emma picks them up and smooths them out.)

      LIZZIE. Why are you leaving me?

      EMMA. I feel like a visit with the girls. Is there something wrong with that?

55   LIZZIE. How can you go now?

      EMMA. I don't know what you're getting at.

      LIZZIE. I heard them. I heard them talking yesterday. Do you know what they're saying?

      EMMA. How could I?

60   LIZZIE. "How could I?" What do you mean "How could I?" Did you know?

      EMMA. No, Lizzie, I did not.

      LIZZIE. *Did-not-what.*

      EMMA. Know.

      LIZZIE. But you know now. How do you know now?

65   EMMA. I've put two and two together and I'm going over to the girls for a visit!

      LIZZIE. Please Emma!

      EMMA. It's too hot.

      LIZZIE. I need you, don't go.

70   EMMA. I've been talking about this trip.

      LIZZIE. That's a lie.

      EMMA. They're expecting me.

      LIZZIE. You're lying to me!

      EMMA. I'm going to the girls' place. You can come if you want, you can stay if you want. I planned this trip and I'm taking it!

      LIZZIE. Stop lying!

      EMMA. If I want to tell a little white lie to avoid an altercation in this house, I'll do so. Other people have been doing it for years!

      LIZZIE. You don't understand, you don't understand anything.

80   EMMA. Oh, I understand enough.

      LIZZIE. You don't! Let me explain it to you. You listen carefully, you listen.... Harry's getting the farm, can you understand that? Harry is here and he's moving on the farm and he's going to be there, on the farm, living on the farm. *Our farm.* Do you understand that? ... Do you understand that!

85   EMMA. Yes.

      LIZZIE. Harry's going to be on the farm. That's the first thing.... No ... no it isn't.... The first thing ... was the mill house, that was the first thing! And *now* the farm. You see there's a pattern, Emma, you can see that, can't you?

EMMA. I don't—

LIZZIE. You can see it! The mill house, then the farm, and the next thing is the papers for the farm—do you know what he's doing, Papa's doing? He's signing the farm over to her. It will never be ours, we will never have it, not ever. It's ours by rights, don't you feel that? \

EMMA. The farm—has always meant a great deal to me, yes.

LIZZIE. Then what are you doing about it! You can't leave me now ... but that's not all. Papa's going to make a will, and you can see the pattern, can't you, and if the pattern keeps on, what do you suppose his will will say. What do you suppose, answer me!

EMMA. I don't know.

LIZZIE. Say it!

EMMA. He'll see we're looked after.

LIZZIE. I don't want to be looked after! What's the matter with you? Do you really want to spend the rest of your life with that cow, listening to her drone on and on for years! That's just what they think you'll do. Papa'll leave you a monthly allowance, just like he'll leave me, just enough to keep us all living together. We'll be worth millions on paper, and be stuck in this house and by and by Papa will die and Harry will move in and you will wait on that cow while she gets fatter and fatter and I—will—sit in my room.

EMMA. Lizzie.

LIZZIE. We have to do something, you can see that. We have to do something!

EMMA. There's nothing we can do.

LIZZIE. Don't say that!

EMMA. Alright, then, what can we do?

LIZZIE. I ... I ... don't know. But we have to do something, you have to help me, you can't go away and leave me alone, you can't do that.

EMMA. Then—

LIZZIE. You know what I thought? I thought you could talk to him, really talk to him, make him understand that we're people. *Individual people*, and we have to live separate lives, and his will should make it possible for us to do that. And the farm can't go to Harry.

EMMA. You know it's no use.

LIZZIE. I can't talk to him anymore. Every time I talk to him I make everything worse. I hate him, no. No I don't. I hate her.

(*Emma looks at her brooch watch.*)

LIZZIE. Don't look at the time.

EMMA. I'll miss my connections.

LIZZIE. No!

EMMA. (*Puts on her gloves.*) Lizzie. There's certain things we have to face. One
130   of them is, we can't change a thing.

LIZZIE. I won't let you go!

EMMA. I'll be back on the weekend.

LIZZIE. He killed my birds! He took the axe and he killed them! Emma, I ran
         out and held them in my hands, I felt their hearts throbbing and pumping
135   and the blood gushed out of their necks, it was all over my hands, don't
         you care about that?

EMMA. I ... I ... have a train to catch.

LIZZIE. He didn't care how much he hurt me and you don't care either. No-
         body cares.

140 EMMA. I ... have to go now.

LIZZIE. That's right. Go away. I don't even like you, Emma. Go away! (*Emma
         leaves, Lizzie runs after her calling.*) I'm sorry for all the things I told you!
         Things I really felt! You pretended to me, and I don't like you!! Go away!!
         (*Lizzie runs to the window and looks out after Emma's departing figure. After
         a moment she slowly turns back into the room. Miss Lizzie/Bridget is there.*)

LIZZIE. I want to die ... I want to die, but something inside won't let me ...
145   inside something says *no*. (*She shuts her eyes.*) I can do anything.

DEFENCE. Miss Borden.

         (*Both Lizzies turn.*)

DEFENCE. Could you describe the sequence of events upon your father's ar-
         rival home?

LIZZIE. (*With no animation.*) Papa came in ... we exchanged a few words ...
150   Bridget and I spoke of the yard goods sale downtown, whether she would
         buy some. She went up to her room....

DEFENCE. And then?

LIZZIE. I went out back ... through the yard ... I picked up several pears from
         the ground beneath the trees ... I went into the shed ... I stood looking out
155   the window and ate the pears ...

DEFENCE. How many?

LIZZIE. Four.

DEFENCE. It wasn't warm, stifling in the shed?

LIZZIE. No, it was cool.

160 DEFENCE. What were you doing, apart from eating the pears?

LIZZIE. I suppose I was thinking. I just stood there, looking out the window,
         thinking, and eating the pears I'd picked up.

DEFENCE. You're fond of pears?

LIZZIE. Otherwise, I wouldn't eat them.

DEFENCE. Go on.   165
LIZZIE. I returned to the house. I found—Papa. I called for Bridget.

(*Mrs. Borden descends the stairs. Lizzie and Bridget turn to look at her.
Mrs. Borden is only aware of Lizzie's stare. Pause.*)

MRS. BORDEN. ... What're you staring at? ... I said what're you staring at?
LIZZIE. (*Continuing to stare at Mrs. Borden.*) Bridget.
BRIDGET. Yes ma'am.

(*Pause.*)

MRS. BORDEN. Just coffee and a biscuit this morning, Bridget, it's too hot for   170
a decent breakfast.
BRIDGET. Yes ma'am.

(*She exits for the biscuit and coffee. Lizzie continues to stare at Mrs. Borden.*)

MRS. BORDEN. ... Tell Bridget I'll have it in the parlour.

(*Lizzie is making an effort to be pleasant, to be "good." Mrs. Borden is more
aware of this as unusual behaviour from Lizzie than were she to be rude,
biting, or threatening. Lizzie, at the same time, feels caught in a dimension
other than the one in which the people around her are operating. For Lizzie,
a bell-jar[1] effect. Simple acts seem filled with significance. Lizzie is trying to
fulfill other people's expectations of "normal."*)

LIZZIE. It's not me, is it?
MRS. BORDEN. What?   175
LIZZIE. You're not moving into the parlour because of me, are you?
MRS. BORDEN. What?
LIZZIE. I'd hate to think I'd driven you out of your own dining room.
MRS. BORDEN. No.
LIZZIE. Oh good, because I'd hate to think that was so.   180
MRS. BORDEN. It's cooler in the parlour.
LIZZIE. You know, you're right.
MRS. BORDEN. Eh?
LIZZIE. It is cooler....

(*Bridget enters with the coffee and biscuit.*)

LIZZIE. I will, Bridget.   185

---

1   *bell-jar* Bell-shaped glass lid placed over objects to isolate, protect, or contain them.

(*She takes the coffee and biscuit, gives it to Mrs. Borden. Lizzie watches her eat and drink. Mrs. Borden eats the biscuit delicately. Lizzie's attention is caught by it.*)

LIZZIE. Do you like that biscuit?
MRS. BORDEN. It could be lighter.
LIZZIE. You're right.

(*Mr. Borden enters, makes his way into the kitchen, Lizzie watches him pass.*)

LIZZIE. You know, Papa doesn't look well, Papa doesn't look well at all. Papa
190   looks sick.
MRS. BORDEN. He had a bad night.
LIZZIE. Oh?
MRS. BORDEN. Too hot.
LIZZIE. But it's cooler in here, isn't it ... (*Not trusting her own evaluation of the*
195   *degree of heat.*) Isn't it?
MRS. BORDEN. Yes, yes, it's cooler in here.

(*Mr. Borden enters with his coffee. Lizzie goes to him.*)

LIZZIE. Papa? You should go in the parlour. It's much cooler in there, really
   it is.

(*He goes into the parlour. Lizzie remains in the dining room. She sits at the table, folds her hands in her lap. Mr. Borden begins to read the paper.*)

MRS. BORDEN. ... I think I'll have Bridget do the windows today ... they
200   need doing ... get them out of the way first thing.... Anything in the paper,
   Andrew?
MR. BORDEN. (*As he continues to read.*) Nope.
MRS. BORDEN. There never is ... I don't know why we buy it.
MR. BORDEN. (*Reading.*) Yup.
205 MRS. BORDEN. You going out this morning?
MR. BORDEN. Business.
MRS. BORDEN. ... Harry must be having a bit of a sleep-in.
MR. BORDEN. Yup.
MRS. BORDEN. He's always up by—(*Harry starts down the stairs.*) Well, speak
210   of the devil—coffee and biscuits?
HARRY. Sounds good to me.

(*Mrs. Borden starts off to get it. Lizzie looks at her, catching her eye. Mrs. Borden stops abruptly.*)

LIZZIE. (*Her voice seems too loud.*) Emma's gone over to visit at the girls' place. (*Mr. Borden lowers his paper to look at her. Harry looks at her. Suddenly aware of the loudness of her voice, she continues softly, too softly.*) ... Till the weekend.

MR. BORDEN. She didn't say she was going, when'd she decide that?   215

(*Lizzie looks down at her hands, doesn't answer. A pause. Then Mrs. Borden continues out to the kitchen.*)

HARRY. Will you be ah ... going down town today?

MR. BORDEN. This mornin'. I got ... business at the bank.

(*A look between them. They are very aware of Lizzie's presence in the dining room.*)

HARRY. This mornin' eh? Well now ... that works out just fine for me. I can ... I got a bill to settle in town myself.

(*Lizzie turns her head to look at them.*)

HARRY. I'll be on my way after that.   220

MR. BORDEN. Abbie'll be disappointed you're not stayin' for lunch.

HARRY. 'Nother time.

MR. BORDEN. (*Aware of Lizzie's gaze.*) I ... I don't know where she is with that coffee. I'll—

HARRY. Never you mind, you sit right there, I'll get it. (*He exits.*)   225

(*Lizzie and Mr. Borden look at each other. The bell-jar effect is lessened.*)

LIZZIE. (*Softly.*) Good mornin' Papa.

MR. BORDEN. Mornin' Lizzie.

LIZZIE. Did you have a good sleep?

MR. BORDEN. Not bad.

LIZZIE. Papa?   230

MR. BORDEN. Yes Lizzie.

LIZZIE. You're a very strong-minded person, Papa, do you think I'm like you?

MR. BORDEN. In some ways ... perhaps.

LIZZIE. I must be like someone.

MR. BORDEN. You resemble your mother.   235

LIZZIE. I look like my mother?

MR. BORDEN. A bit like your mother.

LIZZIE. But my mother's dead.

MR. BORDEN. Lizzie—

LIZZIE. I remember you told me she died because she was sick ... I was born   240 and she died.... Did you love her?

MR. BORDEN. I married her.

LIZZIE. Can't you say if you loved her?

MR. BORDEN. Of course I did, Lizzie.

245   LIZZIE. Did you hate me for killing her?

MR. BORDEN. You don't think of it that way, it was just something that happened.

LIZZIE. Perhaps she just got tired and died. She didn't want to go on, and the chance came up and she took it. I could understand that.... Perhaps she
250   was like a bird, she could see all the blue sky and she wanted to fly away but she couldn't. She was caught, Papa, she was caught in a horrible snare, and she saw a way out and she took it.... Perhaps it was a very brave thing to do, Papa, perhaps it was the only way, and she hated to leave us because she loved us so much, but she couldn't breathe all caught in the snare....
255   (*Long pause.*) Some people have very small wrists, have you noticed? Mine aren't ...

(*There is a murmur from the kitchen, then muted laughter. Mr. Borden looks towards it.*)

LIZZIE. Papa! ... I'm a very strong person.

MRS. BORDEN. (*Off, laughing.*) You're tellin' tales out of school, Harry!

HARRY. (*Off.*) God's truth. You should have seen the buggy when they
260   brought it back.

MRS. BORDEN. (*Off.*) You've got to tell Andrew. (*Pokes her head in.*) Andrew, come on out here, Harry's got a story. (*Off.*) Now you'll have to start at the beginning again. Oh my goodness.

(*Mr. Borden starts for the kitchen. He stops, and looks back at Lizzie.*)

LIZZIE. Is there anything you want to tell me, Papa?

265   MRS. BORDEN. (*Off.*) Andrew!

LIZZIE. (*Softly, an echo.*) Andrew.

MR. BORDEN. What is it, Lizzie?

LIZZIE. If I promised to be a good girl forever and ever, would anything change?

270   MR. BORDEN. I don't know what you're talking about.

LIZZIE. I would be lying ... Papa! ... Don't do any business today. Don't go out. Stay home.

MR. BORDEN. What for?

LIZZIE. Everyone's leaving. Going away. Everyone's left.

275   MRS. BORDEN. (*Off.*) Andrew!

LIZZIE. (*Softly, an echo.*) Andrew.

MR. BORDEN. What is it?

LIZZIE. I'm calling you.

(*Mr. Borden looks at her for a moment, then leaves for the kitchen. Dr. Patrick is heard whistling very softly. Lizzie listens.*)

LIZZIE. Listen ... can you hear it ... can you?

MISS LIZZIE/BRIDGET. I can hear it.... It's stopped.   280

(*Dr. Patrick can't be seen. Only his voice is heard.*)

DR. PATRICK. (*Very low.*) Lizzie?

LIZZIE. (*Realization.*) I could hear it before [*you*]. (*Pause.*) It sounded so sad
    I wanted to cry.

MISS LIZZIE/BRIDGET. You mustn't cry.

LIZZIE. I mustn't cry.   285

DR. PATRICK. I bet you know this one. (*He whistles an Irish jig.*)

LIZZIE. I know that! (*She begins to dance. Dr. Patrick enters. He claps in time
    to the dance. Lizzie finishes the jig.*)

(*Dr. Patrick applauds.*)

DR. PATRICK. Bravo! Bravo!!

LIZZIE. You didn't know I could do that, did you?

DR. PATRICK. You're a woman of many talents, Miss Borden.   290

LIZZIE. You're not making fun of me?

DR. PATRICK. I would never do that.

LIZZIE. I can do anything I want.

DR. PATRICK. I'm sure you can.

LIZZIE. If I wanted to die—I could even do that, couldn't I?   295

DR. PATRICK. Well now, I don't think so.

LIZZIE. Yes, I could!

DR. PATRICK. Lizzie—

LIZZIE. You wouldn't know—you can't see into my heart.

DR. PATRICK. I think I can.   300

LIZZIE. Well you can't.

DR. PATRICK. ... It's only a game.

LIZZIE. I never play games.

DR. PATRICK. Sure you do.

LIZZIE. I hate games.   305

DR. PATRICK. You're playin' one now.

LIZZIE. You don't even know me!

DR. PATRICK. Come on Lizzie, we don't want to fight. I know what we'll do
    ... we'll start all over.... Shut your eyes, Lizzie. (*She does so.*) Good mornin'
    Miss Borden.... Good mornin' Miss Borden....   310

LIZZIE. ... I haven't decided.... (*She slowly opens her eyes.*) ... if it is or it isn't.

DR. PATRICK. Much better ... and now ... would you take my arm, Miss Borden? How about a wee promenade?

LIZZIE. There's nowhere to go.

315 DR. PATRICK. That isn't so.... What about Boston? ... Do you think it's too far for a stroll? ... I know what we'll do, we'll walk 'round to the side and you'll show me your birds. (*They walk.*) ... I waited last night but you never showed up ... there I was, travellin' bag and all, and you never appeared.... I know what went wrong! We forgot to agree on an hour! Next time, Lizzie,

320 you must set the hour.... Is this where they're kept?

(*Lizzie nods, she opens the cage and looks in it.*)

DR. PATRICK. It's empty. (*He laughs.*) And you say you never play games?

LIZZIE. They're gone.

DR. PATRICK. You've been havin' me on again, yes you have.

LIZZIE. They've run away.

325 DR. PATRICK. Did they really exist?

LIZZIE. I had blood on my hands.

DR. PATRICK. What do you say?

LIZZIE. You can't see it now, I washed it off, see?

DR. PATRICK. (*Takes her hands.*) Ah Lizzie....

330 LIZZIE. Would you ... help someone die?

DR. PATRICK. Why do you ask that?

LIZZIE. Some people are better off dead. I might be better off dead.

DR. PATRICK. You're a precious and unique person, Lizzie, and you shouldn't think things like that.

335 LIZZIE. Precious and unique?

DR. PATRICK. All life is precious and unique.

LIZZIE. I am precious and unique? ... I *am* precious and unique. You said that.

DR. PATRICK. Oh, I believe it.

340 LIZZIE. And I am. I know it. People mix things up on you, you have to be careful. I am a person of worth.

DR. PATRICK. Sure you are.

LIZZIE. Not like that fat cow in there.

DR. PATRICK. Her life too is—

345 LIZZIE. No!

DR. PATRICK. Liz—

LIZZIE. Do you know her!

DR. PATRICK. That doesn't matter.

LIZZIE. Yes it does, it does matter.

350 DR. PATRICK. You can't be—

LIZZIE. You're a doctor, isn't that right?

DR. PATRICK. Right enough there.

LIZZIE. So, tell me, tell me, if a dreadful accident occurred ... and two people were dying ... but you could only save one.... Which would you save?

DR. PATRICK. You can't ask questions like that.   355

LIZZIE. Yes I can, come on, it's a game. How does a doctor determine? If one were old and the other were young—would you save the younger one first?

DR. PATRICK. Lizzie.

LIZZIE. You said you liked games! If one were a bad person and the other was good, was trying to be good, would you save the one who was good and   360 let the bad person die?

DR. PATRICK. I don't know.

LIZZIE. Listen! If you could go back in time ... what would you do if you met a person who was evil and wicked?

DR. PATRICK. Who?   365

LIZZIE. I don't know, Attila the Hun!

DR. PATRICK. (*Laughs.*) Oh my.

LIZZIE. Listen, if you met Attila the Hun, and you were in a position to kill him, would you do it?

DR. PATRICK. I don't know.   370

LIZZIE. Think of the suffering he caused, the unhappiness.

DR. PATRICK. Yes, but I'm a doctor, not an assassin.

LIZZIE. I think you're a coward.

(*Pause.*)

DR. PATRICK. What I do is try to save lives ...

LIZZIE. But you put poison out for the slugs in your garden.   375

DR. PATRICK. You got something mixed up.

LIZZIE. I've never been clearer. Everything's clear. I've lived all of my life for this one moment of absolute clarity! If war were declared, would you serve?

DR. PATRICK. I would fight in a war.

LIZZIE. You wouldn't fight, you would kill—you'd take a gun and shoot   380 people, people who'd done nothing to you, people who were trying to be good, you'd kill them! And you say you wouldn't kill Attila the Hun, or that that stupid cow's life is precious—*My life is precious!!*

DR. PATRICK. To you.

LIZZIE. Yes to me, are you stupid!?   385

DR. PATRICK. And hers is to her.

LIZZIE. I don't care about her! (*Pause.*) I'm glad you're not my doctor, you can't make decisions, can you? You are a coward.

(*Dr. Patrick starts off.*)

LIZZIE. You're afraid of your wife ... you can *only* play games.... If I really
wanted to go to Boston, you wouldn't come with me because you're a
coward! *I'm not a coward!!*

(*Lizzie turns to watch Mrs. Borden sit with needlework. After a moment
Mrs. Borden looks at Lizzie, aware of her scrutiny.*)

LIZZIE. ... Where's Papa?

MRS. BORDEN. Out.

LIZZIE. And Mr. Wingate?

MRS. BORDEN. He's out too.

LIZZIE. So what are you going to do ... Mrs. Borden?

MRS. BORDEN. I'm going to finish this up.

LIZZIE. You do that.... (*Pause.*) Where's Bridget?

MRS. BORDEN. Out back washing windows.... You got clean clothes to go
upstairs, they're in the kitchen.

(*Pause.*)

LIZZIE. Did you know Papa killed my birds with the axe? He chopped off
their heads. (*Mrs. Borden is uneasy.*) ... It's alright. At first I felt bad, but I
feel better now. I feel much better now.... I am a woman of decision, Mrs.
Borden. When I decide to do things, I do them, yes, I do. (*Smiles.*) How
many times has Papa said—when Lizzie puts her mind to a thing, she does
it—and I do.... It's always me who puts the slug poison out because they
eat all the flowers and you don't like that, do you? They're bad things, they
must die. You see, not all life is precious, is it?

(*After a moment Mrs. Borden makes an attempt casually to gather together
her things, to go upstairs. She does not want to be in the room with Lizzie.*)

LIZZIE. Where're you going?

MRS. BORDEN. Upstairs.... (*An excuse.*) The spare room needs changing.

(*A knock at the back door.... A second knock.*)

LIZZIE. Someone's at the door.... (*A third knock.*) I'll get it.

(*She exits to the kitchen. Mrs. Borden waits. Lizzie returns. She's a bit out
of breath. She carries a pile of clean clothes which she puts on the table. She
looks at Mrs. Borden.*)

LIZZIE. Did you want something?

MRS. BORDEN. Who was it?—the door?

LIZZIE. Oh yes. I forgot. I had to step out back for a moment and—it's a
note. A message for you.

MRS. BORDEN. Oh.

LIZZIE. Shall I open it?

MRS. BORDEN. That's alright. (*She holds out her hand.*)

LIZZIE. Looks like Papa's handwriting.... (*She passes over the note.*) Aren't you going to open it?   420

MRS. BORDEN. I'll read it upstairs.

LIZZIE. Mrs. Borden! ... Would you mind ... putting my clothes in my room? (*She gets some clothes from the table, Mrs. Borden takes them, something she would never normally do. Before she can move away, Lizzie grabs her arm.*) Just a minute ... I would like you to look into my eyes. What's the matter?   425 Nothing's wrong. It's an experiment.... Look right into them. Tell me ... what do you see ... can you see anything?

MRS. BORDEN. ... Myself.

LIZZIE. Yes. When a person dies, retained on her eye is the image of the last thing she saw. Isn't that interesting? (*Pause.*)   430

(*Mrs. Borden slowly starts upstairs. Lizzie picks up remaining clothes on table. The hand hatchet is concealed beneath them. She follows Mrs. Borden up the stairs.*)

LIZZIE. Do you know something? If I were to kill someone, I would come up behind them very slowly and quietly. They would never even hear me, they would never turn around. (*Mrs. Borden stops on the stairs. She turns around to look at Lizzie who is behind her.*) They would be too frightened to turn around even if they heard me. They would be so afraid they'd see what they   435 feared. (*Mrs. Borden makes a move which might be an effort to go past Lizzie back down the stairs. Lizzie stops her.*) Careful. Don't fall. (*Mrs. Borden turns and slowly continues up the stairs with Lizzie behind her.*) And then, I would strike them down. With them not turning around, they would retain no image of me on their eye. It would be better that way.   440

(*Lizzie and Mrs. Borden disappear at the top of the stairs. The stage is empty for a moment. Bridget enters. She carries the pail for washing the windows. She sets the pail down, wipes her forehead. She stands for a moment looking towards the stairs as if she might have heard a sound. She picks up the pail and exits to the kitchen. Lizzie appears on the stairs. She is carrying the pile of clothes she carried upstairs. The hand hatchet is concealed under the clothes. Lizzie descends the stairs, she seems calm, self-possessed. She places the clothes on the table. She pauses, then she slowly turns to look at Mrs. Borden's chair at the table. After a moment she moves to it, pauses a moment, then sits down in it. She sits there at ease, relaxed, thinking. Bridget enters from the kitchen, she sees Lizzie, she stops, she takes in Lizzie*) *sitting in Mrs. Borden's chair. Bridget glances towards the stairs, back to Lizzie. Lizzie looks, for the first time, at Bridget.)*

LIZZIE. We must hurry before Papa gets home.

BRIDGET. Lizzie?

LIZZIE. I have it all figured out, but you have to help me, Bridget, you have to help me.

445 BRIDGET. What have you done?

LIZZIE. He would never leave me the farm, not with her on his back, but now (*She gets up from the chair*) I will have the farm, and I will have the money, yes, to do what I please! And you too Bridget, I'll give you some of my money but you've got to help me. (*She moves towards Bridget who backs*

450 *away a step.*) Don't be afraid, it's me, it's Lizzie, you like me!

BRIDGET. What have you done! (*Pause. Bridget moves towards the stairs.*)

LIZZIE. Don't go up there!

BRIDGET. You killed her!

LIZZIE. Someone broke in and they killed her.

455 BRIDGET. They'll know!

LIZZIE. Not if you help me.

BRIDGET. I can't Miss Lizzie, I can't!

LIZZIE. (*Grabs Bridget's arm.*) Do you want them to hang me! Is that what you want! Oh Bridget, look! Look! (*She falls to her knees.*) I'm begging for

460 my life, I'm begging. Deny me, and they will kill me. Help me, Bridget, please help me.

BRIDGET. But ... what ... could we do?

LIZZIE. (*Up off her knees.*) Oh I have it all figured out. I'll go down town as quick as I can and you leave the doors open and go back outside and work

465 on the windows.

BRIDGET. I've finished them, Lizzie.

LIZZIE. Then do them again! Remember last year when the burglar broke in? Today someone broke in and she caught them.

BRIDGET. They'll never believe us.

470 LIZZIE. Have coffee with Lucy next door, stay with her till Papa gets home and he'll find her, and then each of us swears she was fine when we left, she was alright when we left!—it's going to work, Bridget, I know it!

BRIDGET. Your papa will guess.

LIZZIE. (*Getting ready to leave for down town.*) If he found me here he might

475 guess, but he won't.

BRIDGET. Your papa will know!

LIZZIE. Papa loves me, if he has another story to believe, he'll believe it. He'd want to believe it, he'd have to believe it.

BRIDGET. Your papa will know.

LIZZIE. Why aren't you happy? I'm happy. We both should be happy! (*Lizzie* 480
embraces Bridget. Lizzie steps back a pace.*) Now—how do I look?

(*Mr. Borden enters. Bridget sees him. Lizzie slowly turns to see what Bridget
is looking at.*)

LIZZIE. Papa?

MR. BORDEN. What is it? Where's Mrs. Borden?

BRIDGET. I ... don't know ... sir ... I ... just came in, sir.

MR. BORDEN. Did she leave the house?   485

BRIDGET. Well, sir ...

LIZZIE. She went out. Someone delivered a message and she left.

(*Lizzie takes off her hat and looks at her father.*)

LIZZIE. ... You're home early, Papa.

MR. BORDEN. I wanted to see Abbie. She's gone out, has she? Which way did
she go? (*Lizzie shrugs, he continues, more thinking aloud.*) Well ... I ... I ...   490
best wait for her here. I don't want to miss her again.

LIZZIE. Help Papa off with his coat, Bridget.... I hear there's a sale of dress
goods on down-town. Why don't you go buy yourself a yard?

BRIDGET. Oh ... I don't know, ma'am.

LIZZIE. You don't want any?   495

BRIDGET. I don't know.

LIZZIE. Then ... why don't you go upstairs and lie down. Have a rest before
lunch.

BRIDGET. I don't think I should.

LIZZIE. Nonsense.   500

BRIDGET. Lizzie, I—

LIZZIE. You go up and lie down. I'll look after things here.

(*Lizzie smiles at Bridget. Bridget starts up the stairs, suddenly stops. She
looks back at Lizzie.*)

LIZZIE. It's alright ... go on ... it's alright. (*Bridget continues up the stairs. For
the last bit of interchange, Mr. Borden has lowered the paper he's reading.
Lizzie looks at him.*) Hello Papa. You look so tired.... I make you unhap-   505
py.... I don't like to make you unhappy. I love you.

MR. BORDEN. (*Smiles and takes her hand.*) I'm just getting old, Lizzie.

LIZZIE. You've got on my ring.... Do you remember when I gave you that?
... When I left Miss Cornelia's—it was in a little blue velvet box, you hid
it behind your back, and you said, "guess which hand, Lizzie!" And I   510
guessed. And you gave it to me and you said, "it's real gold, Lizzie, it's for

you because you are very precious to me." Do you remember, Papa? (*Mr. Borden nods.*) And I took it out of the little blue velvet box, and I took your hand, and I put my ring on your finger and I said "thank you, Papa, I love
515 you." ... You've never taken it off ... see how it bites into the flesh of your finger. (*She presses his hand to her face.*) I forgive you, Papa, I forgive you for killing my birds.... You look so tired, why don't you lie down and rest, put your feet up, I'll undo your shoes for you. (*She kneels and undoes his shoes.*)

MR. BORDEN. You're a good girl.

520 LIZZIE. I could never stand to have you hate me, Papa. Never. I would do anything rather than have you hate me.

MR. BORDEN. I don't hate you, Lizzie.

LIZZIE. I would not want you to find out anything that would make you hate me. Because I love you.

525 MR. BORDEN. And I love you, Lizzie, you'll always be precious to me.

LIZZIE. (*Looks at him, and then smiles.*) Was I—when I had scabs on my knees?

MR. BORDEN. (*Laughs.*) Oh yes. Even then.

LIZZIE. (*Laughs.*) Oh Papa! ... Kiss me! (*He kisses her on the forehead.*) Thank
530 you, Papa.

MR. BORDEN. Why're you crying?

LIZZIE. Because I'm so happy. Now ... put your feet up and get to sleep ... that's right ... shut your eyes ... go to sleep ... go to sleep....

(*She starts to hum, continues humming as Mr. Borden falls asleep. Miss Lizzie/Bridget appears on the stairs unobtrusively. Lizzie still humming, moves to the table, slips her hand under the clothes, withdraws the hatchet. She approaches her father with the hatchet behind her back. She stops humming. A pause, then she slowly raises the hatchet very high to strike him. Just as the hatchet is about to start its descent, there is a blackout. Children's voices are heard singing:*)

"Lizzie Borden took an axe,
535 Gave her Mother forty whacks,
When the job was nicely done,
She gave her father forty-one!
Forty-one!
Forty-one!"

(*The singing increases in volume and in distortion as it nears the end of the verse till the last words are very loud but discernible, just. Silence. Then the sound of slow measured heavy breathing which is growing into a wordless sound of hysteria. Light returns to the stage, dim light from late in the day.*)

The actress stands with the hatchet raised in the same position in which we saw her before the blackout, but the couch is empty. Her eyes are shut. The sound comes from her. Miss Lizzie is at the foot of the stairs. She moves to the actress, reaches up to take the hatchet from her. When Miss Lizzie's hand touches the actress's, the actress releases the hatchet and whirls around to face Miss Lizzie who is left holding the hatchet. The actress backs away from Miss Lizzie. There is a flickering of light at the top of the stairs.)

EMMA. (*From upstairs.*) Lizzie! Lizzie! You're making too much noise!   540

(*Emma descends the stairs carrying an oil lamp. The actress backs away from Lizzie, turns and runs into the kitchen. Miss Lizzie turns to see Emma. The hand hatchet is behind Miss Lizzie's back concealed from Emma. Emma pauses for a moment.*)

EMMA. Where is she?
MISS LIZZIE. Who?
EMMA. (*A pause then Emma moves to the window and glances out.*) It's raining.
MISS LIZZIE. I know.
EMMA. (*Puts the lamp down, sits, lowers her voice.*) Lizzie.   545
MISS LIZZIE. Yes?
EMMA. I want to speak to you, Lizzie.
MISS LIZZIE. Yes Emma.
EMMA. That ... actress who's come up from Boston.
MISS LIZZIE. What about her?   550
EMMA. People talk.
MISS LIZZIE. You needn't listen.
EMMA. In your position you should do nothing to *inspire talk*.
MISS LIZZIE. People need so little in the way of inspiration. And Miss Cornelia's classes didn't cover "Etiquette for Acquitted Persons."   555
EMMA. Common sense should tell you what you ought or ought not do.
MISS LIZZIE. Common sense is repugnant to me. I prefer uncommon sense.
EMMA. I forbid her in this house, Lizzie!

(*Pause.*)

MISS LIZZIE. Do you?
EMMA. (*Backing down, softly.*) It's ... disgraceful.   560
MISS LIZZIE. I see.

(*Miss Lizzie turns away from Emma a few steps.*)

EMMA. I simply cannot—
MISS LIZZIE. You could always leave.
EMMA. Leave?

565 MISS LIZZIE. Move. Away. Why don't you?

EMMA. I—

MISS LIZZIE. You could never, could you?

EMMA. If I only—

MISS LIZZIE. Knew.

570 EMMA. Lizzie, did you?

MISS LIZZIE. Oh Emma, do you intend asking me that question from now till death us do part?

EMMA. It's just—

MISS LIZZIE. For if you do, I may well take something sharp to you.

575 EMMA. Why do you joke like that!

MISS LIZZIE. (*Turning back to Emma who sees the hatchet for the first time. Emma's reaction is not any verbal or untoward movement. She freezes as Miss Lizzie advances on her.*) Did you never stop and think that if I did, then you were guilty too?

580 EMMA. What?

(*The actress will enter unobtrusively on the periphery. We are virtually unaware of her entrance until she speaks and moves forward.*)

MISS LIZZIE. It was you who brought me up, like a mother to me. Almost like a mother. Did you ever stop and think that I was like a puppet, your puppet. My head your hand, yes, your hand working my mouth, me saying all the things you felt like saying, me doing all the things you felt like 585 doing, me spewing forth, me hitting out, and you, you—!

THE ACTRESS. (*Quietly.*) Lizzie.

(*Miss Lizzie is immediately in control of herself.*)

EMMA. (*Whispers.*) I wasn't even here that day.

MISS LIZZIE. I can swear to that.

EMMA. Do you want to drive me mad?

590 MISS LIZZIE. Oh yes.

EMMA. You didn't ... did you?

MISS LIZZIE. Poor ... Emma.

THE ACTRESS. Lizzie. (*She takes the hatchet from Miss Lizzie.*) Lizzie you did.

MISS LIZZIE. I didn't. (*The actress looks to the hatchet—then to the audience.*)
595   You did.

(*Blackout.*)

—1980

Hannah Moscovitch

b. 1978

Toronto-based playwright Hannah Moscovitch, called "the wunderkind of Canadian theatre" by CBC radio, achieved national success early in her career. She made her name by addressing difficult subjects—in her words, finding "unusual slants on old topics, complex stories, and unheard voices"—in a style that often blends satire and dark humour with emotional sensitivity. "The darker the story gets, the funnier it gets," she has said; "that's what life seems like to me."

Moscovitch was born in Ottawa and grew up in a left-leaning, academic environment; her father was a professor of social policy and her mother a labour researcher and writer of feminist non-fiction. After graduating from the National Theatre School of Canada in the acting stream, Moscovitch studied literature at the University of Toronto.

Moscovitch first gained widespread acclaim with the debut of her short plays *Essay* (2005) and *The Russian Play* (2006) at Toronto's SummerWorks festival; *Essay* won the Contra Guys Award for Best New Play, and *The Russian Play* was awarded Jury Prize for Best New Production. *This Is War* (2013) won the Trillium Book Award and the Toronto Critics' Award for Best Canadian Play.

The content of Moscovitch's work is often challenging or controversial: *Essay* confronts issues of gender and power in academia, *East of Berlin* addresses the legacy of the Holocaust, and *This Is War* (2013) is based on a true story involving Canadian soldiers in 2008 Afghanistan. Regarding the social and political complexity of her plays, she says, "I want to ask the audience questions. I get excited by the idea of a character being forced to confront a hostile audience. There's something so fascinating about watching those dynamics play out."

Essay

CHARACTERS

Jeffrey: thirty
Pixie: eighteen
Professor Galbraith: early sixties

SCENE 1

A small office on campus. An open laptop sits on a desk amidst piles of papers, files and books. The greenish hue of fluorescent lighting fills the room. Lights up on Jeffrey, behind the desk, and Pixie, in front of it.

JEFFREY. Just, uh, please take a seat while I finish this paragraph and then I'll leave off.

PIXIE. Am I early ...? Or ...?

JEFFREY. No, no, just finishing up, just finishing up.

(Jeffrey closes his laptop.)

5   Now. Essay proposal, is that right? Essay due on the eighteenth?

PIXIE. Thank you for letting me come and—

JEFFREY. No, please. Just remind me. I rejected your proposal, is that ...?

PIXIE. Uh, yes, you did, but—

JEFFREY. Right. Good. Well, my notes are vague sometimes, and my hand-
10   writing is very bad, so before you raze the field, we might as well take a closer look at it.

PIXIE. *(getting out her essay proposal)* Okay, great, um, well what I wanted to—

JEFFREY. It's usually just a question of coming up with an alteration that will
15   render it—

PIXIE. —um, okay—

JEFFREY. —more precise, more scholarly.

PIXIE. Okay. That's what I wanted to talk to you about.

JEFFREY. Good. Yes. Let's talk!

20 PIXIE. Your objections, because I—I think I can make an argument for this essay proposal.

JEFFREY. This one?

PIXIE. Yeah.

JEFFREY. This essay proposal?

25 PIXIE. Yes?

(Beat.)

JEFFREY. Ah. I see. You've come to contest.

PIXIE. Or at least I just wanted to—

JEFFREY. To make your case, is that it?

PIXIE. I—I just think that—that it's possible—that it's possible to argue, I mean if the problem is just sourcing.

JEFFREY. Let me take a look at it, can I?

(*Pixie hands him the essay proposal.*)

Let's just see what we've got here before we ... (*laughs*) ... have it out.

(*Beat.*)

PIXIE. (*waiting, shifting*) If—if you read the notes you made ...

(*Jeffrey holds out his hand to indicate to Pixie that she should give him a minute to finish reading.*)

(*Beat.*)

JEFFREY. (*scanning*) Elizabeth Farnese.[1] Strategies of, important contributions to. Summary, summary, more summary. Look. What you've got here is very interesting. A very interesting historical figure—

PIXIE. Yeah, well I thought—

JEFFREY. —who no doubt deserves more.... An argument could be made that this is an oversight. The historical record has failed to illuminate this neglected but highly engaging corner of European history.

PIXIE. Unhunh, well—

JEFFREY. Hoards of insensitive historians have obscured a very important character, as it were.

PIXIE. Yeah, well—

JEFFREY. And she is worthy, entitled to, a second glance, now, in our modern era. However, that said—

PIXIE. Unhunh.

JEFFREY. —that said, I'm not sure that for the purposes of this first year course it's—it's—if there would be enough material to support a ten-page essay on the topic.

PIXIE. Yeah, but—

JEFFREY. Ten pages. You'll need more than a cursory—

PIXIE. Yeah.

---

1   *Elizabeth Farnese* Italian noblewoman (1692–1766) and queen consort of Spain. Through her influence over her husband Philip V, she orchestrated Spain's foreign policy, including the country's involvement in several wars. Because Philip already had children by his first wife, Elizabeth's primary ambition was to secure Italian thrones for her sons.

JEFFREY. —more than a brief mention in a larger—

55 PIXIE. Yeah, I have. I have plenty of material. And also, there's one listed at the bottom of the supplementary readings, on page twenty-one.

JEFFREY. One what?

PIXIE. An article on her.

(*Beat.*)

JEFFREY. That's very possible, all right.

60 PIXIE. And I found ample sources in the stacks.

JEFFREY. That's very possible.

PIXIE. And the article was on the list—

JEFFREY. Right, right I see the—now we're getting to the bottom of the—

PIXIE. —and so—

65 JEFFREY. This is progress!

PIXIE. And so, I thought—

JEFFREY. You thought it was on the list, it must be—

PIXIE. Yeah.

JEFFREY. And I want to stress that your idea is not invalid, by any means, all

70 right?

PIXIE. Unhunh.

JEFFREY. At least not in general terms, all right?

PIXIE. Unhunh?

(*Beat.*)

JEFFREY. I'm not the—I don't want to be the big bad—

75 PIXIE. Yeah?

JEFFREY. —the big bad—

PIXIE. Yeah?

JEFFREY. Is that ...? Is it Pixie? Is that your ...?

PIXIE. Yeah. Pixie.

80 JEFFREY. Look, Pixie—

PIXIE. Yeah?

JEFFREY. I understand you feel very passionately about this. Here you are in my office, overflowing with passion ... (*laughs*) ...

(*Pixie shifts away from Jeffrey.*)

No, no, what I mean is you've made the effort to come here, to defend

85 your proposal to me, the topic you've chosen indicates that you're trying to avoid the banal and revitalize history, as it were, and so—

PIXIE. Yeah?

JEFFREY. I want to stress that I appreciate your passion.

(*Beat.*)

PIXIE. But—

JEFFREY. Your topic is frankly.... You see, this is a history course that—   90

PIXIE. And this is history.

JEFFREY. Yes, yes it's history, but Pixie, this course deals with war and state-craft. In the eighteenth and early nineteenth century.

PIXIE. Yeah?

JEFFREY. Eighteenth and early nineteenth century. Now I'm not saying that   95
women haven't, in more recent times, made very valuable contributions to
war efforts. But, in the eighteenth century, women didn't yet—

PIXIE. —unhuhn—

JEFFREY. —possess the freedom of movement, the—the wherewithal to—

PIXIE. —unhuhn—   100

JEFFREY. —and so women couldn't as yet be classified as "military leaders,"
per se.

PIXIE. Okay, but—

JEFFREY. And—just a minute—and that is why I can't allow you to write a
paper on a woman who, while she may be very compelling from a social   105
history perspective—

PIXIE. Yeah, but she—

JEFFREY. —is not an appropriate subject given the requirements of this particular writing assignment. Now I commend you for finding source material. Good work there! But the thing is you're simply not on topic.   110

(*Jeffrey hands back Pixie's essay proposal.*)

If you need to hear this from a higher source, by all means, take it up with
the professor, he is the final word—

PIXIE. No, it's fine, I'm just—I don't know, a little—

JEFFREY. Disappointed, I see that.

PIXIE. No, I'm confused.   115

JEFFREY. Yes. Confused, disappointed, and believe me, I understand. European history is a ... bewildering series of men who prance about, waging
war, and making a nuisance of themselves. And so, you light on Elizabeth
Farnese because you'd like to champion her, establish her worth, she is one
of the unacknowledged greats of history, and that's a very understandable   120
response given the material—

PIXIE. Wait.

JEFFREY. —the time period—

PIXIE. You—wait—you think I picked her because she's a girl? You think I
picked Elizabeth Farnese because she's a girl.   125

(*Beat.*)

JEFFREY. Well, what I was suggesting wasn't quite so simplistic—

PIXIE. I didn't. I really—I'm not a feminist. It said war and strategy and she was a great strategist, really, if you read the material I found.

JEFFREY. I—Pixie, I'm sure she was, but—

130 PIXIE. She was.

JEFFREY. I'm sure she was, but—

PIXIE. She was. She was a great strategist, she played everyone. The French, the Austrians—

JEFFREY. Yes, Pixie, that's the history.

135 PIXIE. Well, that's why I picked her. 'Cause I thought that was on topic.

JEFFREY. I—let's back up here for a moment—

PIXIE. I thought I was on topic.

JEFFREY. Pixie, let's—please, let's back up for a moment—

PIXIE. If I'm not on topic, then—

140 JEFFREY. Pixie! Please. I want to—we must address a statement you made a moment ago. Did I, or am I mistaken, hear you say you're not a feminist?

PIXIE. No, I'm not, I was just doing the assignment.

JEFFREY. Yes, yes, but—

PIXIE. I thought it was just a question of sources. That's what you wrote on my sheet, that's why I came here.

145 JEFFREY. Yes, but Pixie. Feminism—

PIXIE. I'm not a feminist.

JEFFREY. But you ... (*laughs uncomfortably*) ... I don't think you—

PIXIE. I'm not. I took this course. I wanted to take the history of war, I didn't take a women's studies course—

150 JEFFREY. —but—

PIXIE. —I took this course.

JEFFREY. But, Pixie, women's studies is a very valuable body of knowledge, and you are a feminist.

155 PIXIE. No I'm not.

JEFFREY. Yes you ...! Perhaps you don't realize—

PIXIE. I'm not a feminist—

JEFFREY. —because the very fact that you're standing here, before me, in this institution—a hundred years ago, fifty, that would not have been possible, and you would not have received adequate education to be able to argue to me that Elizabeth Farnese is a military leader—

160

PIXIE. No, this is the point. I didn't pick her because she's a girl.

JEFFREY. But Pixie—

PIXIE. I didn't go looking for some girl so I could pick her, so I could make some big point to you to vindicate women or whatever you're thinking—

165

JEFFREY. Why did you pick her, then?

(*Beat.*)

Why pick her?

(*Beat.*)

PIXIE. Okay. Fine. I picked a girl. But the point I was trying to make about not being a feminist was—

JEFFREY. You are a feminist.   170

PIXIE. No I'm not.

JEFFREY. Yes you ...! Pixie, look—

PIXIE. I'm not.

JEFFREY. Look. Take you and I, you and I, Pixie. You believe yourself to be equal to me, don't you?   175

PIXIE. I'm your student.

JEFFREY. Yes, but, aside from our status as—as—I'm a bad example. Take any of your fellow students, the male members of your classes, you believe yourself to be equal to them, don't you?

(*Beat.*)

That's feminism. That is feminism. And so you are, by definition—   180

PIXIE. Fine. Fine. I'm a feminist.

JEFFREY. Now, all right—

PIXIE. I'm a fucking feminist.

JEFFREY. All right. Let's not—let's please—

PIXIE. All I was trying to say was I thought Elizabeth Farnese was really effec- 185
tive and interesting, but I don't care, okay? I'll write on Napoleon.

JEFFREY. Yes, all right.

PIXIE. I'll write on Napoleon like everyone else.

JEFFREY. Pixie. Please, just slow down. Let's not raise our voices please.

(*Beat.*)

PIXIE. (*more confused than sorry*) Sorry.   190

JEFFREY. That's all right.

(*Beat.*)

Napoleon would be a highly appropriate choice, in the context of this ...

(*Pixie has walked out.*)

Pixie, where are you going?

(*Jeffrey walks after her.*)

Can you—can we please finish our ...?

(*Beat.*)

195   Pixie?

(*Pixie is gone. Jeffrey shakes his head, and goes back over to his desk. He crosses off his meeting with Pixie in his date book. Lights out.*)

SCENE 2

Jeffrey's office, a week and a half later. There is a pile of essays on his desk. Jeffrey is marking. Professor Galbraith enters and looks at the office.

GALBRAITH. This is a dismal little office, Jeffrey.

JEFFREY. (*standing*) Professor Galbraith!

GALBRAITH. I haven't been down here since, well, the seventies, and I don't think it's changed.

5 JEFFREY. Thank you for ... stopping by.

GALBRAITH. Who are you sharing it with, some social science ...?

JEFFREY. She's, yes, an anthropology Ph.D., but she's on a very different schedule, opposite hours—

GALBRAITH. Good.

10 JEFFREY. It's worked out well. I barely ever see her.

(*Beat.*)

And I keep meaning to say thank you for finding me this office—

GALBRAITH. So what's the matter, Jeffrey? Hm? Your email, your phone call? I'm sorry I've been unresponsive, the conference—

JEFFREY. Yes, I know, the timing—

15 GALBRAITH. I agreed to moderate a couple of panels, deliver a keynote, and suddenly when the coffee machine breaks down, they all come to me.

JEFFREY. Yes, I can see how that would happen.

GALBRAITH. This is the downside of heading the department. There are upsides! There are upsides!

20 JEFFREY. I'm sure there are.

(*Beat.*)

So, Professor—

GALBRAITH. So what is it, Jeffrey? Hm? You need to consult? You need to be supervised? Someone to hold your hand?

JEFFREY. Well—

25 GALBRAITH. It's difficult, this juncture in the dissertation-writing process.

The tunnel, they call it.

JEFFREY. Uh, no—

GALBRAITH. Which is apt because you're pretty much hunting down your own asshole at this point, excuse the.... Because, once the research is done and you're writing—

JEFFREY. Yes, no, I—

GALBRAITH. —there it is, looming on the horizon, your own anus. That's what a Ph.D. is. An heroic-apocalyptic confrontation with the self.

JEFFREY. Professor, that's very ... funny, and sometimes it does feel as though I'm peering into my own ... but no, it's not my dissertation.

GALBRAITH. Dissertation is going well, is it?

JEFFREY. Yes, it's going, but I've been trying to grade the essays for History 103?

(*Galbraith picks up a pile of essays.*)

GALBRAITH. This them?

JEFFREY. Yes, and what I need to ask you is—

GALBRAITH. Lots of little comments. Good point. This is awkward.

JEFFREY. (*laughs*) Yes.

GALBRAITH. Where's your thesis?

JEFFREY. Yes ... (*laughs*) ... and, uh, Professor, what I wanted to ask you is—

GALBRAITH. I haven't seen you at the conference, by the way.

(*Beat.*)

JEFFREY. No. I haven't been attending. I've been so intent on getting through these—

GALBRAITH. I chaired what turned out to be a very energetic panel on interpretations of Napoleonic law.

JEFFREY. Well, I'm sorry I missed it.

GALBRAITH. Also a lecture on problems of coalition warfare. Quite compelling. A Chicago University professor, Sheila Newbery. Right up your alley, research wise. I hope you weren't grading undergraduate essays rather than attending the conference?

JEFFREY. I—well—I—

GALBRAITH. I hope you were at least chasing—or—what's the euphemism these days for female companionship? The conference falls a little short there. One look at the participants and.... (*laughs*) Don't expect to find love in the history department, Jeffrey.

JEFFREY. I ... won't hold my breath. (*trying to joke*) Perhaps the English department.

GALBRAITH. There's a good hunting ground. The English department!

(*Professor Galbraith and Jeffrey share a laugh. Beat.*)

JEFFREY. Professor, I wanted to ask you—
GALBRAITH. Oh, right, yes, ask me the—
65 JEFFREY. A student of mine, an essay—
GALBRAITH. Right.

(*Jeffrey begins looking through the pile for Pixie's essay.*)

JEFFREY. I'm trying to grade this one paper, but it's very difficult. I rejected
70   this student's essay proposal when she submitted it two weeks ago. We
      discussed it, I thought she'd resolved to write on a more appropriate topic,
      but, as it turns out, she hasn't. She's written on the original.
GALBRAITH. Ah.
JEFFREY. And, yes, and now I'm not sure whether to fail her, or what's the
75   procedure? I told her to come by my office this afternoon, thinking I'd
      have a chance to confer with you first—

(*Jeffrey finds the essay and hands it to Professor Galbraith.*)

The title should give you a good sense of the type of—
GALBRAITH. Cock-up?
JEFFREY. Yes.

(*Beat. Professor Galbraith and Jeffrey look at the title.*)

80 GALBRAITH. Hmmm, yes! Quite the—
JEFFREY. You see the ...

(*Beat.*)

GALBRAITH. (*reading*) Elizabeth Farnese and Napoleon Bonaparte: A Critical
      Comparison of their Wartime Strategies.
JEFFREY. You see the difficulty. And, for grading, it reads like an English
85   paper, all conjecture and—
GALBRAITH. Yes.

(*Beat.*)

JEFFREY. The sources are fine, but—
GALBRAITH. Yes.

(*Beat.*)

Yes, this certainly isn't what I discussed with her. I didn't approve a com-
90   parison. Although, I suppose she was trying to appease you and write on
      her topic. Servant of two masters.

(*Professor Galbraith looks through the essay.*)

JEFFREY. I'm ... sorry. I'm sorry, Professor. You—did she—

GALBRAITH. Didn't I tell you, Jeffrey? This girl came to see me a week, a week and a half ago, asked if she could write on Elizabeth Farnese, Philip the fifth's second wife?   95

JEFFREY. (*to confirm that he knows who she is*) Yes.

GALBRAITH. How Elizabeth Farnese is a military leader ... (*laughs*) ... I'm interested to know.

(*Professor Galbraith flips through the essay.*)

JEFFREY. Yes, but, she's not. I'm sorry, she's not, at least not considered to be—   100

GALBRAITH. Elizabeth Farnese?

JEFFREY. She's not generally considered to be a military leader—

GALBRAITH. No, no, of course not. But, she seemed.... This girl—the girl ...?

JEFFREY. Pixie Findley?

GALBRAITH. She seemed very—I'm probably looking for attractive, but let's   105 say determined for the sake of decorum. I thought, why not let her have a go, she's likely going to argue something preposterous. Has she?

JEFFREY. I—I don't know.

GALBRAITH. I was hoping for something a little risqué, at least euphemistically, as in Elizabeth Farnese's victories were won not on the battlefield but   110 in the bedroom, or Frederick the Great favoured the oblique attack while Elizabeth perfected the horizontal one, something to that effect.

(*Professor Galbraith reads through the essay.*)

JEFFREY. But the guidelines for this essay were very specific—

GALBRAITH. I let the leash out a little.

(*Beat.*)

JEFFREY. I—yes—I can see why you might. I hesitated, uh, briefly before I   115 rejected her proposal. It's sensitive, of course, and highly charged, but the reason why I ultimately did turn her down was—

GALBRAITH. (*referring to Pixie's essay*) This is quite good, this opening.

(*Beat.*)

JEFFREY. The reason, Professor, why I didn't allow Pixie to write on Elizabeth Farnese is that I felt fairly certain that, given the parameters of the assign-   120 ment that you set, military leader, it would result in her producing a very weak essay.

(*Beat.*)

And she has produced a very weak essay. Professor.

GALBRAITH. Ah, now, here we have it! (reading from Pixie's essay) "While
125 Napoleon engaged in warfare to resolve international strife," very nice,
"Elizabeth relied on her feminine wiles."

JEFFREY. Professor.

GALBRAITH. Very nice phrasing. Wiles. Where do you suppose her wiles were
located?

130 JEFFREY. Look, I—

GALBRAITH. Adjacent to her thighs, presumably.

JEFFREY. I—Professor—this is a student's essay!

(*Galbraith stops reading Pixie's essay and looks at Jeffrey.*)

I realize some of it's laughable, but ...

(*Beat.*)

I'm sorry, I'm just a little surprised you allowed a student to write on Eliza-
135 beth Farnese.

GALBRAITH. What are you concerned about, Jeffrey? Her grade?

JEFFREY. Well, yes, her grade, but also—

GALBRAITH. Pass her, write a few comments on it. Good effort. Fails to convince.

140 JEFFREY. I suppose I can do that. This essay certainly doesn't deserve a passing
grade. I don't feel all that comfortable with—

GALBRAITH. Jeffrey—

JEFFREY. —arbitrarily assigning it one.

(*Beat.*)

GALBRAITH. B minus.

(*Beat.*)

145 JEFFREY. No—you—no, the point is, I'm forced to arbitrarily assign her a
grade because she was allowed to write on a, I think, inappropriate ... B
minus. That's at least a firm hold on the material. Look, I—I really don't
like being put in this position at all, I feel very—

GALBRAITH. Jeffrey.

150 JEFFREY. B minus? Based on what criteria?

GALBRAITH. Well, no doubt she learned something while writing it.

JEFFREY. She learned. She learned something. That's your criterion?

GALBRAITH. You don't like my criterion?

JEFFREY. This is a very unconvincing essay!

GALBRAITH. How bad can it be?   155

JEFFREY. It's a terrible essay! It's ridiculous.

GALBRAITH. Jeffrey.

JEFFREY. A short story would be more convincing. A finger-painting!

GALBRAITH. Oh, for Christ's sake, Jeffrey, she wrote a bad essay! The girl is
 seventeen. Eighteen. Let her go skip off and neck in the quad.   160

>   (*Beat.*)

JEFFREY. Neck in the ...!

GALBRAITH. Or what do they say, make out?

>   (*Beat.*)

JEFFREY. Professor, this is the student who argued that Elizabeth Farnese is a
 military leader, and now you're trivializing—

GALBRAITH. All right—   165

JEFFREY. —and—and ridiculing her very earnest attempt—

GALBRAITH. All right!

JEFFREY. —to include women in the history of—

GALBRAITH. Yes, I know, Jeffrey, because I'm the one who let her. I approved
 her essay topic. I said yes. Write on Elizabeth Farnese. Prove she's on par   170
 with Nelson,[1] Napoleon. Set us all straight, us men.

>   (*Beat.*)

(*smiling*) We have to let the girls have their day, Jeffrey.

>   (*Beat.*)

JEFFREY. We have to ... let the girls ...?

>   (*Beat.*)

I'm sorry?

GALBRAITH. In my experience, it's best to just let them, well, have their day. 175

>   (*Beat.*)

JEFFREY. What do you mean?

GALBRAITH. It may make for weak scholarship, but I think it's best to allow
 for it, at the moment, despite its weaknesses.

>   (*Beat.*)

---

1 *Nelson* Viscount Horatio Nelson (1758–1805), famous English admiral responsible for
   British victories in the important naval battles of several wars.

JEFFREY. I—I'm sorry. What—what makes for weak scholarship?

180 GALBRAITH. There's a great deal of so-called research in circulation these days that's entirely based on resentment.

JEFFREY. What are you talking about?

GALBRAITH. Gendered revisionism,[1] Jeffrey. Biographies of Napoleon's lover, James Joyce's wife,[2] the unsung women of history, herstory, all very fash-

185 ionable, but at a certain point ... (*laughs*) ... it fails to convince.

(*Beat.*)

JEFFREY. It—it fails to ... are you joking? Professor?

GALBRAITH. You said it yourself. Pixie's essay is a failure. Why? Because Elizabeth Farnese is, at best, a second-rate figure who cannot yield any important historical insight.

190 JEFFREY. Yes, perhaps in the context of this assignment—

GALBRAITH. And the result, an unscholarly, as you said, paper—

JEFFREY. But not as a general—

GALBRAITH. That you deemed weak—

JEFFREY. I—I wouldn't make that kind of a sweeping—

195 GALBRAITH. That you rejected—

JEFFREY. Yes! I—yes—I rejected her essay proposal, not the whole field of inquiry!

(*Beat.*)

GALBRAITH. All right, Jeffrey, what is history? What is it?

(*Beat.*)

JEFFREY. What is ... history?

200 GALBRAITH. Too broad? What isn't history?

(*Beat.*)

JEFFREY. What is not—

GALBRAITH. What can we say is not history?

(*Beat.*)

Seventeenth, eighteenth century. What are men doing?

---

1   *revisionism* I.e., reinterpretation of history in opposition to conventional approaches; although the term can be value-neutral, it is sometimes used disparagingly to suggest an intellectually unjustified denial of accepted facts.

2   *Napoleon's lover* Napoleon's several lovers included a countess, a queen, and a famous actress; *James Joyce's wife* The Irish novelist James Joyce was married to Nora Barnacle (1884–1951), who inspired the character of Molly Bloom in his novel *Ulysses* (1922).

(*Beat.*)

Revolutionizing warfare. And what are women doing?

JEFFREY. Well, they're—   205

GALBRAITH. Curling their hair, boiling potatoes, et cetera, et cetera. They are not central to the major events. They are—it's unfortunate, it's unlike-able—marginal to them. If we want to include women, we have to reorient history to the mundane, and frankly—

JEFFREY. —uh, Professor—   210

GALBRAITH. —frankly—

JEFFREY. —Professor—

GALBRAITH. —then it's no longer history, is it? It's sociology, anthropology, women's studies-ology.

(*Beat.*)

JEFFREY. Look, Professor, that is all ... very controversial and I—   215

GALBRAITH. What?

JEFFREY. I—I—

GALBRAITH. What?

JEFFREY. —disagree. I think we should be privileging a female discourse, given how excluded and sidelined—   220

GALBRAITH. So Elizabeth Farnese is a military leader.

JEFFREY. No, that's not—that's a bad example.

GALBRAITH. Which is it?

JEFFREY. I don't think it's an either-or—

GALBRAITH. So she is?   225

JEFFREY. Well, one could argue, I mean, as it stands, no.

GALBRAITH. So she isn't.

JEFFREY. No—she—I just—no, I don't think it's that simple. Because—

GALBRAITH. Jeffrey.

JEFFREY. No! Because one could argue, one could radically redefine the term   230
military leader—

GALBRAITH. Yes, and one could write an essay about how Napoleon's horse influenced his decisions. If a horse came to you and asked if it could write that essay, you would probably say, let the horse have its day. Call it horsestory. And it may be true, to a certain extent, that Napoleon's horse   235
did influence his decisions, but who really gives a damn?

(*Beat.*)

JEFFREY. Professor, I'm sorry, are you actually not joking? Because I—I can't believe I'm hearing this.

GALBRAITH. Jeffrey, relax, all right?

240 JEFFREY. I can't believe you just said horsestory.

GALBRAITH. Jeffrey.

JEFFREY. Horsestory? Professor? Horsestory? That's a very pejorative, uh, derisive, misogynist—

GALBRAITH. Misogynist?

245 JEFFREY. I, yes, I think, misogynist—

GALBRAITH. All right, all right, relax, I'm ... what? Toying with your liberal sensibilities? I'm not rejecting all revisionism, per se. However, one gets tired, worn down. The relentless onslaught of victimology. The history department's awash in it. We're being strangled to death by cultural stud-
250 ies. They've got their own fucking department, why do they want mine? What is wrong with Napoleon? Personally, I love the guy. You love the guy!

(*Beat.*)

JEFFREY. Well, yes, but—

GALBRAITH. That's history, Jeffrey. That's history. A love affair with Napoleon.

JEFFREY. I—no, you see—no—I don't agree.

(*Beat.*)

255 I disagree!

GALBRAITH. You're researching Napoleon—

JEFFREY. Yes, fine, I am, but I don't think Napoleon Bonaparte is the only valid ...! I think this whole argument only highlights the fact that we've constructed a false notion of history as male, as centred on male events,
260 male figures, in which case, we should be trying to update, and redress—

GALBRAITH. —yes, fine—

JEFFREY. —to try and right the balance.

GALBRAITH. Yes. You're right.

JEFFREY. And broaden the scope of ...

(*Beat.*)

265 I'm right.

GALBRAITH. Yes, I agree. I agree with you, as in Pixie's case. Pixie got to write her essay. Write on a female figure, have her say—

JEFFREY. No, but, no—

GALBRAITH. Right the balance, redress the what-have-you—

270 JEFFREY. But, no—that's not—no—you think her say has no merit.

(*Beat.*)

You think it's merit-less.

GALBRAITH. So do you.

JEFFREY. But, no, look, that's patronizing.

GALBRAITH. No Jeffrey.

JEFFREY. That's—yes it is. You're humouring her, you're cynically appeasing   275
her—

GALBRAITH. Pixie is happy.

(*Beat.*)

JEFFREY. That's ...! You're patronizing her!

GALBRAITH. I am allowing her to have her say.

JEFFREY. You don't value her say!   280

GALBRAITH. She can't tell the difference. If she can't tell the difference, then—

JEFFREY. What? Then it's not patronizing?

GALBRAITH. Then, no, it's not patronizing, largely because she doesn't feel
patronized.

JEFFREY. Yes, but that's only because—   285

GALBRAITH. Or are you claiming to be better qualified to determine what's
patronizing for Pixie than Pixie is herself?

JEFFREY. No, no I'm not. Except, yes, at this moment, yes, I'm the one who's—

GALBRAITH. What?

JEFFREY. Here! Listening to—privy to—   290

GALBRAITH. What?

JEFFREY. To ..., your—

GALBRAITH. What? Jeffrey?

JEFFREY. —sexism!

(*Long beat.*)

GALBRAITH. Hm.   295

(*Beat.*)

Do you think you might be a little worn down?

JEFFREY. Uh, no, I think I'm fine.

GALBRAITH. (*considering*) Three, four years into your Ph.D. Middle of your
thesis, three tutorials, this little office, working until all hours, you haven't
been attending the conference, leaving me a series of phone and email   300
messages about one undergraduate paper.

(*Beat.*)

JEFFREY. If you're suggesting that—

GALBRAITH. Because it's inadvisable to throw around words like sexist, all
right Jeffrey? Given the current climate in campus politics. And, once

305   you've been in the department a little longer, then you'll start to—

JEFFREY. What? Then I'll what? I'll start referring to my female students as girls and allowing the attractive ones to write personal responses instead of essays. "How do you feel about Napoleon, Pixie?" "Oh, I really like him." B minus!

310 GALBRAITH. (*laughs*) No, but, over time, you will come to realize that students such as Pixie float through here every year on their way to the cultural studies department. Next year she'll switch to commerce, business admin. Why? Because she likes their building better. And then, when you've seen enough Pixies come and go, you'll realize it's best to just let

315   them have their little say.

(*A momentary standoff between the men. Pixie enters at the doorway.*)

PIXIE. Hi! Sorry to interrupt. (*to Galbraith*) Hi Professor. (*to Jeffrey*) I just wanted to let you know I'm here. If you're—uh—in the middle of something, I'll just wait in the hallway until you're—

GALBRAITH. No, Pixie, please, come in.

320 PIXIE. I can just wait in the hallway.

GALBRAITH. No, no, please, come in. Jeffrey and I were just discussing, but please.

JEFFREY. Uh, yes. Come in Pixie.

(*Pixie enters.*)

PIXIE. Am I in trouble ... or ...?

325 JEFFREY. Uh no, no Pixie, I'm sorry, please sit down—

PIXIE. Okay, just with the two of you standing there ...

JEFFREY. Yes, I'm sorry, we were just finishing up. (*to Professor Galbraith*) Professor, I asked Pixie here to talk about her essay.

GALBRAITH. Right, right.

330 JEFFREY. And so I think I should, uh—

GALBRAITH. Right. Well, I'm off. I'll leave you to it.

(*Beat.*)

Jeffrey, the conference resumes at ten tomorrow morning, should you choose to grace us. (*to Pixie*) Pixie. Nice to see you again so soon.

PIXIE. Yeah.

335 GALBRAITH. And the assignment we discussed ...? When was it, a week, a week and a half ago?

PIXIE. Yeah.

GALBRAITH. How did it go? Hm? Did you enjoy writing it?

PIXIE. (*with a quick glance at Jeffrey*) I, yes, I really enjoyed—I learned a lot.

GALBRAITH. That's good. That's good. That's very good.   340

(*Galbraith looks at Jeffrey. So does Pixie, causing Jeffrey to turn away. Beat.*)

There are sources, Pixie, that suggest Elizabeth Farnese may have led the Spanish Army against the French in 1717,[1] not long after her accession.

PIXIE. Yeah, I came across that.

GALBRAITH. (*picturing it*) On horseback, at the head of the Spanish Army, as the formidable Louis XV crossed the Pyrenees.[2]   345

PIXIE. Yes.

GALBRAITH. Quite the—quite the—

PIXIE. Yeah—

GALBRAITH. —feat! For a young ...!

PIXIE. (*with a quick glance at Jeffrey*) Unhunh, yeah, I thought so too.   350

GALBRAITH. A very ambitious young person. Shared a number of qualities with Napoleon Bonaparte.

PIXIE. Uh, yeah! The comparison is kind of a stretch, of course. Napoleon conquered Europe, and Elizabeth got her sons thrones through her diplomacy, but, um, I think it holds.   355

GALBRAITH. (*considering her*) Elizabeth Farnese! It's a shame she wasn't allowed to cultivate her talents more fully. But, in the eighteenth century—

PIXIE. Yeah! I, uh—it's weird. There's not a lot of, um, women in this history we're covering—

GALBRAITH. No.   360

PIXIE. No, and the funny thing is, all term I've had this feeling of being left out. Like, it's all been very interesting, but it doesn't feel like it's about me, or for me, if that makes any sense?

(*Galbraith smiles at her.*)

I thought it might just be because I'm in first year, and everything is a little ...! But I think it's actually the content of the course. (*to Jeffrey*) And I was   365 thinking about, uh, what you asked. Why—why I chose Elizabeth, why I wanted to write on her, and I think that probably, without realizing it, I chose her because—I don't know.

(*Beat.*)

---

1   *Spanish Army ... in 1717*   In 1717, Spain briefly conquered Sardinia, initiating the War of the Quadruple Alliance (1718–20), in which France, Britain, the Netherlands, and the Holy Roman Empire united against Spain.

2   *Louis XV*   King Louis XV of France (1710–74) was still a child when the French army invaded Spain as part of the War of the Quadruple Alliance; *Pyrenees* Mountain range separating France and Spain.

(*to Jeffrey*) Because I wanted to be in it, you know?

(*Beat.*)

370 GALBRAITH. Well, that's very nice, Pixie. That's a very nice sentiment.
PIXIE. Uh, yeah.

(*Beat.*)

JEFFREY. And Pixie, now that you've written on Elizabeth Farnese, do you feel
there is a place for women in history? Or, are they just left out?

(*Beat.*)

PIXIE. Uh, um—
375 GALBRAITH. I'm sorry, Pixie. We're interrogating you. (*to Jeffrey*) Jeffrey, we're
interrogating her, I think we should stop.
PIXIE. No, I just didn't, uh, come prepared to—
GALBRAITH. No, of course you didn't—
JEFFREY. I—I'm sorry Pixie, just the one last question, if you don't mind, and
380 then we'll talk about your essay.

(*Beat.*)

PIXIE. What was the question?
GALBRAITH. Jeffrey, this is getting a little heavy-handed—
JEFFREY. The question was, is there a place for women in history?

(*Beat.*)

PIXIE. Well, from the lectures and the textbooks, I would say women don't
385 have a place in history. But I don't know if I believe that.
JEFFREY. What do you believe?

(*Beat.*)

PIXIE. Is this about my essay?
GALBRAITH. All right, we've asked our questions. I think we should stop now
before Pixie begins to feel put upon—
390 JEFFREY. (*a little too vehement*) She—no—she wants to answer!

(*Beat.*)

I—I'm sorry, is there some reason why Pixie shouldn't be allowed to offer
a response?

(*Beat.*)

GALBRAITH. Pixie, would you please wait in the hallway for a moment—

PIXIE. Uh, okay—

JEFFREY. (*motioning for Pixie to wait*) Uh, no, Pixie. (*to Galbraith*) Professor, 395
why? Is there some reason why Pixie can't answer?

GALBRAITH. She can answer, Jeffrey, it's not a question of whether or not she
can answer—

JEFFREY. Then—

GALBRAITH. I have no objections to hearing Pixie's response— 400

JEFFREY. Then, good! Let's—

GALBRAITH. —but I'm afraid we're overburdening her—

JEFFREY. With one question?

   (*Beat.*)

GALBRAITH. (*to Pixie*) Pixie, I'm sorry, if you could please wait in the hallway
for one moment— 405

PIXIE. Uh, okay—

JEFFREY. I don't see why Pixie should wait in the hallway—

GALBRAITH. (*to Pixie*) Jeffrey and I are ... (*laughs*)—

JEFFREY. (*to Galbraith*)—while we—

GALBRAITH. (*to Pixie*)—in the midst of a.... Your essay raised a number of 410
questions—

JEFFREY. (*to Pixie*)—about women and their under-representation in the historical record, and, Pixie, your essay interests us in that—

GALBRAITH. (*low, to Jeffrey*) Jeffrey—

JEFFREY. (*to Pixie*)—in that it speaks to the deficit of female figures— 415

GALBRAITH. (*low, to Jeffrey*) I'd really prefer if you didn't—

JEFFREY. (*to Pixie*)—as well as history departments' traditional unwillingness
to—

GALBRAITH. (*to Jeffrey*)—extend our argument into student affairs!

JEFFREY. (*to Galbraith*) Extend it into ...! It's about her. Her essay is the sub- 420
ject of the argument!

   (*Beat.*)

GALBRAITH. (*to Pixie*) Thank you, Pixie, it will just be one minute.

PIXIE. Okay—

JEFFREY. (*to Galbraith*) Just now, Professor, Pixie very clearly expressed feelings of exclusion. She's been left out. The subject matter doesn't seem to be 425
addressed to her—

GALBRAITH. Yes, I heard her—

JEFFREY. —the history excludes her.

GALBRAITH. I heard her.

JEFFREY. I'd like to—can we hear her out? Because I don't see how she can be 430
included in the discourse if she's sitting in the hallway.

(*Beat.*)

GALBRAITH. Fine, go ahead.

(*Jeffrey stares at Galbraith.*)

Go ahead.

(*Galbraith indicates that Jeffrey can ask his question.*)

JEFFREY. Pixie, I'm sorry, the question, should women have a place in history?
435   I would very much like to hear your response.

(*Beat.*)

PIXIE. Look, I—I don't know, okay? You're the experts. Why don't you tell
me. I came here to learn, to be taught, so I really don't know.

(*Beat.*)

JEFFREY. Yes—
PIXIE. You're the experts.
440   JEFFREY. Yes, we are, but, we're asking you because you wrote on Elizabeth
Farnese, and, arguably, that makes you an expert. An Elizabeth Farnese
expert.
PIXIE. Okay, but that's a pretty limited, um, field, Elizabeth Farnese. And you
asked me if women should be in history?
445   JEFFREY. Yes.
PIXIE. I think Elizabeth Farnese should be in history, is that what you're asking me?

(*Beat.*)

JEFFREY. Well, Pixie, yes, okay, that's—yes, Elizabeth Farnese is part of this
because you appealed your essay topic to Professor Galbraith, and that was
450   a very strong gesture on your part, and it indicates to me that you are embracing feminist—but I'd like to broaden our discussion from—and talk
about what you said a moment ago—that while taking this course history
seemed closed to, or seemed to leave out, women.

(*Beat.*)

PIXIE. Yeah?
455   JEFFREY. And you said, I don't know if I believe that.

(*Beat.*)

PIXIE. Yeah?

JEFFREY. And you meant ... what?

(*Beat. Pixie shifts, thinks.*)

All right. Pixie, look, the essay topic, military leader, Elizabeth Farnese is not a military leader.

PIXIE. Well—

JEFFREY. Yes! Exactly! You questioned that! And I think this is important, because what you hit upon, Pixie, is that there's a certain amount of exclusivity, a certain sexism built into the terminology, into the wording of the essay questions, which are, of course, formulated by Professor Galbraith.

(*Jeffrey looks at Professor Galbraith, who looks away.*)

And I think this relates to what you said a moment ago, about the textbooks, and the lectures—

PIXIE. —okay—

JEFFREY. —about your growing awareness of the emphasis on male figures—

PIXIE. —okay—

JEFFREY. (*half to Galbraith*)—and of the almost complete absence of female figures—

PIXIE. Yeah, okay—

JEFFREY. —and of the feelings of exclusion generated by what is a pronounced bias in the course material—

PIXIE. —unhunh—

JEFFREY. —as well as your skepticism. Your sense that women are a part of history—

PIXIE. (*soft*)—unhunh—

JEFFREY. —and that—that they would be a part of history if they weren't being under-represented in Professor Galbraith's lectures and on Professor Galbraith's course lists, and that, Pixie, that is what I'd like to hear about!

(*Beat.*)

PIXIE. Why are you yelling at me?

JEFFREY. I'm not ...! (*dropping the intensity level*) I'm not yelling, I'm trying to—

PIXIE. I, no, I don't want to answer this anymore.

(*Beat.*)

JEFFREY. No, Pixie, I'm sorry, let's—please, let's—

PIXIE. I feel uncomfortable answering this.

JEFFREY. But, but, Pixie—

GALBRAITH. Jeffrey—

490 JEFFREY. (*to Galbraith*) No. (*to Pixie*) Pixie—

PIXIE. No. I don't want to—

JEFFREY. But ...! Listen, let's just—

PIXIE. No.

GALBRAITH. Jeffrey—

495 JEFFREY. Look Pixie, let's just—

PIXIE. No.

JEFFREY. But, but Pixie!

PIXIE. You're yelling at me!

JEFFREY. I'm not—I'm not ...! Pixie, just listen for one—

500 PIXIE. No.

JEFFREY. Just for one—

PIXIE. No.

JEFFREY. Please! Pixie! Just for one—

PIXIE. No, I—no. I don't care. I don't care about women in history, okay?
505 This is my fucking elective. I have no idea!

(*Beat.*)

JEFFREY. You don't care.

(*Beat.*)

Doesn't it, for one second, occur to you that I am trying to defend you?

GALBRAITH. Jeffrey, I think we should stop now—

JEFFREY. That more is at stake than just your essay, and your grades—

510 GALBRAITH. Jeffrey, let's stop this right now.

JEFFREY. But, you know what, Pixie? Why don't you just glaze over—

GALBRAITH. —Jeffrey!—

JEFFREY. —while we determine that women and horses have equal historic
significance! Or—or apply your fucking lip gloss one more time—

515 GALBRAITH. All right, Jeffrey!

JEFFREY. —while Professor Galbraith eliminates women from the historical
record!

GALBRAITH. That's enough!

JEFFREY. You are being degraded and—and patronized—

520 GALBRAITH. That's enough, Jeffrey!

JEFFREY. —and you are sitting there like a lobotomized ...! Like a lobotomy
in a ... skirt!

(*Long beat. Long enough for Jeffrey to contemplate the possible ramifications
of his outburst. Very little motion occurs on stage. Pixie begins to cry and
covers her face.*)

I—shit.

(*Beat.*)

I—Pixie—I didn't—I didn't mean to—fuck.

(*Beat.*)

I—I—fuck.   525

GALBRAITH. Hm, yes. Jeffrey? Would you please wait in the hallway for a moment?

JEFFREY. (*half to Galbraith, half to Pixie*) I—no, look, I—I'm sorry—

GALBRAITH. Yes, I know you are—

JEFFREY. I just got—I got—   530

GALBRAITH. Yes, I know. But now I would prefer if you went out into the hallway.

JEFFREY. But—I—Professor, I—

GALBRAITH. Because, as you can see, Pixie is crying, and I think it would be best to give her a chance to collect herself.   535

(*Jeffrey doesn't go.*)

Jeffrey?

JEFFREY. I—yes, I just—I don't feel all that comfortable leaving her ... with ...

GALBRAITH. The head of the department?

(*A standoff between the two men. Beat. Pixie's crying is audible.*)

All right, Jeffrey. Can we please offer Pixie some Kleenex?

(*Jeffrey gets a box of tissues off the bookshelf. Galbraith takes the box of tissues from Jeffrey, and goes over to Pixie. She takes a couple of tissues without looking up. Long beat of crying.*)

PIXIE. I'm just trying to ... (*gestures*) ...   540

GALBRAITH. Please. I think it would be very strange if you weren't crying. I would cry if the dean yelled at me.

(*Galbraith smiles at Pixie. Pixie tries to pull it together again. Another beat of crying.*)

(*with sympathy*) You're upset.

(*Pixie nods.*)

PIXIE. (*quiet*) Yeah.

GALBRAITH. (*with sympathy*) Hm.   545

(*Beat.*)

I'm very sorry about this, Pixie. I shouldn't have let Jeffrey yell at you, I should have ... stepped in. (*for Jeffrey's benefit*) This is not how we encourage our TAs to behave.

(*Beat.*)

Jeffrey hasn't been raising his voice in tutorial, has he?

(*Pixie shakes her head no.*)

550 PIXIE. No.
GALBRAITH. No. Hm.

(*Beat.*)

You should know that we do have a formal complaints procedure at the university, Pixie. There is a women's coordinator. Or, rather, what is the current ...?

(*Beat.*)

555 Jeffrey?
JEFFREY. Yes?
GALBRAITH. What's the new title for the women's coordinator?
JEFFREY. The equity officer?
GALBRAITH. The equity officer. (*to Pixie*) She's in the Office of the Dean of
560 Students. She's a very approachable person, and I'm sure she would help you make your case.

(*Beat.*)

One of the avenues of appeal, when incidents of this type occur, is to come and talk with me. We've bypassed that step, as I witnessed the incident. And, in my experience, handling these types of incidents in the depart-
565 ment, I've found that it's important for the student to hear from the professor, or, in this case, TA, themselves. What's important for the student is to hear the faculty member acknowledge that their behaviour was not ... appropriate. Then, hopefully, a teaching relationship can be re-established.

(*Beat.*)

I know Jeffrey would like to apologize to you. And I will be here supervis-
570 ing, so if anything makes you feel uncomfortable, then we'll stop, and I'll ask Jeffrey to leave.

(*Beat.*)

Hm? Pixie? Is that ...?

(*Pixie shrugs—sure. Galbraith smiles at her.*)

Jeffrey.

(*Galbraith indicates to Jeffrey that he should speak to Pixie.*)

JEFFREY. (*half to Galbraith*) I—I—yes. I'm very sorry. I lost my—I uh—I
shouldn't have used that language to—   575
GALBRAITH. (*sharp*) Are you apologizing to Pixie, Jeffrey?
JEFFREY. (*confused*) Yes?

(*Galbraith indicates that Pixie is over there.*)

(*to Pixie*) Pixie, I shouldn't have used—I was frustrated, and I chose the
wrong words to express that—
PIXIE. You yelled at me!   580
JEFFREY. Yes. I—yes. I'm sorry.
PIXIE. I came here to get my essay. I came here to pick up my essay, so can I
have it please, or are you all on crack?
JEFFREY. Yes, I—I know that this must seem—
PIXIE. You wanted to talk to me about my essay, that's what you said, that's   585
why I came here, to talk about my essay! And then—
JEFFREY. Yes, I know, I see that—
PIXIE. —and then you YELL AT ME!!!
JEFFREY. I—yes, I appreciate that this isn't what you were expecting. You were
expecting a formal discussion of your essay and your grade, but Pixie, we   590
were, in fact, talking about your essay—
PIXIE. No we weren't. You were arguing with Professor Galbraith.

(*Beat.*)

JEFFREY. (*quiet*) But ... (*laughs*) ... Pixie, yes, but—
PIXIE. You were arguing.
JEFFREY. Yes, but, what you don't understand is, I was trying to—I was advo-   595
cating for you, because, you see—
PIXIE. You were in the middle of an argument! You and the Professor were
arguing!
JEFFREY. But—yes—I—yes, but you see, the argument was ... about you.
PIXIE. No it wasn't!   600
JEFFREY. But you don't ...! (*laughs*) It—it—yes, it was about ... you—
PIXIE. No.

(*Beat.*)

JEFFREY. But it—yes—
PIXIE. It wasn't about me!

(*Beat.*)

605 JEFFREY. But—but, okay, Pixie—
PIXIE. This wasn't about me.
JEFFREY. But I was—I was advocating for you. I was trying to advocate for you. You—what do you want? I was trying to—what do you women fucking want!
610 GALBRAITH. Jeffrey!
JEFFREY. I was putting my—I was—fuck—I was advocating for women!
PIXIE. You were arguing with Professor Galbraith! You were arguing with him about women in history. I was just ... in the room!

(*Beat.*)

615 Which is so funny, because in the textbook—the reason—the reason why I wrote the essay is because in the textbook, at the bottom of one of the pages, there's a footnote. Elizabeth Farnese, second wife of Philip the Fifth of Spain, secured her sons the thrones of Parma and Tuscany. She got her sons thrones. How? It doesn't say. There's just the footnote. So I wrote the essay. And I was sitting here, looking at you, and I could tell you wanted 620 me to say certain things for the sake of your argument, and I was thinking, my history TA is yelling at me for no reason and I am pissed off because I am kind of like a footnote here!

(*Beat.*)

"Professor Galbraith and Jeffrey had an argument about whether or not women should be included in history. And by the way, they were arguing because of Pixie Findley." "Pixie Findley? Who's she?" "Let's check the 625 footnote." And somehow, even though you think it's about me, it's not. It's about you. And your argument. I'm just the excuse for you to argue with each other. So I don't care which one of you wins because it's not about me.

(*Beat.*)

630 So ... yeah.

(*Long beat.*)

JEFFREY. I see what you're ... saying, but, Pixie, I didn't mean to.... It's—yes—you're talking about—yes, I see what you're pointing out, and I didn't mean to—to—I—you're right. I shouldn't have—I didn't, uh—I never,

uh, asked you if you wanted me to—but my intention—my intention
wasn't to appropriate, to—uh ... yeah.   635

(*Beat.*)

I'm—Pixie, I'm sorry.

(*Beat.*)

I'm ... sorry.
PIXIE. That's okay.
JEFFREY. I'm sorry. You're right, I—yes. I was—yes.
PIXIE. That's okay.   640
GALBRAITH. Have we, perhaps, resolved this? Pixie?

(*Pixie shrugs, nods.*)

PIXIE. Yeah.
GALBRAITH. Good, good. Good. Then perhaps we can leave this for now?
PIXIE. Yeah.

(*Pixie picks up her bag and Professor Galbraith ushers her to the doorway
over the course of his speech.*)

GALBRAITH. We have a lot to offer here in the history department, Pixie. 645
Perhaps not as much as the business school—that's the large architectural
tribute to Fort Knox and the Playboy Mansion up that way—but we have
a lot to offer. And Pixie? Please come to me if you feel uncomfortable, or if
you would like to discuss this further.
PIXIE. Okay. Thanks.   650

(*Pixie exits. The men look after her for a moment. Beat.*)

GALBRAITH. Off she goes.

(*Long beat.*)

If you were tenured, Jeffrey, I would say, by all means, go ahead and yell
gendered slurs at the female undergraduates. But, at this juncture in your
career ... (*laughs*).

(*Beat.*)

I appreciate that you wanted to argue your point to me. But we're the— 655
you're a Ph.D. candidate, I'm a professor; distinguished, books published,
summa cum laude, et cetera, et cetera. What could Pixie Findley possibly
have contributed to our discussion? Hm?

(*Beat.*)

Connect up the dots for me.

660 JEFFREY. It started off with me trying to defend her—

GALBRAITH. (*sharp*) From?

JEFFREY. Yes, I—I—yes, I'm the one who insulted her, who verbally ... insulted her, in a gendered—in a language that was—I don't know where I—how I—what made me—

665 GALBRAITH. Oh, for Christ's sake, the girl's name is Pixie! Her name is Pixie! She's asking to be patronized.

(*Beat.*)

If you were to crack her skull open, butterflies would flutter out. Or, what did you say? Lobotomy in a skirt?

(*Galbraith laughs, regards Jeffrey, laughs again. Jeffrey stares at Galbraith.*)

Lucky for you. Let's just pray she doesn't pick up Simone de Beauvoir over 670 the weekend, hm?

(*Beat.*)

Let's just pray she sticks to *Cosmopolitan*, or what is it my wife reads? *Vanity Fair.*

(*Beat.*)

And Jeffrey? Give her a B minus.

(*Galbraith hands Jeffrey the essay and exits. Jeffrey holds it for a moment, then he opens it and begins to read. Lights out.*)

—2005

Poetry

Why poetry? Why, when we hear so much of the value of making one's meaning plain to others, of striving for clarity, of avoiding ambiguity, should we pay attention to writing that much of the time seems to willfully ignore all of that? Is poetry important? Is poetry meaningless? What *is* it, anyway! And why should we study it?

If the human animal were so constructed as to always think without feeling, and feel without thinking, the human world would have no place for poetry. In the twenty-first century, what poetry may do best is to explore through words the places where reason and the emotions and senses meet. When we "think" of death, of loss, or of love, our powers of reasoning are unlikely to be untouched by our emotions—or by our senses. And much the same is often true when we think of morning, or of light, or of the sea. Poetry at its best can give full expression to the ways in which our thoughts and feelings come together with our sense impressions—and can itself give rise to powerful sense impressions. Not infrequently, indeed, poetry has been defined by the physical reactions it is capable of producing. "If I read a book and it makes my whole body so cold no fire can ever warm me," wrote the American poet Emily Dickinson, "I know that is poetry." "If I feel physically as if the top of my head were taken off, I know *that* is poetry," she added.

It seems safe to conclude that few lose their heads to poetry in the way Dickinson describes—but a great many others find there is a natural association between poetry and intensity of feeling. Carol Ann Duffy tells us that poems, above all, "are a series of intense moments." Of her own poetry she writes, "I'm not dealing with facts. I'm dealing with emotions." The Australian poet Les Murray suggests that "a true poem is dreamed and danced as well as thought."

Murray knows perfectly well that a poem cannot be danced—not in any literal sense. Like Dickinson, in attempting to describe poetry he has resorted to the language of poetry: language that suggests and likens and associates as it moves toward meaning. Even more than in prose fiction or in drama, language is central to the ways in which poems work. In a poem the connotations of a word or phrase—the things that it is capable of suggesting—are often at least as important as the word's denotative meaning. Poetry works above all through association. Associations of thought and emotion and sense impressions; associations of sound and of sense; associations between physical images; and associations between what we see on a printed page and what goes on in our mind. Let's turn to that last one first.

The Look of the Lines in a Poem

The layers of an onion have frequently been a metaphorical reference point when people talk about trying to get to the centre of something. Let's begin this section by looking at a few lines from a poem about the real thing— "Onions," by Lorna Crozier:

> If Eve had bitten it
> Instead of the apple
> How different
> Paradise

Compare that with how the same words would look on the page written as prose:

> If Eve had bitten it instead of the apple how different paradise.

Why do these words work better set out in the way that Crozier has chosen? Does setting them out this way on the page make them more easily intelligible? In prose, arguably, one would have to add not only punctuation but also extra words to convey the same meaning:

> If Eve had bitten it instead of the apple, how different paradise would have been.

As is often the case, poetry is here a means of expression more concise than prose. It also gives the words different emphases; giving "Paradise" a line on its own draws attention to the notion of paradise itself.

Laying out words in the way that Crozier has done may also encourage the reader to feel suggestions of a variety of meanings; ambiguity, which we generally take to be a fault if it occurs in essay writing, can add interest and richness to poetry. A poem's presence as words and lines upon a page can open up a rich world of suggestion for the reader—and open up too the possibility of surprise. Let's turn to another example. The following lines are taken from a poem by Al Purdy about the experience of pioneers trying to farm in early Ontario, "The Country North of Belleville":

> a lean land
>   not like the fat south
> with inches of black soil on

<pre>
            earth's round belly —
And where the farms are
            it's as if a man stuck
both thumbs in the stony earth and pulled
            it apart
            to make room
enough between the trees
for a wife
            and maybe some cows and
            room for some
of the more easily kept illusions
</pre>

Which are the lines here that end in ways that open up different possible meanings? Where are we surprised? Does that surprise happen differently because the words and lines are laid out in verse? Perhaps the most notable thing about the layout of these lines is the way in which the lines "it apart" and "to make room" are set with plenty of space to each side, suggesting through the look of the words on the page their literal meaning. Do the lines "for a wife" and "of the more easily kept illusions" also surprise? Surely they strike the reader in a slightly different way than they would if they were set out as prose.

Laying the words of a poem out on the page in irregular lines in this way (as **free verse**) has become commonplace—so much so that many now think of it as the primary form in which poetry is written. But until the late nineteenth century in France, and until well into the twentieth century in the English-speaking world, such poetry was unheard of. Before the **imagist** verse of Ezra Pound and of H.D. and, even more influentially, the early poetry of T.S. Eliot, the layout of a poem on the page was typically governed very largely by formal metrical patterns (and also, often, by rhyme)—governed, in short, by structures of sound (these are treated more fully in separate sections).

The **stanza** is another important aspect to the form a poem may take on the page—as well as to the structure of ideas in many poems, and the patterning of sounds. Stanzas are groups of lines into which a poem may be divided. Sometimes a poem's stanzas may each be only two lines long—as they are, for example, in Carol Ann Duffy's "Drunk." Each stanza in Sylvia Plath's "Daddy," on the other hand, is six lines long; W.B. Yeats's "Easter 1916" is made up of four stanzas, the first and the third each sixteen lines long, the second and the fourth each twenty-four lines long.

In many poems each stanza follows a set pattern in its metre and/or in its rhyme scheme. In the most common forms of ballad, for example, the poem is divided into stanzas that each have four lines. (In one common pattern the first and third lines in each stanza rhyme, as do the second and fourth; in another the first and second lines rhyme with each other, as do the third and fourth.) A few stanzas from William Blake's "The Chimney Sweeper" may give a sense of how stanzas may be used in developing a narrative in poetry:

> When my mother died I was very young,
> And my father sold me while yet my tongue
> Could scarcely cry 'weep! 'weep! 'weep! 'weep!
> So your chimneys I sweep, & in soot I sleep.
>
> There's little Tom Dacre, who cried when his head,
> That curl'd like a lamb's back, was shav'd; so I said,
> "Hush Tom! never mind it, for when your head's bare,
> You know that the soot cannot spoil your white hair."
>
> And so he was quiet, & that very night,
> As Tom was a-sleeping he had such a sight!
> That thousands of sweepers, Dick, Joe, Ned, & Jack,
> Were all of them lock'd up in coffins of black;
>
> And by came an Angel who had a bright key,
> And he open'd the coffins & set them all free;
> Then down a green plain leaping, laughing they run,
> And wash in a river and shine in the Sun.

Poetry and Sound

There are many ways in which poetry can be organized according to sound. In a language such as Shona (a Bantu language), tonal patterns may provide the structure; much of Shona poetry is characterized by a drifting downwards in pitch from the beginning to the end of each line. In ancient Greece and Rome the organizing principle was the lengths of the sounds, with each line organized into patterns of alternating long and short sounds. The length of a sound is also referred to as its **quantity**, and poetry based on a system of alternating lengths of sound as **quantitative verse**. The Greeks developed a set of terms to describe sound combinations with this system—terms we still use today (albeit with a twist, as discussed below). A pattern in which short sounds were followed by long sounds was called iambic, and a single grouping of a short sound followed by a long sound was called an **iamb**. Other possible patterns of long and short sounds were similarly categorized. A long sound followed by a short sound was called a **trochee**; a long sound followed by two short sounds was called a **dactyl**; two short sounds followed by a long sound was called an **anapest**; a group of two long sounds together was called a **spondee**, and so on. Each group of sounds was termed a **foot**, and lines of poetry would be formed with a set number of poetic feet. If each line in a poem comprised five iambs in a row, then the **metre**, or pattern of poetic rhythm, was called **iambic pentameter**. The Anglo-Saxon (or Old English) language was organized according to very different structures of sound. What mattered most was not which syllables were long and which were short, but which were **stressed** (or **accented**) and which were not. A line of poetry in Old English is typically divided into two halves, in each of which there are two stressed syllables. Here, for example, are two lines from the most famous poem in Old English, *Beowulf*:

| Swa sceal geong guma | gode gewyrcean |
| Fromum feohgiftum | on faeder bearme |

| So shall [a] young man | good make-happen |
| [with] pious gifts | from [his] father's coffers |

In the first of these lines the syllables "geong" and "gu-" are stressed, as are the syllables "gode" and "wyrc"; in the next line the syllables "From-" and "gift" are stressed, as are the syllables "fae-" and "bear-." It is a structure of sound that does not take into account the *total* number of sounds or syllables in each line; what matters is the number of *stressed* syllables in each line.

Even without any knowledge of Old English, it's easy to notice another way in which sounds connect in these lines: **alliteration**. In Old English poetry there is very frequently alliteration between one or both of the stressed syllables in the first half-line and the first stressed syllable of the second half-line. (There is often also a good deal of alliteration beyond that—as there is here.)

A third way of structuring a poem according to sounds may also be found in Old English poetry, but it appears in only a single poem that has survived. It is a poem known as "The Rhyming Poem," and **rhyme** is indeed its organizing principle, with lines organized into rhyming pairs, or **couplets**. Aside from that one example, rhyme is nowhere present in the Anglo-Saxon literature that has come down to us; rhyme evidently never took hold in Anglo-Saxon poetry. It became a staple of later English poetry due to the influence of French poetry on English—specifically, songs of love and chivalry of the twelfth- and thirteenth-century French poets known as troubadours. Rhyme is a strong presence in the poetry of Geoffrey Chaucer. But there is no uniformity in the sound structures of medieval English poetry; some of the most important medieval poems (notably *Sir Gawain and the Green Knight*) use alliteration very much as it is used in many Old English poems—and are also written in the same metre as is most Old English poetry.

Metre and Rhythm

The English Renaissance of the sixteenth century breathed new life into the ideas and the literary works of ancient Greece and Rome. It also picked up on the literary work and intellectual currents of the Italian Renaissance that had begun more than a century earlier. By the late sixteenth century the metrical patterns of ancient Greek and Latin poetry had become dominant in English poetry as well. But where the ancient Greeks and Romans had structured poetic metre on the basis of *long* and *short* syllables, English substituted a system based on *stressed* and *unstressed* syllables. In ancient Greece a line of iambic pentameter was a line in which a short syllable was followed by a long syllable five times in a row; in Renaissance England it became a line in which an unstressed syllable was followed by a stressed syllable five times in a row. Because it is based on counting the syllables in each line (and in each group of sounds, or poetic foot, within that line), this system of metre is syllabic; because it is also based on stress, or accent, it is accentual. The system, then, is known as **accentual-syllabic verse**.

Given that spoken English tends toward substantial variation in levels of stress (far more so than Greek or Latin or French or Italian), it is not very surprising that English would emphasize alternation between stressed and unstressed syllables rather than between longer and shorter syllables. But the degree to which the new accentual-syllabic approach to structuring the sounds of poetry came to dominate—and the speed with which it came to dominate—is remarkable. At the beginning of the sixteenth century accentual-syllabic poetry was still a rarity in England; by the end of the century virtually all poetry written in English used some form of accentual-syllabic metre.

Where accentual-syllabic metre is strictly adhered to, the alternation of stressed and unstressed syllables follows an absolutely regular pattern. Such is the case, for example, in these lines from Sir Walter Ralegh's "The Nymph's Reply to the Shepherd":

> If all the world and love were young,
> And truth in ev'ry shepherd's tongue,
> These pretty pleasures might me move
> To live with thee and be thy love.

These lines are written in iambic tetrameter—an accentual-syllabic metre in which each line is composed of four iambic feet; that is to say, each group of syllables (or foot) is made up of an unstressed syllable followed by a stressed syllable, with four such groups in every line. Here are the lines again with the feet and the stressed syllables marked:

If **all** / the **world** / and **love** / were **young**,
And **truth** / in **ev'**– / ry **shep**– / herd's **tongue**,
These **pret**– / ty **pleas**– / ures **might** / me **move**
To **live** / with **thee** / and **be** / thy **love**.

Iambic tetrameter is one common accentual-syllabic metre; more common still is iambic pentameter—in which each line has five feet rather than four. The following lines from Phyllis Wheatley's poem "Imagination" are written in iambic pentameter:

Imagination! who can sing thy force?
Or who describe the swiftness of thy course?

Here are the lines again with the feet and stresses marked:

Im- **a-** / gi- **na-** / tion! **who** / can **sing** / thy **force**?
Or **who** / des- **cribe** / the **swift-** / ness of / thy **course**?

Notice here that one poetic foot—the fourth foot of the second line quoted—is irregular, with neither of the two syllables being stressed.

A metre in which the lines have three feet is called **trimeter**; a metre in which the lines have six feet is called **hexameter**.

Together with an accentual-syllabic metre, Ralegh and Wheatley both employ rhyme as a second structure of sound; the lines are in couplets, with the last words in each couplet rhyming (*young* and *tongue*, *force* and *course*) or almost rhyming (*move* and *love*).[1]

It is worth noticing here that in the interests of maintaining the regular pattern of metre and of rhyme, the ordering of the words has been made (to modern ears at least) less regular; Ralegh writes "might me move" instead of using the more common syntactical arrangement "might move me." Such alterations of word order are called **syntactical inversions**.

Rhyme is very commonly used in poems that follow an accentual-syllabic metrical structure, but there is no necessary connection between the two. Indeed, some of the best-known poetry in English is written in **blank verse**—lines in iambic pentameter that do not rhyme. Such verse is found frequently in William Shakespeare's plays and is used throughout John Milton's epic poem *Paradise Lost*. Here are the final four lines of that poem:

The world was all before them, where to choose
Their place of rest, and Providence their guide.

---

1   It is entirely possible that "move" and "love" may have rhymed fully in England in Ralegh's time.

They, hand in hand, with wand'ring steps and slow
Through Eden took their solitary way.

The syllables at the ends of these lines (*choose*, *guide*, *slow*, *way*) do not rhyme—but the lines do follow a regular pattern of unstressed and stressed syllables. Here are the lines again, this time with the feet and the stressed syllables[1] marked:

The **world** / was **all** / be-**fore** / them, **where** / to **choose**
Their **place** / of **rest**, / and **Pro**– /vi- **dence** / their **guide**.
They, **hand** / in **hand**, / with **wand'**– / ring **steps** / and **slow**
Through **E**– /den **took** / their **sol**– / i-**tar**– / y **way**.

The lines have a very different feel to them than do the lines from the Ralegh poem—and that's more than a matter of their being unrhymed, or than their having five feet in each line rather than four. Three of the four lines from the Ralegh poem are **end-stopped**—that is, they end with punctuation such as a comma or period that brings a marked pause in the verse. And none of the Ralegh lines are written with a significant pause in the middle of the line. In contrast, there are significant pauses in the middle of three of the four lines from *Paradise Lost*—and only two of the four are end-stopped. Both these features have names. The practice of carrying sense and grammatical construction past the end of a line in poetry is called **enjambment**; a pause in the middle of a line of poetry is called a **caesura**. By using enjambment and caesura, poets can vary the rhythm of a poem while the underlying metre—the arrangement of stressed and unstressed syllables—remains the same.

The idea that a poem works most effectively when its sounds suggest its sense is an old one; the eighteenth-century poet Alexander Pope gave memorable expression to it in *An Essay on Criticism*, asserting that in poetry, "the sound must seem an echo to the sense." Poets have in many cases continued to strive for these aural effects. The effect they are striving for might perhaps be termed broad onomatopoeia. In an individual word or phrase, **onomatopoeia** occurs when the sounds of the words in themselves seem to imitate the sound they are naming—as do, for example, the words *burst* or *scrape*. A broader sort of imitation is involved in phrases such as Tennyson's "as moving seems asleep," Milton's "with wand'ring steps and slow," or Hardy's "the rain drop ploughs." And something that might be called onomatopoeia may operate more broadly still. Arguably, some form of onomatopoeia—of the sounds of a poem imitating its sense—can operate throughout entire poems, such as Karen Solie's "Sturgeon" and Theodore Roethke's "My Papa's Waltz."

---

1   To some degree the accenting of syllables is subjective, of course. One might, for example, read these lines with a stress placed on *They* at the beginning of the third line.

Rhyme

The examples of patterns of rhyme we have touched on thus far have been rhyming couplets. That is only one way of rhyming; many possible **rhyme schemes** may be used as part of the organizing principle of a poem: rhyming every other line; carrying on patterns of rhyme from one stanza to another; returning at the end of a poem to rhymes used at the beginning.

There are also a number of different types of rhyme. What we tend to think of first when we think of rhyme is the repetition of identical or similar sounds, usually in pairs and generally at the ends of metrical lines. In English, a full rhyme (or "perfect rhyme") must involve vowel as well as consonant sounds. In the following example the ending consonant sounds (-*nd*) match, but the ending vowel sounds are different:

> The grass was dark, the moon was round,
> And he had finally met his end.

In contrast, words such as *sound* and *drowned* and *ground* share both consonant and vowel sounds with the word *round*. The following lines are an example of a full rhyme:

> The grass was dark, the moon was round,
> And he lay dead upon the ground.

A full rhyme in English must also involve the final *stressed* syllable of a line— as it does in the above example, with the last stress of the first line falling on *round* and the last stress of the second line falling on *ground*. In the majority of lines of English poetry the final syllable in a line is, as in this case, also the final stressed syllable of the line—but in many lines that is not the case. In the following example both vowel and consonant sounds match in the final syllables of the lines (in both cases, –*ing*), but the lines nevertheless do not fully rhyme; the final stressed syllables (*go-* and *end-*) have quite different sounds:

> The grass was dark, the light was going,
> And on the ground his life was ending.

In summary, then: for there to be a full rhyme in English, the vowel sounds as well as the ending consonant sounds of the final syllable must match, and the same must be true of the final stressed syllable, if that is different.

To understand something of the workings of full rhyme, however, is only to begin to understand the many ways in which rhyme can operate in English poetry. Many rhyming poets frequently use partial rhymes—of which there are several sorts:

unstressed syllables may match but not stressed ones (e.g., "going" / "ending"; "water" / "flower"); this is also known as "weak" or "unstressed rhyme";

a stressed syllable may be "rhymed" with an unstressed one (e.g., "to sing" / "casing");

one of the rhymed words may have an "extra" syllable at the end (e.g., "clink" / "drinking");

the match in sound may be imperfect (e.g., "grin" / "plain"); this is sometimes referred to as "forced rhyme," or "oblique rhyme";

the consonant sounds of stressed syllables may match, but the vowel sounds may not (e.g., "spoiled" / "spilled," "taint" / "stint"). This form of partial rhyme is sometimes referred to as "slant rhyme"—though *slant rhyme* is also sometimes used as a term to denote any form of partial rhyme.

Ever since the break with the past ushered in by modernism early in the twentieth century, poets in the English-speaking world have often chosen not to rhyme. In North America, rhyme has been imagined to be appropriate to certain forms of music—from folk music to hip-hop—but not necessarily to modern poetry. Too often the thought of rhyming in *poetry* conjures up images of verse that is childish or sentimental or hopelessly old fashioned, or all of the above. Those who disparage rhyming poetry have often pictured it as typically operating in conjunction with a highly regular, even metronomic metre—and of rhymed verse where it may seem the poet has been entirely willing to meddle with normal grammar and syntax for no better purpose than to achieve rhymes at the end of each line. The modernist Ezra Pound was among those who led the way in caricaturing a certain sort of poetry in which, as he put it, "the words are shovelled in to fill a metric pattern or to complete the noise of a rhyme-sound." We should remember that the poetry of William Shakespeare, of John Milton, of Anne Bradstreet—indeed, of virtually every leading poet of the sixteenth, seventeenth, and eighteenth centuries—is similarly twisted syntactically:

> I once that loved the shady woods so well,
> Now thought the rivers did the trees excel,
> And if the sun would ever shine, there would I dwell.
> (Anne Bradstreet, "Contemplations")

What went out of poetic fashion in the twentieth century was not only rhyme and metrical regularity and the sentimental; it was also the use of "poetic language"—a set of syntactical structures as well as of particular words.

These things were frequently interconnected in the criticisms Pound and other modernists levelled against poetic convention. But there is of course no necessary connection among them; rhyme has no necessary connection to particular sentiments or poetic traditions, and it may be used quite independently of any accentual-syllabic metrical system. It may be used loosely in free verse—as T.S. Eliot does in these lines from *The Waste Land*:

> The river sweats
> Oil and tar
> The barges drift
> With the turning tide
> Red sails
> Wide
> To leeward, swing on the heavy spar.

As every child senses intuitively, rhyme gives the human ear an opportunity to recognize and confirm a regular pattern—something the mind delights in. Because it has served this purpose for so long, it's sometimes used by modern and contemporary poets to suggest the very idea of regularity and order—or to suggest a sense of delight.

A more contemporary, and equally inventive, use of rhyme to convey meaning is found in Kim Addonizio's "First Poem for You," which uses the rhyme scheme of the Shakespearian sonnet to perfection, but makes such extensive use of enjambment that the human ear has to strain to actually detect the rhyme. Here's how the poem begins:

> I like to touch your tattoos in complete
> darkness, when I can't see them. I'm sure of
> where they are, know by heart the neat
> lines of lightning pulsing just above
> your nipple,

We may sometimes think of rhyme as being an inherently intrusive aural element in a poem—something that will inevitably draw attention to itself rather than to the meaning of the lines. But if the rhyming syllables are only lightly stressed, as is the case here, rhyme can operate quite unobtrusively. And that is all the more true if, again as here, the poet employs enjambment and caesura, so that the reader never stops and lingers at the rhymes.

In the Shakespearean sonnet form the final two lines are a rhymed couplet—and here too Addonizio holds to the form. But now the poem abandons enjambment; both these final lines are end-stopped, thus giving strong emphasis to each line's final word.

... whatever persists

or turns to pain between us, they will still

be there. Such permanence is terrifying.

So I touch them in the dark; but touch them, trying.

In a poem that seems in large part to be about trying to deal with the terror of permanence in a relationship, it is wonderfully appropriate to have the two words "trying" and "terrifying" rhymed in a couplet at the poem's end. There are many tensions and harmonies in "First Poem for You"—and throughout the poem, sound echoes sense.

• • •

It is sometimes imagined that sound is only an important element of poetry when some sound-related organizing principle is involved—metre, or rhyme, or some wholly different aural principle (such as that involved in Christian Bök's *Eunoia*, in which each section uses one vowel only). But even poets who tend not to organize their poems according to aural principles are often highly attuned to sound. Margaret Atwood is a good example. She remains a poet better known for the striking ways in which her poems lay words out on a page than she is for the sounds of her poems. Yet here is how she responded in 1984 to an interviewer's question about "words on the page":

> First of all, a poem is not words on a page. A poem is words in the air; or I should say words in the ear, because a poem is heard. And the words on the page are a notation like a musical score. We would not say that Beethoven was a bunch of black marks on a page; you would say that Beethoven is what we hear when we transcribe those black marks. And it's the same with a poem; when you are reading a poem the words are in your ear.

Is she right? That may be a question best discussed after listening to a number of poets reading their work. An extraordinary range of such material is now available online, on sites such as that of the Poetry Foundation and the Poetry Archive as well as on YouTube. Certain poets—from Alfred, Lord Tennyson in the nineteenth century to Dylan Thomas in the mid-twentieth century, to Christian Bök and Lillian Allen in our own day—have been renowned as performers of their work, and certainly it can be fascinating to listen to Tennyson reading "The Charge of the Light Brigade" or Allen reading "Social Worker Poem." Listen to how they deal with the ends of lines, with rhyme, with pitch (are there many high notes or low notes in their readings?) as well as to how strongly or lightly they place an emphasis on the stressed syllables in their poems.

Imagery, Metaphor and Simile, Symbol

When readers think of imagery, they often think first of imagist poets such as Ezra Pound, H.D., and William Carlos Williams—poets who use the spacing of the words on the page (and the sounds those words convey) in ways that draw attention to the physical images the words name. This is what Williams does in poems such as "The Red Wheelbarrow" and "This Is Just to Say," poems that offer the reader fragments of experience.

> I have eaten
> the plums
> that were in
> the icebox
>
> and which
> you were probably
> saving
> for breakfast
>
> Forgive me
> they were delicious
> so sweet
> and so cold

It is often imagined that what gives an image specificity must be purely a matter of physical description. But an image may also be made specific by human circumstance; what gives the plums specificity here is not only the physical attributes of sweetness and coldness but also their "history"—the small part they play in the relationship between the speaker and the one he is addressing. It is useful in discussing poetic imagery to distinguish between the two axes concrete/abstract and specific/general. Whereas the opposite of concrete is abstract, the opposite of specific is general. The terms "concrete" and "specific" are often used almost interchangeably in discussing imagery, and certainly there is an overlap between the two. Yet they are in fact distinct from each other. The word "fruit" expresses something concrete but general; the word "nourishment" expresses a far more abstract concept. To speak of "plums" is to be both more specific and more concrete than to speak of "fruit." To speak of "ripe plums" is again both more concrete and more specific. "The plums that were in the icebox," though, is not a more concrete image than "the plums"; it adds a degree of specificity to the image without adding to the concreteness of it.

A related point: poetic imagery may sometimes be used to convey a vivid sense of things that are in many respects imprecise. A good example is the opening section of Audre Lorde's "Outside," a poem about growing up in New York City in the 1930s and 1940s:

> In the centre of a harsh and spectrumed city
> All things natural are strange.
> I grew up in genuine confusion
> between grass and weeds and flowers
> and what coloured meant
> except for clothes you couldn't bleach
> and nobody called me nigger
> until I was thirteen.
> Nobody lynched my momma
> but what she'd never been
> had bleached her face of everything
> but very private furies
> and made the other children
> call me yellow snot at school.

"Between" here is presumably in one sense literal—the child sees these forms of plant life all round—but it also suggests confusion as to categories; what is a flower? What is a weed? Such classification is of course arbitrary, depending on the preferences of the adult humans who draw up the categories, define where one part of the spectrum stops and another begins, make the rules. What did "coloured" mean in the America in which Lorde grew up? From one angle it was a fixed category; if you were labelled as coloured you were subject to discriminatory practices in almost every area of life—even in Northern states. Yet the category itself resisted definition; relatively light-skinned blacks could often "pass" as white; toward the other end of the spectrum, the darker your skin, the greater the level of persecution you would suffer. The child's confusion as to "what coloured meant" thus conveys a vivid sense of illogic as well as the imprecision of the way in which the adult world drew distinctions on the basis of a foundation that was as unstable as it was unjust. There is uncertainty too in the image of bleaching: we are told of the mother that "what she had never been"—her history of unwhiteness, we take it—"had bleached her face of everything but very private furies." In the background here is the widespread practice of using cosmetics—many of them damaging to the skin—to attempt to lighten one's skin colour. Is it suggested that the mother did this? That is not clear—it may be that the "bleaching" is purely metaphorical. But the image takes on added resonance in the context of that history of literal bleaching of black skin. There is of course an underlying clarity to the imprecision here; however much the categories may have been based on imprecision and illogic, the suffering was real—and it has come to be shared too by the child, as the powerful image of a different colour that ends the quoted section of the poem makes clear.

Imagery in poetry is sometimes imagined to consist almost entirely of metaphor or simile—of using figures of speech to liken one thing to another. We will get to those in a moment. But the sorts of description found in poems such as the ones referenced above by Williams and Lorde may help to remind us that metaphor is not everything when it comes to imagery. Another example of how powerful imagery can be without metaphor or simile is Douglas LePan's "The Haystack":

> It doesn't take a Hiroshima to burn a man to a crisp,
> A haystack will do. And what could be more bucolic than that? And
>   you get tired of sleeping in cellars or slit-trenches,
> so why not behind a haystack that has simmered all day
> in the warmth of an Italian summer sun? But at night
> the jackals are ready to spring, the German eighty-eights,
> with their high muzzle velocities and their low trajectories,
> so that the haystack ignites like a torch and a gunner is burnt
> to a crisp. How far back was that? Thirty years? Forty years?
> He doesn't remember. He only remembers the stench of fear, his own
>   fear, and a grey army blanket, and a young
> sunburned back alive on the banks of the Volturno,
> then burning, burning. By dire subtleties such as these he was pre-
>   pared for the carbonization of cities.

This is a poem without the ornamentation of many figures of speech; the images are powerfully direct throughout. There is a likeness drawn between the still-alive soldier writing the poem, with his sunburn, and the soldier immolated by the haystack. And there is a parallel drawn too between the burning of an individual human in these circumstances in Italy and the burning of many tens of thousands (the "carbonization of cities") when atomic bombs were dropped on Hiroshima and Nagasaki. But these are likenesses and parallels—not figures of speech.

If metaphor and simile are not everything when it comes to imagery, they are nevertheless central to a very great deal of what poetry does. In essence, **metaphor** is a way of likening one thing to another thing through language. In its simplest form, the **simile**, the likeness is made explicit through the use of words such as *like* or *as if*. "Like a roe I bounded o'er the mountains" is a simile in which Wordsworth is likening himself to an animal. That example—like the line so often used as the paradigm of a simile, Robert Burns's "My love is like a red, red rose"—offers a likeness that is easy for almost any reader to comprehend. Many similes, though, draw connections that are far more tenuous. Such is the case with the famous simile at the opening of "The Love Song of J. Alfred Prufrock":

> Let us go then, you and I,
> When the evening is spread out against the sky
> Like a patient etherized upon a table;

The suggestive power of a simile can often be arresting in ways that are surprising or puzzling or disturbing; the same is true of other forms of metaphorical language. Sometimes such metaphors may be compressed into a powerful phrase, as is the case when Karen Solie writes of a sturgeon landed on the water's edge being unable to contain

> the old current he had for a mind, its pull
> and his body a muscle called river, called spawn.

Using highly concentrated metaphorical language, Solie likens the fish's body to the river that is its natural home, the fish's mind to the current of the river—and then ends by drawing a further likeness.

Some poems elaborate on a single metaphor in a sustained way over several stanzas. Such is the case with the comparison between two souls and the twin feet of a compass in the final stanzas of John Donne's "A Valediction: Forbidding Mourning." An elaborate and sustained metaphor such as Donne's twin feet is often referred to as a **conceit** or a Petrarchan conceit; many of the poems of Petrarch include this sort of extended metaphor. Indeed, a metaphor may be extended throughout an entire poem—as it is, for example, in Seamus Heaney's "Digging."

When a comparison (metaphorical or otherwise) is made or implied between something with non-human and human qualities, it is often referred to as **personification**. Thus Sir Philip Sidney personifies the moon in this opening to one of his sonnets:

> With how sad steps, O Moon, thou climb'st the skies!
> How silently, and with how wan a face!

And thus Allen Ginsberg personifies his country in his poem "America":

> America, when will you be angelic?
> When will you take off your clothes?

A figure of speech that is sometimes grouped with metaphor and simile is **metonymy**. Like metaphors and similes, metonyms do bring together different things. But whereas with metaphor and simile the connection is a matter of comparison, with metonymy it is a matter of association. The following sentences may clarify the distinction:

Numerous scientists have criticized Ottawa's plan to close the environmental research centre.

What dish are you cooking tonight?

In the first of these examples the word "Ottawa" is standing for "the federal government of Canada"; as the capital, Ottawa is the home of the federal government and is thus naturally associated with it, but it is not being compared to the federal government. Nor, in the second example, is the dish being compared to the food; it is associated with the food rather than likened to it. When T.S. Eliot writes in "The Love Song of J. Alfred Prufrock" of "sawdust restaurants" he is employing metonymy; the restaurants are not being likened to sawdust but rather associated with one particular characteristic: the sawdust on the floor.

A related literary device is **synecdoche**—the practice of referring to a part of something in a way that stands for the whole. If someone asks "Have you got wheels?" the rhetorical device of synecdoche is being used—as it is in a number of vulgar expressions in which a person's sexual organs are named as a way of referring to an entire person ("The prick followed me all the way home"). Synecdoche may be thought of as one form of metonymy: wheels are part of a car and that is one way of being associated with a car. But (unlike with metaphor and simile) they are not being *likened* to a car. "The Love Song of J. Alfred Prufrock" may again provide a poetic example; Eliot employs synecdoche when he writes "after the teacups" rather than saying "after we had finished with the tea and the teacups and the sandwiches...." It is useful to be aware of devices such as metonymy and synecdoche—but it is also useful to be aware that they occur far less frequently in poetry than do metaphor, simile, and personification.

One other concept that is important to the understanding of poetic imagery—and of poetry generally—is **symbol**. This is a term used more loosely than most of the terms discussed above—it is one that may overlap with many of them (a metaphor may act as a symbol, but so may a metonym). In Christian tradition a cross evokes the crucifix but may also symbolize Christianity or Christ's body. The beaver and the maple leaf are symbols of Canada, as the bald eagle is a symbol of the United States. But not all symbols are entrenched in tradition as are these—and not all are cast in stone. A bird is often in poetry a symbol of freedom, but in Edgar Allan Poe's "The Raven," a symbolic bird suggests the inescapability of sorrowful memories. The rose is traditionally a symbol of love, but it may also carry other associations. Even when symbols are broadly similar, they may carry quite different nuances of meaning. Williams's "This Is Just to Say," Ginsberg's "A Supermarket in California," and Eliot's "The Love Song of J. Alfred Prufrock" all arguably evoke the forbidden fruit of the Garden of Eden. But fruit suggests the allure of the forbidden when Williams confesses "I have eaten / the plums," and fruit encapsulates a much more specific nod toward same-sex desire when Ginsberg imagines asking Federico García Lorca what he was "doing down by the watermelons." Many interpretations have been offered for Eliot's musing "Do I dare to eat a peach?"

Meaning

There have also been significant shifts over time in the ways in which poets strive to express meaning—or, in some cases, to problematize the very idea that a poem should have a meaning. One such shift began in France in the second half of the nineteenth century. The young poet Arthur Rimbaud was one who rejected the conventions both of Western poetry and of Western society altogether. Here is how he put it in his 1871 collection *Une Saison en Enfer* (*A Season in Hell*):

> Un soir, j'ai assis la Beauté sur mes genoux—et je l'ai trouvée amère—et je l'ai injuriée. (One night I sat Beauty on my lap—and I found her bitter—and I gave her a rough time.)

When Edgar Allan Poe, writing in 1849, described the poetry of words as "the rhythmical creation of beauty," he was giving memorable expression to an idea that for centuries had been generally assumed to be central to the art of poetry. Rimbaud turned all that on its head: the rejection of any idea that the poet should be creating something beautiful is a consistent theme in his work, with images of vomit and of mucus jostling together with images of children and of the sea. What is the reader to make of such poetry? How are we to construct meaning out of it?

The modernist revolution in English poetry that poets such as Mina Loy and T.S. Eliot ushered in early in the twentieth century has deep roots in the work of nineteenth-century French poets such as Rimbaud, Jules Laforgue, and Stéphane Mallarmé. No longer was it felt that incidents or images should connect clearly and coherently with meaning, or that the images and meanings of one line should follow from that of the previous one in ways that could be clearly understood. "What branches grow / Out of this stony rubbish?" Eliot asked in *The Waste Land*—and answered, "You cannot say, or guess, for you know only / A heap of broken images."

In the Medieval period and through the Renaissance the accepted view was that poetry should have both a clear meaning and a clear moral purpose. One way of conveying a moral message was simply to tell a story, and have the good characters end up rewarded and the bad characters punished—though to put it so crudely is to grossly oversimplify the poetic theory of the time. Even when poetry was not telling a story, it was felt that moral improvement was a natural accompaniment to the art of poetry. Poetry should imitate the world—but in doing so should always make plain the world as it *should* be. As Sir Philip Sidney put it in the late sixteenth century, poetry is "an art of imitation, a speaking picture with this end, to teach and delight."

The consensus that instruction and delight were twin purposes of poetry (and indeed of all literature) remained powerful through to the late eighteenth century, when the French Revolution and the birth of Romanticism brought a shift; the idea that poetry should provide moral instruction began to lose favour, while the idea that poetry should give expression to the truths of nature, and to unbridled human feeling (including feelings of romantic love, certainly, but including as well strong political feeling) came to the fore. It was during this era that Wordsworth defined poetry as "the spontaneous overflow of powerful feelings: it takes its origin from emotion recollected in tranquility." It was in this era too that Percy Shelley argued that poetry had to it "something divine," but that it also could and should be used to further political causes. He wrote with equal passion of the spiritual force of nature and of the oppressive force of the wealthy landlords and heartless manufacturers of the era. Here, for example, is how he addresses the labouring classes in "Song to the Men of England," a poem widely taken up by the British labour movement:

> Men of England, wherefore plough
> For the lords who lay ye low?
> Wherefore weave with toil and care
> The rich robes your tyrants wear?

The notion that conveying a political message can be as appropriate to poetry as conveying thoughts of nature or of love did not begin with Shelley, nor did it end with him; it remained a powerful sub-current in nineteenth-century aesthetics.

The modernism of the early twentieth century, however, was antithetical not only to the notion that poetry should try to teach, but also to the idea that it should have any clear meaning. Perhaps the most extreme expression of this view (on the face of it, at least) appears in "Ars Poetica," a poem by the American modernist Archibald MacLeish, which concludes as follows:

> A poem should be equal to:
> Not true.
> For all the history of grief
> An empty doorway and a maple leaf.
> For love

the leaning grasses and two lights above the sea—
A poem should not mean
But be.

Does MacLeish really mean that a poem should be without meaning? Or is he simply trying to argue that what comes naturally to poetry is suggestion and association—that poetry does not naturally convey meaning in any fixed or conventional sense?

Eliot, the most important figure of modernism, did not go so far as to suggest that a poem should be without meaning. But he did feel that it was natural to the spirit of the age for poetry to be difficult. Here is how he put it in his 1926 essay "The Metaphysical Poets":

> … it appears likely that poets in our civilization, must be difficult.…
> The poet must become more and more comprehensive, more allusive,
> more indirect, in order to force, to dislocate if necessary, language
> into his meaning.

The idea that meanings in poetry should be allusive and indirect—even by their very nature inexpressible in words other than those chosen by the poet—remained strong through the twentieth century and into the twenty-first. It is the governing idea in Les Murray's "The Meaning of Existence":

> Everything except language
> knows the meaning of existence.
> Trees, planets, rivers, time
> know nothing else. They express it
> moment by moment as the universe.
> Even this fool of a body lives it in part, and would
> have full dignity within it
> but for the ignorant freedom
> of my talking mind.

Does language truly get in the way of meaning, as Murray suggests? It is one irony of the poem that, even as it suggests that the meaning of existence is inexpressible through language, it conveys that thought in a wonderfully clear and coherent fashion, through language.

A great many poems from the past hundred years are less paradoxical than this, but also less clear in the ways that they convey meaning. To appreciate them we have to be open to the ways in which meanings can be suggested even when they are not stated clearly. And we must be able to recognize a central truth about poetry: the fact that meaning is not always plain does not mean it is absent.

None of the above should be taken to imply that all twentieth- and twenty-first-century poets eschew plain speaking—far from it. Some strive quite consistently for clarity of meaning in writing about a wide range of topics, while remaining attuned to the ways in which their poems can suggest meanings above and beyond those stated. Others write with a clear ethical or political stance, and have wanted for those reasons to make their meanings plain. It is important not to presume, however, that once one has acknowledged the most transparent meaning of a poem which makes a clear point, nothing is left to be said. Even in a poem that aims to convey a clear political message there may be layered or multiple meanings.

Point of View

One of the most important ways in which the genres of literature differ one from another is in the way that they present human characters. Whereas the presentation of different human characters is central to prose fiction and to drama, it is often much less important to poetry. If one wishes to give direct expression to one's feelings or thoughts about nature, or death, or love, poetry is the natural medium to write in. But it is not always that simple.

As readers, how do we know who is behind a poem? If it is an "I" or a "we"—if it is written in the first person, in other words, how do we know who that "I" or "we" is? Sometimes we may need to bring historical or biographical information to bear. If we read the late nineteenth-century African American poet Paul Laurence Dunbar's "We Wear the Mask" without knowing the identity of "we," we will be missing a detail that greatly affects our reading of the poem. And sometimes the poem will say "I" or "we" but we cannot and should not be confident that the poet means what she says.

To say that poetry is often the most personal of the genres is not to say that we should read all poems as being direct expressions of the poet's thoughts or feelings. When we read a work of prose fiction in which a narrator tells a story, we should never assume that narrator to be the author; very frequently the author narrates a story through a *persona*, in order to provide a particular perspective on the events being narrated. The character of that persona may be very different indeed from that of the author. Much the same can be true in poetry. In some cases the poet may adopt a persona radically different from herself—as Margaret Atwood does, for example, in "Death of a Young Son by Drowning" and the other poems in her book *The Journals of Susanna Moodie*, in which she writes from the point of view of a woman who emigrated to Canada in the nineteenth century.

In *The Journals of Susanna Moodie* it is usually quite obvious who the "I" in the poems is. In other cases it may be much less clear whether the "I" in a poem is a persona. To what extent is the "I" in a love poem by John Donne the poet speaking directly? Or a sonnet by Shakespeare? Or, for that matter, any one of the thousands of love poems written in the first person, with an "I" addressing a "you"? In the case of a poem such as "Tintern Abbey," where there is external evidence that Wordsworth saw the proper function of poetry as being the direct expression of personal feeling, we may be reasonably confident that the "I" of the poem is indeed the poet himself, though even with such a seemingly direct poem, one must refer to the "speaker" in the poem, not the author. Further, poetry that reads as "personal" may be expressing a point of view quite independent from that of the poet. Such may be the case even with poetry that is highly intimate, even confessional (as the poetry of Sylvia Plath is often described as being).

With some poems written in the first person (or the first and second person), we may gradually come to realize as we read the poem not only that the "I" behind the poem is someone other than the poet, but also that this "I" is someone we should not trust. In a dramatic monologue such as d'bi young anitafrika's "foreign mind/local body" we need to pay attention to character in much the same way as we do when trying to respond to a work of prose fiction in which we recognize that the narrator is unreliable. In a poem such as that one, the point of view is maintained consistently throughout the poem. Such is the case as well with dramatic monologues such as Tennyson's "Ulysses." A poem such as "The Love Song of J. Alfred Prufrock," however, begins very much like a dramatic monologue, but then seems to shift from time to time in its point of view. Is the "we" of "We have lingered in the chambers of the sea" near the poem's end written from the same point of view as that of the "I" with which the poem begins—or the "I" of "Do I dare to eat a peach?" a few lines earlier? Or is the viewpoint unstable in a poem such as this one?

One often unappreciated aspect of point of view in poetry is the degree to which a wide range of poems may be written very largely in the second person. This is true of a great deal of love poetry, certainly, and also of many dramatic monologues. It is true as well of a poem such as Tom Wayman's "Did I Miss Anything?"—a poem consisting entirely of a professor's answers to the question posed by a student in the title of the poem. And it is true of Carol Ann Duffy's "The Good Teachers," a very different sort of poem about education, in which "you" is used not in the way we usually use the second person, but in the way we use "one" when speaking in the third person.

Fixed Forms

This introduction has already touched on a number of aspects of the formal properties a poem may exhibit. It may follow a particular metrical form, for example, and it may have a set rhyme scheme. There are also various fixed forms in which complete poems may be written. The most common of these by far in English poetry is the **sonnet**—a poem of 14 lines, usually written in iambic pentameter, and generally following a strict rhyme scheme. Details concerning several of the main types of sonnet (including the **Petrarchan**, the **Spenserian**, the **Shakespearian**, and the **Miltonic**), as well as many more technical aspects of poetry than are dealt with in this introduction, will be found in the glossary.

The sonnet is itself only one of several different complete fixed forms. The **villanelle**, for example, is a poem generally consisting of 19 lines, with 5 tercets rhyming aba followed by a quatrain rhyming abaa. Dylan Thomas's "Do Not Go Gentle into That Good Night" is one example of a villanelle; Elizabeth Bishop's "One Art" is another.

Many other fixed forms—including **ballad**, **ghazal**, **haiku**, **ottava rima**, **rhyme royal**, **rondeau** (and its variant form, the **rondelle**), **sestina**, and **triolet**—are also described in the glossary. So too are various categories of poem—the **elegy**, for example—that are defined less by such characteristics as metre or rhyme scheme than by subject matter and tone. The reader will also find in the glossary far more detail than is provided in this introduction on such things as the various forms of accentual-syllabic metre, the various forms of rhyme, and the various figures of speech commonly used in poetry.

The Sub-Genres of Poetry, and the Subject Matter of Poetry

Almost all of what is said elsewhere in this overview is written with particular reference to **lyric** poetry, the sort of poetry that has been dominant in Western culture since the Renaissance. A lyric is a relatively short poem expressive of an individual's thoughts or feelings, and often appreciated for its aural qualities. Sonnets, elegies, dramatic monologues—all these are different sorts of lyric, as are poems as diverse as Andrew Marvell's "To His Coy Mistress," Emily Dickinson's "[Tell all the Truth, but tell it slant]," E.E. Cummings's "[anyone lived in a pretty how town]," George Elliott Clarke's "blank sonnet," and Gregory Scofield's "Aunty." As a genre, then, "lyric" covers a vast amount of ground. Yet the lyric is only one of several large genres into which poetry may be divided; in other cultures and in other eras epic narratives in poetic form have been of central importance; in others still drama in poetic form has been central.

Nowadays Carol Ann Duffy speaks for a great many poets (and a great many readers of poetry too) in her belief that "poetry's power is not in narrative." To the ancient Greeks, however, the **epic** poem—a long poem telling a story, or a series of stories—was considered the most important form of poetry.

And even today variants of epic poetry continue to be written; Alice Oswald's *Memorial*, a long poem that reimagines Homer's *Iliad* as a memorial to the dead, is a case in point. The ancient Greeks also wrote plays in verse, and most plays in English-speaking cultures were also written largely or entirely in verse until the eighteenth century.

There are often strong associations between certain sorts of poem and certain sorts of subject matter. An epic poem typically tells certain sorts of stories—stories of heroism, of great struggle, of grand loves and of events involving many people in a variety of locations. A ballad typically tells a story too—but in this case the subject matter associated with the form is more likely to involve a much smaller cast of characters, and to be more personal in nature.

There have been sonnets on all subjects over the centuries; the first sonnet sequence in English, for example, Anne Locke's *A Meditation of a Penitent Sinner* (1560), is a sequence of confessional religious poems, as is John Donne's series of Holy Sonnets from early in the next century. But in every age the sonnet form has been strongly associated with love poetry, from the fourteenth-century sonnets of Petrarch to those of Sir Philip Sidney and William Shakespeare in the sixteenth century, to those of Lady Mary Wroth and Sir John Suckling in the seventeenth, to those of Edna St. Vincent Millay and George Elliott Clarke in the twentieth.

Were it not for such strong associations as these, it would not be possible to write poems that go against the grain—as do mock epics such as Alexander Pope's *The Rape of the Lock*, which uses the grand style of epic when the topic is a trivial one. Many sonnets go against the grain as well—playing off the strong association of the genre with romantic love to portray love or sex in a different light. W.B. Yeats's "Leda and the Swan" and Kim Addonizio's "First Poem for You" are two notable examples. Another that goes against the grain in this way is "Against Love Poetry," by the modern Irish poet Eavan Boland—a prose poem, without stanzas, without metre, without rhyme—but printed in fourteen lines, to echo the sonnet form.

In other times and other cultures, even science and philosophy have been thought fit matter for poetry. *De Rerum Natura*, a long Latin poem about the nature of physical things and of life and death by the first century BCE writer Lucretius, is written entirely in verse—some 7,400 lines in total, all in dactylic hexameter. Through to the early modern period poets in English-speaking cultures may also be found using poetry to express scientific ideas. The 1653 atomic poems of Margaret Cavendish are a noteworthy example:

If atoms are as small, as small can be,
They must in quantity of matter all agree:
And if consisting matter of the same (be right,)

Then every atom must weigh just alike.
("The Weight of Atoms")

From certain angles, such poems as *De Rerum Natura* or "The Weight of Atoms" may seem highly remote from twenty-first-century concerns. Yet Cavendish's atomic poems are today being read more widely (and discussed more widely by scholars) than at any other time since they first appeared in the seventeenth century. The importance of Lucretius's work is also being appreciated afresh; the critic and scholar Stephen Greenblatt's *The Swerve* has helped to bring *On The Nature of Things* (as the poem's title translates into English) to the admiring attention of fresh generations of readers, two millennia after it was written. There are fewer limits to the "appropriate subject matter" of poetry than has often been assumed.

[D.L.]

Sir Thomas Wyatt

c. 1503–1542

Thomas Wyatt lived his entire adult life amidst the political intrigue and turmoil that accompanied the reign of King Henry VIII, and was twice imprisoned in the Tower of London. Even his poems on subjects far from the machinations of the king and his courtiers—subjects such as love and idyllic country life—can carry a subtext about the court's political dramas. Wyatt wrote in many poetic forms, but is best known for the artistry of his satires and songs and, along with Henry Howard, Earl of Surrey (1517–47), for introducing the Italian sonnet to England.

Wyatt was born into a family of wealth and status. He was a man of many accomplishments, adept at music and poetry as well as politics, and he soon became a valued member of King Henry VIII's court. He began a diplomatic career in 1526 with missions to France, Rome, and Venice, where he may have acquired his knowledge of Italian sonnets. He was knighted in 1536 but soon afterward had his first falling out with the king and was imprisoned in the Tower of London—possibly because of a past relationship with the queen, Anne Boleyn, who would be executed that year. Wyatt temporarily regained the king's favour, but in 1541 he was imprisoned again, this time on trumped-up charges of treason. He was spared and returned to favour a second time, but died the next year, succumbing to fever in 1542.

Few of Wyatt's poems were printed in his lifetime, but many appeared in Richard Tottel's 1557 volume *Songes and Sonettes* (later to become known as *Tottel's Miscellany*). Some years later, the Elizabethan critic George Puttenham summarized Sir Thomas Wyatt's importance to the English literary tradition in terms that remain broadly accepted today: "[Wyatt and Surrey] travailed into Italie, and there tasted the sweet and stately measures and stile of the Italian Poesie.... They greatly pollished our rude & homely maner of vulgar Poesie, from that it had been before, and for that cause may justly be said the first reformers of our English meetre and stile."

[The long love that in my thought doth harbour][1]

The long love that in my thought doth harbour
And in mine heart doth keep his residence
Into my face presseth with bold pretence
And therein campeth, spreading his banner.
5　She that me learneth° to love and suffer　　　　　　　　　　　*teaches*

1　[*The long love ... doth harbour*] This poem is an adaptation of Sonnet 140 from the Italian poet Petrarch's *Rime sparse* (*Scattered Rhymes*).

And will° that my trust and lust's negligence   *wishes*
Be reined by reason, shame,° and reverence,   *modesty*
With his hardiness° taketh displeasure.   *daring*
Wherewithal unto the heart's forest he fleeth,
Leaving his enterprise with pain and cry,   10
And there him hideth and not appeareth.
What may I do when my master feareth,
But in the field with him to live and die?
For good is the life ending faithfully.

—1557

[They flee from me that sometime did me seek]

They flee from me that sometime did me seek
With naked foot stalking° in my chamber.   *treading softly*
I have seen them gentle, tame, and meek
That now are wild and do not remember
That sometime they put themself in danger   5
To take bread at my hand; and now they range,
Busily seeking with a continual change.

Thanked be fortune it hath been otherwise
Twenty times better; but once in special,
In thin array after° a pleasant guise,°   *in accordance with / style*   10
When her loose gown from her shoulders did fall
And she me caught in her arms long and small,
Therewithal sweetly did me kiss
And softly said, "Dear heart, how like you this?"

It was no dream; I lay broad waking.°   *wide awake*   15
But all is turned, through my gentleness,
Into a strange fashion of forsaking.
And I have leave to go of her goodness,[1]
And she also to use newfangleness.°   *inconstancy*
But since that I so kindly[2] am served,   20
I would fain° know what she hath deserved.   *gladly*
—1557

---

1   *I have ... goodness* I have her permission to go from her.
2   *kindly* Naturally, according to natural laws (i.e., that women are fickle). The word also
     ironically suggests the modern "with kindness." In the original printing after Wyatt's
     death, the text was amended to "unkindly," removing the irony.

[Whoso list to hunt, I know where is an hind][1]

Whoso list° to hunt, I know where is an hind,°   *likes / female deer*
But as for me, alas, I may no more:
The vain travail hath wearied me so sore.
I am of them that farthest cometh behind;
5   Yet may I by no means my wearied mind
Draw from the deer: but as she fleeth afore,
Fainting I follow. I leave off therefore,
Since in a net I seek to hold the wind.
Who list her hunt, I put him out of doubt,
10 As well as I may spend his time in vain:
And, graven with diamonds, in letters plain
There is written her fair neck round about:
"*Noli me tangere*, for Caesar's I am,[2]
And wild for to hold, though I seem tame."

—1557

---

1   *[Whoso list ... an hind]* This poem is an adaptation of Sonnet 190 from Petrarch's *Rime sparse* (*Scattered Rhymes*).
2   *Noli me tangere* Latin: Touch me not; words spoken by Christ after his resurrection; *for Caesar's I am* It was thought that Caesar's deer wore collars with this inscription to ensure they would not be hunted. Wyatt's readers who identified the deer with Anne Boleyn (whom Wyatt knew and perhaps loved) would have read the lines as suggesting that the "hind" belongs to Henry VIII.

Sir Walter Ralegh

c. 1554–1618

Known as an explorer, courtier, writer, and adventurer—and as a knight and captain of the Queen's Guard who was later accused of treason—Sir Walter Ralegh was a controversial figure. A great portion of his writing has been lost over the centuries, but the remaining works reveal a dynamic voice imaginatively relaying his experiences and boldly critiquing the social and political climate in which he lived.

Born in Hayes Barton, Devonshire, Ralegh was a student at Oxford and a soldier in France and Ireland before becoming a favourite of Elizabeth I in the early 1580s. A secret marriage to one of Elizabeth's ladies-in-waiting caused him to fall out of favour, and in 1592 he was imprisoned for several months in the Tower of London—the occasion of his long poem *The Ocean to Cynthia*, lamenting Elizabeth's displeasure. Before and after his imprisonment Ralegh made attempts to establish colonies in what is now Virginia and the Carolinas, and he undertook several expeditions to the New World, including a 1595 voyage to Guiana in search of the legendary golden city of El Dorado. In 1596 he wrote *The Discovery of Guiana*, a vivid and partly fantastical account of his travels that influenced the popular European conception of South America as an exotic locale.

After his tumultuous relationship with Elizabeth I, Ralegh found a less sympathetic ruler in James I, who had him condemned under dubious charges of treason and imprisoned in the Tower from 1603 to 1616. Upon his release Ralegh embarked on another failed search for El Dorado. During this expedition, his crew attacked a Spanish settlement in contradiction of James's diplomatic policy, and when Ralegh returned home he was executed for his defiance.

Ralegh's poetry is characterized by an intensely personal treatment of such conventional themes as love, loss, beauty, and time. The majority of his poems are short lyrics—many of them occasional, written in response to particular events. Although he wrote throughout his eventful life, he was most prolific during the period of his imprisonment, producing poetry, political treatises, and an unfinished *History of the World* intended to chronicle life on Earth from the time of creation to Ralegh's own era.

The Nymph's Reply to the Shepherd[1]

If all the world and love were young,
And truth in every shepherd's tongue,
These pretty pleasures might me move
To live with thee and be thy love.

5 Time drives the flocks from field to fold
When rivers rage and rocks grow cold,
And Philomel becometh dumb;[2]
The rest complains of cares to come.

The flowers do fade, and wanton° fields   *unrestrained, unruly*
10 To wayward winter reckoning yields;
A honey tongue, a heart of gall,°   *bitterness, rancour*
Is fancy's spring, but sorrow's fall.

Thy gowns, thy shoes, thy beds of roses,
Thy cap, thy kirtle,° and thy posies   *tunic or skirt*
15 Soon break, soon wither, soon forgotten—
In folly ripe, in reason rotten.

Thy belt of straw and ivy buds,
Thy coral clasps and amber studs,
All these in me no means can move
20 To come to thee and be thy love.

But could youth last and love still breed,
Had joys no date nor age no need,[3]
Then these delights my mind might move
To live with thee and be thy love.

—1600

---

1   *The Nymph's … Shepherd* Response to Christopher Marlowe's "The Passionate Shepherd to His Love" (1599), also included in this anthology.
2   *Philomel becometh dumb* I.e., the nightingale does not sing. In classical mythology, Philomela, the daughter of the King of Athens, was transformed into a nightingale after being pursued and raped by her brother-in-law, Tereus, who tore out her tongue.
3   *Had joys … no need* If joys had no ending and aging did not bring with it its own needs.

Christopher Marlowe
1564–1593

As Tennyson wrote, "if Shakespeare is the dazzling sun" of the English Renaissance, then his fellow poet-playwright Christopher Marlowe "is certainly the morning star." Marlowe's plays heralded a new dawn for English drama in their use of blank verse (unrhymed iambic pentameter): by demonstrating its potential to capture the dynamic cadence of natural speech in plays such as *Tamburlaine the Great* (1587) and *Doctor Faustus* (1592?), he helped to make blank verse a standard form for playwrights of the period. Marlowe's facility with language extended to poetry, and he was known for his translations of Latin poets as well as for his original work. "The Passionate Shepherd to His Love," based in part on Virgil's Second Eclogue, is perhaps his most famous English poem.

Despite his success as a writer, Marlowe was dogged by controversy throughout his career. Not only was he a party to a homicide (of which he was acquitted on grounds of self-defence), he was also arrested for coining money and arraigned before the Privy Council on charges of blasphemy and heresy, both serious transgressions in Elizabethan England.

Marlowe's troubles came to a brutal head when at 29 he was fatally stabbed in what may have been a planned assassination connected with his apparent service to the Crown as a government agent. The enigmatic circumstances of his life and death have contributed to Marlowe's reputation as a man who—as Thomas Kyd attested—was "intemperate and of a cruel heart," skeptical of religion, scornful of decorum, and bold unto recklessness. Whatever the truth may be, Marlowe produced an extraordinary body of work that emits what William Hazlitt described as "a glow of the imagination, unhallowed by anything but its own energies."

The Passionate Shepherd to His Love

Come live with me and be my love,
And we will all the pleasures prove°   try
That valleys, groves, hills, and fields,
Woods, or steepy mountain yields.

And we will sit upon the rocks,
Seeing the shepherds feed their flocks,   5
By shallow rivers to whose falls
Melodious birds sing madrigals.[1]

---

1   *madrigals* Part-songs for several voices, often with pastoral or amatory associations.

And I will make thee beds of roses
10 And a thousand fragrant posies,
A cap of flowers, and a kirtle° *tunic or skirt*
Embroidered all with leaves of myrtle;

A gown made of the finest wool
Which from our pretty lambs we pull;
15 Fair linèd slippers for the cold,
With buckles of the purest gold;

A belt of straw and ivy buds,
With coral clasps and amber studs:
And if these pleasures may thee move,
20 Come live with me, and be my love.

The shepherd swains° shall dance and sing *rustic lovers*
For thy delight each May morning:
If these delights thy mind may move,
Then live with me and be my love.

—1599

William Shakespeare
1564–1616

As his fellow poet-playwright Ben Jonson declared, William Shakespeare "was not of an age, but for all time." Without doubt, the "Bard of Avon" has proved worthy of this monumental phrase: nearly four centuries after his death, Shakespeare's histories, comedies, tragedies, and romances continue to be staged the world over.

Today, Shakespeare's name is connected less with a flesh-and-blood human being—the son of a glover, born in the small town of Stratford-on-Avon, who left for London to pursue a career in the theatre after fathering three children—than with an extraordinary body of work. Shakespeare's oeuvre includes as many as 38 plays, many of them masterpieces; two narrative poems, *Venus and Adonis* (1593) and *The Rape of Lucrece* (1594), both much admired in Shakespeare's lifetime; and 154 sonnets, which were not necessarily conceived as a sequence but were published as one in 1609, perhaps without Shakespeare's consent.

In the sonnets the chief object of the poet's desire is not a chaste fair-haired lady but an idealized young man who prefers the praises of a rival poet and who occupies the centre of a psychologically complex love triangle in which the poet-speaker and a promiscuous "dark lady" are entangled. Because of their intensely intimate expression of love, lust, jealousy, and shame, the sonnets have been the subject of endless biographical speculation, yet it is by no means certain whether the poet-speaker is Shakespeare himself or a persona constructed for dramatic effect.

The enduring power of the sonnets resides not merely in what they mean but in how they produce meaning, that is, in the emotional and intellectual tensions and continuities between their several interworking parts.

Sonnets

18

Shall I compare thee to a summer's day?
Thou art more lovely and more temperate:
Rough winds do shake the darling buds of May,
And summer's lease hath all too short a date:
Sometime too hot the eye of heaven shines,   5
And often is his gold complexion dimmed;
And every fair° from fair sometime declines,   *beauty*
By chance, or nature's changing course, untrimmed:
But thy eternal summer shall not fade,

10 Nor lose possession of that fair thou ow'st,°   *own*
    Nor shall death brag thou wander'st in his shade
    When in eternal lines to time thou grow'st:
            So long as men can breathe or eyes can see,
            So long lives this, and this gives life to thee.

29

    When in disgrace with fortune and men's eyes
    I all alone beweep my outcast state,
    And trouble deaf heav'n with my bootless° cries,   *unavailing*
    And look upon myself, and curse my fate,
5   Wishing me like to one more rich in hope,
    Featured like him,[1] like him with friends possessed,
    Desiring this man's art° and that man's scope,   *skill*
    With what I most enjoy contented least;
    Yet in these thoughts myself almost despising,
10 Haply° I think on thee, and then my state,   *by chance*
    Like to the lark at break of day arising,
    From sullen° earth sings hymns at heaven's gate;   *dark, gloomy*
            For thy sweet love remembered such wealth brings
            That then I scorn to change my state with kings.

73

    That time of year thou mayst in me behold,
    When yellow leaves, or none, or few do hang
    Upon those boughs which shake against the cold,
    Bare ruined choirs[2] where late the sweet birds sang;
5   In me thou seest the twilight of such day
    As after sunset fadeth in the west,
    Which by and by black night doth take away,
    Death's second self[3] that seals up all in rest;
    In me thou seest the glowing of such fire
10 That on the ashes of his youth doth lie,
    As the deathbed, whereon it must expire,
    Consumed with that which it was nourished by;
            This thou perceiv'st, which makes thy love more strong,
            To love that well, which thou must leave° ere long.   *lose*

---

1   *Featured like him* With physical attractions like his.
2   *choirs* Parts of churches designated for singers.
3   *Death's second self* Sleep.

116

Let me not to the marriage of true minds
Admit impediments;[1] love is not love
Which alters when it alteration finds,
Or bends with the remover[2] to remove.
O no, it is an ever-fixèd mark,   5
That looks on tempests and is never shaken;
It is the star to every wand'ring bark,°   *boat*
Whose worth's unknown, although his height be taken.[3]
Love's not Time's fool, though rosy lips and cheeks
Within his bending sickle's compass° come;   *sweep*   10
Love alters not with his brief hours and weeks,
But bears it out even to the edge of doom.
        If this be error and upon me proved,
        I never writ, nor no man ever loved.

130

My mistress' eyes are nothing like the sun;
Coral is far more red than her lips' red;
If snow be white, why then her breasts are dun;°   *greyish-brown*
If hairs be wires, black wires grow on her head;
I have seen roses damasked,° red and white,   *parti-coloured*   5
But no such roses see I in her cheeks;
And in some perfumes is there more delight
Than in the breath that from my mistress reeks.
I love to hear her speak, yet well I know
That music hath a far more pleasing sound;   10
I grant I never saw a goddess go;°   *walk*
My mistress when she walks treads on the ground.
        And yet, by heaven, I think my love as rare
        As any she[4] belied with false compare.

—1609

---

1   *impediments* Cf. the marriage service in the Book of Common Prayer (c. 1552): "If any
    of you know cause, or just impediment, why these two persons should not be joined
    together in holy Matrimony, ye are to declare it."

2   *remover* One who changes, i.e., ceases to love.

3   *Whose ... taken* Referring to the "star" of the previous line, most likely the North Star,
    whose altitude can be reckoned for navigation purposes using a sextant, but whose es-
    sence remains unknown.

4   *any she* Any woman.

John Donne

1572–1631

John Donne was an innovator who set out to startle readers with his disdain for convention, writing poems that challenged expectations about what was appropriate in poetic subject matter, form, tone, language, and imagery.

As with the speaker of his "Holy Sonnet 19," in Donne "contraries meet in one." Some critics and readers try to resolve these "contraries" by separating Donne's career in two: in early life, a witty man-about-London whose love poems combine erotic energy with high-minded argument; in later life, a learned minister famous for his religious verse and his sermons. But Donne frequently blurs the differences between the sacred and the secular, sometimes presenting erotic love as a form of religious experience, and sometimes portraying religious devotion as an erotic experience. His poetic voice, moreover, ranges across a multitude of roles and postures, from misogynist cynicism to tender idealism and devout religious passion.

Donne was the son of a prosperous ironmonger, and his family was Catholic at a time when the government viewed all Catholics with suspicion. Donne studied at both Oxford and Cambridge but took no degree—perhaps because graduation required accepting the Church of England's 39 "articles of religion." In 1592 he began legal studies in London, and over the next few years wrote many of the love lyrics for which he later became famous; like most of his poems, these were circulated in manuscript but not published during his lifetime.

Donne eventually converted to Anglicanism, and in 1615 he became a clergyman. In 1621, he was appointed Dean of St. Paul's Cathedral in London, where he attracted large audiences for his intellectually challenging and emotionally stirring sermons. His *Poems* first appeared in 1633, two years after his death.

The Flea

Mark but this flea, and mark in this,
How little that which thou deny'st me is;
It sucked me first, and now sucks thee,
And in this flea, our two bloods mingled be;[1]
5   Thou know'st that this cannot be said
A sin, nor shame, nor loss of maidenhead,
    Yet this enjoys before it woo,

---

1   *mingled be* The speaker's subsequent argument hinges on the traditional belief that blood mixed during sexual intercourse.

And pampered swells with one blood made of two
And this, alas, is more than we would do.

Oh stay, three lives in one flea spare,   10
Where we almost, yea more than married are.
This flea is you and I, and this
Our marriage bed, and marriage temple is;
Though parents grudge, and you, we're met,
And cloistered in these living walls of jet.   15
 Though use° make you apt to kill me,   *habit*
 Let not to that, self murder added be,
 And sacrilege, three sins in killing three.

Cruel and sudden, hast thou since
Purpled thy nail, in blood of innocence?   20
Wherein could this flea guilty be,
Except in that drop which it sucked from thee?
Yet thou triumph'st, and sayest that thou
Find'st not thy self, nor me the weaker now;
 'Tis true, then learn how false, fears be;   25
 Just so much honour, when thou yield'st to me,
 Will waste, as this flea's death took life from thee.

       —1633

from *Holy Sonnets*

10

Death be not proud, though some have called thee
Mighty and dreadful, for thou art not so,
For, those, whom thou think'st thou dost overthrow
Die not, poor death, nor yet canst thou kill me.
From rest and sleep, which but thy pictures be,   5
Much pleasure, then from thee, much more must flow,
And soonest our best men with thee do go,
Rest of their bones, and soul's delivery.
Thou art slave to Fate, Chance, kings, and desperate men,
And dost with poison, war, and sickness dwell,   10
And poppy, or charms, can make us sleep as well,
And better than thy stroke; why swell'st thou then?
One short sleep past, we wake eternally,
And death shall be no more; death, thou shalt die.

14

Batter my heart, three personed God; for you
As yet but knock, breathe, shine, and seek to mend;
That I may rise and stand, o'erthrow me, and bend
Your force, to break, blow, burn and make me new.
5 I, like an usurped town, to another due,
Labour to admit You, but oh, to no end,
Reason Your viceroy in me, me should defend,
But is captived, and proves weak or untrue.
Yet dearly I love You, and would be loved fain,
10 But am betrothed unto Your enemy:
Divorce me, untie, or break that knot again,
Take me to you, imprison me, for I
Except you enthrall me, never shall be free,
Nor ever chaste, except you ravish me.

—1633

A Valediction: Forbidding Mourning

As virtuous men pass mildly away,
    And whisper to their souls to go,
Whilst some of their sad friends do say,
    The breath goes now, and some say, no:

5 So let us melt, and make no noise,
    No tear-floods, nor sigh-tempests move,
'Twere profanation of our joys
    To tell the laity our love.

Moving of th'earth° brings harms and fears,   *earthquake*
10   Men reckon what it did and meant,
But trepidation of the spheres,[1]
    Though greater far, is innocent.

---

1   *the spheres* According to Ptolemaic theory, a concentric series of spheres revolved around
the earth; the heavenly bodies were set into these spheres. Enveloping all the rest was an
outer sphere known as the "*Primum Mobile*" ("First Mover"), thought to give motion to
the other spheres, and to introduce variations into the times of the equinoxes.

Dull sublunary[1] lovers' love
    (Whose soul is sense) cannot admit
Absence, because it doth remove   15
    Those things which elemented it.

But we by a love, so much refined,
    That our selves know not what it is,
Inter-assured of the mind,
    Care less, eyes, lips, and hands to miss.   20

Our two souls therefore, which are one,
    Though I must go, endure not yet
A breach, but an expansion,
    Like gold to airy thinness beat.

If they be two, they are two so   25
    As stiff twin compasses[2] are two,
Thy soul, the fixed foot, makes no show
    To move, but doth, if th'other do.

And though it in the centre sit,
    Yet when the other far doth roam,   30
It leans, and hearkens after it,
    And grows erect, as that comes home.

Such wilt thou be to me, who must
    Like th'other foot, obliquely run;
Thy firmness draws my circle just,   35
    And makes me end, where I begun.

                  —1633

---

1   *sublunary* Beneath the moon, hence earthly (as opposed to heavenly) and therefore corruptible and subject to change.

2   *twin compasses* Single drawing compass (with twin "feet").

Lady Mary Wroth

1587–1653?

Lady Mary Wroth wrote the first work of prose romance and the first amatory sonnet sequence published by a woman in English. Her work was admired by a number of poets of her day—Ben Jonson proclaimed that her verse had made him "a better lover, and much better poet"—and although her reputation faded during the ensuing centuries, today she is recognized as a significant Jacobean writer and pioneer.

Born Mary Sidney, Wroth was a member of an illustrious political and literary family. She was educated by tutors and was already an accomplished scholar and musician by the time of her arranged marriage in 1604. The marriage was unhappy; when her husband died in 1614, Wroth was left with crushing debts, but was also free to pursue more openly a long-time illicit affair with her cousin, William Herbert. This affair, and financial constraints, may have limited Wroth's access to court and spurred her to write more seriously.

Wroth published a court romance, *The Countess of Montgomery's Urania*, in 1621. A groundbreaking work, *Urania* exploits a genre traditionally written by men—pastoral romance—in untraditional ways to examine the social situation of women in actual court society. Appended to *Urania* was a sequence of 83 sonnets and 20 songs entitled *Pamphilia to Amphilanthus*. These poems highlight love's tensions and contradictions with great poetic skill; the climax of *Pamphilia to Amphilanthus* is a technical *tour de force*, a "corona" or "crown" of 14 sonnets in which the last line of each poem becomes the first line of the next.

from *Pamphilia to Amphilanthus*

Song [Love, a child, is ever crying]

Love, a child, is ever crying,
    Please him, and he straight is flying;
    Give him, he the more is craving,
    Never satisfied with having.

5 His desires have no measure,
    Endless folly is his treasure;
    What he promiseth he breaketh;
    Trust not one word that he speaketh.

He vows nothing but false matter,
      And to cozen° you he'll flatter;   *deceive*   10
  Let him gain the hand, he'll leave you,
  And still glory to deceive you.

He will triumph in your wailing,
    And yet cause be of your failing:
  These his virtues are, and slighter   15
  Are his gifts, his favours lighter.

Feathers are as firm in staying,
  Wolves no fiercer in their preying.
  As a child then leave him crying,
  Nor seek him, so giv'n to flying.   20

77[1]

In this strange labyrinth how shall I turn?
       Ways° are on all sides while the way I miss: *paths*
  If to the right hand, there in love I burn;
  Let me go forward, therein danger is;
If to the left, suspicion hinders bliss;   5
  Let me turn back, shame cries I ought return,
       Nor faint, though crosses° with my fortunes kiss;   *troubles*
  Stand still is harder, although sure to mourn.[2]
Thus let me take the right, or left-hand way,
  Go forward, or stand still, or back retire: 10
       I must these doubts endure without allay°   *relief*
  Or help, but travail[3] find for my best hire.
Yet that which most my troubled sense doth move,
Is to leave all, and take the thread of Love.[4]

                   —1621

---

1   *77* The first sonnet in the 14-poem sequence *A Crown of Sonnets Dedicated to Love*, part
     of the larger sequence of *Pamphilia to Amphilanthus*.

2   *sure to mourn* Sure to make me mourn.

3   *travail* Take pains to; possibly meant as a pun on "travel," which was the word used in an
     early edition of the poem.

4   *thread of Love* Referring to the myth of Ariadne, who gave her beloved Theseus a spool of
     thread to unwind behind him as he travelled through the labyrinth of the Minotaur; by
     following the thread he could find his way back out.

George Herbert
1593–1633

George Herbert was born in Wales to a well-connected family and was educated at Trinity College in Cambridge, becoming a university orator, a member of Parliament, and later an Anglican priest. Deeply religious, he bemoaned the number of "love poems that are daily writ and consecrated to Venus" and the much smaller number of poems that "look toward God and Heaven." His own work opposed this trend: Herbert is known for devotion poetry that employs varied metre, unusual figurative language, and visual effects in the expression of faith.

Herbert experimented with poetic form: the words of his poem "Easter Wings," for example, are assembled on the page to depict two pairs of wings, while the text of "The Altar" takes the shape of an altar. Such typographical pattern poems influenced nineteenth- and twentieth-century poets such as Lewis Carroll, E.E. Cummings, and bpNichol, among others, and his work is considered a precursor to the "concrete poetry" movement of the 1950s. *The Temple* (1633), Herbert's major collection of poetry, was published in the year of his death.

Herbert had immense influence on the devotional poets of the 1600s, but by the nineteenth century his reputation had waned. In the twentieth century he rejoined the poetic mainstream when T.S. Eliot praised his fusion of emotion and intellect. Herbert was, Eliot wrote, "an anatomist of feeling and a trained theologian too; his mind is working continually both on the mysteries of faith and the motives of the heart."

The Altar

A broken A L T A R, Lord, thy servant rears,
Made of a heart, and cemented with tears:[1]
   Whose parts are as thy hand did frame;
   No workman's tool hath touched the same.[2]
       A H E A R T alone   5
       Is   such   a   stone,
       As   nothing   but
       Thy pow'r doth cut.
     Wherefore° each part   *accordingly*
     Of my hard heart   10
     Meets in this frame,
     To praise thy name.
  That, if I chance to hold my peace,
  These stones to praise thee may not cease.[3]
O let thy blessed S A C R I F I C E be mine,   15
And sanctify this A L T A R to be thine.

—1633

---

1   *A broken … tears* See Psalms 51.17: "The sacrifices of God are a broken spirit: a broken
    and a contrite heart, O God, thou wilt not despise."
2   *No … same* See Exodus 20.25: "And if thou wilt make me an altar of stone, thou shalt
    not build it of hewn stone: for if thou lift up thy tool upon it, thou hast polluted it."
3   *That … cease* In Luke 19.40, Jesus says of his disciples, "if these should hold their peace,
    the stones would immediately cry out."

Easter Wings

Lord, who createdst man in wealth and store,
Though foolishly he lost the same,
Decaying more and more,
Till he became
Most poor:
With thee
O let me rise
As larks, harmoniously,
And sing this day thy victories:
Then shall the fall further the flight in me.

My tender age in sorrow did begin:
And still with sicknesses and shame
Thou didst so punish sin,
That I became
Most thin.
With thee
Let me combine,
And feel this day thy victory:
For, if I imp[1] my wing on thine,
Affliction shall advance the flight in me.

—1633

1   *imp* Graft feathers from one falcon onto the wing of another, a technique used in falconry to mend damaged wings and improve flight.

John Milton
1608–1674

Missionary poet, Puritan sage, and radical champion of religious, domestic, and civil liberties, John Milton is among the most influential figures in English literature, a writer who, as the critic Matthew Arnold wrote, was "of the highest rank in the great style." In *Paradise Lost* (1667), his culminating achievement, Milton at once works within and transforms the epic tradition of Homer, Virgil, and Dante, casting off "the troublesome and modern bondage of rhyming" for majestic blank verse (unrhymed lines of iambic pentameter).

Milton was a Puritan, a Protestant who wanted to "purify" and simplify English religion, and, like other Puritans during the English Civil Wars (1642–51), he supported rebellion against the king—a support he expressed in an array of tracts and polemics. However, his religious opinions diverged from Puritanism to become increasingly heretical in his later years. Denounced for his pamphlets advocating divorce, which were prompted by his troubled marriage, Milton wrote the *Areopagitica* (1644), one of history's most rousing defences of a free press. He later reconciled with his wife only to lose her in childbirth, the first in a series of personal crises that saw the death of his son, his second wife, and their infant daughter, as well as the complete loss of his sight. Despite these blows, Milton continued late into his life to produce poetry of vast ambition.

On Shakespeare

What needs my Shakespeare for his honoured bones
The labour of an age in pilèd stones,
Or that his hallowed relics should be hid
Under a star-ypointing pyramid?
Dear son of memory,[1] great heir of Fame,   5
What need'st thou such weak witness of thy name?
Thou in our wonder and astonishment
Hast built thyself a livelong monument.
For whilst to th'shame of slow-endeavouring art,
Thy easy numbers flow, and that each heart   10
Hath from the leaves of thy unvalued° Book   *invaluable*
Those Delphic[2] lines with deep impression took,

---

1   *memory* Mnemosyne, mother of the muses.
2   *Delphic* Apollo, god of poetry, had his temple at Delphi.

Then thou our fancy of itself bereaving,
Dost make us marble with too much conceiving;
15 And so sepùlchered in such pomp dost lie,
That kings for such a tomb would wish to die.

—1632

[When I consider how my light is spent][1]

When I consider how my light is spent,
    Ere half my days, in this dark world and wide,
    And that one talent[2] which is death to hide,
    Lodged with me useless, though my soul more bent
5 To serve therewith my maker, and present
    My true account, lest he returning chide,
    Doth God exact day-labour, light denied,
    I fondly° ask; but patience to prevent   *foolishly*
That murmur, soon replies, God doth not need
10   Either man's work or his own gifts; who best
    Bear his mild yoke, they serve him best, his state
Is kingly. Thousands at his bidding speed
    And post° o'er land and ocean without rest: *ride*
    They also serve who only stand and wait.

—1673 (written c. 1652–55)

---

1   *[When ... spent]* Milton became blind in 1651.
2   *talent* Reference to the biblical parable of the talents; see Matthew 25.14–30. In this parable, a master gives varying amounts of money to three servants: five talents, two talents, and one talent, respectively. The servants that received larger sums invest the money, double it, and are celebrated, while the servant with one talent buries it for safekeeping and is punished for his failure to collect interest.

Anne Bradstreet
1612–1672

A member of an affluent and well-connected English family, Anne Bradstreet was well read and well learned in languages and literatures. At 18, she left England with her husband and parents aboard the *Arbella*, a ship headed for Massachusetts. Twenty years later, Bradstreet would become the first published female writer in the new colonies with her poetry collection *The Tenth Muse Lately Sprung Up in America* (1650).

Bradstreet's early writing bears the impress of her education, but her later poetry was also deeply influenced by her new life in America. Initially, she wrote, her "heart rose up" in protest at the "new world and new manners" that she found there. However, she continued to write under the difficult conditions of colonial life, while also raising eight children in the country so different from her birthplace. Her poetry conveyed familial devotion toward her husband and children as well as documenting the hardships endured by early settlers. Much of Bradstreet's poetry expressed strong Puritan faith, and the ornate diction and forms of her earlier work gave way to mature work distinguished by a lyrical voice, biblical themes, and biblical language.

The Tenth Muse was admired upon its publication, and Bradstreet has long been counted among the early literary lights of American poetry.

The Author to Her Book[1]

Thou ill-formed offspring of my feeble brain,
Who after birth didst by my side remain,
Till snatched from thence by friends, less wise than true
Who thee abroad, exposed to public view,
Made thee in rags, halting to th' press to trudge,   5
Where errors were not lessened (all may judge).
At thy return my blushing was not small,
My rambling brat (in print) should mother call,
I cast thee by as one unfit for light,
Thy visage° was so irksome in my sight;   *face*   10
Yet being mine own, at length affection would
Thy blemishes amend, if so I could:

---

1   *The Author to Her Book* These lines are thought to be a preface intended for a new edition of Bradstreet's collection *The Tenth Muse*, which was first published without her permission.

I washed thy face, but more defects I saw,
And rubbing off a spot still made a flaw.

15 I stretched thy joints to make thee even feet,
Yet still thou run'st more hobbling than is meet;°   *appropriate*
In better dress to trim thee was my mind,
But nought save homespun cloth i' th' house I find.
In this array 'mongst vulgars may'st thou roam.

20 In critic's hands beware thou dost not come,
And take thy way where yet thou art not known;
If for thy father asked, say thou hadst none;
And for thy mother, she alas is poor,
Which caused her thus to send thee out of door.

—1678

Andrew Marvell

1621–1678

Andrew Marvell's poems are complex, full of paradox and irony, and frequently employ naïve or ambivalent personae who present debates or balance competing claims. His poem "An Horation Ode upon Cromwell's Return from Ireland" (1650), for example, oscillates between admiration for King Charles I and praise for (and veiled criticism of) Oliver Cromwell, who choreographed the abolition of the monarchy through the English Civil Wars (1642–51), executing Charles I in the process. Marvell was known primarily as a politician and satirist during his lifetime, and his reputation as one of the best lyric poets of his era was not fully established until the twentieth century.

The son of a clergyman, Marvell grew up in Hull in northeast England. At age 12 he was admitted to the University of Cambridge, where he studied for seven years and where he published his first poems, written in Latin and Greek. Instead of completing his degree, Marvell left England in 1642 for four years of travel in continental Europe, perhaps to wait out the period of the English Civil Wars. In 1650, he began working as a tutor to the 12-year-old daughter of Thomas, Lord Fairfax, the recently retired Commander-in-Chief of Cromwell's army. It was likely during his two years on the Fairfax estate that Marvell composed many of his most famous works, including the sensuous and witty "To His Coy Mistress."

Marvell served in Cromwell's government as Latin Secretary and was elected in 1659 as Member of Parliament for Hull, a seat he would maintain until his death. He was highly critical of Charles II (who was restored to the monarchy in 1660 after the collapse of Cromwell's Commonwealth), but Marvell's harshest criticisms were published anonymously. When he died in 1678, there was still an outstanding government reward offered for the name of the man who had written "An Account of the Growth of Popery and Arbitrary Government in England" a year earlier.

To His Coy Mistress

Had we but world enough, and time,
This coyness Lady were no crime.
We would sit down, and think which way
To walk, and pass our long love's day.
Thou by the Indian Ganges' side
Should'st rubies find: I by the tide
Of Humber[1] would complain. I would

5

---

1   *Humber* River in northern England; it flows alongside Hull, Marvell's home town.

Love you ten years before the Flood:
And you should, if you please, refuse
Till the conversion of the Jews.[1]
10 My vegetable love should grow[2]
Vaster than empires, and more slow.
An hundred years should go to praise
Thine eyes, and on thy forehead gaze.
Two hundred to adore each breast:
15 But thirty thousand to the rest.
An age at least to every part,
And the last age should show your heart.
For Lady you deserve this state;
Nor would I love at lower rate.
20 But at my back I always hear,
Time's wingèd chariot hurrying near:
And yonder all before us lie
Deserts of vast eternity.
Thy beauty shall no more be found;
25 Nor, in thy marble vault, shall sound
My echoing song; then worms shall try
That long preserved virginity:
And your quaint honour turn to dust;
And into ashes all my lust.
30 The grave's a fine and private place,
But none I think do there embrace.
Now therefore, while the youthful glew
Sits on thy skin like morning dew,[3]
And while thy willing soul transpires
35 At every pore with instant fires,
Now let us sport us while we may;
And now, like am'rous birds of prey,
Rather at once our time devour,

---

1   *conversion of the Jews* Event supposed to usher in the final millennium leading to the end
     of time.
2   *vegetable love should grow* His love (or its physical manifestation) would grow slowly and
     steadily: Aristotle (384–322 BCE) defined the vegetative part of the soul as that character-
     ized only by growth.
3   *youthful glew ... morning dew* This wording is as it appears in Marvell's original manu-
     script, but there are many early variants on the final words in each line of this couplet.
     Most of these changes occurred in printer's attempts to correct "glew" (which may mean
     "sweat," or be a variant spelling of "glow").

Than languish in his slow-chapt[1] pow'r.
Let us roll all our strength, and all   40
Our sweetness, up into one ball:
And tear our pleasures with rough strife,
Thorough° the iron gates[2] of life.   *through*
Thus, though we cannot make our sun
Stand still,[3] yet we will make him run.   45

—1681

---

1   *slow-chapt* Slowly devouring; "chaps" are jaws.
2   *gates* "Grates" in the 1681 printed edition with manuscript corrections, but many editors
    see "gates of life" as a typically Marvellian inversion of the biblical "gates of death" (see
    Psalm 9.13).
3   *sun / Stand still* Refers both to the love poetry convention in which lovers ask for time to
    stop when they are together, and to Joshua 10.12–14, in which Joshua made the sun and
    moon stand still while his army slaughtered the Amorites.

Anna Laetitia Barbauld

1743–1825

Anna Laetitia Barbauld's diverse accomplishments established her as a leading figure in London's intellectual life: she was as an educational reformer, critic, editor, radical political writer, and well-regarded poet of early Romanticism and children's literature. Her career as a published poet began in 1773 with her wide-ranging debut collection *Poems*, which was so popular that it would be re-issued and revised several times over the next 20 years. The varied subject matter of her work reflects a wide range of interests, from politics to animal rights to religious devotion.

Barbauld's father superintended one of the Protestant alternatives to England's exclusive Anglican schools; from him she learned languages such as Greek and Latin and received an education in literary classics. She followed in her father's footsteps when she and her husband co-founded their own boarding school for boys. Her work there inspired her *Lessons for Children* (1778–79) and *Hymns in Prose for Children* (1781), primers with literacy and faith as their respective goals. The large type in these small texts was an innovation that popularized children's books, and *Lessons* and *Hymns* were influential in both England and the newly formed United States.

Barbauld was also a political writer whose essays, pamphlets, and persuasive verse addressed topics such as freedom of religion, the abolition of slavery, and Britain's engagement in the Napoleonic Wars.

The Caterpillar

No, helpless thing, I cannot harm thee now;
Depart in peace, thy little life is safe,
For I have scanned thy form with curious eye,
Noted the silver line that streaks thy back,
5 The azure and the orange that divide
Thy velvet sides; thee, houseless wanderer,
My garment has enfolded, and my arm
Felt the light pressure of thy hairy feet;
Thou hast curled round my finger; from its tip,
10 Precipitous descent! with stretched out neck,
Bending thy head in airy vacancy,
This way and that, inquiring, thou hast seemed
To ask protection; now, I cannot kill thee.
Yet I have sworn perdition° to thy race,   *damnation, destruction*

And recent from the slaughter am I come   15
Of tribes and embryo nations: I have sought
With sharpened eye and persecuting zeal,
Where, folded in their silken webs they lay
Thriving and happy; swept them from the tree
And crushed whole families beneath my foot;   20
Or, sudden, poured on their devoted heads
The vials of destruction.[1]—This I've done,
Nor felt the touch of pity: but when thou—
A single wretch, escaped the general doom,
Making me feel and clearly recognize   25
Thine individual existence, life,
And fellowship of sense with all that breathes—
Present'st thyself before me, I relent,
And cannot hurt thy weakness.—So the storm
Of horrid war, o'erwhelming cities, fields,   30
And peaceful villages, rolls dreadful on:
The victor shouts triumphant; he enjoys
The roar of cannon and the clang of arms,
And urges, by no soft relentings stopped,
The work of death and carnage. Yet should one,   35
A single sufferer from the field escaped,
Panting and pale, and bleeding at his feet,
Lift his imploring eyes—the hero weeps;
He is grown human, and capricious Pity,
Which would not stir for thousands, melts for one   40
With sympathy spontaneous: 'Tis not Virtue,
Yet 'tis the weakness of a virtuous mind.

                                                           —1825

---

1   *vials of destruction* I.e., pesticides.

Phillis Wheatley

1753–1784

The first black person of African heritage to have a book published, Phillis Wheatley gained an international readership for her poetry, yet died impoverished and largely forgotten. During her lifetime, she published some 50 poems in American newspapers, an exceptional number for the time, and had a collection of poetry, *Poems on Various Subjects, Religious and Moral* (1773), published in London.

Born in Africa, Wheatley was transported to the British colonies in America on the slave ship *Phillis* in 1761. She was purchased as a slave-servant by a businessman and his wife, John and Susannah Wheatley, who gave her an education in English, Latin, classics, and the Bible. Her first published poem appeared in a Rhode Island newspaper when she was only 14 years old.

The 38 *Poems on Various Subjects* include several on nature and morality, a number of poems written to mark specific occasions (called occasional poems), and a racially self-conscious poem on religious transformation, "On Being Brought from Africa to America." Many of the poems are elegies for the dead, which display a reluctance to mourn and instead celebrate the passage of the departed to a happier and better life.

Wheatley gained her freedom in 1778, and in the same year she married a free black man. They lived in extreme poverty, which contributed to the death of all three of her children in infancy—and to Wheatley's own premature death at age 31.

On Being Brought from Africa to America

'Twas mercy brought me from my Pagan land,
Taught my benighted soul to understand
That there's a God, that there's a Saviour too:
Once I redemption neither sought nor knew.
5 Some view our sable race with scornful eye—
"Their colour is a diabolic dye."
Remember, Christians, Negroes, black as Cain,[1]
May be refined, and join th' angelic train.

—1773

---

1   *Cain* In Genesis 4.1–15, the son of Adam and Eve, who murdered his brother Abel and was cursed and marked by God as punishment. A popular interpretation of this story was that the mark of Cain turned his skin dark.

William Blake
1757–1827

"I labour upwards into futurity," wrote William Blake on the back of one of the "tablets" of his visionary art. Blake's genius was largely unrecognized during his own lifetime, but the mysterious and powerful poetry that he crafted—perhaps most memorably in *Songs of Innocence and Experience* (1789, 1794)—would eventually be recognized as having revolutionary significance.

As a child living above his parents' hosiery shop in London, Blake once received a thrashing for declaring he had seen the face of God. Apprenticed at 14 to a highly respected engraver, he spent seven years learning the trade that would earn him his keep. As an adult, Blake claimed to communicate daily with the spirit of his brother Robert, who had died of tuberculosis; the unique style of "illuminated printing" that Blake later devised came to him in a visitation from Robert. Etching words backwards into copper plates so that they would reverse to normal upon printing, Blake in 1788 created his first illuminated texts. Over the next 20 years he would produce an extraordinary series of works in which he used both words and images to express his artistic vision.

The Bible was a tremendous imaginative reserve upon which Blake drew all of his life, and one vision to which he often returns is that of an earthly Eden triumphing over forces of repression. He also had associations with decidedly non-mystical movements calling for political reforms, although he never fully participated in any organization, religious or political.

Blake found his soul mate in Catherine Boucher, a market gardener's daughter whom he taught to read and trained in the printing business. Catherine was evidently a submissive, devoted wife, and some have denigrated Blake's approach to marriage, citing his pronouncement that "the female … lives from the light of the male." But at the same time, Blake abjured sexual domination and celebrated "the moment of desire!" as a portal to the divine.

Against the grain of the times—he lived during the Industrial Revolution—Blake continued producing labour-intensive, elaborately illustrated books, none of which was commercially successful. Only 20 copies of *Songs of Experience* had been sold at the time of his death.

from *Songs of Innocence*

The Lamb

Little lamb, who made thee?
Dost thou know who made thee,
Gave thee life & bid thee feed
By the stream & o'er the mead—

William Blake, "The Lamb," Songs of Innocence, *1789. Blake produced his illuminated books, including* Songs of Innocence *and* Songs of Experience, *by etching both text and illustrations onto copper plates, which he then used for printing. Often, he coloured the printed images by hand.*

5   Gave thee clothing of delight,
     Softest clothing, woolly bright,
     Gave thee such a tender voice,
     Making all the vales rejoice?
         Little lamb, who made thee,
10   Dost thou know who made thee?

     Little lamb, I'll tell thee,
     Little lamb, I'll tell thee!

He is called by thy name,
For he calls himself a Lamb;
He is meek & he is mild,[1]   15
He became a little child:
I a child, & thou a lamb,
We are called by his name.
    Little lamb, God bless thee,
    Little lamb, God bless thee!   20

—1789

from *Songs of Experience*

London

I wander thro' each charter'd[2] street
Near where the charter'd Thames does flow,
And mark in every face I meet
Marks of weakness, marks of woe.

In every cry of every Man,   5
In every Infant's cry of fear,
In every voice, in every ban,
The mind-forg'd manacles I hear.

How the Chimney-sweeper's cry
Every black'ning Church appalls,   10
And the hapless Soldier's sigh
Runs in blood down Palace walls.

But most thro' midnight streets I hear
How the youthful Harlot's curse[3]
Blasts the new-born Infant's tear,[4]
And blights with plagues the marriage hearse.   15

—1794

---

1   *He is ... is mild* See Charles Wesley's hymn "Gentle Jesus, Meek and Mild" (1742).
2   *charter'd* Licensed. Charters grant freedoms, often for a select minority (such as merchants).
3   *Harlot's curse* Referring to both the oaths she utters and the venereal diseases she spreads.
4   *Blasts ... tear* Reference to the blindness caused in infants if they contract certain venereal diseases (such as gonorrhea) from their mother.

William Wordsworth
1770–1850

William Wordsworth is often credited with initiating the shifts in poetic form and content that characterized the Romantic era in British poetry. The most frequent subjects of his poems are nature, the sublime, and the lives of ordinary country people—of interest because, according to Wordsworth, in "low and rustic life ... the essential passions of the heart find a better soil in which they can attain their maturity, are less under restraint, and speak a plainer and more emphatic language." Wordsworth himself viewed poetry as a divine gift and, in addition to celebrating "rustic living" and nature, many of his poems celebrate the imaginative capacity of the author.

Wordsworth was born in the English Lake District. His parents were both dead by the time he was 13, and he was sent by relatives to be educated at a boarding school, later completing his degree at Cambridge. He spent parts of his young adulthood walking throughout Europe, an experience which deepened his interest in politics as well as in nature; his time spent in Revolutionary France had an especially profound impact on his poetry. After these travels were concluded, Wordsworth would spend much of the rest of his life sharing a home with his "beloved sister" Dorothy, whom he described as one of "the two beings to whom my intellect is most indebted" (the other was his friend and fellow poet Samuel Taylor Coleridge).

Lyrical Ballads (1798), which Wordsworth co-authored with Coleridge, is often considered the most important single volume of poetry of the period. Wordsworth's self-stated ambition to write about "incidents and situations from common life" in "language really used by men" was a shift from the impersonal, formulaic poetry of the eighteenth century. This deviation stirred up a great deal of criticism, but by the last decades of his life, Wordsworth's skill and mastery as a poet were widely acknowledged. He was awarded the title of Poet Laureate at the age of 73. In the year after his death, his long poem *The Prelude* was published; originally written in 1798–99, and expanded then revised over the next 40 years, it is often regarded as Wordsworth's crowning achievement.

Lines Written a Few Miles above Tintern Abbey

On Revisiting the Banks of the Wye during a Tour, July 13, 1798 [1]

Five years have passed; five summers, with the length
Of five long winters! and again I hear
These waters, rolling from their mountain-springs
With a sweet inland murmur.[2] Once again
Do I behold these steep and lofty cliffs,　　　　　　　　　　　5
Which on a wild secluded scene impress
Thoughts of more deep seclusion; and connect
The landscape with the quiet of the sky.
The day is come when I again repose
Here, under this dark sycamore, and view　　　　　　　　　　10
These plots of cottage-ground, these orchard-tufts,
Which, at this season, with their unripe fruits,
Among the woods and copses lose themselves,
Nor, with their green and simple hue, disturb
The wild green landscape. Once again I see　　　　　　　　　15
These hedge-rows, hardly hedge-rows, little lines
Of sportive wood run wild; these pastoral farms
Green to the very door; and wreaths of smoke
Sent up, in silence, from among the trees,
With some uncertain notice, as might seem,　　　　　　　　　20
Of vagrant dwellers in the houseless woods,
Or of some hermit's cave, where by his fire
The hermit sits alone.

　　　　　　　　　Though absent long,
These forms of beauty have not been to me,　　　　　　　　　25
As is a landscape to a blind man's eye:
But oft, in lonely rooms, and 'mid the din
Of towns and cities, I have owed to them,
In hours of weariness, sensations sweet,
Felt in the blood, and felt along the heart,　　　　　　　　　30

1　[Wordsworth's note] No poem of mine was composed under circumstances more
　　pleasant for me to remember than this. I began it upon leaving Tintern, after crossing
　　the Wye, and concluded it just as I was entering Bristol in the evening, after a ramble
　　of 4 or 5 days, with my sister. Not a line of it was altered, and not any part of it was
　　written down till I reached Bristol.
2　[Wordsworth's note] The river is not affected by the tides a few miles above Tintern.

And passing even into my purer mind
With tranquil restoration—feelings too
Of unremembered pleasure; such, perhaps,
As may have had no trivial influence
35 On that best portion of a good man's life;
His little, nameless, unremembered acts
Of kindness and of love. Nor less, I trust,
To them I may have owed another gift,
Of aspect more sublime; that blessed mood,
40 In which the burthen of the mystery,
In which the heavy and the weary weight
Of all this unintelligible world
Is lighten'd—that serene and blessed mood,
In which the affections gently lead us on,
45 Until, the breath of this corporeal frame,
And even the motion of our human blood
Almost suspended, we are laid asleep
In body, and become a living soul:
While with an eye made quiet by the power
50 Of harmony, and the deep power of joy,
We see into the life of things.

               If this
Be but a vain belief, yet, oh! how oft,
In darkness, and amid the many shapes
55 Of joyless day-light; when the fretful stir
Unprofitable, and the fever of the world,
Have hung upon the beatings of my heart,
How oft, in spirit, have I turned to thee
O sylvan° Wye! Thou wanderer through the woods,   *wooded*
60 How often has my spirit turned to thee!

And now, with gleams of half-extinguish'd thought,
With many recognitions dim and faint,
And somewhat of a sad perplexity,
The picture of the mind revives again:
65 While here I stand, not only with the sense
Of present pleasure, but with pleasing thoughts
That in this moment there is life and food
For future years. And so I dare to hope
Though changed, no doubt, from what I was, when first

I came among these hills; when like a roe°   *deer*   70
I bounded o'er the mountains, by the sides
Of the deep rivers, and the lonely streams,
Wherever nature led; more like a man
Flying from something that he dreads, than one
Who sought the thing he loved. For nature then   75
(The coarser pleasures of my boyish days,
And their glad animal movements all gone by)
To me was all in all. I cannot paint
What then I was. The sounding cataract
Haunted me like a passion: the tall rock,   80
The mountain, and the deep and gloomy wood,
Their colours and their forms, were then to me
An appetite: a feeling and a love,
That had no need of a remoter charm,
By thought supplied, or any interest   85
Unborrowed from the eye. That time is past,
And all its aching joys are now no more,
And all its dizzy raptures. Not for this
Faint[1] I, nor mourn nor murmur: other gifts
Have followed, for such loss, I would believe,   90
Abundant recompense. For I have learned
To look on nature, not as in the hour
Of thoughtless youth, but hearing oftentimes
The still, sad music of humanity,
Not harsh nor grating, though of ample power   95
To chasten and subdue. And I have felt
A presence that disturbs me with the joy
Of elevated thoughts; a sense sublime
Of something far more deeply interfused,
Whose dwelling is the light of setting suns,   100
And the round ocean, and the living air,
And the blue sky, and in the mind of man,
A motion and a spirit, that impels
All thinking things, all objects of all thought,
And rolls through all things. Therefore am I still   105
A lover of the meadows and the woods,
And mountains; and of all that we behold
From this green earth; of all the mighty world

---

1   *Faint* Lose heart; grow weak.

Of eye and ear, both what they half create,
110 And what perceive; well pleased to recognize
In nature and the language of the sense,
The anchor of my purest thoughts, the nurse,
The guide, the guardian of my heart, and soul
Of all my moral being.

115   Nor, perchance,
If I were not thus taught, should I the more
Suffer my genial° spirits to decay: *creative*
For thou art with me, here, upon the banks
Of this fair river; thou, my dearest Friend,[1]
120 My dear, dear Friend, and in thy voice I catch
The language of my former heart, and read
My former pleasures in the shooting lights
Of thy wild eyes. Oh! yet a little while
May I behold in thee what I was once,
125 My dear, dear Sister! And this prayer I make,
Knowing that Nature never did betray
The heart that loved her; 'tis her privilege,
Through all the years of this our life, to lead
From joy to joy: for she can so inform
130 The mind that is within us, so impress
With quietness and beauty, and so feed
With lofty thoughts, that neither evil tongues,
Rash judgments, nor the sneers of selfish men,
Nor greetings where no kindness is, nor all
135 The dreary intercourse of daily life,
Shall e'er prevail against us, or disturb
Our cheerful faith that all which we behold
Is full of blessings. Therefore let the moon
Shine on thee in thy solitary walk;
140 And let the misty mountain winds be free
To blow against thee: and in after years,
When these wild ecstasies shall be matured
Into a sober pleasure, when thy mind
Shall be a mansion for all lovely forms,
145 Thy memory be as a dwelling-place
For all sweet sounds and harmonies; Oh! then,

---

1   *my dearest Friend* I.e., Dorothy Wordsworth, the poet's sister.

If solitude, or fear, or pain, or grief,
Should be thy portion, with what healing thoughts
Of tender joy wilt thou remember me,
And these my exhortations! Nor, perchance,   150
If I should be, where I no more can hear
Thy voice, nor catch from thy wild eyes these gleams
Of past existence, wilt thou then forget
That on the banks of this delightful stream
We stood together; and that I, so long   155
A worshipper of Nature, hither came,
Unwearied in that service: rather say
With warmer love, oh! with far deeper zeal
Of holier love. Nor wilt thou then forget,
That after many wanderings, many years   160
Of absence, these steep woods and lofty cliffs,
And this green pastoral landscape, were to me
More dear, both for themselves, and for thy sake.

—1798

[The world is too much with us]

The world is too much with us; late and soon,
Getting and spending, we lay waste our powers:
Little we see in nature that is ours;
We have given our hearts away, a sordid boon!°   *gift*
The Sea that bares her bosom to the moon;   5
The Winds that will be howling at all hours
And are up-gathered now like sleeping flowers;
For this, for every thing, we are out of tune;
It moves us not. Great God! I'd rather be
A Pagan suckled in a creed outworn;   10
So might I, standing on this pleasant lea,
Have glimpses that would make me less forlorn;
Have sight of Proteus[1] coming from the sea;
Or hear old Triton[2] blow his wreathed horn.

—1807

---

1   *Proteus* Shape-changing sea god.
2   *Triton* Sea god with the head and torso of a man and the tail of a fish. He was fre-
     quently depicted blowing on a conch shell.

Samuel Taylor Coleridge
1772–1834

Coleridge wrote in a 1796 letter, "I am, and ever have been, a great reader, and have read almost everything—a library-cormorant." His own work was similarly wide-ranging and prolific; Coleridge's collected writings comprise 50 volumes and reveal his interest in a myriad of subjects from history and politics to science and literary criticism. He is chiefly remembered, however, for his significant contribution to English Romantic poetry: poems such as "The Rime of the Ancient Mariner" and "Kubla Khan" that have remained fresh and affecting for generations of readers.

The son of a school headmaster, Coleridge received a robust classical education and later briefly attended Cambridge, although he left without taking a degree. After several false starts—he joined the army, and upon his release concocted an ill-fated plan to move to America to found a communal society—he began to publish his writing. His second book of poetry was *Lyrical Ballads* (1798), a collaboration with his friend William Wordsworth; it opened with "The Rime of the Ancient Mariner," which remains Coleridge's most critically lauded single poem.

Coleridge composed little poetry during the last 35 years of his life. His most important writing from this period is the two-volume *Biographia Literaria* (1817), a work of autobiography and literary criticism in which he anatomizes both poetry and poetic production, considering not only formal elements but also the psychology of the creative process.

Frost at Midnight

The Frost performs its secret ministry,
Unhelped by any wind. The owlet's cry
Came loud—and hark, again! loud as before.
The inmates of my cottage, all at rest,
5   Have left me to that solitude, which suits
Abstruser musings: save that at my side
My cradled infant slumbers peacefully.
'Tis calm indeed! so calm, that it disturbs
And vexes meditation with its strange
10   And extreme silentness. Sea, hill, and wood,
This populous village! Sea, and hill, and wood,
With all the numberless goings-on of life,
Inaudible as dreams! the thin blue flame
Lies on my low-burnt fire, and quivers not;

Only that film,[1] which fluttered on the grate,   15
Still flutters there, the sole unquiet thing.
Methinks, its motion in this hush of nature
Gives it dim sympathies with me who live,
Making it a companionable form,
Whose puny flaps and freaks the idling Spirit   20
By its own moods interprets, every where
Echo or mirror seeking of itself,
And makes a toy of Thought.

                       But O! how oft,
How oft, at school, with most believing mind,   25
Presageful, have I gazed upon the bars,
To watch that fluttering *stranger*! and as oft
With unclosed lids, already had I dreamt
Of my sweet birth-place, and the old church-tower,
Whose bells, the poor man's only music, rang   30
From morn to evening, all the hot Fair-day,
So sweetly, that they stirred and haunted me
With a wild pleasure, falling on mine ear
Most like articulate sounds of things to come!
So gazed I, till the soothing things, I dreamt,   35
Lulled me to sleep, and sleep prolonged my dreams!
And so I brooded all the following morn,
Awed by the stern preceptor's° face, mine eye   *teacher's*
Fixed with mock study on my swimming book:
Save if the door half opened, and I snatched   40
A hasty glance, and still my heart leaped up,
For still I hoped to see the *stranger's* face,
Townsman, or aunt, or sister more beloved,
My play-mate when we both were clothed alike!

         Dear Babe, that sleepest cradled by my side,   45
Whose gentle breathings, heard in this deep calm,
Fill up the interspersèd vacancies
And momentary pauses of the thought!
My babe so beautiful! it thrills my heart
With tender gladness, thus to look at thee,   50
And think that thou shalt learn far other lore,

---

1   [Coleridge's note] In all parts of the kingdom these films are called *strangers* and sup-
    posed to portend the arrival of some absent friend.

And in far other scenes! For I was reared
In the great city, pent 'mid cloisters dim,
And saw nought lovely but the sky and stars.
55 But *thou*, my babe! shalt wander like a breeze
By lakes and sandy shores, beneath the crags
Of ancient mountain, and beneath the clouds,
Which image in their bulk both lakes and shores
And mountain crags: so shalt thou see and hear
60 The lovely shapes and sounds intelligible
Of that eternal language, which thy God
Utters, who from eternity doth teach
Himself in all, and all things in himself.
Great universal Teacher! he shall mould
65 Thy spirit, and by giving make it ask.

   Therefore all seasons shall be sweet to thee,
Whether the summer clothe the general earth
With greenness, or the redbreast sit and sing
Betwixt the tufts of snow on the bare branch
70 Of mossy apple-tree, while the nigh thatch
Smokes in the sun-thaw; whether the eave-drops fall
Heard only in the trances of the blast,
Or if the secret ministry of frost
Shall hang them up in silent icicles,
75 Quietly shining to the quiet Moon.

             —1798

Kubla Khan

Or, A Vision in a Dream. A Fragment[1]

In Xanadu did Kubla Khan
A stately pleasure-dome decree:
Where Alph, the sacred river, ran
Through caverns measureless to man
5 Down to a sunless sea.

---

1 [Coleridge's note] The following fragment is here published at the request of a poet [Lord Byron] of great and deserved celebrity, and as far as the Author's own opinions are concerned, rather as a psychological curiosity, than on the ground of any supposed poetic merits.

  In the summer of the year 1797, the Author, then in ill health, had retired to a lonely farmhouse between Porlock and Linton, on the Exmoor confines of Somerset and

So twice five miles of fertile ground
With walls and towers were girdled round:
And there were gardens bright with sinuous rills,°   *brooks*
Where blossomed many an incense-bearing tree;
And here were forests ancient as the hills,   10
Enfolding sunny spots of greenery.

But oh! that deep romantic chasm which slanted
Down the green hill athwart a cedarn cover!
A savage place! as holy and enchanted
As e'er beneath a waning moon was haunted   15

Devonshire. In consequence of a slight indisposition [dysentery], an anodyne [opium] had been prescribed, from the effects of which he fell asleep in his chair at the moment that he was reading the following sentence, or words of the same substance, in *Purchas's Pilgrimage*: "Here the Khan Kubla commanded a palace to be built, and a stately garden thereunto. And thus ten miles of fertile ground were inclosed with a wall." The author continued for about three hours in a profound sleep, at least of the external senses, during which time he has the most vivid confidence, that he could not have composed less than from two to three hundred lines, if that indeed can be called composition in which all the images rose up before him as things, with a parallel production of the correspondent expressions, without any sensation or consciousness of effort. On awaking he appeared to himself to have a distinct recollection of the whole, and taking his pen, ink, and paper, instantly and eagerly wrote down the lines that are here preserved. At this moment he was unfortunately called out by a person on business from Porlock, and detained by him above an hour, and on his return to his room, found to his no small surprise and mortification, that though he still retained some vague and dim recollection of the general purpose of the vision, yet, with the exception of some eight or ten scattered lines and images, all the rest had passed away like the images on the surface of a stream into which a stone has been cast, but, alas! without the after restoration of the latter!

> Then all the charm
> Is broken—all that phantom-world so fair
> Vanishes, and a thousand circlets spread,
> And each mis-shape the other. Stay awhile,
> Poor youth! who scarcely dar'st lift up thine eyes—
> The stream will soon renew its smoothness, soon
> The visions will return! And lo, he stays,
> And soon the fragments dim of lovely forms
> Come trembling back, unite, and now once more
> The pool becomes a mirror.

[from Coleridge's "The Picture, or the Lover's Resolution" (1802), 69–78]

Yet from the still surviving recollections in his mind, the Author has frequently purposed to finish for himself what had been originally, as it were, given to him. Σαμερον αδιον ασω [from Theocritus's *Idyll* 1.145]: but the tomorrow is yet to come.

As a contrast to this vision, I have annexed a fragment of a very different character [Coleridge's poem "The Pains of Sleep," not included in this anthology], describing with equal fidelity the dream of pain and disease.

By woman wailing for her demon-lover!
And from this chasm, with ceaseless turmoil seething,
As if this earth in fast thick pants were breathing,
A mighty fountain momently was forced:
20 Amid whose swift half-intermitted burst
Huge fragments vaulted like rebounding hail,
Or chaffy grain beneath the thresher's flail:
And 'mid these dancing rocks at once and ever
It flung up momently the sacred river.
25 Five miles meandering with a mazy° motion   *labyrinthine*
Through wood and dale the sacred river ran,
Then reached the caverns measureless to man,
And sank in tumult to a lifeless ocean:
And 'mid this tumult Kubla heard from far
30 Ancestral voices prophesying war!
         The shadow of the dome of pleasure
         Floated midway on the waves;
         Where was heard the mingled measure
         From the fountain and the caves.
35 It was a miracle of rare device,
A sunny pleasure-dome with caves of ice!
         A damsel with a dulcimer
         In a vision once I saw:
         It was an Abyssinian maid,
40   And on her dulcimer she played,
         Singing of Mount Abora.
         Could I revive within me
         Her symphony and song,
         To such a deep delight 'twould win me,
45 That with music loud and long,
I would build that dome in air,
That sunny dome! those caves of ice!
And all who heard should see them there,
And all should cry, Beware! Beware!
50 His flashing eyes, his floating hair!
Weave a circle round him thrice,
And close your eyes with holy dread,
For he on honey-dew hath fed,
And drunk the milk of Paradise.

—1816 (written 1798)

Percy Bysshe Shelley
1792–1822

Although he was born into wealth and privilege, Percy Bysshe Shelley opposed the powerful, especially the Tory government and press whom he believed were responsible for the oppression of the working classes. He was called "Mad Shelley" at Oxford not only for his political radicalism but also for his vocal atheism and his intense interest in science. These intellectual passions underwrite a body of remarkable visionary poetry characterized by an elegance and complexity that is at once very wonderful and very difficult.

Shelley, heir to the estate and title of his baronet father and grandfather, attended Eton College, and was still a student there when he published *Zastrozzi* (1810), a Gothic romance novel. He continued to publish during his short stint at the University of Oxford, from which he and a friend were expelled for co-authoring a pamphlet entitled *The Necessity of Atheism* (1811). In 1813 Shelley published his first important work: *Queen Mab*, a poetic utopian dream-vision that vilified conventional morality and institutional religion.

In 1819–20 Shelley wrote his greatest utopian fantasy, *Prometheus Unbound*, which imagined a world grown young again as human beings unlearn historically acquired fear and hatred in favour of love, which Shelley called "the great secret" of all morality. A year later, he penned perhaps his best-known prose work, *A Defence of Poetry* (1821), which famously ends with the bold claim, "Poets are the unacknowledged legislators of the world."

Shelley's reputation was marred by personal as well as political scandal, not least because he abandoned his wife for Mary Godwin (later Mary Shelley, the author of *Frankenstein*), whom he married when his first wife committed suicide. Although he enjoyed scant fame or immediate influence during his lifetime, he has long been recognized as one of the most important poets of the Romantic era.

Ozymandias[1]

I met a traveller from an antique land
Who said: Two vast and trunkless legs of stone
Stand in the desert ... Near them, on the sand,
Half sunk, a shattered visage lies, whose frown,

---

1   *Ozymandias* Greek name for King Ramses II of Egypt (1304–1237 BCE). First century BCE Greek historian Diodorus Siculus records the story of this monument (Ozymandias's tomb was in the shape of a male sphinx) and its inscription, which Diodorus says reads: "King of Kings am I, Ozymandias. If anyone would know how great I am and where I lie, let him surpass one of my exploits."

5 And wrinkled lip, and sneer of cold command,
Tell that its sculptor well those passions read
Which yet survive, stamped on these lifeless things,
The hand that mocked them, and the heart that fed:
And on the pedestal these words appear:
10 "My name is Ozymandias, king of kings:
Look on my works, ye Mighty, and despair!"
Nothing beside remains. Round the decay
Of that colossal wreck, boundless and bare
The lone and level sands stretch far away.

—1818

Ode to the West Wind[1]

1

O Wild West Wind, thou breath of Autumn's being,
Thou, from whose unseen presence the leaves dead
Are driven, like ghosts from an enchanter fleeing,

Yellow, and black, and pale, and hectic° red,   *feverish*
5 Pestilence-stricken multitudes: O thou,
Who chariotest to their dark wintry bed

The wingèd seeds, where they lie cold and low,
Each like a corpse within its grave, until
Thine azure sister of the Spring shall blow

10 Her clarion[2] o'er the dreaming earth, and fill
(Driving sweet buds like flocks to feed in air)
With living hues and odours plain and hill:

Wild Spirit, which art moving everywhere;
Destroyer and Preserver; hear, oh, hear!

---

1 [Shelley's note] This poem was conceived and chiefly written in a wood that skirts the
   Arno, near Florence, and on a day when that tempestuous wind, whose temperature is
   at once mild and animating, was collecting the vapours which pour down the autumnal
   rains. They began, as I foresaw, at sunset with a violent tempest of hail and rain, attended by that magnificent thunder and lightning peculiar to the Cispaline regions.
2 *clarion* High-pitched trumpet.

2

Thou on whose stream, 'mid the steep sky's commotion,   15
Loose clouds like earth's decaying leaves are shed,
Shook from the tangled boughs of Heaven and Ocean,

Angels° of rain and lightning: there are spread   *harbingers*
On the blue surface of thine aëry surge,
Like the bright hair uplifted from the head   20

Of some fierce Mænad,[1] even from the dim verge
Of the horizon to the zenith's height,
The locks of the approaching storm. Thou dirge

Of the dying year, to which this closing night
Will be the dome of a vast sepulchre,   25
Vaulted with all thy congregated might

Of vapours,° from whose solid atmosphere   *clouds*
Black rain, and fire, and hail will burst: oh, hear!

3

Thou who didst waken from his summer dreams
The blue Mediterranean, where he lay,   30
Lulled by the coil of his chrystàlline streams,[2]

Beside a pumice isle in Baiae's bay,[3]
And saw in sleep old palaces and towers
Quivering within the wave's intenser day,

All overgrown with azure moss and flowers   35
So sweet, the sense faints picturing them! Thou
For whose path the Atlantic's level powers

---

1   *Mænad* Female attendant of Bacchus, the Greek god of wine.
2   *coil ... streams* Currents of the Mediterranean, the colours of which are often different
     from the surrounding water.
3   *pumice* Porous stone made from cooled lava; *Baiae's bay* Bay west of Naples that con-
     tains the ruins of several imperial villas.

Cleave themselves into chasms, while far below
The sea-blooms and the oozy woods which wear
40 The sapless foliage of the ocean, know

Thy voice, and suddenly grow grey with fear,
And tremble and despoil themselves:[1] oh, hear!

4

If I were a dead leaf thou mightest bear;
If I were a swift cloud to fly with thee;
45 A wave to pant beneath thy power, and share

The impulse of thy strength, only less free
Than thou, O uncontrollable! If even
I were as in my boyhood, and could be

The comrade of thy wanderings over Heaven,
50 As then, when to outstrip thy skiey° speed   *lofty*
Scarce seemed a vision; I would ne'er have striven

As thus with thee in prayer in my sore need.
Oh! lift me as a wave, a leaf, a cloud!
I fall upon the thorns of life! I bleed!

55 A heavy weight of hours has chained and bowed
One too like thee: tameless, and swift, and proud.

5

Make me thy lyre,[2] even as the forest is:
What if my leaves are falling like its own!
The tumult of thy mighty harmonies

---

1   [Shelley's note] The phenomenon alluded to at the conclusion of the third stanza is well known to naturalists. The vegetation at the bottom of the sea, of rivers, and of lakes, sympathizes with that of the land in the change of seasons, and is consequently influenced by the winds which announce it.

2   *lyre* Aeolian harp, a stringed instrument that produces music when exposed to wind.

Will take from both a deep, autumnal tone,   60
Sweet though in sadness. Be thou, Spirit fierce,
My spirit! Be thou me, impetuous one!

Drive my dead thoughts over the universe
Like withered leaves to quicken a new birth!
And, by the incantation of this verse,   65

Scatter, as from an unextinguished hearth
Ashes and sparks, my words among mankind!
Be through my lips to unawakened Earth

The trumpet of a prophecy! O, Wind,
If Winter comes, can Spring be far behind?
                                                              70
                              —1820

John Keats

1795–1821

John Keats has come to epitomize the popular conception of the Romantic poet as a passionate dreamer whose intense, sensuous poetry celebrates the world of the imagination over that of everyday life. Keats published only 54 poems in his short lifetime, but his work ranges across a number of poetic genres, including sonnets, odes, romances, and epics. His poetry often seeks a beauty and truth that will transcend the world of suffering, and often questions its own process of interpretation.

Keats, who died of tuberculosis at 25, often despaired of achieving the immortality he wanted for his work. In a note to his beloved, Fanny Brawne, he expresses regret that, "if I should die ... I have left no immortal work behind me—nothing to make my friends proud of my memory—but I have loved the principle of beauty in all things, and if I had had time I would have made myself remembered." Keats had scarcely a year to live when he wrote these words, but already he had completed, in an extraordinary surge of creativity, almost all the poetry on which his reputation rests, including "The Eve of St. Agnes," "La Belle Dame sans Merci," "Lamia," and his "great Odes," which remain among the highest expressions of the form in English.

Keats was also a highly skilled letter-writer, and his extensive correspondence, in which he reflects on aesthetics, the social role of the poet, and his own sense of poetic mission, reveals a nature acutely alive to the extremes of joy and heartbreak.

When I Have Fears that I May Cease to Be

When I have fears that I may cease to be
    Before my pen has glean'd my teeming brain,
Before high pilèd books, in charact'ry,[1]
    Hold like rich garners° the full-ripen'd grain;   *granaries*
5 When I behold, upon the night's starr'd face,
    Huge cloudy symbols of a high romance,
And think that I may never live to trace
    Their shadows, with the magic hand of chance;
And when I feel, fair creature of an hour!
10   That I shall never look upon thee more,
Never have relish in the fairy power
    Of unreflecting love;—then on the shore

---

1   *charact'ry* Symbols or letters.

Of the wide world I stand alone, and think
    Till love and fame to nothingness do sink.

           —1848 (written 1818)

La Belle Dame sans Merci:[1] A Ballad

O what can ail thee, knight-at-arms,
    Alone and palely loitering?
The sedge[2] has wither'd from the lake,
    And no birds sing.

O what can ail thee, knight-at-arms,   5
    So haggard and so woe-begone?
The squirrel's granary is full,
    And the harvest's done.

I see a lily[3] on thy brow
    With anguish moist and fever dew,   10
And on thy cheeks a fading rose
    Fast withereth too.

I met a lady in the meads,°   *meadows*
    Full beautiful, a fairy's child;
Her hair was long, her foot was light,   15
    And her eyes were wild.

I made a garland for her head,
    And bracelets too, and fragrant zone;°   *belt, girdle*
She look'd at me as she did love,
    And made sweet moan.   20

I set her on my pacing steed,
    And nothing else saw all day long,
For sidelong would she bend, and sing
    A faery's song.

---

1   *La Belle Dame sans Merci* French: The Beautiful Lady without Pity. This original version of the poem, found in a journal letter to George and Georgiana Keats, was first published in 1848. Keats's revised version was published in 1820.
2   *sedge* Rush-like grass.
3   *lily* Flower traditionally associated with death.

25 She found me roots of relish sweet,
　　　And honey wild, and manna dew,[1]
And sure in language strange she said
　　　"I love thee true."

She took me to her elfin grot,°　　　　　　　　　　　　　*grotto*
30　　　And there she wept, and sigh'd full sore,
And there I shut her wild wild eyes
　　　With kisses four.

And there she lulled me asleep,
　　　And there I dream'd—Ah! woe betide!
35 The latest° dream I ever dream'd　　　　　　　　　　　　*last*
　　　On the cold hill side.

I saw pale kings, and princes too,
　　　Pale warriors, death pale were they all;
They cried, "La belle dame sans merci
40　　　Hath thee in thrall!"

I saw their starv'd lips in the gloom°　　　　　　*gloaming, twilight*
　　　With horrid warning gaped wide,
And I awoke and found me here
　　　On the cold hill's side.

45 And this is why I sojourn here,
　　　Alone and palely loitering,
Though the sedge is wither'd from the lake,
　　　And no birds sing.

　　　　　　　　　　　　　　　—1848 (written 1819)

1　*manna dew* See Exodus 16, in which God provides the Israelites with a food that falls
　　from heaven, called manna.

Ode to a Nightingale

1

My heart aches, and a drowsy numbness pains
    My sense, as though of hemlock° I had drunk,   *poison*
    Or emptied some dull opiate to the drains
    One minute past, and Lethe-wards[1] had sunk:
'Tis not through envy of thy happy lot,   5
    But being too happy in thine happiness—
        That thou, light-winged Dryad° of the trees,   *wood-nymph*
           In some melodious plot
Of beechen green, and shadows numberless,
    Singest of summer in full-throated ease.   10

2

O, for a draught of vintage! that hath been
    Cool'd a long age in the deep-delved earth,
Tasting of Flora[2] and the country green,
    Dance, and Provençal[3] song, and sunburnt mirth!
O for a beaker full of the warm South,   15
    Full of the true, the blushful Hippocrene,[4]
        With beaded bubbles winking at the brim,
           And purple-stained mouth;
That I might drink, and leave the world unseen,
    And with thee fade away into the forest dim: 20

3

Fade far away, dissolve, and quite forget
    What thou among the leaves hast never known,
The weariness, the fever, and the fret
    Here, where men sit and hear each other groan;
Where palsy shakes a few, sad, last grey hairs,   25
    Where youth grows pale, and spectre-thin, and dies;
        Where but to think is to be full of sorrow
           And leaden-eyed despairs,

1   *Lethe-wards* In classical myth, Lethe was a river in Hades, the waters of which brought
    forgetfulness.
2   *Flora* Roman goddess of flowers.
3   *Provençal* From Provence, the region in France associated with troubadours.
4   *Hippocrene* Water from the spring on Mount Helicon, sacred to the Muses.

Where Beauty cannot keep her lustrous eyes,
30   Or new Love pine at them beyond to-morrow.

4

Away! away! for I will fly to thee,
      Not charioted by Bacchus and his pards,[1]
But on the viewless wings of Poesy,
      Though the dull brain perplexes and retards:
35 Already with thee! tender is the night,
      And haply° the Queen-Moon is on her throne,   *perhaps*
            Cluster'd around by all her starry Fays;°   *fairies*
                  But here there is no light,
Save what from heaven is with the breezes blown
40   Through verdurous glooms and winding mossy ways.

5

I cannot see what flowers are at my feet,
      Nor what soft incense hangs upon the boughs,
But, in embalmed° darkness, guess each sweet   *fragrant, perfumed*
      Wherewith the seasonable month endows
45 The grass, the thicket, and the fruit-tree wild;
      White hawthorn, and the pastoral eglantine;
            Fast fading violets cover'd up in leaves;
                  And mid-May's eldest child,
The coming musk-rose, full of dewy wine,
50   The murmurous haunt of flies on summer eves.

6

Darkling[2] I listen; and, for many a time
      I have been half in love with easeful Death,
Call'd him soft names in many a mused rhyme,
      To take into the air my quiet breath;
55 Now more than ever seems it rich to die,
      To cease upon the midnight with no pain,
            While thou art pouring forth thy soul abroad
                  In such an ecstasy!

---

1   *Bacchus and his pards* Bacchus, the Roman god of wine, rides a chariot drawn by leop-
    ards.
2   *Darkling* In the dark.

Still wouldst thou sing, and I have ears in vain—
    To thy high requiem become a sod.   60

7

Thou wast not born for death, immortal Bird!
    No hungry generations tread thee down;
The voice I hear this passing night was heard
    In ancient days by emperor and clown:°   *rustic*
Perhaps the self-same song that found a path   65
    Through the sad heart of Ruth,[1] when, sick for home,
        She stood in tears amid the alien corn;
           The same that oft-times hath
Charm'd magic casements, opening on the foam
    Of perilous seas, in faery lands forlorn.   70

8

Forlorn! the very word is like a bell
    To toll me back from thee to my sole self!
Adieu! the fancy cannot cheat so well
    As she is fam'd to do, deceiving elf.
Adieu! adieu! thy plaintive anthem fades   75
    Past the near meadows, over the still stream,
        Up the hill-side; and now 'tis buried deep
          In the next valley-glades:
Was it a vision, or a waking dream?
    Fled is that music—Do I wake or sleep?   80

                                 —1819

Ode on a Grecian Urn

1

Thou still unravish'd bride of quietness,
    Thou foster-child of silence and slow time,
Sylvan° historian, who canst thus express   *woodland*
    A flowery tale more sweetly than our rhyme:
What leaf-fring'd legend haunts about thy shape   5
    Of deities or mortals, or of both,

---

1   *Ruth* In the biblical story the widowed Ruth leaves her native Moab for Judah, there
helping her mother-in-law by working in the fields at harvest time.

In Tempe or the dales of Arcady?[1]
What men or gods are these? What maidens loth?°   *reluctant*
What mad pursuit? What struggle to escape?
10   What pipes and timbrels?° What wild ecstasy?[2]   *tambourines*

2

Heard melodies are sweet, but those unheard
   Are sweeter; therefore, ye soft pipes, play on;
Not to the sensual ear, but, more endear'd,
   Pipe to the spirit ditties of no tone:
15 Fair youth, beneath the trees, thou canst not leave
   Thy song, nor ever can those trees be bare;
      Bold lover, never, never canst thou kiss,
Though winning near the goal—yet, do not grieve;
   She cannot fade, though thou hast not thy bliss,
20   For ever wilt thou love, and she be fair!

3

Ah, happy, happy boughs! that cannot shed
   Your leaves, nor ever bid the Spring adieu;
And, happy melodist, unwearied,
   For ever piping songs for ever new;
25 More happy love! more happy, happy love!
   For ever warm and still to be enjoy'd,
      For ever panting, and for ever young;
All breathing human passion far above,
   That leaves a heart high-sorrowful and cloy'd,
30   A burning forehead, and a parching tongue.

4

Who are these coming to the sacrifice?
   To what green altar, O mysterious priest,
Lead'st thou that heifer lowing at the skies,
   And all her silken flanks with garlands drest?
35 What little town by river or sea shore,
   Or mountain-built with peaceful citadel,
      Is emptied of this folk, this pious morn?

---

1   *Tempe* Valley in ancient Greece renowned for its beauty; *Arcady* Ideal region of rural life, named for a mountainous district in Greece.
2   *What pipes ... ecstasy* This side of the vase seems to depict a Dionysian ritual, in which participants sometimes attained a state of frenzy.

And, little town, thy streets for evermore
    Will silent be, and not a soul to tell
        Why thou art desolate, can e'er return.   40

5

O Attic[1] shape! Fair attitude! with brede°   *interwoven design*
    Of marble men and maidens overwrought,°   *overlaid*
With forest branches and the trodden weed;
    Thou, silent form, dost tease us out of thought
As doth eternity: Cold Pastoral!   45
    When old age shall this generation waste,
        Thou shalt remain, in midst of other woe
Than ours, a friend to man, to whom thou say'st,
    "Beauty is truth, truth beauty,"—that is all
        Ye know on earth, and all ye need to know.   50

        —1820

To Autumn

1

Season of mists and mellow fruitfulness,
    Close bosom-friend of the maturing sun;
Conspiring with him how to load and bless
    With fruit the vines that round the thatch-eves run;
To bend with apples the moss'd cottage-trees,   5
    And fill all fruit with ripeness to the core;
        To swell the gourd, and plump the hazel shells
With a sweet kernel; to set budding more,
    And still more, later flowers for the bees,
    Until they think warm days will never cease,   10
        For Summer has o'er-brimm'd their clammy cells.

2

Who hath not seen thee oft amid thy store?
    Sometimes whoever seeks abroad may find
Thee sitting careless on a granary floor,
    Thy hair soft-lifted by the winnowing wind;   15
Or on a half-reap'd furrow sound asleep,

---

1   *Attic* From Attica, the region around Athens.

Drows'd with the fume of poppies, while thy hook°   *scythe*
    Spares the next swath and all its twined flowers:
And sometimes like a gleaner thou dost keep
20   Steady thy laden head across a brook;
    Or by a cyder-press, with patient look,
        Thou watchest the last oozings hours by hours.

3

Where are the songs of Spring? Ay, where are they?
    Think not of them, thou hast thy music too—
25 While barred clouds bloom the soft-dying day,
    And touch the stubble-plains with rosy hue;
Then in a wailful choir the small gnats mourn
    Among the river sallows,° borne aloft   *willows*
        Or sinking as the light wind lives or dies;
30 And full-grown lambs loud bleat from hilly bourn;°   *realm*
    Hedge-crickets sing; and now with treble soft
    The red-breast whistles from a garden-croft;°   *enclosed garden*
        And gathering swallows twitter in the skies.

—1820

Elizabeth Barrett Browning
1806–1861

Once considered for the position of Poet Laureate of England, Elizabeth Barrett Browning was a writer of tremendous versatility. Best known for her sonorous love poetry, she was also one of the foremost political poets of the nineteenth century.

When she was a child in Herefordshire, England, Barrett Browning's love of reading and writing was fostered by her parents. As an adolescent, she developed an unknown illness and became dependent on the opium she was prescribed, but in 1826 she published her first collection, *An Essay on Mind and Other Poems*. By the time she published her next book, *The Seraphim and Other Poems* (1838), she had begun to suffer from either bronchiectasis or tuberculosis. However, she continued to write prolifically and to maintain an active correspondence with other writers and critics; the scholar Marjorie Stone claims that "she literally wrote herself back to life."

Barrett Browning gained international recognition for her *Poems* (1844), admiration for which motivated her future husband, the poet Robert Browning, to write to her. The love poems published as *Sonnets from the Portuguese* (1850) were written during their courtship; though they were relatively unnoticed at first, before long they became her most famous work.

Barrett Browning also published several long poems, the most significant of which was the "verse-novel" *Aurora Leigh* (1856). An epic poem focused on the character of a woman writer, it encompasses Barrett Browning's convictions on desire, power, art, love, romance, race, class structures, and the subjugation of women. Although it was her most controversial work, the poem's many admirers included George Eliot and the critic John Ruskin, who called it the "greatest poem" of the century.

from *Sonnets from the Portuguese*

Sonnet 22

When our two souls stand up erect and strong,
Face to face, silent, drawing nigh and nigher,
Until the lengthening wings break into fire
At either curvèd point—what bitter wrong
Can the earth do to us, that we should not long   5
Be here contented? Think. In mounting higher,
The angels would press on us and aspire
To drop some golden orb of perfect song
Into our deep, dear silence. Let us stay

10 Rather on earth, Belovèd—where the unfit
   Contrarious moods of men recoil away
   And isolate pure spirits, and permit
   A place to stand and love in for a day,
   With darkness and the death-hour rounding it.

Sonnet 24

Let the world's sharpness like a clasping knife
Shut in upon itself and do no harm
In this close hand of Love, now soft and warm,
And let us hear no sound of human strife
5 After the click of the shutting. Life to life—
I lean upon thee, Dear, without alarm,
And feel as safe as guarded by a charm
Against the stab of worldlings, who if rife
Are weak to injure. Very whitely still
10 The lilies of our lives may reassure
Their blossoms from their roots, accessible
Alone to heavenly dews that drop not fewer;
Growing straight, out of man's reach, on the hill.
God only, who made us rich, can make us poor.

Sonnet 43

How do I love thee? Let me count the ways.
I love thee to the depth and breadth and height
My soul can reach, when feeling out of sight
For the ends of Being and ideal Grace.
5 I love thee to the level of everyday's
Most quiet need, by sun and candlelight.
I love thee freely, as men strive for Right;
I love thee purely, as they turn from Praise.
I love thee with the passion put to use
10 In my old griefs, and with my childhood's faith.
I love thee with a love I seemed to lose
With my lost saints—I love thee with the breath,
Smiles, tears, of all my life!—and, if God choose,
I shall but love thee better after death.

—1850

Edgar Allan Poe
1809–1849

Edgar Allan Poe is one of antebellum America's most famous and controversial literary figures. Dubbed "the Leader of the Cult of the Unusual" by Jules Verne, Poe continues to be regarded as a haunted and enigmatic outcast, a public image he himself cultivated following his childhood hero, the poet Lord Byron.

Contemporary reviewers often identified Poe with the manic, mentally unhinged narrators of stories such as "The Tell-Tale Heart" (1843) and "The Black Cat" (1843), attributing his preoccupation with the perverse impulses and abysmal depths of the mind to a moral defect in his character. A notorious obituary by his literary executor, which depicted him as a mad and melancholy lost soul, his "heart gnawed by anguish," his "face shrouded in gloom," did much to establish the legend of Poe as an erratic and disturbed outsider. More recently, psychoanalytic critics—not least Freud himself—have made prooftexts of his poems and tales, speculating that Poe, who famously declared the death of a beautiful woman "the most poetical topic in the world," never overcame the loss of his mother, foster mother, and young wife, whose ghosts return in works such as "Ligeia" (1838), "The Raven" (1845), and "Annabel Lee" (1849).

Of all Poe's poetic creations, "The Raven" remains the best known and most beloved. Widely reprinted and parodied in his lifetime, the poem made him famous but did little to relieve his near constant poverty. Poe offered a meticulous, if at times tongue-in-cheek, account of the poem's construction in "The Philosophy of Composition," an essay in which he rejects the Romantic notion that poetry is born of a "fine frenzy" of spontaneous creativity. The burnished formalism of "The Raven"—its incantatory metre, sonorous diction, tightly controlled rhyme scheme, and famous refrain—is a testament to Poe's belief in the primacy of method and craft over "ecstatic intuition."

The Raven

Once upon a midnight dreary, while I pondered, weak and weary,
Over many a quaint and curious volume of forgotten lore—
While I nodded, nearly napping, suddenly there came a tapping,
As of some one gently rapping, rapping at my chamber door.
"'Tis some visitor," I muttered, "tapping at my chamber door—   5
          Only this and nothing more."

Ah, distinctly I remember it was in the bleak December,
And each separate dying ember wrought its ghost upon the floor.

Eagerly I wished the morrow;—vainly I had sought to borrow
10   From my books surcease of sorrow—sorrow for the lost Lenore[1]—
For the rare and radiant maiden whom the angels name Lenore—
                  Nameless here for evermore.

And the silken sad uncertain rustling of each purple curtain
Thrilled me—filled me with fantastic terrors never felt before;
15   So that now, to still the beating of my heart, I stood repeating
"'Tis some visitor entreating entrance at my chamber door—
Some late visitor entreating entrance at my chamber door;—
                  This it is and nothing more."

Presently my soul grew stronger; hesitating then no longer;
20   "Sir," said I, "or Madam, truly your forgiveness I implore;
But the fact is I was napping, and so gently you came rapping,
And so faintly you came tapping, tapping at my chamber door,
That I scarce was sure I heard you"—here I opened wide the door;—
                  Darkness there and nothing more.

25   Deep into that darkness peering, long I stood there wondering, fearing,
Doubting, dreaming dreams no mortal ever dared to dream before;
But the silence was unbroken, and the stillness gave no token,
And the only word there spoken was the whispered word, "Lenore!"
This *I* whispered, and an echo murmured back the word "Lenore!"
30   Merely this and nothing more.

Back into the chamber turning, all my soul within me burning,
Soon again I heard a tapping somewhat louder than before.
"Surely," said I, "surely that is something at my window lattice;
Let me see, then, what thereat is, and this mystery explore—
35   Let my heart be still a moment and this mystery explore;—
                  'Tis the wind and nothing more!"

Open here I flung the shutter, when, with many a flirt and flutter,
In there stepped a stately raven of the saintly days of yore;
Not the least obeisance made he; not a minute stopped or stayed he;
40   But, with mien of lord or lady, perched above my chamber door—
Perched upon a bust of Pallas[2] just above my chamber door—
                  Perched, and sat, and nothing more.

---

1   *Lenore* Poe's poem "Lenore" (1831) dramatizes the death of a young woman mourned by her lover.
2   *Pallas* Pallas Athena, Greek goddess of wisdom.

Then this ebony bird beguiling my sad fancy into smiling,
By the grave and stern decorum of the countenance it wore,
"Though thy crest be shorn and shaven, thou," I said, "art sure no craven,   45
Ghastly grim and ancient raven wandering from the Nightly shore—
Tell me what thy lordly name is on the Night's Plutonian[1] shore!"
                              Quoth the raven "Nevermore."

Much I marvelled this ungainly fowl to hear discourse so plainly,
Though its answer little meaning—little relevancy bore;   50
For we cannot help agreeing that no living human being
Ever yet was blessed with seeing bird above his chamber door—
Bird or beast upon the sculptured bust above his chamber door,
                              With such name as "Nevermore."

But the raven, sitting lonely on the placid bust, spoke only   55
That one word, as if his soul in that one word he did outpour.
Nothing farther then he uttered—not a feather then he fluttered—
Till I scarcely more than muttered "Other friends have flown before—
On the morrow *he* will leave me, as my hopes have flown before."
                              Then the bird said "Nevermore."   60

Startled at the stillness broken by reply so aptly spoken,
"Doubtless," said I, "what it utters is its only stock and store
Caught from some unhappy master whom unmerciful Disaster
Followed fast and followed faster till his songs one burden[2] bore—
Till the dirges of his Hope that melancholy burden bore   65
                              Of 'Never—nevermore.'"

But the raven still beguiling all my sad soul into smiling.
Straight I wheeled a cushioned seat in front of bird, and bust and door;
Then, upon the velvet sinking, I betook myself to linking
Fancy unto fancy, thinking what this ominous bird of yore—   70
What this grim, ungainly, ghastly, gaunt, and ominous bird of yore
                              Meant in croaking "Nevermore."

This I sat engaged in guessing, but no syllable expressing
To the fowl whose fiery eyes now burned into my bosom's core;
This and more I sat divining, with my head at ease reclining   75
On the cushion's velvet lining that the lamplight gloated° o'er,   *refracted*
But whose velvet violet lining with the lamplight gloating o'er,
                              She shall press, ah, nevermore!

---

1   *Plutonian* In Roman mythology, Pluto is god of the underworld.
2   *burden* Theme; in a poem or song, chorus or refrain.

Then, methought, the air grew denser, perfumed from an unseen censer
80 Swung by angels whose faint foot-falls tinkled on the tufted[1] floor.
"Wretch," I cried, "thy God hath lent thee—by these angels he hath
       sent thee
Respite—respite and nepenthe[2] from thy memories of Lenore!
Quaff, oh quaff this kind nepenthe and forget this lost Lenore!"
                             Quoth the raven "Nevermore."

85 "Prophet!" said I, "thing of evil!—prophet still, if bird or devil!—
Whether Tempter sent, or whether tempest tossed thee here ashore,
Desolate yet all undaunted, on this desert land enchanted—
On this home by Horror haunted—tell me truly, I implore—
Is there—*is* there balm in Gilead?[3]—tell me—tell me, I implore!"
90   Quoth the raven "Nevermore."

"Prophet!" said I, "thing of evil!—prophet still, if bird or devil!
By that Heaven that bends above us—by that God we both adore—
Tell this soul with sorrow laden if, within the distant Aidenn,°   *Eden*
It shall clasp a sainted maiden whom the angels name Lenore—
95 Clasp a rare and radiant maiden whom the angels name Lenore."
                             Quoth the raven "Nevermore."

"Be that word our sign of parting, bird or fiend!" I shrieked, upstarting—
"Get thee back into the tempest and the Night's Plutonian shore!
Leave no black plume as a token of that lie thy soul hath spoken!
100 Leave my loneliness unbroken!—quit the bust above my door!
Take thy beak from out my heart, and take thy form from off my door!"
                             Quoth the raven "Nevermore."

And the raven, never flitting, still is sitting, *still* is sitting
On the pallid bust of Pallas just above my chamber door;
105 And his eyes have all the seeming of a demon's that is dreaming,
And the lamp-light o'er him streaming throws his shadow on the floor;
And my soul from out that shadow that lies floating on the floor
                             Shall be lifted—nevermore!

                                                      —1845

---

1   *tufted* I.e., carpeted.
2   *nepenthe* Drink supposed to banish sorrow by inducing forgetfulness.
3   *Is there … Gilead* See Jeremiah 8.22: "Is there no balm in Gilead?"; *balm* Soothing oint-
     ment; *Gilead* In the Bible, the land east of the River Jordan.

Alfred, Lord Tennyson
1809–1892

More than any other poet, Alfred, Lord Tennyson gave voice to the ambitions, anxieties, and myths of the Victorian era; he was Poet Laureate of the United Kingdom for 42 years.

Born in 1809 to a privileged, somewhat eccentric family, Tennyson decided early on that poetry was his true vocation. He left the University of Cambridge without taking a degree and devoted himself to writing in a variety of poetic forms, among them dramatic monologues (such as "Ulysses," 1842), short lyrics (such as "Tears, Idle Tears," 1847), and retellings of Arthurian narratives (such as "The Lady of Shalott," 1832). The year 1850 was trebly significant for Tennyson: after a 14-year courtship, he married Emily Sellwood; he was named Poet Laureate; and he published *In Memoriam A.H.H.*, a long, reflective poem in memory of his friend Arthur Hallam that was immediately recognized as his most important work.

Tennyson's appearance conveyed a solemn sense of respectability, and his poetry often deals with issues such as the individual's responsibility to society. But both his personality and his poetry are multi-dimensional; in much of his work, anxieties over sexuality, violence, and death lie close to the surface. Perhaps because of his engagement with such concepts, Tennyson was no stranger to controversy. For example, his long poem *Maud* (1855), which ends with the tormented protagonist departing for the Crimea and "the blood-red blossom of war," was attacked by several reviewers (the writer George Eliot notable among them) for allegedly expressing a "hatred of peace."

Tennyson's verse has often been praised for its "verbal music," although his reading voice was an urgent rattle. His voice may still be heard: not long before he died, he was recorded by Thomas Edison reading "The Charge of the Light Brigade" and a few other poems.

The Lady of Shalott[1]

PART 1

On either side the river lie
Long fields of barley and of rye,
That clothe the wold° and meet the sky;   *plain*
And through the field the road runs by

---

1   *The Lady of Shalott* Elaine of the Arthurian romances, who dies of love for Lancelot; she is called "the lily maid of Astolat" in Malory's *Morte Darthur* (1485). Tennyson first encountered the story, however, in a medieval Italian romance called "La Donna di Scalotta" and changed the name to Shalott for a softer sound.

5   To many-towered Camelot;
And up and down the people go,
Gazing where the lilies blow
Round an island there below,
       The island of Shalott.

10 Willows whiten,[1] aspens quiver,
Little breezes dusk° and shiver   *darken*
Through the wave that runs for ever
By the island in the river
       Flowing down to Camelot.
15 Four grey walls, and four grey towers,
Overlook a space of flowers,
And the silent isle imbowers°   *encloses*
       The Lady of Shalott.

By the margin, willow-veiled,
20 Slide the heavy barges trailed
By slow horses; and unhailed
The shallop[2] flitteth silken-sailed
       Skimming down to Camelot:
But who hath seen her wave her hand?
25 Or at the casement seen her stand?
Or is she known in all the land,
       The Lady of Shalott?

Only reapers, reaping early
In among the bearded barley,
30 Hear a song that echoes cheerly
From the river winding clearly,
       Down to towered Camelot:
And by the moon the reaper weary,
Piling sheaves in uplands airy,
35 Listening, whispers "'Tis the fairy
       Lady of Shalott."

PART 2

There she weaves by night and day
A magic web with colours gay.
She has heard a whisper say,
40 A curse is on her if she stay

---

1   *Willows whiten* I.e., the wind exposes the white undersides of the leaves.
2   *shallop* Light open boat for use in shallow water.

To look down to Camelot.
She knows not what the curse may be,
And so she weaveth steadily,
And little other care hath she,
    The Lady of Shalott.   45

And moving through a mirror clear
That hangs before her all the year,
Shadows of the world appear.
There she sees the highway near
    Winding down to Camelot: 50
There the river eddy whirls,
And there the surly village-churls,
And the red cloaks of market girls,
    Pass onward from Shalott.

Sometimes a troop of damsels glad,   55
An abbot on an ambling pad,°   *horse*
Sometimes a curly shepherd-lad,
Or long-haired page in crimson clad,
    Goes by to towered Camelot;
And sometimes through the mirror blue   60
The knights come riding two and two:
She hath no loyal knight and true,
    The Lady of Shalott.

But in her web she still delights
To weave the mirror's magic sights,
For often through the silent nights   65
A funeral, with plumes and lights
    And music, went to Camelot:
Or when the moon was overhead,
Came two young lovers lately wed;   70
"I am half sick of shadows," said
    The Lady of Shalott.

PART 3

A bow-shot from her bower-eaves,
He rode between the barley-sheaves,
The sun came dazzling through the leaves,   75
And flamed upon the brazen greaves[1]
    Of bold Sir Lancelot.

---

1 *greaves* Armour worn below the knee.

A red-cross knight for ever kneeled
To a lady in his shield,
80 That sparkled on the yellow field,
    Beside remote Shalott.

The gemmy° bridle glittered free,   *brilliant*
Like to some branch of stars we see
Hung in the golden Galaxy.
85 The bridle bells rang merrily
    As he rode down to Camelot:
And from his blazoned baldric° slung   *shoulder-strap*
A mighty silver bugle hung,
And as he rode his armour rung,
90   Beside remote Shalott.

All in the blue unclouded weather
Thick-jewelled shone the saddle-leather,
The helmet and the helmet-feather
Burned like one burning flame together,
95   As he rode down to Camelot.
As often through the purple night,
Below the starry clusters bright,
Some bearded meteor, trailing light,
    Moves over still Shalott.

100 His broad clear brow in sunlight glowed;
On burnished hooves his war-horse trode;
From underneath his helmet flowed
His coal-black curls as on he rode,
    As he rode down to Camelot.
105 From the bank and from the river
He flashed into the crystal mirror,
"Tirra lirra," by the river
    Sang Sir Lancelot.

She left the web, she left the loom,
110 She made three paces through the room,
She saw the water-lily bloom,
She saw the helmet and the plume,
    She looked down to Camelot.
Out flew the web and floated wide;
115 The mirror cracked from side to side;
"The curse is come upon me," cried
    The Lady of Shalott.

PART 4

In the stormy east-wind straining,
The pale yellow woods were waning,
The broad stream in his banks complaining,   120
Heavily the low sky raining
    Over towered Camelot;
Down she came and found a boat
Beneath a willow left afloat,
And round about the prow she wrote   125
    The Lady of Shalott.

And down the river's dim expanse
Like some bold seer in a trance,
Seeing all his own mischance—
With a glassy countenance   130
    Did she look to Camelot.
And at the closing of the day
She loosed the chain, and down she lay;
The broad stream bore her far away,
    The Lady of Shalott.   135

Lying, robed in snowy white
That loosely flew to left and right—
The leaves upon her falling light—
Through the noises of the night
    She floated down to Camelot: 140
And as the boat-head wound along
The willowy hills and fields among,
They heard her singing her last song,
    The Lady of Shalott.

Heard a carol, mournful, holy,   145
Chanted loudly, chanted lowly,
Till her blood was frozen slowly,
And her eyes were darkened wholly,
    Turned to towered Camelot.
For ere she reached upon the tide   150
The first house by the water-side,
Singing in her song she died,
    The Lady of Shalott.

Under tower and balcony,
By garden-wall and gallery,   155

A gleaming shape she floated by,
Dead-pale between the houses high,
　　Silent into Camelot.
Out upon the wharfs they came,
160　Knight and burgher, lord and dame,
And round the prow they read her name,
　　The Lady of Shalott.

Who is this? and what is here?
And in the lighted palace near
165　Died the sound of royal cheer;
And they crossed themselves for fear,
　　All the knights at Camelot:
But Lancelot mused a little space;
He said, "She has a lovely face;
170　God in his mercy lend her grace,
　　The Lady of Shalott."

　　　　　　　　　　　　—1832 (revised 1842)

John William Waterhouse, The Lady of Shalott, 1888. *The Lady of Shalott was a frequent subject for art in the nineteenth century; perhaps the most famous example is Waterhouse's painting.*

Ulysses[1]

It little profits that an idle king,
By this still hearth, among these barren crags,
Matched with an agèd wife, I mete and dole
Unequal laws unto a savage race,
That hoard, and sleep, and feed, and know not me.   5
I cannot rest from travel: I will drink
Life to the lees:° all times I have enjoyed   *dregs*
Greatly, have suffered greatly, both with those
That loved me, and alone; on shore, and when
Thro' scudding drifts the rainy Hyades[2]   10
Vexed the dim sea: I am become a name;
For always roaming with a hungry heart
Much have I seen and known; cities of men
And manners, climates, councils, governments,
Myself not least, but honoured of them all;   15
And drunk delight of battle with my peers,
Far on the ringing plains of windy Troy.
I am a part of all that I have met;
Yet all experience is an arch wherethrough
Gleams that untravelled world, whose margin° fades   *horizon*   20
For ever and for ever when I move.
How dull it is to pause, to make an end,
To rust unburnished, not to shine in use!
As though to breathe were life. Life piled on life
Were all too little, and of one to me   25
Little remains: but every hour is saved
From that eternal silence, something more,
A bringer of new things; and vile it were
For some three suns to store and hoard myself,
And this grey spirit yearning in desire   30
To follow knowledge like a sinking star,
Beyond the utmost bound of human thought.

     This is my son, mine own Telemachus,
To whom I leave the sceptre and the isle—

---

1   *Ulysses* Latin name for Odysseus, the protagonist of Homer's *Odyssey*. Here, long after
     the adventures recounted in that poem, the aged, yet restless Ulysses prepares to em-
     bark on one last voyage.
2   *Hyades* Group of stars near the constellation Taurus and associated with rainstorms.

35 Well-loved of me, discerning to fulfil
    This labour, by slow prudence to make mild
    A rugged people, and through soft degrees
    Subdue them to the useful and the good.
    Most blameless is he, centred in the sphere
40 Of common duties, decent not to fail
    In offices of tenderness, and pay
    Meet° adoration to my household gods,   *appropriate*
    When I am gone. He works his work, I mine.

        There lies the port; the vessel puffs her sail:
45 There gloom the dark broad seas. My mariners,
    Souls that have toiled, and wrought, and thought with me—
    That ever with a frolic welcome took
    The thunder and the sunshine, and opposed
    Free hearts, free foreheads—you and I are old;
50 Old age hath yet his honour and his toil;
    Death closes all: but something ere the end,
    Some work of noble note, may yet be done,
    Not unbecoming men that strove with Gods.
    The lights begin to twinkle from the rocks:
55 The long day wanes: the slow moon climbs: the deep
    Moans round with many voices. Come, my friends,
    'Tis not too late to seek a newer world.
    Push off, and sitting well in order smite
    The sounding furrows; for my purpose holds
60 To sail beyond the sunset, and the baths
    Of all the western stars, until I die.
    It may be that the gulfs will wash us down:
    It may be we shall touch the Happy Isles,[1]
    And see the great Achilles,[2] whom we knew.
65 Though much is taken, much abides; and though
    We are not now that strength which in old days
    Moved earth and heaven; that which we are, we are;
    One equal temper of heroic hearts,
    Made weak by time and fate, but strong in will
70 To strive, to seek, to find, and not to yield.

                                        —1842 (written 1833)

---

1   *Happy Isles* Elysium, or Isles of the Blessed, where heroes enjoyed the afterlife.
2   *Achilles* Hero from Greek mythology, also the central character of Homer's *Iliad*.

The Charge of the Light Brigade[1]

1

Half a league,[2] half a league,
Half a league onward,
All in the valley of Death
    Rode the six hundred.[3]
"Forward, the Light Brigade!   5
Charge for the guns!" he said:
Into the valley of Death
    Rode the six hundred.

2

"Forward, the Light Brigade!"
Was there a man dismayed?   10
Not though the soldier knew
    Some one had blundered:
Theirs not to make reply,
Theirs not to reason why,
Theirs but to do and die: 15
Into the valley of Death
    Rode the six hundred.

3

Cannon to right of them,
Cannon to left of them,
Cannon in front of them   20
    Volleyed and thundered;
Stormed at with shot and shell,
Boldly they rode and well,

---

1   *The Charge ... Brigade* Written some weeks after a disastrous engagement during the
    Crimean War. At the Battle of Balaclava on 25 October 1854, the 700 cavalrymen of
    the Light Brigade, acting on a misinterpreted order, directly charged the Russian artil-
    lery.
2   *league* About three miles.
3   *six hundred* The initial newspaper account read by Tennyson mentioned "607 sabres,"
    and he retained the number even when the correct number was discovered to be con-
    siderably higher because "six is much better than seven hundred ... metrically" (*Letters*
    2.101).

Into the jaws of Death,
25 Into the mouth of Hell
    Rode the six hundred.

4

Flashed all their sabres bare,
Flashed as they turned in air
Sabring the gunners there,
30 Charging an army, while
    All the world wondered:
Plunged in the battery-smoke
Right through the line they broke;
Cossack and Russian
35 Reeled from the sabre-stroke
    Shattered and sundered.
Then they rode back, but not
    Not the six hundred.

5

Cannon to right of them,
40 Cannon to left of them,
Cannon behind them
    Volleyed and thundered;
Stormed at with shot and shell,
While horse and hero fell,
45 They that had fought so well
Came through the jaws of Death,
Back from the mouth of Hell,
All that was left of them,[1]
    Left of six hundred.

6

50 When can their glory fade?
O the wild charge they made!
    All the world wondered.
Honour the charge they made!
Honour the Light Brigade,
55   Noble six hundred!

—1854

---

1   *All ... them* 118 men were killed and 127 wounded; after the charge, only 195 men were still with their horses.

Roger Fenton, Cookhouse of the 8th Hussars, *1855. In the Crimean War (1853–56), waged primarily on the Crimean Peninsula in Eastern Europe, the Russian Empire fought a group of allies that included the French, British, and Ottoman Empires. The Crimean War was the first to be photographed extensively, but both the technology of the time and the demands of Victorian taste prevented photographers from shooting scenes of battle directly. This photograph depicts the 8th Hussars, a regiment of Irish cavalry, preparing a meal.*

Roger Fenton, Valley of the Shadow of Death, *1855. This image, one of the most famous photographs of the Crimean War, came to be closely associated with Tennyson's famous 1854 poem "The Charge of the Light Brigade." The valley in the photograph is not the place where the charge occurred but another valley in the vicinity—one that soldiers had begun to call "the valley of the shadow of death" (in an echo both of Tennyson's poem and of the Bible) because of the frequency with which the Russians shelled it.*

Robert Browning

1812–1889

Robert Browning was not a popular poet for much of his lifetime. His poetry, in the eyes of many of his contemporaries, was far too obscure, littered as it was with recondite historical and literary references and with dubious subject matter—husbands murdering their wives, artists frolicking with prostitutes. Fame did come, however, and scholars now credit Browning for having realized new possibilities in the dramatic monologue, a form of poetry that, like a monologue in a dramatic production, showcases the speech of a character to an implied or imaginary audience.

Browning was born to a relatively wealthy family, and his father provided him with a rich home education, an extensive personal library, and financial support that allowed him to dedicate himself to writing. He gained moderate critical attention with the dramatic poem *Paracelsus* (1835), but most found his next long narrative poem, *Sordello* (1840), to be incomprehensible. His next volume, *Dramatic Lyrics* (1842), was more successful; it included now-famous shorter poems such as "My Last Duchess" and "Porphyria's Lover."

In 1845 Browning began corresponding with the poet Elizabeth Barrett, and the following year they eloped to Italy. Although their marriage was a happy and intensely devoted one, Browning wrote little during this time, with the notable exception of the short collection *Men and Women* (1855).

After his wife's death in 1861, Browning returned to London society, where he produced several volumes that would at last make him popular among British readers. These works included his 12-part epic "murder-poem" (as Browning called it), *The Ring and the Book* (1868–69), which told the story of a 1698 Italian murder trial in the voices of multiple characters. The 1879–80 volumes of *Dramatic Idyls* brought the poet even greater fame, both in England and internationally. Browning was at the peak of his popularity during the last decade of his life.

My Last Duchess[1]

Ferrara

That's my last Duchess painted on the wall,
Looking as if she were alive. I call
That piece a wonder, now: Fra Pandolf's[2] hands
Worked busily a day, and there she stands.
Will't please you sit and look at her? I said   5
"Fra Pandolf" by design, for never read
Strangers like you that pictured countenance,
The depth and passion of its earnest glance,
But to myself they turned (since none puts by
The curtain I have drawn for you, but I)   10
And seemed as they would ask me, if they durst,
How such a glance came there; so, not the first
Are you to turn and ask thus. Sir, 'twas not
Her husband's presence only, called that spot
Of joy into the Duchess' cheek: perhaps   15
Fra Pandolf chanced to say "Her mantle laps
Over my lady's wrist too much," or "Paint
Must never hope to reproduce the faint
Half-flush that dies along her throat": such stuff
Was courtesy, she thought, and cause enough   20
For calling up that spot of joy. She had
A heart—how shall I say?—too soon made glad,
Too easily impressed; she liked whate'er
She looked on, and her looks went everywhere.
Sir, 'twas all one! My favour at her breast,[3]   25
The dropping of the daylight in the West,
The bough of cherries some officious fool
Broke in the orchard for her, the white mule
She rode with round the terrace—all and each
Would draw from her alike the approving speech,   30
Or blush, at least. She thanked men—good! but thanked

---

1   *My Last Duchess* Based on events in the life of Alfonso II, first Duke of Ferrara, Italy, whose first wife died in 1561 under suspicious circumstances after three years of marriage. Upon her death, the Duke entered into negotiations with an agent of Count Ferdinand I of Tyrol, whose daughter he married in 1565.

2   *Fra Pandolf* Brother Pandolf, an imaginary painter, just as "Claus of Innsbruck" (line 56) is an imaginary sculptor.

3   *My favour at her breast* I.e., a scarf or ribbon decorated with the Duke's heraldic colours or armorial bearings.

Somehow—I know not how—as if she ranked
My gift of a nine-hundred-years-old name
With anybody's gift. Who'd stoop to blame
35 This sort of trifling? Even had you skill
In speech—(which I have not)—to make your will
Quite clear to such an one, and say, "Just this
Or that in you disgusts me; here you miss,
Or there exceed the mark"—and if she let
40 Herself be lessoned so, nor plainly set
Her wits to yours, forsooth, and made excuse,
—E'en then would be some stooping; and I choose
Never to stoop. Oh sir, she smiled, no doubt,
Whene'er I passed her; but who passed without
45 Much the same smile? This grew; I gave commands;
Then all smiles stopped together. There she stands
As if alive. Will't please you rise? We'll meet
The company below, then. I repeat,
The Count your master's known munificence
50 Is ample warrant that no just pretence
Of mine for dowry will be disallowed;
Though his fair daughter's self, as I avowed
At starting, is my object. Nay, we'll go
Together down, sir. Notice Neptune,[1] though,
55 Taming a sea-horse, thought a rarity,
Which Claus of Innsbruck cast in bronze for me!

—1842

---

1   *Neptune* Roman god of the sea, who rides in a chariot pulled by seahorses.

Emily Brontë
1818–1848

It would seem that there were two Emily Brontës: one a shy, introverted, and unremarkable young woman, and the other the strong-willed, brilliant, and legendary woman who became almost a mythic figure after her death at the age of 30. Both versions develop from the impressions her sister Charlotte gave of her in the preface to the 1850 edition of Emily's only novel, *Wuthering Heights*. For many years it was this work for which she was best known; it was not until the start of the twentieth century that her poetry began to receive serious critical attention.

The fifth of six children born to a literary-minded Anglican clergyman, Brontë grew up in a village in the moors of West Yorkshire—a landscape that is frequently reflected in her poetic imagery. Her literary talent flourished in a house of creative writers that included her sisters Charlotte (author of *Jane Eyre*) and Anne (author of *The Tenant of Wildfell Hall*). As adults, the three sisters collaborated on a volume of poetry, which they published pseudonymously as *The Poems of Currer, Ellis, and Acton Bell* (1846); though its significance is recognized today, the edition published by the sisters sold only two copies.

Wuthering Heights and much of Brontë's poetry share a bleak tone and a preoccupation with passion, loss, and death, yet her poems exhibit a degree of tenderness not evident in her novel. Many explore an existence free of the restraints of everyday life, though attainable only through imagination—a tendency that connects Brontë to her Romantic predecessors more than to her Victorian contemporaries.

Brontë died of tuberculosis in December 1848, only one year after the publication of *Wuthering Heights*. Charlotte Brontë championed her sister's poetic reputation after Emily's death, arguing that the poems evoke the stirrings of the "heart like the sound of a trumpet."

[Ah! why, because the dazzling sun]

Ah! why, because the dazzling sun
Restored my earth to joy
Have you departed, every one,
And left a desert sky?

5 All through the night, your glorious eyes
Were gazing down in mine,
And with a full heart's thankful sighs

I blessed that watch divine!

I was at peace, and drank your beams
10 As they were life to me
And revelled in my changeful dreams
Like petrel[1] on the sea.

Thought followed thought—star followed star
Through boundless regions on,
15 While one sweet influence, near and far,
Thrilled through and proved us one.

Why did the morning rise to break
So great, so pure a spell,
And scorch with fire the tranquil cheek
20 Where your cool radiance fell?

Blood-red he rose, and arrow-straight,
His fierce beams struck my brow;
The soul of Nature sprang elate,
But mine sank sad and low!

25 My lids closed down—yet through their veil
I saw him blazing still;
And bathe in gold the misty dale,
And flash upon the hill.

I turned me to the pillow then
30 To call back Night, and see
Your worlds of solemn light, again
Throb with my heart and me!

It would not do—the pillow glowed
And glowed both roof and floor,
35 And birds sang loudly in the wood,
And fresh winds shook the door.

The curtains waved, the wakened flies
Were murmuring round my room,

---

1   *petrel* Type of seabird, such as a storm petrel or an albatross.

Imprisoned there, till I should rise
And give them leave to roam.   40

O Stars and Dreams and Gentle Night;
O Night and Stars return!
And hide me from the hostile light
That does not warm, but burn—

That drains the blood of suffering men;   45
Drinks tears, instead of dew:
Let me sleep through his blinding reign,
And only wake with you!

                                                —1846

[No coward soul is mine]

No coward soul is mine
No trembler in the world's storm-troubled sphere
I see Heaven's glories shine
And Faith shines equal arming me from Fear

O God within my breast   5
Almighty ever-present Deity
Life, that in me hast rest
As I Undying Life, have power in Thee

Vain are the thousand creeds
That move men's hearts, unutterably vain,   10
Worthless as withered weeds
Or idlest froth amid the boundless main°   *sea*

To waken doubt in one
Holding so fast by thy infinity
So surely anchored on   15
The steadfast rock of Immortality.

With wide-embracing love
Thy spirit animates eternal years
Pervades and broods above,
Changes, sustains, dissolves, creates and rears   20

Though Earth and moon were gone
And suns and universes ceased to be
And thou wert left alone
Every Existence would exist in thee

25 There is not room for Death
Nor atom that his might could render void
Since thou art Being and Breath
And what thou art may never be destroyed.

—1850 (written 1846)

[Often rebuked, yet always back returning][1]

Often rebuked, yet always back returning
    To those first feelings that were born with me,
And leaving busy chase of wealth and learning
    For idle dreams of things which cannot be:

5 Today, I will seek not the shadowy region;
    Its unsustaining vastness waxes drear;
And visions rising, legion after legion,
    Bring the unreal world too strangely near.

I'll walk, but not in old heroic traces,
10   And not in paths of high morality,
And not among the half-distinguished faces,
    The clouded forms of long-past history.

I'll walk where my own nature would be leading:
    It vexes me to choose another guide:
15 Where the grey flocks in ferny glens are feeding;
    Where the wild wind blows on the mountain side.

What have those lonely mountains worth revealing?
    More glory and more grief than I can tell:
The earth that wakes *one* human heart to feeling
20   Can centre both the worlds of Heaven and Hell.

—1850

---

1   [*Often ... returning*] The authorship of this poem has been variously credited to Emily,
    Charlotte, and Anne Brontë; when the poem was first printed, under the title "Stanzas,"
    it was recorded as having been written by Emily.

[I'll come when thou art saddest]

I'll come when thou art saddest,
Laid alone in the darkened room;
When the mad day's mirth has vanished.
And the smile of joy is banished
From evening's chilly gloom.   5

I'll come when the heart's real feeling
Has entire, unbiased sway,
And my influence o'er thee stealing,
Grief deepening, joy congealing,
Shall bear thy soul away.   10

Listen! 'tis just the hour,
The awful time for thee:
Dost thou not feel upon thy soul
A flood of strange sensations roll,
Forerunners of a sterner power,   15
Heralds of me?

—1902 (written 1837)

Walt Whitman
1819–1892

An essayist, journalist, school teacher, nurse, wanderer, and lover of the natural world, Walt Whitman is best known for his ground-breaking and influential work of poetry, *Leaves of Grass* (1855–92). Although it addresses universal subjects such as selfhood, nature, and the body, Whitman intended his work primarily as a contribution to the establishment of a uniquely American literature "with neither foreign spirit, nor imagery nor form, but adapted to our case, ... strengthening and intensifying the national soul."

Whitman was born to working-class parents near Hempstead, Long Island, and the family moved to Brooklyn when he was still a child. He received six years of public school education before providing himself with an informal education in a variety of subjects using publicly available resources in New York City. As a young man, he worked as a journalist and editor and became involved with the Democratic Party; this background is reflected in the frequent political focus of *Leaves of Grass*.

A provocative work in its time, *Leaves of Grass* was criticized for its informal diction, nontraditional metre, and overt references to sex and the body, but it was also recognized by a few as a literary masterwork. Whitman sent copies of the first edition to well-known writers of the day, including John Greenleaf Whittier, who is said to have thrown his copy in the fire. Ralph Waldo Emerson, however, wrote Whitman in praise of the book.

Leaves of Grass remained an amorphous work in progress, published in a sequence of editions with Whitman's own substantial changes and additions; the first edition contained 12 poems, while the last contained more than 350.

from *Song of Myself*

1

I celebrate myself, and sing myself,
And what I assume you shall assume,
For every atom belonging to me as good belongs to you.

I loafe and invite my soul,
5 I lean and loafe at my ease observing a spear of summer grass.

My tongue, every atom of my blood, form'd from this soil, this air,
Born here of parents born here from parents the same, and their
    parents the same,
I, now thirty-seven years old in perfect health begin,

Hoping to cease not till death.
Creeds and schools in abeyance,   10
Retiring back a while sufficed at what they are, but never forgotten,
I harbour for good or bad, I permit to speak at every hazard,
Nature without check with original energy.

—1855, 1881

I Hear America Singing

I hear America singing, the varied carols I hear;
Those of mechanics, each one singing his as it should be blithe and strong,
The carpenter singing his as he measures his plank or beam,
The mason singing his as he makes ready for work, or leaves off work.
The boatman singing what belongs to him in his boat, the deckhand   5
    singing on the steamboat deck,
The shoemaker singing as he sits on his bench, the hatter singing as he
    stands,
The wood-cutter's song, the ploughboy's on his way in the morning, or
    at noon intermission or at sundown,
The delicious singing of the mother, or of the young wife at work, or of
    the girl sewing or washing,
Each singing what belongs to him or her and to none else,
The day what belongs to the day—at night the party of young fellows,   10
    robust, friendly,
Singing with open mouths their strong melodious songs.

—1860

When I Heard the Learn'd Astronomer

When I heard the learn'd astronomer,
When the proofs, the figures, were ranged in columns before me,
When I was shown the charts and diagrams, to add, divide, and
    measure them,
When I sitting heard the astronomer where he lectured with much
    applause in the lecture-room,
How soon unaccountable I became tired and sick,   5
Till rising and gliding out I wander'd off by myself,
In the mystical moist night-air, and from time to time,
Look'd up in perfect silence at the stars.

—1865

Emily Dickinson
1830–1886

Emily Dickinson is often compared to Walt Whitman; they are the leading figures of mid-nineteenth-century American literature, and both exerted enormous influence on the writing of later generations. But whereas Whitman was an exuberantly public figure, Dickinson was intensely private. Whitman strove continually to make a mark; Dickinson remained all but unknown until after her death.

Dickinson was one of three children of Emily and Edward Norcross of Amherst, Massachusetts; her father was an officer of Amherst College and a representative in Congress. She was educated at Amherst Academy and, briefly, at nearby Mount Holyoke College; after one year at Mount Holyoke, however, she returned to Amherst, and from the age of 18 onward she again lived with her family, allowing very few people to visit her. After reaching 30, she became a recluse. Although she acknowledged the appeal of fame and public recognition, she criticized it often in her poems; in one it was "a bright but tragic thing," in another "a fickle food / Upon a shifting plate."

Dickinson's work has a deeply personal flavour to it, but her subject matter is wide-ranging—as was her knowledge of classical and English literature. Her poems often engage with religious themes, yet they also at times suggest a profound religious skepticism. The voice we hear in her poetry is often forceful and direct—yet the poems are filled with ambiguities of syntax and of punctuation.

Dickinson wrote more than 1,700 poems, but most of these did not circulate while she was alive, even in manuscript; only a handful were published during her lifetime. The majority were discovered in a trunk in her bedroom after her death. They were first published in edited versions that regularized and "corrected" many of the eccentricities of Dickinson's punctuation; only in recent decades have readers been able to read the poems as Dickinson wrote them.

249

Wild Nights—Wild Nights!
Were I with thee
Wild Nights should be
Our luxury!

5 Futile—the Winds—
To a Heart in port—

Done with the Compass—
Done with the Chart!

Rowing in Eden—
Ah, the Sea!   10
Might I but moor—Tonight—
In Thee!

—1891 (written c. 1861)

288

I'm Nobody! Who are you?
Are you—Nobody—Too?
Then there's a pair of us!
Don't tell! they'd advertise—you know!

How dreary—to be—Somebody!   5
How public—like a Frog—
To tell one's name—the livelong June—
To an admiring Bog!

—1891 (written c. 1861)

341

After great pain, a formal feeling comes—
The Nerves sit ceremonious, like Tombs—
The stiff Heart questions was it He, that bore,
And Yesterday, or Centuries before?

The Feet, mechanical, go round—   5
Of Ground, or Air, or Ought—
A Wooden way
Regardless grown,
A Quartz contentment, like a stone—

This is the Hour of Lead—   10
Remembered, if outlived,
As Freezing persons, recollect the Snow—
First—Chill—then Stupor—then the letting go—

—1929 (written c. 1862)

465

I heard a Fly buzz—when I died—
The Stillness in the Room
Was like the Stillness in the Air—
Between the Heaves of Storm—

5   The Eyes around—had wrung them dry—
And Breaths were gathering firm
For that last Onset—when the King
Be witnessed—in the Room—

I willed my Keepsakes—Signed away
10 What portion of me be
Assignable—and then it was
There interposed a Fly—

With Blue—uncertain stumbling Buzz—
Between the light—and me—
15 And then the Windows failed—and then
I could not see to see—

—1896 (written c. 1862)

712

Because I could not stop for Death—
He kindly stopped for me—
The Carriage held but just Ourselves—
And Immortality.

5   We slowly drove—He knew no haste
And I had put away
My labour and my leisure too,
For His Civility—

We passed the School, where Children strove
10 At Recess—in the Ring—
We passed the Fields of Gazing Grain—
We passed the Setting Sun—

Or rather—He passed Us—
The Dews drew quivering and chill—
For only Gossamer,[1] my Gown—   15
My Tippet°—only Tulle—   *shawl*

We paused before a House that seemed
A Swelling of the Ground—
The Roof was scarcely visible—
The Cornice[2]—in the Ground—   20

Since then—'tis Centuries—and yet
Feels shorter than the Day
I first surmised the Horses' Heads
Were toward Eternity—

                         —1890 (written c. 1863)

754

My Life had stood—a Loaded Gun—
In Corners—till a Day
The Owner passed—identified—
And carried Me away—

And now We roam in Sovereign Woods—   5
And now We hunt the Doe—
And every time I speak for Him—
The Mountains straight reply—

And do I smile, such cordial light
Upon the Valley glow—   10
It is as a Vesuvian[3] face
Had let its pleasure through—

And when at Night—Our good Day done—
I guard My Master's Head—

---

1 *Gossamer* Fine, sheer fabric.
2 *Cornice* Decorative moulding that runs along the top of a building's exterior wall where
   it meets the roof.
3 *Vesuvian* Refers to Mount Vesuvius, a volcano in Italy.

15 'Tis better than the Eider-Duck's[1]
Deep Pillow—to have shared—

To foe of His—I'm deadly foe—
None stir the second time—
On whom I lay a Yellow Eye—
20 Or an emphatic Thumb—

Though I than He—may longer live
He longer must—than I—
For I have but the power to kill,
Without—the power to die—

—1929 (written c. 1863)

1129

Tell all the Truth but tell it slant—
Success in Circuit lies
Too bright for our infirm Delight
The Truth's superb surprise

5 As Lightning to the Children eased
With explanation kind
The Truth must dazzle gradually
Or every man be blind—

—1945 (written c. 1868)

---

1   *Eider-Duck* Duck whose down feathers are used to stuff pillows.

Christina Rossetti

1830–1894

To the late-Victorian critic Edmund Gosse, Christina Rossetti was "one of the most perfect poets of the age." Her melding of sensuous imagery and stringent form earned her the admiration and devotion of many nineteenth-century readers, and the ease of her lyric voice remains apparent in works as diverse as the sensual "Goblin Market" and the subtle religious hymns she penned throughout her career.

Rossetti was born in London in 1830. Her father, a scholar and Italian expatriate, and her mother, who had been a governess before her marriage, inculcated in each of their four children a love of language, literature, and the arts. In 1850 several of her poems were published in *The Germ*, the journal of the Pre-Raphaelite Brotherhood founded in part by her two brothers, Dante Gabriel and William Michael. Although Rossetti was not formally a member of the Brotherhood, her aesthetic sense—and especially her attention to colour and detail—link her to the movement. Other Pre-Raphaelite values were also central to Rossetti's poetic vision, including a devotion to the faithful representation of nature and, at the same time, a penchant for symbols.

Rossetti first gained attention in the literary world with her 1862 publication of *Goblin Market and Other Poems*. The vast majority of her Victorian critics praised the volume for what one reviewer called its "very decided character and originality, both in theme and treatment," and "Goblin Market" remains among her most discussed works. Few readers have believed William Michael Rossetti's insistence that his sister "did not mean anything profound" by "Goblin Market," but many have found the precise nature of its deep suggestiveness elusive.

In 1871, Rossetti was stricken with Graves's disease, a thyroid problem, which led her to retreat even further into an already quiet life. She continued, however, to publish poetry, including *Sing-Song* (1872), a children's collection; *A Pageant and Other Poems* (1881); and *Verses* (1893). In 1892 she was among those mentioned as a possible successor to Tennyson as England's Poet Laureate. She died in 1894 as a result of breast cancer.

Goblin Market

Morning and evening
Maids heard the goblins cry:
"Come buy our orchard fruits,
Come buy, come buy:

5 Apples and quinces,
Lemons and oranges,
Plump unpecked cherries,
Melons and raspberries,
Bloom-down-cheeked peaches,
10 Swart°-headed mulberries,   *dark*
Wild free-born cranberries,
Crabapples, dewberries,
Pine-apples, blackberries,
Apricots, strawberries;—
15 All ripe together
In summer weather,—
Morns that pass by,
Fair eves that fly;
Come buy, come buy:
20 Our grapes fresh from the vine,
Pomegranates full and fine,
Dates and sharp bullaces,
Rare pears and greengages,
Damsons[1] and bilberries
25 Taste them and try:
Currants and gooseberries,
Bright-fire-like barberries,
Figs to fill your mouth,
Citrons from the South,
30 Sweet to tongue and sound to eye;
Come buy, come buy."

Evening by evening
Among the brookside rushes,
Laura bowed her head to hear,
35 Lizzie veiled her blushes:
Crouching close together
In the cooling weather,
With clasping arms and cautioning lips,
With tingling cheeks and finger tips.
40 "Lie close," Laura said,
Pricking up her golden head:
"We must not look at goblin men,

---

1   *bullaces ... Damsons* Bullaces, greengages, and damsons are all varieties of plums.

We must not buy their fruits:
Who knows upon what soil they fed
Their hungry thirsty roots?"   45
"Come buy," call the goblins
Hobbling down the glen.
"Oh," cried Lizzie, "Laura, Laura,
You should not peep at goblin men."
Lizzie covered up her eyes,   50
Covered close lest they should look;
Laura reared her glossy head,
And whispered like the restless brook:
"Look, Lizzie, look, Lizzie,
Down the glen tramp little men.   55
One hauls a basket,
One bears a plate,
One lugs a golden dish
Of many pounds weight.
How fair the vine must grow   60
Whose grapes are so luscious;
How warm the wind must blow
Through those fruit bushes."
"No," said Lizzie: "No, no, no;
Their offers should not charm us,   65
Their evil gifts would harm us."
She thrust a dimpled finger
In each ear, shut eyes and ran:
Curious Laura chose to linger
Wondering at each merchant man.   70
One had a cat's face,
One whisked a tail,
One tramped at a rat's pace,
One crawled like a snail,
One like a wombat prowled obtuse and furry,   75
One like a ratel° tumbled hurry skurry.   *badger*
She heard a voice like voice of doves
Cooing all together:
They sounded kind and full of loves
In the pleasant weather.   80

Laura stretched her gleaming neck
Like a rush-imbedded swan,

Like a lily from the beck,°   *stream*
Like a moonlit poplar branch,
85 Like a vessel at the launch
When its last restraint is gone.

Backwards up the mossy glen
Turned and trooped the goblin men,
With their shrill repeated cry,
90 "Come buy, come buy."
When they reached where Laura was
They stood stock still upon the moss,
Leering at each other,
Brother with queer brother;
95 Signalling each other,
Brother with sly brother.
One set his basket down,
One reared his plate;
One began to weave a crown
100 Of tendrils, leaves, and rough nuts brown
(Men sell not such in any town);
One heaved the golden weight
Of dish and fruit to offer her:
"Come buy, come buy," was still their cry.
105 Laura stared but did not stir,
Longed but had no money:
The whisk-tailed merchant bade her taste
In tones as smooth as honey,
The cat-faced purr'd,
110 The rat-paced spoke a word
Of welcome, and the snail-paced even was heard;
One parrot-voiced and jolly
Cried "Pretty Goblin" still for "Pretty Polly";—
One whistled like a bird.

115 But sweet-tooth Laura spoke in haste:
"Good Folk, I have no coin;
To take were to purloin:
I have no copper in my purse,
I have no silver either,
120 And all my gold is on the furze°   *evergreen shrub*
That shakes in windy weather

Above the rusty heather."
"You have much gold upon your head,"
They answered all together:
"Buy from us with a golden curl."   125
She clipped a precious golden lock,
She dropped a tear more rare than pearl,
Then sucked their fruit globes fair or red.
Sweeter than honey from the rock,[1]
Stronger than man-rejoicing wine,   130
Clearer than water flowed that juice;
She never tasted such before,
How should it cloy with length of use?
She sucked and sucked and sucked the more
Fruits which that unknown orchard bore;   135
She sucked until her lips were sore;
Then flung the emptied rinds away
But gathered up one kernel-stone,
And knew not was it night or day
As she turned home alone.   140

Lizzie met her at the gate
Full of wise upbraidings:
"Dear, you should not stay so late,
Twilight is not good for maidens;
Should not loiter in the glen   145
In the haunts of goblin men.
Do you not remember Jeanie,
How she met them in the moonlight,
Took their gifts both choice and many,
Ate their fruits and wore their flowers   150
Plucked from bowers
Where summer ripens at all hours?
But ever in the moonlight
She pined and pined away;
Sought them by night and day,   155
Found them no more but dwindled and grew grey;
Then fell with the first snow,
While to this day no grass will grow
Where she lies low:

---

1   *honey from the rock* See Deuteronomy 32.13.

160 I planted daisies there a year ago
    That never blow.
    You should not loiter so."
    "Nay, hush," said Laura:
    "Nay, hush, my sister:
165 I ate and ate my fill,
    Yet my mouth waters still;
    Tomorrow night I will
    Buy more": and kissed her:
    "Have done with sorrow;
170 I'll bring you plums tomorrow
    Fresh on their mother twigs,
    Cherries worth getting;
    You cannot think what figs
    My teeth have met in,
175 What melons icy cold
    Piled on a dish of gold
    Too huge for me to hold,
    What peaches with a velvet nap,
    Pellucid° grapes without one seed: *translucent*
180 Odorous indeed must be the mead°   *meadow*
    Whereon they grow, and pure the wave they drink
    With lilies at the brink,
    And sugar-sweet their sap."

    Golden head by golden head,
185 Like two pigeons in one nest
    Folded in each other's wings,
    They lay down in their curtained bed:
    Like two blossoms on one stem,
    Like two flakes of new-fall'n snow,
190 Like two wands of ivory
    Tipped with gold for awful° kings.   *awe-inspiring*
    Moon and stars gazed in at them,
    Wind sang to them lullaby,
    Lumbering owls forbore to fly,
195 Not a bat flapped to and fro
    Round their rest:
    Cheek to cheek and breast to breast
    Locked together in one nest.

Early in the morning
When the first cock crowed his warning,   200
Neat like bees, as sweet and busy,
Laura rose with Lizzie:
Fetched in honey, milked the cows,
Aired and set to rights the house,
Kneaded cakes of whitest wheat,   205
Cakes for dainty mouths to eat,
Next churned butter, whipped up cream,
Fed their poultry, sat and sewed;
Talked as modest maidens should:
Lizzie with an open heart,   210
Laura in an absent dream,
One content, one sick in part;
One warbling for the mere bright day's delight,
One longing for the night.

At length slow evening came: 215
They went with pitchers to the reedy brooks;
Lizzie most placid in her look,
Laura most like a leaping flame.
They drew the gurgling water from its deep.
Lizzie plucked purple and rich golden flags,   220
Then turning homeward said: "The sunset flushes
Those furthest loftiest crags;
Come Laura, not another maiden lags.
No wilful squirrel wags,
The beasts and birds are fast asleep."   225
But Laura loitered still among the rushes,
And said the bank was steep.

And said the hour was early still,
The dew not fall'n, the wind not chill;
Listening ever, but not catching   230
The customary cry,
"Come buy, come buy,"
With its iterated jingle
Of sugar-baited words:
Not for all her watching   235
Once discerning even one goblin
Racing, whisking, tumbling, hobbling—

Let alone the herds
That used to tramp along the glen,
240 In groups or single,
Of brisk fruit-merchant men.
Till Lizzie urged, "O Laura, come;
I hear the fruit-call, but I dare not look:
You should not loiter longer at this brook:
245 Come with me home.
The stars rise, the moon bends her arc,
Each glowworm winks her spark,
Let us get home before the night grows dark:
For clouds may gather
250 Though this is summer weather,
Put out the lights and drench us thro';
Then if we lost our way what should we do?"

Laura turned cold as stone
To find her sister heard that cry alone,
255 That goblin cry,
"Come buy our fruits, come buy."
Must she then buy no more such dainty fruit?
Must she no more such succous° pasture find,   *juicy*
Gone deaf and blind?
260 Her tree of life drooped from the root:
She said not one word in her heart's sore ache;
But peering through the dimness, nought discerning,
Trudged home, her pitcher dripping all the way;
So crept to bed, and lay
265 Silent till Lizzie slept;
Then sat up in a passionate yearning,
And gnashed her teeth for baulked desire, and wept
As if her heart would break.

Day after day, night after night,
270 Laura kept watch in vain
In sullen silence of exceeding pain.
She never caught again the goblin cry,
"Come buy, come buy"—
She never spied the goblin men
275 Hawking their fruits along the glen:
But when the noon waxed bright

Her hair grew thin and grey;
She dwindled, as the fair full moon doth turn
To swift decay and burn
Her fire away.   280

One day remembering her kernel-stone
She set it by a wall that faced the south;
Dewed it with tears, hoped for a root,
Watched for a waxing shoot,
But there came none.   285
It never saw the sun,
It never felt the trickling moisture run:
While with sunk eyes and faded mouth
She dreamed of melons, as a traveller sees
False waves in desert drouth°   *drought* 290
With shade of leaf-crowned trees,
And burns the thirstier in the sandful breeze.

She no more swept the house,
Tended the fowl or cows,
Fetched honey, kneaded cakes of wheat,   295
Brought water from the brook:
But sat down listless in the chimney-nook
And would not eat.

Tender Lizzie could not bear
To watch her sister's cankerous care,   300
Yet not to share.
She night and morning
Caught the goblins' cry:
"Come buy our orchard fruits,
Come buy, come buy":—   305
Beside the brook, along the glen,
She heard the tramp of goblin men,
The voice and stir
Poor Laura could not hear;
Longed to buy fruit to comfort her,   310
But feared to pay too dear.
She thought of Jeanie in her grave,
Who should have been a bride;
But who for joys brides hope to have

315 Fell sick and died
In her gay prime,
In earliest winter time,
With the first glazing rime,°   *hoar frost*
With the first snow-fall of crisp Winter time.

320 Till Laura dwindling
Seemed knocking at Death's door.
Then Lizzie weighed no more
Better and worse;
But put a silver penny in her purse,
325 Kissed Laura, crossed the heath with clumps of furze
At twilight, halted by the brook:
And for the first time in her life
Began to listen and look.

Laughed every goblin
330 When they spied her peeping:
Came towards her hobbling,
Flying, running, leaping,
Puffing and blowing,
Chuckling, clapping, crowing.
335 Clucking and gobbling,
Mopping and mowing,
Full of airs and graces,
Pulling wry faces,
Demure grimaces,
340 Cat-like and rat-like,
Ratel- and wombat-like,
Snail-paced in a hurry,
Parrot-voiced and whistler,
Helter skelter, hurry skurry,
345 Chattering like magpies,
Fluttering like pigeons,
Gliding like fishes,—
Hugged her and kissed her:
Squeezed and caressed her:
350 Stretched up their dishes,
Panniers, and plates:
"Look at our apples
Russet and dun,°   *dark*

Bob at our cherries,
Bite at our peaches,
Citrons and dates,
Grapes for the asking,
Pears red with basking
Out in the sun,
Plums on their twigs;
Pluck them and suck them,—
Pomegranates, figs."

355

360

Dante Gabriel Rossetti, frontispiece to Goblin Market and Other Poems, *1862. The first edition of* Goblin Market *appeared with illustrations by Christina Rossetti's brother, the Pre-Raphaelite painter and poet Dante Gabriel Rossetti. In this frontispiece, the round inset above the drawing of sisters Laura and Lizzie depicts the goblins carrying their fruits to market.*

"Good folk," said Lizzie,
Mindful of Jeanie:
365 "Give me much and many"—
Held out her apron,
Tossed them her penny.
"Nay, take a seat with us,
Honour and eat with us,"
370 They answered grinning:
"Our feast is but beginning.
Night yet is early,
Warm and dew-pearly,
Wakeful and starry:
375 Such fruits as these
No man can carry;
Half their bloom would fly,
Half their dew would dry,
Half their flavour would pass by.
380 Sit down and feast with us,
Be welcome guest with us,
Cheer you and rest with us."—
"Thank you," said Lizzie: "But one waits
At home alone for me:
385 So without further parleying,°   *discussion*
If you will not sell me any
Of your fruits though much and many,
Give me back my silver penny
I tossed you for a fee."—
390 They began to scratch their pates,°   *heads*
No longer wagging, purring,
But visibly demurring,
Grunting and snarling.
One called her proud,
395 Cross-grained, uncivil;
Their tones waxed loud,
Their looks were evil.
Lashing their tails
They trod and hustled her,
400 Elbowed and jostled her,
Clawed with their nails,
Barking, mewing, hissing, mocking,
Tore her gown and soiled her stocking,

Twitched her hair out by the roots,
Stamped upon her tender feet,   405
Held her hands and squeezed their fruits
Against her mouth to make her eat.

White and golden Lizzie stood,
Like a lily in a flood,—
Like a rock of blue-veined stone   410
Lashed by tides obstreperously,—
Like a beacon left alone
In a hoary roaring sea,
Sending up a golden fire,—
Like a fruit-crowned orange tree   415
White with blossoms honey-sweet
Sore beset by wasp and bee,—
Like a royal virgin town
Topped with gilded dome and spire
Close beleaguered by a fleet   420
Mad to tug her standard down.

One may lead a horse to water,
Twenty cannot make him drink.
Though the goblins cuffed and caught her,
Coaxed and fought her,   425
Bullied and besought her,
Scratched her, pinched her black as ink,
Kicked and knocked her,
Mauled and mocked her,
Lizzie uttered not a word;   430
Would not open lip from lip
Lest they should cram a mouthful in:
But laughed in heart to feel the drip
Of juice that syruped all her face,
And lodged in dimples of her chin,   435
And streaked her neck which quaked like curd.
At last the evil people,
Worn out by her resistance,
Flung back her penny, kicked their fruit
Along whichever road they took,   440
Not leaving root or stone or shoot;
Some writhed into the ground,

Some dived into the brook
With ring and ripple,
445 Some scudded on the gale without a sound,
Some vanished in the distance.

In a smart, ache, tingle,
Lizzie went her way;
Knew not was it night or day;
450 Sprang up the bank, tore through the furze,
Threaded copse and dingle,°   *dell*
And heard her penny jingle
Bouncing in her purse,—
Its bounce was music to her ear.
455 She ran and ran
As if she feared some goblin man
Dogged her with gibe or curse
Or something worse:
But not one goblin skurried after,
460 Nor was she pricked by fear;
The kind heart made her windy-paced
That urged her home quite out of breath with haste
And inward laughter.

She cried, "Laura," up the garden,
465 "Did you miss me?
Come and kiss me.
Never mind my bruises,
Hug me, kiss me, suck my juices
Squeezed from goblin fruits for you,
470 Goblin pulp and goblin dew.
Eat me, drink me, love me;
Laura, make much of me;
For your sake I have braved the glen
And had to do with goblin merchant men."

475 Laura started from her chair,
Flung her arms up in the air,
Clutched her hair:
"Lizzie, Lizzie, have you tasted
For my sake the fruit forbidden?
480 Must your light like mine be hidden,

Your young life like mine be wasted,
Undone in mine undoing,
And ruined in my ruin,
Thirsty, cankered, goblin-ridden?"—
She clung about her sister,   485
Kissed and kissed and kissed her:
Tears once again
Refreshed her shrunken eyes,
Dropping like rain
After long sultry drouth;   490
Shaking with aguish° fear, and pain,   *feverish*
She kissed and kissed her with a hungry mouth.

Her lips began to scorch,
That juice was wormwood to her tongue,
She loathed the feast: 495
Writhing as one possessed she leaped and sung,
Rent all her robe, and wrung
Her hands in lamentable haste,
And beat her breast.
Her locks streamed like the torch   500
Borne by a racer at full speed,
Or like the mane of horses in their flight,
Or like an eagle when she stems the light
Straight toward the sun,
Or like a caged thing freed,   505
Or like a flying flag when armies run.

Swift fire spread through her veins, knocked at her heart,
Met the fire smouldering there
And overbore its lesser flame;
She gorged on bitterness without a name: 510
Ah! fool, to choose such part
Of soul-consuming care!
Sense failed in the mortal strife:
Like the watchtower of a town
Which an earthquake shatters down,   515
Like a lightning-stricken mast,
Like a wind-uprooted tree
Spun about,
Like a foam-topped waterspout

520 Cast down headlong in the sea,
    She fell at last;
    Pleasure past and anguish past,
    Is it death or is it life?

    Life out of death.
525 That night long Lizzie watched by her,
    Counted her pulse's flagging stir,
    Felt for her breath,
    Held water to her lips, and cooled her face
    With tears and fanning leaves.
530 But when the first birds chirped about their eaves,
    And early reapers plodded to the place
    Of golden sheaves,
    And dew-wet grass
    Bowed in the morning winds so brisk to pass,
535 And new buds with new day
    Opened of cup-like lilies on the stream,
    Laura awoke as from a dream,
    Laughed in the innocent old way,
    Hugged Lizzie but not twice or thrice;
540 Her gleaming locks showed not one thread of grey,
    Her breath was sweet as May,
    And light danced in her eyes.

    Days, weeks, months, years
    Afterwards, when both were wives
545 With children of their own;
    Their mother-hearts beset with fears,
    Their lives bound up in tender lives;
    Laura would call the little ones
    And tell them of her early prime,
550 Those pleasant days long gone
    Of not-returning time:
    Would talk about the haunted glen,
    The wicked quaint fruit-merchant men,
    Their fruits like honey to the throat
555 But poison in the blood;
    (Men sell not such in any town):
    Would tell them how her sister stood
    In deadly peril to do her good,

And win the fiery antidote:
Then joining hands to little hands 560
Would bid them cling together,—
"For there is no friend like a sister
In calm or stormy weather;
To cheer one on the tedious way,
To fetch one if one goes astray, 565
To lift one if one totters down,
To strengthen whilst one stands."

—1862 (written 1859)

Laurence Housman, illustration from Goblin Market, *1893. A very popular edition of* Goblin Market, *released about three decades after the poem was first published, featured art nouveau illustrations by the writer and artist Laurence Housman.*

Gerard Manley Hopkins
1844–1889

Although Gerard Manley Hopkins lived and worked during the Victorian period, his poems were not published until 1918, when they were released by his literary executor and gained him posthumous fame. That some critics treated Hopkins as a modernist poet is not only a matter of this timing; indeed, the close observations and fine descriptions found in his poetry do resemble the singular sensory images of modernist literature. As the reviewer Arthur Clutton-Brock wrote in 1919, Hopkins's "poems are crowded with objects sharply cut, and with sounds no less sharp and clashing."

Hopkins was educated at Oxford, where the poet and cultural critic Matthew Arnold (1822–88) was one of his teachers. In 1866, Hopkins entered the Roman Catholic Church, eventually becoming a Jesuit priest and, later, a professor of classics at University College in Dublin. He burned his early efforts at poetry (imitations of Keats written during the 1860s), but went on to write poems in his own distinctive style—syntactically disjunctive, highly alliterative, and densely rhyming—that often aim to celebrate the spiritual and the divine. His few poetry submissions to journals were rejected; uncertain about the quality of his work, and struggling with the fear that a religious life was incompatible with any attempt at artistic fame, he soon stopped trying to publish his poems.

Much of Hopkins's historical importance as a poet comes from his experimentation with metre and form. He devised a precursor to free verse that he called "sprung rhythm," a style of metre in which only the number of stressed syllables in each line is fixed, while the number of unstressed syllables can vary; Hopkins included frequent stress marks in his own verse to clarify the intended rhythm. He also used invented compound words (such as "piece-bright" and "blue-bleak") to link an object's striking characteristics. Such compounds represent an attempt to convey "inscape," a term Hopkins coined to refer to the dynamic, individual design or essence specific to each object in the world.

God's Grandeur

The world is charged with the grándeur of God.
　　It will flame out, like shining from shook foil;[1]

1　[Hopkins's note] I mean foil in its sense of leaf or tinsel.... Shaken goldfoil gives off broad glares like sheet lightning and also, and this is true of nothing else, owing to its zigzag dints and creasings and network of small many cornered facets, a sort of fork lightning too.

It gathers to a greatness, like the ooze of oil
Crushed.[1] Why do men then now not reck° his rod?   *regard*
Génerátions have trod, have trod, have trod;   5
     And all is seared with trade; bleared, smeared, with toil;
     And wears man's smudge and shares man's smell: the soil
Is bare now, nor can foot feel, being shod.

Ánd, for° all this, náture is never spent;   *despite*
     There lives the dearest freshness deep down things;   10
And though the last lights off the black West went
     Oh, morning, at the brown brink eastward, springs—
Because the Holy Ghost óver the bent
     World broods with warm breast and with ah! bright wings.
                   —1918 (written 1877)

The Windhover[2]

To Christ Our Lord

I caught this morning morning's minion, king-
     dom of daylight's dauphin,[3] dapple-dáwn-drawn Falcon,
         in his riding
     Of the rólling level únderneáth him steady air, and striding
High there, how he rung upon the rein of a wimpling° wing   *rippling*
In his écstasy! then off, off forth on swing,
     As a skate's heel sweeps smooth on a bow-bend: the hurl and gliding   5
     Rebuffed the bíg wind. My heart in hiding
Stírred for a bird,—the achieve of, the mástery of the thing!

Brute beauty and valour and act, óh, air, pride, plúme, here
     Buckle! AND the fire that breaks from thee then, a billion   10
Tímes told lovelier, more dangerous, O my chevalier!°   *horseman*

     No wónder of it: shéer plód makes plóugh down síllion°   *furrows*
Shíne, and blue-bleak embers, ah my dear,
     Fall, gáll themsélves, and gásh góld-vermílion.
                   —1918 (written 1877)

---

1   *oil / Crushed* I.e., as olive oil.
2   *Windhover* Another name for a kestrel, a small falcon that appears to hover in the
     wind.
3   *dauphin* Title of the eldest son of the king of France—the heir.

W.B. Yeats
1865–1939

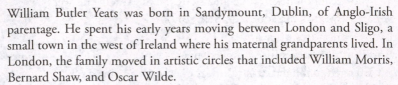

William Butler Yeats was born in Sandymount, Dublin, of Anglo-Irish parentage. He spent his early years moving between London and Sligo, a small town in the west of Ireland where his maternal grandparents lived. In London, the family moved in artistic circles that included William Morris, Bernard Shaw, and Oscar Wilde.

His early work is imbued with what he saw as the mystery and beauty of Irish myth and landscape. When Yeats's father saw his son's first poem, he declared that Yeats had "given tongue to the sea-cliffs." The early poems also contain some of the most memorable love poetry in English. In 1899, Yeats was involved in the foundation of the Irish National Theatre; he would become its director and write more than 20 plays that were performed there. But he also continued to write poetry, developing a more dramatic, collo- quial, and compact voice. Beginning with the volume *Responsibilities* (1914), he began to explore increasingly complex themes and poetic forms as he sought to give voice to the "blood-dimmed tide" of modern experience.

Yeats was deeply interested in the occult and explored the symbolic worlds of astrology, Theosophism, the tarot, and alchemy. He developed his own system of symbols and conception of history; the poems "Leda and the Swan" and "The Second Coming" are both, for example, influenced by his idea that civilizations are born cyclically, through violent, mystical, and sexual encounters.

Yeats was a formative influence on modern poetry and on the cultural and political history of Ireland; T.S. Eliot described him as "part of the consciousness of an age which cannot be understood without him." Yeats worked all his life to foster an Irish national literature, and in 1923 he was the first writer from Ireland to receive the Nobel Prize.

Easter 1916[1]

I have met them at close of day
Coming with vivid faces
From counter or desk among grey
Eighteenth-century houses.
5 I have passed with a nod of the head
Or polite meaningless words,

---

1   *Easter 1916* On Easter Monday, 24 April 1916, Irish nationalists instigated an unsuc- cessful rebellion against the British government (which was then at war with Ger- many); the Easter Rebellion lasted until 29 April. Many of the Irish nationalist leaders were executed that May.

Or have lingered awhile and said
Polite meaningless words,
And thought before I had done
Of a mocking tale or a gibe   10
To please a companion
Around the fire at the club,
Being certain that they and I
But lived where motley° is worn: *jester's costume*
All changed, changed utterly: 15
A terrible beauty is born.

That woman's days were spent
In ignorant good-will,
Her nights in argument
Until her voice grew shrill.[1]   20
What voice more sweet than hers
When, young and beautiful,
She rode to harriers?[2]
This man had kept a school
And rode our wingèd horse;[3]   25
This other his helper and friend[4]
Was coming into his force;
He might have won fame in the end,
So sensitive his nature seemed,
So daring and sweet his thought.   30
This other man I had dreamed
A drunken, vainglorious lout.[5]
He had done most bitter wrong
To some who are near my heart,

---

1   *That woman's ... shrill* Countess Markiewicz, née Constance Gore-Booth (1868–1927), played a central role in the Easter Rebellion; she was arrested and sentenced to death (though the death sentence was later commuted). Yeats later wrote a poem about her and her Irish-nationalist sister, "In Memory of Eva Gore-Booth and Con Markiewicz" (1929).

2   *rode to harriers* Went hunting with hounds.

3   *This man ... wingèd horse* Pádraic Pearse (1879–1916) founded St. Enda's School near Dublin. He was a leader in the effort to revive the Gaelic language, and wrote both Irish and English poetry; *wingèd horse* Refers to Pegasus, the horse of the Muses.

4   *This other his helper and friend* Thomas MacDonagh (1878–1916), an Irish poet and playwright who also taught school.

5   *vainglorious lout* Major John MacBride (1865–1916), estranged husband of Irish nationalist Maud Gonne; their separation just two years after marriage was due in part to his drinking bouts.

35 Yet I number him in the song;
He, too, has resigned his part
In the casual comedy;
He, too, has been changed in his turn,
Transformed utterly:
40 A terrible beauty is born.

Hearts with one purpose alone
Through summer and winter seem
Enchanted to a stone
To trouble the living stream.
45 The horse that comes from the road,
The rider, the birds that range
From cloud to tumbling cloud,
Minute by minute they change;
A shadow of cloud on the stream
50 Changes minute by minute;
A horse-hoof slides on the brim,
And a horse plashes within it;
The long-legged moor-hens dive,
And hens to moor-cocks call;
55 Minute by minute they live:
The stone's in the midst of all.

Too long a sacrifice
Can make a stone of the heart.
O when may it suffice?
60 That is Heaven's part, our part
To murmur name upon name,
As a mother names her child
When sleep at last has come
On limbs that had run wild.
65 What is it but nightfall?
No, no, not night but death;
Was it needless death after all?
For England may keep faith
For all that is done and said.[1]
70 We know their dream; enough
To know they dreamed and are dead;

---

1   *For England ... said* England had originally granted Ireland Home Rule in 1913, but
then postponed it due to World War I, promising to institute it after the war.

And what if excess of love
Bewildered them till they died?
I write it out in a verse—
MacDonagh and MacBride   75
And Connolly and Pearse[1]
Now and in time to be,
Wherever green is worn,
Are changed, changed utterly:
A terrible beauty is born.   80

—1916

The Second Coming[2]

Turning and turning in the widening gyre[3]
The falcon cannot hear the falconer;
Things fall apart; the centre cannot hold;
Mere anarchy is loosed upon the world,
The blood-dimmed tide is loosed, and everywhere   5
The ceremony of innocence is drowned;
The best lack all conviction, while the worst
Are full of passionate intensity.

Surely some revelation is at hand;
Surely the Second Coming is at hand.   10
The Second Coming! Hardly are those words out
When a vast image out of *Spiritus Mundi*[4]
Troubles my sight: somewhere in sands of the desert
A shape with lion body and the head of a man,[5]
A gaze blank and pitiless as the sun,   15
Is moving its slow thighs, while all about it
Reel shadows of the indignant desert birds.
The darkness drops again; but now I know
That twenty centuries of stony sleep

---

1   *Connolly* James Connolly (1868–1916), Irish socialist; *MacDonagh ... Pearse* All four
     men were executed for their involvement in the Easter Rebellion of 1916.
2   *The Second Coming* The return of Christ, as predicted in the New Testament. See Reve-
     lation 1.7: "Behold, he cometh with clouds; and every eye shall see him."
3   *gyre* Spiral formed from concentric circles.
4   *Spiritus Mundi* Latin: Spirit of the World; universal spirit that houses the images of
     civilization's past memories and provides divine inspiration for the poet. The human
     race is a connected whole in the *spiritus mundi*.
5   *shape ... man* The Egyptian Sphinx.

20   Were vexed to nightmare by a rocking cradle,[1]
And what rough beast, its hour come round at last,
Slouches towards Bethlehem to be born?

—1920

Leda and the Swan[2]

A sudden blow: the great wings beating still
Above the staggering girl, her thighs caressed
By the dark webs, her nape caught in his bill,
He holds her helpless breast upon his breast.

5   How can those terrified vague fingers push
The feathered glory from her loosening thighs?
And how can body, laid in that white rush,
But feel the strange heart beating where it lies?

A shudder in the loins engenders there
10 The broken wall, the burning roof and tower
And Agamemnon dead.[3]
                                    Being so caught up,
So mastered by the brute blood of the air,
Did she put on his knowledge with his power
15 Before the indifferent beak could let her drop?

—1924

Sailing to Byzantium[4]

1

That is no country for old men. The young
In one another's arms, birds in the trees

---

1   *rocking cradle* Cradle of the Christ Child.
2   *Leda and the Swan* In Greek mythology, Leda was visited by Zeus in the form of a swan, who in some versions of the story seduced her and in other versions raped her. From this union she bore two eggs, one becoming the twins Castor and Pollux, the other Helen (whose abduction later initiated the Trojan War).
3   *broken wall … Agamemnon dead* Events during and after the Trojan War.
4   *Byzantium* Ancient city eventually renamed Constantinople (now Istanbul), capital of the Eastern Roman Empire. In *A Vision*, Yeats envisioned Byzantium as a centre for artists: "The painter, the mosaic worker, the worker in gold and silver, the illuminator of sacred books were almost impersonal, almost perhaps without the consciousness of individual design, absorbed in their subject matter and that the vision of a whole people."

—Those dying generations—at their song,
The salmon-falls, the mackerel-crowded seas,
Fish, flesh, or fowl, commend all summer long   5
Whatever is begotten, born, and dies.
Caught in that sensual music all neglect
Monuments of unageing intellect.

2

An aged man is but a paltry thing,
A tattered coat upon a stick, unless   10
Soul clap its hands and sing, and louder sing
For every tatter in its mortal dress,
Nor is there singing school but studying
Monuments of its own magnificence;
And therefore I have sailed the seas and come   15
To the holy city of Byzantium.

3

O sages standing in God's holy fire
As in the gold mosaic of a wall,
Come from the holy fire, perne in a gyre,[1]
And be the singing-masters of my soul.   20
Consume my heart away; sick with desire
And fastened to a dying animal
It knows not what it is; and gather me
Into the artifice of eternity.

4

Once out of nature I shall never take   25
My bodily form from any natural thing,
But such a form as Grecian goldsmiths make
Of hammered gold and gold enamelling
To keep a drowsy Emperor awake;
Or set upon a golden bough to sing[2]   30
To lords and ladies of Byzantium
Of what is past, or passing, or to come.

—1927

---

1   *perne in a gyre* Rotate in a spiral; the literal definition of "perne" is "bobbin."
2   [Yeats's note] I have read somewhere that in the Emperor's palace at Byzantium was a
    tree made of gold and silver, and artificial birds that sang.

Paul Laurence Dunbar
1872–1906

Born in Dayton, Ohio, to parents who had both been slaves in the American South, Paul Laurence Dunbar is considered the first African American poet to have been read widely in both white and African American communities. His second book of poetry, *Majors and Minors* (1896), brought him to national attention, particularly because of that collection's "minors," poems composed in African American dialect. (The "majors" were more traditional poems influenced by the Romantic tradition and by Dunbar's contemporaries.) Though Dunbar's traditional poetic works were more numerous, it was the dialect poems that caught the public's imagination—to a degree that troubled both Dunbar and some of his critics.

Though known primarily as a poet, Dunbar worked in a wide variety of genres. In addition to poetry, he founded a newspaper and wrote short stories, novels, song lyrics, a libretto for an operetta, and the lyrics to the first all-black musical on Broadway, *In Dahomey* (1902). Gavin Jones has characterized Dunbar as "a wily manipulator of the conventions, a subtle overturner of racist stereotypes, a sensitive renderer of the multiple facets of Black consciousness at the turn of the twentieth century."

We Wear the Mask

We wear the mask that grins and lies,
It hides our cheeks and shades our eyes,—
This debt we pay to human guile;
With torn and bleeding hearts we smile,
5   And mouth with myriad subtleties.

Why should the world be over-wise,
In counting all our tears and sighs?
Nay, let them only see us, while
     We wear the mask.

10 We smile, but, O great Christ, our cries
To thee from tortured souls arise.
We sing, but oh the clay is vile
Beneath our feet, and long the mile;
But let the world dream otherwise,
15   We wear the mask!

—1895

Robert Frost
1874–1963

Though Robert Frost's career spanned the modernist period and displays modernist influences, his work is not so easily categorized. Unlike many of his contemporaries, Frost insisted on observing rules of traditional verse—he relied on regular metre and rhyme in crafting his work—and famously said that "writing free verse is like playing tennis with the net down." A merging of traditional form with colloquial speech is the hallmark of Frost's style.

Born in San Francisco in 1874, Frost moved to New England at the age of 11. He began writing poetry while still in high school; he attended both Dartmouth College and Harvard University but never completed a degree. In 1912, Frost and his family relocated to England, a move that would prove to be a turning point in his career. While in London, he published *A Boy's Will* (1913) and *North of Boston* (1914), two full-length collections that earned Frost critical acclaim and attracted the attention of well-known poets such as Ezra Pound. By the time of Frost's return to the United States in 1915, he was established as a serious poet. Over the following decades, his reputation would grow even further with the publication of four Pulitzer Prize-winning collections: *New Hampshire: A Poem with Notes and Grace Notes* (1924), *Collected Poems* (1931), *A Further Range* (1937), and *A Witness Tree* (1943).

When Frost died in 1963, President John F. Kennedy said that the poet's death left "a vacancy in the American spirit." His epitaph reads: "I Had A Lover's Quarrel With The World."

The Road Not Taken

Two roads diverged in a yellow wood,
And sorry I could not travel both
And be one traveller, long I stood
And looked down one as far as I could
To where it bent in the undergrowth;   5

Then took the other, as just as fair,
And having perhaps the better claim,
Because it was grassy and wanted wear;
Though as for that, the passing there
Had worn them really about the same,   10

And both that morning equally lay
In leaves no step had trodden black.
Oh, I kept the first for another day!
Yet knowing how way leads on to way,
15 I doubted if I should ever come back.

I shall be telling this with a sigh
Somewhere ages and ages hence:
Two roads diverged in a wood, and I—
I took the one less travelled by,
20 And that has made all the difference.

—1916

Stopping by Woods on a Snowy Evening

Whose woods these are I think I know.
His house is in the village, though;
He will not see me stopping here
To watch his woods fill up with snow.

5 My little horse must think it queer
To stop without a farmhouse near
Between the woods and frozen lake
The darkest evening of the year.

He gives his harness bells a shake
10 To ask if there is some mistake.
The only other sound's the sweep
Of easy wind and downy flake.

The woods are lovely, dark, and deep,
But I have promises to keep,
15 And miles to go before I sleep,
And miles to go before I sleep.

—1923

Wallace Stevens

1879–1955

"Life," Wallace Stevens wrote, "consists of propositions about life." His work reflects this idea insofar as it examines the relationship between the human understanding of reality—an ever-shifting product of perception and imagination—and reality itself. Although he was strongly influenced by Romanticism's emphases on nature and poetic imagination, Stevens was modernist in his concern with the role of poetry in the spiritually disillusioned world of the twentieth century.

Stevens was born in Pennsylvania and attended Harvard, where he edited the *Harvard Monthly* but left before completing a degree. After a brief and unsatisfying period as a journalist, Stevens became a lawyer. He would spend the rest of his life working in insurance firms, eventually becoming vice president of the Hartford Accident and Indemnity Company. But he also continued to write, and in his thirties he began to publish plays and some of the individual poems that would appear in his first collection, *Harmonium* (1923).

Harmonium contains some of what would become Stevens's best-known work, though its initial critical reception was lukewarm. With later volumes such as *Ideas of Order* (1935) and *The Man with the Blue Guitar* (1937), he attracted more attention, but some critics found his work too abstract and difficult, and he was disparaged for not engaging directly with the political concerns of his time. Stevens received much more profound and favourable recognition, however, toward the end of his career, when he won two National Book Awards: one for *The Auroras of Autumn* (1951), and another for his *Collected Poems* (1954), which was also awarded the Pulitzer Prize.

Thirteen Ways of Looking at a Blackbird

I

Among twenty snowy mountains,
The only moving thing
Was the eye of the blackbird.

II

I was of three minds,
Like a tree
In which there are three blackbirds.

5

III

The blackbird whirled in the autumn winds.
It was a small part of the pantomime.

IV

A man and a woman
10 Are one.
A man and a woman and a blackbird
Are one.

V

I do not know which to prefer,
The beauty of inflections
15 Or the beauty of innuendoes,
The blackbird whistling
Or just after.

VI

Icicles filled the long window
With barbaric glass.
20 The shadow of the blackbird
Crossed it, to and fro.
The mood
Traced in the shadow
An indecipherable cause.

VII

25 O thin men of Haddam,[1]
Why do you imagine golden birds?
Do you not see how the blackbird
Walks around the feet
Of the women about you?

VIII

30 I know noble accents
And lucid, inescapable rhythms;
But I know, too,
That the blackbird is involved
In what I know.

---

1 *Haddam* Town in Connecticut.

IX

When the blackbird flew out of sight,   35
It marked the edge
Of one of many circles.

X

At the sight of blackbirds
Flying in a green light,
Even the bawds° of euphony°   *brothel operators / pleasant sound*   40
Would cry out sharply.

XI

He rode over Connecticut
In a glass coach.
Once, a fear pierced him,
In that he mistook   45
The shadow of his equipage[1]
For blackbirds.

XII

The river is moving.
The blackbird must be flying.

XIII

It was evening all afternoon.   50
It was snowing
And it was going to snow.
The blackbird sat
In the cedar-limbs.

—1917

---

1   *equipage* Horses and carriage.

William Carlos Williams
1883–1963

A major poet of the twentieth century, William Carlos Williams was also a working medical doctor who spent most of his life in his birthplace, Ruther-ford, New Jersey. As a poet, his primary allegiance was to American culture, and he strove to capture quintessentially American ideas and experiences in colloquial language: "not the speech of English country people ... but language modified by ... the American environment." Although he is most remembered for his poetry, it comprised only half of his more than 40 pub-lished works, which also included critical prose, short stories, novels, plays, and letters.

Of Williams's many friends in the artistic and literary avant-gardes of New York and Europe, the most significant to his career was undoubtedly fellow poet Ezra Pound, a leader in the imagist movement in which Williams became a major participant. Williams's early style was profoundly shaped by imagism's quest to capture impressions through precise, concentrated lan-guage, and this influence remains in the direct and unornamented spirit of his later work. However, he also continued to evolve as a poet, experimenting with form and idiom throughout his career.

Perhaps because of his work's deceptively easy style, critics did not begin to count Williams among the best poets of his era until the last decades of his life. The rise of his reputation began with the publication of the first book of *Paterson* (1946–63), a long poem that explores the city of Paterson (near Rutherford) from diverse angles, in both poetry and prose. Despite failing health, Williams continued writing until his death in 1963, and was posthumously awarded the Pulitzer Prize for his final collection, *Pictures from Brueghel and Other Poems* (1962).

The Red Wheelbarrow

so much depends
upon

a red wheel
barrow

5 glazed with rain
water

beside the white
chickens

—1923

Spring and All

By the road to the contagious hospital
under the surge of the blue
mottled clouds driven from the
northeast—a cold wind. Beyond, the
waste of broad, muddy fields   5
brown with dried weeds, standing and fallen

patches of standing water
the scattering of tall trees

All along the road the reddish
purplish, forked, upstanding, twiggy   10
stuff of bushes and small trees
with dead, brown leaves under them
leafless vines—

Lifeless in appearance, sluggish
dazed spring approaches—   15

They enter the new world naked,
cold, uncertain of all
save that they enter. All about them
the cold, familiar wind—

Now the grass, tomorrow   20
the stiff curl of wildcarrot leaf

One by one objects are defined—
It quickens: clarity, outline of leaf

But now the stark dignity of
entrance—Still, the profound change   25
has come upon them: rooted they
grip down and begin to awaken

                                        —1923

This Is Just to Say

I have eaten
the plums
that were in
the icebox

5   and which
you were probably
saving
for breakfast

Forgive me
10   they were delicious
so sweet
and so cold

—1934

Landscape with the Fall of Icarus[1]

According to Brueghel
when Icarus fell
it was spring

a farmer was ploughing
5   his field
the whole pageantry

of the year was
awake tingling
near

10   the edge of the sea
concerned
with itself

sweating in the sun
that melted
15   the wings' wax

unsignificantly
off the coast
there was

a splash quite unnoticed
20   this was
Icarus drowning

—1962

---

1   *Landscape … of Icarus* Painting (c. 1555) by Pieter Brueghel the Elder based on an ancient Greek story. Wearing wings made by his father Daedalus, Icarus flew too close to the
sun; the wax on the wings melted, and Icarus fell to his death. In Brueghel's painting, an
ordinary farmer ploughing on a hill dominates the foreground, while Icarus's drowning
body appears very small in the ocean below, next to a much larger ship.

Ezra Pound
1885–1972

A modernist poet, editor, and critic, Ezra Pound promoted novelty and formal experimentation in poetry, contributing to the rise of free verse and strongly influencing the development of the twentieth-century literary avant-garde. Pound's early views were unequivocal: "no good poetry is ever written in a manner twenty years old, for to write in such a manner shows conclusively that the writer thinks from books, convention and cliché, and not from life."

Born in Indiana, in 1908 Pound moved to Europe, where he became the centre of a literary circle that included established writers such as W.B. Yeats, as well as talented new writers such as T.S. Eliot and James Joyce, whose work Pound promoted. His first collection of poetry, *Personae* (1909), a mix of traditional and newer forms of expression, was well-received by critics; his next books, however, lost critical favour due to their non-traditional nature.

In 1924 Pound moved to Italy, where he became involved in fascist politics and, during World War II, broadcast fascist and anti-Semitic propaganda for the Italian government. During the American occupation of Italy, he was arrested for treason and imprisoned in a US military camp, where he suffered a mental breakdown; declared unfit for trial, he spent the following decade in an American psychiatric hospital. Despite the controversy surrounding his politics, Pound was awarded the Bollingen Prize in 1948 for his *Pisan Cantos* (1924–48), a self-contained section of his major work, the unfinished long poem *The Cantos* (1917–69).

Pound was a leading force behind the poetic movement known as imagism. Partly drawn from tenets of classical Chinese and Japanese poetry—of which Pound was a translator—imagism departs from the elaborate style and regular metre of Victorian poetry, instead advocating the clear, precise, and economical use of language for what Pound called "the direct treatment of the 'thing'."

The River-Merchant's Wife: A Letter[1]

While my hair was still cut straight across my forehead
I played about the front gate, pulling flowers.
You came by on bamboo stilts, playing horse,
You walked about my seat, playing with blue plums.
And we went on living in the village of Chōkan:[2]   5
Two small people, without dislike or suspicion.

---

1   *The River-Merchant's ... Letter* Pound's adaptation of a poem by the Chinese poet Li Po (701–62 CE), whose name is given in its Japanese form ("Rihaku") at the end of the poem.
2   *Chōkan* Suburb of Nanking.

At fourteen I married My Lord you.
I never laughed, being bashful.
Lowering my head, I looked at the wall.
10 Called to, a thousand times, I never looked back.

At fifteen I stopped scowling,
I desired my dust to be mingled with yours
Forever and forever and forever.
Why should I climb the look out?

15 At sixteen you departed,
You went into far Ku-tō-en,[1] by the river of swirling eddies,
And you have been gone five months.
The monkeys make sorrowful noise overhead.

You dragged your feet when you went out.
20 By the gate now, the moss is grown, the different mosses,
Too deep to clear them away!
The leaves fall early this autumn, in wind.
The paired butterflies are already yellow with August
Over the grass in the West garden;
25 They hurt me. I grow older.
If you are coming down through the narrows of the river Kiang,
Please let me know beforehand,
And I will come out to meet you
            As far as Chō-fū-Sa.[2]

                                        Rihaku
                                        —1915

In a Station of the Metro

The apparition of these faces in the crowd;
Petals on a wet, black bough.

                    —1916 (earlier version published 1913)

---

1   *Ku-tō-en* Chang Jiang, a Chinese river, also called the Yangtze Kiang.
2   *Chō-fū-Sa* Chang-feng Sha, a beach located in Anhui several hundred miles upriver.

Marianne Moore

1887–1972

Born in Kirkwood, Missouri, Marianne Moore was raised by her mother in the home of her grandfather, a Presbyterian pastor. Her family moved to Pennsylvania, where she received her BA from Bryn Mawr College and subsequently became a teacher at a boarding school for Indigenous children. In 1918, she moved with her mother to New York City, where she was soon noticed in literary circles. Some of her work was published in the journal *Dial*, which she eventually edited from 1925 until 1929.

Moore is known for poems grounded in the observation of nature, and for her deft experimentation with form and metre. She is also famous for revising her work long after publication; for instance, "Poetry," 29 lines long in 1921, is reduced to three lines in the final version published in 1967. Moore's revisions have not always been well-received, but her modest attitude toward writing suggests her rationale for revisiting works: "I'm a happy hack as a writer.... I never knew anyone with a passion for words who had as much difficulty in saying things as I do. I seldom say them in a manner I like."

Moore's *Collected Poems* (1951) was awarded the National Book Award, the Pulitzer Prize, and the Bollingen Prize. The poet James Dickey has written in praise of her style that "every poem of hers lifts us towards our own discovery-prone lives. It does not state, in effect, that I am more intelligent than you, more creative because I found this item and used it and you didn't. It seems to say, rather, I found this, and what did you find? Or, a better, what can you find?"

Poetry

I, too, dislike it: there are things that are important beyond all this fiddle.
   Reading it, however, with a perfect contempt for it, one discovers in
     it after all, a place for the genuine.
       Hands that can grasp, eyes
    that can dilate, hair that can rise
       if it must, these things are important not because a   5

high-sounding interpretation can be put upon them but because they are
   useful. When they become so derivative as to become unintelligible,
    the same thing may be said for all of us, that we
      do not admire what
     we cannot understand: the bat   10
       holding on upside down or in quest of something to

eat, elephants pushing, a wild horse taking a roll, a tireless wolf under
    a tree, the immovable critic twitching his skin like a horse that feels
        a flea, the base-
15 ball fan, the statistician—
      nor is it valid
        to discriminate against "business documents and

schoolbooks":[1] all these phenomena are important. One must make
      a distinction
    however: when dragged into prominence by half poets, the result
      is not poetry,
20 nor till the poets among us can be
      "literalists of
    the imagination"[2]—above
      insolence and triviality and can present

for inspection, "imaginary gardens with real toads in them,"[3] shall we have
25 it. In the meantime, if you demand on the one hand,
    the raw material of poetry in
      all its rawness and
    that which is on the other hand
      genuine, then you are interested in poetry.

                                 —1921

Poetry (Revised version)

I, too, dislike it.
    Reading it, however, with a perfect contempt for it, one discovers in
    it, after all, a place for the genuine.

                                   —1967

---

1   *business documents and / schoolbooks* Moore's note quotes from the *Diaries of Tolstoy* (1917), in which Tolstoy considers the boundary between poetry and prose: "Poetry is verse: prose is not verse. Or else poetry is everything with the exception of business documents and schoolbooks."

2   *literalists of the imagination* In *Ideas of Good and Evil* (1903), W.B. Yeats calls William Blake "a too literal realist of imagination as others are of nature."

3   *imaginary gardens … in them* No source has been found for this phrase; despite the quotation marks, it is generally thought to be Moore's.

T.S. Eliot
1888–1965

No twentieth-century writer did more to shape the direction of modern poetry and criticism than T.S. Eliot. In poems such as "The Love Song of J. Alfred Prufrock" (1915) and *The Waste Land* (1922), Eliot founded a radical new poetical idiom to express the alienation and the "chaotic, irregular, fragmentary" experience of the modern mind, which he considered disconnected from any meaningful sense of tradition. Eliot's many essays and reviews, notably "Tradition and the Individual Talent" (1919) and "The Metaphysical Poets" (1921), were scarcely less influential. Such writings not only provided a theoretical foundation for New Criticism, one of the most prominent critical schools of the early to mid-twentieth century; they also introduced new terms and concepts—"objective correlative," "the dissociation of sensibility," the ideal development of the poet as a "continual extinction of personality"—that have enriched the study of modern literature, not least by illuminating Eliot's own complex poetics.

Eliot's poetry is challenging, but in his reckoning it could hardly be otherwise, for he believed that "poets in our civilization, as it exists at present, must be *difficult*. Our civilization comprehends great variety and complexity, and this variety and complexity, playing upon a refined sensibility, must produce various and complex results." Among the most striking of these results is the absence—particularly in his early poetry—of fluid transitions: images are precise but often jarring and incongruous, arrestingly juxtaposed to suggest broader patterns of meaning. At once colloquial and erudite, fragmentary and unified, much of Eliot's poetry relies on ironies, tensions, and paradoxes. These qualities are ideally suited to the rigorous methodology of close reading championed by the New Critics, who focused not on the mind of the poet or the external conditions of the text's creation but on the details of the text itself.

Eliot's thought and technique evolved over his career, particularly following his conversion to Anglo-Catholicism, when—as in "Journey of the Magi" (1927) and *Four Quartets* (1943)—he began to explore more religious themes. Although his poetic output was relatively modest, his body of work occupies the very centre of literary modernism. As Northrop Frye remarked, "a thorough knowledge of Eliot is compulsory for anyone interested in contemporary literature. Whether he is liked or disliked is of no importance, but he must be read."

The Love Song of J. Alfred Prufrock[1]

> *S'io credesse che mia risposta fosse*
> *A persona che mai tornasse al mondo,*
> *Questa fiamma staria senza piu scosse.*
> *Ma perciocche giammai di questo fondo*
> 5 *Non torno viva alcun, s'i'odo il vero,*
> *Senza tema d'infamia ti rispondo.*[2]

Let us go then, you and I,
When the evening is spread out against the sky
Like a patient etherized upon a table;
10 Let us go, through certain half-deserted streets,
The muttering retreats
Of restless nights in one-night cheap hotels
And sawdust restaurants with oyster-shells:
Streets that follow like a tedious argument
15 Of insidious intent
To lead you to an overwhelming question …
Oh, do not ask, "What is it?"
Let us go and make our visit.

In the room the women come and go
20 Talking of Michelangelo.

The yellow fog that rubs its back upon the window-panes,
The yellow smoke that rubs its muzzle on the window-panes
Licked its tongue into the corners of the evening,
Lingered upon the pools that stand in drains,
25 Let fall upon its back the soot that falls from chimneys,
Slipped by the terrace, made a sudden leap,
And seeing that it was a soft October night,
Curled once about the house, and fell asleep.

And indeed there will be time
30 For the yellow smoke that slides along the street,

---

1 *J. Alfred Prufrock* The name is likely taken from the The Prufrock-Littau Company, a furniture dealer located in St. Louis, Eliot's birthplace.

2 *S'io credesse … ti rispondo* Italian: "If I thought that my reply were given to anyone who might return to the world, this flame would stand forever still; but since never from this deep place has anyone ever returned alive, if what I hear is true, without fear of infamy I answer thee," Dante's *Inferno* 27.61–66; Guido da Montefeltro's speech as he burns in Hell.

Rubbing its back upon the window panes;
There will be time, there will be time[1]
To prepare a face to meet the faces that you meet
There will be time to murder and create,
And time for all the works and days[2] of hands   35
That lift and drop a question on your plate;
Time for you and time for me,
And time yet for a hundred indecisions,
And for a hundred visions and revisions,
Before the taking of a toast and tea.   40

In the room the women come and go
Talking of Michelangelo.

And indeed there will be time
To wonder, "Do I dare?" and, "Do I dare?"
Time to turn back and descend the stair,   45
With a bald spot in the middle of my hair—
(They will say: "How his hair is growing thin!")
My morning coat,[3] my collar mounting firmly to the chin,
My necktie rich and modest, but asserted by a simple pin—
(They will say: "But how his arms and legs are thin!")   50
Do I dare
Disturb the universe?
In a minute there is time
For decisions and revisions which a minute will reverse.

For I have known them all already, known them all—   55
Have known the evenings, mornings, afternoons,
I have measured out my life with coffee spoons;
I know the voices dying with a dying fall[4]
Beneath the music from a farther room.
     So how should I presume?   60

And I have known the eyes already, known them all—
The eyes that fix you in a formulated phrase,

---

1   *there will be time* See Ecclesiastes 3.1–8: "To everything there is a season, and a time to
    every purpose under heaven: A time to be born, and a time to die; a time to plant, and
    a time to pluck up that which is planted; a time to kill, and a time to heal...."
2   *works and days* Title of a poem by eighth-century BCE Greek poet Hesiod.
3   *morning coat* Formal coat with tails.
4   *with a dying fall* In Shakespeare's *Twelfth Night* 1.1.1–15 Duke Orsino commands,
    "That strain again, it had a dying fall."

And when I am formulated, sprawling on a pin,
When I am pinned and wriggling on the wall,
65 Then how should I begin
To spit out all the butt-ends of my days and ways?
  And how should I presume?

And I have known the arms already, known them all—
Arms that are braceleted and white and bare
70 (But in the lamplight, downed with light brown hair!)
Is it perfume from a dress
That makes me so digress?
Arms that lie along a table, or wrap about a shawl.
  And should I then presume?
75   And how should I begin?

  *   *   *

Shall I say, I have gone at dusk through narrow streets
And watched the smoke that rises from the pipes
Of lonely men in shirt-sleeves, leaning out of windows? ...[1]

I should have been a pair of ragged claws
80 Scuttling across the floors of silent seas.[2]

  *   *   *

And the afternoon, the evening, sleeps so peacefully!
Smoothed by long fingers,
Asleep ... tired ... or it malingers,
Stretched on the floor, here beside you and me.
85 Should I, after tea and cakes and ices,
Have the strength to force the moment to its crisis?
But though I have wept and fasted, wept and prayed,
Though I have seen my head (grown slightly bald) brought in
  upon a platter,[3]
I am no prophet[4]—and here's no great matter;

---

1 ... The ellipsis here makes note of a 38 line insertion written by Eliot, entitled *Pru-frock's Pervigilium*. The subtitle and 33 of the lines were later removed.

2 *I should ... seas* See Shakespeare's *Hamlet* 2.2, in which Hamlet tells Polonius, "for you yourself, sir, should be old as I am, if like a crab you could go backwards."

3 *brought in upon a platter* Reference to Matthew 14.1–12, in which the prophet John the Baptist is beheaded at the command of Herod, and his head presented to Salomé upon a platter.

4 *I am no prophet* See Amos 7.14. When commanded by King Amiziah not to proph-esize, the Judean Amos answered: "I was no prophet, neither was I a prophet's son; but I was a herdsman, and a farmer of sycamore fruit."

I have seen the moment of my greatness flicker,   90
And I have seen the eternal Footman hold my coat, and snicker,
And in short, I was afraid.

And would it have been worth it, after all,
After the cups, the marmalade, the tea,
Among the porcelain, among some talk of you and me,   95
Would it have been worth while,
To have bitten off the matter with a smile,
To have squeezed the universe into a ball[1]
To roll it toward some overwhelming question,
To say: "I am Lazarus,[2] come from the dead,   100
Come back to tell you all, I shall tell you all"—
If one, settling a pillow by her head,
    Should say: "That is not what I meant at all;
    That is not it, at all."

And would it have been worth it, after all,   105
Would it have been worth while,
After the sunsets and the dooryards and the sprinkled streets,[3]
After the novels, after the teacups, after the skirts that trail along
    the floor—
And this, and so much more?—
It is impossible to say just what I mean!   110
But as if a magic lantern[4] threw the nerves in patterns on a screen:
Would it have been worth while
If one, settling a pillow or throwing off a shawl,
And turning toward the window, should say:
    "That is not it at all,   115
    That is not what I meant, at all."

    *   *   *

No! I am not Prince Hamlet, nor was meant to be;
Am an attendant lord, one that will do
To swell a progress,[5] start a scene or two,
Advise the prince; no doubt, an easy tool,   120

---

1   *squeezed ... ball* See Andrew Marvell's "To His Coy Mistress," 41–42: "Let us roll our
    strength and all / Our sweetness up into one ball."
2   *Lazarus* Raised from the dead by Jesus in John 11.1–44.
3   *sprinkled streets* Streets sprayed with water to keep dust down.
4   *magic lantern* In Victorian times, a device used to project images painted on glass onto
    a blank screen or wall.
5   *progress* Journey made by royalty through the country.

Deferential, glad to be of use,
Politic, cautious, and meticulous;
Full of high sentence,[1] but a bit obtuse;
At times, indeed, almost ridiculous—
125 Almost, at times, the Fool.

I grow old ... I grow old ...
I shall wear the bottoms of my trousers rolled.

Shall I part my hair behind? Do I dare to eat a peach?
I shall wear white flannel trousers, and walk upon the beach.
130 I have heard the mermaids singing,[2] each to each.

I do not think that they will sing to me.

I have seen them riding seaward on the waves
Combing the white hair of the waves blown back
When the wind blows the water white and black.

135 We have lingered in the chambers of the sea
By sea-girls wreathed with seaweed red and brown
Till human voices wake us, and we drown.

—1915, 1917

Journey of the Magi[3]

"A cold coming we had of it,
Just the worst time of the year
For a journey, and such a long journey:
The ways deep and the weather sharp,
5 The very dead of winter."[4]
And the camels galled, sore-footed, refractory,
Lying down in the melting snow.
There were times we regretted
The summer palaces on slopes, the terraces,
10 And the silken girls bringing sherbet.

---

1 *high sentence* Serious, elevated sentiments or opinions.
2 *I have ... singing* See John Donne's "Song": "Teach me to hear the mermaids singing."
3 *Magi* Three wise men who journeyed to Bethlehem to honour Jesus at his birth (see Matthew 2.1–12).
4 *A cold ... winter* Adapted from a sermon given by Anglican preacher Lancelot Andrews on Christmas Day, 1622.

Then the camel men cursing and grumbling
And running away, and wanting their liquor and women,
And the night-fires going out, and the lack of shelters,
And the cities hostile and the towns unfriendly
And the villages dirty and charging high prices: 15
A hard time we had of it.
At the end we preferred to travel all night,
Sleeping in snatches,
With the voices singing in our ears, saying
That this was all folly.   20

Then at dawn we came down to a temperate valley,
Wet, below the snow line, smelling of vegetation;
With a running stream and a water-mill beating the darkness,
And three trees[1] on the low sky,
And an old white horse[2] galloped away in the meadow.   25
Then we came to a tavern with vine-leaves over the lintel,°   *doorframe*
Six hands at an open door dicing for pieces of silver,[3]
And feet kicking the empty wine-skins.
But there was no information, and so we continued
And arrived at evening, not a moment too soon   30
Finding the place; it was (you may say) satisfactory.

All this was a long time ago, I remember,
And I would do it again, but set down
This set down
This: were we led all that way for   35
Birth or Death? There was a Birth, certainly,
We had evidence and no doubt. I had seen birth and death,
But had thought they were different; this Birth was
Hard and bitter agony for us, like Death, our death.
We returned to our places, these Kingdoms,   40
But no longer at ease here, in the old dispensation,
With an alien people clutching their gods.
I should be glad of another death.

—1927

---

1   *three trees* Suggests the three crosses on Calvary, on which Christ and two criminals
    were crucified (see Luke 23.32–43).
2   *white horse* Ridden by Christ in Revelation 6.2 and 19.11–14.
3   *dicing … silver* Allusion to Judas's betrayal of Jesus for 30 pieces of silver, and to the
    soldiers who played dice for the robes of Christ at his crucifixion (Matthew 26.14 and
    27.35).

Edna St. Vincent Millay

1892–1950

Edna St. Vincent Millay wrote the iconic line "My candle burns at both ends" in her poem "First Fig" (1920)—a poem that inspired the imaginations of an emerging generation of sexually liberated American women. This American poet and playwright embodied the spirit of romantic rebellion characteristic of the 1920s and, throughout her career, remained a powerful presence in American public consciousness.

Millay demonstrated a talent for writing poetry at an early age, her first published poem appearing in a children's magazine when she was 14. Following her graduation from Vassar College, Millay published her first book, *Renascence and Other Poems* (1917), and moved to Greenwich Village in New York. Over the next few years her growing reputation as a poet was matched by her reputation as a freethinker in the realm of sexual politics. Two of her most significant verse collections date from this period: *A Few Figs from Thistles* (1920) and *The Harp-Weaver and Other Poems* (1923), which won the Pulitzer Prize for poetry.

Although Millay's fame was earned primarily during the early years of her career, she remained active and innovative well into the 1940s, and her work became more politically and emotionally intense. The 52 sonnets in her collection *Fatal Interview* (1931) were widely admired for their mastery of the form; the sequence draws on centuries of poetic tradition, but was reviewed as expressing "the thoughts of a new age."

[I, being born a woman and distressed]

I, being born a woman and distressed
By all the needs and notions of my kind,
Am urged by your propinquity° to find   *proximity*
Your person fair, and feel a certain zest
5 To bear your body's weight upon my breast:
So subtly is the fume of life designed,
To clarify the pulse and cloud the mind,
And leave me once again undone, possessed.
Think not for this, however, the poor treason
10 Of my stout blood against my staggering brain,
I shall remember you with love, or season
My scorn with pity,—let me make it plain:
I find this frenzy insufficient reason
For conversation when we meet again.

—1923

[What lips my lips have kissed, and where, and why]

What lips my lips have kissed, and where, and why,
I have forgotten, and what arms have lain
Under my head till morning; but the rain
Is full of ghosts tonight, that tap and sigh
Upon the glass and listen for reply,   5
And in my heart there stirs a quiet pain
For unremembered lads that not again
Will turn to me at midnight with a cry.
Thus in winter stands the lonely tree,
Nor knows what birds have vanished one by one,   10
Yet knows its boughs more silent than before:
I cannot say what loves have come and gone;
I only know that summer sang in me
A little while, that in me sings no more.

—1923

Wilfred Owen
1893–1918

One of 16 World War I poets commemorated in Westminster Abbey's Poet's Corner, Wilfred Owen is best remembered for poems such as "Anthem for Doomed Youth" and "Dulce et Decorum Est" (1920), in which he offers searing indictments of those who would send young men to war.

Owen began to experiment with poetry as a teenager. He spent the years prior to the war working as a lay assistant to the vicar of Dunsden, and later as a private tutor in Bordeaux, France. In 1915, he enlisted in the army and was commissioned as second lieutenant in the Manchester Regiment. The trauma he experienced on the front haunted Owen, who once spent days trapped in a dugout with the remains of a fellow officer. Diagnosed with shell shock in 1917, the poet was sent to recuperate at Craiglockhart War Hospital near Edinburgh. His biographer Jon Stallworthy suggests that the nightmares that are a symptom of shellshock were "a principal factor in the liberation and organization of [Owen's work].... The realities of battle, banished from his waking mind, […] erupt into his dreams and into his poems."

At the War Hospital, he met fellow patient and recently published poet Siegfried Sassoon, who became a mentor to Owen. Up to this point, Owen's style had reflected his admiration of Romantic poets such as John Keats and Percy Shelley, but with Sassoon's encouragement, he abandoned Romantic poetics for a colloquial style similar to Sassoon's. Almost all of his best-known work was composed in the year before he was discharged from the War Hospital and sent back to France in August 1918.

Owen was killed in action one week before the end of the war.

Anthem for Doomed Youth

What passing-bells for these who die as cattle?
Only the monstrous anger of the guns.
Only the stuttering rifles' rapid rattle
Can patter out their hasty orisons.°   *prayers*
5 No mockeries for them from prayers or bells,
Nor any voice of mourning save the choirs,—
The shrill, demented choirs of wailing shells;
And bugles calling for them from sad shires.

What candles may be held to speed them all?
10 Not in the hands of boys, but in their eyes
Shall shine the holy glimmers of good-byes.

The pallor of girls' brows shall be their pall;[1]
Their flowers the tenderness of silent minds,
And each slow dusk a drawing-down of blinds.

—1920

Dulce et Decorum Est[2]

Bent double, like old beggars under sacks,
Knock-kneed, coughing like hags, we cursed through sludge,
Till on the haunting flares we turned our backs,
And towards our distant rest began to trudge.
Men marched asleep. Many had lost their boots,   5
But limped on, blood-shod. All went lame, all blind;
Drunk with fatigue; deaf even to the hoots
Of gas-shells dropping softly behind.
Gas! GAS! Quick, boys!—An ecstasy of fumbling,
Fitting the clumsy helmets just in time,   10
But someone still was yelling out and stumbling
And flound'ring like a man in fire or lime—
Dim, through the misty panes[3] and thick green light,
As under a green sea, I saw him drowning.

In all my dreams before my helpless sight   15
He plunges at me, guttering, choking, drowning.

If in some smothering dreams, you too could pace
Behind the wagon that we flung him in,
And watch the white eyes writhing in his face,
His hanging face, like a devil's sick of sin;   20
If you could hear, at every jolt, the blood
Come gargling from the froth-corrupted lungs,
Bitter as the cud
Of vile, incurable sores on innocent tongues,—
My friend, you would not tell with such high zest   25
To children ardent for some desperate glory,
The old Lie: Dulce et decorum est
Pro patria mori.

—1920

---

1   *pall* Cloth spread over a coffin, hearse, or tomb.
2   *Dulce et Decorum Est* Owen's poem takes its title from a famous line from the Roman
     poet Horace's *Odes* (3.2): "*Dulce et decorum est pro patria mori*" (Latin: "Sweet and fitting
     it is to die for one's country").
3   *panes* Visors of gas masks.

E.E. Cummings
1894–1962

Edward Estlin Cummings is best known for his avant-garde poetry, in which he experiments with syntax, grammar, and punctuation. Cummings's work found an unusually large popular audience; according to poet and critic Randall Jarrell, "No one else has ever made avant-garde, experimental poems so attractive to the general and the specific reader."

Cummings grew up in an intellectual home in Cambridge, Massachusetts, and attended Harvard University, where several of his poems were published in the anthology *Eight Harvard Poets* (1917). Upon graduating from university during World War I, Cummings went to France to be an ambulance driver, but instead was put into an internment camp for "suspicious" foreigners. He fictionalized this experience in the prose work *The Enormous Room* (1922), which was much admired by other young writers.

This was followed in 1923 by his first book of poetry, *Tulips and Chimneys*, showcasing his facility with typographical experimentation and invented language. The characteristic poem "[in Just-]," for example, describes a children's world using vibrant and playful terms such as "mud- / luscious," "balloonMan," and "puddle-wonderful." Cummings continued to write prolifically for the next several decades, producing 15 books of poems ranging from lyrical love poetry to cynical criticism of the modern world.

In 1931, Cummings visited the Soviet Union. He had been hoping to find that communism had created an ideal society, but was disillusioned by his experience, and wrote a travelogue, *Eimi* (1933), strongly critical of the Soviet regime.

[in Just-]

in Just-
spring   when the world is mud-
luscious the little
lame balloonman

5 whistles   far   and wee

and eddieandbill come
running from marbles and
piracies and it's
spring

when the world is puddle-wonderful   10

the queer
old balloonman whistles
far   and   wee
and bettyandisbel come dancing

from hop-scotch and jump-rope and   15

it's
spring
and

    the

        goat-footed   20

balloonMan   whistles
far
and
wee

                          —1923

[somewhere i have never travelled,gladly beyond]

somewhere i have never travelled,gladly beyond
any experience,your eyes have their silence:
in your most frail gesture are things which enclose me,
or which i cannot touch because they are too near

your slightest look easily will unclose me   5
though i have closed myself as fingers,
you open always petal by petal myself as Spring opens
(touching skilfully,mysteriously)her first rose

or if your wish be to close me,i and
my life will shut very beautifully,suddenly,   10
as when the heart of this flower imagines
the snow carefully everywhere descending;

nothing which we are to perceive in this world equals
the power of your intense fragility:whose texture
compels me with the colour of its countries,   15
rendering death and forever with each breathing

(i do not know what it is about you that closes
and opens;only something in me understands
the voice of your eyes is deeper than all roses)
20 nobody,not even the rain,has such small hands

—1931

anyone lived in a pretty how town

anyone lived in a pretty how town
(with up so floating many bells down)
spring summer autumn winter
he sang his didn't he danced his did.

5   Women and men(both little and small)
cared for anyone not at all
they sowed their isn't they reaped their same
sun moon stars rain

children guessed(but only a few
10 and down they forgot as up they grew
autumn winter spring summer)
that noone loved him more by more

when by now and tree by leaf
she laughed his joy she cried his grief
15 bird by snow and stir by still
anyone's any was all to her

someones married their everyones
laughed their cryings and did their dance
(sleep wake hope and then)they
20 said their nevers they slept their dream

stars rain sun moon
(and only the snow can begin to explain
how children are apt to forget to remember
with up so floating many bells down)

25 one day anyone died i guess
(and noone stooped to kiss his face)

busy folk buried them side by side
little by little and was by was

all by all and deep by deep
and more by more they dream their sleep
noone and anyone earth by april   30
wish by spirit and if by yes.

Women and men(both dong and ding)
summer autumn winter spring
reaped their sowing and went their came
sun moon stars rain   35

—1940

Langston Hughes
1902–1967

In his first autobiography, *The Big Sea* (1940), Langston Hughes wrote, "my best poems were all written when I felt the worst. When I was happy, I didn't write anything." His career produced many lyric poems that have the sadness but also the vitality of jazz, blues, and bebop, and that participate in an African American tradition of struggle for positive social change. Hughes contributed to American letters not only as a poet but also as a playwright, journalist, short story writer, novelist, historian, and translator.

In the early 1920s Hughes worked odd jobs—including a stint on an American freighter travelling the African coastline—as he began to publish his work in magazines. His first poetry collection, *Weary Blues* (1926), established him as a major figure in the Harlem Renaissance, a movement of African American writers, artists, and musicians that flourished in the 1920s and 1930s. Even more than some of his Harlem Renaissance contemporaries, Hughes celebrated black working-class culture and experience in his writing.

Hughes became a Marxist in the 1930s, and he spent time in Haiti, Cuba, and the USSR learning about alternatives to American politics and economics. He also began to address contemporary urban politics more directly in his work, pronouncing his faith in Marxism in poems such as "Goodbye Christ" (1932): "And nobody's gonna sell ME / To a king, or a general, / Or a millionaire." Hughes abandoned communism after World War II but continued to write on political themes; his last work, for example, *The Panther and the Lash* (1967), was a collection of poetry focused on the civil rights movement.

The Negro Speaks of Rivers

(*To W.E.B. Du Bois*)[1]

I've known rivers:
I've known rivers ancient as the world and older than the flow of human
    blood in human veins.
My soul has grown deep like the rivers.

---

1   *W.E.B. Du Bois* American activist (1868–1963) and one of the founders of the NAACP (National Association for the Advancement of Colored People).

I bathed in the Euphrates when dawns were young.
I built my hut near the Congo and it lulled me to sleep.   5
I looked upon the Nile and raised the pyramids above it.
I heard the singing of the Mississippi when Abe Lincoln went down
      to New Orleans,[1] and I've seen its muddy bosom turn all golden
      in the sunset.

I've known rivers:
Ancient, dusky rivers.

My soul has grown deep like the rivers.   10

                                                —1926

Harlem (2)

What happens to a dream deferred?

    Does it dry up
    like a raisin in the sun?
    Or fester like a sore—
    And then run?
    Does it stink like rotten meat?   5
    Or crust and sugar over—
    like a syrupy sweet?
    Maybe it just sags
    like a heavy load.   10

    Or does it explode?

                                                  —1951

---

1   *when Abe ... New Orleans* In 1831, Lincoln travelled down the Mississippi to New Orleans, where he witnessed the brutality of the slave market there. Some biographers suggest that this experience consolidated his opinion against slavery.

Stevie Smith

1902–1971

Stevie Smith's poetry is deceptively simple. Its plain language, playful rhymes, odd syntax, and repetitive, singsong rhythms convey a child-like sensibility—one accentuated by the bizarre "doodles" of men, women, and animals that she included with her writing. Beneath her poetry's light-hearted and humorous surface, however, is a serious engagement with such concepts as loneliness, religion, suicide, and death. As poet Peter Porter suggests, Smith was not the "naive writer" she appeared to be; on the contrary, "her unshockable eye and brilliant ear enabled her to cover almost all the unmentionable topics."

Smith lived most of her life in London, where she worked as a secretary. Her first published work was a novel entitled *Novel on Yellow Paper* (1936); its commercial success enabled her to publish her first volume of poems, *A Good Time Was Had by All* (1937). Smith would go on to write seven more poetry collections, as well as short stories, essays, literary reviews, and two more novels.

Skilled at performing her own verse, Smith was a popular figure at poetry readings in the 1960s. Although she had a large and admiring readership, for most of her career she did not receive a great deal of approval from critics, who were put off by the atypical, apparently frivolous tone of her work. However, she had gained respect as a serious poet by the time her *Selected Poems* was published in 1962, and in the last years of her life she received the Queen's Gold Medal for Poetry (1969).

Not Waving but Drowning

Nobody heard him, the dead man,
But still he lay moaning:
I was much further out than you thought
And not waving but drowning.

5 Poor chap, he always loved larking
And now he's dead
It must have been too cold for him his heart gave way,
They said.

Oh, no no no, it was too cold always
10 (Still the dead one lay moaning)
I was much too far out all my life
And not waving but drowning.

—1957

Earle Birney

1904–1995

A mountain climber, travel writer, and political activist as well as an important Canadian poet, Earle Birney was as adventurous in his work as he was in his life. He experimented with compound nouns (e.g., "seajet"), syntax and sound, and unconventional punctuation, and he frequently changed his style during his long career. As the critic George Woodcock writes, Birney possessed an "openness to the new and the unorthodox" that enabled him to create "the special voice and form appropriate to each situation."

Raised in Alberta and British Columbia, Birney attended university in Vancouver and Toronto; he lived for brief periods in England and in Utah before returning to Canada to teach at the University of British Columbia—and to publish poetry. He was an immediate success: his first collection, *David and Other Poems* (1942), won a Governor General's Award. He spent the next several decades writing prolifically and teaching, and in 1965 established Canada's first Creative Writing program.

Birney addressed many topics and adopted many different poetic styles over his long career. His work often engages with the issues of the day— Birney was a Marxist when young, and always remained strongly on the left politically—and it engages experimentally with several poetic movements, including sound poetry and concrete poetry.

Vancouver Lights

About me the night   moonless   wimples[1] the mountains
wraps ocean   land   air   and mounting
sucks at the stars   The city   throbbing below
webs the sable peninsula   The golden
strands overleap the seajet   by bridge and buoy   5
vault the shears of the inlet   climb the woods
toward me   falter   and halt   Across to the firefly
haze of a ship on the gulf's erased horizon
roll the lambent° spokes of a lighthouse   *radiant*

Through the feckless years we have come to the time   10
when to look on this quilt of lamps is a troubling delight
Welling from Europe's bog   through Africa flowing

---

1   *wimples* I.e., covers; a wimple is the head covering traditionally worn by nuns.

and Asia   drowning the lonely lumes[1] on the oceans
tiding up over Halifax   now to this winking
15 outpost comes flooding the primal ink

On this mountain's brutish forehead with terror of space
I stir   of the changeless night and the stark ranges
of nothing   pulsing down from beyond and between
the fragile planets   We are a spark beleaguered
20 by darkness   this twinkle we make in a corner of emptiness
how shall we utter our fear that the black Experimentress
will never in the range of her microscope find it?   Our Phoebus[2]
himself is a bubble that dries on Her slide   while the Nubian[3]
wears for an evening's whim a necklace of nebulae

25 Yet we must speak   we the unique glowworms
Out of the waters and rocks of our little world
we conjured these flames   hooped these sparks
by our will   From blankness and cold we fashioned stars
to our size   and signalled Aldebaran[4]
30 This must we say   whoever may be to hear us
if murk devour   and none weave again in gossamer:

These rays were ours
we made and unmade them   Not the shudder of continents
doused us   the moon's passion   nor crash of comets
35 In the fathomless heat of our dwarfdom   our dream's combustion
we contrived the power   the blast that snuffed us
No one bound Prometheus[5]   Himself he chained
and consumed his own bright liver   O stranger
Plutonian   descendant   or beast in the stretching night—
40 there was light.

—1948

---

1   *lumes* Variant form of "leams," meaning lights or rays.
2   *Phoebus* Epithet of Apollo, god of the sun; here, the sun itself.
3   *Nubian* Inhabitant of the African region of Nubia.
4   *Aldebaran* Red star of the first magnitude, in the constellation of Taurus.
5   *Prometheus* In Greek myth, the Titan who stole fire from Heaven to give to humankind;
     for this, his punishment was to be chained to a rock while an eagle devoured his liver each
     day.

The Bear on the Delhi Road

Unreal   tall as a myth
by the road the Himalayan bear
is beating the brilliant air
with his crooked arms
About him two men   bare   5
spindly as locusts   leap

One pulls on a ring
in the great soft nose   His mate
flicks   flicks with a stick
up at the rolling eyes   10

They have not led him here
down from the fabulous hills
to this bald alien plain
and the clamorous world   to kill
but simply to teach him to dance   15

They are peaceful both   these spare
men of Kashmir   and the bear
alive is their living   too
If   far on the Delhi way
around him galvanic they dance   20
it is merely to wear   wear
from his shaggy body the tranced
wish forever to stay
only an ambling bear
four-footed in berries   25

It is no more joyous for them
in this hot dust to prance
out of reach of the praying claws
sharpened to paw for ants
in the shadows of deodars[1]   30
It is not easy to free
myth from reality
or rear this fellow up
to lurch   lurch with them
in the tranced dancing of men   35

—1973

---

1   *deodars* Indian cedars.

W.H. Auden

1907–1973

W.H. Auden's poetry documents the changing political, social, and psychological landscape of his time, describing society's material troubles and seeking a clear understanding of human existence. His work often couples contemporary speech with more traditional, structured verse forms.

Born in York, England, Wystan Hugh Auden spent his childhood in Birmingham. He won a scholarship to study natural science at Oxford, but a developing passion for poetry soon led him to transfer to English. At university, he became the central member of a cohort of writers known as the "Oxford Group," and soon after graduation he published his first major volume, *Poems* (1930).

In the thirties, Auden travelled extensively and worked variously as a schoolmaster, a university lecturer, a writer of nonfiction and experimental drama, and a verse commentator on documentary films. Though he was gay, in 1935 he entered into a marriage of convenience with Erika Mann, daughter of the German novelist Thomas Mann, to enable her escape from Nazi Germany. During the Spanish Civil War (1936–39), Auden volunteered as a propaganda writer on the side of the left—an experience that left him somewhat disillusioned with socialist politics.

In 1939, Auden moved to New York, where he settled for most of his later life. A year later he published *Another Time* (1940), which includes some of his best-known poems, such as "Musée des Beaux Arts" and "September 1, 1939." From then on, his work began to take on more subjective overtones, often with religious themes (he had abandoned Anglicanism as a youth, but returned to it in 1941). While his earlier poetry had examined concrete social ills, his later poetry developed a more complex worldview, often casting social problems in terms of personal responsibility.

With *The Collected Poetry* (1945), Auden began revising his earlier work, a task that included rewriting and even suppressing some of his most left-wing poems. When he was awarded the National Medal for Literature in 1967, the committee declared that Auden's work, "branded by the moral and ideological fires of our age, breathes with eloquence, perception, and intellectual power."

Funeral Blues[1]

Stop all the clocks, cut off the telephone,
Prevent the dog from barking with a juicy bone,
Silence the pianos and with muffled drum
Bring out the coffin, let the mourners come.

Let aeroplanes circle moaning overhead   5
Scribbling on the sky the message He is Dead,
Put crêpe bows[2] round the white necks of the public doves,
Let the traffic policemen wear black cotton gloves.

He was my North, my South, my East and West,
My working week and my Sunday rest,   10
My noon, my midnight, my talk, my song;
I thought that love would last forever: I was wrong.

The stars are not wanted now; put out every one;
Pack up the moon and dismantle the sun;
Pour away the ocean and sweep up the wood;   15
For nothing now can ever come to any good.

—1936, 1940

Musée des Beaux Arts

About suffering they were never wrong,
The Old Masters: how well they understood
Its human position; how it takes place
While someone else is eating or opening a window or just walking
      dully along;
How, when the aged are reverently, passionately waiting   5
For the miraculous birth, there always must be
Children who did not specially want it to happen, skating
On a pond at the edge of the wood:

---

1 *Funeral Blues* This poem first appeared in *The Ascent of F6* (1936), a play co-written by
   Auden and Christopher Isherwood. A revised version with the present title later appeared
   in Auden's 1940 collection *Another Time*. The original 1936 version has five stanzas and
   is considerably more satirical.
2 *crêpe bows* Black crêpe, a woven fabric with a wrinkled surface, is often associated with
   mourning.

They never forgot
10 That even the dreadful martyrdom must run its course
Anyhow in a corner, some untidy spot
Where the dogs go on with their doggy life and the torturer's horse
Scratches its innocent behind on a tree.

In Brueghel's *Icarus*[1] for instance: how everything turns away
15 Quite leisurely from the disaster; the ploughman may
Have heard the splash, the forsaken cry,
But for him it was not an important failure; the sun shone
As it had to on the white legs disappearing into the green
Water; and the expensive delicate ship that must have seen
20 Something amazing, a boy falling out of the sky,
Had somewhere to get to and sailed calmly on.

—1940

September 1, 1939[2]

I sit in one of the dives
On Fifty-second Street
Uncertain and afraid
As the clever hopes expire
5 Of a low dishonest decade:
Waves of anger and fear
Circulate over the bright
And darkened lands of the earth,
Obsessing our private lives;
10 The unmentionable odour of death
Offends the September night.

Accurate scholarship can
Unearth the whole offence

---

1   *Brueghel's Icarus* The reference is to *Landscape with the Fall of Icarus* (c. 1555), a painting
    by Pieter Brueghel the Elder. It references an ancient Greek story in which Daedalus and
    his son Icarus tried to escape from Crete, where they were imprisoned, using wings of
    feathers and wax. Icarus flew too high, the wax melted, and he drowned. In Brueghel's
    painting, an ordinary farmer ploughing on a hill dominates the foreground, while Icarus's
    drowning body appears very small in the ocean below, next to a much larger ship.
2   *September 1, 1939* Date of Hitler's invasion of Poland; France and Britain declared war
    on Germany two days later. Auden had left England to take up residence in the United
    States the previous January.

From Luther[1] until now
That has driven a culture mad,
Find what occurred at Linz,[2]
What huge imago[3] made
A psychopathic god:
I and the public know
What all schoolchildren learn,
Those to whom evil is done
Do evil in return.

Exiled Thucydides[4] knew
All that a speech can say
About Democracy,
And what dictators do,
The elderly rubbish they talk
To an apathetic grave;
Analysed all in his book,
The enlightenment driven away,
The habit-forming pain,
Mismanagement and grief:
We must suffer them all again.

Into this neutral air
Where blind skyscrapers use
Their full height to proclaim
The strength of Collective Man,
Each language pours its vain
Competitive excuse:
But who can live for long

---

1   *Luther* Martin Luther (1483–1546), the German religious leader whose attacks on ecclesiastical corruption began the Protestant Reformation in Europe. Luther's writings grew markedly more anti-Semitic as he aged; in his book *Mein Kampf*, Hitler ranks Martin Luther as a great German cultural hero.
2   *Linz* Capital of upper Austria where Hitler grew up.
3   *imago* Psychoanalytic term for an idealized image of a person; imagos are formed in childhood and influence adult behaviour.
4   *Thucydides* Athenian historian (c. 460–c. 395 BCE) whose failure as a naval commander led to his 20-year exile, during which time he wrote *The History of the Peloponnesian War*. In his *History*, Thucydides records Pericles's funeral oration for the dead Athenian soldiers, which outlines the dangers and benefits of democracy. Elected 16 times to the position of general, Pericles instituted many democratic reforms while retaining a significant degree of personal power.

40 In an euphoric dream;
Out of the mirror they stare,
Imperialism's face
And the international wrong.

Faces along the bar
45 Cling to their average day:
The lights must never go out,
The music must always play,
All the conventions conspire
To make this fort assume
50 The furniture of home;
Lest we should see where we are,
Lost in a haunted wood,
Children afraid of the night
Who have never been happy or good.

55

The windiest militant trash
Important Persons shout
Is not so crude as our wish:
What mad Nijinsky[1] wrote
About Diaghilev
60 Is true of the normal heart;
For the error bred in the bone
Of each woman and each man
Craves what it cannot have,
Not universal love
65 But to be loved alone.

From the conservative dark
Into the ethical life
The dense commuters come,
Repeating their morning vow;
70 "I *will* be true to the wife,
I'll concentrate more on my work,"
And helpless governors wake

---

1   *Nijinsky* Vaslav Nijinsky (1890–1950), Russian ballet dancer and choreographer, worked
     with the Russian ballet producer Sergei Diaghilev (1872–1929) until their falling out in
     1913. In 1917 Nijinsky's mental instability forced him into permanent retirement. In his
     diary, published in 1937, Nijinsky wrote: "Some politicians are hypocrites like Diaghilev,
     who does not want universal love, but to be loved alone. I want universal love."

To resume their compulsory game:
Who can release them now,
Who can reach the deaf,
Who can speak for the dumb?

Defenceless under the night
Our world in stupor lies;
Yet, dotted everywhere,
Ironic points of light
Flash out wherever the Just
Exchange their messages:
May I, composed like them
Of Eros[1] and of dust,
Beleaguered by the same
Negation and despair,
Show an affirming flame.

          —1940

The Unknown Citizen

(To JS/07/M/378
This Marble Monument
Is Erected by the State)

He was found by the Bureau of Statistics to be
One against whom there was no official complaint,
And all the reports on his conduct agree
That, in the modern sense of an old-fashioned word, he was a saint,
For in everything he did he served the Greater Community.
Except for the War till the day he retired
He worked in a factory and never got fired,
But satisfied his employers, Fudge Motors Inc.
Yet he wasn't a scab[2] or odd in his views,
For his Union reports that he paid his dues,
(Our report on his Union shows it was sound)
And our Social Psychology workers found
That he was popular with his mates and liked a drink.

---

1   *Eros* In contrast to the New Testament *agape*, or Christian love, *eros* represents earthly, or
      sexual love. In Greek myth, the winged Eros, son of Aphrodite, is the god of love.
2   *scab* Someone who works during a strike or refuses to join a union.

The Press are convinced that he bought a paper every day
And that his reactions to advertisements were normal in every way.
15 Policies taken out in his name prove that he was fully insured,
And his Health-card shows he was once in hospital but left it cured.
Both Producers Research and High-Grade Living declare
He was fully sensible to the advantages of the Instalment Plan
And had everything necessary to the Modern Man,
20 A phonograph, a radio, a car and a frigidaire.
Our researchers into Public Opinion are content
That he held the proper opinions for the time of year;
When there was peace, he was for peace; when there was war, he
    went.
He was married and added five children to the population,
25 Which our Eugenist[1] says was the right number for a parent of his
    generation.
And our teachers report that he never interfered with their education.
Was he free? Was he happy? The question is absurd:
Had anything been wrong, we should certainly have heard.

—1940

---

1   *Eugenist* Scientist who studies the development of physically or mentally improved human beings through selective breeding. Eugenics has played a key role in legitimizing racist ideologies such as Nazism.

Theodore Roethke

1908–1963

Known for his introspective verse, Theodore Roethke was both praised and criticized for his focus on the self. Some critics saw his personal exploration as a means to valuable insight into the human body and the unconscious mind, but others considered his scope too limited and irrelevant to the political and social concerns of the day. Despite the inward focus of his poetry, Roethke read widely, and his style was strongly influenced by the poets he admired, such as William Blake, T.S. Eliot, and W.B. Yeats. He also formed literary friendships with fellow poets W.H. Auden, Dylan Thomas, and William Carlos Williams.

Born in Michigan into a German-American family, Roethke had ambivalent childhood memories of his horticulturalist father that centred on the family's extensive greenhouses. Images of growth, decay, and death recur in his poetry, especially in what he referred to as the "greenhouse poems" included in *The Lost Son and Other Poems* (1948). By contrast, joyful love is the subject of "I Knew a Woman" from *Words for the Wind* (1958), published after his marriage to Beatrice O'Connell. *Words for the Wind* marked a new direction for Roethke, who frequently returned to love poetry in his later work.

Roethke taught at Michigan State College and was very dedicated to his teaching; however, he was dismissed after the first of what became a series of mental breakdowns and psychiatric hospitalizations. He then taught at the University of Washington where, although he was often unwell, he was valued for both his teaching and his writing. Roethke's honours include the Pulitzer Prize, two National Book Awards, and the Shelley Memorial Award.

My Papa's Waltz

The whiskey on your breath
Could make a small boy dizzy;
But I hung on like death:
Such waltzing was not easy.

We romped until the pans
Slid from the kitchen shelf;
My mother's countenance
Could not unfrown itself.

5

The hand that held my wrist
10 Was battered on one knuckle;
At every step you missed
My right ear scraped a buckle.

You beat time on my head
With a palm caked hard by dirt,
15 Then waltzed me off to bed
Still clinging to your shirt.

—1948

I Knew a Woman

I knew a woman, lovely in her bones,
When small birds sighed, she would sigh back at them;
Ah, when she moved, she moved more ways than one:
The shapes a bright container can contain!
5 Of her choice virtues only gods should speak,
Or English poets who grew up on Greek
(I'd have them sing in chorus, cheek to cheek).

How well her wishes went! She stroked my chin,
She taught me Turn, and Counter-turn, and Stand;[1]
10 She taught me Touch, that undulant white skin;
I nibbled meekly from her proffered hand;
She was the sickle; I, poor I, the rake,
Coming behind her for her pretty sake
(But what prodigious mowing we did make).

15 Love likes a gander, and adores a goose:
Her full lips pursed, the errant note to seize;
She played it quick, she played it light and loose;
My eyes, they dazzled at her flowing knees;
Her several parts could keep a pure repose,
20 Or one hip quiver with a mobile nose
(She moved in circles, and those circles moved).

---

1   *Turn, and Counter-turn, and Stand* Allusion to *strophe, antistrophe,* and *epode,* the three
parts of a typical Greek ode.

Let seed be grass, and grass turn into hay:
I'm martyr to a motion not my own;
What's freedom for? To know eternity.
I swear she cast a shadow white as stone.   25
But who would count eternity in days?
These old bones live to learn her wanton ways:
(I measure time by how a body sways).

—1958

Elizabeth Bishop

1911–1979

Although respected by her contemporaries and honoured with a host of prestigious appointments, prizes, awards, and fellowships, Elizabeth Bishop came to be recognized only posthumously as a major American poet on the strength of a small but scrupulously crafted body of work. That she published just 101 poems in a cluster of slender volumes is a testament to the pains she took with her art. According to the poet Robert Lowell, with whom she shared a close friendship, she was "an unerring Muse" who made "the casual perfect."

Born in Massachusetts, Bishop was raised there and in Nova Scotia, and during her adult life she travelled extensively. She lived in Brazil from 1951 to 1966, for most of that time with architect Lota de Macedo Soares. In 1956 she received the Pulitzer Prize for a collection of poetry, *Poems: North & South/A Cold Spring*; thereafter she was frequently a recipient of honours and awards.

As one who spent much of her life roving from country to country, Bishop explained her "passion for accuracy" in the following terms: "since we do float on an unknown sea I think we should examine the floating things that come our way very carefully; who knows what might depend on it?" Some of Bishop's poems, such as "First Death in Nova Scotia," draw on elements of her personal life. But she remained wary of confessional poetry, believing that a poem that luxuriates in the feelings of the poet must be of diminished significance to other readers. She made a discipline of reticence and discretion, striving never to fall into sentimental self-pity or intrude too much of herself in order that the particular might serve to illuminate and bear the weight of the universal.

Sestina

September rain falls on the house.
In the failing light, the old grandmother
sits in the kitchen with the child
beside the Little Marvel[1] Stove,
5 reading the jokes from the almanac,[2]
laughing and talking to hide her tears.

---

1   *Little Marvel* Brand of cast-iron stove.
2   *almanac* Yearly calendar that includes information about weather patterns and astronomical data.

She thinks that her equinoctial[1] tears
and the rain that beats on the roof of the house
were both foretold by the almanac,
but only known to a grandmother.   10
The iron kettle sings on the stove.
She cuts some bread and says to the child,

It's time for tea now; but the child
is watching the teakettle's small hard tears
dance like mad on the hot black stove,   15
the way the rain must dance on the house.
Tidying up, the old grandmother
hangs up the clever almanac

on its string. Birdlike, the almanac
hovers half open above the child,   20
hovers above the old grandmother
and her teacup full of dark brown tears.
She shivers and says she thinks the house
feels chilly, and puts more wood in the stove.

It was to be, says the Marvel Stove.   25
I know what I know, says the almanac.
With crayons the child draws a rigid house
and a winding pathway. Then the child
puts in a man with buttons like tears
and shows it proudly to the grandmother.   30

But secretly, while the grandmother
busies herself about the stove,
the little moons fall down like tears
from between the pages of the almanac
into the flower bed the child   35
has carefully placed in the front of the house.

Time to plant tears, says the almanac.
The grandmother sings to the marvelous stove
and the child draws another inscrutable house.

—1956

---

1   *equinoctial* Related to or occurring at the time of the equinox. The term can also refer to
    an "equinoctial gale," a storm occurring near the equinox (which was believed to cause an
    increase in intense weather).

First Death in Nova Scotia

In the cold, cold parlour
my mother laid out Arthur
beneath the chromographs:
Edward, Prince of Wales,
5 with Princess Alexandra,
and King George with Queen Mary.[1]
Below them on the table
stood a stuffed loon
shot and stuffed by Uncle
10 Arthur, Arthur's father.

Since Uncle Arthur fired
a bullet into him,
he hadn't said a word.
He kept his own counsel
15 on his white, frozen lake,
the marble-topped table.
His breast was deep and white,
cold and caressable;
his eyes were red glass,
20 much to be desired.

"Come," said my mother,
"Come and say good-bye
to your little cousin Arthur."
I was lifted up and given
25 one lily of the valley
to put in Arthur's hand.
Arthur's coffin was
a little frosted cake,
and the red-eyed loon eyed it
30 from his white, frozen lake.

---

1   *chromographs* Coloured prints; *Edward, Prince ... Queen Mary* Members of the British
    royal family. Edward VII was Prince of Wales when he married Alexandra of Denmark in
    1863. They became king and queen consort in 1901 and were succeeded by King George
    V and Mary of Teck in 1910.

Arthur was very small.
He was all white, like a doll
that hadn't been painted yet.
Jack Frost had started to paint him
the way he always painted   35
the Maple Leaf (Forever).[1]
He had just begun on his hair,
a few red strokes, and then
Jack Frost had dropped the brush
and left him white, forever.   40

The gracious royal couples
were warm in red and ermine;
their feet were well wrapped up
in the ladies' ermine trains.
They invited Arthur to be   45
the smallest page at court.
But how could Arthur go,
clutching his tiny lily,
with his eyes shut up so tight
and the roads deep in snow?   50

—1962

One Art

The art of losing isn't hard to master;
so many things seem filled with the intent
to be lost that their loss is no disaster.

Lose something every day. Accept the fluster
of lost door keys, the hour badly spent.   5
The art of losing isn't hard to master.

Then practice losing farther, losing faster:
places, and names, and where it was you meant
to travel. None of these will bring disaster.

---

1   *the Maple Leaf (Forever)* Reference to "The Maple Leaf Forever" (1867), an unofficial
    Canadian anthem.

10   I lost my mother's watch. And look! my last, or
next-to-last, of three loved houses went.
The art of losing isn't hard to master.

I lost two cities, lovely ones. And, vaster,
some realms I owned, two rivers, a continent.
15   I miss them, but it wasn't a disaster.

—Even losing you (the joking voice, a gesture
I love) I shan't have lied. It's evident
the art of losing's not too hard to master
though it may look like (*Write* it!) like disaster.

—1976

Dylan Thomas
1914–1953

Dylan Thomas was a raucous fixture in the taverns of London's Soho-Fitzrovia district, and he haunted the rural hills and seashores of Wales. Influenced by a romantic sensibility, he sought to articulate his sense that life and death were rolled together in nature's driving "green fuse."

Thomas was born in Swansea, Wales, and his youth and childhood there would be a recurring subject in his poetry. His father was a teacher at Swansea Grammar School, which Thomas attended and where he was far from a prize pupil; as a teenager, he regularly cut classes to work on his own poetry. His first published work, "And Death Shall Have No Dominion" (1933), was printed in a literary magazine when he was only 18.

When Thomas's *18 Poems* was published the following year, the strange and disturbing power of his verse woke up London's literary establishment. The cool, controlled style of T.S. Eliot, which conditioned poetic attitudes well into the 1950s, appeared subdued next to what one critic called Thomas's "belligerent syntax." While fresh and vital, Thomas's poems are also complex, built of dense interlocking images, and tightly structured: "Do Not Go Gentle into That Good Night" (1951), for example, adopts the restrictive form of a villanelle.

Despite his heavy drinking and a turbulent marriage, Thomas continued to publish poems—as well as short stories and radio plays—until the end of his life. Constant money troubles were lessened when he began making recordings of his poetry and touring to give public readings, which were enormously popular in Europe, and even more so in the United States. He was 39 when he died in New York of problems related to alcoholism.

Do Not Go Gentle into That Good Night

Do not go gentle into that good night,
Old age should burn and rave at close of day;
Rage, rage against the dying of the light.

Though wise men at their end know dark is right,
Because their words had forked no lightning they
Do not go gentle into that good night.

Good men, the last wave by, crying how bright
Their frail deeds might have danced in a green bay,
Rage, rage against the dying of the light.

5

10 Wild men who caught and sang the sun in flight,
   And learn, too late, they grieved it on its way,
   Do not go gentle into that good night.

   Grave men, near death, who see with blinding sight
   Blind eyes could blaze like meteors and be gay,
15 Rage, rage against the dying of the light.

   And you, my father, there on the sad height,
   Curse, bless, me now with your fierce tears, I pray.
   Do not go gentle into that good night.
   Rage, rage against the dying of the light.

   —1951

P.K. Page
1916–2010

Although she was also a visual artist of no small talent and an accomplished writer of fiction and non-fiction, P.K. Page is best known as a visionary poet with a gift for fusing the physical and the metaphysical through an elaborate system of evocative imagery.

After emigrating from her native England at a young age, Page grew up on the Canadian prairies, eventually settling in Montreal. Over the course of her long career, she explored a vast intellectual terrain, from ancient philosophy and mysticism to modern psychology and neuroscience, in a style that became increasingly spare and transparent. For this reason, and because Page was a significant part of the movement to modernize Canadian poetry, she is known as a modernist poet, though her frequent use of densely patterned imagery also affiliates her with Symbolism.

Following the publication of her Governor General's Award-winning collection *The Metal and the Flower* (1954), Page lapsed into a 13-year poetic silence while accompanying her husband to Australia, Brazil, Mexico, and Guatemala on his political and diplomatic appointments. Whereas the early poems have been described as aloof portraits that observe and ruminate in a spirit of analytical detachment, the work she wrote after her return to Canada is often regarded as an attempt to move beyond aesthetic portraiture, to transcend what she called the "tyranny of subjectivity" for a more compassionate, expansive, even mystical vision of the world.

Page continued to write until her death at the age of 93. In 1998 she was made a Companion of the Order of Canada, and in 2003 her collection *Planet Earth: Poems Selected and New* was shortlisted for the Griffin Prize.

The Stenographers

After the brief bivouac[1] of Sunday,
their eyes, in the forced march of Monday to Saturday,
hoist the white flag, flutter in the snow-storm of paper,
haul it down and crack in the mid-sun of temper.

In the pause between the first draft and the carbon
they glimpse the smooth hours when they were children—
the ride in the ice-cart, the ice-man's name,
the end of the route and the long walk home;

5

---

1   *bivouac* Military camp made without covered shelters.

remember the sea where floats at high tide
10 were sea marrows growing on the scatter-green vine
or spools of grey toffee, or wasps' nests on water;
remember the sand and the leaves of the country.

Bell rings and they go and the voice draws their pencil
like a sled across snow; when its runners are frozen
15 rope snaps and the voice then is pulling no burden
but runs like a dog on the winter of paper.

Their climates are winter and summer—no wind
for the kites of their hearts—no wind for a flight;
a breeze at the most, to tumble them over
20 and leave them like rubbish—the boy-friends of blood.

In the inch of the noon as they move they are stagnant.
The terrible calm of the noon is their anguish;
the lip of the counter, the shapes of the straws
like icicles breaking their tongues, are invaders.

25 Their beds are their oceans—salt water of weeping
the waves that they know—the tide before sleep;
and fighting to drown they assemble their sheep
in columns and watch them leap desks for their fences
and stare at them with their own mirror-worn faces.

30 In the felt of the morning the calico-minded,
sufficiently starched, insert papers, hit keys,
efficient and sure as their adding machines;
yet they weep in the vault, they are taut as net curtains
stretched upon frames. In their eyes I have seen
35 the pin men of madness in marathon trim
race round the track of the stadium pupil.

—1946

Stories of Snow

Those in the vegetable rain retain
an area behind their sprouting eyes
held soft and rounded with the dream of snow
precious and reminiscent as those globes—
souvenir of some never nether land—   5
which hold their snowstorms circular, complete,
high in a tall and teakwood cabinet.

In countries where the leaves are large as hands
where flowers protrude their fleshy chins
and call their colours   10
an imaginary snowstorm sometimes falls
among the lilies.
And in the early morning one will waken
to think the glowing linen of his pillow
a northern drift, will find himself mistaken   15
and lie back weeping.
And there the story shifts from head to head,
of how, in Holland, from their feather beds
hunters arise and part the flakes and go
forth to the frozen lakes in search of swans—   20
the snow light falling white along their guns,
their breath in plumes.
While tethered in the wind like sleeping gulls
ice boats await the raising of their wings
to skim the electric ice at such a speed   25
they leap jet strips of naked water,
and how these flying, sailing hunters feel
air in their mouths as terrible as ether.
And on the story runs that even drinks
in that white landscape dare to be no colour;   30
how, flasked and water clear, the liquor slips
silver against the hunters' moving hips.
And of the swan in death these dreamers tell
of its last flight and how it falls, a plummet,
pierced by the freezing bullet   35
and how three feathers, loosened by the shot,
descend like snow upon it.

While hunters plunge their fingers in its down
deep as a drift, and dive their hands
40 up to the neck of the wrist
in that warm metamorphosis of snow
as gentle as the sort that woodsmen know
who, lost in the white circle, fall at last
and dream their way to death.

45 And stories of this kind are often told
in countries where great flowers bar the roads
with reds and blues which seal the route to snow
as if, in telling, raconteurs unlock
the colour with its complement and go
50 through to the area behind the eyes
where silent, unrefractive whiteness lies.

—1946

Al Purdy

1918–2000

Al Purdy was a staunch Canadian nationalist whose love of country was an overwhelming presence in his poetic works. Purdy wrote realistically about Canada's geography and regional history, drawing on material ranging from the lives of the long-dead Dorset Inuit to his own formative experiences train-hopping across the country, to his great love for the rock-strewn, formidable landscape of Eastern Ontario where he spent much of his life. His rough, sometimes self-deprecating poetic persona is distinctly Canadian, too, as is the colloquial style he evolved over the course of his career to reflect everyday Canadian speech. Of his writing, Purdy's friend and collaborator Doug Beardsley said, "He spoke to us, for us, he gave articulation to our lives as Canadians. He consciously set out to map this country with poetry and he did that."

Born in 1918, Purdy dropped out of school and, during his youth, spent time travelling across the country. He served in the Royal Canadian Air Force during World War II, and went on to become a cab driver and a mattress factory employee. In 1944 he published his first collection of poetry, *The Enchanted Echo*; he would later decry his early works, claiming that it was not until 1965 that he was truly a poet. That year he won his first Governor General's Award for *The Cariboo Horses*, and in 1986 he would receive another for *The Collected Poems of Al Purdy, 1956–1986*. Over the course of his career, Purdy published over 30 volumes of poetry and championed the work of other Canadian poets in his work as an editor and anthologist.

Trees at the Arctic Circle

(*Salix Cordifolia*—Ground Willow)

They are 18 inches long
or even less
crawling under rocks
grovelling among the lichens
bending and curling to escape   5
making themselves small
finding new ways to hide
Coward trees
I am angry to see them
like this   10
not proud of what they are

bowing to weather instead
careful of themselves
worried about the sky
15   afraid of exposing their limbs
like a Victorian married couple

I call to mind great Douglas Firs
I see tall maples waving green
and oaks like gods in autumn gold
20   the whole horizon jungle dark
and I crouched under that continual night
But these
even the dwarf shrubs of Ontario
mock them
25   Coward trees

And yet—and yet—
their seed pods glow
like delicate grey earrings
their leaves are veined and intricate
30   like tiny parkas
They have about three months
to ensure the species does not die
and that's how they spend their time
unbothered by any human opinion
35   just digging in here and now
sending their roots down down down
And you know it occurs to me
about 2 feet under
those roots must touch permafrost
40   ice that remains ice forever
and they use it for their nourishment
they use death to remain alive

I see that I've been carried away
in my scorn of the dwarf trees
45   most foolish in my judgments
To take away the dignity
of any living thing
even tho it cannot understand
the scornful words

is to make life itself trivial 50
and yourself the Pontifex Maximus° *High Priest*
    of nullity
I have been stupid in a poem
I will not alter the poem
but let the stupidity remain permanent 55
as the trees are
in a poem
the dwarf trees of Baffin Island

Pangnirtung[1]

—1967

Lament for the Dorsets[2]

(Eskimos extinct in the 14th century AD)

Animal bones and some mossy tent rings
scrapers and spearheads carved ivory swans
all that remains of the Dorset giants
who drove the Vikings back to their long ships[3]
talked to spirits of earth and water 5
—a picture of terrifying old men
so large they broke the backs of bears
so small they lurk behind bone rafters
in the brain of modern hunters
among good thoughts and warm things 10
and come out at night
to spit on the stars

The big men with clever fingers
who had no dogs and hauled their sleds
over the frozen northern oceans 15
awkward giants
        killers of seal
they couldn't compete with little men

---

1   *Pangnirtung* Hamlet on Baffin Island.
2   *Dorsets* Dorset people lived in the central and eastern Canadian Arctic until about 500 years ago.
3   *drove the ... long ships* In the late tenth century, Norse people briefly established temporary settlements in North America.

who came from the west with dogs
Or else in a warm climatic cycle
20   the seals went back to cold waters
and the puzzled Dorsets scratched their heads
with hairy thumbs around 1350 A.D.
—couldn't figure it out
went around saying to each other plaintively
25   "What's wrong? What happened?
                     Where are the seals gone?"
And died

Twentieth-century people
apartment dwellers
30   executives of neon death
warmakers with things that explode
—they have never imagined us in their future
how could we imagine them in the past
squatting among the moving glaciers
35   six hundred years ago
with glowing lamps?
As remote or nearly
as the trilobites and swamps
when coal became
40   or the last great reptile hissed
at a mammal the size of a mouse
that squeaked and fled

Did they ever realize at all
what was happening to them?
45   Some old hunter with one lame leg
a bear had chewed
sitting in a caribou-skin tent
—the last Dorset?
Let's say his name was Kudluk
50   and watch him sitting there
carving 2-inch ivory swans
for a dead grand-daughter
taking them out of his mind
the places in his mind
55   where pictures are
He selects a sharp stone tool

to gouge a parallel pattern of lines
on both sides of the swan
holding it with his left hand
bearing down and transmitting   60
his body's weight
from brain to arm and right hand
and one of his thoughts
turns to ivory
The carving is laid aside   65
in beginning darkness
at the end of hunger
and after a while wind
blows down the tent and snow
begins to cover him   70

After 600 years
the ivory thought
is still warm

—1968

Allen Ginsberg
1926–1997

Along with writers Jack Kerouac and William S. Burroughs, Allen Ginsberg was one of the most prominent writers of the 1950s "Beat Generation," remembered for their literary rebellion against middle-class values and formalist poetry.

Ginsberg is perhaps best known for his poem "Howl," first delivered at a poetry reading in San Francisco in 1955 and published the following year. Drawing on influences from Jewish liturgy to William Blake, the long poem condemns American society's repressive attitudes toward homosexuality, drug use, and mental illness, presenting the demonic god Moloch as an embodiment of America's obsession with money and order. Because the poem makes explicit references to drug use and homosexuality at a time when both were illegal, the publishers of "Howl" were charged with distributing obscene literature, and Ginsberg's poem became the centrepiece of a landmark obscenity trial in the United States. The publishers and the poem ultimately triumphed.

After the Beat era, Ginsberg continued to write until his death, publishing letters and essays as well as poetry. His interest in religion and philosophy, especially Hindu and Buddhist thought, provided an increasingly important focus in his later work. Like "Howl," his post-Beat poems are often politically motivated; *Wichita Vortex Sutra* (1966), for example, censures the Vietnam War, against which Ginsberg was an effective and dedicated activist.

A Supermarket in California

What thoughts I have of you tonight, Walt Whitman,[1] for I walked down the sidestreets under the trees with a headache self-conscious looking at the full moon.

In my hungry fatigue, and shopping for images, I went into the neon fruit
5 supermarket, dreaming of your enumerations!

What peaches and what penumbras![2] Whole families shopping at night! Aisles full of husbands! Wives in the avocados, babies in the tomatoes!—and you, García Lorca,[3] what were you doing down by the watermelons?

---

1   *Walt Whitman* American poet (1819–92), one of Ginsberg's major influences. "A Supermarket in California" was written in 1955, 100 years after Whitman published the first edition of his collection *Leaves of Grass*.

2   *penumbras* Partially shaded regions at the edges of a shadow.

3   *García Lorca* Federico García Lorca (1899–1936), Spanish poet and dramatist.

I saw you, Walt Whitman, childless, lonely old grubber, poking among the meats in the refrigerator and eyeing the grocery boys.[1]

I heard you asking questions of each: Who killed the pork chops? What price bananas? Are you my Angel?

I wandered in and out of the brilliant stacks of cans following you, and followed in my imagination by the store detective. We strode down the open corridors together in our solitary fancy tasting artichokes, possessing every frozen delicacy, and never passing the cashier.

Where are we going, Walt Whitman? The doors close in an hour. Which way does your beard point tonight?

(I touch your book and dream of our odyssey in the supermarket and feel absurd.)

Will we walk all night through solitary streets? The trees add shade to shade, lights out in the houses, we'll both be lonely.

Will we stroll dreaming of the lost America of love past blue automobiles in driveways, home to our silent cottage?

Ah, dear father, greybeard, lonely old courage-teacher, what America did you have when Charon[2] quit poling his ferry and you got out on a smoking bank and stood watching the boat disappear on the black waters of Lethe?[3]

—1956 (written 1955)

---

1   *I saw you ... grocery boys* Although the full nature of his sexuality is still debated, most scholars believe that Whitman was gay.

2   *Charon* In Greek mythology, the boatman who ferried the souls of the dead across the River Styx to Hades.

3   *Lethe* River in Hades, the waters of which brought forgetfulness.

Adrienne Rich

1929–2012

Adrienne Rich was born in Baltimore, Maryland. Over her long career, she published more than sixteen volumes of poetry and five volumes of critical prose, most recently *Tonight No Poetry Will Serve: Poems 2007–2010*, *A Human Eye: Essays on Art in Society*, and *Later Poems: Selected and New 1971–2012*, published posthumously. She edited Muriel Rukeyser's *Selected Poems* for the Library of America. Among numerous other recognitions, Rich was the 2006 recipient of the National Book Foundation's Medal for Distinguished Contribution to American Letters. Her poetry and essays have been widely translated and published internationally.[1]

Aunt Jennifer's Tigers

Aunt Jennifer's tigers prance across a screen,
Bright topaz denizens of a world of green.
They do not fear the men beneath the tree;
They pace in sleek chivalric certainty.

5 Aunt Jennifer's fingers fluttering through her wool
Find even the ivory needle hard to pull.
The massive weight of Uncle's wedding band
Sits heavily upon Aunt Jennifer's hand.

When Aunt is dead, her terrified hands will lie
10 Still ringed with ordeals she was mastered by.
The tigers in the panel that she made
Will go on prancing, proud and unafraid.

—1951

---

1   Editors' note: This author biography was provided by the rights holders of Adrienne Rich's poetry, and is included at their request. Its relative brevity in no way reflects the editors' views as to the importance of Rich's work.

Living in Sin

She had thought the studio would keep itself;
no dust upon the furniture of love.
Half heresy, to wish the taps less vocal,
the panes relieved of grime. A plate of pears,
a piano with a Persian shawl, a cat   5
stalking the picturesque amusing mouse
had risen at his urging.
Not that at five each separate stair would writhe
under the milkman's tramp; that morning light
so coldly would delineate the scraps   10
of last night's cheese and three sepulchral bottles;
that on the kitchen shelf among the saucers
a pair of beetle-eyes would fix her own—
envoy from some black village in the mouldings ...
Meanwhile, he, with a yawn,   15
sounded a dozen notes upon the keyboard,
declared it out of tune, shrugged at the mirror,
rubbed at his beard, went out for cigarettes;
while she, jeered by the minor demons,
pulled back the sheets and made the bed and found   20
a towel to dust the table-top,
and let the coffee-pot boil over on the stove.
By evening she was back in love again,
though not so wholly but throughout the night
she woke sometimes to feel the daylight coming   25
like a relentless milkman up the stairs.

—1955

Diving into the Wreck

First having read the book of myths,
and loaded the camera,
and checked the edge of the knife-blade,
I put on
the body-armour of black rubber   5
the absurd slippers
the grave and awkward mask.
I am having to do this

not like Cousteau[1] with his
10 assiduous team
aboard the sun-flooded schooner
but here alone.

There is a ladder.
The ladder is always there
15 hanging innocently
close to the side of the schooner.
We know what it is for,
we who have used it.
Otherwise
20 it's a piece of maritime floss
some sundry equipment.

I go down.
Rung after rung and still
the oxygen immerses me
25 the blue light
the clear atoms
of our human air.
I go down.
My flippers cripple me,
30 I crawl like an insect down the ladder
and there is no one
to tell me when the ocean
will begin.

First the air is blue and then
35 it is bluer and then green and then
black I am blacking out and yet
my mask is powerful
it pumps my blood with power
the sea is another story
40 the sea is not a question of power
I have to learn alone
to turn my body without force
in the deep element.

---

1   *Cousteau* Jacques Cousteau (1910–97), well-known oceanographer and undersea explorer.

And now: it is easy to forget
what I came for   45
among so many who have always
lived here
swaying their crenellated fans
between the reefs
and besides   50
you breathe differently down here.

I came to explore the wreck.
The words are purposes.
The words are maps.
I came to see the damage that was done   55
and the treasures that prevail.
I stroke the beam of my lamp
slowly along the flank
of something more permanent
than fish or weed   60

the thing I came for:
the wreck and not the story of the wreck
the thing itself and not the myth
the drowned face always staring
toward the sun   65
the evidence of damage
worn by salt and sway into this threadbare beauty
the ribs of the disaster
curving their assertion
among the tentative haunters.   70

This is the place.
And I am here, the mermaid whose dark hair
streams black, the merman in his armoured body
We circle silently
about the wreck   75
we dive into the hold.
I am she: I am he

whose drowned face sleeps with open eyes
whose breasts still bear the stress

80 whose silver, copper, vermeil[1] cargo lies
    obscurely inside barrels
    half-wedged and left to rot
    we are the half-destroyed instruments
    that once held to a course
85 the water-eaten log
    the fouled compass

    We are, I am, you are
    by cowardice or courage
    the one who find our way
90 back to this scene
    carrying a knife, a camera
    a book of myths
    in which
    our names do not appear.

—1973

---

1   *vermeil* Gold plate over silver.

Ted Hughes

1930–1998

With bold metaphors and forceful rhythms, poet Ted Hughes paints grim, often violent, visions of human existence. At the same time, he celebrates the power of nature and attempts to reunite humanity with the natural world. Hughes's first volume of poetry, *The Hawk in the Rain* (1957), received critical praise for its strong, earthy language and intense natural imagery. He further established his reputation as a major new poet with his second book, *Lupercal* (1960), and he continued to write prolifically, producing many volumes of poetry as well as verse for children, radio plays, and translations.

In 1956 Hughes married the American poet Sylvia Plath (1932–63); the couple separated in 1962, and Plath committed suicide less than a year later. Hughes put his own poetry on hold to focus on editing and publishing his wife's poems and journals, and the editorial decisions he made as her executor received intense criticism from some of her admirers. Hughes would say very little regarding his relationship with Plath until his 1998 publication of *Birthday Letters*, a series of poems addressed to her.

Wodwo (1967), Hughes's return to poetry after Plath's death, signalled a change in direction from his earlier work. A marked interest in anthropology—and especially in occult, mythic, and folktale sources—began to colour his writing. Several of his volumes were produced in collaboration with visual artists, such as photographer Fay Godwin, with whom he created *Remains of Elmet* (1979), an exploration of the history and landscape of his native West Yorkshire from ancient to industrial times.

Hughes was Britain's Poet Laureate from 1984 until his death in 1998. British poet and critic Dick Davis has offered this explanation for the continuing appeal of Hughes's poetry: "He brings back to our suburban, centrally-heated and, above all, *safe* lives reports from an authentic frontier of reality and the imagination."

The Thought-Fox

I imagine this midnight moment's forest:
Something else is alive
Beside the clock's loneliness
And this blank page where my fingers move.

Through the window I see no star:
Something more near
Though deeper within darkness
Is entering the loneliness:

Cold, delicately as the dark snow
10 A fox's nose touches twig, leaf;
Two eyes serve a movement, that now
And again now, and now, and now

Sets neat prints into the snow
Between trees, and warily a lame
15 Shadow lags by stump and in hollow
Of a body that is bold to come

Across clearings, an eye,
A widening deepening greenness,
Brilliantly, concentratedly,
20 Coming about its own business

Till, with a sudden sharp hot stink of fox,
It enters the dark hole of the head.
The window is starless still; the clock ticks,
The page is printed.

—1957

Pike[1]

Pike, three inches long, perfect
Pike in all parts, green tigering the gold.
Killers from the egg: the malevolent aged grin.
They dance on the surface among the flies.

5 Or move, stunned by their own grandeur,
Over a bed of emerald, silhouette
Of submarine delicacy and horror.
A hundred feet long in their world.

In ponds, under the heat-struck lily pads—
10 Gloom of their stillness:
Logged on last year's black leaves, watching upwards.
Or hung in an amber cavern of weeds

---

1   *Pike* Family of freshwater fish, some species of which can grow longer than two metres.
Considered unusually aggressive predators, they eat other fish, amphibians, small mam-
mals, birds, and sometimes each other.

The jaws' hooked clamp and fangs
Not to be changed at this date;
A life subdued to its instrument; 15
The gills kneading quietly, and the pectorals.

Three we kept behind glass,
Jungled in weed: three inches, four,
And four and a half: fed fry to them—
Suddenly there were two. Finally one. 20

With a sag belly and the grin it was born with.
And indeed they spare nobody.
Two, six pounds each, over two feet long,
High and dry and dead in the willow-herb—

One jammed past its gills down the other's gullet: 25
The outside eye stared: as a vice locks—
The same iron in this eye
Though its film shrank in death.

A pond I fished, fifty yards across,
Whose lilies and muscular tench[1] 30
Had outlasted every visible stone
Of the monastery that planted them—

Stilled legendary depth:
It was as deep as England. It held
Pike too immense to stir, so immense and old 35
That past nightfall I dared not cast

But silently cast and fished
With the hair frozen on my head
For what might move, for what eye might move.
The still splashes on the dark pond, 40

Owls hushing the floating woods
Frail on my ear against the dream
Darkness beneath night's darkness had freed,
That rose slowly towards me, watching.

—1959

---

1   *tench* Fish similar to carp.

Derek Walcott

1930–2017

In 1992, Derek Walcott became the first Caribbean writer to receive the Nobel Prize in Literature. Throughout his career, he grappled with the central issues of twentieth- and twenty-first-century Caribbean writing: the use of the English language versus that of Creole; the effects of a history of slavery and colonization on the region; and the deep-seated ambivalence toward English culture that results from that history.

Walcott's personal background reflects the cultural complexities of the Caribbean. A descendant both of Europeans and of former slaves, he was born into an English-speaking family on the predominantly French Creole-speaking island of St. Lucia, and lived there or in Trinidad for most of his life. In his Nobel acceptance speech he expressed his wish that the people of the Caribbean would move beyond their painful history, claiming that "[we] make too much of that long groan which underlines the past." He proffered instead a vision of Caribbean poetry as a route to rebuilding and celebrating Caribbean culture: "the fate of poetry is to fall in love with the world, in spite of History."

Some Caribbean intellectuals have criticized Walcott's attitude toward the colonial past, arguing for an unequivocal return to African traditions or for a turning away from the English language in favour of Creole. In response to criticism of his decision to write in English, Walcott has argued that the language is shaped by those who use it.

Walcott's more than 20 books of poetry include the epic *Omeros* (1990), which merges Homer's *Odyssey* with the history of St. Lucia, and the T.S. Eliot Prize-winning collection *White Egrets* (2011). Walcott was also a prolific playwright whose work was instrumental to the development of indigenous theatre in Trinidad.

A Far Cry from Africa

A wind is ruffling the tawny pelt
Of Africa. Kikuyu,[1] quick as flies,
Batten upon[2] the bloodstreams of the veldt.°   *open country*
Corpses are scattered through a paradise.
5 Only the worm, colonel of carrion, cries:
"Waste no compassion on these separate dead!"

---

1   *Kikuyu* Bantu-speaking people of Kenya who fought against British colonial settlers as part of the eight-year Mau Mau uprising of the 1950s.

2   *Batten upon* Thrive on; revel in.

Statistics justify and scholars seize
The salients of colonial policy.
What is that to the white child hacked in bed?
To savages, expendable as Jews?   10

Threshed out by beaters, the long rushes break
In a white dust of ibises[1] whose cries
Have wheeled since civilization's dawn
From the parched river or beast-teeming plain.
The violence of beast on beast is read   15
As natural law, but upright man
Seeks his divinity by inflicting pain.
Delirious as these worried beasts, his wars
Dance to the tightened carcass of a drum,
While he calls courage still that native dread   20
Of the white peace contracted by the dead.

Again brutish necessity wipes its hands
Upon the napkin of a dirty cause, again
A waste of our compassion, as with Spain,[2]
The gorilla wrestles with the superman.   25
I who am poisoned with the blood of both,
Where shall I turn, divided to the vein?
I who have cursed
The drunken officer of British rule, how choose
Between this Africa and the English tongue I love?   30
Betray them both, or give back what they give?
How can I face such slaughter and be cool?
How can I turn from Africa and live?

—1962

---

1   *ibises* Long-legged, stork-like birds that inhabit lakes and swamps.
2   *Spain* I.e., the Spanish Civil War (1936–39). Many foreign volunteers participated in
     the Civil War, perceiving it as a way to resist the international rise of fascism. After bru-
     tality on both sides, the war ended with the establishment of a dictatorship supported
     by the German Nazis and the Italian Fascists.

Arun Kolatkar

1932–2004

A prolific writer of Marathi and English poems, Indian poet Arun Kolatkar was described by the novelist Amit Chaudhuri as "the poet who deserves to be as well-known as Salman Rushdie." Despite being recognized within India as one of the foremost artistic talents of his time, Kolatkar was a notorious recluse, who refused to own a telephone, avoided speaking to the press, and published most of his work in low-circulation magazines. "I try to not limit myself with theoretical speculations about what poetry should be," Kolatkar told an interviewer in 2004. "I keep my ideas and attitudes in a limbo, in a suspension, without firming them up, so that when I write I feel free."

Born in Kolhapur, in the Indian state of Maharashtra, Kolatkar had a successful career in the advertising industry of Bombay (now Mumbai). In the late 1950s and 1960s, he composed a series of avant-garde poems synthesizing a wide range of artistic influences including surrealism, American beat poetry, Indian mythology, and traditional Marathi devotional poetry. Though the poems of this period were written primarily in Marathi, a dominant language of Maharashtra, when he wrote his first published collection in the 1970s, he did so in English. This book, *Jejuri* (1976), named for a famous pilgrimage town that provides a setting for the poems, remains his best-known work. Scorned by the Indian critical establishment for its refusal to, as Kolatkar phrased it, "take a position about God one way or the other," *Jejuri* left an indelible imprint upon fellow Indian authors Nissim Ezekiel and Salman Rushdie.

Despite influencing some of the leading figures of Indian postmodernism, Kolatkar remained on the fringes of the Indian poetic scene for the remainder of his life. He is remembered for his deadpan sense of humour, as well as for his virtuosity in both English and Marathi verse. "Why I write one group of poems in one language rather than the other—the answer may be interesting but I don't have it," Kolatkar explained. "As long as I'm writing, I'm fine."

Yeshwant Rao[1]

Are you looking for a god?
I know a good one.
His name is Yeshwant Rao
and he's one of the best.
5   Look him up
when you are in Jejuri next.

---

1   *Yeshwant Rao* Minor Hindu deity with a shrine located in Jejuri, outside the walls of the city's primary temple, which is dedicated to the deity Khandoba.

Of course he's only a second class god
and his place is just outside the main temple.
Outside even of the outer wall.
As if he belonged   10
among the tradesmen and the lepers.

I've known gods
prettier faced
or straighter laced.
Gods who soak you for your gold.   15
Gods who soak you for your soul.
Gods who make you walk
on a bed of burning coal.
Gods who put a child inside your wife.
Or a knife inside your enemy.   20
Gods who tell you how to live your life,
double your money
or triple your land holdings.
Gods who can barely suppress a smile
as you crawl a mile for them.   25
Gods who will see you drown
if you won't buy them a new crown.
And although I'm sure they're all to be praised,
they're either too symmetrical
or too theatrical for my taste.   30

Yeshwant Rao,
mass of basalt,
bright as any post box,
the shape of protoplasm
or king size lava pie   35
thrown against the wall,
without an arm, a leg
or even a single head.

Yeshwant Rao.
He's the god you've got to meet.   40
If you're short of a limb,[1]

---

1   *If you're ... limb* Among the offerings commonly left at Yeshwant Rao's shrine are wooden
    arms and legs placed there as requests for healing.

Yeshwant Rao will lend you a hand
and get you back on your feet.

Yeshwant Rao
45 Does nothing spectacular.
He doesn't promise you the earth
Or book your seat on the next rocket to heaven.
But if any bones are broken,
you know he'll mend them.
50 He'll make you whole in your body
and hope your spirit will look after itself.
He is merely a kind of a bone setter.
The only thing is,
as he himself has no heads, hands and feet,
55 he happens to understand you a little better.

—1976

Yeshwant Rao, outside the main temple of Jejurī, Maharashtra.

Pictures from a Marathi Alphabet Chart

Pineapple. Mother. Pants. Lemon.
Mortar. Sugarcane. Ram.
How secure they all look
each ensconced in its own separate square.

Mango. Anvil. Cup. Ganapati.[1] Cart. House.   5
Medicine Bottle. Man Touching his Toes.
All very comfortable,
they all know exactly where they belong.

Spoon. Umbrella. Ship. Frock.
Watermelon. Rubberstamp. Box. Cloud. Arrow.   10
Each one of them seems to have found
Its own special niche, a sinecure.[2]

Sword. Inkwell. Tombstone. Longbow. Watertap.
Kite. Jackfruit. Brahmin.[3] Duck. Maize.
Their job is just to go on being themselves   15
and their appointment is for life.

Yajna.[4] Chariot. Garlic. Ostrich.
Hexagon. Rabbit. Deer. Lotus. Archer.
No, you don't have to worry.
There's going to be no trouble in this peaceable kingdom.   20

The mother will not pound the baby with a pestle.
The Brahmin will not fry the duck in garlic.
That ship
will not crash against the watermelon.

If the ostrich won't eat the child's frock,   25
The archer won't shoot an arrow in Ganapati's stomach.
And as long as the ram resists the impulse
of butting him from behind

---

1   *Ganapati* Hindu deity with an elephant head, also known as Ganesha.
2   *sinecure* Job that requires little effort but is still profitable.
3   *Brahmin* Member of the highest-ranking Hindu caste, which traditionally consists of
    priests and teachers.
4   *Yajna* Hindu ritual involving a sacred fire.

what possible reason
30 could the Man-Touching-his-Toes have
to smash the cup
on the tombstone?

—1977

Marathi alphabet chart.

Sylvia Plath
1932–1963

Sylvia Plath's early life was, outwardly, one of upper middle-class privilege. The daughter of a Boston University professor and his wife, Plath was an excellent student both in school and later at Smith, a prestigious liberal arts college for women, where she became a prolific writer of poems and short stories. Inwardly, however, she had been profoundly affected by the death of her father when she was eight, and became deeply conflicted over the roles young women in the 1950s were expected to fulfill. Following her third year at Smith she was awarded a guest editorship at the young women's magazine *Mademoiselle*; the experience was a disappointment, however, and Plath fell into a deep depression. She attempted suicide that August, and spent many months thereafter in psychiatric care.

Plath recovered, and in 1955 was awarded a scholarship to Cambridge University, where her talents as a writer began to be more widely recognized—and where she met and soon married the British poet Ted Hughes. The couple both published well-received volumes of poetry (Plath's *The Colossus* appeared in 1960) and they had two children together, but their relationship was sometimes strained and Plath continued to suffer from depression. In 1962, following Plath's discovery that Hughes had been having an affair, the two separated. Between that time and Plath's suicide in February of 1963, living with the children in a bitterly cold flat in London, she wrote the extraordinary body of work on which her reputation now rests. These poems (published posthumously in 1965 in the volume *Ariel*) are spare and controlled in their form but entirely unsparing in the searing intensity with which they explore human strangeness and savagery—perhaps most memorably, the savagery of the Holocaust.

Plath's one novel, *The Bell Jar* (1963), is highly autobiographical, and, given the sensational aspects of her life, it is not surprising that her poetry is often discussed in relation to her life. But, as Catriona O'Reilly has observed, it will not do to regard Plath's work as "an extended suicide note." Her strongest poems are almost universally accorded a vital place in the history of poetry in the twentieth century.

Daddy

You do not do, you do not do
Any more, black shoe
In which I have lived like a foot
For thirty years, poor and white,
5   Barely daring to breathe or Achoo.

Daddy, I have had to kill you.
You died before I had time—
Marble-heavy, a bag full of God,
Ghastly statue with one grey toe[1]
10 Big as a Frisco seal

And a head in the freakish Atlantic
Where it pours bean green over blue
In the waters off beautiful Nauset.[2]
I used to pray to recover you.
15 Ach, du.[3]

In the German tongue, in the Polish town[4]
Scraped flat by the roller
Of wars, wars, wars.
But the name of the town is common.
20 My Polack friend

Says there are a dozen or two.
So I never could tell where you
Put your foot, your root,
I never could talk to you.
25 The tongue stuck in my jaw.

It stuck in a barb wire snare
Ich, ich, ich, ich,[5]

---

1   *Ghastly … grey toe* Plath's father, Otto Plath (1885–1940), died from complications due
    to untreated diabetes. Before he died, his toe became gangrenous and his leg was ampu-
    tated.
2   *Nauset* Beach in Orleans, Massachusetts.
3   *Ach, du* German: Oh, you.
4   *Polish town* Otto Plath emigrated to the US from the Polish town of Grabow.
5   *Ich, ich, ich, ich* German: I, I, I, I.

I could hardly speak.
I thought every German was you.
And the language obscene   30

An engine, an engine
Chuffing me off like a Jew.
A Jew to Dachau, Auschwitz, Belsen.[1]
I began to talk like a Jew.
I think I may well be a Jew.   35

The snows of the Tyrol,[2] the clear beer of Vienna
Are not very pure or true.
With my gypsy ancestress and my weird luck
And my Taroc° pack and my Taroc pack   *Tarot*
I may be a bit of a Jew.   40

I have always been scared of *you*,
With your Luftwaffe,[3] your gobbledygoo.
And your neat moustache
And your Aryan eye, bright blue.
Panzer-man,[4] panzer-man, O You—   45

Not God but a swastika
So black no sky could squeak through.
Every woman adores a Fascist,
The boot in the face, the brute
Brute heart of a brute like you.   50

You stand at the blackboard,[5] daddy,
In the picture I have of you,
A cleft in your chin instead of your foot
But no less a devil for that, no not
Any less the black man who   55

---

1   *Dachau, Auschwitz, Belsen* Sites of Nazi concentration camps during World War II.
2   *Tyrol* State in Austria.
3   *Luftwaffe* German air force during World War II.
4   *Panzer-man* "Panzers" were German armoured vehicles.
5   *You … blackboard* Otto Plath taught biology and German at Boston University.

Bit my pretty red heart in two.
I was ten when they buried you.
At twenty I tried to die
And get back, back, back to you.
60 I thought even the bones would do.

But they pulled me out of the sack,
And they stuck me together with glue.
And then I knew what to do.
I made a model of you,
65 A man in black with a Meinkampf[1] look

And a love of the rack and the screw.
And I said I do, I do.
So daddy, I'm finally through.
The black telephone's off at the root,
70 The voices just can't worm through.

If I've killed one man, I've killed two—
The vampire who said he was you
And drank my blood for a year,
Seven years, if you want to know.
75 Daddy, you can lie back now.

There's a stake in your fat black heart
And the villagers never liked you.
They are dancing and stamping on you.
They always *knew* it was you.
80 Daddy, daddy, you bastard, I'm through.

—1965 (written 1962)

Lady Lazarus[2]

I have done it again.
One year in every ten
I manage it—

---

1   *Meinkampf* Adolf Hitler's book *Mein Kampf* (1924) outlines his political philosophy.
2   *Lazarus* Man brought back to life by Jesus after being dead for four days. See John 11.1–44.

A sort of walking miracle, my skin
Bright as a Nazi lampshade,[1]
My right foot   5

A paperweight,
My featureless, fine
Jew linen.

Peel off the napkin   10
O my enemy.
Do I terrify?—

The nose, the eye pits, the full set of teeth?
The sour breath
Will vanish in a day.   15

Soon, soon the flesh
The grave cave ate will be
At home on me

And I a smiling woman.
I am only thirty.   20
And like the cat I have nine times to die.

This is Number Three.
What a trash
To annihilate each decade.

What a million filaments.   25
The peanut-crunching crowd
Shoves in to see

Them unwrap me hand and foot—
The big strip tease.
Gentlemen, ladies   30

---

1   *Nazi lampshade* Some Nazi officials allegedly created leather souvenirs, such as lamp-
     shades, using the skin of concentration camp victims.

These are my hands
My knees.
I may be skin and bone,

Nevertheless, I am the same, identical woman.
35 The first time it happened I was ten.
It was an accident.

The second time I meant
To last it out and not come back at all.
I rocked shut

40 As a seashell.
They had to call and call
And pick the worms off me like sticky pearls.

Dying
Is an art, like everything else.
45 I do it exceptionally well.

I do it so it feels like hell.
I do it so it feels real.
I guess you could say I've a call.

It's easy enough to do it in a cell.
50 It's easy enough to do it and stay put.
It's the theatrical

Comeback in broad day
To the same place, the same face, the same brute
Amused shout:

55 "A miracle!"
That knocks me out.
There is a charge

For the eyeing of my scars, there is a charge
For the hearing of my heart—
60 It really goes.

And there is a charge, a very large charge
For a word or a touch
Or a bit of blood

Or a piece of my hair or my clothes.
So, so, Herr[1] Doktor.
So, Herr Enemy.   65

I am your opus,
I am your valuable,
The pure gold baby

That melts to a shriek.   70
I turn and burn.
Do not think I underestimate your great concern.

Ash, ash—
You poke and stir.
Flesh, bone, there is nothing there—   75

A cake of soap,[2]
A wedding ring,
A gold filling.

Herr God, Herr Lucifer
Beware   80
Beware.

Out of the ash
I rise with my red hair
And I eat men like air.

—1965 (written 1962)

---

1   *Herr* German: Sir, Lord, Mister.
2   *cake of soap* During and after the war, it was widely believed that the bodies of the dead
    from concentration camps were used to mass produce soap; historians have not found
    evidence to substantiate this rumour.

Lucille Clifton
1936–2010

Lucille Clifton consciously broke from poetic conventions in her work, which celebrates family life, the female body, biblical characters (often envisioned as Caribbean or African), and African American history, including the history of her own family. She addressed these subjects in personal, evocative, and straightforward language. Clifton tidily expressed her impatience with conventional images of the poet with a few comments in her final interview: "There's a way you're supposed to look if you're an American poet. There's a way you're supposed to sound…. And I think it's hogwash."

Born Thelma Lucille Sayles, Clifton grew up in Buffalo, New York; her working-class parents exposed their large family to an abundance of literature. She attended university and teacher's college, but dropped out to work on her writing. A few years later, she gave birth to the first of her six children; although she claimed that at home she was "wife and mama mostly," she also said that her experience as a mother was an important source of poetic inspiration. When Clifton published her first poetry collection, *Good Times*, in 1969, it was named by *The New York Times* as one of the year's ten best books.

Clifton received the National Book Award for *Blessing the Boats: New and Selected Poems, 1988–2000* (2000), and was posthumously awarded the Frost Medal in 2010. In addition to writing more than ten poetry books for adults, Clifton was also a prolific author of children's literature that often addressed difficult subjects such as death, history, and abuse.

miss rosie

when i watch you
wrapped up like garbage
sitting, surrounded by the smell
of too old potato peels
5 or
when i watch you
in your old man's shoes
with the little toe cut out
sitting, waiting for your mind
10 like next week's grocery
i say
when i watch you
you wet brown bag of a woman

who used to be the best looking gal in georgia
used to be called the Georgia Rose   15
i stand up
through your destruction
i stand up

—1969

the lost baby poem

the time i dropped your almost body down
down to meet the waters under the city
and run one with the sewage to the sea
what did i know about waters rushing back
what did i know about drowning   5
or being drowned

you would have been born into winter
in the year of the disconnected gas
and no car   we would have made the thin
walk over genesee hill into the canada wind   10
to watch you slip like ice into strangers' hands
you would have fallen naked as snow into winter
if you were here i could tell you these
and some other things

if i am ever less than a mountain   15
for your definite brothers and sisters
let the rivers pour over my head
let the sea take me for a spiller
of seas   let black men call me stranger
always   for your never named sake   20

—1987

Margaret Atwood
b. 1939

In a career spanning half a century and virtually all genres, Margaret Atwood has risen to become one of Canada's most visible and versatile literary figures. Her work, which is as frequently found on best-seller lists as on academic syllabi, has been translated into over 35 languages. But despite her international appeal, Atwood remains a self-consciously Canadian writer.

Atwood writes within and across many traditional forms and categories. Although best known for novels such as *The Handmaid's Tale* (1985) and *Oryx and Crake* (2003), she initially established her reputation as a poet. Her first major collection, *The Circle Game* (1966) is concerned with national identity, particularly as it relates to Canada's natural landscape. Atwood explored similar themes in *The Animals in That Country* (1968) and *The Journals of Susanna Moodie* (1970), in which stark, precise, tightly controlled poems explore the artificial constructs that we attempt to impose on the uncontrollable, mysterious natural forces that inhabit and surround us.

The poems in her many collections range widely; national and feminist concerns are among the subjects she touches on, as are mythology, environmentalism, and old age and death. Regardless of their subject, her poems engage consistently with language itself; in Atwood's view, fiction "is the guardian of the moral and ethical sense" of a society, while "poetry is the heart of the language, the activity through which language is renewed and kept alive."

Death of a Young Son by Drowning[1]

He, who navigated with success
the dangerous river of his own birth
once more set forth

on a voyage of discovery
5 into the land I floated on
but could not touch to claim.

---

1   *Death of … Drowning* From *The Journals of Susanna Moodie* (1970), a collection Atwood based on the life and work of Susanna Moodie, author of the 1852 pioneer memoir *Roughing It in the Bush.* Moodie's son drowned in the Moira River in Upper Canada, where the family had settled.

His feet slid on the bank,
the currents took him;
he swirled with ice and trees in the swollen water

and plunged into distant regions,   10
his head a bathysphere;[1]
through his eyes' thin glass bubbles

he looked out, reckless adventurer
on a landscape stranger than Uranus
we have all been to and some remember.   15

There was an accident; the air locked,
he was hung in the river like a heart.
They retrieved the swamped body,

cairn of my plans and future charts,
with poles and hooks   20
from among the nudging logs.

It was spring, the sun kept shining, the new grass
leapt to solidity;
my hands glistened with details.

After the long trip I was tired of waves.   25
My foot hit rock. The dreamed sails
collapsed, ragged.

      I planted him in this country
      like a flag.

—1970

[you fit into me]

you fit into me
like a hook into an eye

a fish hook
an open eye

—1971

---

1   *bathysphere* Spherical diving-bell for deep-sea observation.

Variation on the Word *Sleep*

I would like to watch you sleeping,
which may not happen.
I would like to watch you,
sleeping. I would like to sleep
5   with you, to enter
your sleep as its smooth dark wave
slides over my head

and walk with you through that lucent°   *shining*
wavering forest of bluegreen leaves
10 with its watery sun & three moons
towards the cave where you must descend,
towards your worst fear
I would like to give you the silver
branch, the small white flower, the one
15 word that will protect you
from the grief at the centre
of your dream, from the grief
at the centre. I would like to follow
you up the long stairway
20 again & become
the boat that would row you back
carefully, a flame
in two cupped hands
to where your body lies
25 beside me, and you enter
it as easily as breathing in

I would like to be the air
that inhabits you for a moment
only. I would like to be that unnoticed
30 & that necessary.

—1981

Frank Bidart
b. 1939

Frank Bidart's poetry, according to *New York Times* critic Major Jackson, offers "a wholly new approach to autobiographical material, chiefly by giving voice to the inner travails of other people's lives, both real and imagined, while also laying bare" the difficulties of his own life. Strongly influenced by the autobiographical "confessional" poets of twentieth-century America, Bidart's work engages with philosophical dilemmas about desire, mortality, guilt, and art itself that, Jackson writes, allow him to escape the limitations of the merely biographical "by ennobling thought itself."

Born and raised in Bakersfield, California, Bidart initially hoped to be a director or actor, but began to write poetry in his twenties. He attended the University of California, Riverside, and then Harvard, where he formed a close friendship and working relationship with the poet Robert Lowell and, through Lowell, his colleague Elizabeth Bishop. In addition to these influences, Bidart also drew inspiration from the modernist poets T.S. Eliot and Ezra Pound.

Bidart's first book of poetry, *Golden State*, was published in 1973; though this was well received, it was his third collection, *Sacrifice* (1983), that cemented his reputation. These early volumes include dramatic monologues featuring such varied characters as a child-killing pedophile and the prominent dancer and choreographer Vaslav Nijinsky. *In the Western Night: Collected Poems 1965–1990* (1990) includes poems addressing the AIDS crisis— a recurring subject in Bidart's work, whose personal life as a gay man was profoundly affected by it.

Bidart continues to receive acclaim for his later works, including *Half-Light: Collected Poems 1965–2016* (2017), a retrospective collection that also includes new poetry. Bidart has received the Bobbitt Prize for poetry, and was awarded the 2017 National Book Award for poetry and the Griffin Poetry Prize lifetime achievement award. Griffin Prize trustee Mark Doty described his work as "ferocious": Bidart, he said, writes "with an eye always on what is at stake, which is everything."

Queer

Lie to yourself about this and you will
forever lie about everything.

Everybody already knows everything

so you can
5 lie to them. That's what they want.

But lie to yourself, what you will

lose is yourself. Then you
turn into them.

                    •

For each gay kid whose adolescence

10 was America in the forties or fifties
the primary, the crucial

scenario

forever is coming out—
or not. Or not. Or not. Or not. Or not.

                    •

15 Involuted[1] velleities[2] of self-erasure.

                    •

Quickly after my parents
died, I came out. Foundational narrative

designed to confer existence.

If I had managed to come out to my
20 mother, she would have blamed not

me, but herself.

The door through which you were shoved out
into the light

---

1   *Involuted* Complicated, inward-turning.
2   *velleities* Inclinations.

was self-loathing and terror.

·

Thank you, terror!   25

You learned early that adults' genteel
fantasies about human life

were not, for you, life. You think sex

is a knife
driven into you to teach you that.   30

—2013

Half-light

That crazy drunken night I
maneuvered you out into a field outside of

Coachella[1]—I'd never seen a sky
so full of stars, as if the dirt of our lives

still were sprinkled with glistening   5
white shells from the ancient seabed

beneath us that receded long ago.
Parallel. We lay in parallel furrows.

—That suffocated, fearful
look on your face.   10

Jim, yesterday I heard your wife on the phone
tell me you died almost nine months ago.

Jim, now we cannot ever. Bitter
that we cannot ever have

---

1   *Coachella* Valley in the inland area of Southern California; it is the site of an annual
     music festival of the same name.

15 the conversation that in
nature and alive we never had. Now not ever.

We have not spoken in years. I thought
perhaps at ninety or a hundred, two

broken-down old men, we wouldn't
20 give a damn, and find speech.

When I tell you that all the years we were
undergraduates I was madly in love with you

you say you
knew. I say I knew you

25 knew. You say
There was no place in nature we could meet.

You say this as if you need me to
admit something. *No place*

in nature, given our natures. Or is this
30 warning? I say what is happening now is

happening only because one of us is
dead. You laugh and say, Or both of us!

Our words
will be weirdly jolly.

35 That light I now envy
exists only on this page.

—2014

Seamus Heaney

1939–2013

Born to farmers in County Derry, just outside Belfast, Seamus Heaney grew up in a Roman Catholic household in a predominantly Protestant part of Northern Ireland. He remained unmarked in childhood by the strife that would later affect the region; instead, he experienced a community that lived in harmony, regardless of religious affiliation. Heaney frequently draws on his roots for poetic inspiration, and many of his poems recall his childhood or draw on the activities of rural life—such as digging potatoes or churning milk—to comment on universal issues.

Much of Heaney's poetry concerns the political and sectarian violence that rocked Northern Ireland during the second half of the twentieth century. He has been criticized both for his allegedly ambivalent attitude toward the conflict and for his decision to leave Northern Ireland for the relatively stable Republic of Ireland in 1972. Heaney did not, however, forget the political turmoil of his birthplace, and in the decade following his move he wrote some of his most political works, including *North* (1975) and *Field Work* (1979).

The death of Heaney's mother in 1984 was the occasion for some of his most poignant poetry, published in *The Haw Lantern* (1987). When questioned about his memorializing of lost friends and family, Heaney responded: "The elegiac Heaney? There's nothing else." Heaney's poems addressing the past often comment indirectly on the present; among the best-known examples of this approach are his "bog poems" about the preserved bodies of ancient sacrificial victims discovered in the peat bogs of Denmark.

Heaney combined writing with an academic career that included guest lectureships at Harvard and Oxford. He also wrote translations from ancient and medieval languages, among them a critically acclaimed translation of *Beowulf* (2000). In 1995, Heaney was awarded the Nobel Prize in Literature; the committee cited his "works of lyrical beauty and ethical depth, which exalt everyday miracles and the living past."

Digging

Between my finger and my thumb
The squat pen rests; as snug as a gun.

Under my window a clean rasping sound
When the spade sinks into gravelly ground:
My father, digging. I look down 5

Till his straining rump among the flowerbeds
Bends low, comes up twenty years away
Stooping in rhythm through potato drills[1]
Where he was digging.

10 The coarse boot nestled on the lug, the shaft
Against the inside knee was levered firmly.
He rooted out tall tops, buried the bright edge deep
To scatter new potatoes that we picked
Loving their cool hardness in our hands.

15 By God, the old man could handle a spade,
Just like his old man.

My grandfather could cut more turf[2] in a day
Than any other man on Toner's bog.
Once I carried him milk in a bottle
20 Corked sloppily with paper. He straightened up
To drink it, then fell to right away
Nicking and slicing neatly, heaving sods
Over his shoulder, digging down and down
For the good turf. Digging.

25 The cold smell of potato mould, the squelch and slap
Of soggy peat, the curt cuts of an edge
Through living roots awaken in my head.
But I've no spade to follow men like them.

Between my finger and my thumb
30 The squat pen rests.
I'll dig with it.

—1966

---

1   *potato drills* Rows of sown potatoes.
2   *turf* Slabs of peat.

Mid-Term Break[1]

I sat all morning in the college sick bay
Counting bells knelling classes to a close.
At two o'clock our neighbors drove me home.

In the porch I met my father crying—
He had always taken funerals in his stride—   5
And Big Jim Evans saying it was a hard blow.

The baby cooed and laughed and rocked the pram
When I came in, and I was embarrassed
By old men standing up to shake my hand

And tell me they were "sorry for my trouble,"   10
Whispers informed strangers I was the eldest,
Away at school, as my mother held my hand

In hers and coughed out angry tearless sighs.
At ten o'clock the ambulance arrived
With the corpse, stanched and bandaged by the nurses.   15

Next morning I went up into the room. Snowdrops
And candles soothed the bedside; I saw him
For the first time in six weeks. Paler now,

Wearing a poppy bruise on his left temple,
He lay in the four foot box as in his cot.   20
No gaudy scars, the bumper knocked him clear.

A four foot box, a foot for every year.

—1966

---

1   *Mid-Term Break*   While Heaney was at boarding school in 1953, his four-year-old brother
    Christopher was killed in a car accident.

The Grauballe Man[1]

As if he had been poured
in tar, he lies
on a pillow of turf
and seems to weep

5   the black river of himself.
The grain of his wrists
is like bog oak,[2]
the ball of his heel

like a basalt egg.
10 His instep has shrunk
cold as a swan's foot
or a wet swamp root.

His hips are the ridge
and purse of a mussel,
15 his spine an eel arrested
under a glisten of mud.

The head lifts,
the chin is a visor
raised above the vent
20 of his slashed throat

that has tanned and toughened.
The cured wound
opens inwards to a dark
elderberry place.

25 Who will say "corpse"
to his vivid cast?
Who will say "body"
to his opaque repose?

---

1   *Grauballe Man* Man from the third century BCE whose preserved remains were found in
    1952, in a peat bog near the village of Grauballe, Denmark.
2   *bog oak* Wood of an oak tree preserved in a peat bog.

P.V. Glob, "The First Picture of the Grauballe Man," 1965. The Grauballe Man is one of hundreds of well-preserved ancient corpses that have been discovered in peat bogs in Northern Europe. In his book The Bog People: Iron Age Man Preserved (Mose-folket: Jernalderens Mennesker bevaret I 2000 År, *1965), the Danish archaeologist P.V. Glob argued that most of these "bog people" were victims of ritual sacrifice. The* Bog People *and the photographs it contained were a source of inspiration for a number of poems by Seamus Heaney, including "The Grauballe Man."*

And his rusted hair,
a mat unlikely
as a foetus's.
I first saw his twisted face   30

in a photograph,
a head and shoulder
out of the peat,
bruised like a forceps baby,   35

but now he lies
perfected in my memory,
down to the red horn
40 of his nails,

hung in the scales
with beauty and atrocity:
with the Dying Gaul[1]
too strictly compassed

45 on his shield,
with the actual weight
of each hooded victim,
slashed and dumped.

—1975

Cutaways

i

Children's hands in close-up
On a bomb site, picking and displaying
Small shrapnel curds for the cameramen

Who stalk their levelled village. *Ferrum*
5 and *rigor* and *frigor*[2] of mouse grey iron,
The thumb and finger of my own right hand

Closing around old hard plasticine
Given out by Miss Walls, thumbing it
To nests no bigger than an acorn cup,

10 Eggs no bigger than a grain of wheat,
Pet pigs with sausage bellies, belly-buttoned
Fingerprinted sausage women and men.

---

1 *Dying Gaul* Roman copy of a lost Greek statue (c. 230–220 BCE) depicting a Gallic
   (French) warrior dying in battle.
2 *Ferrum* Latin: iron; *rigor* Latin: stiffness; *frigor* Latin: cold.

ii

Or trigger-fingering a six-gun stick,
Cocking a stiff hammer-thumb above
A sawn-off kitchen chair leg; or flying round   15

A gable, the wingspan of both arms
At full stretch and a-tilt, the left hand tip
Dangerously near earth, the air-shearing right

Describing arcs—angelic potential
Fleetly, unforgettably attained: 20
Now in richochets that hosannah[1] through

The backyard canyons of Mossbawn,[2]
Now a head and shoulders dive
And skive as we hightail it up and away

iii

To land hard back on heels, like the charioteer   25
Holding his own at Delphi,[3] his six horses
And chariot gone, his left hand lopped off

A wrist protruding like a waterspout,
The reins astream in his right
Ready at any moment to curb and grapple   30

Bits long fallen away.
The cast of him on a postcard was enough
To set me straight once more between two shafts,

Another's hand on mine to guide the plough,
Each slither of the share, each stone it hit   35
Registered like a pulse in the timbered grips.

—2008

---

1   *hosannah* Exclamation of praise used in Jewish and Christian worship.
2   *Mossbawn* Farmhouse where Heaney was born.
3   *charioteer ... Delphi* Bronze statue found at the temple of Apollo at Delphi and one of the best known surviving examples of ancient Greek sculpture (c. 475 BCE).

Gwendolyn MacEwen

1941–1987

One of Canada's most accomplished poets, Gwendolyn MacEwen ventured in many of her best-known poems into what she called the "elementary world" of myth, dream, and the unconscious mind. As she explained in her essay "A Poet's Journey into the Interior" (1986), "I tend to regard poetry in much the same way as the ancients regarded the chants or hymns used in holy festivals—as a means of invoking the mysterious forces which move the world, inform our deepest and most secret thoughts, and often visit us in sleep."

MacEwen's volumes of poetry include the Governor General's Award-winning collections *The Shadow-Maker* (1969) and *Afterworlds* (1987). Margaret Atwood has praised her ability to create, "in a remarkably short time, a complete and diverse poetic universe and a powerful and unique voice, by turns playful, extravagant, melancholy, daring, and profound." MacEwen's work displays remarkable breadth of tone and style, but in its subject matter returns repeatedly to a cluster of themes, among them the nature of time and memory, alchemy and mysticism, the transcendent power of imagination, the interplay—and interdependence—of darkness and light, and the subterranean truths and terrors of dreams.

Dark Pines Under Water

This land like a mirror turns you inward
And you become a forest in a furtive lake;
The dark pines of your mind reach downward,
You dream in the green of your time,
5 Your memory is a row of sinking pines.

Explorer, you tell yourself this is not what you came for
Although it is good here, and green;
You had meant to move with a kind of largeness,
You had planned a heavy grace, an anguished dream.

10 But the dark pines of your mind dip deeper
And you are sinking, sinking, sleeper
In an elementary world;
There is something down there and you want it told.

—1969

The Discovery

do not imagine that the exploration
ends, that she has yielded all her mystery
or that the map you hold
cancels further discovery

I tell you her uncovering takes years,   5
takes centuries, and when you find her naked
look again,
admit there is something else you cannot name,
a veil, a coating just above the flesh
which you cannot remove by your mere wish   10

when you see the land naked, look again
(burn your maps, that is not what I mean),
I mean the moment when it seems most plain
is the moment when you must begin again

—1969

Sharon Olds
b. 1942

Sharon Olds's poems are notable for their intimate portrayals of taboo subjects such as family abuse, sexuality, violence, and the human body; she is often compared to an earlier generation of confessional poets such as Sylvia Plath and Anne Sexton. Olds herself describes her work as "apparently personal." Whether autobiographical or not, her poetry boldly examines many of life's fundamental experiences. Poet Tony Hoagland praises Olds's "empathetic insight" and describes her work as "an extended, meticulous, passionate, often deeply meditative testament about the 'central meanings'; skilled dramatic expressions of the most archetypal templates, obstructions and liberations of one human life."

Born in San Francisco, Olds studied at Stanford University, and she completed a PhD in English at Columbia University in 1972. Her first collection, *Satan Says* (1980), received the San Francisco Poetry Center Award, while her next, *The Dead and the Living* (1983), received the National Book Critics Circle Award. She is also a recipient of the T.S. Eliot Prize, for which she has been shortlisted multiple times: after being shortlisted for *The Father* (1992), a themed collection about an alcoholic father's death from cancer, and for *One Secret Thing* (2008), which addresses parenthood, sexuality, and past traumas, she won for *Stag's Leap* (2012), a volume centred on her experience of divorce.

The One Girl at the Boys Party

When I take my girl to the swimming party
I set her down among the boys. They tower and
bristle, she stands there smooth and sleek,
her math scores unfolding in the air around her.
5 They will strip to their suits, her body hard and
indivisible as a prime number,
they'll plunge in the deep end, she'll subtract
her height from ten feet, divide it into
hundreds of gallons of water, the numbers
10 bouncing in her mind like molecules of chlorine
in the bright blue pool. When they climb out,
her ponytail will hang its pencil lead
down her back, her narrow silk suit
with hamburgers and french fries printed on it

will glisten in the brilliant air, and they will   15
see her sweet face, solemn and
sealed, a factor of one, and she will
see their eyes, two each,
their legs, two each, and the curves of their sexes,
one each, and in her head she'll be doing her   20
wild multiplying, as the drops
sparkle and fall to the power of a thousand from her body.

—1983

Sex without Love

How do they do it, the ones who make love
without love? Beautiful as dancers,
gliding over each other like ice-skaters
over the ice, fingers hooked
inside each other's bodies, faces   5
red as steak, wine, wet as the
children at birth whose mothers are going to
give them away. How do they come to the
come to the   come to the   God   come to the
still waters,[1] and not love   10
the one who came there with them, light
rising slowly as steam off their joined
skin? These are the true religious,
the purists, the pros, the ones who will not
accept a false Messiah, love the   15
priest instead of the God. They do not
mistake the lover for their own pleasure,
they are like great runners: they know they are alone
with the road surface, the cold, the wind,
the fit of their shoes, their over-all cardio-   20
vascular health—just factors, like the partner
in the bed, and not the truth, which is the
single body alone in the universe
against its own best time.

—1984

---

1   *still waters* See Psalm 23.2: "he leadeth me beside the still waters."

Eavan Boland

b. 1944

Eavan Boland has developed the concept of "dailiness," a focus on the ordinary minutiae of life, as a theme throughout her work. Beginning her career at a time when, she says, "nobody thought a suburb could be a visionary place for a poet" and "nobody thought a daily moment could be [poetic]," she was inspired by "a great tenderheartedness toward these things that were denied their visionary life." Her work also draws deeply on the past: she weaves scenes of the everyday together with re-imagined figures and motifs from mythology, and she examines Irish history with particular attention to its legacy of women's oppression. Boland does not shy away from the harsh realities of women's lives—past or present; domestic violence and anorexia are among the subjects addressed in her poems.

Born in 1944, Boland grew up in London and Ireland. She attended Trinity College in Dublin, and has since taught there and at other universities, including Bowdoin College and Stanford University. Since her first collection, *23 Poems* (1962), Boland has published ten volumes of poetry, among them *In a Time of Violence* (1994), which won the Lannan Award and was shortlisted for the T.S. Eliot Award. Her anthology *New Collected Poems* (2008), containing previously unpublished works as well as a selection of her early poems, has cemented her place as a leading contemporary Irish writer. In her collection of essays *A Journey with Two Maps: Becoming a Woman Poet* (2011), Boland reflects on her identity as a woman and a poet, and on the construction of those identities by others.

Night Feed

This is dawn.
Believe me
This is your season, little daughter.
The moment daisies open,
5 The hour mercurial rainwater
Makes a mirror for sparrows.
It's time we drowned our sorrows.

I tiptoe in.
I lift you up
10 Wriggling
In your rosy, zipped sleeper.
Yes, this is the hour

For the early bird and me
When finder is keeper.

I crook the bottle.   15
How you suckle!
This is the best I can be,
Housewife
To this nursery
Where you hold on,   20
Dear life.

A slit of milk.
The last suck.
And now your eyes are open,
Birth-coloured and offended.   25
Earth wakes.
You go back to sleep.
The feed is ended.

Worms turn.
Stars go in.   30
Even the moon is losing face.
Poplars stilt for dawn
And we begin
The long fall from grace.
I tuck you in.   35

—1982

Against Love Poetry

We were married in summer, thirty years ago. I have loved you deeply from that moment to this. I have loved other things as well. Among them the idea of women's freedom. Why do I put these words side by side? Because I am a woman. Because marriage is not freedom. Therefore, every word here is written against love poetry. Love poetry can do no justice to this. Here, 5 instead, is a remembered story from a faraway history: A great king lost a war and was paraded in chains through the city of his enemy. They taunted him. They brought his wife and children to him—he showed no emotion. They brought his former courtiers—he showed no emotion. They brought his old servant—only then did he break down and weep.[1] I did not find my 10 womanhood in the servitudes of custom. But I saw my humanity look back at me there. It is to mark the contradictions of a daily love that I have written this. Against love poetry.

—2001

---

1   *a remembered ... and weep* From Herodotus, *The Histories* 3.14. The defeated king explains, "my private sorrows were too great for tears, but the troubles of my companion deserved them."

bpNichol

1944–1988

As George Bowering wrote, bpNichol "did not sound like the rest of the poets of his time." One of Canada's most important avant-garde poets, he experimented not only with lyric and narrative poetry but also with the visual and auditory aspects of language. The range of his work encompassed both concrete poetry—a visual form in which the words form an image that contributes to the poem's meaning—and sound poetry, a spoken form that engages with the sounds of speech, usually independent of actual words.

Barrie Phillip Nichol was born in Vancouver, British Columbia. His first collection, *bp* (1967), challenged the notion of the book: it was published in the form of a box containing a book, a collection of loose visual poems, a record, and a flipbook, with a "Statement" printed on the back of the box. In 1970, Nichol won the Governor General's Award for four volumes published that year: *Still Water, The true eventual story of Billie the Kid, Beach Head*, and *The Cosmic Chief*. His experiments with form and genre were continued in works such as *The Captain Poetry Poems* (1971), a convergence of pop art, concrete and lyric poetry, and myth. Of his more than 30 books and filmed or recorded performances, perhaps the most impressive is *The Martyrology* (1972–92), a "life-long" poem spanning nine books in six volumes.

Nichol often worked collaboratively; he was a member of the famed sound poetry group The Four Horsemen and a co-founder of *grOnk*, a magazine with a focus on concrete poetry. With a fellow member of The Four Horsemen, he produced theoretical writing under the pseudonym "Toronto Research Group." He was also a writer for Jim Henson's television show *Fraggle Rock* (1983–87).

Blues

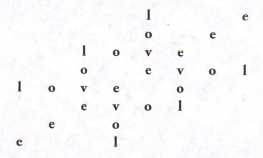

5

—1966

[dear Captain Poetry]

dear Captain Poetry,
your poetry is trite.
you cannot write a sonnet
tho you've tried to every night
5 since i've known you.
we're thru!!
        madame X

dear madame X

        Look how the sun leaps now upon our faces
10   Stomps & boots our eyes into our skulls
        Drives all thot to weird & foreign places
        Till the world reels & the kicked mind dulls,
        Drags our hands up across our eyes
        Sends all white hurling into black
15   Makes the inner cranium our skies
        And turns all looks sent forward burning back.
        And you, my lady, who should be gentler, kind,
        Have yet the fiery aspect of the sun
        Sending words to burn into my mind
20   Destroying all my feelings one by one;
            You who should have tiptoed thru my halls
            Have slammed my doors & smashed me into walls.

                love
                Cap Poetry
                —1970

Tom Wayman
b. 1945

Tom Wayman's poetry depicts the challenges of daily life and work with humour and honesty, addressing the commonplace in colloquial, conversational language. In his work, Wayman writes, he strives to "provide an accurate depiction of our common everyday life" and to help us "consider how our jobs shape us"—a consideration which requires that we recognize the relative "state of unfreedom" in which most of us lead our working lives. Much of his writing relates to working-class employment such as factory labour and construction, but some of his best-known poems are about the everyday experience of the university.

Born in Ontario in 1945 and raised in British Columbia, Wayman holds a BA from the University of British Columbia and an MFA from the University of California. His first collection, *Waiting for Wayman*, was published in 1973; it has been followed by more than a dozen volumes of poetry, as well as by short fiction, critical essays, drama, and a novel.

Wayman has edited several anthologies, often with a focus on work writing, and has been a teacher and a writer-in-residence at many Canadian universities. Among other awards, he has received the Canadian Authors' Association Poetry Award and the A.J.M. Smith Prize for distinguished achievement in Canadian poetry. His poetry collection *My Father's Cup* (2002) was shortlisted for the Governor General's Award.

Did I Miss Anything?

*Question frequently asked by
students after missing a class*

Nothing. When we realized you weren't here
we sat with our hands folded on our desks
in silence, for the full two hours

    Everything. I gave an exam worth
    40 per cent of the grade for this term
    and assigned some reading due today
    on which I'm about to hand out a quiz
    worth 50 per cent

5

Nothing. None of the content of this course
10 has value or meaning
Take as many days off as you like:
any activities we undertake as a class
I assure you will not matter either to you or me
and are without purpose

15   Everything. A few minutes after we began last time
            a shaft of light descended and an angel
            or other heavenly being appeared
            and revealed to us what each woman or man must do
            to attain divine wisdom in this life and
20   the hereafter
            This is the last time the class will meet
            before we disperse to bring this good news to all people on earth

Nothing. When you are not present
how could something significant occur?

25   Everything. Contained in this classroom
            is a microcosm of human existence
            assembled for you to query and examine and ponder
            This is not the only place such an opportunity has been gathered

            but it was one place

30   And you weren't here

                                                —1994

Robert Bringhurst
b. 1946

Robert Bringhurst spent ten years studying a variety of subjects—including physics, architecture, linguistics, and philosophy—at multiple universities before completing a BA in Comparative Literature from Indiana University. Since then he has published more than 15 collections of poetry and more than ten works of prose, including a canonical text on book design and typography, *Elements of Typographical Design* (1992).

Kate Kellaway of *The Observer* has commented that Bringhurst "has the curiosity of a scientist…. His writing is at once lyrical and spartan. And yet he is witty. And while he has no taste for lamentation, many a poem catches, calmly, at the heart." Interested in escaping what he calls "the prison of time" and "the prison of personality" through his work, Bringhurst tends not to focus on self-exploration but rather to explore larger topics: nature, timeless philosophical questions, mythology and literature (including the literature of the Bible, ancient Greek literature, and North American indigenous oral literature). He is well known for his work as a translator of Haida myths and narrative poems; that work has inspired controversy (he has been criticized for appropriating First Nations traditions), but it has also been widely praised for contributing to the preservation and promotion of Haida culture.

Bringhurst has received several prestigious awards for his works, including the Macmillan Poetry Prize (1975) and a Guggenheim Fellowship (1988), and was shortlisted for the prestigious Griffin Poetry Prize (2001). He lives on Quadra Island, British Columbia.

Leda and the Swan[1]

for George Faludy

Before the black beak reappeared
like a grin from in back of a drained cup,
letting her drop,
she fed at the sideboard of his thighs,
the lank air tightening in the sunrise,   5
yes. But no, she put on no knowledge

---

1   *Leda and the Swan* In Greek mythology, Leda was visited by Zeus in the form of a swan, who in some versions of the story raped her and in other versions seduced her. From their union she bore two eggs; one produced the twins Castor and Pollux, the other Helen (whose abduction later initiated the Trojan War). See W.B. Yeats's "Leda and the Swan," also included in this anthology.

with his power. And it was his power alone
that she saved of him for her daughter.
Not his knowledge.
10 No.
He was the one who put on knowledge.
He was the one who looked down out of heaven
with a dark croak, knowing more
than he had ever known before,
15 and knowing he knew it:

knowing the xylophone of her bones,
the lute of her back and the harp of her belly,
the flute of her throat,
woodwinds and drums of her muscles,
20 knowing the organ pipes of her veins;

knowing her as a man knows mountains he has hunted
naked and alone in—
knowing the fruits, the roots and the grasses,
the tastes of the streams
25 and the depths of the mosses,
knowing as he moves in the darkness he is also
resting at noon in the shade of her blood—
leaving behind him in the sheltered places
glyphs[1] meaning mineral and moonlight and mind
30 and possession and memory,
leaving on the outcrops signs meaning mountain
and sunlight and lust and rest and forgetting.

Yes. And the beak that opened to croak
of his knowing that morning creaked like a rehung
35 door and said nothing, felt nothing. The past
is past. What is known is as lean
as the day's edge and runs
one direction. The truth floats
down, out of fuel,
40 indigestible, like a feather. The lady
herself, though—whether
or not she was truth or untruth, or both, or was neither—

---

1   *glyphs* Carved figures or characters.

she dropped through the air like a looped rope,
a necklace of meaning, remembering
everything forward and backward—   45
the middle, the end, the beginning—
and lit like a fishing skiff gliding aground.

That evening, of course, while her husband, to whom
she told nothing, strode like the king
of Lakonia[1] through the orchestra   50
pit of her body, touching
this key and that string in his passing,
she lay like so much
green kindling,
fouled tackle and horse harness under his hands   55
and said nothing, felt
nothing, but only
lay thinking
not flutes, lutes and xylophones,
no: thinking soldiers   60
and soldiers and soldiers and soldiers
and daughters,
the rustle of knives in his motionless wings.

—1982

---

1   *Lakonia* Region in ancient Greece, of which Sparta was the principal city.

Marilyn Nelson
b. 1946

The author of dozens of poetry collections, translations, and children's books, Marilyn Nelson is a prolific contributor to American literature. While her poetry traverses a range of subjects from marriage and motherhood to Christian spirituality, much of Nelson's work narrates American history, especially black history. Such volumes include *The Homeplace* (1990), which recounts her family history beginning with her great-great-grandmother; *Carver: A Life in Poems* (2001), about celebrated African American scientist George Washington Carver; and the sonnet crown *A Wreath for Emmett Till* (2005), about a teenager whose lynching galvanized the civil rights movement. Yet Nelson is more storyteller than political historian, creating poems that, as fellow poet Daniel Hoffman has said, "reach past feminist anguish and black rage" and "spring from her own sources." Some of Nelson's works are published as young adult books, but even these invite a broader audience; she explained that she wrote *Carver*, for example, "as I always do, striving for clarity and truthfulness, and imagining an audience of grown-ups."

Nelson is professor emerita at the University of Connecticut and also served as the state's Poet Laureate from 2001 to 2006. In 2004, she founded Soul Mountain Retreat, a writer's colony with special interest in "traditionally underrepresented racial and cultural groups." In 2012 Nelson received the Frost Medal for "distinguished lifetime achievement in poetry."

Minor Miracle

Which reminds me of another knock-on-wood
memory. I was cycling with a male friend,
through a small midwestern town. We came to a 4-way
stop and stopped, chatting. As we started again,
a rusty old pick-up truck, ignoring the stop sign,
hurricaned past scant inches from our front wheels.
My partner called, "Hey, that was a 4-way stop!"
The truck driver, stringy blond hair a long fringe
under his brand-name beer cap, looked back and yelled,
     "You fucking niggers!"
And sped off.
My friend and I looked at each other and shook our heads.
We remounted our bikes and headed out of town.
We were pedalling through a clear blue afternoon

between two fields of almost-ripened wheat   15
bordered by cornflowers and Queen Anne's lace
when we heard an unmuffled motor, a honk-honking.
We stopped, closed ranks, made fists.
It was the same truck. It pulled over.
A tall, very much in shape young white guy slid out: 20
greasy jeans, homemade finger tattoos, probably
a Marine Corps boot-camp footlockerful
of martial arts techniques.

"What did you say back there!" he shouted.
My friend said, "I said it was a 4-way stop.   25
You went through it."
"And what did I say?" the white guy asked.
"You said: 'You fucking niggers.'"
The afternoon froze.

"Well," said the white guy,   30
shoving his hands into his pockets
and pushing dirt around with the pointed toe of his boot,
"I just want to say I'm sorry."
He climbed back into his truck
and drove away.   35

—1994

Lorna Crozier
b. 1948

One of Canada's most celebrated poets, Lorna Crozier is well known for the musical simplicity of her language and her artful way of approaching complex subjects in a style that is at once forthright and sly. According to Crozier, the poet is a conduit who must develop an alertness to the world's sensory details so as to recreate them in the "small charged world of the poem." In her view, "the poem is in the details," and though experience may resist or elude language, it is the task of the poet to "circle what can't be said until something of its smell, sound, taste, and gesture appears on the page."

Crozier was born in Swift Current, Saskatchewan. Much of her work is informed by the atmosphere and culture of small-town prairie life—notably *Inventing the Hawk* (1992), winner of a Governor General's Award; *A Saving Grace* (1996), inspired by Sinclair Ross's prairie novel *As for Me and My House* (1941); and the memoir *Small Beneath the Sky* (2009). But such localism is by no means narrow or restrictive: Crozier frequently takes up broad political, spiritual, and philosophical questions. Through her poetic retellings of scripture, for example, she interrogates a Judeo-Christian vision of the world.

Critics have approached Crozier's work from many different angles. Some focus on her intimate connection to the Canadian prairies or her concern with social injustice; others explore her fascination with the gaps in our stories and experiences, with absence, silence, loss, and all that which "can't be said."

from *The Sex Lives of Vegetables*

Carrots

Carrots are fucking
the earth. A permanent
erection, they push deeper
into the damp and dark.
5   All summer long
they try so hard to please.
Was it good for you,
was it good?

Perhaps because the earth won't answer
they keep on trying.   10
While you stroll through the garden
thinking *carrot cake*,
carrots and onions in beef stew,
carrot pudding with caramel sauce,
they are fucking their brains out   15
in the hottest part of the afternoon.

Onions

The onion loves the onion.
It hugs its many layers,
saying O, O, O,
each vowel smaller
than the last.   5

Some say it has no heart.
It doesn't need one.
It surrounds itself,
feels whole. Primordial.
First among vegetables.   10

If Eve had bitten it
instead of the apple,
how different
Paradise.

—1985

When I Come Again to My Father's House

When I come again to my father's house
I will climb wide wooden steps
to a blue door. Before I knock
I will stand under the porchlight and listen.
My father will be sitting in a plaid shirt,   5
open at the throat, playing his fiddle—
something I never heard in our other life.

Mother told me his music stopped
when I was born. He sold the fiddle
to buy a big console radio.   10

One day when I was two
I hit it with a stick,
I don't know why, Mother covering
the scratches with a crayon
15 so Father wouldn't see.
It was the beginning of things
we kept from him.

Outside my father's house
it will be the summer
20 before the drinking starts,
the jobs run out, the bitterness
festers like a sliver buried
in the thumb, too deep under the nail
to ever pull it out. The summer
25 before the silences, the small
hard moons growing in his throat.

When I come again to my father's house
the grey backdrop of the photos
my mother keeps in a shoebox
30 will fall away, the one sparse tree
multiply, branches green with rain.
My father will stand in his young man's pose
in front of a car, foot on the runningboard,
sleeves rolled up twice on each forearm.

35 I will place myself beside him.
The child in me will not budge
from this photograph,
will not leave my father's house
unless my father as he was
40 comes with me, throat swollen
with rain and laughter,
young hands full of music,
the slow, sweet song of his fiddle
leading us to my mother's
45 home.

—1995

Agha Shahid Ali

1949–2001

Agha Shahid Ali was a Shia Muslim born in predominantly Hindu New Delhi, raised in Sunni Kashmir, and later educated in the United States, where he lived and worked for many years as an academic, poet, and translator. He drew inspiration from his diverse cultural heritage and literary influences, finding fertile ground for his imagination in both his native and adopted homelands. He was raised, he wrote, "a bilingual, bicultural (but never rootless) being," and his loyalties to English and Urdu were so deeply felt and closely joined that they "led not to confusion, but to a strange, arresting clarity."

In collections such as *The Half-Inch Himalayas* (1987), Ali often looks back on the past and dwells on the experience of living apart from one's history. But, in taking stock of what he has left behind, the poet also comes to better represent his own nature and place in the world. In *A Walk through the Yellow Pages* (1987) and *A Nostalgist's Map of America* (1991), Ali does not simply write poems about the vast and varied landscapes of the United States and the American Southwest; he writes as an American poet, working in the tradition of the American sublime.

Among Ali's most significant literary contributions are his translations of the celebrated Urdu poet Faiz Ahmed Faiz. Before Ali published *The Rebel's Silhouette* (1991), both Faiz's poetry and the *ghazal*, a Persian lyric form consisting of rhymed, thematically self-contained couplets, were little known in the West. Here as in much of his work, Ali was keen to experiment with ways to, as he phrased it, "make English behave outside its aesthetic habits."

Postcard from Kashmir

Kashmir shrinks into my mailbox,
my home a neat four by six inches.

I always loved neatness. Now I hold
the half-inch Himalayas in my hand.
This is home. And this the closest
I'll ever be to home. When I return,
the colours won't be so brilliant,
the Jhelum's[1] waters so clean,

5

---

1   *Jhelum* River originating in the Himalayas in Kashmir.

so ultramarine. My love
10 so overexposed.
And my memory will be a little
out of focus, in it
a giant negative, black
and white, still undeveloped.

—1987

The Wolf's Postscript to "Little Red Riding Hood"

First, grant me my sense of history:
I did it for posterity,
for kindergarten teachers
and a clear moral:
5 Little girls shouldn't wander off
in search of strange flowers,
and they mustn't speak to strangers.

And then grant me my generous sense of plot:
Couldn't I have gobbled her up
10 right there in the jungle?
Why did I ask her where her grandma lived?
As if I, a forest-dweller,
didn't know of the cottage
under the three oak trees
15 and the old woman lived there
all alone?
As if I couldn't have swallowed her years before?

And you may call me the Big Bad Wolf,
now my only reputation.
20 But I was no child-molester
though you'll agree she was pretty.

And the huntsman:
Was I sleeping while he snipped
my thick black fur
and filled me with garbage and stones?[1]   25
I ran with that weight and fell down,
simply so children could laugh
at the noise of the stones
cutting through my belly,
at the garbage spilling out   30
with a perfect sense of timing,
just when the tale
should have come to an end.

—1987

---

1   *And the ... stones* In the version of the Red Riding Hood story that appears in *Grimms'*
    Fairy Tales (1812–15), a huntsman discovers the wolf asleep and cuts its stomach open.
    He rescues the child and her grandmother, who are still alive inside, and they kill the wolf
    by filling its stomach with stones.

Anne Carson

b. 1950

Hailed by Michael Ondaatje as "the most exciting poet writing in English today," Anne Carson is known for formally experimental work that draws on a deep knowledge of literary history, from ancient Greek poetry and medieval mysticism to modernism and contemporary psychoanalysis. Her many accolades include the Griffin Prize for Poetry, the T.S. Eliot Prize for Poetry, and the Order of Canada.

Carson is a professor of classics, and her academic work and her poetry strongly influence each other. These talents most clearly overlap in her Greek translation work, including *If Not, Winter: Fragments of Sappho* (2002) and the three-play collection *An Oresteia* (2009). Captivated by the mindset of ancient Greek culture, Carson says that "what's entrancing about the Greeks is that you get little glimpses, little latches of similarity [to contemporary culture], embedded in unbelievable otherness." Her own poems often view the ancient through a contemporary lens; *Autobiography of Red: A Novel in Verse* (1998), for example, transforms the Greek story of Herakles' battle with the monster Geryon into a story of troubled love between twentieth-century men.

Carson's style is distinctive for its blending of genres, often occupying the borders between poetry and prose. Her first book of poetry, *Short Talks* (1992), is presented as a compilation of miniature lectures, while works such as *Plainwater* (1995) and *Men in the Off Hours* (2000) include poetic essays alongside more traditional lyric poetry. She is also known for her novels in free verse, such as *Autobiography of Red* and *The Beauty of the Husband: A Fictional Essay in 29 Tangos* (2001). With *Nox* (2010), Carson revives her first love—visual art—to memorialize the life of her brother through an interweaving of translation, original poetry, and photographic collage.

from *Short Talks*

On Rain

It was blacker than olives the night I left. As I
ran past the palaces, oddly joyful, it began to
rain. What a notion it is, after all—these small
shapes! I would get lost counting them. Who
5 first thought of it? How did he describe it to
the others? Out on the sea it is raining too.
It beats on no one.

On Sylvia Plath[1]

Did you see her mother on television? She said
plain, burned things. She said I thought it an
excellent poem but it hurt me. She did not say
jungle fear. She did not say jungle hatred wild
jungle weeping chop it back chop it. She said   5
self-government she said end of the road. She
did not say humming in the middle of the air[2]
what you came for chop.

On Walking Backwards

My mother forbade us to walk backwards. That
is how the dead walk, she would say. Where did
she get this idea? Perhaps from a bad translation. The dead, after all, do not walk backwards
but they do walk behind us. They have no lungs   5
and cannot call out but would love for us to
turn around. They are victims of love, many of
them.

—1992

---

1   *Sylvia Plath* (1932-63), American poet and author. The mother in her semi-autobiographical novel *The Bell Jar* (1963) and many of the mother figures in her poetry are
portrayed with hostility.

2   *in the middle of the air* See Plath's poem "The Disquieting Muses" (1960): "I woke one
day to see you, mother, / Floating above me in bluest air."

Lillian Allen

b. 1951

An avowed feminist and political radical, Canadian dub poet and musician Lillian Allen considers poetry to be one of the most potent weapons available to the disenfranchised. "Poetry is the deprogramming faculty we have as humans," she has suggested, with which "we can create community, name the nameless and put out a point of view."

Born in Kingston, Jamaica, Allen grew up in Spanish Town. In 1969, she attended the University of Waterloo, and then moved to New York City, where she first achieved fame with the publication of her poem "I Fight Back" (1970). She then returned to Canada, where she completed her BA at York University. In 1978, Allen met Oku Onuora, a founding figure of dub poetry. Inspired by Onuora's performances, Allen became a leading figure among Toronto dub poets who, she has said, "set out to ... increase the dynamism of poetry, to increase its impact and immediacy." She published her first chapbook, *Rhythm an' Hardtimes* (1982), and soon afterward released her first audio recording, *Dub Poet: The Poetry of Lillian Allen* (1983).

Throughout the 1980s and 1990s, Allen became a central figure of Canadian reggae with albums such as *Revolutionary Tea Party* (1986) and *Conditions Critical* (1988), both of which received Juno awards. During this period she continued to publish printed collections, some written for the page and some adapted from spoken performance. Allen also co-directed and co-produced the film *Blak Wi Blakk* (1993) and hosted the CBC radio spoken-word series WORDBEAT (2004).

In 1992, Allen became a Professor of Creative Writing at OCAD University, a position from which she has advocated for the artistic, political, and intellectual importance of Canadian dub poetry. Dub poets, she has said, make "art part and parcel of political work."

One Poem Town

Hey!   Hey!   Hey!
this is a one poem town
this is a one poem town

ride in on your macrame verses
5   through barber-green minds
keep it kool! kool! kool!
on the page
'cause, if yu bring one in

any other way
we'll shoot you with metaphors   10
tie you cordless
hang you high in ironies
drop a pun 'pon yu toe
and run you down, down, down
and out of town   15
'cause, this is a one poem town

and hey! what yu doing here anyway?

so don't come with no pling, ying, jing
ding something
calling it poetry
'cause, this is a one poem town   20
and you're not here to stay

Are you?

—1993

Dionne Brand

b. 1953

For Dionne Brand, poetry is "a philosophical mode for thinking through how one lives in the world and one's relation to other human beings." Her poetry frequently engages with issues of race (and racism), and of gender and sexuality, at times bringing acutely personal perspectives into play to explore these facets of existence.

While Brand has written acclaimed novels, short stories, non-fiction prose, and documentaries, she remains best known as a poet. Her collections include *Chronicles of a Hostile Sun* (1984), a book of poems based on her experience working for a non-government organization in Grenada; *Land to Light On* (1997), a Governor General's Award-winning volume that focuses on experiences of displacement and homelessness, linking them to histories of slavery, colonialism, and migration; and *thirsty* (2002), a book-length poem set in the city of Toronto. She received a Griffin Poetry Prize for *Ossuaries* (2011), another long poem, which the award judges praised for "fulfilling the novelistic narrative ambition of her work, [without] sacrific[ing] the tight lyrical coil of the poetic line."

Born in Trinidad, Brand immigrated to Canada in 1970. She earned a BA at the University of Toronto (1975) and, later, an MA at the Ontario Institute for Studies in Education (1989). She has held a number of prestigious university positions including Distinguished Visiting Scholar at St. Lawrence University and University Research Chair at the University of Guelph. Brand was named Poet Laureate of Toronto in 2009.

from *thirsty*

30

Spring darkness is forgiving. It doesn't descend
abruptly before you have finished work,
it approaches palely waiting for you
to get outside to witness another illumined hour

5 you feel someone brush against you,
on the street, you smell leather, the lake,
the coming leaves, the rain's immortality
pierces you, but you will be asleep when it arrives

you will lie in the groove of a lover's neck
unconscious, translucent, tendons singing,   10
and that should be enough, the circumference
of the world narrowed to your simple dreams

Days are perfect, that's the thing about them,
standing here in half darkness, I think this.
It's difficult to rise to that, but I expect it   15
I expect each molecule of my substance to imitate that

I can't of course, I can't touch syllables
tenderness, throats.
Look it's like this, I'm just like the rest,
limping across the city, flying when I can   20

32

Every smell is now a possibility, a young man
passes wreathed in cologne, that is hope;
teenagers, traceries of marijuana, that is hope too, utopia;

smog braids the city where sweet grass used to,
yesterday morning's exhaust, this day's   5
breathing by the lightness, the heaviness of the soul.

Every night the waste of the city is put out and taken away
to suburban landfills and recycling plants,
and that is the rhythm everyone would prefer in their life,

that the waste is taken out, that what may be useful   10
be saved and the rest, most of it, the ill of it,
buried.

Sometimes the city's stink is fragrant offal,
sometimes it is putrid. All depends on what wakes you up,
the angular distance of death or the elliptic of living.   15

—2002

Louise Bernice Halfe
b. 1953

Louise Halfe, also known by the name Sky Dancer, is a Cree and Canadian poet who served as the Poet Laureate of Saskatchewan from 2005 to 2006. Halfe's poetry addresses the enduring legacy of the Canadian residential schools, describing the trauma of cultural erasure. "My parents both went to residential school, and they took with them a lot of the culture," she told an interviewer from the CBC. "I've had to be like a ground squirrel, scrounging for crumbs and tidbits so that I can start feeling a little bit whole in my Indianness."

Born in Two Hill, Alberta, Halfe grew up on the Saddle Lake Indian Reserve, and was compelled to attend the Blue Quills Residential School. After leaving Blue Quills, Halfe studied social work at the University of Regina and earned a certificate in addictions counselling. While studying at a satellite campus in Northern Saskatchewan, Halfe travelled three hours a day in order to attend her classes. During these long commutes, she wrote continuously in her journal, a text that would eventually become the foundation of her first book of poetry, *Bear Bones & Feathers* (1994). "I didn't choose poetry," Halfe explains. "Poetry came nodding its head in when I was keeping a journal. The journal writing kept calling to me and was reinforced by dreams and ceremony."

Since the first publication of her work in the anthology *Writing the Circle: Native Women of Western Canada* (1990), Halfe has become an established figure in the Canadian poetry scene. Her second collection, *Blue Marrow* (1998), was short-listed for the Governor General's Award, and her third, *The Crooked Good* (2007), received The First Peoples Publishing Award. Her 2016 work, *Burning in this Midnight Dream*, was written in response to the Truth and Reconciliation Commission's collection of the testimonies of thousands of people impacted by residential schools. George Elliott Clarke praised Halfe's text as "a canonical work of Anglo-Canadian letters, one that will always be as relevant as the Constitution and First Nations and Crown Treaties."

Halfe describes her poetry as a contribution to the ongoing work of decolonization and reconciliation. "When one tends to an open sore/wound on their body with tenderness and consideration … the wound heals," she reflects. "It is the same when dealing with the spirit and the heart. Perhaps as we dialogue with one another this malaise will lighten."

wêpinâson[1]

Two women stare at each other.
Grunts, groans, rippling, meowing and cawing,
they spin these songs:
Of a brook searching. A crane meditating
A frog croaking. A mantis sucking on a fly.   5
A beaver caught in an iron jaw.
Thunder shuddered. A pair of lovers parted under a tree.
Lightning smiled through one's heart.
Dew rolled into the woman's basket.

The Inuit voices bounced, echoed against   10
their lodge, wet with death.

A deer rubbed her nose into her mate,
pranced into the meadow,
fell as an arrow flew.
Her robe sliced with fluttering hands.   15
Her bones become the scraper, skinning knife, needles
and flute. Her sinew thread, rawhide bowls, folding boxes,
drums and medicine bags.
Her skin a lodge of sticks and hide. Her hair, a mattress.
Close by, fur-covered men sat drumming.   20
This I saw, *ê-kwêskît*[2] — Turn Around Woman. I am she.

—2007

ê-kwêskît — **Turn-Around Woman**

When I was growing up in the bush, on the hillside,
I watched the sun arrive from the dark, watch her slip
into the dark. I travelled. I didn't know the world back then.
I just travelled. I was afraid

---

1   *wêpinâson* 1. ceremonial cloth, cloth offering; 2. prayer cloth, an offering. Without being disrespectful, the closest translation is an offering, in particular, a cloth that is being thrown away but in gesture of a give-away or offering more than the actual casting away. Perhaps more specifically, a sacred offering/throw away which flies in the wind. [All translations are taken from the glossary that appears in Halfe's collection *The Crooked Good* (2007).]

2   *ê-kwêskît* 1. S/he turns around; 2. personal name given to a female: Turn-Around Woman.

5 I would never return. I tumbled that hillside
back into myself.

You can tell me
after you hear this story
if my name suits me.
10 I've yet to figure it out.

In Rib Woman
stories are born.
The Old Man called it psychology. Me,
I just dream it.

15   *These gifted mysterious people of long ago,*
          kayâs kî-mamâhtâwisiwak iyiniwak,[1]

my mother, Gone-For-Good, would say.

          They never died. They are scattered here, there,
          everywhere, somewhere. They know the language,
20   *the sleep, the dream, the laws, these singers, these healers,*
          âtayôhkanak,[2] *these ancient story keepers.*

I, Turn-Around, am not one of them.

I was taught by Old people.
An Indian Man, a White Man.
25 An Indian Woman, a White Woman.
They worked in lairs, in the full veins of
Rib Woman.
I sat in their thicket, wailing.
The old ones navigated through my dreams.
30 Sometimes they dragged, scolded, cajoled,
cheered and celebrated.
I wanted to be with them. Like them.

---

1   *kayâs … iyiniwak* A long time ago people were filled the gift of Mystery—spiritual gifts
     that materialize in gifted people.
2   *âtayôhkanak* Spirit beings; spiritual entities; ancient legend spirits (pl).

I am not a saint. I am a crooked good.
My cousins said I was easy, therefore
I've never been a maiden.   35
I am seventy, but still
I carry my sins. Brothers-in-law
I meet for the first time wipe their hands
as if I am still among the maggots. I didn't
know their women wept when their men   40
slept in my bed. I am not a saint.

I married Abel, a wide green-eyed man. Fifty years now.
Inside Rib Woman I shook hands with promise.
Promise never forgot, trailed me year after year.
His Big Heavens a morning lake   45
drowns me in my lair.
I learned how to build Rib Woman
one willow at a time, one skin at a time.
I am only half done. This is part of the story.

I, *ê-kwêskît*, am a dreamer.   50
I dream awake. Asleep. On paper.
The Old Man said the universe,
the day, was the story. So,
every day I am born.
The Old White Man taught me   55
to unfold night visits.
The Old Woman taught me
all of it was real.
The Old White Woman helped me
to cry with the Thunder.   60

—2007

Harryette Mullen
b. 1953

Scholar Elisabeth A. Frost describes American poet Harryette Mullen as a pioneer of "her own form of bluesy, disjunctive lyric poetry, combining a concern for the political issues raised by identity politics with a poststructualist emphasis on language." Her challenging work draws together a vast body of influences: the avant-garde, allusive wordplay of modernist writers such as Gertrude Stein; the rhythmic, auditory qualities of spoken-word poetry; and the critical approaches offered by the civil rights movement, feminism, and postmodern philosophy.

Mullen was raised in Texas, and was still in high school when she had her first poem published in a local newspaper. She began her academic studies at the University of Texas at Austin, where she was deeply influenced by the Black Power, Chicano, and Black Arts movements of the 1960s and 1970s. Reviewer Stephen Yenser describes one of her earliest volumes of poetry, *Tree Tall Woman* (1981), as "an ebulliently feminist, black and bluesy, bebop, wicked, scatty, addictive sequence of mazy prose poems, ostensibly about wardrobe accessories and the ramifications thereof, and in fact about language and semiotics in general." Much of her work similarly exploits the language of popular culture to address matters such as consumerism and social inequality.

In 1990, Mullen completed a PhD at the University of California, Santa Cruz, where she studied slave narratives, and in 1995 she joined the English faculty at the University of California, Los Angeles. While publishing as an academic, she has continued to write volumes of poetry. Perhaps her most critically acclaimed is the 2002 collection *Sleeping with the Dictionary*, which was a finalist for the National Book Award, National Book Critics Circle Award, and Los Angeles Times Book Prize. These poems, according to a *New York Times* reviewer, "prove that wordplay can be serious business."

Dim Lady[1]

My honeybunch's peepers are nothing like neon. Today's special at Red Lobster is redder than her kisser. If Liquid Paper is white, her racks are institutional beige. If her mop were Slinkys, dishwater Slinkys would grow on her noggin. I have seen tablecloths in Shakey's Pizza Parlors, red and white, but no such picnic colors do I see in her mug. And in some minty-fresh mouthwashes there is more sweetness than in the garlic breeze my

---

1   *Dim Lady* See Sonnet 130 by William Shakespeare (page 477).

main squeeze wheezes. I love to hear her rap, yet I'm aware that
Muzak has a hipper beat. I don't know any Marilyn Monroes.
My ball and chain is plain from head to toe. And yet, by gosh,   10
my scrumptious twinkie has as much sex appeal for me as any
lanky model or platinum movie idol who's hyped beyond belief.

—2002

Black Nikes[1]

We need quarters like King Tut needed a boat. A slave could
row him to heaven from his crypt in Egypt full of loot. We've
lived quietly among the stars, knowing money isn't what matters. We only bring enough to tip the shuttle driver when we
hitch a ride aboard a trailblazer of light. This comet could scour   5
the planet. Make it sparkle like a fresh toilet swirling with blue.
Or only come close enough to brush a few lost souls. Time is
rotting as our bodies wait for now I lay me down to earth.
Noiseless patient spiders[2] paid with dirt when what we want is
star dust. If nature abhors an expensive appliance, why does the   10
planet suck ozone? This is a big ticket item, a thickety ride.
Please page our home and visit our sigh on the wide world's
ebb. Just point and cluck at our new persuasion shoes. We're
opening the gate that opens our containers for recycling. Time
to throw down and take off on our launch. This flight will nail   15
our proof of pudding. The thrill of victory is, we're exiting
earth. We're leaving all this dirt.

—2002

---

1 *Nikes* In Greek mythology, Nike is the goddess of victory, usually depicted with wings.
   (The running shoe and sports equipment company is named for the goddess.)
2 *Noiseless patient spiders* Reference to Walt Whitman's 1891 poem "A Noiseless Patient
   Spider," in which a spider ejecting thread into "the vacant vast surrounding" is likened to
   the soul's attempts to engage with the universe.

from *Muse & Drudge*

[marry at a hotel, annul 'em][1]

marry at a hotel, annul 'em
nary hep male rose sullen
let alley roam, yell melon
dull normal fellow hammers omelette

5 divine sunrises
Osiris's[2] irises
his splendid mistress
is his sis Isis[3]

creole cocoa loca
10 crayon gumbo boca
crayfish crayola[4]
jumbo mocha-cola

warp maid fresh
fetish coquettish
15 a voyeur leers
at X-rated reels

—2006

---

1   [*marry at a hotel, annul 'em*] Anagram of "Harryette Mullen."
2   *Osiris* Egyptian god of death, resurrection, and the afterlife.
3   *Isis* Egyptian goddess associated with magic and nature; she is the wife and sister of
     Osiris.
4   *loca … crayola* loca: Spanish for crazy; boca: Spanish for mouth: crayola: Spanish for
     crayon.

Kim Addonizio

b. 1954

Known for her direct and empathetic depictions of love, loss, desire, and struggle, Kim Addonizio has achieved recognition for her poetry and novels, as well as for public readings in which she often blends poetry with the sounds of the blues harmonica. Her many honours include a Guggenheim Fellowship, a Pushcart Prize, and two National Endowment for the Arts Fellowships.

Born in Washington, DC, Addonizio obtained a BA and an MA from San Francisco State University, then worked as a lecturer at several colleges while she began to pursue her writing career. Her first collection, *Three West Coast Women* (1987), was a collaboration with fellow poets Laurie Duesing and Dorianne Laux. Several solo volumes followed, including *The Philosopher's Club* (1994), *Tell Me* (2000), and *Lucifer at the Starlite* (2009). As a poet, Addonizio is notable for writing both in free verse and in fixed forms (including the sonnet and a variant of the sonnet that she invented, the sonnenizio); her work displays an abiding interest in the interplay of syntax and rhythm, and a highly developed (if often unobtrusive) talent for rhyme.

With Dorianne Laux, Addonizio co-authored *The Poet's Companion: A Guide to the Pleasures of Writing Poetry* (1997); in 2009, she released *Ordinary Genius: A Guide for the Poet Within*, her own collection of writing exercises and personal insights. Addonizio has taught writing at Goddard College, at San Francisco State University, and through private workshops.

First Poem for You

I like to touch your tattoos in complete
darkness, when I can't see them. I'm sure of
where they are, know by heart the neat
lines of lightning pulsing just above
your nipple, can find, as if by instinct, the blue   5
swirls of water on your shoulder where a serpent
twists, facing a dragon. When I pull you
to me, taking you until we're spent
and quiet on the sheets, I love to kiss
the pictures in your skin. They'll last until   10
you're seared to ashes; whatever persists
or turns to pain between us, they will still
be there. Such permanence is terrifying.
So I touch them in the dark; but touch them, trying.

—1994

Carol Ann Duffy

b. 1955

As Jeanette Winterson has written, Carol Ann Duffy is Britain's "favourite poet after Shakespeare." In 2009, when Duffy was appointed the first female Poet Laureate of the United Kingdom, Prime Minister Gordon Brown described her as "a truly brilliant modern poet who has stretched our imaginations by putting the whole range of human experiences into lines that capture emotions perfectly." She is also (to quote Winterson once more) "political in that she wants to change things, [and] idealistic in that she believes she—and poetry—can change things. And, of course, she's a woman, she's a Celt, and she's gay."

Duffy was born in Glasgow, Scotland, and raised in Staffordshire, England. She graduated from the University of Liverpool in 1977 with an honours degree in philosophy, and over the following decade she wrote a number of radio plays and collections of poems. Her talent with a variety of poetic forms and her reluctance to shy away from disturbing content are both evident in her first book, *Standing Female Nude* (1985), which included, for example, a first-person poem from the point of view of a burgeoning murderer and an unflinching depiction of a Holocaust scene. In 1999, Duffy published *The World's Wife*, a series of dramatic monologues written in the voices of the wives of famous historical and fictional figures. *Mean Time* (1993), a volume of poems about the emotional struggles and triumphs of adolescence, won the Whitbread Poetry Award. In 2005, Duffy received the T.S. Eliot Award for *Rapture*, a semi-autobiographical collection recounting a love story from first sight to eventual collapse. Her 2011 work *The Bees* incorporates poems on war and climate change alongside lyrics on the death of the poet's mother.

Duffy's work is extraordinary not least of all for its formal artistry; she is renowned as a master of poetic rhythm and of rhyme as much as of image and metaphor. In her discussions of poetry as well as in the poems themselves, she draws connections between sounds and their human meanings: a poem, she has said, "is the place in language [where] we are most human and we can see ourselves fully—far more than prose in fiction. A poem is able to hold so much in so little space."

Drunk

Suddenly the rain is hilarious.
The moon wobbles in the dusk.

What a laugh. Unseen frogs
belch in the damp grass.

The strange perfumes of darkening trees.   5
Cheap red wine

and the whole world a mouth.
Give me a double, a kiss.

—1993

Crush

The older she gets,
the more she awakes
with somebody's face strewn in her head
like petals which once made a flower.

What everyone does   5
is sit by a desk
and stare at the view, till the time
where they live reappears. Mostly in words.

Imagine a girl
turning to see   10
love stand by a window, taller,
clever, anointed with sudden light.

Yes, like an angel then,
to be truthful now.
At first a secret, erotic, mute;   15
today a language she cannot recall.

And we're all owed joy,
sooner or later.
The trick's to remember whenever
it was, or to see it coming.   20

—1998

Marilyn Dumont

b. 1955

For Marilyn Dumont, poetry is a form of activism: beginning with her first collection, *A Really Good Brown Girl* (1997), she has evocatively told the neglected stories of Canadian Indigenous experience. Her following works, *green girl dreams mountains* (2001) and *that tongued belonging* (2007), have been commended for their exploration of poverty, femininity, and the effects of colonization in Canada.

Although Dumont's commitment to Canadian Indigenous issues has not changed, her approach to writing has developed in the course of her poetic career. *A Really Good Brown Girl*, she says, directly expresses "anger, shame, hurt, disillusionment and grief about the subjugation and mistreatment of Aboriginal peoples and traditions in Canada." Since then, however, she has found it more effective to communicate similar concepts "in different ways—through humour, through pathos, through sleight of hand, through elegance." Both approaches have attracted critical acclaim: Dumont received a Gerald Lampert Memorial Award for *A Really Good Brown Girl*, and *that tongued belonging* was chosen as Aboriginal Book of the Year by McNally Robinson and Poetry Book of the Year at the Ânskohk Aboriginal Literature Festival.

Dumont was born in northeastern Alberta in 1955 and spent her youth living in logging camps in the Alberta foothills. She is Métis and Cree, a descendant of Gabriel Dumont (a leader of Métis forces during the North-west Rebellion of 1885), and was raised in a bilingual Cree and English household. She has been Writer-in-Residence at several institutions (among them the University of Alberta, the University of Windsor, Grant MacEwan University, and Athabasca University), and has also taught in the Aboriginal Emerging Writers Program at the Banff Centre for the Arts.

Not Just a Platform for My Dance

this land is not
just a place to set my house my car my fence

this land is not
just a plot to bury my dead my seed

5 this land is
my tongue   my eyes   my mouth
this headstrong grass and relenting willow

these flat-footed fields and applauding leaves
these frank winds and electric sky lines
are my prayer   10
they are my medicine
and they become my song
this land is not
just a platform for my dance

—1996

The White Judges

We lived in an old schoolhouse, one large room that my father converted
into two storeys with a plank staircase leading to the second floor. A single
window on the south wall created a space that was dimly lit even at midday.
All nine kids and the occasional friend slept upstairs like cadets in rows of
shared double beds, ate downstairs in the kitchen near the gas stove and   5
watched TV near the airtight heater in the adjacent room. Our floors were
worn linoleum and scatter rugs, our walls high and bare except for the
family photos whose frames were crowded with siblings waiting to come of
age, marry or leave. At supper eleven of us would stare down a pot of moose
stew, bannock and tea, while outside the white judges sat encircling our   10
house.

And they waited to judge

waited till we ate tripe
watched us inhale its wild vapour
sliced and steaming on our plates,   15
watched us welcome it into our being,
sink our teeth into its rubbery texture
chew and roll each wet and tentacled piece
swallow its gamey juices
until we had become it and it had become us.   20

Or waited till the cardboard boxes
were anonymously dropped at our door, spilling with clothes
waited till we ran swiftly away from the windows and doors
to the farthest room for fear of being seen
and dared one another to   25
'open it'
'no you open it'

'no you'
someone would open it
30   cautiously pulling out a shirt
that would be tried on
then passed around till somebody claimed it by fit
then sixteen or eighteen hands would be pulling out
skirts, pants, jackets, dresses from a box transformed now
35   into the Sears catalogue.

Or the white judges would wait till twilight
and my father and older brothers
would drag a bloodstained canvas
heavy with meat from the truck onto our lawn, and
40   my mother would lift and lay it in place
like a dead relative,
praying, coaxing and thanking it
then she'd cut the thick hair and skin back
till it lay in folds beside it like carpet

45   carving off firm chunks
until the marble bone shone out of the red-blue flesh
long into the truck-headlight-night she'd carve
talking in Cree to my father and in English to my brothers
long into the dark their voices talking us to sleep
50   while our bellies rested in the meat days ahead.

Or wait till the guitars came out
and the furniture was pushed up against the walls
and we'd polish the linoleum with our dancing
till our socks had holes.

55   Or wait till a fight broke out
and the night would settle in our bones
and we'd ache with shame
for having heard or spoken
that which sits at the edge of our light side
60   that which comes but we wished it hadn't
like 'settlement' relatives who would arrive at Christmas and
leave at Easter.

—1996

Li-Young Lee
b. 1957

When Li-Young Lee was two years old his Chinese family fled persecution in Indonesia, travelling through Hong Kong, Macau, and Japan before they reached the United States in 1964. Lee's work often focuses on his personal life, including his relationships with his wife and children; the most frequently recurring figure is his father, who had been Mao Zedong's personal physician, but in the United States became a Presbyterian minister. Lee strives to unite his examination of personal memories with a more universal exploration of selfhood and spirituality, describing himself as "an amateur mystic."

Although Lee is often pigeonholed as an immigrant writer and acknowledges the influence of Imperial-era Chinese poets such as Tu Fu and Su Tung-po, he also cites the influence of his father's Christianity on his work—and the influence of writers such as John Keats, Walt Whitman, and Cynthia Ozick. Resisting pressure to identify his poetry as "Asian," "American," or even "Asian-American," Lee says, "I want to be a global poet."

Lyrical and elegant in his handling of themes of exile, identity, and mortality, Lee has received critical acclaim since the publication of his first book, *Rose* (1986). Although his reputation rests primarily on poetry collections such as *The City in Which I Love You* (1990) and *Behind My Eyes* (2008), he has also published an American Book Award-winning prose memoir, *The Winged Seed* (1995).

Persimmons

In sixth grade Mrs. Walker
slapped the back of my head
and made me stand in the corner
for not knowing the difference
between *persimmon* and *precision*.   5
How to choose

persimmons. This is precision.
Ripe ones are soft and brown-spotted.
Sniff the bottoms. The sweet one
will be fragrant. How to eat: 10
put the knife away, lay down newspaper.
Peel the skin tenderly, not to tear the meat.
Chew the skin, suck it,

and swallow. Now, eat
15 the meat of the fruit,
    so sweet,
    all of it, to the heart.

    Donna undresses, her stomach is white.
    In the yard, dewy and shivering
20 with crickets, we lie naked,
    face-up, face-down.
    I teach her Chinese.
    Crickets: *chiu chiu*. Dew: I've forgotten.
    Naked: I've forgotten.
25 *Ni, wo*: you and me.
    I part her legs,
    remember to tell her
    she is beautiful as the moon.

    Other words
30 that got me into trouble were
    fight and *fright*, *wren* and *yarn*.
    Fight was what I did when I was frightened,
    Fright was what I felt when I was fighting.
    Wrens are small, plain birds,
35 yarn is what one knits with.
    Wrens are soft as yarn.
    My mother made birds out of yarn.
    I loved to watch her tie the stuff;
    a bird, a rabbit, a wee man.

40 Mrs. Walker brought a persimmon to class
    and cut it up
    so everyone could taste
    a *Chinese apple*. Knowing
    it wasn't ripe or sweet, I didn't eat
45 but watched the other faces.

    My mother said every persimmon has a sun
    inside, something golden, glowing,
    warm as my face.

    Once, in the cellar, I found two wrapped in newspaper,
50 forgotten and not yet ripe.
    I took them and set both on my bedroom windowsill,

where each morning a cardinal
sang, *The sun, the sun.*

Finally understanding
he was going blind,   55
my father sat up all one night
waiting for a song, a ghost.
I gave him the persimmons,
swelled, heavy as sadness,
and sweet as love.   60

This year, in the muddy lighting
of my parents' cellar, I rummage, looking
for something I lost.
My father sits on the tired, wooden stairs,
black cane between his knees,   65
hand over hand, gripping the handle.
He's so happy that I've come home.
I ask how his eyes are, a stupid question.
All gone, he answers.

Under some blankets, I find a box.   70
Inside the box I find three scrolls.
I sit beside him and untie
three paintings by my father:
Hibiscus leaf and a white flower.
Two cats preening.   75
Two persimmons, so full they want to drop from the cloth.

He raises both hands to touch the cloth,
asks, *Which is this?*

This is persimmons, Father.

Oh, the feel of the wolftail on the silk,   80
the strength, the tense
precision in the wrist.
I painted them hundreds of times
eyes closed. These I painted blind.
Some things never leave a person: 85
scent of the hair of one you love,
the texture of persimmons,
in your palm, the ripe weight.

—1986

George Elliott Clarke
b. 1960

George Elliott Clarke is a playwright, academic, critic, and poet known for the power and lyricism of his language. His poetry draws on biblical stories, oral narratives, and music, especially jazz and the blues. He often uses linked poems as a mode of storytelling; speaking of the story-in-verse, Clarke has said that a "lyric poem—even a haiku—is always a little drama, a little story—just as every snapshot is a truncated tale. So, as soon as one compiles a bunch of lyrics, they almost always begin to comprise a narrative."

A political and cultural activist as well as a writer, Clarke frequently addresses the history and experiences of black Canadians in his work; he especially interested in Maritimers of African descent, whom he refers to as "Africadians." Clarke's interests in black history and narrative poetry come together in works such as his verse novel *Whylah Falls* (1990), set in the 1930s in the fictional black Nova Scotian community of Whylah Falls.

Clarke himself is a seventh-generation Canadian and the descendant of black Loyalists who settled in Nova Scotia in 1783. He holds degrees from the University of Waterloo (BA), Dalhousie University (MA), and Queen's University (PhD). He was named the E.J. Pratt Professor of Canadian Literature at the University of Toronto in 2003 and Poet Laureate of Toronto in 2012. Among Clarke's many awards are numerous honorary doctorates, the Governor General's Award for his collection *Execution Poems* (2001), the Martin Luther King, Jr. Achievement Award (2004), the Pierre Elliott Trudeau Fellows Prize (2005), and the Order of Canada (2008).

from *Whylah Falls*

Blank Sonnet

The air smells of rhubarb, occasional
Roses, or first birth of blossoms, a fresh,
Undulant hurt, so body snaps and curls
Like flower. I step through snow as thin as script,
5   Watch white stars spin dizzy as drunks, and yearn
To sleep beneath a patchwork quilt of rum.
I want the slow, sure collapse of language
Washed out by alcohol. Lovely Shelley,[1]

---

1   *Shelley* The speaker's lover.

I have no use for measured, cadenced verse
If you won't read. Icarus-like,[1] I'll fall   10
Against this page of snow, tumble blackly
Across vision to drown in the white sea
That closes every poem—the white reverse
That cancels the blackness of each image.

Look Homeward, Exile

I can still see that soil crimsoned by butchered
Hog and imbrued with rye, lye, and homely
Spirituals everybody must know,
Still dream of folks who broke or cracked like shale:
Pushkin, who twisted his hands in boxing,   5
Marrocco, who ran girls like dogs and got stabbed,
Lavinia, her teeth decayed to black stumps,
Her lovemaking still in demand, spitting
Black phlegm—her pension after twenty towns,
And Toof; suckled on anger that no Baptist   10
Church could contain, who let wrinkled Eely
Seed her moist womb when she was just thirteen.
          And the tyrant sun that reared from barbed-wire
Spewed flame that charred the idiot crops
To Depression, and hurt my granddaddy   15
To bottle after bottle of sweet death,
His dreams beaten to one, tremendous pulp,
Until his heart seized, choked; his love gave out.
          But Beauty survived, secreted
In freight trains snorting in their pens, in babes   20
Whose faces were coal-black mirrors, in strange
Strummers who plucked Ghanaian banjos, hummed
Blind blues—precise, ornate, rich needlepoint,
In sermons scorched with sulphur and brimstone,
And in my love's dark, orient skin that smelled   25
Like orange peels and tasted like rum, good God!
          I remember my Creator in the old ways:
I sit in taverns and stare at my fists;

---

1   *Icarus* Ancient Greek mythological character who flew using wings made of feathers and
     wax. When Icarus flew too close to the sun, the wax melted, and he fell into the ocean
     and drowned.

I knead earth into bread, spell water into wine.
30 Still, nothing warms my wintry exile—neither
Prayers nor fine love, neither votes nor hard drink:
For nothing heals those saints felled in green beds,
Whose loves are smashed by just one word or glance
Or pain—a screw jammed in thick, straining wood.

—1990

Casualties

January 16, 1991[1]

Snow annihilates all beauty
this merciless January.
A white blitzkrieg,[2] Klan—cruel,
arsons and obliterates.

5 Piercing lies numb us to pain.
Nerves and words fail so we
can't feel agony or passion,
so we can't flinch or cry,

when we spy blurred children's
10 charred bodies protruding
from the smoking rubble
of statistics or see a man

stumbling in a blizzard
of bullets. Everything is
15 normal, absurdly normal.
We see, as if through a snow-

---

1   *January 16, 1991* Date of the beginning of the Gulf War (January–February 1991), in which the United States and its allies expelled the Iraqi military from Kuwait, which Iraq had invaded the previous year. The war demonstrated the power of American military technology; there were fewer than 500 casualties on the side of the American-led coalition, but tens of thousands of civilian casualties and as many as 100,000 casualties among Iraqi soldiers. The war also created millions of refugees.

2   *blitzkrieg* Intensive war strategy that combines aerial bombing and mechanized ground troops to surprise and overwhelm an enemy; the American-led coalition used this sort of strategy in the Gulf War.

storm, darkly. Reporters
rat-a-tat-tat tactics,
stratagems. Missiles bristle
behind newspaper lines.   20

Our minds chill; we weather
the storm, huddle in dreams.
Exposed, though, a woman,
lashed by lightning, repents

of her flesh, becomes a living   25
X-ray, "collateral damage."
The first casualty of war
is language.

                                                    —1992

Jackie Kay
b. 1961

Deemed "one of the most sure-footed voices in contemporary literature" by *The Guardian*, Jackie Kay is a writer of poetry, fiction, children's books, drama, and autobiography. She began writing in her late teens, she has said, because, as a black lesbian growing up in Scotland, she found "there wasn't anybody else saying the things I wanted to say.... I started out of that sense of wanting to create some images for myself."

Born to a Nigerian father and Scottish mother, Kay was adopted and raised in Glasgow by white parents—an experience that has informed much of her writing, including poetry collections such as *The Adoption Papers* (1991) and *Fiere* (2011) as well as her 2010 prose memoir *Red Dust Road*. "I sometimes take my own experience as a diving board to jump off into the pool of my imagination," Kay has said of her work, which often delves into aspects of identity, including race, culture, and sexuality. Her novel *Trumpet* (1998), for example, concerns a biological woman who lives his life as a man, while her BBC radio play *The Lamplighter* (2007) examines the history of the Atlantic slave trade.

Kay has more than 15 publications to her credit and is the recipient of numerous awards. She won the *Guardian* Fiction Prize for *Trumpet* and the CLPE Poetry Award for her children's poetry collection *Red, Cherry Red* (2007), and in 2006 she was made a Member of the Order of the British Empire for services to literature. She teaches creative writing at Newcastle University.

In My Country

Walking by the waters
down where an honest river
shakes hands with the sea,
a woman passed round me
5 in a slow watchful circle,
as if I were a superstition;

or the worst dregs of her imagination,
so when she finally spoke
her words spliced into bars
10 of an old wheel. A segment of air.
"*Where do you come from?*"
"Here," I said. "Here. These parts."

—1991

Her

I had been told about her
How she would always, always
How she would never, never
I'd watched and listened
But I still fell for her   5
How she always, always
How she never, never

In the small brave night
Her lips, butterfly moments
I tried to catch her and she laughed   10
A loud laugh that cracked me in two
But then I had been told about her
How she would always, always
How she would never, never

We two listened to the wind   15
We two galloped a pace
We two, up and away, away, away.
And now she's gone
Like she said she would go
But then I had been told about her   20
How she would always, always.

—2005

Gregory Scofield
b. 1966

Gregory Scofield is a poet whose work is heavily influenced by his Métis heritage and upbringing. Alongside allusions to popular culture, his writing often incorporates Cree language, rhythm, and story-telling traditions. Scofield also draws on his own experiences of Vancouver street life and Canadian gay culture, as well as his late-in-life discovery of his Jewish paternal ancestry. "Scofield's range of subject, work, and style dazzles," wrote the judges who awarded him the 2016 Writers' Trust Poetry Prize.

Scofield was raised in Canada's North, first by his mother, then by an aunt, and finally in several foster homes. Throughout his youth, he faced hardships related to poverty, discrimination, and abuse. Once grown, he worked in social outreach, providing support to troubled youth living on the streets of Vancouver. His debut poetry collection, *The Gathering: Stones for the Medicine Wheel* (1993), was well-received by Canadian critics and was awarded the Dorothy Livesay Poetry Prize in 1994. In 1996 Scofield won the Canadian Authors Association's award for most promising young writer. He has since published many more volumes of poetry, while also teaching literature and serving as writer-in-residence at a series of Canadian universities.

Scofield uses his own experience as inspiration not only for his poetry but also for other art forms. In 1999, he published a memoir, *Thunder Through My Veins*, in which he recounts some of the most painful episodes of his past. He was also the subject of a 2007 documentary entitled *Singing Home the Bones: A Poet Becomes Himself.*

Scofield is a vocal advocate for gay and Indigenous rights. In 2015, he began a social media campaign called "Name A Day," in which he regularly tweeted the name and image of a different murdered or missing Indigenous woman. His political passions also inspire his poetry; for example, missing and murdered Indigenous women are a central subject of his book *Witness, I Am* (2016).

Not All Halfbreed Mothers

for Mom, Maria

Not all halfbreed mothers

drink

red rose, blue ribbon,
Kelowna Red, Labatt's Blue.[1]

Not all halfbreed mothers
wear cowboy shirts or hats,
flowers behind their ears
or moccasins
sent from up north.

Not all halfbreed mothers
crave wild meat,
settle for hand-fed rabbits
from Superstore.[2]

Not all halfbreed mothers
pine over lost loves,
express their heartache
with guitars, juice harps,[3]
old records shoved
into the wrong dustcover.

Not all halfbreed mothers
read *The Star, The Enquirer,*
The Tibetan Book of the Dead
or Edgar Cayce,[4]
know the Lady of Shalott[5]
like she was a best friend
or sister.

---

1   *red rose* Iconic Canadian brand of tea; *blue ribbon* Brand of tea that was common in western Canada in the twentieth century; *Kelowna Red* The Okanagan region is a centre of Canadian wine production; *Labatt's Blue* Beer brand that is widely available in Canada.
2   *Superstore* Grocery chain.
3   *juice harps* Also known as Jew's harps or jaws harps; small instruments played by holding the reed in one's mouth and plucking at the metal frame.
4   *Edgar Cayce* American mystic (1877–1945).
5   *the Lady of Shalott* Title character of a poem by Alfred, Lord Tennyson (see page 531).

Not all halfbreed mothers
speak like a dictionary
or Cree hymn book,
30   tell stories
about faithful dogs
or bears
that hung around or sniffed
in the wrong place.

35   Not all halfbreed mothers
know how to saddle
and ride a horse,
how to hot-wire a car
or siphon gas.

40   Not all halfbreed mothers

drink

red rose, blue ribbon,
Kelowna Red, Labatt's Blue.

Mine just happened
45   to like it

Old Style.[1]

—1999

Aunty

No matter how
young or old,
sober, half-cut
or gone

5   she'd fluff the pillows,
spread and tuck
her homemade quilts
under my chin,

count the patches in Cree

---

1   *Old Style* Brand of western Canadian beer.

starting sometimes at nine,
ten to see if I was listening,
if I'd laugh and say,
"Keeskwiyan,"
just the way she taught me,
mischievously,
knitting my brows together,
mouth tight and puckered
so she'd say,
"Ma, tapway chee?"
"E-he," I'd nod
and wait, the song
a bluebird on her lips
lifting me to dreams

    Sleep baby sleepy
    Close your bright eyes
    Listen to your mother, dear
    Sing these lullabies.
    Sleep baby sleepy
    While angels watch over you
    Listen to your mother, dear
    While she sings to you...
        —Jimmie Rodgers,[1] from re-recorded
        cassette by Georgina Houle Young[2]

Keeskwiyan: You're crazy
Ma, tapway chee?: Oh my, is that right?
E-he: Yes[3]

                                       —1999

---

1   *Jimmie Rodgers* American country singer (1897–1933). The paraphrased song, "Sleep Baby Sleep," was written by S.A. Emery in the mid-nineteenth century and recorded by Rodgers in 1927.
2   *Georgina Houle Young* Scofield's aunt.
3   Note to readers: the glosses of Cree words appear at the end of the original poem, as they do here.

Wrong Image

Yeah, their necks were stiff
From watching Indians downtown
who'd piss in the back alley
closing time.
5 From their cars
They were safe, those honkies.
We knew they were there
Skulking around
Like a weak species
10 Trying to build themselves up.

In high school
Emma and me
Were the only Indians.
We started hanging out together
15 Formed the very first
Least likely to succeed club.
None of those white kids
Could down a mickey
Of rye like us.
20 We didn't even need a mixer—
Just pop off the cap
And chug-a-lug.

Sometimes they'd stand
Out on the street
25 Straining to hear our drunk talk.
We spoked pretty broken
So when dey mimicked our dalk
It was authentic not Hollywood.
They joked about our appearance
30 Said we picked
Leftovers at Sally Ann.
Once at recess
we overheard them laughing
And gave each one
35 a damn good wallop.

In the school library
where I thought and brooded
a long time
I crouched over history books
staring sullen   40
at those stoical faces.
Me and Emma
got names too.
I was her chief
and she my squaw—   45
only she humped anything
I was too stupid to notice.

Last summer
I spent the afternoon with a journalist.
I wore linen and leather sandals,   50
spoke of racism and class
and why I began writing.
The interview was about survival
and healing.
In the article   55
I read he was disturbed
by the predominance of alcohol
in my work—
how I perpetuated
the negative image of native people.   60

Walking the beach later
So many white skins
sprawled and craving
earth colouring, a cool beer
I smiled stupid and wondered   65
whatever became of Emma.

—2000

Karen Solie
b. 1966

The subject matter of Karen Solie's poetry spans great distances: from the rural landscapes of Saskatchewan where she was born and raised to the bars and hotels of urban Canada; from the scientific terms of physics and biology to the emotional language of disappointment and desire. Fellow poet Don McKay has described her work as "fierce writing of quickness and edge that can take on just about anything ... with candour and a trenchant humour that's the cutting edge of intelligence."

Karen Solie worked for three years as a reporter in Lethbridge, Alberta, before completing a BA from the University of Lethbridge. Her career as a published poet began when her work was included in the anthology *Breathing Fire: Canada's New Poets* (1995), and six years later she released her first collection, *Short Haul Engine*, which won the Dorothy Livesay Poetry Prize. Solie then moved from Alberta to Toronto, where she further established herself as an important voice in Canadian poetry with her next collections, *Modern and Normal* (2005) and *Pigeon* (2009). *Pigeon* won several awards, including the Trillium Award and the Griffin Poetry Prize; the Griffin judges noted Solie's ability to "pull great wisdom from the ordinary" and "to see at once into and through our daily struggle, often thwarted by our very selves, toward something like an honourable life."

Solie has taught poetry at the Banff Centre for the Arts, been writer-in-residence at several Canadian universities, and held the first International Writer's Residency at the University of St. Andrews in Scotland.

Sturgeon

Jackfish and walleye circle like clouds as he strains
the silt floor of his pool, a lost lure in his lip,
Five of Diamonds, River Runt, Lazy Ike,[1]
or a simple spoon, feeding
5 a slow disease of rust through his body's quiet armour.
Kin to caviar, he's an oily mudfish. Inedible.
Indelible. Ancient grunt of sea
in a warm prairie river, prehistory a third eye in his head.
He rests, and time passes as water and sand
10 through the long throat of him, in a hiss, as thoughts
of food. We take our guilts

---

1   *Five of Diamonds ... Lazy Ike* Popular fishing lures. "Spoon" is also a type of lure.

to his valley and dump them in,
give him quicksilver° to corrode his fins, weed killer,   *mercury*
gas oil mix, wrap him in poison arms.
Our bottom feeder,   15
sin-eater.

On an afternoon mean as a hook we hauled him
up to his nightmare of us and laughed
at his ugliness, soft sucker mouth opening,
closing on air that must have felt like ground glass,   20
left him to die with disdain
for what we could not consume.
And when he began to heave and thrash over yards of rock
to the water's edge and, unbelievably, in,
we couldn't hold him though we were teenaged   25
and bigger than everything. Could not contain
the old current he had for a mind, its pull,
and his body a muscle called river, called spawn.

—2001

Nice

> "I think I'm kind of two-faced. I'm very ingratiating. It really kind
> of annoys me. I'm just sort of a little too nice. Everything is Oooo."
> —Diane Arbus[1]

Still dark, but just. The alarm
kicks on. A voice like a nice hairdo
squeaks *People, get ready*
for another nice one. Low 20s,
soft breeze, ridge of high pressure   5
settling nicely. Songbirds swallowing, ruffling,
starting in. Does anyone curse
the winter wren, calling in Christ's name
for just one bloody minute of silence?
Of course not. They sound nice.   10
I pull away and he asks why I can't
be nicer to him. Well,
I have to work, I say, and wouldn't it be nice

---

1   *Diane Arbus* (1923–71), American photographer.

if someone made some money today?
15   Very nice, he quavers, rolling
his face to the wall. A nice face.
A nice wall. We agreed on the green
down to hue and shade straight away.
That was a very nice day.

—2003

Self-Portrait in a Series of Professional Evaluations

An excellent vocabulary, but spatial skills
are lacking. Poor in math. A bit uncoordinated,
possibly the inner ear? An eye exam
may be required. Not what you'd call a natural
5   athlete. Doesn't play well with others. Tries hard.

Fine sense of melody but a weak left hand. For God's sake
practice with a metronome. Your Chopin
is all over the place. Test scores indicate aptitude
for a career in the secretarial sciences. Handwriting
10   suggests some latent hostility. A diligent worker,
though often late. Please note:

an AC/DC t-shirt does not constitute professional
attire. You drove *how* long on the spare?
A good grasp of theory, though many sentence fragments
15   and an unusual fondness for semicolons; a tendency
toward unsubstantiated leaps. A black aura.

Needs to stroke essence of tangerine through the aura.
Should consider regular facials. Most people walk around
dehydrated all the time and don't even know it.
20   Normal. Negative. This month, avoid air travel
and dark-haired men. Focus on career goals.
Make a five-year plan.

—2005

Arundhathi Subramaniam

b. 1967

■ Arundhathi Subramaniam's poetry often addresses philosophical, political, or spiritual questions at the level of the local, the individual, and the everyday—an approach frequently inflected by Subramaniam's complex relationship with her home city of Mumbai. Her first two books of poetry, *On Cleaning Bookshelves* (1991) and *Where I Live* (2005), were published in English in her native India; her third collection, *Where I Live: New & Selected Poems* (2009), was published in the United Kingdom. In response to what she calls "the increasing spirit of cultural nativism … [that interprets] the use of English as a reactionary throwback to the imperial past," she has defended her choice of language, arguing that "English is Indian—period. It's as Indian as cricket and democracy."

Subramaniam's commitment to the sincere consideration of spiritual matters has found expression not only in her poetry but also in her account of the Buddha's life, *The Book of Buddha* (2005), and her biography of contemporary yogi Jaggi Vasudev, *Sadhguru* (2010). In 2003, she received the Charles Wallace Fellowship at the University of Stirling, and in 2009 was given the Raza Award for Poetry. She has worked for the National Centre for the Performing Arts in Mumbai and was for many years a member of Mumbai's Poetry Circle.

To the Welsh Critic Who Doesn't Find Me Identifiably Indian

You believe you know me,
wide-eyed Eng Lit type
from a sun-scalded colony,
reading my Keats[1]—or is it yours—
while my country detonates   5
on your television screen.

You imagine you've cracked
my deepest fantasy—
oh, to be in an Edwardian[2] vicarage,
living out my dharma[3]   10

---

1   *Keats* John Keats (1795–1821), English poet.
2   *Edwardian* Characteristic of England during King Edward VII's reign (1901–10).
3   *dharma* In various Indian religions, the inherent nature and order of the universe, and a person's actions which uphold that order.

with every sip of dandelion tea
and dreams of the weekend jumble sale ...

You may have a point.
I know nothing about silly mid-offs,[1]
15 I stammer through my Tamil,[2]
and I long for a nirvana
that is hermetic,
odour-free,
bottled in Switzerland,
20 money-back-guaranteed.

This business about language,
how much of it is mine,
how much yours,
how much from the mind,
25 how much from the gut,
how much is too little,
how much too much,
how much from the salon,
how much from the slum,
30 how I say verisimilitude,
how I say Brihadaranyaka,[3]
how I say vaazhapazham[4]—
it's all yours to measure,
the pathology of my breath,
35 the halitosis of gender,
my homogenised plosives[5]
about as rustic
as a mouth-freshened global village.

Arbiter of identity,
40 remake me as you will.
Write me a new alphabet of danger,
a new patois to match

---

1   *mid-offs* Cricket term referring to the left side of the field.
2   *Tamil* Language spoken by the Tamil people in parts of India and Sri Lanka.
3   *Brihadaranyaka* Brihadaranyaka Upanishad, one of the Sanskrit texts that form the phil-
     osophical basis of the Hindu religion.
4   *vaazhapazham* Tamil: banana.
5   *plosives* Consonant sounds (such as *b*, *d*, and *p*), created by briefly halting airflow.

the Chola[1] bronze of my skin.
Teach me how to come of age
in a literature you've bark-scratched   45
into scripture.
Smear my consonants
with cow-dung and turmeric and godhuli.[2]
Pity me, sweating,
rancid, on the other side of the counter.   50
Stamp my papers,
lease me a new anxiety,
grant me a visa
to the country of my birth.
Teach me how to belong,   55
the way you do,
on every page of world history.

—2005

---

1   *Chola* Chola dynasty, a long-ruling Tamil dynasty that rose to power in southern India
     during the Middle Ages.
2   *godhuli* Urdu or Sanskrit: dùsk; in Sanskrit, literally "the dust raised by the feet of cattle."

Rita Wong
b. 1968

Rita Wong describes the subject matter of her poetry as "scary, interrelated phenomena like social and environmental injustice, pollution, and global warming." Her poems often condemn the impact big corporations have on human rights and on the food system, but Wong also emphasizes her readers' collective responsibility to the often geographically distant people who face intolerable working conditions or the consequences of environmental damage. Environmental concerns are, for Wong, inextricable from concerns of race, class, and gender; her poetry is powerfully focused on globalization and the legacy of colonization.

A writer who makes frequent use of puns and other language play and often omits punctuation, Wong is experimental in her approach to poetry—an attitude that extends from the layout of words on the page to the writing process itself. Many of her poems include, as marginalia, Chinese characters or hand-written political or cultural statements, sometimes quotations from other thinkers that inform her work. Her long poem *sybil unrest* (2009), a collaboration with fellow Vancouver writer Larissa Lai, was composed over email.

Wong was raised in Calgary and received a PhD from Simon Fraser University, where she studied Asian North American literature. Her first book of poetry, *monkeypuzzle*, was published in 1998; her next, *forage* (2007), received the Dorothy Livesay Poetry Prize and was the winner of Canada Reads Poetry 2011. Wong is an associate professor at the Emily Carr University of Art and Design, where she teaches Critical and Cultural Studies.

opium[1]

chemical history narcopolemics
attempted genocide call it crack war
alcohol white powder suffocates
shades of deep brown earth red desert
yellow skin dependency myths who   5
needs the high of trying to kill the other?
racist gaze tingles on my skin induced
economic muscle flexes to displace
millions rifles fire behind the dollar
signs & still the underground pulses   10
suffering blue veins seek the
transformative heart as ordnance° drops   *artillery*
on embassies and arteries cry for kin

                        —2007

"Queen Victoria waged war twice... in order to ensure the free commerce of opium."
—Avital Ronell

---

1   The handwritten quotation is from American philosopher and critical theorist Avital
     Ronell's *Crack Wars: Literature, Addiction, Mania* (1992). Britain conducted two
     "Opium Wars" (1839–42 and 1856–60) to force the Chinese government to legalize the
     importation of opium; trading opium for tea and other Chinese luxuries was important
     to the British economy.

nervous organism[1]

jellyfish potato/ jellypo fishtato/ glow in the pork toys/
nab your crisco while it's genetically cloudy boys/
science lab in my esophagus/ what big beakers you have
sir/ all the better to mutate you with my po monster/
po little jelly-kneed demonstrator/ throws flounder-crossed
tomatoes/ hafta nasty nafta[2] through mexico,
california, oregon, washington, canada/ hothoused
experiment nestled beside basketballs of lettuce,
avocado bullets/ industrial food defeats nutrition/
immune systems attrition/ soil vampires call/ shiny
aisles all touch and no contact/ jellypish for tato smack/
your science experiment snack yields slugfish arteries
brain murmurs tumour precipitation whack

—2007

---

1   The handwritten quotation is from Canadian literary critic Northrop Frye's *Anatomy of Criticism* (1957); *cri de coeur* French: cry of the heart.

2   *nafta* North American Free Trade Agreement, a free trade pact between the United States, Canada, and Mexico that took effect in 1994.

Victoria Chang

b. 1970

Victoria Chang is an American poet, editor, children's writer, and business consultant. Her poems, which touch upon such concepts as family, history, economics, gender, and warfare, have been praised for their vitality, wit, and fast-paced juxtaposition of seemingly disparate concepts. "For me," she writes, "poetry is about mystery and surprise, and the collision of different ideas and different things that might never otherwise come together. I think that is ... the fun of poetry."

Born in Detroit, Michigan, to a family of Taiwanese immigrants, Chang graduated from the University of Michigan and Harvard University with degrees in Asian Studies, as well as from Stanford University with an MBA. Unable to leave her workplace to pursue a creative writing MFA in a traditional university program, Chang received a Holden Scholarship to study at the low-residency Warren Wilson MFA Program for Writers. First receiving recognition for her poetry collection Circle (2005), Chang received a Book Award from the Association for Asian American Studies in 2007. She then went on to release the critically acclaimed poetry collections *Salvinia molesta* (2008) and *The Boss* (2013), as well as the irreverent children's book *Is Mommy?* (2015) in collaboration with Marla Frazee. She was awarded a Guggenheim Fellowship in 2017.

Chang is notable for producing much of her poetry while working full-time in an office setting, and her poetry frequently addresses her struggle to reconcile the distinct cultural worlds she negotiates as a businessperson, mother, child of immigrants, and poet. The resulting work frequently investigates the nature of hierarchy and power. "We're all just a part of this large, spiraling, constantly fluid hierarchy," she suggests. "At some points in your life, you feel crushed by that."

Mr. Darcy[1]

In the end she just wanted the house
      and a horse not much more what
   if he didn't own the house or worse
      not even a horse how do we

---

1   *Mr. Darcy* Character in Jane Austen's novel *Pride and Prejudice* (1813).

5   separate the things from a man the man from
                 the things is a man still the same
           without his reins here it rains every fifteen
                 minutes it would be foolish to

     marry a man without an umbrella did
10   Cinderella really love the prince or
           just the prints on the curtains in the
                       ballroom once I went window-

     shopping but I didn't want a window when
                 do you know it's time to get a new
15   man one who can win more things at the
                       fair I already have four stuffed

     pandas from the fair I won fair and square
                 is it time to be less square to wear
           something more revealing in North and
20   South[1] she does the dealing gives him

     the money in the end but she falls in love
                 with him when he has the money when
           he is still running away if the water is
                       running in the other room is it wrong

25 for me to not want to chase it because it owns
                 nothing else when I wave to a man I
           love what happens when another man with
                 a lot more bags waves back

                                                    —2015

---

1   *North and South* 1855 novel by Elizabeth Gaskell.

Sharon Harris

b. 1972

Sharon Harris is a Canadian artist whose work combines a range of forms and mediums, including poetry, prose, photography, sculpture, and painting. Influenced by the poet bpNichol, much of her work has a significant visual dimension and depends for its effect on the interplay of word and image. In her concrete poems, the typographical characteristics and arrangement of the words on the page become part of the overall sense-making apparatus.

Harris's first full-length poetry collection, *AVATAR* (2006), is a blended, hybrid work that mingles figures and letters to create meaning. In it, she experiments with an array of devices and ideas, from pataphysics—the fictional science of imaginary phenomena—to the limits of art and language. This latter idea is a problem to which she returns repeatedly, both throughout the collection and in her work more generally: how does one write about things and places beyond words? *AVATAR* is preoccupied with the nature and uses of the phrase "I love you," which is at once ubiquitous and elusive, full of power and void of meaning.

At once playful and thoughtful, Harris's work invites the reader/viewer to look again at familiar words and phrases and see the concepts they gesture toward in an altogether different light.

99. Where Do Poems Come From?

Moisten your finger and hold it straight up in the air. You will notice at once that one side of the finger is cold. This is the direction from which the poem is coming.

—2005

5

FIGURE L

70. Why Do Poems Make Me Cry?

Reading a poem releases noxious
gases into your environment. The
brain reacts by telling your tear
ducts to produce water, to dilute the
5 irritating acid so the eyes are protected. Your other reaction is probably to rub your eyes, but this will
make the irritation a lot worse if you
have poem juices all over your
10 hands.

There are all kinds of remedies for
dealing with this irritating phenomenon, some more effective than
others. As a general rule, move your
15 head as far away from the poem
as you can, so the gas will mostly dis-
perse before it reaches your eyes. The
simplest solution might be to not
date poets.

—2005

d'bi.young anitafrika
b. 1977

d'bi.young anitafrika[1] is a Jamaican-Canadian dub poet, playwright, performer, and educator. Through her own writing and as artistic director of the Watah Theatre, anitafrika uses art as a tool to "centre black women, queer-identifying people, working class people, and LGBT people." From her performances with the band d'bi. & the 333 to her authorship of plays such as *Lukumi: A Dub Opera* (2017), she sees all her work as animated by the same artistic, political, and ethical principles. "The elements that I use to engage the audience as a dubpoet are the same elements I use to engage the audience as a playwright," she writes. "It's all storytelling."

The daughter of dub poet Anita Stewart, anitafrika was born in Kingston, Jamaica, and given the name Debbie Young. In 1993, she moved to Toronto. As a student at McGill University and Concordia University, anitafrika became established in Montreal's dub poetry community, and in 2000 she released her first recording, *when the love is not enough*.

Throughout the 2000s, anitafrika grew rapidly in stature as an actor, playwright, and poet. She released two collections of dub poetry, *art on black* (2006) and *rivers…and other blackness…between us* (2007). In 2005, she first staged her her semiautobiographical one-person show *bloodclaat: one oomaan story*, for which she received two Dora awards: one for her performance and one for the play itself. *bloodclaat* became the first play in the trilogy *sankofa*, which remains her best-known work; anitafrika completed the trilogy with *androgyne* (2006) and *benu* (2009).

"Mentoring is integral to my creative process," says anitafrika. In 2008, she founded the anitafrika dub theatre program, which offered creativity workshops to black artists. Through this program, she developed a framework for employing "creative discovery for self and collective empowerment"; this approach, which she calls the Sorplusi method, has been employed by such organizations as The Stephen Lewis Foundation and the University of Toronto. The method's name is an acronym expressing the values she also uses to guide her own writing and performance: "self-knowledge, orality, rhythm, political content and context, language, urgency, sacredness, and integrity." She writes that these guiding principles "form a comprehensive eco-system of accountability and responsibility between my audiences and me."

---

1   This anthology follows anitafrika's own practices of capitalization for her name and any quotations from her written work.

self-esteem (ii)

paranoia
has
lessened
since
5 my
return

work makes
normal
people
10 of us all[1]

—2007

foreign mind/local body

for n.k.m.

me friend deh a foreign fi di last two weeks
one place call montreal
everytime mi ask har if dat mean seh
she deh close to brooklyn new york
5 she tell me seh she nuh know
well foreign a foreign
an who cyaan guh a foreign a bat
me dun know seh
me have one whole heap a family a foreign
10 me have family a florida
a atlanta
even a new york
me have family inna a brooklyn
nyc represent!
15 well mi best friend
we been bes friend fi
mek me see
bout thirteen years
since wi a three years old

---

1   *work makes ... us all* See *Hamlet* 3.1.84: "Thus conscience does make cowards of us all."

we used to give each oddah everyting   20
from ice cream
to blouse and skirt
to book and pencil
wi did even guh a di same basic school together
me best friend tell me dat   25
when she get pan har feet at
foreign
she a sen me new shoes
and clothes
and nuff panty an brief   30
well di brief dem a fi mi breddah Jacob
him a seven now
just turn seven last week

mi hear seh foreign nice enuh
tings free   35
di street dem pave wid gold
and money grow pon tree basically
yuh tink inna foreign people live inna zinc house
a brick dem live inna
like inna di story book dem   40
hansel and gretel
people nuh live inna poverty and degradation like we do
all di cussing and fighting
looting and murdering nuh gwaan a foreign
inna jam dung life hard   45
an people wi do anyting fi backbite yuh

inna foreign
everybody live inna one white picket fence
wid house
and land and cyar   50
and dog
and two point three pickney[1]
dem even have washing machine and dryer
dem even have machine fi wash up dem cup and plate
a laziness dat if yuh ask me   55
but nobody nevah ask

---

1   *pickney* Caribbean English term for a child.

mi soon gawn a foreign
but me best friend gone quicker dan mi

but wait how come she
60 nuh write mi back yet
after she dun tell me seh
she is me bes frien
yuh know weh dem seh bout people like dat
dem get rich an switch
65 yes
she gawn a foreign and get rich and switch

—2007

love speak

what language have i
to transcend the treachery
of miscommunication
should poetry give name to
5 thought
then courage births revolushunaries
of love
these silent spaces sprout seeds
for a mute beginning
10 and I am left at the end of the circle
contemplating running the track of
my choices yet again

breathless
from fear

—2007

Hai-Dang Phan
b. 1980

Vietnamese-American academic, poet, and translator Hai-Dang Phan is, in the words of poet Edward Hirsch, "a gifted poet of dislocation, migration and inheritance." Many of his poems address global politics, sometimes in the context of his family's own experience of immigration.

Phan was born in Vietnam shortly after the Vietnam War. His father, having been an officer in the South Vietnamese Navy, was imprisoned in a "re-education camp" by the new communist government. When Phan was only a year old, his family escaped Vietnam and emigrated as refugees to the United States, where, once settled, Phan's father attended college and became a computer programmer. Years later, Phan went on to study creative writing at the University of Florida and completed a PhD in literary studies at the University of Wisconsin-Madison. In 2012, he joined the faculty at Grinnell College, Iowa, where he had been an undergraduate student.

Phan's poetry has been published in *The New Yorker*, the *New England Review*, and *Poetry* magazine. He has also translated several contemporary Vietnamese poets, such as Phan Nhiên Hạo and Nguyễn Quốc Chánh. In 2016, he won the *New England Review* Award for Emerging Writers; the following year, he received a National Endowment for the Arts Fellowship in Creative Writing.

Phan wrote "My Father's 'Norton Introduction to Literature,' Third Edition (1981)" (2015) after finding one of his father's old English Literature textbooks in his parents' home. This poem, which Phan describes as "my marginalia on his marginalia," won the Frederick Bock Prize and was selected for entry into *The Best American Poetry 2016*. The poem is also included in Phan's first collection, the short chapbook *Small Wars: Poems* (2016).

My Father's "Norton Introduction to Literature," Third Edition (1981)

Certain words give him trouble: *cannibals, puzzles, sob,*
bosom, martyr, deteriorate, shake, astonishes, vexed, ode ...
These he looks up and studiously annotates in Vietnamese.
Ravish means *cướp đoạt*; *shits* is like when you have to *đi ỉa*;
mourners are those whom we say are full of *buồn rầu.*
For "even the like precurse of feared events"[1] think *báo trước.*

5

---

1   *even ... events* From *Hamlet* 1.1.

Its thin translucent pages are webbed with his marginalia,
graphite ghosts of a living hand, and the notes often sound
just like him: "All depend on how look at thing," he pencils
10 after "I first surmised the Horses' Heads/Were toward Eternity —"[1]
His slanted handwriting is generally small, but firm and clear.
His pencil is a No. 2, his preferred Hi-Liter, arctic blue.

I can see my father trying out the tools of literary analysis.
He identifies the "turning point" of "The Short and Happy Life
15 of Francis Macomber";[2] underlines the simile in "Both the old man
and the child stared ahead <u>as if</u> they were awaiting an apparition."[3]
My father, as he reads, continues to notice relevant passages
and to register significant reactions, but increasingly sorts out

his ideas in English, shaking off those Vietnamese glosses.
20 1981 was the same year we *vượt biển* and came to America,
where my father took Intro Lit ("for fun"), Comp Sci ("for job").
"Stopping by Woods on a Snowy Evening,"[4] he murmurs
something about the "dark side of life how awful it can be"
as I begin to track silence and signal to a cold source.

25 Reading Ransom's[5] "Bells for John Whiteside's Daughter,"
a poem about a "young girl's death," as my father notes,
how could he not have been "<u>vexed</u> at her brown study/
Lying so primly propped," since he never properly observed
(I realize this just now) his own daughter's wake.
30 *Lấy làm ngạc nhiên về* is what it means to be astonished.

Her name was Đông Xưa, Ancient Winter, but at home she's Bebe.
"There was such speed in her <u>little body</u>,/And such lightness
in her footfall,/It is no wonder her brown study/Astonishes
us all." In the photo of her that hangs in my parents' house
35 she is always fourteen months old and staring into the future.
In "reeducation camp" he had to believe she was alive

---

1   *I first ... Eternity* See Emily Dickinson's poem 712, "Because I could not stop for Death"
     (page 554).
2   *"The Short ... Macomber"* 1936 short story by Ernest Hemingway.
3   *Both ... apparition* From Flannery O'Connor's "A Good Man is Hard to Find" (1953).
4   *"Stopping by Woods on a Snowy Evening"* 1923 poem by Robert Frost (see page 584).
5   *Ransom* American poet John Crowe Ransom (1888–1974).

because my mother on visits "took arms against her shadow."[1]
Did the memory of those days sweep over him like a leaf storm
from the pages of a forgotten autumn? Lost in the margins,
I'm reading the way I discourage my students from reading.   40
But this is "how we deal with death," his black pen replies.
Assume there is a reason for everything, instructs a green asterisk.

Then between pp. 896–97, opened to Stevens' "Sunday Morning,"[2]
I pick out a newspaper clipping, small as a stamp, an old listing
from the 404-Employment Opps State of Minnesota, and read: 45
For current job opportunities dial (612) 297-3180. Answered 24 hrs.
When I dial, the automated female voice on the other end
tells me I have reached a non-working number.

                                                    —2015

---

1   *took arms ... shadow* Reference to "Bells for John Whiteside's Daughter" by John Crowe
     Ransom, which in turn references Shakespeare's *Hamlet*.
2   *"Sunday Morning"* 1915 poem by Wallace Stevens.

Jordan Abel
b. 1985

Poet Jordan Abel has been called "a master carver of the page" by poet Susan Holbrook, a descriptor that references both the sculpture-like visual qualities of his work and his use of found materials as the building blocks of his poetry. A Nisga'a writer born in British Columbia and raised in Ontario, Abel has been praised by critic Neal McLeod for his "new and vibrant Indigenous poetic consciousness." His work often disassembles and reworks colonialist writings to reveal and resist the racism that underlies them.

In his first book, *The Place of Scraps* (2013), Abel draws on the writing and photography of the white anthropologist Marius Barbeau (1883–1969), who believed himself to be preserving coastal First Nations cultures by moving totem poles and other objects to museums—a practice now termed salvage anthropology and viewed as a form of colonial aggression. Inspired by the work of such writers as M. NourbeSe Philip and Anne Carson, both of whom have also engaged with history through found text, Abel transforms the text of Barbeau's book *Totem Poles* through interjection, rewriting, and, perhaps most importantly, the removal of words. As Abel puts it, "[f]or me, erasure is the poem. There is no book without it." *The Place of Scraps* was nominated for the Gerald Lampert Memorial Award and won the Dorothy Livesay Poetry Prize.

Abel followed *The Place of Scraps* with *Un/inhabited* (2015) and the Griffin Prize-winning long poem *Injun* (2017). Both texts were published as he pursued a PhD at Simon Fraser University combining Indigenous literary studies with digital humanities—a field in which digital technologies are used to open up new approaches to literature and other arts. Both *Un/inhabited* and *Injun* employ large numbers of public-domain western novels as their sources. Abel compiled these novels, then searched the texts for key words—such as, for his 2017 poem, "injun"—and used the sentences surrounding those words as raw material for his work.

from *The Place of Scraps*

"*A feud over this pole.* Old chief Mountain or Sakau'wan, some time before his death in 1928, gave an account of the rivalry between the Eagle-Raven clan and the Killer-Whales or Gispewudwades of Nass River, over the size of their new totems.[1] In summary here it is.

The Killer-Whale chief, Sispagut, who headed the faction of the earlier occupants on the river, announced his determination to put up the tallest pole ever seen in the country. Its name was to be Fin-of-the-Killer-Whale. However, instead of selecting for its carver Hladerh whose right it was to do the work, he chose Oyai of the canyon. Hladerh naturally felt slighted and confided his grudge to Sakau'wan, chief of the Eagles, and his friend. From then on the Eagles and the Wolves of their own day were to be closely allied, as the ancestors of both had moved in from Alaska and at one time had been allies.

[1] For a fuller account see *Alaska Beckons* by Marius Barbeau. The Caxton Printers, Caldwell, Idaho and the Macmillan Company of Canada, 1947, pp. 127–136"

Marius Barbeau, *Totem Poles*, vol. 1 (1950), 29.

                                                or Sakau'wan

        and

                            Sispagut
        the river
            the country

                        the canyon

allied

                    by Marius Barbeau

his

new totems

his determination

his
Eagles and   Wolves

an account
or
summary

was to be
carve   d

from Alaska'

his

his

    their   s[1]   h   is

h   i   s   h

       his   i

       s

H   i s   H   i s

   h   i   s

his   his

     h   i   s

      h   i   s

h   i s

[1] For a fuller account see *Alaska Beckons* by Marius Barbeau.

In summary

,   his

"*The pole transported to Toronto.* To remove this huge totem pole from the Nass, and transfer it to a museum thousands of miles away was not an easy job. Taking it down to the ground and shifting it into the water taxed the ingenuity of a railway engineer and his crew of Indians. It leaned sharply, face forwards, and had it fallen, its carvings would have been damaged. But the work was successfully carried out and after a few days the pole with two others was towed down Portland Canal, on its way south along the coast to Prince Rupert. As it floated in the water, several men could walk on it without feeling a tremor under their feet; it was so large that a few hundred pounds made no difference. When it reached Prince Rupert, it had to be cut, as it lay in the water, into three sections, for the longest railway cars are 50 feet. Nor were all difficulties overcome after the three sections had reached Toronto."

Marius Barbeau, *Totem Poles*, vol. 1 (1950), 34.

  remove

                transfer

                                            shift

        face forwards
                    work

                                    down
                                        float   in
                    feel
                        no difference
                        in the water
                            or
                    Toronto

       his   totem

                 the water
   his   Indians

    carried
down Portland Canal,

         their feet

lay in the water

                    remove
               thousands of

                            Indians

          successfully

without feeling a tremor

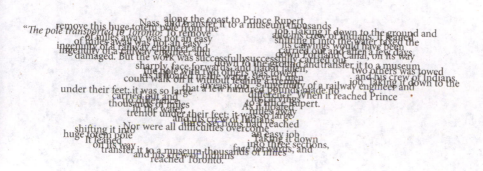

—2013

Literary Non-Fiction

Literary non-fiction is a diverse genre with a long history—yet its nature is hard to pin down. A work of literary non-fiction is nowadays almost always written in prose, but it may be an essay, a memoir, or a piece of journalism. It may be written for any one of a wide range of purposes. It may be as short as a page or two, or it may be of book length.

No work that calls itself "non-fiction" can be the product of pure invention—if you make up the story, you are writing fiction. Yet the line that separates fiction from non-fiction may sometimes be hard to determine. Many authors of literary non-fiction consider it a legitimate practice to shape the presentation of events or characters in an essay or a memoir in ways that deviate from the specifics of what actually happened. George Orwell, one of the most highly acclaimed writers of literary non-fiction of the twentieth century, is known to have done this frequently. So too does Barack Obama, who, in the preface to *Dreams from My Father*, candidly acknowledges that at least part of what he has written is, in some sense, fiction:

> Although much of this book is based on contemporaneous journals or the oral histories of my family, the dialogue is necessarily an approximation of what was actually said or relayed to me. For the sake of compression, some of the characters that appear are composites of people I've known, and some events appear out of precise chronology.

In other words, the writer has felt at liberty to sift and shape the material to give a personal view of what seems to him to be, in his words, "some granite slab of truth." Critics may reach different conclusions as to whether or not the picture that emerges in such writing does in fact present "some granite slab of truth," but what is equally necessary in this genre is that the writing itself is worthy of critical attention—that it be thought of as literature.

Literary Non-Fiction and Academic Non-Fiction

The form that literary non-fiction most frequently takes is that of the essay. But an *essay* in this sense is something very different from the kind of essay that university students are asked to read (and, usually, to write) when they take courses in academic subjects. For the most part, students are taught that an academic essay should be distanced and impersonal. It should be structured according to established conventions of its academic discipline. And according to these conventions, the academic essay should strive for objectivity; subjective reflections have little place in this kind of writing. The task of the essay writer is not to sway the reader through description or narration or emotional appeal of any sort, but rather to analyze evidence in support of an argument. Whether that argument is made inductively or deductively, an academic essay should display careful reasoning. It should also cite references to support its argument—and to enable others to verify the evidence and use it in their own scholarship.

The sort of essay that constitutes a work of literary non-fiction is none of these things. Though it may sometimes marshal evidence in support of a reasoned argument, it may also employ narration and description and emotional appeal. It may be loosely structured. It is more likely to be personal in tone. And it will normally not include any cited sources. Whereas the academic essay is generally addressed to an audience within a particular scholarly academic discipline, literary non-fiction is typically addressed to a broad audience. It aims to interest and entice readers and to give them pleasure, in the way that literature gives pleasure—through the use of well-crafted images, figurative language, and symbols, by ordering events to create suspense, and by creating interesting non-fictional "characters" to engage us.

Such pleasure is not contingent on the writer's topic being pleasurable. Just as a novel about horrific events can be, *as literature*, enjoyable as well as interesting to read, so too a piece of literary non-fiction about horrific events can be, *as literature*, enjoyable. Conveying in memorable and affecting ways the "unspeakable" is an important function of literature. Philip Gourevitch's piece in this volume, reflecting on the nature of genocide and on having seen the aftermath of a massacre, falls squarely into this category. But if, as a general question, we ask what sorts of topics literary non-fiction addresses, there is no simple answer. The writer may work through any one of a wide range of structures in trying to mediate a reader's understanding of an endless variety of topics. Examples in this volume include an exploration of a father's life (Miriam Toews's memoir); an explanation of the conventions of comics (Scott McCloud); a memoir of growing up and understanding gender (Ivan Coyote); and an exploration of what it means to have brown skin in a world that values whiteness (Kamal Al-Solaylee).

History of the Genre

Given that literary non-fiction has only recently begun to receive considerable attention as a distinct literary genre, one might easily imagine that writing of this sort would be a relatively recent phenomenon. In fact, its roots go almost as far back as do those of poetry and drama. Like them, the genre of literary non-fiction has strong roots in the classical cultures of ancient Greece and Rome. The ancients referred to the process of communication as *rhetoric*. Broadly defined, rhetoric may be said to be involved in almost anything to do with the study of cultural messages, with any communication that attempts to persuade, with almost every human effort to express thoughts coherently so as to communicate them to others. In practice, the Greeks and Romans defined rhetoric much more narrowly. Classical rhetoric was an art whose precepts were designed to help orators (*rhetors*) organize and deliver their arguments in a methodical, articulate, and persuasive way. That may sound a long way from the literary non-fiction of today—may sound, indeed, of more relevance to the roots of the modern academic essay than to those of literary non-fiction. And there can be no question of the relevance of classical rhetoric to the history of academic argument. But historians suggest that the modern essay as a work of literary non-fiction may also be found in embryonic form in the works of some classical writers—not least of all in a work now almost two thousand years old, the *Moral Letters* of the Roman Stoic philosopher Lucius Annaeus Seneca (usually known simply as Seneca).

Though the 124 pieces that make up the *Moral Letters* are written as letters to the then-governor of Sicily, Lucilius—each one begins "Seneca greets his Lucilius"—in every other respect the epistles far more closely resemble what we now call literary non-fiction than they do modern-day personal letters. They are personal in tone, to be sure, but they include little or nothing relating to the particulars of the personal relationship between Seneca and Lucilius. They seem rather to address a general audience. They sometimes try to persuade, and at others, offer rich description (as when Seneca gives us a picture of the dining table or describes the master whose greed has filled his distended belly). They as often appeal to the senses and to the emotions as to reason. And the topics tend to be broad and range widely, from drunkenness to scientific invention, to how a love of sports can become excessive, to the issue of equality between men and women. Seneca is thought of today primarily as a philosopher, but in the Moral Letters his writing is far closer to that of today's writer of literary essays than it is to the writing of most contemporary philosophers.

In the post-medieval era the literary essay is generally said to have begun with the sixteenth-century French writer Michel de Montaigne, known in his day as the "French Seneca." Like Seneca, Montaigne wrote short pieces on a wide variety of broad topics ranging from marriage to study, education, and various aspects of current affairs. But Montaigne's pieces tend to be both more closely reasoned than those of Seneca, and looser in structure. More often than not they explore an idea rather than set out an argument in favour of a predetermined position. Montaigne saw writing of this sort less as a means of persuading the reader to accept a certain conclusion than as a means of trying to grope one's way toward understanding. Hence the name he gave to these short pieces—*essais*, or, in English, *attempts* or *tries*. (The connection is a direct one; among its definitions of *essay* the *Oxford English Dictionary* offers the following: "the action or process of trying or testing.") And always, while attempting to understand some aspect of an idea or of the world, Montaigne was attempting to understand himself—reflecting on his own thoughts, impulses, and desires. In the preface to the *Essais* Montaigne famously declares, "lecteur, je suis moi-même la matière de mon livre" ("reader, I am myself the subject of my book"). In all these respects—the looseness of structure, the vision of writing as a means of groping toward understanding, the tendency to use the essay to explore the outside world and the self simultaneously—Montaigne's writing continues to exert an influence on literary non-fiction.

The history of the literary essay in English is extraordinarily varied. It is often said to begin in early seventeenth-century England with the essays of Francis Bacon. With the eighteenth century came the pointed political and literary essays of Samuel Johnson and Jonathan Swift, and the beginnings of literary journalism. The nineteenth century brought the cultural criticism of Charles Dickens, Matthew Arnold, and George Eliot in Britain, and the personal-philosophic essays of Henry David Thoreau and Ralph Waldo Emerson in the United States. In the twentieth century the range of literary non-fiction became broader still, from Virginia Woolf's essays on gender and society and George Orwell's explorations of politics and culture, to the fresh approaches to form and the tremendous variety of subject matter that characterize the literary non-fiction of late twentieth- and early twenty-first-century writers from every corner of the globe. Across this diversity, though, direct links to the traditions of Montaigne and Seneca remain—in tone, style, structure, and rhetorical strategies.

Style and Structure, Argument, and Rhetoric

Let's return to our comparison of how arguments are presented in the modern academic essay versus literary non-fiction. As we have said, reason and logic are central to what the writer of the academic essay strives for, and the logic of the argument is made overt through such conventions as thesis statements and topic sentences. Anything that might impede an impersonal and objective presentation of a reasoned argument is often said to be inappropriate in an academic essay. Rhetorical flourishes are kept to a minimum. The structure in which an argument is presented tends to be standardized. The pronoun "I" is often said to have no place here, and the same is said of personal details or reflections. Style and structure, in short, are conventionalized in order for the writer to be as unobtrusive as possible—and in order to allow reasoned argument to shine through.

In literary non-fiction, on the other hand, a range of structures is available to the writer, and the adoption of a personal tone and a unique style are often very much a part of the presentation of the "argument." Why is the word "argument" put in quotation marks here? To make clear that, in the context of literary non-fiction, *argument* is not to be taken in the same sense as it is with most academic non-fiction. The argument of a piece of literary non-fiction is the line along which ideas are connected; it may be much looser and less overt than the argument of the typical academic paper of today, and its logic may be implicit, to be sought out by the reader.

Whether we are looking at non-literary academic arguments or those of literary non-fiction, the vocabulary of classical rhetoric remains highly useful when it comes to naming the elements of argument. According to one of the most influential classical rhetorical manuals, *Rhetorica ad Herennium* (which dates from the first century BCE), rhetoric has five canons or general, fundamental principles: invention, arrangement, style, memory, and delivery. As may readily be inferred from the last two items on that list, the expectation was that rhetorical arguments would be delivered orally through a speech (by a *rhetor*) rather than in writing. But the strength and originality of the ideas (invention), the way in which they are arranged, and the style with which they are presented are concepts that remain relevant to non-fiction writing of all sorts.

The *Rhetorica ad Herennium* also sets out guidelines for the layout of an argument (in classical terminology, its *disposition*), specifying that it should include the following elements:

- exordium (introduces the argument)

- narration (states the issue; may supply background or explore the history of the issue)

- division (separates and lists the parts under discussion)

- confirmation (elaborates and supports the *rhetor*'s position)

- confutation (refutes opposing arguments)

- peroration (conclusion)

We may observe these elements in Seneca's writing (see sites.broadviewpress.com/BIL)—how he separates the parts under discussion, how he anticipates (and refutes) the arguments of his opponents. Aside perhaps from *exordium* and *peroration*, though, it may well be thought that such concepts are of limited use in analyzing the contemporary literary essay. But from time to time they may indeed be useful in discussing academic non-fiction. We may see traces of the classical rhetorical strategies of narration and division, for example, in the way in which Scott McCloud separates and defines the elements of comic art.

Ancient guides to rhetoric also often considered arguments as belonging to one of three types: deliberative (concerned with the future), judicial (sometimes referred to as forensic; concerned with the past), and epideictic (celebratory arguments). These classifications too may sometimes be helpful in discussions of literary non-fiction. When Mark Twain addresses an imaginary audience in "Advice to Youth," he creates an epideictic argument. Roland Barthes, as he explores "The World of Wrestling," makes a judicial or forensic argument (as do several of the other selections). Deliberative arguments in anything close to a pure form, however, are rarely found in literary non-fiction; they occur far more frequently in politicians' speeches, in the arguments of newspaper and television commentators—or in the world of advertising.

Perhaps of greater relevance to today's literary non-fiction are the three categories of appeal that are set out in classical rhetoric (from the early Greek philosopher Aristotle on down): *logos*, *pathos*, and *ethos*. All three are widely and usefully employed in many discussions of literary writing today.

Logos is often translated as *logic*, and to a large extent appeals based on *logos* may indeed be appeals that are logical in nature. But in the world of rhetoric such appeals are not always made according to the principles of inductive or deductive logic that apply to most academic essays. The meaning of *logos* in the ancient world was multi-faceted; it could mean *reason* or *logic*, but it could also simply mean *word*; in the context of literary non-fiction, an appeal based on *logos* may perhaps best be understood as an appeal based on the ideas that the words hold. The rational arguments that Seneca makes—appealing to the principle of fairness and citing the benefits of treating one's slaves or servants well—represent appeals to *logos*. Much the same can be said of Barthes's arguments about the moral content of wrestling. These are arguments that in large part make appeals to *logos* based on traditional principles of logical reasoning. But Miriam Toews also makes an appeal to *logos* when she recounts the history in the Mennonite church of shunning those "out of faith"—a category that included those suffering from depression or despair—and then writes that she "can't help thinking" that this history of shunning had "just a little to do with" the ways in which her father tried to deal with his depression. Toews's line of reasoning cannot be said to follow the same sorts of logical steps that the arguments of Barthes do—and she makes no claims to have reached an airtight conclusion. Yet her appeal to *logos* may be more powerful than that of any of the other pieces included here. Rather than establishing the tenets of and the conclusion to an argument, her appeal to *logos* suggests connections.

And rather than demonstrating irrefutably that those connections exist, she persuades us that they are likely to have played a real part in what happened to her father. Giving readers freedom in this way to discern an argument's logic by forging connections for themselves is one important way in which the genre of literary non-fiction may exert powerful effects.

The word *pathos* is sometimes thought to hold pejorative connotations, describing an appeal to the emotions that is too contrived, blatant, or superficial. Appeals to the emotions may surely be all of those things. But they need not be any of them and certainly the term *pathos*, properly used, carries much the same meaning today as it did for the ancients, referring to any appeal to the emotions. Such appeals have a legitimate place in most forms of argumentation, given that our responses to experiences inevitably involve both heart and head; indeed, many would argue that the direction our reason takes is always informed at some level by our initial, emotional responses. Such appeals may take many forms. When you read Orwell's "Shooting an Elephant," you will likely be moved by the full sweep of the experience the writer is recounting. Toews's "A Father's Faith" is another example of a piece in which an appeal to *pathos* arguably runs throughout the essay. But appeals to *pathos* may be embedded even in very brief descriptions that have strong emotive content.

For Aristotle and other ancient Greek authorities, an appeal to *ethos* was one based on the character of the person presenting the argument, whether that might have to do with the speaker's position of authority, his or her perceived honesty, or other ethical virtues. In modern usage, *ethos* is still used to refer to the character of the person putting forward an argument, but there may be more factors that come into play today in determining this character. The idea of authority is a case in point. Though our society's more populist impulses may make us less inclined to judge the merits of a given argument on the basis of the writer's credentials, reputation still influences the willingness many of us have to extend faith to authors. The idea of virtue today is somewhat more complicated: it is now quite widely accepted that we do not in fact have reliable information as to the virtues—or lack thereof—of the writer of an essay. Yet we can gain a sense of whether a writer seems virtuous or not from any number of tiny cues—in the compassion we may sense in an author's treatment of a subject, or, by contrast, in his or her failure to judge others generously. What this means is that, generally speaking, appeals to *ethos* may be considered to rest on a wider range of characteristics today, for instance on our knowledge of a given speaker and the way in which speakers present themselves, or on the overall personality that we sense behind a particular piece of writing.

Unlike the structural elements of logical arguments (whether as set out according to the principles of classical rhetoric, or according to those of modern manuals for academic essay writing), the sorts of appeals that literary non-fiction makes (to *logos*, *pathos*, and *ethos*) are unlikely ever to follow one upon the other in a predictable order. Appeals to logic may alternate with appeals to emotion, just as narrative and descriptive and argumentative passages may be interspersed one with another. Such alternation is a continual feature of a number of the pieces of literary non-fiction included here, including those by Orwell, Toews, and Al-Solaylee. Arguments that are almost academic in their tone may alternate with paragraphs in which appeals to *ethos* and *pathos* come to the fore. There may be sudden turns; surprise is a strategy that we tend to associate with narrative fiction but also one that may feature prominently in literary non-fiction.

I end this introduction with one more glance in the direction of the two points of comparison we've used throughout: the principles of classical rhetoric and those of modern academic essay writing. Both those sets of principles are prescriptive: the precepts of classical rhetoric were designed to help orators organize and deliver their speeches in a methodical, articulate way. Similarly, modern manuals of essay writing are designed to help students follow the established conventions of an academic discipline. It is more difficult—perhaps impossible—to provide a blueprint for how to write literary non-fiction—and certainly this introduction makes no attempt to do so. It aims to be descriptive rather than prescriptive—to give some sense of the history and characteristics of the genre of literary non-fiction. While the selections here don't aim to trace the historical development of the genre, they do provide some sense of this burgeoning genre's diversity and versatility.

[P.L.]

Jonathan Swift
1667–1745

Although the art of literary satire traces its origins to antiquity, its golden age is often said to have occurred in the late seventeenth and eighteenth centuries—the time of Molière, Dryden, Pope, and Voltaire. Among the many gifted satirical minds that set out during this period to lash the vices and follies of mankind, none was more adept than Jonathan Swift, who aimed to "vex the world" into reform but acknowledged the limitations of satire as a "glass wherein beholders do generally discover everybody's face but their own."

Swift is best known as the author of *Gulliver's Travels* (1726), but he initially rose to prominence—first with the Whigs, then with the Tories—as one of the most brilliant political writers of his day. Ordained as a priest in the Anglican Church, Swift entertained hopes for ecclesiastical preferment in England, but when in 1714 the Tory ministry fell with the death of Queen Anne, he reluctantly retreated to his native Ireland, where he had been appointed dean of St. Patrick's Cathedral in Dublin. Here Swift came face to face with the appalling conditions of the Irish poor, whose hardships were much exacerbated by English economic policy. To this day Swift is regarded as a national hero for the many letters and pamphlets—published anonymously though their authorship was generally known—in which he championed Irish political and economic independence, discharging his "savage indignation" in some of the finest prose ever written.

Swift was moved to write much of his satire in response to particular events and circumstances, but the objects of his attack—above all the moral and intellectual failings of the human race—are perennial. "A Modest Proposal" (1729), his darkest, most disturbingly cynical work, appeared at the height of Ireland's wretchedness, a time of rampant inflation, poverty, famine, homelessness, and unemployment.

A Modest Proposal

For Preventing the Children of Poor People in Ireland from Being a Burden to Their Parents or the Country, and for Making Them Beneficial to the Public

It is a melancholy object to those who walk through this great town,[1] or travel in the country, when they see the streets, the roads, and cabin doors crowded with beggars of the female sex, followed by three, four, or six children, all in

---

1   *this great town* I.e., Dublin.

rags and importuning every passenger[1] for an alms. These mothers, instead of being able to work for their honest livelihood, are forced to employ all their time in strolling[2] to beg sustenance for their helpless infants, who, as they grow up, either turn thieves for want of work, or leave their dear native country to fight for the Pretender in Spain, or sell themselves to the Barbados.[3]

I think it is agreed by all parties that this prodigious number of children in the arms, or on the backs, or at the heels of their mothers, and frequently of their fathers, is, in the present deplorable state of the kingdom, a very great additional grievance; and therefore, whoever could find out a fair, cheap, and easy method of making these children sound and useful members of the commonwealth would deserve so well of the public as to have his statue set up for a preserver of the nation.

But my intention is very far from being confined to provide only for the children of professed beggars; it is of a much greater extent, and shall take in the whole number of infants at a certain age who are born of parents in effect as little able to support them as those who demand our charity in the streets.

As to my own part, having turned my thoughts for many years upon this important subject and maturely weighed the several schemes of other projectors,[4] I have always found them grossly mistaken in their computation. 'Tis true, a child just dropped from its dam may be supported by her milk for a solar year with little other nourishment, at most not above the value of two shillings, which the mother may certainly get, or the value in scraps, by her lawful occupation of begging; and it is exactly at one year old that I propose to provide for them in such a manner as, instead of being a charge upon their parents or the parish, or wanting food and raiment for the rest of their lives, they shall on the contrary contribute to the feeding, and partly to the clothing, of many thousands.

There is likewise another great advantage in my scheme, that it will prevent those abortions, and that horrid practice of women murdering their bastard children, alas, too frequent among us, sacrificing the poor innocent babes, I doubt,[5] more to avoid the expense than the shame, which would move tears and pity in the most savage and inhuman breast.

---

1   *passenger* Passerby.
2   *strolling* Wandering, roving.
3   *the Pretender* James Francis Edward Stuart, son of James II who was deposed from the throne in the Glorious Revolution due to his overt Catholicism. Catholic Ireland was loyal to Stuart, and the Irish were often recruited by France and Spain to fight against England; *Barbados* Because of the extreme poverty in Ireland, many Irish people emigrated to the West Indies, selling their labour to sugar plantations in advance to pay for the voyage.
4   *projectors* Those who design or propose experiments or projects.
5   *doubt* Think.

The number of souls in this kingdom being usually reckoned one million and a half, of these I calculate there may be about two hundred thousand couples whose wives are breeders, from which number I subtract thirty thousand couples who are able to maintain children, although I apprehend there cannot be as many under the present distresses of the kingdom; but this being granted, there will remain one hundred and seventy thousand breeders.

I again subtract fifty thousand for those women who miscarry, or whose children die by accident or disease within the year. There only remain one hundred and twenty thousand children of poor parents annually born. The question therefore is how this number shall be reared and provided for, which, as I have already said, under the present situation of affairs is utterly impossible by all the methods hitherto proposed. For we can neither employ them in handicraft or agriculture; we neither build houses (I mean in the country) nor cultivate land.[1] They can very seldom pick up a livelihood by stealing till they arrive at six years old, except where they are of towardly parts,[2] although I confess they learn the rudiments much earlier, during which time they can however be properly looked upon only as probationers, as I have been informed by a principal gentleman in the county of Cavan, who protested to me that he never knew above one or two instances under the age of six, even in a part of the kingdom so renowned for the quickest proficiency in that art.

I am assured by our merchants that a boy or a girl before twelve years old is no saleable commodity; and even when they come to this age, they will not yield above three pounds, or three pounds and half a crown at most, on the Exchange, which cannot turn to account[3] either to the parents or the kingdom, the charge of nutriment and rags having been at least four times that value.

I shall now therefore humbly propose my own thoughts, which I hope will not be liable to the least objection.

I have been assured by a very knowing American[4] of my acquaintance in London that a young healthy child well nursed is at a year old a most delicious, nourishing, and wholesome food, whether stewed, roasted, baked, or boiled; and I make no doubt that it will equally serve in a fricassee or a ragout.[5]

I do therefore humbly offer it to public consideration that of the hundred and twenty thousand children already computed, twenty thousand may be

---

1   *neither build ... land* The British placed numerous restrictions on the Irish agricultural industry, retaining the majority of land for the grazing of sheep. The vast estates of British absentee landlords further contributed to Ireland's poverty.

2   *of towardly parts* Exceptionally able.

3   *on the Exchange* At the market; *turn to account* Result in profit.

4   *American* I.e., Native American.

5   *fricassee or a ragout* Stews.

reserved for breed, whereof only one fourth part to be males, which is more than we allow to sheep, black cattle, or swine, and my reason is that these children are seldom the fruits of marriage, a circumstance not much regarded by our savages; therefore, one male will be sufficient to serve four females. That the remaining hundred thousand may at a year old be offered in sale to the persons of quality and fortune through the kingdom, always advising the mother to let them suck plentifully of the last month, so as to render them plump and fat for a good table. A child will make two dishes at an entertainment for friends, and when the family dines alone, the fore or hind quarter will make a reasonable dish, and seasoned with a little pepper or salt will be very good boiled on the fourth day, especially in winter.

I have reckoned upon a medium that a child just born will weigh twelve pounds, and in a solar year if tolerably nursed increase to twenty-eight pounds.

I grant this food will be somewhat dear,[1] and therefore very proper for landlords, who, as they have already devoured most of the parents, seem to have the best title to the children.

Infants' flesh will be in season throughout the year, but more plentiful in March, and a little before and after. For we are told by a grave author, an eminent French physician, that, fish being a prolific[2] diet, there are more children born in Roman Catholic countries about nine months after Lent than at any other season; therefore, reckoning a year after Lent, the markets will be more glutted than usual because the number of popish[3] infants is at least three to one in this kingdom, and therefore it will have one other collateral advantage by lessening the number of papists among us.

I have already computed the charge of nursing a beggar's child (in which list I reckon all cottagers,[4] labourers, and four fifths of the farmers) to be about two shillings per annum, rags included, and I believe no gentleman would repine to give ten shillings for the carcass of a good fat child, which, as I have said, will make four dishes of excellent nutritive meat when he hath only some particular friend or his own family to dine with him. Thus the squire[5] will learn to be a good landlord and grow popular among his tenants; the mother will have eight shillings net profit and be fit for work till she produces another child.

---

1   *dear* Expensive.
2   *grave author* Sixteenth-century satirist François Rabelais. See his *Gargantua and Pantagruel*; *prolific* I.e., causing increased fertility.
3   *popish* Derogatory term meaning "Catholic."
4   *cottagers* Country dwellers.
5   *squire* Owner of a country estate.

Those who are more thrifty (as I must confess the times require) may flay the carcass, the skin of which, artificially[1] dressed, will make admirable gloves for ladies and summer boots for fine gentlemen.

As to our city of Dublin, shambles[2] may be appointed for this purpose in the most convenient parts of it, and butchers we may be assured will not be wanting, although I rather recommend buying the children alive and dressing them hot from the knife, as we do roasting pigs.

A very worthy person, a true lover of his country, and whose virtues I highly esteem, was lately pleased, in discoursing on this matter, to offer a refinement upon my scheme. He said that, many gentlemen of this kingdom having of late destroyed their deer, he conceived that the want of venison might be well supplied by the bodies of young lads and maidens, not exceeding fourteen years of age nor under twelve, so great a number of both sexes in every county being now ready to starve for want of work and service; and these to be disposed of by their parents if alive, or otherwise by their nearest relations. But with due deference to so excellent a friend and so deserving a patriot, I cannot be altogether in his sentiments; for as to the males, my American acquaintance assured me from frequent experience that their flesh was generally tough and lean, like that of our schoolboys, by continual exercise, and their taste disagreeable, and to fatten them would not answer the charge. Then as to the females, it would, I think with humble submission, be a loss to the public because they soon would become breeders themselves. And besides, it is not improbable that some scrupulous people might be apt to censure such a practice (although indeed very unjustly) as a little bordering upon cruelty, which, I confess, hath always been with me the strongest objection against any project, however well intended.

But in order to justify my friend, he confessed that this expedient was put into his head by the famous Psalmanazar,[3] a native of the island of Formosa, who came from thence to London above twenty years ago, and in conversation told my friend that in his country, when any young person happened to be put to death the executioner sold the carcass to persons of quality as a prime dainty, and that in his time the body of a plump girl of fifteen, who was crucified for an attempt to poison the emperor, was sold to his Imperial Majesty's Prime Minister of State and other great Mandarins of the court, in joints from the

---

1 *artificially* Artfully, skillfully.
2 *shambles* Slaughterhouses.
3 *Psalmanazar* George Psalmanazar, a French adventurer who pretended to be a Formosan and published an account of Formosan customs, *Historical and Geographical Description of Formosa* (1704), which was later exposed as fraudulent. The story Swift recounts here is found in the second edition of Psalmanazar's work.

gibbet,[1] at four hundred crowns. Neither indeed can I deny that if the same use were made of several plump young girls in this town who, without one single groat to their fortunes, cannot stir abroad without a chair,[2] and appear at the playhouse and assemblies in foreign fineries which they never will pay for, the kingdom would not be the worse.

Some persons of a desponding spirit are in great concern about that vast number of poor people who are aged, diseased, or maimed, and I have been desired to employ my thoughts what course may be taken to ease the nation of so grievous an encumbrance. But I am not in the least pain upon that matter because it is very well known that they are every day dying and rotting by cold and famine, and filth and vermin, as fast as can be reasonably expected. And as to the younger labourers, they are now in almost as hopeful a condition. They cannot get work, and consequently pine away for want of nourishment to a degree that if at any time they are accidentally hired to common labour, they have not strength to perform it; and thus the country and themselves are happily delivered from the evils to come.

I have too long digressed, and therefore shall return to my subject. I think the advantages by the proposal which I have made are obvious and many, as well as of the highest importance.

For first, as I have already observed, it would greatly lessen the number of papists, with whom we are yearly overrun, being the principal breeders of the nation as well as our most dangerous enemies, and who stay at home on purpose with a design to deliver the kingdom to the Pretender, hoping to take their advantage by the absence of so many good Protestants, who have chosen rather to leave their country than stay at home and pay tithes against their conscience to an Episcopal curate.[3]

Secondly, the poorer tenants will have something valuable of their own, which by law may be made liable to distress[4] and help to pay their landlord's rent, their corn and cattle being already seized, and money a thing unknown.

Thirdly, whereas the maintenance of an hundred thousand children from two years old and upwards cannot be computed at less than ten shillings apiece per annum, the nation's stock will be thereby increased fifty thousand pounds per annum, besides the profit of a new dish introduced to the tables of all gentlemen of fortune in the kingdom who have any refinement in taste,

---

1   *gibbet* Gallows.
2   *groat* Silver coin equal in value to four pence. It was removed from circulation in 1662, and thereafter "a groat" was used metaphorically to signify any very small sum; *chair* Sedan chair, which seated one person and was carried on poles by two men.
3   *Episcopal curate* I.e., Anglican church official.
4   *distress* Seizure of property for the payment of debt.

and the money will circulate among ourselves, the goods being entirely of our own growth and manufacture.

Fourthly, the constant breeders, besides the gain of eight shillings sterling per annum by the sale of their children, will be rid of the charge of maintaining them after the first year.

Fifthly, this food would likewise bring great customs to taverns, where the vintners will certainly be so prudent as to procure the best receipts[1] for dressing it to perfection, and consequently have their houses frequented by all the fine gentlemen who justly value themselves upon their knowledge in good eating. And a skillful cook who understands how to oblige his guests will contrive to make it as expensive as they please.

Sixthly, this would be a great inducement to marriage, which all wise nations have either encouraged by rewards or enforced by laws and penalties. It would increase the care and tenderness of mothers toward their children, when they were sure of a settlement for life to the poor babes, provided in some sort by the public, to their annual profit instead of expense. We should soon see an honest emulation[2] among the married women, which of them could bring the fattest child to market. Men would become as fond of their wives during the time of their pregnancy as they are now of their mares in foal, their cows in calf, or sows when they are ready to farrow, nor offer to beat or kick them (as it is too frequent a practice) for fear of a miscarriage.

Many other advantages might be enumerated: for instance, the addition of some thousand carcasses in our exportation of barrelled beef; the propagation of swine's flesh and improvement in the art of making good bacon, so much wanted among us by the great destruction of pigs, too frequent at our tables, which are no way comparable in taste or magnificence to a well-grown, fat yearling child, which, roasted whole, will make a considerable figure at a Lord Mayor's feast or any other public entertainment. But this and many others I omit, being studious of brevity.

Supposing that one thousand families in this city would be constant customers for infants' flesh, besides others who might have it at merry-meetings, particularly weddings and christenings, I compute that Dublin would take off annually about twenty thousand carcasses, and the rest of the kingdom (where probably they will be sold somewhat cheaper) the remaining eighty thousand.

I can think of no one objection that will possibly be raised against this proposal, unless it should be urged that the number of people will be thereby much lessened in the kingdom. This I freely own, and it was indeed one principal design in offering it to the world. I desire the reader will observe

---

1   *receipts* Recipes.
2   *emulation* Rivalry.

that I calculate my remedy for this one individual kingdom of Ireland, and for no other that ever was, is, or, I think, ever can be upon earth. Therefore let no man talk to me of other expedients:[1] of taxing our absentees at five shillings a pound; of using neither clothes nor household furniture, except what is of our own growth and manufacture; of utterly rejecting the materials and instruments that promote foreign luxury; of curing the expensiveness of pride, vanity, idleness, and gaming[2] in our women; of introducing a vein of parsimony, prudence, and temperance; of learning to love our country, wherein we differ even from Laplanders and the inhabitants of Topinamboo; of quitting our animosities and factions, nor act any longer like the Jews, who were murdering one another at the very moment their city was taken;[3] of being a little cautious not to sell our country and consciences for nothing; of teaching landlords to have at least one degree of mercy toward their tenants; lastly, of putting a spirit of honesty, industry, and skill into our shopkeepers, who, if a resolution could now be taken to buy only our native goods, would immediately unite to cheat and exact upon us in the price, the measure, and the goodness, nor could ever yet be brought to make one fair proposal of just dealing, though often in earnest invited to it.

Therefore I repeat, let no man talk to me of these and the like expedients till he hath at least some glimpse of hope that there will ever be some hearty and sincere attempt to put them in practice.

But as to myself, having been wearied out for many years with offering vain, idle, visionary thoughts, and at length utterly despairing of success, I fortunately fell upon this proposal, which, as it is wholly new, so it hath something solid and real, of no expense and little trouble, full in our own power, and whereby we can incur no danger in disobliging England. For this kind of commodity will not bear exportation, the flesh being of too tender a consistence to admit a long continuance in salt, although perhaps I could name a country[4] which would be glad to eat up our whole nation without it.

After all, I am not so violently bent upon my own opinion as to reject any offer, proposed by wise men, which shall be found equally innocent, cheap, easy, and effectual. But before something of that kind shall be advanced in

---

1   *other expedients* All of which Swift had already proposed in earnest attempts to remedy Ireland's poverty. See, for example, his *Proposal for the Universal Use of Irish Manufactures.* In early editions the following proposals were italicized to show the suspension of Swift's ironic tone.

2   *gaming* Gambling.

3   *Topinamboo* District in Brazil; *Jews ... was taken* According to the history of Flavius Josephus, Roman Emperor Titus's invasion and capture of Jerusalem in 70 BCE was aided by the fact that factional fighting had divided the city.

4   *a country* I.e., England.

contradiction to my scheme, and offering a better, I desire the author or authors will be pleased maturely to consider two points.

First, as things now stand, how they will be able to find food and raiment for one hundred thousand useless mouths and backs.

And secondly, there being a round million of creatures in human figure throughout this kingdom whose whole subsistence, put into a common stock, would leave them in debt two million of pounds sterling, adding those who are beggars by profession to the bulk of farmers, cottagers, and labourers with their wives and children, who are beggars in effect.

I desire those politicians who dislike my overture, and may perhaps be so bold to attempt an answer, that they will first ask the parents of these mortals whether they would not at this day think it a great happiness to have been sold for food at a year old in the manner I prescribe, and thereby have avoided such a perpetual scene of misfortunes as they have since gone through by the oppression of landlords, the impossibility of paying rent without money or trade, the want of common sustenance, with neither house nor clothes to cover them from the inclemencies of the weather, and the most inevitable prospect of entailing[1] the like or greater miseries upon their breed forever.

I profess in the sincerity of my heart that I have not the least personal interest in endeavoring to promote this necessary work, having no other motive than the public good of my country by advancing our trade, providing for infants, relieving the poor, and giving some pleasure to the rich. I have no children by which I can propose to get a single penny, the youngest being nine years old, and my wife past childbearing.

—1729

---

1   *entailing* Bestowing, conferring.

Virginia Woolf
1882–1941

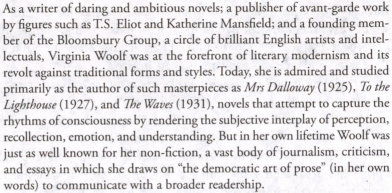 As a writer of daring and ambitious novels; a publisher of avant-garde work by figures such as T.S. Eliot and Katherine Mansfield; and a founding member of the Bloomsbury Group, a circle of brilliant English artists and intellectuals, Virginia Woolf was at the forefront of literary modernism and its revolt against traditional forms and styles. Today, she is admired and studied primarily as the author of such masterpieces as *Mrs Dalloway* (1925), *To the Lighthouse* (1927), and *The Waves* (1931), novels that attempt to capture the rhythms of consciousness by rendering the subjective interplay of perception, recollection, emotion, and understanding. But in her own lifetime Woolf was just as well known for her non-fiction, a vast body of journalism, criticism, and essays in which she draws on "the democratic art of prose" (in her own words) to communicate with a broader readership.

Two of Woolf's longer non-fiction works, *A Room of One's Own* (1929) and *Three Guineas* (1938), are now acknowledged as ground-breaking feminist studies of the social, psychological, and political effects of patriarchy. But many critics have tended to treat Woolf's essays as incidental works, interesting only insofar as they illuminate her fictional theory and practice. Woolf herself distinguished between professional and creative writing—the one a means to an income, the other part of a broader artistic project. The essays tend to be more formally conventional than the novels, but many of them are nonetheless remarkable for their expression of personality and their open engagement with ideas. Amiable and urbane, more exploratory than authoritative, they wander from topic to topic, full of idiosyncratic asides and digressions. Through her engagingly forthright tone Woolf often achieves a remarkable intimacy with the reader. She considered the possibility for creating such intimacy to be a chief virtue of the form: as she observed, a good essay "must draw its curtain round us, but it must be a curtain that shuts us in, not out."

The Death of the Moth

Moths that fly by day are not properly to be called moths; they do not excite that pleasant sense of dark autumn nights and ivy-blossom which the commonest yellow-underwing asleep in the shadow of the curtain never fails to rouse in us. They are hybrid creatures, neither gay like butterflies nor sombre like their own species. Nevertheless the present specimen, with his narrow hay-coloured wings, fringed with a tassel of the same colour, seemed to be content with life. It was a pleasant morning, mid–September, mild, benignant, yet with a keener breath than that of the summer months. The plough was already scoring the field opposite the window, and where the share[1] had been, the earth was pressed flat and gleamed with moisture. Such vigour came rolling in from the fields and the down beyond that it was difficult to keep the eyes strictly turned upon the book. The rooks too were keeping one of their annual festivities; soaring round the tree tops until it looked as if a vast net with thousands of black knots in it had been cast up into the air; which, after a few moments sank slowly down upon the trees until every twig seemed to have a knot at the end of it. Then, suddenly, the net would be thrown into the air again in a wider circle this time, with the utmost clamour and vociferation, as though to be thrown into the air and settle slowly down upon the tree tops were a tremendously exciting experience.

The same energy which inspired the rooks, the ploughmen, the horses, and even, it seemed, the lean bare-backed downs, sent the moth fluttering from side to side of his square of the window-pane. One could not help watching him. One was, indeed, conscious of a queer feeling of pity for him. The possibilities of pleasure seemed that morning so enormous and so various that to have only a moth's part in life, and a day moth's at that, appeared a hard fate, and his zest in enjoying his meagre opportunities to the full, pathetic. He flew vigorously to one corner of his compartment, and, after waiting there a second, flew across to the other. What remained for him but to fly to a third corner and then to a fourth? That was all he could do, in spite of the size of the downs, the width of the sky, the far-off smoke of houses, and the romantic voice, now and then, of a steamer out at sea. What he could do he did. Watching him, it seemed as if a fibre, very thin but pure, of the enormous energy of the world had been thrust into his frail and diminutive body. As often as he crossed the pane, I could fancy that a thread of vital light became visible. He was little or nothing but life.

Yet, because he was so small, and so simple a form of the energy that was rolling in at the open window and driving its way through so many narrow and intricate corridors in my own brain and in those of other human beings, there was something marvellous as well as pathetic about him. It was as if someone had taken a tiny bead of pure life and decking it as lightly as possible with down and feathers, had set it dancing and zig-zagging to show us the true nature of life. Thus displayed one could not get over the strangeness of it. One is apt to forget all about life, seeing it humped and bossed and garnished and cumbered so that it has to move with the greatest circumspection and dignity. Again, the thought of all that life might have been had he been born in any other shape caused one to view his simple activities with a kind of pity.

---

1   *share* Blade of a plough.

After a time, tired by his dancing apparently, he settled on the window ledge in the sun, and, the queer spectacle being at an end, I forgot about him. Then, looking up, my eye was caught by him. He was trying to resume his dancing, but seemed either so stiff or so awkward that he could only flutter to the bottom of the window-pane; and when he tried to fly across it he failed. Being intent on other matters I watched these futile attempts for a time without thinking, unconsciously waiting for him to resume his flight, as one waits for a machine, that has stopped momentarily, to start again without considering the reason of its failure. After perhaps a seventh attempt he slipped from the wooden ledge and fell, fluttering his wings, on to his back on the window sill. The helplessness of his attitude roused me. It flashed upon me that he was in difficulties; he could no longer raise himself; his legs struggled vainly. But, as I stretched out a pencil, meaning to help him to right himself, it came over me that the failure and awkwardness were the approach of death. I laid the pencil down again.

The legs agitated themselves once more. I looked as if for the enemy against which he struggled. I looked out of doors. What had happened there? Presumably it was midday, and work in the fields had stopped. Stillness and quiet had replaced the previous animation. The birds had taken themselves off to feed in the brooks. The horses stood still. Yet the power was there all the same, massed outside indifferent, impersonal, not attending to anything in particular. Somehow it was opposed to the little hay-coloured moth. It was useless to try to do anything. One could only watch the extraordinary efforts made by those tiny legs against an oncoming doom which could, had it chosen, have submerged an entire city, not merely a city, but masses of human beings; nothing, I knew, had any chance against death. Nevertheless after a pause of exhaustion the legs fluttered again. It was superb this last protest, and so frantic that he succeeded at last in righting himself. One's sympathies, of course, were all on the side of life. Also, when there was nobody to care or to know, this gigantic effort on the part of an insignificant little moth, against a power of such magnitude, to retain what no one else valued or desired to keep, moved one strangely. Again, somehow, one saw life, a pure bead. I lifted the pencil again, useless though I knew it to be. But even as I did so, the unmistakable tokens of death showed themselves. The body relaxed, and instantly grew stiff. The struggle was over. The insignificant little creature now knew death. As I looked at the dead moth, this minute wayside triumph of so great a force over so mean an antagonist filled me with wonder. Just as life had been strange a few minutes before, so death was now as strange. The moth having righted himself now lay most decently and uncomplainingly composed. O yes, he seemed to say, death is stronger than I am.

—1942

Zora Neale Hurston
1891–1960

Today critics often speak of the resurrection of Zora Neale Hurston. Although among the most prolific African American writers of her generation, she spent her latter years in obscurity, earning a paltry and irregular subsistence as a maid, supply teacher, and sometime journalist. When she died in a county welfare home in Florida, she was buried in an unmarked grave, her achievements largely ignored or forgotten. It was not until 1975, when Alice Walker published her essay "In Search of Zora Neale Hurston," that the author of *Jonah's Gourd Vine* (1934) and *Their Eyes Were Watching God* (1937) was restored to her rightful place and recognized as "the intellectual and spiritual foremother of a generation of black women writers."

Many commentators on Hurston's novels, short stories, and pioneering studies of African folklore have been struck by what Walker describes as their exuberant "racial health—a sense of black people as complete, complex, *undiminished* human beings, a sense that is lacking in so much black writing and literature." Informed by the myths, rituals, and storytelling traditions that she documented in her anthropological work, Hurston's fiction celebrates black culture and the nuance and vitality of black vernacular speech. But her reluctance to use her art to "lecture on the race problem" or to give a politicized, sociological account of "the Negro" alienated many other prominent authors and intellectuals of the Harlem Renaissance. In a rancorous review of *Their Eyes Were Watching God*, Richard Wright accused Hurston of perpetuating a degrading minstrel tradition, dismissing her masterpiece as an exercise in "facile sensuality" that "carries no theme, no message, no thought."

Ever an individualist, Hurston refused to write resentful novels of social protest in which "black lives are only defensive reactions to white actions." As she declared in her essay "How It Feels to Be Coloured Me" (1928), "I do not belong to that sobbing school of Negrohood who hold that nature somehow has given them a lowdown dirty deal." Hurston's position was controversial, particularly in the era of Jim Crow segregation laws, but she sought after her own fashion to overcome what W.E.B. Du Bois called "the problem of the colour line" by opening up the souls of black men and women so as to reveal their common humanity and individual strength.

How It Feels to Be Coloured Me

I am coloured but I offer nothing in the way of extenuating circumstances except the fact that I am the only Negro in the United States whose grandfather on the mother's side was *not* an Indian chief.[1]

I remember the very day that I became coloured. Up to my thirteenth year I lived in the little Negro town of Eatonville, Florida. It is exclusively a coloured town. The only white people I knew passed through the town going to or coming from Orlando. The native whites rode dusty horses, the Northern tourists chugged down the sandy village road in automobiles. The town knew the Southerners and never stopped cane chewing when they passed. But the Northerners were something else again. They were peered at cautiously from behind curtains by the timid. The more venturesome would come out on the porch to watch them go past and got just as much pleasure out of the tourists as the tourists got out of the village.

The front porch might seem a daring place for the rest of the town, but it was a gallery[2] seat for me. My favourite place was atop the gate-post. Proscenium box for a born first-nighter.[3] Not only did I enjoy the show, but I didn't mind the actors knowing that I liked it. I usually spoke to them in passing. I'd wave at them and when they returned my salute, I would say something like this: "Howdy-do-well-I-thank-you-where-you-goin'?" Usually the automobile or the horse paused at this, and after a queer exchange of compliments, I would probably "go a piece of the way" with them, as we say in farthest Florida. If one of my family happened to come to the front in time to see me, of course negotiations would be rudely broken off. But even so, it is clear that I was the first "welcome-to-our-state" Floridian, and I hope the Miami Chamber of Commerce will please take notice.

During this period, white people differed from coloured to me only in that they rode through town and never lived there. They liked to hear me "speak pieces" and sing and wanted to see me dance the parse-me-la, and gave me generously of their small silver for doing these things, which seemed strange to me for I wanted to do them so much that I needed bribing to stop. Only they didn't know it. The coloured people gave no dimes. They deplored any joyful tendencies in me, but I was their Zora nevertheless. I belonged to them, to the nearby hotels, to the county—everybody's Zora.

---

1   *I am ... Indian chief* An improbably high number of African Americans claimed to have Native American heritage, which was prestigious in African American communities at this time.

2   *gallery* Theatre seating area situated in an elevated balcony.

3   *Proscenium box* Theatre seating area near the proscenium, the frame of the stage; *first-nighter* Person who frequently appears in the audience of opening night performances.

But changes came in the family when I was thirteen, and I was sent to school in Jacksonville. I left Eatonville, the town of the oleanders, as Zora. When I disembarked from the river-boat at Jacksonville, she was no more. It seemed that I had suffered a sea change. I was not Zora of Orange County any more, I was now a little coloured girl. I found it out in certain ways. In my heart as well as in the mirror, I became a fast[1] brown—warranted not to rub nor run.

But I am not tragically coloured. There is no great sorrow dammed up in my soul, nor lurking behind my eyes. I do not mind at all. I do not belong to the sobbing school of Negrohood who hold that nature somehow has given them a lowdown dirty deal and whose feelings are all hurt about it. Even in the helter-skelter skirmish that is my life, I have seen that the world is to the strong regardless of a little pigmentation more or less. No, I do not weep at the world—I am too busy sharpening my oyster knife.

Someone is always at my elbow reminding me that I am the granddaughter of slaves. It fails to register depression with me. Slavery is sixty years in the past.[2] The operation was successful and the patient is doing well, thank you. The terrible struggle that made me an American out of a potential slave said "On the line!" The Reconstruction[3] said "Get set!"; and the generation before said "Go!" I am off to a flying start and I must not halt in the stretch to look behind and weep. Slavery is the price I paid for civilization, and the choice was not with me. It is a bully[4] adventure and worth all that I have paid through my ancestors for it. No one on earth ever had a greater chance for glory. The world to be won and nothing to be lost. It is thrilling to think—to know that for any act of mine, I shall get twice as much praise or twice as much blame. It is quite exciting to hold the centre of the national stage, with the spectators not knowing whether to laugh or to weep.

The position of my white neighbour is much more difficult. No brown spectre pulls up a chair beside me when I sit down to eat. No dark ghost thrusts its leg against mine in bed. The game of keeping what one has is never so exciting as the game of getting.

---

1   *fast* Adjective applied to dyes that will not run or change colour.
2   *Slavery is … the past* In 1863, the Emancipation Proclamation legally ended slavery in America.
3   *Reconstruction* Period of recovery (1865–77) after the American Civil War. During Reconstruction, the Southern states adjusted to an economy without legal slavery and rebuilt infrastructure that had been damaged by the war.
4   *bully* Merry, splendid.

I do not always feel coloured. Even now I often achieve the unconscious Zora of Eatonville before the Hegira.[1] I feel most coloured when I am thrown against a sharp white background.

For instance at Barnard.[2] "Beside the waters of the Hudson"[3] I feel my race. Among the thousand white persons, I am a dark rock surged upon, and overswept, but through it all, I remain myself. When covered by the waters, I am; and the ebb but reveals me again.

Sometimes it is the other way around. A white person is set down in our midst, but the contrast is just as sharp for me. For instance, when I sit in the drafty basement that is The New World Cabaret with a white person, my colour comes. We enter chatting about any little nothing that we have in common and are seated by the jazz waiters. In the abrupt way that jazz orchestras have, this one plunges into a number. It loses no time in circumlocutions, but gets right down to business. It constricts the thorax and splits the heart with its tempo and narcotic harmonies. This orchestra grows rambunctious, rears on its hind legs and attacks the tonal veil with primitive fury, rending it, clawing it until it breaks through to the jungle beyond. I follow those heathen—follow them exultingly. I dance wildly inside myself; I yell within, I whoop; I shake my assegai[4] above my head, I hurl it true to the mark *yeeeeooww*! I am in the jungle and living in the jungle way. My face is painted red and yellow and my body is painted blue. My pulse is throbbing like a war drum. I want to slaughter something—give pain, give death to what, I do not know. But the piece ends. The men of the orchestra wipe their lips and rest their fingers. I creep back slowly to the veneer we call civilization with the last tone and find the white friend sitting motionless in his seat smoking calmly.

"Good music they have here," he remarks, drumming the table with his fingertips.

Music. The great blobs of purple and red emotion have not touched him. He has only heard what I felt. He is far away and I see him but dimly across the ocean and the continent that have fallen between us. He is so pale with his whiteness then and I am *so* coloured.

At certain times I have no race, I am *me*. When I set my hat at a certain angle and saunter down Seventh Avenue, Harlem City, feeling as snooty as the lions

1   *Hegira* I.e., journey; refers to Mohammed's journey from Mecca to Medina, which marks the beginning of the current era in the Islamic calendar.
2   *Barnard* Women's liberal arts college in New York City, affiliated with Columbia University.
3   *Beside … Hudson* Barnard school song.
4   *assegai* Spear made of a tree of the same name, used by people of southern Africa.

in front of the Forty-Second Street Library, for instance. So far as my feelings are concerned, Peggy Hopkins Joyce on the Boule Mich[1] with her gorgeous raiment, stately carriage, knees knocking together in a most aristocratic manner, has nothing on me. The cosmic Zora emerges. I belong to no race nor time. I am the eternal feminine with its string of beads.

I have no separate feeling about being an American citizen and coloured. I am merely a fragment of the Great Soul that surges within the boundaries. My country, right or wrong.

Sometimes, I feel discriminated against, but it does not make me angry. It merely astonishes me. How *can* any deny themselves the pleasure of my company? It's beyond me.

But in the main, I feel like a brown bag of miscellany propped against a wall. Against a wall in company with other bags, white, red and yellow. Pour out the contents, and there is discovered a jumble of small things priceless and worthless. A first-water[2] diamond, an empty spool, bits of broken glass, lengths of string, a key to a door long since crumbled away, a rusty knife-blade, old shoes saved for a road that never was and never will be, a nail bent under the weight of things too heavy for any nail, a dried flower or two still a little fragrant. In your hand is the brown bag. On the ground before you is the jumble it held—so much like the jumble in the bags, could they be emptied, that all might be dumped in a single heap and the bags refilled without altering the content of any greatly. A bit of coloured glass more or less would not matter. Perhaps that is how the Great Stuffer of Bags filled them in the first place—who knows?

—1928

---

1   *Peggy Hopkins Joyce* White American actress (1893–1957) known for her extravagant lifestyle; *Boule Mich* Boulevard Saint-Michel, a major street in Paris.

2   *first-water* Best quality of diamond or other gem.

George Orwell

1903–1950

George Orwell is best known to modern readers for two works: the anti-Stalinist allegory *Animal Farm* (1945) and the dystopian nightmare *1984* (1949). It was with reference to these two novels that the word "Orwellian" entered the English language as a signifier for any oppressive, invasive, and manipulative practice that seems to threaten the freedom of a society. Orwell was also a successful and prolific writer of non-fiction: full-length works of political and social criticism (notably *The Road to Wigan Pier*, *Down and Out in Paris and London*, and *Homage to Catalonia*) as well as essays of a variety of sorts (memoir, literary criticism, political journalism). The imprint he left on English literary non-fiction may be even deeper than that which he left on English fiction; the scholar Leo Rockas has said that "Orwell's style is probably more admired and pointed to as a model than any other modern prose style, primarily for its no-nonsense approach."

Eric Arthur Blair, the man who would become famous as George Orwell, was born in the Indian municipality of Motihari to an English father employed in the Indian Civil Service. His mother had grown up in Burma, where her French father pursued his business interests. When he was one year old, his mother took him and his older sister to live in England; there, Orwell attended a number of boarding schools, including Eton, in preparation for a university career. His Eastern origins, however, exerted a strong influence on the young man, and in 1922 Orwell left England to begin service with the Indian Imperial Police in Burma.

Orwell's time in Burma would inform his art and politics for the rest of his life. Most directly, he would draw on his experiences in writing essays such as "Shooting an Elephant" (1936). Beyond that, the distaste he developed in Burma for the imperial project continued to inform Orwell's treatment of the themes of authority, oppression, and moral conscience—in the novels *Animal Farm* and *1984* as well as in his non-fiction.

Shooting an Elephant

In Moulmein, in Lower Burma, I was hated by large numbers of people—the only time in my life that I have been important enough for this to happen to me. I was sub-divisional police officer of the town, and in an aimless, petty kind of way anti-European feeling was very bitter. No one had the guts to raise a riot, but if a European woman went through the bazaars alone somebody would probably spit betel[1] juice over her dress. As a police officer I was an ob-

---

1   *betel* Leaf and nut mixture that is chewed as a stimulant, common in Southeast Asia.

vious target and was baited whenever it seemed safe to do so. When a nimble Burman tripped me up on the football field and the referee (another Burman) looked the other way, the crowd yelled with hideous laughter. This happened more than once. In the end the sneering yellow faces of young men that met me everywhere, the insults hooted after me when I was at a safe distance, got badly on my nerves. The young Buddhist priests were the worst of all. There were several thousands of them in the town and none of them seemed to have anything to do except stand on street corners and jeer at Europeans.

All this was perplexing and upsetting. For at that time I had already made up my mind that imperialism was an evil thing and the sooner I chucked up my job and got out of it the better. Theoretically—and secretly, of course—I was all for the Burmese and all against their oppressors, the British. As for the job I was doing, I hated it more bitterly than I can perhaps make clear. In a job like that you see the dirty work of Empire at close quarters. The wretched prisoners huddling in the stinking cages of the lock-ups, the grey, cowed faces of the long-term convicts, the scarred buttocks of the men who had been flogged with bamboos—all these oppressed me with an intolerable sense of guilt. But I could get nothing into perspective. I was young and ill-educated and I had had to think out my problems in the utter silence that is imposed on every Englishman in the East. I did not even know that the British Empire is dying, still less did I know that it is a great deal better than the younger empires that are going to supplant it. All I knew was that I was stuck between my hatred of the empire I served and my rage against the evil-spirited little beasts who tried to make my job impossible. With one part of my mind I thought of the British Raj as an unbreakable tyranny, as something clamped down, *in saecula saeculorum*,[1] upon the will of prostrate peoples; with another part I thought that the greatest joy in the world would be to drive a bayonet into a Buddhist priest's guts. Feelings like these are the normal by-products of imperialism; ask any Anglo-Indian official, if you can catch him off duty.

One day something happened which in a roundabout way was enlightening. It was a tiny incident in itself, but it gave me a better glimpse than I had had before of the real nature of imperialism—the real motives for which despotic governments act. Early one morning the sub-inspector at a police station the other end of the town rang me up on the phone and said that an elephant was ravaging the bazaar. Would I please come and do something about it? I did not know what I could do, but I wanted to see what was happening and I got on to a pony and started out. I took my rifle, an old .44 Winchester and much too small to kill an elephant, but I thought the noise might be useful *in*

---

1   *in saecula saeculorum* Latin: for centuries upon centuries; forever. This phrase appears frequently in the New Testament.

terrorem.[1] Various Burmans stopped me on the way and told me about the elephant's doings. It was not, of course, a wild elephant, but a tame one which had gone "must."[2] It had been chained up, as tame elephants always are when their attack of "must" is due, but on the previous night it had broken its chain and escaped. Its mahout,[3] the only person who could manage it when it was in that state, had set out in pursuit, but had taken the wrong direction and was now twelve hours' journey away, and in the morning the elephant had suddenly reappeared in the town. The Burmese population had no weapons and were quite helpless against it. It had already destroyed somebody's bamboo hut, killed a cow and raided some fruit-stalls and devoured the stock; also it had met the municipal rubbish van and, when the driver jumped out and took to his heels, had turned the van over and inflicted violences upon it.

The Burmese sub-inspector and some Indian constables were waiting for me in the quarter where the elephant had been seen. It was a very poor quarter, a labyrinth of squalid bamboo huts, thatched with palmleaf, winding all over a steep hillside. I remember that it was a cloudy, stuffy morning at the beginning of the rains. We began questioning the people as to where the elephant had gone and, as usual, failed to get any definite information. That is invariably the case in the East; a story always sounds clear enough at a distance, but the nearer you get to the scene of events the vaguer it becomes. Some of the people said that the elephant had gone in one direction, some said that he had gone in another, some professed not even to have heard of any elephant. I had almost made up my mind that the whole story was a pack of lies, when we heard yells a little distance away. There was a loud, scandalized cry of "Go away, child! Go away this instant!" and an old woman with a switch in her hand came round the corner of a hut, violently shooing away a crowd of naked children. Some more women followed, clicking their tongues and exclaiming; evidently there was something that the children ought not to have seen. I rounded the hut and saw a man's dead body sprawling in the mud. He was an Indian, a black Dravidian coolie,[4] almost naked, and he could not have been dead many minutes. The people said that the elephant had come suddenly upon him round the corner of the hut, caught him with its trunk, put its foot on his back and ground him into the earth. This was the rainy season and the ground was soft, and his face had scored a trench a foot deep and a couple of yards long. He was lying on his belly with arms crucified and head sharply twisted to one side. His face was coated with mud, the eyes wide open, the

---

1   *in terrorem* Legal term for a warning; literally, Latin phrase meaning "in fear or alarm."

2   *must* Condition characterized by aggressive behaviour brought on by a surge in testosterone.

3   *mahout* Elephant trainer or keeper.

4   *Dravidian coolie* I.e., southern Indian manual labourer.

teeth bared and grinning with an expression of unendurable agony. (Never tell me, by the way, that the dead look peaceful. Most of the corpses I have seen looked devilish.) The friction of the great beast's foot had stripped the skin from his back as neatly as one skins a rabbit. As soon as I saw the dead man I sent an orderly to a friend's house nearby to borrow an elephant rifle. I had already sent back the pony, not wanting it to go mad with fright and throw me if it smelt the elephant.

The orderly came back in a few minutes with a rifle and five cartridges, and meanwhile some Burmans had arrived and told us that the elephant was in the paddy fields below, only a few hundred yards away. As I started forward practically the whole population of the quarter flocked out of the houses and followed me. They had seen the rifle and were all shouting excitedly that I was going to shoot the elephant. They had not shown much interest in the elephant when he was merely ravaging their homes, but it was different now that he was going to be shot. It was a bit of fun to them, as it would be to an English crowd; besides they wanted the meat. It made me vaguely uneasy. I had no intention of shooting the elephant—I had merely sent for the rifle to defend myself if necessary—and it is always unnerving to have a crowd following you. I marched down the hill, looking and feeling a fool, with the rifle over my shoulder and an ever-growing army of people jostling at my heels. At the bottom, when you got away from the huts, there was a metalled road and beyond that a miry waste of paddy fields a thousand yards across, not yet ploughed but soggy from the first rains and dotted with coarse grass. The elephant was standing eight yards from the road, his left side towards us. He took not the slightest notice of the crowd's approach. He was tearing up bunches of grass, beating them against his knees to clean them and stuffing them into his mouth.

I had halted on the road. As soon as I saw the elephant I knew with perfect certainty that I ought not to shoot him. It is a serious matter to shoot a working elephant—it is comparable to destroying a huge and costly piece of machinery—and obviously one ought not to do it if it can possibly be avoided. And at that distance, peacefully eating, the elephant looked no more dangerous than a cow. I thought then and I think now that his attack of "must" was already passing off; in which case he would merely wander harmlessly about until the mahout came back and caught him. Moreover, I did not in the least want to shoot him. I decided that I would watch him for a little while to make sure that he did not turn savage again, and then go home.

But at that moment I glanced round at the crowd that had followed me. It was an immense crowd, two thousand at the least and growing every minute. It blocked the road for a long distance on either side. I looked at the sea of yellow faces above the garish clothes—faces all happy and excited over this bit of fun, all certain that the elephant was going to be shot. They were watching me as they would watch a conjurer about to perform a trick. They did not like me, but with the magical rifle in my hands I was momentarily worth watching. And suddenly I realized that I should have to shoot the elephant after all. The people expected it of me and I had got to do it; I could feel their two thousand wills pressing me forward, irresistibly. And it was at this moment, as I stood there with the rifle in my hands, that I first grasped the hollowness, the futility of the white man's dominion in the East. Here was I, the white man with his gun, standing in front of the unarmed native crowd—seemingly the leading actor of the piece; but in reality I was only an absurd puppet pushed to and fro by the will of those yellow faces behind. I perceived in this moment that when the white man turns tyrant it is his own freedom that he destroys. He becomes a sort of hollow, posing dummy, the conventionalized figure of a sahib.[1] For it is the condition of his rule that he shall spend his life in trying to impress the "natives," and so in every crisis he has got to do what the "natives" expect of him. He wears a mask, and his face grows to fit it. I had got to shoot the elephant. I had committed myself to doing it when I sent for the rifle. A sahib has got to act like a sahib; he has got to appear resolute, to know his own mind and do definite things. To come all that way, rifle in hand, with two thousand people marching at my heels, and then to trail feebly away, having done nothing—no, that was impossible. The crowd would laugh at me. And my whole life, every white man's life in the East, was one long struggle not to be laughed at.

But I did not want to shoot the elephant. I watched him beating his bunch of grass against his knees, with that preoccupied grandmotherly air that elephants have. It seemed to me that it would be murder to shoot him. At that age I was not squeamish about killing animals, but I had never shot an elephant and never wanted to. (Somehow it always seems worse to kill a *large* animal.) Besides, there was the beast's owner to be considered. Alive, the elephant was worth at least a hundred pounds; dead, he would only be worth the value of his tusks, five pounds, possibly. But I had got to act quickly. I turned to some experienced-looking Burmans who had been there when we arrived, and asked them how the elephant had been behaving. They all said the same thing: he took no notice of you if you left him alone, but he might charge if you went too close to him.

It was perfectly clear to me what I ought to do. I ought to walk up to within, say, twenty-five yards of the elephant and test his behaviour. If he charged, I could shoot; if he took no notice of me, it would be safe to leave

---

1   *sahib* I.e., colonial Englishman; this title of respect was used to address European men in colonial India.

him until the mahout came back. But also I knew that I was going to do no such thing. I was a poor shot with a rifle and the ground was soft mud into which one would sink at every step. If the elephant charged and I missed him, I should have about as much chance as a toad under a steam-roller. But even then I was not thinking particularly of my own skin, only of the watchful yellow faces behind. For at that moment, with the crowd watching me, I was not afraid in the ordinary sense, as I would have been if I had been alone. A white man mustn't be frightened in front of "natives"; and so, in general, he isn't frightened. The sole thought in my mind was that if anything went wrong those two thousand Burmans would see me pursued, caught, trampled on and reduced to a grinning corpse like that Indian up the hill. And if that happened it was quite probable that some of them would laugh. That would never do.

There was only one alternative. I shoved the cartridges into the magazine and lay down on the road to get a better aim. The crowd grew very still, and a deep, low, happy sigh, as of people who see the theatre curtain go up at last, breathed from innumerable throats. They were going to have their bit of fun after all. The rifle was a beautiful German thing with cross-hair sights. I did not then know that in shooting an elephant one would shoot to cut an imaginary bar running from ear-hole to ear-hole. I ought, therefore, as the elephant was sideways on, to have aimed straight at his ear-hole, actually I aimed several inches in front of this, thinking the brain would be further forward.

When I pulled the trigger I did not hear the bang or feel the kick—one never does when a shot goes home—but I heard the devilish roar of glee that went up from the crowd. In that instant, in too short a time, one would have thought, even for the bullet to get there, a mysterious, terrible change had come over the elephant. He neither stirred nor fell, but every line of his body had altered. He looked suddenly stricken, shrunken, immensely old, as though the frightful impact of the bullet had paralysed him without knocking him down. At last, after what seemed a long time—it might have been five seconds, I dare say—he sagged flabbily to his knees. His mouth slobbered. An enormous senility seemed to have settled upon him. One could have imagined him thousands of years old. I fired again into the same spot. At the second shot he did not collapse but climbed with desperate slowness to his feet and stood weakly upright, with legs sagging and head drooping. I fired a third time. That was the shot that did for him. You could see the agony of it jolt his whole body and knock the last remnant of strength from his legs. But in falling he seemed for a moment to rise, for as his hind legs collapsed beneath him he seemed to tower upward like a huge rock toppling, his trunk reaching skyward like a tree. He trumpeted, for the first and only time. And then down he came, his belly towards me, with a crash that seemed to shake the ground even where I lay.

I got up. The Burmans were already racing past me across the mud. It was obvious that the elephant would never rise again, but he was not dead. He was breathing very rhythmically with long rattling gasps, his great mound of a side painfully rising and falling. His mouth was wide open—I could see far down into caverns of pale pink throat. I waited a long time for him to die, but his breathing did not weaken. Finally I fired my two remaining shots into the spot where I thought his heart must be. The thick blood welled out of him like red velvet, but still he did not die. His body did not even jerk when the shots hit him, the tortured breathing continued without a pause. He was dying, very slowly and in great agony, but in some world remote from me where not even a bullet could damage him further. I felt that I had got to put an end to that dreadful noise. It seemed dreadful to see the great beast lying there, powerless to move and yet powerless to die, and not even to be able to finish him. I sent back for my small rifle and poured shot after shot into his heart and down his throat. They seemed to make no impression. The tortured gasps continued as steadily as the ticking of a clock.

In the end I could not stand it any longer and went away. I heard later that it took him half an hour to die. Burmans were bringing dahs[1] and baskets even before I left, and I was told they had stripped his body almost to the bones by the afternoon.

Afterwards, of course, there were endless discussions about the shooting of the elephant. The owner was furious, but he was only an Indian and could do nothing. Besides, legally I had done the right thing, for a mad elephant has to be killed, like a mad dog, if its owner fails to control it. Among the Europeans opinion was divided. The older men said I was right, the younger men said it was a damn shame to shoot an elephant for killing a coolie, because an elephant was worth more than any damn Coringhee[2] coolie. And afterwards I was very glad that the coolie had been killed; it put me legally in the right and it gave me a sufficient pretext for shooting the elephant. I often wondered whether any of the others grasped that I had done it solely to avoid looking a fool.

—1936

---

1   *dahs* Short swords or knives.
2   *Coringhee* From Coringha, a town on the coast of India.

Richard Wagamese

1955–2017

In an interview with *The Globe and Mail*, Ojibwe novelist, memoirist, and journalist Richard Wagemese said, "I get my inspiration from the knowledge that there is someone out there in the world who is just like me—curious and desiring more and more knowledge of the world and her people." Wagamese's writing offers not only compelling testimony of the intergenerational trauma caused by colonization, but also powerful meditations on ways to heal those who have been wounded. He has been praised for the "pervasive humanity" his prose style brings to this project: his writing, critics have said, displays "a level of artistry so superb that the personal becomes eternal."

Wagamese was born in 1955 on the Wabaseemoong First Nation into a family haunted by their experiences in residential schools. "Each of the adults had suffered in an institution that tried to scrape the Indian out of their insides," he explained. "[T]hey came back to the bush raw, sore and aching." At the age of two, Wagamese was taken into custody by the Children's Aid Society. After going through three foster homes, he was adopted by a family of strict Presbyterians, who moved him to St. Catharines, Ontario. At age 16, Wagamese left his adoptive home and spent years living on the street. Finding refuge in a library, he received encouragement from the library staff and educated himself in literature, music, mathematics, and science. "The only thing I've taken is the open opportunity that lay between the open covers of a book," Wagamese noted. "I read and read, and by sheer volume alone, I found out what a good sentence was."

In 1979, Wagamese secured a journalist position with *The New Breed*, an Indigenous newspaper in Regina. He would later write as an Indigenous-affairs columnist for *The Calgary Herald*, for which he received a National Newspaper Award in 1991. He received immediate critical acclaim for his first novel, *The Keeper'n Me* (1994). He is perhaps best known for his 2012 novel *Indian Horse*, which was a finalist on the CBC program *Canada Reads*, although Wagamese believed his final novel, *Medicine Walk* (2014), to be his best; it has indeed received wide acclaim for its "sly humour, sharp, believable dialogue and superb storytelling."

Finding Father

In the dream I am running. There's a dim trail through the trees making the footing dangerous. Everywhere there are humped and snaking roots of trees and rocks broad across the back as bread loaves and tall ferns and saplings that whip across my face. But I'm moving as fast as I can. The oversized gumboots I wear make speed even more treacherous. They slap and clap against my shins and flap around my foot at every stride. Still I run. There's a break in the trees and I can see the flash of white water from the rapids and I can hear the river's churning. From behind me I hear my pursuer. Heavy footfalls. Ravaged breath. I run hunched over trying to keep the gumboots on my feet fleeing for the safety of the river.

When I burst clear of the trees the sudden flare of light blinds me. But I sprint out onto the long, flat white peninsula of granite that pokes out into the river above the rapids. There are canoes there. I hope to jump into one and push it out into the current and down the chute of the rapids. I never get that chance.

Giant hands sweep me up. I'm spun in a wild circle. Large, strong arms enfold me. All I see is a whirl of long black hair like a curtain descending around me, falling over me, removing me from the world, the scent of wood smoke, bear grease and tanned hide, then deep laughter and the feel of a large palm at the back of my head. I'm laughing too as the gumboots fall from my feet. The world becomes the heat of the sun on my back and the feel of a big, warm heart beating against my tiny chest.

That dream is all I ever knew of my father.

I am Ojibway. My people occupy the large northern reaches of Ontario. We are bush people, river people, hunters, trappers and fishermen. I was born in a canvas army tent on a trap line. The first sounds I heard were an eagle's cry, the slap of a beaver's tail, the crackle of a fire and soft roll of Ojibway as my family talked and told stories around that fire. I was born to be one of them. But time and politics and history prevented that from happening.

I became one of the disappeared ones. I became one of the thousands of Aboriginal children across Canada swept up in the Sixties Scoop. This was an action by the government in conjunction with foster-care agencies to arbitrarily remove kids from their people. We were transplanted hundreds and thousands of miles away from our home territories. Some were even sent to different continents. We were routinely sold to outside foster-care agencies. I was one of those disenfranchised kids. I disappeared into non-native care before I was even two. I never made it home until I was twenty-four. Most of us never did.

My father's name was Stanley Raven. There were a number of men who adopted the name and role of father in my life when I was disappeared. None of them affected permanence. None of them fit the parameters of my dream. Stanley Raven was my one and only father and he died in a fall from a railway bridge the year before I made it home. There are few pictures of him. A bush-man's life seldom includes photographs and all I learned of my father were stories my mother and elder sister told. He lives for me in the rough and tangle of the northern Ontario landscape. I hear his voice in the rush of rapids, in the pastoral stillness of a northern lake at sunset, in the rutting call of a moose and the haunting soliloquy of a lone wolf howling at a gibbous moon rising above the trees and ridges. Stanley Raven. In those four syllables lays a history I can never reclaim and a connection to this earth, to the territory of my people I can never fully forge—and in this my wound became geography.

The land itself haunted me. I couldn't walk the Winnipeg River without an all consuming tide of loss washing over me, could never stand on that railway bridge without scanning the rocks and trees for the dim path that might lead me to the camp he had set in the bush beyond it, could never hunt without the idea of him guiding me, teaching me, assuring me, could never watch the moon rise there without a wild keening rising from the depths of me.

So I set out to find him in the early fall of 1983.

"Where was the camp where I was born?" I asked my sister Jane.

"I don't think I could even find it," she said. "But it's across the bay from Minaki.[1] There's a long narrow cove with big birches at the end of it. It's somewhere back there." In a landscape of bush and rivers it was an inadequate description. "Who's taking you there?" she asked.

"Just me," I said. "Something I gotta do alone."

She looked at me searchingly. Then she nodded. "Picking up the trail," she said.

I nodded. She never asked me any questions after that. Instead she helped me fill a backpack with things I would need for a couple days in the bush and arranged for a family friend to loan me a boat motor for the trip. When I pushed off from the dock she stood there and watched and waved until I disappeared around a bend in the river.

Our family name, Wagamese, means crooked water. It's in reference to the Winnipeg River. It refers specifically to my great grandfather who worked a trap line through sixty miles of bush that ran along that river. It's my family's territory and my legacy even though we were all removed from it by the fall of 1983. But setting out alone on that river felt right to me and trailing a hand over the gunwale of the boat I felt a connection to its tea coloured depths. If history has a smell then the mineral scent of that river on my hand is mine. If time can be erased and geography can return us to the people we were born to be then the wash of that water across my face was my act of reclamation and redemption. All through that trip downriver, around the cascade of rapids, into the long, sleek, flat muscle of channels, around the hem of islands jutted with white pine and birch and thrusts of pink granite, I let it seep into me and found release in the sudden spray of heron from a tree, the sovereign stance

---

1   *Minaki* Community in northwestern Ontario.

of a moose knee deep in shallows eating lily pads, and the dark punctuation of a bear against the loose paragraph of the hills.

It took hours to get to Minaki. Then I turned south and west into a broad bay and began searching its far shore for the inlet my sister described. I found it just as evening was beginning to fall. There was just enough time to set up camp and light a fire before the thick dark blanket of night fell over everything. I sat up late. When the moon rose I walked to the shore and looked up at millions of stars. I stood in the presence of a deep and profound silence and did not feel the least bit lonely.

In the morning I found an old pit. I dragged a log over and sat on it. I had no idea if it marked the site I was looking for, had no idea if it was my father's hands that had built it. But in the dappled light of that small clearing I chose to believe he had. I chose to believe that he'd held me in that clearing, clasped me to his chest and cried tears of welcome then raised me up to the universe and spoke my name to it, introduced me to both it and the land around me in the language of my people, gave me both blessing and purpose right there in that small clearing so many years before. I sat there for a long time until the shifting light told me it was time to go.

I found my father on that journey. Found him in the shards of rock around an old fire. Found him in the scent of a river, in the ragged spire of granite cliffs, in the depths of the bush and in the image of a ragged white pine perched alone at the top of a cliff lurched leeward by persistent winds, standing alone against time and circumstance, proudly like a prodigal returned to the land that spawned him.

I still have the dream only now we run together into the light.

—2015

Scott McCloud
b. 1960

Scott McCloud is an American cartoonist and author best known for his pioneering work in the theorization of comics: as one critic has commented, "What Aristotle did" for Ancient Greek theatre, "McCloud has done for the neglected form of comics." Addressing a medium that was long dismissed as a childish distraction undeserving of critical analysis, McCloud has made a compelling case for regarding comics as serious works of art. In his seminal text *Understanding Comics* (1993), McCloud developed a sophisticated framework for examining the unique possibilities offered by the comic medium.

Growing up in Lexington, Massachusetts, McCloud began producing comic art in high school. "As soon as I started making my own comics," he recalled, "I began coming up with ideas for how comics worked." Unable to study comics in university, he majored in illustration, producing a portfolio that secured him a job at DC Comics, where he wrote for the *Superman Adventures* series as well as other DC projects.

McCloud defends the comic as a distinct medium of art with its own aesthetic criteria, "visual vocabulary," and methods for representing space and time. In *Understanding Comics*, he offers a tentative theoretical definition of the form, suggesting that comics should be broadly conceptualized as "juxtaposed pictorial and other images in deliberate sequence, intended to convey information and/or produce an aesthetic response in the reader." McCloud has since published other comics examining the medium, including *Reinventing Comics* (2000) and *Making Comics* (2006).

Throughout his career, McCloud has tested the boundaries of the comic medium and defied conventional wisdom about the "right" way to produce comics. In 1984, he created *Zot!*, a playful take on the superhero comic, which eschewed the violence and pessimism that was typical of mainstream comics at the time. Beginning in 1998, McCloud released a succession of "infinite canvas" comics, which took advantage of electronic technologies that have obviated the need to divide comics into pages.

McCloud has already left an enduring legacy as one of the first figures to acknowledge comics as generative objects of study. As one critic put it, "If you want to read ambitious comics and graphic novels, you have many choices, but if you want to learn how to read them, you probably have to start with Scott McCloud."

from *Understanding Comics*

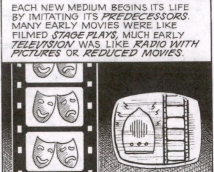

WORDS AND PICTURES IN COMBINATION MAY NOT BE MY *DEFINITION* OF COMICS, BUT THE COMBINATION HAS HAD *TREMENDOUS INFLUENCE* ON ITS *GROWTH.*

com·ics (kom'iks) n. [ ] form, used with a singular [ ] Juxtaposed pictori[ ] images in deliberate [ ]ence, intended to conv[ ] and/or to prod[ ] response in the [ ] **2.** Superheroes [ ] costumes; fight[ ] villains who want [ ] worlds in violent [ ]

A HUGE RANGE OF HUMAN EXPERIENCES CAN BE *PORTRAYED* IN COMICS THROUGH EITHER WORDS OR PICTURES.

AS A RESULT--AND DESPITE ITS MANY *OTHER* POTENTIAL USES -- COMICS HAVE BECOME *FIRMLY IDENTIFIED* WITH THE ART OF *STORYTELLING.*

AND *INDEED*, WORDS AND PICTURES HAVE *GREAT* POWERS TO TELL STORIES WHEN CREATORS FULLY EXPLOIT THEM *BOTH.*

DADA
BIOGRAPHY   HORROR
ROMANCE   SURREALISM
BLANK VERSE
EPIC POETRY   HISTORICAL FICTION
SOCIAL ALLEGORY   FOLK TALES
       EROTICA
SEQUENTIAL ART   MYSTERY
ADAPTATIONS   RELIGIOUS TOPICS
STREAM OF CONSCIOUSNESS
SATIRE

AND SO FAR, WE'VE ONLY SEEN THE *TIP OF THE ICEBERG!*

AS CHILDREN, WE "SHOW AND TELL" *INTERCHANGEABLY*, WORDS AND IMAGES COMBINING TO TRANSMIT A *CONNECTED SERIES OF IDEAS.*

IT'S GOT ONE OF *THESE* THINGS.

THE DIFFERENT WAYS IN WHICH WORDS AND PICTURES CAN *COMBINE* IN COMICS IS VIRTUALLY *UNLIMITED.*

BUT LET'S TRY TO BREAK IT DOWN INTO SOME DISTINCT *CATEGORIES.*

ANOTHER TYPE IS THE *ADDITIVE* COMBINATION WHERE WORDS *AMPLIFY* OR *ELABORATE* ON AN IMAGE OR *VICE VERSA.*

MY HEAD FEELS LIKE A *SMASHED PUMPKIN!*

HOW D'YA LIKE MY *NEW THREADS,* BABE?

IS THIS THE SAME *JUPITER* OF MY YOUTH?

IN *PARALLEL* COMBINATIONS, WORDS AND PICTURES SEEM TO FOLLOW VERY DIFFERENT COURSES--WITHOUT *INTERSECTING.*

"TALKED TO *BILL* YET?"

"*SALLY* DID. *WHY?*"

"THE *TEST RESULTS* CAME BACK. ALL *NEGATIVE.*"

"*REALLY?* THAT'S *GREAT!*"

WELL...

PEPPER.

CEREAL.

MILK.   BUTTER.

LIGHT BULBS.

STILL ANOTHER OPTION IS THE *MONTAGE* WHERE WORDS ARE TREATED AS INTEGRAL *PARTS* OF THE PICTURE.

CASH   PUBL
FLOW BOTTOM
LINE

ANNUAL
REPORT

H
A
P
P
Y!

PERHAPS THE MOST *COMMON* TYPE OF WORD/PICTURE COMBINATION IS THE *INTER-DEPENDENT,* WHERE WORDS AND PICTURES GO *HAND IN HAND* TO CONVEY AN IDEA THAT NEITHER COULD CONVEY *ALONE.*

MEANWHILE...

DID ANYONE *SEE* YOU?

THIS IS ALL I NEED TO *STOP* HIM!

I ASK YOU, DOES THIS GUY LOOK LIKE A *C.E.O.* TO *YOU* ??

"AND JUST *GUESS* WHO DROVE UP IN BOB'S TRUCK AN HOUR LATER!"

HEY, MARGE!

OH, MY GOD!

"AFTER COLLEGE, I PURSUED A CAREER IN *HIGH FINANCE.*"

HE'S LYING.

UH-HUH.

HURRY UP, WILLYA ?!

INTERDEPENDENT COMBINATIONS AREN'T ALWAYS AN *EQUAL BALANCE* THOUGH AND MAY FALL *ANYWHERE* ON A SCALE BETWEEN TYPES ONE AND TWO.

GENERALLY SPEAKING, THE MORE IS SAID WITH *WORDS,* THE MORE THE PICTURES CAN BE FREED TO GO EXPLORING AND *VICE VERSA.*

$$\frac{P}{W}$$

$$\frac{W}{P}$$

—1994

Kamal Al-Solaylee
b. 1964

A Canadian author and professor of journalism at Ryerson University, Kamal Al-Solaylee is also a political activist who seeks to lend his voice to the "millions of darker-skinned people who ... have missed out on the economic and political gains of the post-industrial world and are now clamouring for their fair share of the social mobility, equality, and freedom." His journalism, which includes extensive TV, film, and theatre criticism as well as reportage on international political events, has appeared in *The Globe and Mail*, the *Toronto Star*, the *National Post*, and *The Walrus*.

Although born in the city of Aden, which is now a part of Yemen, Al-Solaylee grew up in Beirut and Cairo as the youngest of 11 children. He returned briefly to Yemen at age 22, but soon left for London, England, both to complete his PhD in English and to escape Yemen's homophobic laws. Al-Solaylee's first book, *Intolerable: A Memoir of Extremes* (2012), recounts his experiences as a gay man growing up in the Middle East in the midst of political changes that brought increasing violence and repression. In this text, he urges young people struggling to live within intolerant environments to remain hopeful in spite of the challenges they face on a daily basis. "You can overcome all that—unfortunately, you may have to get away, as you can't expect the whole culture to change around you."

Al-Solaylee's second book, *Brown: What Being Brown in the World Today Means (to Everyone)* (2016), contemplates brownness as a racial identity and addresses the precarious situation of brown people in the contemporary world. *Brown* was shortlisted for the Governor General's Award.

from *Brown: What Being Brown in the World Today Means (to Everyone)*

I remember the moment I realized I was brown. My brown face, my brown legs and my curly black hair began to weigh on my mind in a way they never had before. Let me take you back to Cairo, early 1974. For several days, one of Egypt's two state television channels had been promoting the small-screen premiere of *Oliver!*, the 1968 film version of the British musical. It was a big deal in Cairo, and probably an omen for a city whose future poverty levels and income inequality would make Victorian London look like a socialist paradise. I write that with the full benefit of hindsight. I was a nine-year-old boy growing up as part of an expatriate Yemeni family, so I can't say that I knew much about the economy or the distribution of wealth back then.

I can't remember why I decided to stay up so late on a school night to watch a period musical about English orphans, pickpocketing gangs and prostitutes with teachable-moment altruism. I had but a passing familiarity with the story, and Western musicals were an artistic taste I had yet to acquire. (I caught up with them as part of an education in all things camp and old Hollywood when I came out as a gay man in my early twenties.)

The film aired just a few months short of my tenth birthday. Life in Egypt had returned to normal after three weeks of fighting and humiliating—or so the propaganda machine would have Egyptians believe—the Israeli army in a war that had started on October 6, 1973.[1] The end of hostilities meant a return to regular programming and a break from the rotation of military- and nationalist-themed songs and documentaries. My father, a lifelong anglophile, probably insisted that we children watch this slice of Merrie Olde England—a display of all things English that only a hardcore colonial like him was permitted to find jolly or nostalgic.

About twenty minutes into the film, though, he lost interest. You could always tell when something he longed for turned out to be a dud, because he'd start talking through it. Probably he hadn't realized that this was a musical version of Dickens's *Oliver Twist*. He didn't particularly like musicals, unless they starred Fred Astaire and Ginger Rogers,[2] his childhood idols.

I, on the other hand, trembled on the inside as I watched the film. My world tilted in that moment, and I'm not sure it's been set right since.

Every time the camera zoomed in on the face of the young actor playing Oliver, Mark Lester, I became painfully aware of how different my own face looked. As the youngest child in a large family, I was adored by my older siblings—the sweet baby boy. But the more I gazed at Lester's face, the less I felt any kind of pride in my looks, and my innocence slipped from under me in the process. He was just too beautiful, too angelic-looking. It defied the laws of nature as I knew them then. I don't think I viewed him in any sexual terms, even though my own awareness of my same-sex desire predated that evening by a few years. I saw it as a skin-to-skin and not boy-to-boy attraction. He had what, all of a sudden, I desired.

If my lifelong journey with physical insecurities and differences in skin colours can be traced to a single moment in time, it is that one. Most children in my immediate circle in downtown Cairo looked like variations of me. Sure,

---

1   *a war that ... October 6, 1973* The 1973 Arab-Israeli War, also called the Yom Kippur War, was a 20-day conflict between Israel and an alliance of primarily Egyptian and Syrian forces. Though Israel is generally recognized as having won the war, Egypt and Syria saw significant victories early in the conflict.

2   *Fred Astaire and Ginger Rogers* Famous dance partners who starred in a series of Hollywood musicals in the 1930s and 1940s.

some bragged about their very light complexion or their ash-blond hair, but no one came close to Mark Lester in brightness, whiteness, holiness. Looking at him, I felt like a lost soul, forever damned by a dark skin.

To be beautiful—to be adorably mischievous—a person needed to look like Lester. His light, shiny hair and his perfectly proportioned features forced me to rush to the bathroom to look at my own face and tousle my own hair. Probably for the first time in my life, all I saw reflected in that mirror was a black, dandruff-prone and curly mane; a big, flat nose; and ears that looked more clown-like than child-like. The hair could be trimmed or straightened, I consoled myself, and perhaps my nose and ears weren't all that unshapely. But there was one thing I couldn't rationalize away: my brown skin. What was I to do with this dark mass? How could I ever catch up with Lester's whiteness, which was the essence of his impossible beauty? If I scrubbed my face with soap ten, twenty times a day, would it get lighter and whiter? What about the rest of my body? How many showers a day would that be? How do you wash the brown away?

I needed answers. I needed help. I got neither.

I felt cursed with this brownness that I'd inherited from my passes-for-white father and my dark brown mother, who came from a Bedouin sheep-tending family in the southern tip of Yemen. My ten siblings displayed a variety of skin shades—some closer to my father's, some to my mother's. I came in between. Standard brown. Egyptians had coined a word for people like me: *asmarany*. It meant someone with a dark complexion, possibly from sustained exposure to the sun, and probably from working cotton fields or construction sites. There was pride in being sun-kissed—it was a symbol of hard work and stamina. In the nationalist period immediately after the 1952 revolution, which eventually severed the country's ties to the British and Ottoman empires, popular musicians wrote songs about the beauty of *asmarany* people. I recently came across one from the late Lebanese singer Sabah, in which she defended her love for an Egyptian *asmarany* man by insisting that his dark skin was actually the secret to his beauty. The song title translates to "So What If He's Brown-Skinned?"

But I didn't comprehend brown skin in that positive sense that night in 1974, or in the many years that followed. Popular music aside, Egypt was teeming with images that not so subtly equated lighter skin with social refinement and physical perfection—possibly, and with hindsight again, my first encounter with white privilege. It's still difficult to fathom how a country at the heart of the Middle East—one that led the way in pan-Arabism and post-colonialism—would be the custodian of a tradition in which the predominant skin colour was relegated to an inferior social position. To be white or very fair-skinned was to win the genetic lottery, and the few who claimed their tickets ensured that social traditions perpetuated this "understanding." Egyptian cinema, the Hollywood of the Arab world, featured a number of leading men and women whose lighter skin was the most desirable part of their physical package.

Egyptian TV commercials and print advertisements of the time sold a bourgeois, consumer-friendly lifestyle through lighter skin, which they promoted as aspirational for the millions of rich *and* poor locals. I don't recall seeing brown-skinned women or men—certainly no dark brown or Nubian-black models—in any of the advertising I grew up watching in the Middle East. Only *National Geographic*-style travel posters in hotels or airports sold an "authentic" Egyptian experience to Western tourists. With the exception of their white teeth, those smiling faces were enveloped in darkness, as if to fulfill tourist fantasies of an exotic journey into the tip of Africa. From my travels over the past few years, I can safely say that selling whiteness and selling out brownness is a long and still-thriving tradition in the Middle East, the Gulf and Southeast Asia. In Dubai, white, European-looking faces promote everything from multimillion-dollar condos to fast-fashion outlets like Zara and H&M. In the odd instance when advertisers deign to use Arab models, it looks like a generous dollop of white paint has been applied to their faces. Not even white people are *that* white.

Many of these images, I suppose, had entered my subconscious before that night watching *Oliver!* Yet somehow those close-ups of Lester's face served as the catalyst, triggering a lifelong awareness of my skin colour as my gateway to seeing the world and being seen by it. This played out in a variety of social and political contexts over decades and across many countries. Wherever I lived or travelled to, my skin awareness followed, a shadow of my shadow. I don't think I'll ever be able to separate myself from it, but I can unpack its meanings, or at least some of them, with a look back at my own and other people's journeys with brownness.

Around 1979, when I was in high school and trying (and failing dismally) to experiment with heterosexuality, a beautiful young Egyptian girl made it clear that we couldn't date—and I use that very North American term loosely and anachronistically—because her mother would find me too dark. My skin tones would pollute the gene pool of a bourgeois Egyptian family that took pride in its lighter skin, its biggest asset in the marriage and social markets.

As a teenager, I lived in fear of being given any item of clothing in red. My parents had taught me and my siblings to show gratitude by using gifts from family and friends as soon as possible. But a popular Egyptian saying at the time went something like this: "Get an *asmarany* to wear red and you'll make people laugh at him." In plainer words, he'll look like a monkey's behind.

The association strikes me as profoundly racist now, but what really sank in for me at the time was the idea that some colours were off limits for me—not because they didn't complement my skin tones but because they made me look like a beast.

My awareness of being brown would become entrenched a few years later, when I moved to the West. As a foreign student in the United Kingdom in the early 1990s, I was called "Paki" more than once. I often wanted to shout back that I wasn't actually Pakistani. It had never occurred to me that I would be lumped with South Asians on the racial-slur spectrum, because I had thought of myself as lighter-skinned than most of them. They were dark brown; I was light brown. Couldn't these racists tell the difference?

As a Canadian citizen in the aftermath of September 11, I learned to accept racial profiling as part of my everyday reality as a brown male—at least until I reached my late forties and started looking too haggard to be a troublemaker or a jihadist. Terrorism is a young man's business.

When I was a (younger) gay man visiting largely white bars and clubs in North America and Europe, I felt either desired or rejected because of my skin tone. (It depended on the evening and the crowd.) Even during a brief 2008 visit to Buenos Aires, the heart of what I thought was brown Latino country, I apparently went to the wrong bar, the one frequented by Argentines of European descent. I'd never felt more like a pariah in my entire life, and that included the time I went on a London-bound bus trip to visit the British Parliament with a group of Young Conservatives in 1991. Getting ignored in bars didn't rankle me that much in general, but this felt more like invisibility—a complete erasure of every part of me, not just my skin. An Argentine friend told me the next day that I should have gone to a more working-class bar where brown and black gay men, local and international, socialized. Being of a lower class made it acceptable to be of darker skin, too.

As a gay man who came of age in the 1980s, between the AIDS epidemic and the perfect-body cult with its white assumptions, I had already found it hard to avoid pondering how skin colour set people apart from (or invited them into) the inner circles of fabulousness. Whenever the models for crotch-enhancing underwear or phone sex in bar rags weren't white, they were black. *Very* black. Desire came in two colours only, and mine wasn't one of them. And although many white gay men of my generation fetishized darker-skinned males, projecting images of hyper-masculinity on, say, Latinos and Middle Easterners, the latter rarely crossed over from the "ethnic porn" aisle to the mainstream of gay sexuality.

Not all my personal experiences of being brown have carried negative undertones, however. In the winter, my white friends tell me they envy my complexion because it doesn't turn as pasty and washed-out as theirs does. (I never notice the difference and have always thought they were being too self-conscious about their own skin, the poor dears.) In parts of New York, I often take advantage of being perceived as *not black*. I've had no problem hailing cabs late at night in Manhattan or asking for directions from passersby. In the hierarchy of skin shades, being brown occupies the comfortable middle space, the buffer—we are not as privileged as whites but not as criminalized as blacks.

My own shade of brown is not fixed—it gets darker in the summer and lighter in the winter. Like many middle-class people who trace their origins to the Global South, I tend to avoid the sun wherever I go. (I used to wonder why white people went to such great lengths to get a tan. All those hours on the beach, and for what?) I'm over fifty now and have never once sunbathed in a park on a summer day, taken a beach holiday or set foot inside a tanning salon. It's a brown-people thing. And a class one, too. The darker you turn, the more you look like the working masses—or so I've been trained to think since childhood. More than forty years later, I can still hear my sister Hoda admonishing me for playing under Cairo's blazing sun: "You'll look like a *khadaam* [a servant]." Summer or winter, it didn't matter—the sun became a year-round enemy to the lightness of our skin. Whenever my brother Wahby, the darkest of the eleven children, misbehaved or showed his stubborn streak, my mother would chide him with the word *abd*, Arabic for "slave."

If you're brown, it's hard to deprogram yourself from thinking such seemingly superficial but nonetheless existential questions as: Am I too dark? If I get darker, will I lose my social position? If I avoid the sun forever, will I pass for white, or at least southern European? Brown people can turn their in-between skin into a back door to Europeanness and whiteness. They just need to stick to the very southern parts of the continent.

Over the years, I've heard similar stories from several Hispanic, Arab, South and East Asian, and North African friends. We live in our skin, our largest human organ—and possibly the biggest prison of them all.

I recall a Syrian student who refused to join a picnic with other doctoral candidates from the graduate club at Nottingham University (where I was doing my PhD in Victorian literature) because the sun was too bright that particular July weekend. It was the very reason the British students had planned the outing. Another friend of Indian descent invited me to a curry restaurant in her hometown of Leicester, where she proceeded to treat the dark-skinned waiter—Bangladeshi, if I remember correctly—abominably, dismissing my concerns on the grounds that "darkies" like him were used to this abusive behaviour from the community. It was the first time I'd heard the word "darkie." It never left my consciousness. It had a negativity that my then favourite word, "swarthy," didn't. Swarthy implied exoticism, even desire.

In 2004, when I told an Indian friend in Toronto that I'd booked my first-ever trip to Southeast Asia, she asked if I could bring her back some skin-whitening creams. (The Toronto summer sun turned her brown skin a shade too dark for her comfort.) Had I known such concoctions existed, I would have forked over all my allowances and begged for more to get hold of them in the post-*Oliver!* years. I spent three weeks travelling through the gorgeous landscapes of Singapore, Malaysia and Thailand on that trip, but I tracked the journey less by the change in scenery and local cultures and more by the gradual darkening of my skin. I didn't want to be a darkie.

Facing a mirror and examining not just my hair but my exact shade of brown turned into a lifelong preoccupation. You may think that I'm operating at the shallow end of life. But I know I'm not alone. Who hasn't obsessed about their body, hair, face, skin—whatever colour the latter may be? Didn't James Joyce write that "modern man has an epidermis rather than a soul"?[1]

It took time to see beyond the exterior. But over many years, I've identified with and felt strengthened by narratives that transcended appearance, including the civil rights, feminist, gay liberation and social justice movements. I experienced a political awakening from the outside in. And while this book is not a chronicle of that journey, it wouldn't have been written without the realization that my struggles to feel at ease in the skin I'm in reflect global issues and trends that go beyond the personal. Everywhere I looked, every story I heard, all but confirmed the prejudices and advantages that a skin tone can inflict or bestow on individuals, communities and nations. The concept of race as biologically determined may have been banished from all but the most extreme corners of politics, but the experiences of racialization, of being judged—literally, in the case of the US legal system—on the colour of one's skin, continue. And the closer I looked, the more I noticed the unique place that brown skin occupied in the global story of race relations and perceptions.

I believe there's a certain collective experience that unites people of brown skin—brown people—despite their geographic, ethnic, national and cultural differences. We are united (and divided) by the fact that we're not white. Or black. Millions of us may be living in East Asia, but we're not ethnic Chinese either. We are billions of people spread across the world and better known as Middle Easterners, Latin Americans, North Africans, and South and Southeast Asians.

To be brown in the world today is to recognize narratives and life experiences that unfold with striking similarities despite different settings and

---

1   *modern man ... a soul* See Joyce's essay "The Universal Literary Influence of the Renaissance" (1912).

contexts. These are not exclusive to brown people, but they take place with such frequency and in such concentration among us that we can claim some ownership of them. Uppermost among them—and a particular focus of this book [*Brown*]—are the experiences of the brown migrant and immigrant. Although each term refers to a specific group of people—migrants move out of desperation, while immigrants relocate in pursuit of better lives—the lines between the two continue to be blurred as war and ecological disasters ravage parts of the Global South.

We're on the move, uprooted, always elsewhere, a sizable portion of 244 million people living outside our countries of birth (a figure, the UN projects, that will reach 590 million by 2050). You'll find us at airports, border crossings and ports, aboard trains, ferries and cars, with our luggage and boxes held together by duct tape and sheer willpower. Our dreams and trepidations dominate this endless journey. Some of us may have our papers in order as we cross borders, but many of us hope to enter other countries, other worlds, using false claims (visiting family) or on humanitarian grounds (seeking refugee status at point of entry). Some of us are surgeons, university professors, investors, tech wizards and creative artists, but many, many more have found a calling in life by doing the work that affluent local people no longer wish to do. We're here to build high-rises, work in kitchens, clean homes, tend to the young and elderly, pick fruits and vegetables from fields (and stock them in supermarkets), and drive everyone home after a night of boozing.

The brown immigrants trigger conversations and political strategies from which their black, East Asian and white counterparts are spared—at least at this moment in time. Those of us who are Muslim live under constant suspicion for the religion we follow. As the 2015 federal elections in Canada proved, when a political party lags behind in the polls, nothing whips its base into a frenzy of racial discrimination faster than depicting Muslims as a stain on Canadian values.[1]

The association of brown people with transient labour is not limited to the white, developed world. As I will show in this book, the lives of some brown migrant workers reach certain intensity in places as far apart as the Caribbean and the Far East, and even *within* other brown nations. It's hard not to think of the brown South Asian worker without considering the thousands of construction workers from Nepal, Sri Lanka and Bangladesh whose blood and sweat have gone into virtually every building, high- or low-rise, in Dubai and Qatar. It's in Dubai, too, that middle-class immigrants from the Middle East

---

1   *2015 federal elections … values* The then-ruling Conservative party promised to establish a police hotline to allow citizens to report "barbaric cultural practices." This proposal was widely condemned as Islamophobic.

and the South Asian subcontinent have for decades kept the schools, banks, hospitals, hotels, food courts and malls running—without ever being afforded the benefits of citizenship.

We are lured to do the work in good times—until the economic bubble bursts. Then we turn into the job stealers, the welfare scammers and the undocumented. Two days before Christmas 2014, the Malaysian government mobilized its military aircraft to deport hundreds of undocumented Indonesian workers. Other illegal workers in Malaysia come from India, Bangladesh and Nepal, and at least one report estimates their numbers at six million. The boom in the Malaysian economy in the decades prior to the financial crisis of 2008 led to a vast improvement in lifestyle for locals. Millions joined the middle classes (by Malaysian standards), and then farmed out work on plantations and in restaurants and homes to other, less privileged brown people from the region. Many collected garbage or cleaned bathrooms in the upscale malls that earned Kuala Lumpur a spot on CNN's list of the top-five shopping destinations in Asia. In early 2015, Indonesian diplomats formally protested to the Malaysian government after a print ad for a vacuum cleaner featured the tagline "Fire Your Indonesian Maid Now."

Men made up the majority of the deported, but brown women are on the move, too. The brown migrant worker, whether in the West or the Gulf States or East Asia, is best symbolized by the millions of Filipina nannies, caregivers and domestic workers. Their tales of family separation, harsh living conditions, exploitation and physical abuse transcend borders. According to one labour organization, employers and recruiters who underpay or fail to pay domestics walk away with about $8 billion a year in illegal profits. As one domestic in Hong Kong told me, the jackpot was a permit to work for a white family in the United States or Canada. (In the informal poll of worst-possible destinations that I conducted with a group of domestic workers, also in Hong Kong, Saudi Arabia topped the list.)

But even in open, tolerant Canada, assumptions about skin colour and specific lines of work are made. I learned that while taking my dog for a walk a few days after moving into my condo building in midtown Toronto. A resident stopped me to ask if I had a business card. I couldn't understand why until it dawned on me that she thought I was a dog walker. Her mind couldn't conceive of the possibility that I was also a resident. She read my skin tone as my identity: worker, and low-paid at that. Many of my aging neighbours rely on a revolving cast of caregivers, helpers and cleaners—most of whom are brown. They hail from the Philippines, Central or South America, and occasionally Somalia or Ethiopia. I see and say hello to so many of them every morning, but I've never once learned their names and have often mixed up which caregiver works for which neighbour on my own floor.

I suspect I'm not alone. How many of us know the name of the Colombian or Nepalese cleaning lady we see only when we work late in the office? Brown people are everywhere and yet somehow remain invisible or nameless. But life and the global economy would come to a halt if the mass relocation of these workers—cleaners, domestic workers, security guards, maintenance staff, cooks, pedicurists, construction workers, farmhands and cashiers who ask for your loyalty card when you pay for toothpaste and toilet paper—were to stop. We keep the world running as we ourselves are run out from one spot to another. The words "work permit," "legal status" and "permanent visa" are music to our brown ears. The notes get discordant when we hear "minimum wage or below," "dormitory-style accommodation," "withholding passports" or "deportation." Our lives unfold as a constant battle to move from the second set of words to the first, to lend legitimacy and a home base to our journeys.

We know (or at least hope) that legitimacy brings with it political recognition and social acceptance. Others in the Western world have reached a similar conclusion.

—2016

Miriam Toews
b. 1964

"This town is so severe. And silent. It makes me crazy, the silence." So the teenaged Nomi Nickel describes her home town, the Mennonite community of East Village, in Miriam Toews's fourth novel, *A Complicated Kindness* (2004). That book, which was a best-seller and winner of the Governor General's Award, established Toews as a major figure on the Canadian literary landscape. Like most of her other work, it draws powerfully upon Toews's experience growing up in the town of Steinbach, Manitoba. In Toews's fiction the currents of comedy are often as powerful as those of sadness or despair—and both often spring from her religious upbringing. "We're Mennonites," Nomi tells the reader: "As far as I know, we are the most embarrassing sub-sect of people to belong to if you're a teenager."

Toews is known for her sure touch with wry comedy, but her life and her work have also been touched by tragedy. In 1998, Toews's father committed suicide after a lifelong battle with bipolar disorder. Toews paid tribute to him in an essay on the connections between his Mennonite beliefs and his struggles with depression; "A Father's Faith" (1999) was first published in a magazine, and later reprinted in an anthology of women's writing, *Dropped Threads* (2001). Her full-length memoir, *Swing Low: A Life* (2000), was told from the point of view of her father. Her 2008 novel, *The Flying Troutmans*, also centres on mental illness. It tells the story of narrator Hattie's road trip with her niece and nephew, whose mother (Hattie's sister) suffers from severe depression.

In 2007 Toews was asked to star in Mexican director Carlo Reygadas' *Silent Light* (2007), a film set in a Mennonite community in Northern Mexico. Toews drew on that experience for her 2011 novel, *Irma Voth*, which concerns two young women whose family has moved from the Canadian prairie to a Mennonite community in Mexico; the arrival of a film crew who plan to make a film about the community becomes the catalyst for change.

In describing what she writes about, Toews has sometimes emphasized simple contrasts. In a 2008 interview with *Quill & Quire*, for example, she summed things up in this way: "Life is funny and life is sad. Life is comic and life is tragic. It's a breeze and it's hell." In "A Father's Faith," though—as in the best of her fiction—the interest comes less from simple oppositions than from Toews's sure feel for complications and for subtleties.

A Father's Faith

On the morning of May 13, 1998, my father woke up, had breakfast, got dressed and walked away from the Steinbach Bethesda Hospital, where he had been a patient for two and a half weeks. He walked through his beloved hometown, along Hespeler Road, past the old farmhouse where his mother had lived with her second husband, past the water tower, greeting folks in his loud, friendly voice, wishing them well. He passed the site on First Street where the house in which my sister and I grew up once stood. He walked down Main Street, past the Mennonite church where, throughout his life, he had received countless certificates for perfect attendance, past Elmdale School where he had taught grade six for forty years.

As he walked by his home on Brandt Road, he saw his old neighbour Bill sitting in his lawn chair. He waved and smiled again, then he continued on past the cemetery where his parents were buried, and the high school his daughters had attended, and down Highway 52, out of town, past the Frantz Motor Inn, which is just outside the town limits because it serves alcohol and Steinbach is a dry town. He kept walking until he got too tired, so he hitched a ride with a couple of guys who were on their way to buy a fishing licence in the small village of Woodridge on the edge of the Sandilands Forest.

The sun would have been very warm by the time they dropped him off, and he would have taken off his stylish cap and wiped his brow with the back of his hand. I'm sure he thanked them profusely, perhaps offering them ten dollars for their trouble, and then he walked the short distance to the café near the railroad tracks, the place he and my mom would sometimes go for a quiet coffee and a change of scenery. He would have been able to smell the clover growing in the ditches beside the tracks and between the ties. He may have looked down the line and remembered that the train would be coming from Ontario, through Warroad, Minnesota, on its way to Winnipeg.

A beautiful young woman named Stephanie was just beginning her shift and she spoke to him through the screen door at the side of the restaurant. Yes, she said, the train will be here soon. And my dad smiled and thanked her, and mentioned that he could hear the whistle. Moments later, he was dead.

Steinbach is an easy forty-minute drive from Winnipeg, east on the Trans-Canada, then south on Highway 12. On the way into town there's a sign proclaiming "Jesus Saves." On the way back to the city just off Highway 12 there's another that says, "Satan is Real. You Can't Be Neutral. Choose Now." The town has recently become a city of 8,500 people, two-thirds of whom are Mennonite, so it's not surprising that about half of the twenty-four churches are Mennonite and conservative. There is a Catholic church too, but it's new and I'm not sure exactly where it is. A little way down from the bowling alley

I can still make out my name on the sidewalk, carved in big bold letters when I was ten and marking my territory.

My town made sense to me then. For me it was a giant playground where my friends and I roamed freely, using the entire town in a game of arrows—something like hide-and-seek—for which my dad, the teacher, provided boxes and boxes of fresh new chalk and invaluable tips. He had, after all, played the same game in the same town many years before.

At six p.m. the siren would go off at the firehall, reminding all the kids to go home for supper, and at nine p.m. it was set off again, reminding us to go home to bed. I had no worries, and no desire ever to leave this place where everyone knew me. If they couldn't remember my name, they knew I was the younger daughter of Mel and Elvira Toews, granddaughter of C.T. Loewen and Henry Toews, from the Kleine Gemeinde congregation, and so on and so on. All the kids in town, other than the church-sponsored Laotians who came over in the seventies, could be traced all the way back to the precise Russian veldt their great-grandparents had emigrated from. They were some of the thousands of Mennonites who came to Manitoba in the late 1800s to escape religious persecution. They were given free land and a promise that they could, essentially, do their own thing without interference. They wanted to keep the world away from their children and their children away from the world. Naturally it was an impossible ideal.

As I grew older, I became suspicious and critical and restless and angry. Every night I plotted my escape. I imagined that Barkman's giant feed mill on Main Street, partially visible from my bedroom window, was a tall ship that would take me away some day. I looked up places like Hollywood and Manhattan and Venice and Montreal in my Childcraft encyclopedias. I begged my sister to play, over and over, the sad songs from her Jacques Brel piano book, and I'd light candles and sing along, wearing a Pioneer Girls tam[1] on my head, using a chopstick as a cigarette holder, pretending I was Jackie Brel, Jacques's long-lost but just as world-weary Mennonite twin. I couldn't believe that I was stuck in a town like Steinbach, where dancing was a sin and serving beer a felony.

There were other things I became aware of as well. That my grandmother was a vanilla alcoholic who believed she was a teetotaller. That seventy-five-year-old women who had borne thirteen children weren't allowed to speak to the church congregation, but that fifteen-year-old boys were. That every family had a secret. And I learned that my dad had been depressed all his life.

1　*Jacques Brel* Belgian singer-songwriter (1929–78) who became famous performing his poetic ballads in Paris clubs; *tam* Scottish soft hat similar to a beret.

I had wondered, when I was a kid, why he spent so much of the weekend in bed and why he didn't talk much at home. Occasionally he'd tell me, sometimes in tears, that he loved me very much and that he wished he were a better father, that he were more involved in my life. But I never felt the need for an apology. It made me happy and a bit envious to know that my dad's students were able to witness his humour and intelligence firsthand, to hear him expound on his favourite subjects: Canadian history, Canadian politics and Canadian newspapers. I remember watching him at work and marvelling at his energy and enthusiasm. I thought he looked very handsome when he rolled up his sleeves and tucked his tie in between the buttons of his shirt, his hands on his hips, all ready for business and hard work.

Teaching school—helping others make sense of the world—was a good profession for a man who was continuously struggling to find meaning in life. I think he needed his students as much as they needed him. By fulfilling his duties, he was also shoring up a psyche at risk of erosion.

Four years before his death he was forced to retire from teaching because of a heart attack and some small strokes. He managed to finish the book he was writing on Canada's prime ministers, but then he seemed to fade away. He spent more and more of his time in bed, in the dark, not getting up even to eat or wash, not interested in watching TV or listening to the radio. Despite our pleading and cajoling, despite the medication and visits to various doctors' offices, appointments he dutifully kept, and despite my mother's unwavering love, we felt we were losing him.

I know about brain chemistry and depression, but there's still a part of me that blames my dad's death on being Mennonite and living in that freaky, austere place where this world isn't good enough and admission into the next one, the perfect one, means everything, where every word and deed gets you closer to or farther away from eternal life. If you don't believe that then nothing Steinbach stands for will make sense. And if life doesn't make sense you lose yourself in it, your spirit decays. That's what I believed had happened to my dad, and that's why I hated my town.

In the weeks and months after his death, my mom and my sister and I tried to piece things together. William Ashdown, the executive director of the Mood Disorders Association of Manitoba, told us the number of mentally ill Mennonites is abnormally high. "We don't know if it's genetic or cultural," he said, "but the Steinbach area is one that we're vitally concerned about."

"It's the way the church delivers the message," says a Mennonite friend of mine, "the message of sin and accountability. To be human, basically, is to be a sinner. So a person, a real believer, starts to get down on himself, and where does it end? They say self-loathing is the cornerstone of depression, right?"

Years ago, the Mennonite Church practised something called "shunning," whereby if you were to leave your husband, or marry outside the Church, or elope, or drink, or in some way contravene the Church's laws or act "out of faith," you could be expelled from the Church and ignored, shunned by the entire community, including your own family. Depression or despair, as it would have been referred to then, was considered to be the result of a lack of faith and therefore could be another reason for shunning.

These days most Mennonites don't officially practise shunning, although William Ashdown claims there are still Mennonites from extreme conservative sects who are being shunned and shamed into silence within their communities for being mentally ill. Certainly Arden Thiessen, the minister of my dad's church, and a long-time friend of his, is aware of the causes of depression and the pain experienced by those who suffer from it. He doesn't see it as a lack of faith, but as an awful sickness.

But I can't help thinking that that history had just a little to do with my alcoholic grandmother's insisting that she was a non-drinker, and my dad's telling his doctors, smiling that beautiful smile of his, that he was fine, just fine.

Not long before he died my dad told me about the time he was five and was having his tonsils out. Just before the operation began he was knocked out with ether and he had a dream that he was somersaulting through the hospital walls, right through, easily, he said, moving his hands in circles through the air. It was wonderful. He told me he would never forget that feeling.

But mostly, the world was a sad and unsafe place for him, and his town provided shelter from it. Maybe he saw this as a gift, while I came to see it as oppression. He could peel back the layers of hypocrisy and intolerance and see what was good, and I couldn't. He believed that it mattered what he did in life, and he believed in the next world, one that's better. He kept the faith of his Mennonite forebears to the very end, or what he might call the beginning, and removed himself from this world entirely.

Stephanie, the waitress in the café in Woodridge, told my mother that my dad was calm and polite when he spoke to her, as if he were about to sit down to a cup of tea. She told her that he hadn't seemed at all afraid. But why would you be if you believed you were going to a place where there is no more sadness?

My dad never talked to us about God or religion. We didn't have family devotion like everybody else. He never quoted out loud from the Bible or lectured us about not going to church. In fact his only two pieces of advice to me were "Be yourself" and "You can do anything."

But he still went to church. It didn't matter how low he felt, or how cold it was outside. He would put on his suit and tie and stylish cap and walk the seven or eight blocks to church. He always walked, through searing heat or sub-arctic chill. If he was away on holidays he would find a church and go to it. At the lake he drove forty miles down gravel roads to attend an outdoor church in the bush. I think he needed church like a junkie needs a fix: to get him through another day in a world of pain.

What I love about my town is that it gave my dad the faith that stopped him from being afraid in those last violent seconds he spent on earth. And the place in my mind where we meet is on the front steps of my dad's church, the big one on Main Street across from Don's Bakery and the Goodwill store. We smile and talk for a few minutes outside, basking in the warmth of the summer sun he loved so much. Then he goes in and I stay outside, and we're both happy where we are.

—1999

Ivan Coyote
b. 1969

Ivan Coyote is a storyteller, performer, filmmaker, and author of more than ten books of fiction, non-fiction, and poetry. They[1] are a popular public speaker and an occasional commentator on transgender issues, including a widely viewed TED Talk on the need for gender-neutral bathrooms. Constantly on the road as a storyteller, entertainer, and public speaker, Coyote does not separate performance from writing, finding that the two are closely related: "Live performance has become the backbone of my editing process."

Coyote, whose gender is non-binary, is a self-proclaimed "gender failure," a phrase also used as the title of a collaborative show and book they created with the singer and writer Rae Spoon. Coyote's work has been praised for its portrayal of trans experience, as well as its "quietly radical" refusal "to centre trans-ness as the single primary concern in trans lives." They have also expressed frustration at the treatment of their work as a form of education or activism: "What would I be free to write and talk about if I wasn't always expected to change the world? What if I was just allowed to live and create in it?"

Coyote's writing, which includes memoir as well as fiction, is often inspired by their working-class upbringing in Whitehorse and, in their teenage years, Vancouver Island. Their Irish Catholic extended family also influenced the style of what Coyote calls their "kitchen table stories," intimate and funny narratives with roots in oral storytelling. The resulting work combines a down-to-earth tone with artistic sophistication: as one reviewer commented, "Coyote is poetic in their phrasing and plain spoken with their truths." Coyote's novel *Bow Grip* won the 2007 ReLit Award, and their short story collection *Close to Spider Man* was a finalist for the Danuta Gleed Award for Short Fiction.

Tomboys Still

Linda Gould was a friend of my mom's. Linda was from somewhere not here, somewhere not the Yukon, she had family down south and she had raven black hair. One time I asked my mom why Linda's name was Linda Gould but her husband was still called Don Dixon. My mom told me that some women chose not to take their husband's last name when they got married. It was 1974 and this impressed me for reasons I did not fully comprehend just yet.

Linda and Don lived in a rented house next to the clay cliffs downtown, and had one wall in their living room covered in that mural type of wallpaper,

---

1   Coyote's pronouns are they/them.

depicting a picture of a forest of giant pine trees. Linda wouldn't let Don paint over that wallpaper or tear it down; she said it reminded her of California.

I was a Yukon kid and had never seen a real tree that big in my life, I could only imagine them.

Linda played hockey, and she also coached a girl's ringette team. As soon as I turned five years old I was allowed to join up. I had never really heard of the game called ringette but wanted to be good at it because Linda was good at it. It turned out ringette was kind of like hockey light, but only girls played it. It wasn't as much fun as hockey looked like it was, but I kept going to practices because my mom had spent all that money on skates and a helmet for me. There were barely enough girls to make one team so we never got to play a real game, we mostly skated around and practiced stopping. That's the truth, and also a metaphor. Some of the girls came in figure skates, but not me.

One day Don Dixon showed up early at practice and watched us run a passing drill for a while. He told Linda after practice that I was already a better skater than half the boys on the Squirts team he coached and so did I want to come and play with the boys? he asked.

I didn't even have to think before I said yes. My mom said hold on, she had to talk it over with my dad, who was only half listening because he was reading that book *Shogun*[1] and it was a super good book he said, and my mom said yes, I guess, you can play hockey, but be careful out there. Linda taught me how to do a slap shot and told me never to skate with my head down. I was the only girl playing in the Whitehorse Minor Hockey League for eleven years after that. I made it all the way up to junior hockey. Left wing.

When I turned sixteen they wouldn't let me play hockey with the boys anymore. I was now a legal liability, they told my parents, and the minor hockey league just couldn't afford that kind of insurance, and besides, what if I got hurt, the boys were so much bigger now, plus body-checking. Come and play on the women's team with us, Linda said, and so I did.

That was how I met Donna Doucette, who played defence and worked as a bartender at the Kopper King on the Alaska Highway. Donna Doucette wore her long brown hair in a whip-like braid that swung between her shoulder blades when she skated back hard for the puck. I think I pretty much fell in love with Donna Doucette the first time I saw her spit perfectly through the square holes in the face mask on her helmet. She just curled her tongue into a tube and horked unapologetically right through her mask. It shot like a bullet, about fifteen feet, straight out onto the ice. I had never seen a woman do anything like that before, I could only imagine the back-of-the-head slap

---

1   *Shogun* 1975 novel by James Clavell.

my gran would lay on me if I ever dared to spit anywhere in public, much less turn it into an art form like Donna Doucette did.

I remember hearing her playing fastball one midnight sunny summer evening; I was playing softball on the field next to the women's league. All the women on my hockey team played ball together in the summer; like serious fast pitch, they were not fooling around. Hockey was for sport but fast pitch was for keeps. Donna Doucette played shortstop and would spare no skin to make a catch, and she spat all over the goddamn place out there on the field too, and cussed and catcalled. Hey batter batta batta swing batta batta. I remember her in silhouette, bobbing back and forth on the toes of her cleats, all backlit by the sun and gum a-chew, a mouthy shadow, punching the pocket of her gloved hand with her red-nailed fingertips coiled into a fist.

That's the thing about Linda and Donna. They weren't like me. Linda wore sapphire studs in her ears and a red red dress to our Christmas party. Donna swore and stole third base wearing what my mother claimed to be too much eye makeup for daylight hours, which even back then I thought was kind of harsh, it being summer in the Yukon and it never really getting dark and all.

Donna and Linda. My memories of them are sharp, hyper-focused. I was paying attention to every detail of them, I was searching them for clues to who I wanted to be, but I already knew I couldn't be like them. I wanted something else. Something close to what they had. They hinted at a kind of freedom, a kind of just not giving a fuck what anyone said about them that made me want things I didn't know the words for.

Theresa Turner drove her two-stroke dirt bike to school every day we were in grade eleven, appearing out of the willows and trailing a tail of dust as she gunned the throttle and skidded to a stop by the tree line at the edge of our high school parking lot. She would dismount and stomp her kickstand down with the heel of her buckled biker boot and shake her mane of mahogany ringlets loose from under her helmet and strut in her skin-tight Levi 501s past the heads smoking cigarettes by the back double doors to the wood shop. Fuck you looking at? she would sneer at them. This for some reason made them blush, and pretend they weren't watching her ass swing as the door hissed shut behind her. I was old enough by then to be full-on smitten.

Carolyn O'Hara was Theresa Turner's very best friend from Cedar. Cedar was a suburb of the pulp mill town of Nanaimo where I was living with my grandmother. Theresa Turner and Carolyn O'Hara had grown up out there together and had known each other all their lives. They also knew all about all the boys from the rural working class outskirts of Nanaimo. Knew all the boys who had to skip school in the fall to bring in the hay and miss entire weeks in the spring when the lambs came.

They knew all about the boys with the jean jacket vests with ZZ Top or Judas Priest[1] album covers recreated in ballpoint ink. Houses of the Holy.[2] The boys whose older brothers were doing time.

Carolyn O'Hara had a necklace strung of these diamonds in the rough, these boys who would punch locker doors and prick the skin in between their forefinger and thumb and rub ink into it in the shape of a broken heart all for the love of Carolyn O'Hara. She had her brother who died in a motorcycle accident's acoustic guitar and she would play "Walk on the Wild Side" by Lou Reed at lunch. I remember her swinging her honey-brown hair in the sun in the front seat of Eddie Bartolo's midnight blue Nova with the windows rolled down and saying, "So what if I am on the rag, you asshole. I'd like to see you go to gym class and do your fucking flexed arm hang exercises if you'd been bleeding out of your ass like it's going out of goddamn style for the last three fucking days. You going to smoke that thing or pass it on, you selfish bastard?"

Carolyn O'Hara could out-swear even Theresa Turner, it's why they were the perfect pair. Carolyn O'Hara was gorgeous. Could have been a model, everybody said so, but she was very practical and took the dental hygienist's program up at the college right after we graduated.

I ran into Theresa one day about five years ago, on my way to Vancouver Island for a gig. Theresa was wearing false eyelashes and an orange reflective vest at the same time, which I thought was awesome. Hugged me hard and told me she had been working for BC Ferries for seventeen years now, doing what my gran had always said was a good, clean, union job if you liked people. Said Carolyn O'Hara had opened her own dog grooming business. A real cool place where you can drop your dog off to get groomed, or rent a big tub and wash your own dog in the back. She said they were both happy, they still kept in real good touch, in fact they were going for mani-pedis for their fortieth birthdays just next week.

Mia Telerico. Fall of 1992, she had just moved to town from Toronto. I met her in my friend's coffee shop on the Drive, she smoked Du Maurier Light King Size and I smoked Player's Light regulars. I, for reasons unexamined by me at the time, I guess I was trying to impress her, so I spontaneously leapt up and did a dramatic reading for her of *The Cat in the Hat,* and we briefly became lovers, and then, so far, life-long friends. Mia Telerico said in my kitchen one night that first winter It's E-Talian, not Eye-Talian, you sound like a redneck if you say it wrong, and then she showed me how to peel a bunch of garlic all at once by crushing it with the side of the butcher knife.

---

1   *ZZ Top ... Judas Priest* Bands that became popular in the early 1970s.
2   *Houses of the Holy* 1973 album by Led Zeppelin.

How many ways do I love Mia Telerico? I love that she refinishes furniture and owns all her own power tools and that it takes hours for her curls to dry so she has special hair-washing days, because washing her hair is like, a thing, right, and she is missing part of a finger from an accident she had cleaning the chain on her motorcycle and she is tough as nails but with the softest heart and bosom, can I even use the word "bosom" anymore? I don't know. Her hugs feel better than nearly anything is all I'm saying, and when she lets me rest my head there for a second I feel so untouchable, so unhurtable somehow, so magically protected by her soft cheek and rough hands ever capable. I called her just now and left a message asking her if it was okay if I called her a femme tomboy, how does she feel about me pinning those words on her femme tomboy, but really, all I'm trying to do here is broaden the joining, I tell her voice mail. All I want to do is honour all the femme tomboys I have ever loved, and thank them for showing me the possibilities. Anyway. Mia's father was from Malta and her mother is Italian and her dad was a janitor and her ma worked in a chocolate factory just like I Love Lucy and Ethel[1] except less funny and for decades until it wrecked her back.

I left Mia Telerico a message but I haven't heard back yet. I hear through the grapevine that she is going through a breakup and, well, I guess I am too, and both of us, we take these things pretty hard, artist's hearts pumping just beneath the skin of our chests like they do.

—2016

---

1   *I Love Lucy and Ethel* Reference to a popular episode of the *I Love Lucy* sitcom (1951–57), in which Lucy and Ethel struggle to keep up with the assembly line in a chocolate factory.

Glossary

Absurdist: characterized by a minimalist style and bleak worldview. The term is most frequently used with reference to certain plays of the post-World-War-II period (notable examples include Samuel Beckett's *Waiting for Godot* and Tom Stoppard's *Rosencrantz and Guildenstern Are Dead*). Such works seem set in a world stripped of faith in god or a rational cosmos, in which idealism has been lost, and human action and communication are futile. Absurdist characters are often portrayed as trapped in a pointless round of trivial, self-defeating acts of comical repetitiveness. For this reason, absurdism can verge on *farce* or *black comedy*. See also *existentialism*.

Accent: in poetry the natural emphasis (stress) speakers place on a syllable.

Accentual Verse: poetry in which a line is measured only by the number of accents or stresses, not by the number of syllables.

Accentual-Syllabic Verse: poetry in which a line is measured by the number of syllables and by the pattern of accented (stressed) and unaccented (unstressed) syllables. This is the most common metrical system in traditional English verse.

Act [of a play]: the sections into which a play or other theatrical work have been divided, either by the playwright or a later editor. Dividing plays into five acts became popular during the Renaissance in imitation of Roman tragedy; modern works are sometimes divided into three.

Aesthetes: members of a late nineteenth-century movement that valued "art for art's sake"—for its purely aesthetic qualities, as opposed to valuing art for the moral content it may convey, for the intellectual stimulation it may provide, or for a range of other qualities.

Allegory: a narrative with both a literal meaning and secondary, often symbolic meaning or meanings. Allegory frequently employs personification to give concrete embodiment to abstract concepts or entities, such as feelings or personal qualities. It may also present one set of characters or events in the guise of another, using implied parallels for the purposes of satire or political comment.

Alliteration: the grouping of words with the same initial consonant (e.g., "break, blow, burn, and make me new"). See also *assonance* and *consonance*.

Alliterative Verse: poetry that employs alliteration of stressed syllables in each line as its chief structural principle.

Allusion: a reference, often indirect or unidentified, to a person, thing, or event. A reference in one literary work to another literary work, whether to its content or its form, also constitutes an allusion.

Ambiguity: an "opening" of language created by the writer to allow for multiple meanings or differing interpretations. In literature, ambiguity may be deliberately employed by the writer to enrich meaning; this differs from any unintentional, unwanted ambiguity in non-literary prose.

Anachronism: accidentally or intentionally attributing people, things, ideas, and events to historical periods in which they do not and could not possibly belong.

Analepsis: see *flashback*.

Analogy: a broad term that refers to our processes of noting similarities among things or events. Specific forms of analogy in poetry include *simile* and *metaphor*.

Anapaest: a metrical foot containing two unstressed syllables followed by one stressed syllable: xx / (e.g., underneath, intervene).

Antistrophe: from Greek drama, the chorus's countermovement or reply to an initial movement (*strophe*). See *ode*.

Apostrophe: a figure of speech (a *trope*; see *figures of speech*) in which a writer directly addresses an object—or a dead or absent person—as if the imagined audience were actually listening.

Apron: the part of a stage that extends into the auditorium or audience beyond the *proscenium* arch; sometimes called a *forestage* or a *thrust stage*.

Archetype: in literature and mythology, a recurring idea, symbol, motif, character, or place. To some scholars and psychologists, an archetype represents universal human thought-patterns or experiences.

Arena Theatre: see *theatre-in-the-round*.

Asides: words delivered by actors to the audience, or by characters to themselves, which by *convention* are treated as if they were inaudible to the other characters on stage.

Assonance: the repetition of identical or similar vowel sounds in stressed syllables in which the surrounding consonants are different: for example, "shame" and "fate"; "gale" and "cage"; or the long "i" sounds in "Beside the pumice isle...."

Atmosphere: see *tone*.

Aubade: a lyric poem that greets or laments the arrival of dawn.

Ballad: a folk song, or a poem originally recited to an audience, which tells a dramatic story based on legend or history.

Ballad Stanza: a quatrain with alternating four-stress and three-stress lines, rhyming *abcb*. A variant is "common measure," in which the alternating lines are strictly iambic, and rhyme *abab*.

Baroque: powerful and heavily ornamented in style. "Baroque" is a term from the history of visual art and of music that is sometimes also used to describe certain literary styles.

Bathos: an anticlimactic effect brought about by a writer's descent from an elevated subject or tone to the ordinary or trivial.

Black Comedy: humour based on death, horror, or any incongruously macabre subject matter.

Blank Verse: unrhymed lines written in iambic pentameter. (A form introduced to English verse by Henry Howard, Earl of Surrey, in his translation of parts of Virgil's *Aeneid* in 1547.)

Bombast: inappropriately inflated or grandiose language.

Broken Rhyme: a kind of rhyme in which a multi-syllable word is split at the end of a line and continued onto the next, to allow an end-rhyme with the split syllable.

Burlesque: satire of an exaggerated sort, particularly that which ridicules its subject by emphasizing its vulgar or ridiculous aspects.

Caesura: a pause or break in a line of verse occurring where a phrase, clause, or sentence ends, and indicated in scansion by the mark ||. If it occurs in the middle of the line, it is known as a "medial" caesura.

Canon: in literature, those works that are commonly accepted as possessing authority or importance. In practice, "canonical" texts or authors are those that are discussed most frequently by scholars and taught most frequently in university courses.

Canto: a sub-section of a long (usually epic) poem.

Canzone: a short song or poem, with stanzas of equal length and an *envoy*.

Caricature: an exaggerated and simplified depiction of character; the reduction of a personality to one or two telling traits at the expense of all other nuances and contradictions.

Carpe Diem: Latin (from Horace) meaning "seize the day." The idea of enjoying the moment is a common one in Renaissance love poetry. See, for example, Marvell's "To His Coy Mistress."

Catalexis: the omission of unstressed syllables from a line of verse (such a line is referred to as "catalectic"). In iambic verse it is usually the first syllable of the line that is omitted; in trochaic, the last. For example, in the first stanza of Housman's "To an Athlete Dying Young" the third line is catalectic: i.e., it has dropped the first, unstressed syllable called for by the poem's iambic tetrameter form: "The time you won your town the race / We chaired you through the market-place; / Man and boy stood cheering by, / And home we brought you shoulder-high."

Catharsis: the arousal through the performance of a dramatic tragedy of "emotions of pity and fear" to a point where "purgation" or "purification" occurs and the feelings are released or transformed. The concept was developed by Aristotle in his *Poetics* from an ancient Greek medical concept, and adapted by him into an aesthetic principle.

Characterization: the means by which an author develops and presents a character's personality qualities and distinguishing traits. A character may be established in the story by descriptive commentary or may be developed less directly—for example, through his or her words, actions, thoughts, and interactions with other characters.

Chiasmus: a figure of speech (a scheme) that reverses word order in successive parallel clauses. If the word order is A-B-C in the first clause, it becomes C-B-A in the second: for example, Donne's line "She is all states, and all princes, I" ("The Sun Rising") incorporates this reversal.

Chorus: originally, the choir of singing, dancing, masked young men who performed in ancient Greek tragedy and comedy. It gradually disappeared from tragedy and comedy, but many attempts have been made to revive some version of it, notably during the Italian and English Renaissance, under Weimar Classicism, and by such twentieth-century playwrights as Jean Anouilh, T.S. Eliot, and Michel Tremblay.

Chronology: the way a story is organized in terms of time. Linear narratives run continuously from one point in time to a later point, while non-linear narratives are non-continuous and may jump forward and backward in time. A *flashback*, in which a story jumps to a scene previous in time, is an example of non-linearity.

Classical: originating in or relating to ancient Greek or Roman culture. As commonly conceived, *classical* implies a strong sense of formal order. The term *neoclassical* is often used with reference to literature of the Restoration and eighteenth century that was strongly influenced by ancient Greek and Roman models.

Closet Drama: a play (typically in verse) written to be read rather than performed. The term came into use in the first half of the nineteenth century.

Closure: the sense of completion evoked at the end of a story when all or most aspects of the major conflicts have been resolved. An example of the resolution of an internal conflict in Charlotte Perkins Gilman's "The Yellow Wallpaper" is the narrator's "merging" with the woman behind the paper. Not every story has a strong sense of closure.

Coloured Narrative: alternative term for *free indirect discourse*.

Comedy: as a literary term, used originally to denote that class of ancient Greek drama in which the action ends happily. More broadly the term has been used to describe a wide variety of literary forms of a more or less light-hearted character.

Comedy of Manners: a type of comic play that flourished in the late seventeenth century in London, and elsewhere since, which bases its humour on the sexual and marital intrigues of "high society." It is sometimes contrasted with "comedy of character" as its *satire* is directed at the social habits and conventional hypocrisy of the whole leisured class. Also called Restoration comedy; exemplified by the plays of Aphra Behn, William Wycherley, and William Congreve.

Commedia dell'arte: largely improvised comic performances conducted by masked performers and involving considerable physical activity. The genre of *commedia dell'arte* originated in Italy in the sixteenth century; it was influential throughout Europe for more than two centuries thereafter.

Conceit: an unusually elaborate metaphor or simile that extends beyond its original tenor and vehicle, sometimes becoming a "master" analogy for the entire poem (see, for example, Donne's "The Flea"). Ingenious or fanciful images and comparisons were especially popular with the *metaphysical poets* of the seventeenth century, giving rise to the term "metaphysical conceit."

Concrete Poetry: an experimental form, most popular during the 1950s and 1960s, in which the printed type itself forms a visual image of the poem's key words or ideas. See also *pattern poetry*.

Conflict: struggles between characters and opposing forces. Conflict can be internal (psychological) or external (conflict with another character, for instance, or with society or nature).

Connotation: the implied, often unspoken meaning(s) of a given word, as distinct from its *denotation*, or literal meaning. Connotations may have highly emotional undertones and are usually culturally specific.

Consonance: the pairing of words with similar initial and ending consonants, but with different vowel sounds (live/love, wander/wonder). See also *alliteration*.

Convention: aesthetic approach, technique, or practice accepted as characteristic and appropriate for a particular form. It is a convention of certain sorts of plays, for example, that the characters speak in blank verse, of other sorts of plays that characters speak in rhymed couplets, and of still other sorts of dramatic performances that characters frequently break into song to express their feelings.

Couplet: a pair of rhyming lines, usually in the same metre. If they form a complete unit of thought and are grammatically complete, the lines are known as a closed couplet. See also *heroic couplet*.

Dactyl: a metrical foot containing one strong stress followed by two weak stresses: / xx (e.g., muttering, helplessly). A minor form known as "double dactyls" makes use of this metre for humorous purposes, e.g., "Jiggery pokery" or "Higgledy Piggledy."

Denotation: see *connotation*.

Dénouement: that portion of a narrative that follows a dramatic climax, in which conflicts are resolved and the narrative is brought to a close. Traditional accounts of narrative structure often posit a triangle or arc, with rising action followed by a climax and then by a dénouement. (Such accounts bear little relation, however, to the ways in which most actual narratives are structured—particularly most twentieth- and twenty-first-century literary fictions.)

Dialogue: words spoken by characters to one another. (When a character is addressing him or her self or the audience directly, the words spoken are referred to as a *soliloquy*.)

Diction: word choice. Whether the diction of a literary work (or of a literary character) is colloquial, conversational, formal, or of some other type contributes significantly to the tone of the text as well as to characterization.

Didacticism: aesthetic approach emphasizing moral instruction.

Dimeter: a poetic line containing two metrical feet.

Dirge: a song or poem that mourns someone's death. See also *elegy* and *lament*.

Dissonance: harsh, unmusical sounds or rhythms that writers may use deliberately to achieve certain effects. Also known as cacophony.

Dramatic Irony: this form of *irony* occurs when an audience has access to information not available to the character.

Dramatic Monologue: a lyric poem that takes the form of an utterance by a single person addressing a silent listener. The speaker may be an historical personage (as in some of Robert Browning's dramatic monologues), or a figure drawn from myth or legend (as in some of Tennyson's).

Dub Poetry: a form of protest poetry originating in Jamaica, with its roots in dance rhythms, especially reggae, and often accompanied in performance by drums and music. See also *rap*.

Duple Foot: a duple foot of poetry has two syllables. The possible duple forms are *iamb* (in which the stress is on the second of the two syllables), *trochee* (in which the stress is on the first of the two syllables), *spondee* (in which both are stressed equally), and *pyrrhic* (in which both syllables are unstressed).

Eclogue: now generally used simply as an alternative name for a pastoral poem. In classical times and in the early modern period, however, an *eclogue* (or *idyll*) was a specific type of pastoral poem—a dialogue or dramatic monologue involving rustic characters. (The other main sub-genre of the pastoral was the *georgic*.)

Elegiac Stanza: a quatrain of iambic pentameters rhyming *abab*, often used in poems meditating on death or sorrow. The best-known example is Thomas Gray's "Elegy Written in a Country Churchyard."

Elegy: a poem which formally mourns the death of a particular person (e.g., Tennyson's "In Memoriam") or in which the poet meditates on other serious subjects (e.g., Gray's "Elegy"). See also *dirge*.

Elision: omitting or suppressing a letter or an unstressed syllable at the beginning or end of a word, so that a line of verse may conform to a given metrical scheme. For example, the three syllables at the beginning of Shakespeare's sonnet 129 are reduced to two by the omission of the first vowel: "Th' expense of spirit in a waste of shame." See also *syncope*.

Ellipsis: the omission of a word or words necessary for the complete grammatical construction of a sentence, but not necessary for our understanding of the sentence.

Embedded Narrative: a story contained within another story.

End-Rhyme: see *rhyme*.

End-Stopped: a line of poetry is said to be end-stopped when the end of the line coincides with a natural pause in the syntax, such as the conclusion of a sentence; e.g., in this couplet from Pope's "Essay on Criticism," both lines are end-stopped: "A little learning is a dangerous thing; / Drink deep, or taste not the Pierian spring." Compare this with *enjambment*.

Enjambment: the "running-on" of the sense from one line of poetry to the next, with no pause created by punctuation or syntax.

Envoy (Envoi): a stanza or half-stanza that forms the conclusion of certain French poetic forms, such as the *sestina* or the *ballade*. It often sums up or comments upon what has gone before.

Epic: a lengthy narrative poem, often divided into books and sub-divided into cantos. It generally celebrates heroic deeds or events, and the style tends to be lofty and grand. Examples in English include Spenser's *The Faerie Queene* and Milton's *Paradise Lost*.

Epic Simile: an elaborate simile, developed at such length that the vehicle of the comparison momentarily displaces the primary subject with which it is being compared.

Epigram: a very short poem, sometimes in closed couplet form, characterized by pointed wit.

Epigraph: a quotation placed at the beginning of a work to indicate or foreshadow the theme.

Epiphany: a moment at which matters of significance are suddenly illuminated for a literary character (or for the reader), typically triggered by something small and seemingly of little import. The term first came into wide currency in connection with the fiction of James Joyce.

Episodic Plot: plot comprising a variety of episodes that are only loosely connected by threads of story material (as opposed to plots that present one or more continually unfolding narratives, in which successive episodes build one on another).

Epithalamion: a poem celebrating a wedding. The best-known example in English is Edmund Spenser's "Epithalamion" (1595).

Epode: the third part of an *ode*, following the *strophe* and *antistrophe*.

Ethos: the perceived character, trustworthiness, or credibility of a writer or narrator.

Eulogy: text expressing praise, especially for a distinguished person recently deceased.

Euphemism: mode of expression through which aspects of reality considered to be vulgar, crudely physical, or unpleasant are referred to indirectly rather than named explicitly. A variety of euphemisms exist for the processes of urination and defecation; *passed away* is often used as a euphemism for *died*.

Euphony: pleasant, musical sounds or rhythms—the opposite of *dissonance*.

Existentialism: a philosophical approach according to which the meaning of human life is derived from the actual experience of the living individual. The existential worldview, in which life is assumed to have no essential or pre-existing meanings other than those we personally choose to endow it with, can produce an *absurdist* sensibility.

Exposition: the setting out of material in an ordered (and usually concise) form, either in speech or in writing. In a play those parts of the action that do not occur on stage but are rather recounted by the characters are frequently described as being presented in exposition. Similarly, when the background narrative is filled in near the beginning of a novel, such material is often described as having been presented in exposition.

Eye-Rhyme: see *rhyme*.

Fable: a short *allegorical* tale that conveys an explicit moral lesson. The characters are often animals or objects with human speech and mannerisms. See *parable*.

Fantasy: in fiction, a sub-genre characterized by the presence of magical or miraculous elements—usually acknowledged as such by the characters and the narrative voice. In *magic realism*, by contrast, miraculous occurrences tend to be treated by the characters and/or the narrative voice as if they were entirely ordinary. In fantasy (also in contrast to magic realism), the fictional world generally has an internal consistency to it that precludes any sense of absurdity on the part of the reader; and the plot tends to build a strong sense of expectation in the reader.

Farce: sometimes classed as the "lowest" form of *comedy*. Its humour depends not on verbal wit, but on physicality and sight gags.

Feminine Rhyme: see *rhyme*.

Fiction: imagined or invented narrative. In literature, the term is usually used to refer to prose narratives (such as novels and short stories).

Figures of Speech: deliberate, highly concentrated uses of language to achieve particular purposes or effects on an audience. There are two kinds of figures: schemes and *tropes*. Schemes involve changes in word-sound and word-order, such as *alliteration* and *chiasmus*. Tropes play on our understandings of words to extend, alter, or transform meaning, as in *metaphor* and *personification*.

First-Person Narrative: narrative recounted using *I* and *me*. See also *narrative perspective*.

Fixed Forms: the term applied to a number of poetic forms and stanzaic patterns, many derived from French models, such as *ballade, rondeau, sestina, triolet,* and *villanelle*. Other "fixed forms" include the *sonnet, rhyme royal, haiku,* and *ottava rima*.

Flashback: in fiction, the inclusion in the primary thread of a story's narrative of a scene (or scenes) from an earlier point in time. Flashbacks may be used to revisit from a different viewpoint events that have already been recounted in the main thread of narrative; to present material that has been left out in the initial recounting; or to present relevant material from a time before the beginning of the main thread of narrative. The use of flashbacks in fiction is sometimes referred to as *analepsis*.

Flashforward: the inclusion in the primary thread of a story's narrative of a scene (or scenes) from a later point in time. See also *prolepsis*.

Flat Character: the opposite of a *round character*, a flat character is defined by a small number of traits and does not possess enough complexity to be psychologically realistic. "Flat character" can be a disparaging term, but need not be; flat characters serve different purposes in a fiction than round characters, and are often better suited to some types of literature, such as allegory or farcical comedy.

Foil: in literature, a character whose behaviour and/or qualities set in relief for the reader or audience those of a strongly contrasting character who plays a more central part in the story.

Foot: a unit of a line of verse that contains a particular combination of stressed and unstressed syllables. Dividing a line into metrical feet (*iambs, trochees,* etc.), then counting the number of feet per line, is part of *scansion*. See also *metre*.

Foreshadowing: the inclusion of elements in a story that hint at some later development(s) in the same story. For example, in Flannery O'Connor's "A Good Man Is Hard to Find," the old family burying ground that the family sees on their drive foreshadows the violence that follows.

Found Space: a site that is not normally a theatre but is used for the staging of a theatrical production. Often, the choice of found space can reflect the play's setting or thematic content.

Free Indirect Discourse: a style of third-person narration that takes on characteristics of first-person narration, thus making it difficult to discern whether the reader is receiving the impressions of the character, the narrator, or some combination of the two.

Free Verse: poetry that does not follow any regular metre, line length, or rhyming scheme. In many respects, though, free verse follows the complex natural "rules" and rhythmic patterns (or cadences) of speech.

Freytag's Pyramid: a model of plot structure developed by the German novelist, playwright, and critic Gustav Freytag and introduced in his book *Die Technik des Dramas* (1863). In the pyramid, five stages of plot are identified as occurring in the following order: exposition, rising action, climax, falling action, and *dénouement*. Freytag intended his pyramid to diagram the structure of classical five-act plays, but it is also used as a tool to analyze other forms of fiction (even though many individual plays and stories do not follow the structure outlined in the pyramid).

Genre: a class or type of literary work. The concept of genre may be used with different levels of generality. At the most general, poetry, drama, and prose fiction are distinguished as separate genres. At a lower level of generality various sub-genres are frequently distinguished, such as (within the genre of prose fiction) the novel, the novella, and the short story; and, at a still lower level of generality, the mystery novel, the detective novel, the novel of manners, and so on.

Georgic: (from Virgil's *Georgics*) a poem that celebrates the natural wealth of the countryside and advises how to cultivate and live in harmony with it. Pope's *Windsor Forest* and James Thomson's *Seasons* are classed as georgics. Georgics were often said to make up, with *eclogues*, the two alliterative forms of pastoral poetry.

Ghazal: derived from Persian and Indian precedents, the ghazal presents a series of thoughts in closed couplets usually joined by a simple rhyme-scheme such as: *a/a b/a c/a d/a, ab bb cb eb fb*, etc.

Gothic: in architecture and the visual arts, a term used to describe styles prevalent from the twelfth to the fourteenth centuries, but in literature a term used to describe work with a sinister or grotesque tone that seeks to evoke a sense of terror on the part of the reader or audience. Gothic literature originated as a genre in the eighteenth century with works such as Horace Walpole's *The Castle of Otranto*. To some extent the notion of the medieval itself then carried with it associations of the dark and the grotesque, but from the beginning an element of intentional exaggeration (sometimes verging on self-parody) attached itself to the genre. The Gothic trend of youth culture that began in the late twentieth century is less clearly associated with the medieval, but shares with the various varieties of Gothic literature (from Walpole in the eighteenth century, to Bram Stoker in the early twentieth, to Stephen King and Anne Rice in the late twentieth) a fondness for the sensational and the grotesque, as well as a propensity to self-parody.

Grotesque: literature of the grotesque is characterized by a focus on extreme or distorted aspects of human characteristics. (The term can also refer particularly to a character who is odd or disturbing.) This focus can serve to comment on and challenge societal norms. The story "A Good Man Is Hard to Find" employs elements of the grotesque.

Haiku: a Japanese poetic form with three unrhymed lines of typically five, seven, and five syllables. Conventionally, it uses precise, concentrated images to suggest states of feeling.

Heptameter: a line containing seven metrical feet.

Heroic Couplet: a pair of rhymed iambic pentameters, so called because the form was much used in seventeenth- and eighteenth-century poems and plays on heroic subjects.

Hexameter: a line containing six metrical feet.

Horatian Ode: inspired by the work of the Roman poet Horace, an ode that is usually calm and meditative in tone, and homostrophic (i.e., having regular stanzas) in form. Keats's odes are English examples.

Hymn: a song whose theme is usually religious, in praise of divinity. Literary hymns may praise more secular subjects.

Hyperbole: a *figure of speech* (a *trope*) that deliberately exaggerates or inflates meaning to achieve particular effects, such as the irony in A.E. Housman's claim (from "Terence, This Is Stupid Stuff") that "malt does more than Milton can / To justify God's ways to man."

Iamb: the most common metrical foot in English verse, containing one unstressed syllable followed by a stressed syllable: x / (e.g., between, achieve).

Idyll: traditionally, a short pastoral poem that idealizes country life, conveying impressions of innocence and happiness.

Image: a representation of a sensory experience or of an object that can be known by the senses.

Imagery: the range of images in a given work. We can gain much insight into works by looking for patterns of imagery. For example, the imagery of spring (budding trees, rain, singing birds) in Kate Chopin's "The Story of an Hour" reinforces the suggestions of death and rebirth in the plot and theme.

Imagism: a poetic movement that was popular mainly in the second decade of the twentieth century. The goal of imagist poets (such as H.D. and Ezra Pound in their early work) was to represent emotions or impressions through highly concentrated imagery.

Implied Author: see *narrator*.

Improvisation: the seemingly spontaneous invention of dramatic dialogue and/or a dramatic plot by actors without the assistance of a written text.

Incantation: a chant or recitation of words that are believed to have magical power. A poem can achieve an "incantatory" effect through a compelling rhyme scheme and other repetitive patterns.

Interlocking Rhyme: see *rhyme*.

Interlude: a short and often comical play or other entertainment performed between the *acts* of a longer or more serious work, particularly during the later Middle Ages and early Renaissance.

Internal Rhyme: see *rhyme*.

Intertextuality: the act of bringing one cultural text into relationship with another, as when a writer references a painting, a song title or lyric, another novel, poem, or play, a famous theoretical work, etc. A literary text may connect with other cultural texts via *allusion*, *parody*, or *satire*, or in a variety of other ways.

Irony: the use of irony draws attention to a gap between what is said and what is meant, or what appears to be true and what is true. Types of irony include verbal irony (which includes *hyberbole*, *litotes*, and *sarcasm*), *dramatic irony*, and structural irony (in which the gap between what is "said" and meant is sustained throughout an entire piece, as when an author makes use of an unreliable narrator or speaker—see Robert Browning's "My Last Duchess").

Lament: a poem that expresses profound regret or grief either because of a death, or because of the loss of a former, happier state.

Language Poetry: a movement that defies the usual lyric and narrative conventions of poetry, and that challenges the structures and codes of everyday language. Often seen as both politically and aesthetically subversive, its roots lie in the works of modernist writers such as Ezra Pound and Gertrude Stein.

Litotes: a *figure of speech* (a *trope*) in which a writer deliberately uses understatement to highlight the importance of an argument, or to convey an ironic attitude.

Liturgical Drama: drama based on and/or incorporating text from the liturgy—the text recited during religious services.

Lyric: a poem, usually short, expressing an individual speaker's feelings or private thoughts. Originally a song performed with accompaniment on a lyre, the lyric poem is often noted for musicality of rhyme and rhythm. The lyric genre includes a variety of forms, including the *sonnet*, the *ode*, the *elegy*, the *madrigal*, the *aubade*, the *dramatic monologue*, and the *hymn*.

Madrigal: a lyric poem, usually short and focusing on pastoral or romantic themes. A madrigal is often set to music.

Magic Realism: a style of fiction in which miraculous or bizarre things often happen but are treated in a matter-of-fact fashion by the characters and/or the narrative voice. There is often an element of the absurd to magic realist narratives, and they tend not to have any strong plot structure generating expectations in the reader's mind. See also *fantasy*.

Masculine Ending: a metrical line ending on a stressed syllable.

Masculine Rhyme: see *rhyme*. An alternative term is hard landing.

Melodrama: originally a term used to describe nineteenth-century plays featuring sensational story lines and a crude separation of characters into moral categories, with the pure and virtuous pitted against evil villains. Early melodramas employed background music throughout the action of the play as a means of heightening the emotional response of the audience. By extension, certain sorts of prose fictions or poems are often described as having melodramatic elements.

Metafiction: fiction that calls attention to itself as fiction. Metafiction is a means by which authors render us conscious of our status as readers, often in order to explore the relationships between fiction and reality.

Metaphor: a *figure of speech* (in this case, a *trope*) in which a comparison is made or identity is asserted between two unrelated things or actions without the use of "like" or "as."

Metaphysical Poets: a group of seventeenth-century English poets, notably Donne, Cowley, Marvell, and Herbert, who employed unusual, difficult imagery and *conceits* in order to develop intellectual and religious themes. The term was first applied to these writers to mark as far-fetched their use of philosophical and scientific ideas in a poetic context.

Metonymy: a *figure of speech* (a *trope*), meaning "change of name," in which a writer refers to an object or idea by substituting the name of another object or idea closely associated with it: for example, the substitution of "crown" for monarchy, "the press" for journalism, or "the pen" for writing. *Synecdoche* is a kind of metonymy.

Metre: the pattern of stresses, syllables, and pauses that constitutes the regular rhythm of a line of verse. The metre of a poem written in the English accentual-syllabic tradition is determined by identifying the stressed and unstressed syllables in a line of verse, and grouping them into recurring units known as feet. See *accent*, *accentual-syllabic*, *caesura*, *elision*, and *scansion*. For some of the better-known metres, see *iamb*, *trochee*, *dactyl*, *anapaest*, and *spondee*. See also *monometer*, *dimeter*, *trimeter*, *tetrameter*, *pentameter*, and *hexameter*.

***Mise en scène*:** French expression, literally meaning "the putting on stage," which has been adopted in other languages to describe the sum total of creative choices made in the staging of a play.

Mock-Heroic: a style applying the elevated diction and vocabulary of epic poetry to low or ridiculous subjects. An example is Alexander Pope's "The Rape of the Lock."

Modernism: in the history of literature, music, and the visual arts, a movement that began in the early twentieth century, characterized by a thoroughgoing rejection of the then-dominant conventions of literary plotting and characterization, of melody and harmony, and of perspective and other naturalistic forms of visual representation. In literature (as in music and the visual arts), modernists endeavoured to represent the complexity of what seemed to them to be an increasingly fragmented world by adopting techniques of presenting story material, illuminating character, and employing imagery that emphasized (in the words of Virginia Woolf) "the spasmodic, the obscure, the fragmentary."

Monologue: an extended speech by a single speaker or character in a poem or play. Unlike a *soliloquy*, a dramatic monologue has an implied listener.

Monometer: a line containing one metrical foot.

Mood: this can describe the writer's attitude, implied or expressed, toward the subject (see *tone*); or it may refer to the atmosphere that a writer creates in a passage of description or narration.

Motif: pattern formed by the recurrence of an idea, image, action, or plot element throughout a literary work, creating new levels of meaning and strengthening structural coherence. The term is taken from music, where it describes recurring melodies or themes. See also *theme*.

Motivation: the forces that seem to cause characters to act, or reasons why characters do what they do.

Narration: the process of disclosing information, whether fictional or non-fictional.

Narrative Perspective: in fiction, the point of view from which a story is narrated. A first-person narrative is recounted using *I* and *me*, whereas a third-person narrative is recounted using *he, she, they*, and so on. When a narrative is written in the third person and the narrative voice evidently "knows" all that is being done and thought, the story is typically described as being recounted by an "omniscient narrator." Second-person narratives, in which the narrative is recounted using *you*, are very rare.

Narrator: the voice (or voices) disclosing information. In fiction, the narrator is distinguished from both the author (a real, historical person) and the implied author (whom the reader imagines the author to be). Narrators can also be distinguished according to the degree to which they share the reality of the other characters in the story and the extent to which they participate in the action; according to how much information they are privy to (and how much of that information they are willing to share with the reader); and according to whether or not they are perceived by the reader as reliable or unreliable sources of information. See also *narrative perspective*.

Neoclassical Dramaturgy: the principles, rules, and *conventions* of writing plays according to the precepts and ideals of *neoclassicism*. Often based on the so-called *unities* of time, place, and action.

Neoclassicism: literally the "new classicism," the aesthetic style that dominated high culture in Europe through the seventeenth and eighteenth centuries, and in some places into the nineteenth century. Its subject matter was often taken from Greek and Roman myth and history; in *style*, it valued order, reason, clarity, and moderation.

Nonsense Verse: light, humorous poetry that contradicts logic, plays with the absurd, and invents words for amusing effects. Lewis Carroll is one of the best-known practitioners of nonsense verse.

Octave: also known as "octet," the first eight lines in certain forms of sonnet—notably the *Italian/Petrarchan*, in which the octet rhymes *abbaabba*. See also *sestet* and *sonnet*.

Octosyllabic: a line of poetry with eight syllables, as in iambic tetrameter.

Ode: originally a classical poetic form, used by the Greeks and Romans to convey serious themes. English poetry has evolved three main forms of ode: the Pindaric (imitative of the odes of the Greek poet Pindar); the Horatian (modelled on the work of the Roman writer Horace); and the irregular ode. The Pindaric ode has a tripartite structure of *strophe, antistrophe*, and *epode* (meaning turn, counterturn, and stand), modelled on the songs and movements of the *Chorus* in Greek drama. The Horatian ode is more personal, reflective, and literary, and employs a pattern of repeated stanzas. The irregular ode, as its name implies, avoids a recurrent stanza pattern, and is sometimes irregular in line length also (for example, Wordsworth's "Ode: Intimations of Immortality").

Omniscient Narrator: see *narrative perspective*.

Onomatopoeia: a *figure of speech* (a scheme) in which a word "imitates" a sound, or in which the sound of a word seems to reflect its meaning.

Orchestra: literally, "the dancing place." In the ancient world it was the lower, flat, circular surface-area of the outdoor theatre where the *chorus* danced and sang.

Ottava Rima: an eight-line stanza, usually in iambic pentameter, with the rhyme scheme *abababcc*. For an example, see Yeats's "Sailing to Byzantium."

Oxymoron: a *figure of speech* (a *trope*) in which two words whose meanings seem contradictory are placed together; we see an example in Shakespeare's *Twelfth Night*, when Orsino refers to the "sweet pangs" of love.

Pantoum: linked quatrains in a poem that rhymes *abab*. The second and fourth lines of one stanza are repeated as the first and third lines of the stanza that follows. In the final stanza the pattern is reversed: the second line repeats the third line of the first stanza, the fourth and final line repeats the first line of the first stanza.

Parable: a story told to illustrate a moral principle. It differs from *allegory* in being shorter and simpler: parables do not generally function on two levels simultaneously.

Parody: a close, usually mocking imitation of a particular literary work, or of the well-known style of a particular author, in order to expose or magnify weaknesses. Parody is a form of *satire*—that is, humour that may ridicule and scorn its object.

Pastiche: a discourse that borrows or imitates other writers' characters, forms, style, or ideas, sometimes creating something of a literary patchwork. Unlike a parody, a pastiche can be intended as a compliment to the original writer.

Pastoral: in general, pertaining to country life; in prose, drama, and poetry, a stylized type of writing that idealizes the lives and innocence of country people, particularly shepherds and shepherdesses. See also *eclogue, georgic, idyll*.

Pastoral Elegy: a poem in which the poet uses the pastoral style to lament the death of a friend, usually represented as a shepherd. Milton's "Lycidas" provides a good example of the form, including its use of such conventions as an invocation of the muse and a procession of mourners.

Pathetic Fallacy: a form of *personification* in which inanimate objects are given human emotions: for example, rain clouds "weeping." The word "fallacy" in this connection is intended to suggest the distortion of reality or the false emotion that may result from an exaggerated use of personification.

Pathos: the emotional quality of a discourse; or the ability of a discourse to appeal to our emotions. It is usually applied to the mood conveyed by images of pain, suffering, or loss that arouse feelings of pity or sorrow in the reader.

Pattern Poetry: a predecessor of modern *concrete poetry* in which the shape of the poem on the page is intended to suggest or imitate an aspect of the poem's subject. George Herbert's "Easter Wings" is an example of pattern poetry.

Pentameter: verse containing five metrical feet in a line.

Performance Poetry: poetry composed primarily for oral performance, often very theatrical in nature. See also *dub poetry* and *rap*.

Persona: the assumed identity or "speaking voice" that a writer projects in a discourse. The term "persona" literally means "mask."

Personification: a *figure of speech* (a *trope*), also known as "prosopopoeia," in which a writer refers to inanimate objects, ideas, or non-human animals as if they were human, or creates a human figure to represent an abstract entity such as Philosophy or Peace.

Phoneme: a linguistic term denoting the smallest unit of sound that it is possible to distinguish. The words *fun* and *phone* each have three phonemes, though one has three letters and one has five.

Plot: the organization of story materials within a literary work. Matters of plotting include the order in which story material is presented; the inclusion of elements that allow or encourage the reader or audience to form expectations as to what is likely to happen; and the decision to present some story material through exposition rather than present it directly to the reader as part of the narrative.

Point of View: see *narrative perspective*.

Postmodernism: in literature and the visual arts, a movement influential in the late twentieth and early twenty-first centuries. In some ways postmodernism represents a reaction to modernism, in others an extension of it. With roots in the work of French philosophers such as Jacques Derrida and Michel Foucault, it is deeply coloured by theory; indeed, it may be said to have begun at the "meta" level of theorizing rather than at the level of practice. Like modernism, postmodernism embraces difficulty and distrusts the simple and straightforward. More broadly, postmodernism is characterized by a rejection of absolute truth or value, of closed systems, of grand unified narratives.

Postmodernist fiction is characterized by a frequently ironic or playful tone in dealing with reality and illusion; by a willingness to combine different styles or forms in a single work (just as in architecture the postmodernist spirit embodies a willingness to borrow from seemingly disparate styles in designing a single structure); and by a highly attuned awareness of the problematized state of the writer, artist, or theorist as observer.

Prolepsis: originally a rhetorical term used to refer to the anticipation of possible objections by someone advancing an argument, prolepsis is used in discussions of fiction to refer to elements in a narrative that anticipate the future of the story. The *flashforward* technique of storytelling is often described as a form of prolepsis; the inclusion in a narrative of material that foreshadows future developments is also sometimes treated as a form of prolepsis.

Proscenium: a Latin architectural term derived from the Greek *proskenion*, the frontmost section of the theatre building as it developed in the post-Classical, Hellenistic period. Stages on which a pictorial illusion is created with the help of a border or frame are called "proscenium arch" or "picture-frame" theatres; they reached their heyday during the nineteenth century, the age of *realism*.

Prose Poem: a poetic discourse that uses prose formats (e.g., it may use margins and paragraphs rather than line breaks or stanzas) yet is written with the kind of attention to language, rhythm, and cadence that characterizes verse.

Prosody: the study and analysis of metre, rhythm, rhyme, stanzaic pattern, and other devices of versification.

Protagonist: the central character in a literary work.

Prothalamion: a wedding song; a term coined by the poet Edmund Spenser, adapted from *epithalamion*.

Pun: a play on words, in which a word with two or more distinct meanings, or two words with similar sounds, may create humorous ambiguities. Also known as "paranomasia."

Pyrrhic: a metrical foot containing two weak stresses.

Quantitative Metre: a metrical system used by Greek and Roman poets, in which a line of verse was measured by the "quantity," or length of sound of each syllable. A foot was measured in terms of syllables classed as long or short.

Quantity: duration of syllables in poetry. The line "There is a Garden in her face" (the first line from the poem of the same name by Thomas Campion) is characterized by the short quantities of the syllables. The last line of Thomas Hardy's "During Wind and Rain" has the same number of syllables as the line by Campion, but the quantities of the syllables are much longer—in other words, the line takes much longer to say: "Down their carved names the rain drop ploughs."

Quatrain: a four-line stanza.

Quintet: a five-line stanza. Sometimes given as "quintain."

Rap: originally coined to describe informal conversation, "rap" now usually describes a style of performance poetry in which a poet will chant rhymed verse, sometimes improvised and usually with musical accompaniment that has a heavy beat.

Realism: as a literary term, the presentation through literature of material closely resembling real life. As notions both of what constitutes "real life" and of how it may be most faithfully represented in literature have varied widely, "realism" has taken a variety of meanings. The term "naturalistic" has sometimes been used as a synonym for *realistic*; naturalism originated in the nineteenth century as a term denoting a form of realism focusing in particular on grim, unpleasant, or ugly aspects of the real.

Refrain: one or more words or lines repeated at regular points throughout a poem, often at the end of each stanza or group of stanzas. Sometimes a whole stanza may be repeated to create a refrain, like the chorus in a song.

Rhetoric: in classical Greece and Rome, the art of persuasion and public speaking. From the Middle Ages onwards, the study of rhetoric gave greater attention to style, particularly *figures of speech*. Today in poetics, the term rhetoric may encompass not only figures of speech, but also the persuasive effects of forms, sounds, and word choices.

Rhyme: the repetition of identical or similar sounds, usually in pairs and generally at the ends of metrical lines.

End-Rhyme: a rhyming word or syllable at the end of a line.

Eye-Rhyme: rhyming that pairs words whose spellings are alike but whose pronunciations are different: for example, though/slough.

Feminine Rhyme: a two-syllable (also known as "double") rhyme. The first syllable is stressed and the second unstressed: for example, hasty/ tasty. See also *triple rhyme*.

Interlocking Rhyme: the repetition of rhymes from one stanza to the next, creating links that add to the poem's continuity and coherence. Examples may be found in Shelley's use of *terza rima* in "Ode to the West Wind" and in Dylan Thomas's *villanelle* "Do Not Go Gentle into That Good Night."

Internal Rhyme: the placement of rhyming words within lines so that at least two words in a line rhyme with each other.

Masculine Rhyme: a correspondence of sound between the final stressed syllables at the end of two or more lines, as in grieve/leave, ar-rive/sur-vive.

Slant Rhyme: an imperfect or partial rhyme (also known as "near" or "half" rhyme) in which the consonant sounds of stressed syllables match but the vowel sounds do not. E.g., spoiled/spilled, taint/stint.

Triple Rhyme: a three-syllable rhyme in which the first syllable of each rhyme-word is stressed and the other two unstressed (e.g., lottery/coterie).

True Rhyme: a rhyme in which everything but the initial consonant matches perfectly in sound and spelling.

Rhyme Royal: a stanza of seven iambic pentameters, with a rhyme-scheme of *ababbcc*. This is also known as the Chaucerian stanza, as Chaucer was the first English poet to use this form. See also *septet*.

Rhythm: in speech, the arrangement of stressed and unstressed syllables creates units of sound. In song or verse, these units may be shaped into a regular rhythmic pattern, described in prosody as *metre*.

Romance: a dreamlike genre of fiction or storytelling in which the ordinary laws of nature are suspended—in which, for example, statues come to life, or shipwrecked men emerge from the sea unharmed.

Romanticism: a major social and cultural movement, originating in Europe, that shaped much of Western artistic thought in the late eighteenth and nineteenth centuries. Opposing the ideal of controlled, rational order associated with the Enlightenment, Romanticism emphasizes the importance of spontaneous self-expression, emotion, and personal experience in producing art. In Romanticism, the "natural" is privileged over the conventional or the artificial.

Rondeau: a 15-line poem, generally octosyllabic, with only two rhymes throughout its three stanzas, and an unrhymed refrain at the end of the ninth and fifteenth lines, repeating part of the opening line.

Round Character: a complex and psychologically realistic character, often one who changes as a work progresses. The opposite of a round character is a *flat character*.

Sarcasm: a form of *irony* (usually spoken) in which the meaning is conveyed largely by the tone of voice adopted; something said sarcastically is meant to imply its opposite.

Satire: literary work designed to make fun of or seriously criticize its subject. According to many literary theories of the Renaissance and neoclassical periods, the ridicule through satire of a certain sort of behaviour may function for the reader or audience as a corrective of such behaviour.

Scansion: the formal analysis of patterns of rhythm and rhyme in poetry. Each line of accentual-syllabic verse will have a certain number of fairly regular "beats" consisting of alternating stressed and unstressed syllables. To "scan" a poem is to count the beats in each line, to mark stressed and unstressed syllables and indicate their combination into "feet," to note pauses, and to identify rhyme schemes with letters of the alphabet.

Scheme: see *figures of speech*.

Septet: a stanza containing seven lines.

Sestet: a six-line stanza. A sestet forms the second grouping of lines in an *Italian/Petrarchan sonnet*, following the octave. See *sonnet* and *sestina*.

Sestina: an elaborate unrhymed poem with six six-line stanzas and a three-line *envoy*.

Setting: the time, place, and cultural environment in which a story or work takes place.

Simile: a *figure of speech* (a *trope*) which makes an explicit comparison between a particular object and another object or idea that is similar in some (often unexpected) way. A simile always uses "like" or "as" to signal the connection. Compare with *metaphor*.

Soliloquy: in drama (or, less often, poetry), a speech in which a character, usually alone, reveals his or her thoughts, emotions, and/or motivations without being heard by other characters. The convention was frequently employed during the Elizabethan era, and many of the best-known examples are from Shakespeare; for example, Hamlet's "To be, or not to be" speech is a soliloquy. Soliloquies differ from *dramatic monologues* in that dramatic monologues address an implied listener, while the speaker of a soliloquy thinks aloud or addresses the audience.

Sonnet: a highly structured lyric poem, which normally has 14 lines of iambic pentameter. We can distinguish four major variations of the sonnet.

> **Italian/Petrarchan:** named for the fourteenth-century Italian poet Petrarch, has an octave rhyming *abbaabba*, and a sestet rhyming *cdecde*, or *cdcdcd* (other arrangements are possible here). Usually, a turn in argument takes place between the octave and sestet.

> **Miltonic:** developed by Milton and similar to the Petrarchan in rhyme scheme, but eliminating the turn after the octave, thus giving greater unity to the poem's structure of thought.

> **Shakespearean:** often called the English sonnet, this form has three quatrains and a couplet. The quatrains rhyme internally but do not interlock: *abab cdcd efef gg*. The turn may occur after the second quatrain, but is usually revealed in the final couplet. Shakespeare's sonnets are the best-known examples of this form.

Spenserian: after Edmund Spenser, who developed the form in his sonnet cycle *Amoretti*. This sonnet form has three quatrains linked through interlocking rhyme, and a separately rhyming couplet: *abab bcbc cdcd ee*.

Spenserian Stanza: a nine-line stanza, with eight iambic pentameters and a concluding 12-syllable line, rhyming *ababbcbcc*.

Spondee: a metrical foot containing two strong stressed syllables: // (e.g., blind mouths).

Sprung Rhythm: a modern variation of accentual verse, created by the English poet Gerard Manley Hopkins, in which rhythms are determined largely by the number of strong stresses in a line, without regard to the number of unstressed syllables. Hopkins felt that sprung rhythm more closely approximated the natural rhythms of speech than did conventional poetry.

Stanza: any lines of verse that are grouped together in a poem and separated from other similarly structured groups by a space. In metrical poetry, stanzas share metrical and rhyming patterns; however, stanzas may also be formed on the basis of thought, as in irregular odes. Conventional stanza forms include the *tercet*, the *quatrain*, *rhyme royal*, the *Spenserian stanza*, the *ballad stanza*, and *ottava rima*.

Stock Character: a character defined by a set of characteristics that are stereotypical and/or established by literary convention; examples include the "wicked stepmother" and the "absent-minded professor."

Story: narrative material, independent of the manner in which it may be presented or the ways in which the narrative material may be organized. Story is thus distinct from *plot*.

Stream of Consciousness: a narrative technique that conveys the inner workings of a character's mind, in which a character's thoughts, feelings, memories, and impressions are related in an unbroken flow, without concern for *chronology* or coherence.

Stress: see *accent*.

Strophe: a *stanza*. In a Pindaric *ode*, the *strophe* is the first stanza. This is followed by an *antistrophe*, which presents the same metrical pattern and rhyme scheme, and finally by an *epode*, differing in metre from the preceding stanzas. Upon completion of this "triad," the entire sequence can recur.

Style: a distinctive or specific use of language and form.

Sublime: a concept, popular in eighteenth-century England, that sought to capture the qualities of grandeur, power, and awe that may be inherent in or produced by undomesticated nature or great art. The sublime was thought of as higher and loftier than something that is merely beautiful.

Subplot: a line of story that is subordinate to the main storyline of a narrative. (Note that properly speaking a subplot is a category of story material, not of plot.)

Substitution: a deliberate change from the dominant pattern of stresses in a line of verse to create emphasis or variation. Thus the first line of Shakespeare's sonnet "Shall I compare thee to a summer's day?" is decidedly iambic in metre (x/x/x/x/x/), whereas the second line substitutes a trochee (/x) in the opening foot: "Thou art more lovely and more temperate."

Subtext: implied or suggested meaning of a passage of text, or of an entire work.

Surrealism: Surrealism incorporates elements of the true appearance of life and nature, combining these elements according to a logic more typical of dreams than waking life. Isolated aspects of surrealist art may create powerful illusions of reality, but the effect of the whole is usually to disturb or question our sense of reality rather than to confirm it.

Suspension of Disbelief: a willingness on the part of the audience member or reader to temporarily accept the fictional world presented in a narrative.

Syllabic Verse: poetry in which the length of a line is measured solely by the number of syllables, regardless of accents or patterns of stress.

Syllable: vocal sound or group of sounds forming a unit of speech; a syllable may be formed with a single effort of articulation. Some syllables consist of a single phoneme (e.g., the word *I*, or the first syllable in the word *u-ni-ty*) but others may be made up of several phonemes (as with one-syllable words such as *lengths*, *splurged*, and *through*). By contrast, the much shorter words *ago*, *any*, and *open* each have two syllables.

Symbol: something that represents itself but goes beyond this in suggesting other meanings. Like metaphor, the symbol extends meaning; but while the tenor and vehicle of metaphor are bound in a specific relationship, a symbol may have a range of connotations. For example, the image of a rose may call forth associations of love, passion, transience, fragility, youth, and beauty, among others. Depending upon the context, such an image could be interpreted in a variety of ways, as in Blake's lyric, "The Sick Rose."

Syncope: in poetry, the dropping of a letter or syllable from the middle of a word, as in "trav'ller." Such a contraction allows a line to stay within a metrical scheme. See also *catalexis* and *elision*.

Synecdoche: a kind of *metonymy* in which a writer substitutes the name of a part of something to signify the whole: for example, "sail" for ship or "hand" for a member of the ship's crew.

Syntax: the ordering of words in a sentence.

Tercet: a group, or stanza, of three lines, often linked by an interlocking rhyme scheme as in *terza rima*. See also *triplet*.

Terza Rima: an arrangement of tercets interlocked by a rhyme scheme of *aba bcb cdc ded*, etc., and ending with a couplet that rhymes with the second-last line of the final tercet (for example, *efe, ff*). See, for example, Percy Shelley's "Ode to the West Wind."

Tetrameter: a line of poetry containing four metrical feet.

Theatre-in-the-Round: a type of staging in which seating for the audience surrounds the stage on all (or at least most) of its sides. This approach was common in ancient Greek, ancient Roman, and medieval theatre; it was not often used after the seventeenth century, but in the mid-twentieth century its popularity increased, especially in experimental theatre. Also called "arena theatre."

Theme: in general, an idea explored in a work through character, action, and/ or image. To be fully developed, however, a theme must consist of more than a single concept or idea: it should also include an argument about the idea. Thus if a poem examines the topic of jealousy, we might say the theme is that jealousy undermines love or jealousy is a manifestation of insecurity. Few, if any, literary works have single themes.

Third-Person Narrative: see *narrative perspective*.

Thrust Stage: see *apron*.

Tone: the writer's attitude toward a given subject or audience, as expressed through an authorial persona or "voice." Tone can be projected through particular choices of wording, imagery, figures of speech, and rhythmic devices. Compare *mood*.

Tragedy: in the traditional definition originating in discussions of ancient Greek drama, a serious narrative recounting the downfall of the protagonist, usually a person of high social standing. More loosely, the term has been applied to a wide variety of literary forms in which the tone is predominantly a dark one and the narrative does not end happily.

Tragicomedy: a genre of drama in which many elements of *tragedy* are present, but which generally has a happy end, or—more generally—which includes both serious and comic components.

Trimeter: verse containing three metrical feet in a line.

Triolet: a French form in which the first line appears three times in a poem of only eight lines. The first line is repeated at lines four and seven; the second line is repeated in line eight. The triolet has only two rhymes: *abaaabab*.

Triple Foot: poetic foot of three syllables. The possible varieties of triple foot are the anapest (in which two unstressed syllables are followed by a stressed syllable), the dactyl (in which a stressed syllable is followed by two unstressed syllables), and the mollossus (in which all three syllables are stressed equally). English poetry tends to use *duple* rhythms far more frequently than triple rhythms.

Triplet: a group of three lines with the same end-rhyme, much used by eighteenth-century poets to vary or punctuate the flow of couplets. See also *tercet*.

Trochee: a metrical foot containing one strong stress followed by one weak stress.

Trope: any figure of speech that plays on our understandings of words to extend, alter, or transform "literal" meaning. Common tropes include *metaphor, simile, personification, hyperbole, metonymy, oxymoron, synecdoche*, and *irony*. See also *figures of speech*.

Turn (Italian "volta"): the point in a *sonnet* where the mood or argument changes. The turn may occur between the octave and sestet, i.e., after the eighth line, or in the final couplet, depending on the kind of sonnet.

Unities: Many literary theorists of the late sixteenth through late eighteenth centuries held that a play should ideally be presented as representing a single place, and confining the action to a single day and a single dominant event. They disapproved of plots involving gaps or long periods of time, shifts in place, or subplots. These concepts, which came to be referred to as the unities of space, time, and action, were based on a misreading of classical authorities (principally of Aristotle).

Unreliable Narrator: a narrator whose reporting or understanding of events invites questioning from the reader. Narrators may be considered unreliable if they lack sufficient intelligence or experience to understand events, or if they have some reason to misrepresent events. See also *narrative perspective*.

Vers libre (French): see *free verse*.

Verse: a general term for works of poetry, usually referring to poems that incorporate some kind of metrical structure. The term may also describe a line of poetry, though more frequently it is applied to a stanza.

Villanelle: a poem usually consisting of 19 lines, with five three-line stanzas (tercets) rhyming *aba*, and a concluding quatrain rhyming *abaa*. The first and third lines of the first tercet are repeated at fixed intervals throughout the rest of the poem. See, for example, Dylan Thomas's "Do Not Go Gentle into That Good Night."

Volta: See *turn*.

Zeugma: a *figure of speech* (*trope*) in which one word links or "yokes" two others in the same sentence, often to comic or ironic effect. For example, a verb may govern two objects, as in Pope's line "Or stain her honour, or her new brocade."

Acknowledgement: The glossary for *The Broadview Introduction to Literature* incorporates some material initially prepared for the following Broadview anthologies: *The Broadview Anthology of Poetry*, edited by Herbert Rosengarten and Amanda Goldrick-Jones; *The Broadview Anthology of Drama*, edited by Jennifer Wise and Craig Walker; *The Broadview Anthology of Short Fiction*, edited by Julia Gaunce et al.; *The Broadview Anthology of British Literature*, edited by Joseph Black et al. The editors gratefully acknowledge the contributions of the editors of these other anthologies. Please note that all material in the glossary, whether initially published in another Broadview anthology or appearing here for the first time, is protected by copyright.

Permissions Acknowledgements

Abel, Jordan. Excerpt from *The Place of Scraps*. Copyright © 2013 by Jordan Abel. Talonbooks, Vancouver. Reprinted with the permission of Talonbooks.

Achebe, Chinua. "Dead Men's Path," from *Girls at War and Other Stories*. Copyright © 1972, 1973 Chinua Achebe. Reprinted with the permission of The Wylie Agency LLC.

Agha Shahid Ali. "Postcard from Kashmir," from *The Half-Inch Himalayas*. Copyright © 1987 by Agha Shahid Ali. Published by Wesleyan University Press and reprinted with permission. www.wesleyan.edu/wespress. "The Wolf's Postscript to 'Little Red Riding Hood,'" from *The Veiled Suite: The Collected Poems*. Copyright © 1987 by Agha Shahid Ali. Reprinted with the permission of W.W. Norton & Company, Inc.

Al-Solaylee, Kamal. Excerpt from *Brown: What Being Brown in the World Today Means (to Everyone)*. Copyright © 2016 by Kamal Al-Solaylee. Published by HarperCollins Publishers Ltd. All rights reserved.

Allen, Lillian. "One Poem Town," from *Women Do This Every Day*. Women's Press, 1993. Reprinted with the permission of Lillian Allen.

Anitafrika, D'bi Young. "self-esteem (ii)"; "foreign mind/local body"; and "love speak"; from *Rivers and Other Blackness Between Us*. Canadian Scholars Press, 2007. Reprinted with the permission of D'bi Young Anitafrika.

Atwood, Margaret. "Happy Endings," from *Murder in the Dark*. Copyright © 1983 by Margaret Atwood, 1997 by O.W. Toad Ltd. Reprinted by permission of McClelland & Stewart, a division of Penguin Random House Canada Limited. All rights reserved. Any third party use of this material, outside of this publication, is prohibited. Interested parties must apply directly to Penguin Random House Canada Limited for permission. "Death of a Young Son by Drowning," and "Variation on the Word Sleep," from *Selected Poems 1966–1984*. Copyright © Oxford University Press Canada, 1990. Reprinted with the permission of the publisher. "You Fit into Me," from *Power Politics*. Copyright © 1971, 1996 by Margaret Atwood. Reprinted by permission of House of Anansi Press Inc., Toronto. www.houseofanansi.com.

Auden, W.H. "Funeral Blues," "Musée des Beaux Arts," "The Unknown Citizen," and "September 1, 1939," from *Collected Poems* by W.H. Auden. Copyright © 1940 and © renewed 1968 by W.H. Auden. Used by permission of Random House LLC. All rights reserved.

sion of The Permissions Company Inc., on behalf of BOA Editions Ltd., www.boaeditions.org.

Coady, Lynn. "Hellgoing," from *Hellgoing*. Copyright © 2013 by Lynn Coady. Reprinted by permission of House of Anansi Press Inc., Toronto. www.houseofanansi.com.

Coyote, Ivan. "Tomboys Still," from *Tomboy Survival Guide*. Arsenal Pulp Press, 2016. Reprinted with the permission of Arsenal Pulp Press.

Crozier, Lorna. "Carrots," and "Onions," from *The Blue Hour of the Day: Selected Poems*. Copyright © 2007 by Lorna Crozier. Reprinted by permission of McClelland & Stewart, a division of Penguin Random House Canada Limited. All rights reserved. Any third party use of this material, outside of this publication, is prohibited. Interested parties must apply directly to Penguin Random House Canada Limited for permission. "When I Come Again to My Father's House," from *Everything Arrives at the Light*. McClelland & Stewart, 1995. Reprinted with the permission of Lorna Crozier.

Duffy, Carol Ann. "Crush," and "Drunk," from *Mean Time*, published by Anvil Press Poetry, 1993. Copyright © Carol Ann Duffy. Reproduced by permission of the author c/o Rogers, Coleridge & White Ltd., 20 Powis Mews, London W11 1JN.

Dumont, Marilyn. "Not Just a Platform for My Dance," and "White Judges," from *A Really Good Brown Girl: Brick Books Classics 4*. Brick Books, 2015. Reprinted with the permission of Brick Books.

Ginsberg, Allen. "A Supermarket in California," from *Collected Poems 1947–1980*. Copyright © 1955 by Allen Ginsberg. Reprinted by permission of HarperCollins Publishers.

Gowdy, Barbara. "We So Seldom Look on Love," from *We So Seldom Look on Love*. Copyright © 1992 by Barbara Gowdy. Published by HarperCollins Publishers Ltd. All rights reserved.

Halfe, Louise Bernice. "wêpinâson," and "ê-kwêskît, Turn-Around Woman," from *The Crooked Good*. Copyright © 2007, Louise Bernice Halfe. Reprinted with the permission of Coteau Books.

Harris, Sharon. "Where do poems come from?" and "Why do poems make me cry?" from *Fun With 'Pataphysics*. BookThug, 2004. Reprinted with the permission of Sharon Harris.

Heaney, Seamus. "Digging," "Mid-Term Break," and "Grauballe Man," from *Opened Ground: Selected Poems 1966–1996*, published by Faber and Faber Ltd. Reprinted with the permission of Faber and Faber Ltd. "Cutaways," originally published in *Irish Pages*, Volume 2 Number 2, 2008. Reprinted with the permission of Faber and Faber Ltd.

Hughes, Ted. "Pike," and "The Thought-Fox," from *Collected Poems*, edited by Paul Keegan. Faber and Faber, 2003. Reprinted with the permission of Faber and Faber Ltd.

Ishiguro, Kazuo. "A Family Supper," published by *Quarter Magazine*, 1980. Copyright © Kazuo Ishiguro. Reproduced with the permission of the author c/o Rogers, Coleridge & White Ltd., 20 Powis Mews, London W11 1JN.

Kay, Jackie. "Her," and "In My Country," from *Darling: New and Selected Poems*. Bloodaxe Books, 2007. Reproduced with the permission of Bloodaxe Books. www.bloodaxebooks.com.

Kolatkar, Arun. "Yeshwant Rao," and "Pictures from a Marathi Alphabet Chart," from *Collected Poems in English*. Bloodaxe, 2010. Reprinted with the permission of Bloodaxe Books. www.bloodaxebooks.com.

Le Guin, Ursula K. "The Ones Who Walk Away from Omelas," copyright © 1973 by Ursula K. Le Guin. First published in *New Dimensions* 3, 1973; subsequently published in *The Wind's Twelve Quarters*. HarperCollins, 1975. Reprinted with the permission of Curtis Brown, Ltd.

Lee, Li-Young. "Persimmons," from *Rose*. Copyright © 1986 by Li-Young Lee. Reprinted with the permission of The Permissions Company Inc., on behalf of BOA Editions Ltd., www.boaeditions.org.

MacEwen, Gwendolyn. "Dark Pines under Water," and "The Discovery," from *The Shadow-Maker*. Toronto: Macmillan, 1969. Reprinted with the permission of David MacKinnon.

MacLeod, Alistair. "As Birds Bring Forth the Sun," from *As Birds Bring Forth the Sun and Other Stories*. Copyright © 1986 by Alistair MacLeod. Reprinted by permission of McClelland & Stewart, a division of Penguin Random House Canada Limited. All rights reserved. Any third party use of this material, outside of this publication, is prohibited. Interested parties must apply directly to Penguin Random House Canada Limited for permission.

McCloud, Scott. Excerpt from *Understanding Comics*, copyright © 1993, 1994 by Scott McCloud. Reprinted with the permission of HarperCollins Publishers.

Mistry, Rohinton. "Squatter," from *Tales from Firozsha Baag*. Copyright © 1987 by Rohinton Mistry. Reprinted by permission of Emblem/McClelland & Stewart, a division of Penguin Random House Canada Limited. All rights reserved. Any third party use of this material, outside of this publication, is prohibited. Interested parties must apply directly to Penguin Random House Canada Limited for permission.

Moore, Marianne. "Poetry" (1921 and 1967) from *The Collected Poems of Marianne Moore*. Copyright © 1935 by Marianne Moore. Copyright renewed 1963 by Marianne Moore. Reprinted with the permission of Scribner, a division of Simon & Schuster, Inc. All rights reserved.

Moscovitch, Hannah. "Essay," copyright © 2008. Reprinted with the permission of Playwrights Canada Press.

Mullen, Harryette. "[marry at a hotel, annul 'em]," from *Recyclopedia*. Copyright © 2006 by Harryette Mullen. Reprinted with the permission of The Permissions Company, Inc., on behalf of Graywolf Press, www.graywolfpress.org. "black nikes," and "Dim Lady," from *Sleeping with the Dictionary*. Copyright © 2002 by the Regents of the University of California. Reprinted with the permission of The University of California Press via Copyright Clearance Center, Inc.

Munro, Alice. "Friend of My Youth," from *Friend of My Youth*. Copyright © 1990 by Alice Munro. Reprinted by permission of McClelland & Stewart, a division of Penguin Random House Canada Limited. All rights reserved. Any third party use of this material, outside of this publication, is prohibited. Interested parties must apply directly to Penguin Random House Canada Limited for permission.

Murakami, Haruki. "Seeing the 100% Perfect Girl One Beautiful April Morning," from *The Elephant Vanishes: Stories*. Copyright © 1993 by Haruki Murakami. Reprinted with the permission of Alfred A. Knopf, an imprint of the Knopf Doubleday Publishing Group, a division of Penguin Random House LLC. All rights reserved. Any third party use of this material, outside of this publication, is prohibited. Interested parties must apply directly to Penguin Random House LLC for permission.

Nelson, Marilyn. "Minor Miracle," from *The Fields of Praise*. Louisiana State University Press, 1997. Reprinted with the permission of Louisiana State University Press.

Nilsen, Anders. "Towards a Conceptual Framework for Understanding Your Individual Relationship to the Totality of the Universe in Four Simple Diagrams." Copyright © Anders Nilsen. First published in *The New York Times*, September 24, 2014.

Olds, Sharon. "Sex without Love," and "The One Girl at the Boys' Party," from *The Dead and The Living*. Copyright © 1975, 1978, 1979, 1980, 1981, 1982, 1983 by Sharon Olds. Used by permission of Alfred A. Knopf, an imprint of the Knopf Doubleday Publishing Group, a division of Penguin Random House LLC. All rights reserved.

Page, P.K. "Stories of Snow," and "The Stenographers," from *The Hidden Room* (in two volumes). Erin, ON: The Porcupine's Quill, 1997. Reprinted with permission.

Phan, Hai-Dang. "My Father's 'Norton Introduction to Literature,' Third Edition (1981)," first published in *Poetry Magazine*, November 2015. Reprinted with the permission of Hai-Dang Phan.

Pollock, Sharon. "Blood Relations" (1980) from *Blood Relations and Other Plays* (revised edition). NeWest Press, 2002. Reprinted with the permission of Sharon Pollock and NeWest Press.

Pound, Ezra. "In a Station of the Metro," and "The River-Merchant's Wife: A Letter," from *Personae*, copyright © 1926 by Ezra Pound. Reprinted with the permission of New Directions Publishing Corp.

Purdy, Al. "Lament for the Dorsets," and "Trees at the Arctic Circle," from *Beyond Remembering: The Collected Poems of Al Purdy*, edited by Sam Solecki. Harbour Publishing, 2000, www.harbourpublishing.com; reprinted with permission.

Rich, Adrienne. "Aunt Jennifer's Tigers," copyright © 2016 by the Adrienne Rich Literary Trust. Copyright © 1951 by Adrienne Rich. "Diving into the Wreck,"

Photograph

Hardy, Friedhelm. Photograph of Yeshwant Rao, outside the main temple of Jejuri, Maharashtra, from *The Religious Culture of India: Power, Love, and Wisdom* by Friedhelm Hardy. Copyright © Cambridge University Press, 1994. Reproduced with the permission of Cambridge University Press.

Website

Foer, Jonathan Safran. "A Primer for the Punctuation of Heart Disease," first published by *The New Yorker*, June 10, 2002. Displayed by permission of Jonathan Safran Foer and Aragi Inc.

Kavanagh, Geoff. "Ditch," from *Staging the North: Twelve Canadian Plays*, edited by Grace et al. Playwrights Union of Canada/Hushion House, 1999. Reprinted with the permission of Geoff Kavanagh.

McEwan, Ian. "Last Day of Summer," from *First Love, Last Rites*. Published by Jonathan Cape, 1975. Copyright © Ian McEwan. Reproduced with the permission of the author c/o Rogers, Coleridge & White Ltd., 20 Powis Mews, London W11 1JN.

The publisher has endeavoured to contact rights holders for all copyrighted material, and would appreciate receiving any information as to errors and omissions.

Index of First Lines

A broken A L T A R, Lord, thy servant rears   485

A cold coming we had of it   600

A sudden blow: the great wings beating still   580

A wind is ruffling the tawny pelt   652

About me the night moonless wimples the mountains   613

About suffering they were never wrong   617

According to Brueghel   590

After great pain, a formal feeling comes—   553

After the brief bivouac of Sunday   633

Ah! why, because the dazzling sun   545

Among twenty snowy mountains   585

An excellent vocabulary, but spatial skills   740

Animal bones and some mossy tent rings   639

anyone lived in a pretty how town   608

Are you looking for a god?   654

As if he had been poured   678

As virtuous men pass mildly away   480

Aunt Jennifer's tigers prance across a screen   644

Batter my heart, three personed God; for you   480

Because I could not stop for Death—   554

Before the black beak reappeared   693

Bent double, like old beggars under sacks   605

Between my finger and my thumb   675

By the road to the contagious hospital   589

Carrots are fucking   698

Certain words give him trouble: cannibals, puzzles, sob   755

chemical history narcopolemics   745

Children's hands in close-up   680

Come live with me and be my love   473

dear Captain Poetry   690

Death be not proud, though some have called thee   479

Did you see her mother on television? She said   705

Do not go gentle into that good night   631

do not imagine that the exploration   683

Every smell is now a possibility, a young man   709

First having read the book of myths   645

First, grant me my sense of history   702

Five years have passed; five summers, with the length   501

Had we but world enough, and time   491

Half a league, half a league   539

He was found by the Bureau of Statistics to be   621

He, who navigated with success   668

Hey! Hey! Hey!   706

How do I love thee? Let me count the ways   526

How do they do it, the ones who make love   685

I can still see that soil crimsoned by butchered   727

I caught this morning morning's minion, king-   575

I celebrate myself, and sing myself   550

I had been told about her   731

871

I have done it again   662
I have eaten   589
I have met them at close of day   576
I hear America singing, the varied carols
　　I hear   551
I heard a Fly buzz—when I died—   554
I imagine this midnight moment's
　　forest: 649
I knew a woman, lovely in her
　　bones   624
I like to touch your tattoos in
　　complete   717
I met a traveller from an antique
　　land   511
I sat all morning in the college sick
　　bay   677
I sit in one of the dives   618
I wander thro' each charter'd
　　street   499
I would like to watch you
　　sleeping   670
I, being born a woman and
　　distressed   602
I, too, dislike it   594
I, too, dislike it: there are things that
　　are important beyond all this
　　fiddle   593
I'll come when thou art saddest   549
I'm Nobody! Who are you?   553
I've known rivers   610
If all the world and love were
　　young   472
in Just-   606
In sixth grade Mrs. Walker   723
In the cold, cold parlour   628
In the end she just wanted the
　　house   747
In this strange labyrinth how shall I
　　turn?   483
In Xanadu did Kubla Khan   508
It little profits that an idle king   537
It was blacker than olives the night I
　　left. As I   704
Jackfish and walleye circle like clouds as
　　he strains   738

jellyfish potato/ jellypo fishtato/ glow in
　　the pork toys/   746
Kashmir shrinks into my mailbox   701
l e   689
Let me not to the marriage of true
　　minds   477
Let the world's sharpness like a clasping
　　knife   526
Let us go then, you and I   596
Lie to yourself about this and you
　　will   671
Little lamb, who made thee?   497
Lord, who createdst man in wealth and
　　store   486
Love, a child, is ever crying   482
Mark but this flea, and mark in
　　this   478
marry at a hotel, annul 'em   716
me friend deh a foreign fi di last two
　　weeks   752
Moisten your finger and hold it   749
Morning and evening   557
My heart aches, and a drowsy numbness
　　pains   519
My honeybunch's peepers are nothing
　　like neon. Today's spe-   714
My Life had stood—a Loaded
　　Gun—   555
My mistress' eyes are nothing like the
　　sun   477
My mother forbade us to walk
　　backwards. That   705
No coward soul is mine   547
No matter how   734
No, helpless thing, I cannot harm thee
　　now   494
Nobody heard him, the dead man   612
Not all halfbreed mothers   733
Nothing. When we realized you weren't
　　here   691
O what can ail thee, knight-at-arms   517
O Wild West Wind, thou breath of
　　Autumn's being   512
Often rebuked, yet always back
　　returning   548

On either side the river lie   531

Once upon a midnight dreary, while I
    pondered, weak and weary   527

paranoia   752

Pike, three inches long, perfect   650

Pineapple. Mother. Pants. Lemon   657

Reading a poem releases noxious   750

S'io credesse che mia risposta fosse   596

Season of mists and mellow
    fruitfulness   523

September rain falls on the house
    626

Shall I compare thee to a summer's
    day?   475

She had thought the studio would keep
    itself   645

Snow annihilates all beauty   728

so much depends   588

somewhere i have never travelled,gladly
    beyond   607

Spring darkness is forgiving. It doesn't
    descend   708

Still dark, but just. The alarm   739

Stop all the clocks, cut off the
    telephone   617

Suddenly the rain is hilarious   718

Tell all the Truth but tell it
    slant—   556

That crazy drunken night I   673

That is no country for old men. The
    young   580

That time of year thou mayst in me
    behold   476

That's my last Duchess painted on the
    wall   543

The air smells of rhubarb,
    occasional   726

The apparition of these faces in the
    crowd   592

The art of losing isn't hard to
    master   629

The Frost performs its secret
    ministry   506

The long love that in my thought doth
    harbour   468

The older she gets   719

The onion loves the onion   699

the time i dropped your almost body
    down   667

The whiskey on your breath   623

The world is charged with the grándeur
    of God   574

The world is too much with us; late and
    soon   505

They are 18 inches long   637

They flee from me that sometime did
    me seek   469

This is dawn   686

this land is not   720

This land like a mirror turns you
    inward   682

Those in the vegetable rain retain   635

Thou ill-formed offspring of my feeble
    brain   489

Thou still unravish'd bride of
    quietness   521

Turning and turning in the widening
    gyre   579

'Twas mercy brought me from my
    Pagan land   496

Two roads diverged in a yellow
    wood   583

Two women stare at each other   711

Unreal tall as a myth   615

Walking by the waters   730

We lived in an old schoolhouse,
    one large room that my father
    converted   721

We need quarters like King Tut needed
    a boat. A slave could   715

We wear the mask that grins and
    lies   582

We were married in summer, thirty
    years ago. I have loved you deeply
    from   688

What happens to a dream
    deferred?   611

what language have i   754

What lips my lips have kissed, and
    where, and why   603

What needs my Shakespeare for his
    honoured bones   487
What passing-bells for these who die as
    cattle?   604
What thoughts I have of you tonight,
    Walt Whitman, for I walked
    down   642
When I come again to my father's
    house   699
When I consider how my light is
    spent   488
When I have fears that I may cease to
    be   516
When I heard the learn'd
    astronomer   551
When I take my girl to the swimming
    party   684
When I was growing up in the bush, on
    the hillside   711

when i watch you   666
When in disgrace with fortune and
    men's eyes   476
When our two souls stand up erect and
    strong   525
Which reminds me of another knock-
    on-wood   696
While my hair was still cut straight
    across my forehead   591
Whose woods these are I think I
    know   584
Whoso list to hunt, I know where is an
    hind   470
Wild Nights—Wild Nights!   552
Yeah, their necks were stiff   736
You believe you know me   741
You do not do, you do not do   660
you fit into me   669

Index of Authors and Titles

30 [Spring darkness is forgiving. It doesn't descend] 708

32 [Every smell is now a possibility, a young man] 709

Abel, Jordan 758

Achebe, Chinua 98

Addonizio, Kim 717

[After great pain, a formal feeling comes] 553

Against Love Poetry 688

[Ah! Why, because the dazzling sun] 545

Al-Solaylee, Kamal 816

Ali, Agha Shahid 701

Allen, Lillian 706

Altar, The 485

anitafrika, d'bi young 751

Anthem for Doomed Youth 604

[anyone lived in a pretty how town] 608

Araby 53

As Birds Bring Forth the Sun 120

Atrophy 43

Atwood, Margaret 127, 668

Auden, W.H. 616

Aunt Jennifer's Tigers 644

Aunty 734

Author to Her Book, The 489

Barbauld, Anna Laetitia 494

[Batter my heart, three-personed God; for you] 480

Bear on the Delhi Road, The 615

[Because I could not stop for Death] 554

Bezmozgis, David 213

Bidart, Frank 671

Big Water 210

Birney, Earle 613

Bishop, Elizabeth 626

Black Nikes 715

Black Cat, The 16

Blake, William 497

Blank Sonnet 726

Blasim, Hassan 225

Blood Relations 365

Blues 689

Boland, Eavan 686

Bradstreet, Anne 489

Brand, Dionne 708

Bringhurst, Robert 693

Brontë, Emily 545

Brown 816

Browning, Elizabeth Barrett 525

Browning, Robert 542

Butler, Octavia 134

Carrots 698

Carson, Anne 704

Casualties 728

Caterpillar, The 494

Chang, Victoria 747

Charge of the Light Brigade, The 539

Chopin, Kate 25

Clarke, George Elliott 726

Clean, Well-Lighted Place, A 73

Clifton, Lucille 666

Coady, Lynn 202

Coleridge, Samuel Taylor 506

Coyote, Ivan 832

Crozier, Lorna 698

Crush 719

Cummings, E.E. 606

Cutaways 680

Daddy 660

Dark Pines Under Water 682

Dead Men's Path 98

[dear Captain Poetry] 690

[Death be not proud, though some have called thee] 479

Death of a Young Son by Drowning 668

Death of the Moth, The 790

Dickinson, Emily 552

Did I Miss Anything? 691

Digging 675

Dim Lady 714

Discovery, The 683

Diving into the Wreck 645
Do Not Go Gentle into That Good
    Night 631
Doll's House, A 249
Donne, John 478
Drunk 718
Duffy, Carol Ann 718
Dulce et Decorum Est 605
Dumont, Marilyn 720
Dunbar, Paul Laurence 582
Easter 1916 576
Easter Wings 486
ê-kwêskît — Turn-Around Woman 711
Eliot, T.S. 595
Essay 414
Family Supper, A 185
Far Cry from Africa, A 652
Father's Faith, A 827
Finding Father 805
First Death in Nova Scotia 628
First Poem for You 717
Flea, The 478
foreign mind/local body 752
Friend of My Youth 102
Frost at Midnight 506
Frost, Robert 583
Funeral Blues 617
Garden Party, The 59
Gilman, Charlotte Perkins 28
Ginsberg, Allen 642
Goblin Market 557
God's Grandeur 574
Good Man Is Hard to Find, A 77
Gowdy, Barbara 152
Grauballe Man, The 678
Half-Light 673
Halfe, Louise Bernice 710
Happy Endings 127
Harlem (2) 611
Harris, Sharon 749
Heaney, Seamus 675
Hellgoing 202
Hemingway, Ernest 72
Her 731
Herbert, George 484

Hopkins, Gerard Manley 574
[How do I love thee? Let me count the
    ways] 526
How It Feels to Be Coloured Me 794
Hughes, Langston 610
Hughes, Ted 649
Hurston, Zora Neale 793
[I celebrate myself, and sing myself]
    550
I Hear America Singing 551
[I heard a Fly buzz—when I died] 554
I Knew a Woman 624
[I, being born a woman and distressed]
    602
[I'll come when thou art saddest] 549
[I'm Nobody! Who are you?] 553
Ibsen, Henrik 248
Importance of Being Earnest, The 310
In a Station of the Metro 592
[in Just-] 606
In My Country 730
[in this strange labyrinth how shall I
    turn?] 483
Ishiguro, Kazuo 185
Journey of the Magi 600
Joyce, James 53
Kay, Jackie 730
Keats, John 516
King, Thomas 131
Kolatkar, Arun 654
Kubla Khan 508
La Belle Dame sans Merci: A Ballad 517
Lady Lazarus 662
Lady of Shalott, The 531
Lamb, The 497
Lament for the Dorsets 639
Landscape with the Fall of Icarus 590
Le Guin, Ursula K. 91
Leda and the Swan 580
Leda and the Swan 693
Lee, Li-Young 723
[Let the world's sharpness like a clasping
    knife] 526
Lines Written a Few Miles above
    Tintern Abbey 501

Living in Sin 645

London 400

Look Homeward, Exile 727

lost baby poem, the 667

Love Song of J. Alfred Prufrock, The 596

love speak 754

MacEwen, Gwendolyn 682

MacLeod, Alistair 120

Mansfield, Katherine 69

Marlowe, Christopher 473

[marry at a hotel, annul 'em] 716

Marvell, Andrew 491

McCloud, Scott 809

Mid-Term Break 677

Milton, John 487

Minor Miracle 696

miss rosie 666

Mistry, Rohinton 163

Modest Proposal, A 781

Moore, Marianne 593

Moscovitch, Hannah 413

Mr. Darcy 747

Mullen, Harryette 714

Munro, Alice 102

Murakami, Haruki 147

Musée des Beaux Arts 617

My Father's 'Norton Introduction to Literature,' Third Edition (1981) 755

My Last Duchess 543

[My Life had stood—a Loaded Gun] 555

My Papa's Waltz 623

Negro Speaks of Rivers, The 610

Nelson, Marilyn 696

nervous organism 746

Nice 739

Nichol, bp 689

Night Feed 686

Nightmare of Carlos Fuentes, The 225

Nilsen, Anders 232

[No coward soul is mine] 547

Not All Half-Breed Mothers 733

Not Just a Platform for My Dance 720

Not Waving but Drowning 612

Nymph's Reply to the Shepherd, The 472

O'Connor, Flannery 77

Ode on a Grecian Urn 521

Ode to a Nightingale 519

Ode to the West Wind 512

[Often rebuked, yet always back returning] 548

Olds, Sharon 684

On Being Brought from Africa to America 496

On Rain 704

On Shakespeare 487

On Sylvia Plath 705

On Walking Backwards 705

One Art 629

One Girl at the Boys Party, The 684

One Poem Town 706

Ones Who Walk Away from Omelas, The 92

Onions 699

opium 745

Orwell, George 798

Owen, Wilfred 604

Ozymandias 511

Page, P.K. 633

Passionate Shepherd to His Love, The 473

Persimmons 723

Phan, Hai-Dang 755

Pictures from a Marathi Alphabet Chart 657

Pike 650

Place of Scraps, The 759

Plath, Sylvia 659

Poe, Edgar Allan 16, 527

Poetry 593

Poetry (revised version) 594

Pollock, Sharon 364

Postcard from Kashmir 701

Pound, Ezra 591

Purdy, Al 736

Queer 671

Ralegh, Sir Walter 471

Raven, The 527

Red Wheelbarrow, The 588
Rich, Adrienne 644
River-Merchant's Wife: Letter, The 591
Road Not Taken, The 583
Robinson, Eden 194
Roethke, Theodore 623
Rossetti, Christina 557
Sailing to Byzantium 580
Scofield, Gregory 732
Second Coming, The 579
Seeing the 100% Perfect Girl One
    Beautiful April Morning 147
self-esteem (ii) 752
Self-Portrait in a Series of Professional
    Evaluations 740
September 1, 1939 618
Sestina 626
Sex without Love 685
Shakespeare, William 475
Shelley, Percy Bysshe 511
Shooting an Elephant 798
Short History of Indians in Canada, A
    131
Simpson, Leanne Betasamosake 209
Smith, Stevie 612
Solie, Karen 738
[somewhere i have never travelled,gladly
    beyond] 607
Song [Love, a child, is ever crying] 482
Sonnet 10 [Death be not proud, though
    some have called thee] 479
Sonnet 14 [Batter my heart, three
    personed God; for you] 480
Sonnet 18 [Shall I compare thee to a
    summer's day?] 475
Sonnet 22 [When our two souls stand
    up erect and strong] 525
Sonnet 24 [Let the world's sharpness
    like a clasping knife] 526
Sonnet 29 [When in disgrace with
    fortune and men's eyes] 476
Sonnet 43 [How do I love thee? Let me
    count the ways] 526
Sonnet 73 [That time of year thou
    mayst in me behold] 476

Sonnet 77 [In this strange labyrinth
    how shall I turn?] 483
Sonnet 116 [Let me not to the marriage
    of true minds] 477
Sonnet 130 [My mistress' eyes are
    nothing like the sun] 477
Speech Sounds 134
Spring and All 589
Squatter 163
St. Vincent Millay, Edna 602
Stenographers, The 633
Stevens, Wallace 585
Stopping by Woods on a Snowy
    Evening 584
Stories of Snow 635
Story of an Hour, The 25
Sturgeon 738
Subramaniam, Arundhathi 741
Supermarket in California, A 642
Swift, Jonathan 781
Tapka 213
[Tell all the Truth but tell it slant] 556
Tennyson, Alfred Lord 531
Terminal Avenue 194
[The long love that in my thought doth
    harbour] 468
[The world is too much with us] 505
[They flee from me that sometime did
    me seek] 469
Thirteen Ways of Looking at a
    Blackbird 585
This Is Just to Say 589
Thomas, Dylan 631
Thought-Fox, The 649
To Autumn 523
To His Coy Mistress 491
To the Welsh Critic Who Doesn't Find
    Me Identifiably Indian 741
Toews, Miriam 826
Tomboy's Survival Guide 832
Toward a Conceptual Framework for
    Understanding Your Individual
    Relationship to the Totality of the
    Universe in Four Simple Diagrams
    233

Trees at the Arctic Circle 637
Ulysses 537
Understanding Comics 810
Unknown Citizen, The 621
Valediction: Forbidding Mourning, A 480
Vancouver Lights 613
Variation on the Word Sleep 670
Wagamese, Richard 805
Walcott, Derek 652
Wayman, Tom 691
We So Seldom Look on Love 152
We Wear the Mask 582
wêpinâson 711
Wharton, Edith 43
[What lips my lips have kissed, and where, and why] 603
Wheatley, Phillis 496
When I Come Again to My Father's House 699
[When I consider how my light is spent] 488
When I Have Fears that I May Cease to Be 516
When I Heard the Learn'd Astronomer 551

[When our two souls stand up erect and strong] 525
Where Do Poems Come From? 749
White Judges, The 721
Whitman, Walt 550
[Whoso list to hunt, I know where is an hind] 470
Why Do Poems Make Me Cry? 750
[Wild Nights—Wild Nights!] 552
Wilde, Oscar 309
Williams, William Carlos 588
Windhover, The 575
Wolf's Postscript to 'Little Red Riding Hood,' The 702
Wong, Rita 744
Woolf, Virginia 790
Wordsworth, William 500
Wrong Image 736
Wroth, Lady Mary 482
Wyatt, Sir Thomas 468
Yeats, W.B. 576
Yellow Wallpaper, The 28
Yeshwant Rao 654
[you fit into me] 669

From the Publisher

A name never says it all, but the word "Broadview" expresses a
good deal of the philosophy behind our company. We are open to
a broad range of academic approaches and political viewpoints.
We pay attention to the broad impact book publishing and book
printing has in the wider world; we began using recycled stock
more than a decade ago, and for some years now we have used
100% recycled paper for most titles. Our publishing program is
internationally oriented and broad-ranging. Our individual titles
often appeal to a broad readership too; many are of interest as
much to general readers as to academics and students.

Founded in 1985, Broadview remains a fully independent
company owned by its shareholders—not an imprint
or subsidiary of a larger multinational.

For the most accurate information on our books (including
information on pricing, editions, and formats) please visit our
website at www.broadviewpress.com. Our print books
and ebooks are also available for sale on our site.

broadview press

www.broadviewpress.com